RESOURCE MANUAL FOR
GUIDELINES
FOR
EXERCISE TESTING
AND
PRESCRIPTION

EDITORS

Steven N. Blair, P.E.D.
Director, Epidemiology
Institute for Aerobics Research
Dallas, TX

Patricia Painter, Ph.D.
Exercise Physiologist
Satellite Dialysis Centers
Redwood City, CA

Russell R. Pate, Ph.D.
Director, Human Performance Laboratory
Department of Physical Education
Professor, College of Health
University of South Carolina
Columbia, SC

L. Kent Smith, M.D., M.P.H.
Medical Director, Cardiac Rehabilitation
and Preventive Medicine Programs
Arizona Heart Institute
Phoenix, AZ

C. Barr Taylor, M.D.
Associate Professor of Psychiatry
Department of Psychiatry and Behavioral Medicine
Stanford University School of Medicine
Stanford, CA

RESOURCE MANUAL FOR GUIDELINES FOR EXERCISE TESTING AND PRESCRIPTION

AMERICAN COLLEGE OF SPORTS MEDICINE

Lea & Febiger

Philadelphia

Lea & Febiger
600 Washington Square
Philadelphia, PA   19106-4198
U.S.A.
(215) 922-1330

LIBRARY OF CONGRESS
Library of Congress Cataloging-in-Publication Data

Resource manual for Guidelines for exercise testing and prescription/American College of
   Sports Medicine; editors, Steven N. Blair . . . [et al.].
      p.   cm.
   Includes bibliographies and index.
   ISBN 0-8121-1109-5
   1. Exercise therapy.   2. Exercise tests.   I. Blair, Steven N.   II. American College of
Sports Medicine.   III. Guidelines for exercise testing and prescription.
   [DNLM: 1. Exercise Test.   2. Exercise Therapy.   3. Exertion.   WE
103 A514g 1986 Suppl.]
RM725.R42 1988
615.8′24 — dc19
DNLM/DLC
for Library of Congress   88-3004
                                                                                    CIP

Printed in the United States of America
Print Number: 5 4 3 2

FOREWORD

The science and art of implementing effective and safe exercise programs for enhancing health and performance capacity in clinically healthy people and selected patients has steadily evolved over the past 30 years. Our understanding of how much of what type of exercise needs to be performed and how often to produce the desired results continues to develop, but substantially more research is required before this pharmacopeia of exercise is complete. Even with our limited fund of knowledge, however, an enormous gap remains between what has been scientifically established and the nature of the information that frequently is provided to the public. Given the increasingly important role that exercise plays in health promotion, medical therapy, and rehabilitation, the need is great for scientifically based educational materials for exercise/health professionals who increasingly will provide exercise program guidance to the public.

During this next decade, a major challenge is to develop approaches to exercise that will result in a substantial increase in physical activity by those individuals who have not yet incorporated appropriate exercise into their usual routine. High-priority target groups include adults over age 50 years, those of low socioeducational status, and those with medical problems that require special guidance for safe and effective exercise. Our ability to meet this challenge successfully will, in part, depend on those individuals now training to become health/fitness professionals. The American College of Sports Medicine (ACSM) has spearheaded the preparation of these personnel through its certification program for exercise professionals. This program will have an even greater impact as the number of certified personnel increases and greater emphasis is placed on individuals conducting preventive programs. The *Resource Manual* is a major contribution to enhancing the effectiveness of the ACSM certification program as well as for use in general continuing education. It provides an extensive overview of the major topics that form the scientific foundations for the implementation of health-oriented physical activity.

Stanford University   William L. Haskell
Stanford, CA

v

FOREWORD

The unprecedented increase in the number of exercise facilities designed to provide preventive and rehabilitative cardiovascular exercise therapy has gone hand in hand with the increasing national awareness of the benefits of exercise in combating cardiovascular disease and other health problems. Other areas of concern must include pulmonary rehabilitation and the rehabilitation of the structurally injured, i.e., physical medicine. Initially, the Preventive and Rehabilitative Exercise Program Committee produced the successful *Guidelines for Graded Exercise Testing and Exercise Prescription* as a support manual for their certification tracks in Cardiac Rehabilitation. The College has committed to an expansion of certifications, however, to include use of exercise as a preventive measure in the fight to improve health for all citizens. In support of this expansion, the Preventive and Rehabilitative Exercise Program Committee recognized the need to provide a resource manual for practitioners delivering preventive and rehabilitative programs. In this manual, a multitude of recognized experts in their individual fields of endeavor provide some 48 chapters of information that support the Behavioral Guidelines and objectives of the Preventive and Rehabilitative Exercise Program Committee's definition of a complete exercise therapy program. By drawing together this vast collection of information into one book, the College intends to provide a resource manual for the student and the practitioner to use for years to come. The careful editing of the Editorial Committee as well as the unrewarded efforts of the authors, members of the College, deserves recognition.

As the current President of the American College of Sports Medicine, I am proud to be associated with our College members in producing such a far-reaching resource.

President,   Peter B. Raven, Ph.D.
American College
of Sports Medicine

FOREWORD

In the September, 1986 edition of the Gallup Poll, the following statement was made: "Americans' preoccupation with physical fitness shows no signs of letting up, with a 51% majority of U.S. adults currently claiming to follow some kind of daily regime — aside from their jobs or housework — that helps them stay in shape. This is roughly the same proportion recorded in Gallup surveys over the last decade, but twice the rate of a generation ago. In Gallup's first (1961) fitness audit, only 24% exercised daily."

The actual number of adults who currently exercise regularly is highly debatable, probably grossly exaggerated, and among those who exercise, only a small percentage exercise enough to gain any significant cardiovascular benefit. Yet, the important point is that "twice as many people are exercising as there were a generation ago," and that translates to millions of Americans.

Many books have been written for the lay person proclaiming the benefits of regular exercise, and even a few books recount its dangers. But the overwhelming conclusion is that as Americans began exercising in unprecedented numbers, the incidence of sudden deaths and deaths from heart attacks did not increase, as was predicted initially by the critics. Likewise, no decrease in life expectancy ensued, which was "bound to occur" according to other critics. To the contrary, coupled with more people exercising, a remarkable decrease in the number of deaths from cardiovascular disease and an unprecedented increase in longevity occurred. Admittedly, these beneficial changes cannot all be attributed to the exercising habits of the American people, but obviously exercise did not cause adverse effects. An obvious conclusion drawn from the published results of many longitudinal studies is that regular exercise is a major factor in reducing coronary risk factors and ultimately cardiovascular deaths. In one study, researchers even documented a prolongation of life in conjunction with regular physical activity.

Throughout this "exercise revolution," the practice of medicine has not been able to keep up with the enthusiasm of the exercising patient. Consequently, a knowledge gap has occurred, which has been filled by many unqualified and untrained people. As could be predicted, problems ensued that in many cases were avoidable. During these years, an authoritative text was urgently needed that could be used to advise all levels of professionals from the physical education student to the practicing physician. The need arose for a text that could not only provide knowledge in the areas of exercise physiology, applied anatomy, and pathophysiology, but also give specific recommendations in the more applied fields of stress testing and exercise prescription. To accomplish such an important goal adequately would require the contributions and cooperation of a large group of international specialists. In this reference manual, that goal has been admirably achieved. For the student, the instructor, or the practicing physician, this book should be required reading, and if its guidelines and recommendations are followed, the exercising person will be the benefactor. Hopefully, the millions of Americans already exercising will find a more highly qualified professional to work with them in their exercise programs and millions more will discover the joys and benefits of exercise. Ultimately, all Americans should benefit by having a healthier and more productive society.

President and Founder   Kenneth H. Cooper
The Aerobics Center
Dallas, TX

PREFACE

The American College of Sports Medicine certification programs began in 1975 with the publication of *Guidelines for Graded Exercise Testing and Exercise Prescription (Guidelines)* and subsequent examinations of certification candidates. The *Guidelines* presented behavioral objectives for the several certification tracks. Candidates were expected to master these objectives and be able to pass written and oral examinations on the content. In the early years of the certification process, candidates were given no assistance in finding educational materials to provide the necessary information relative to the objectives. Later, the Preventive and Rehabilitative Exercise Programs Committee (P & R) developed study packets consisting of reference lists, review papers, and study suggestions to help candidates prepare for the examinations. The P & R Committee also developed manuals for the certification workshops. The P & R Committee thought that the study packets and workshop manuals were helpful but were not entirely adequate to meet the needs of the certification candidates due to the tremendous breadth of material covered in the objectives. No single resource is currently available to meet these diverse needs. The third edition of the *Guidelines* was published in 1986. This edition contains expanded behavioral objectives to include certification tracks in preventive exercise programming. The rehabilitative exercise certifications were expanded with additional objectives for inpatient cardiac rehabilitation and exercise testing and prescription for pulmonary patients.

The P & R Committee decided to produce *Resource Manual for Guidelines for Exercise Testing and Prescription (Resource Manual)* to provide certification candidates with appropriate information relative to the behavioral objectives found in the *Guidelines*. We view the *Resource Manual* as a companion textbook to the *Guidelines*, and we expect it to be a valuable aid in preparing for certification. The *Resource Manual* addresses a broad array of topics. Although no single source will provide all available information on exercise testing and exercise prescription, the *Resource Manual* is a comprehensive and authoritative book. More than 90% of the behavioral objectives in the *Guidelines* are addressed in the *Resource Manual*.

In the early stages of planning for the *Resource Manual*, the Editorial Committee reviewed all behavioral objectives in the *Guidelines*. Objectives were grouped into topics and an outline of the chapters was developed. Behavioral objectives were specifically assigned to authors of the chapters. Authors were asked to write at a level appropriate for persons beginning graduate studies in the health sciences and related areas. Authors were also asked to include key information relevant to the behavioral objectives they were assigned. They were asked to distill their knowledge into a few main points, yet provide sufficient detail to avoid a superficial treatment of the topic. Similar objectives appear in the different certification levels. For example, the exercise test technologist is expected to be able to describe the effect of different drugs on heart rate and blood pressure. The exercise program director must also be able to describe the mechanism of action of a drug and list its major side effects. Behavioral objectives for both of these examples were assigned to a single chapter in the *Resource Manual.* Thus, each chapter has a coherent theme, but is useful for different certification levels. Candidates should read the material with this thought in mind. Candidates preparing for the health fitness instructor certification, for example, should expect to encounter material in the *Resource Manual* that is more advanced than they need. In general, the chapters contain only the most important references and items suggested for further reading.

The material in each chapter represents the opinions of the authors, who were chosen for their expertise in the topic presented. Many areas in exercise science of course remain con-troversial. Experts may disagree on important issues. Therefore, candidates should view the *Resource Manual* as an important guide, but should not expect it to provide answers to all examination questions. The Editorial Committee is confident, however, that the *Resource Manual* is an authoritative source, and candidates who know the material therein will do well on the examination.

The primary value of the *Resource Manual* is that it provides a great deal of information on the behavioral objectives in one place. To extract information on a particular certification process, a candidate should carefully study the behavioral objectives, and then use the Table of Contents and the Index to locate the appropriate material. Remember that more information may be available than you need for your certification. If a behavioral objective requires listing of certain items, simply learn the items to list. If higher levels of knowledge are required by an objective, more complete study of the chapter, and possibly other references, may be necessary.

The Editorial Committee hopes this book proves useful to ACSM certification candidates and to other students of exercise science. Good luck with your studies.

Editorial Committee

ACKNOWLEDGMENTS

The editors thank those individuals who contributed to this book by reviewing manuscripts and providing editorial assistance.

Gary Adams, Ph.D.
Chris Aguiar, Ph.D.
Kathryn Henry
Robert B. Armstrong, Ph.D.
Anne. E. Atwater, Ph.D.
Kathy Berra, R.N.
Gordon Blackburn, Ph.D.
John Cantwell, M.D.
William Day, Ph.D.
Robert F. Debusk, M.D.
Carl Foster, Ph.D.
Barry A. Franklin, Ph.D.
Larry W. Gibbons, M.D., M.P.H.
William L. Haskell, Ph.D.
William G. Herbert, Ph.D.
Robert G. Holly, Ph.D.
David Hyman, M.D.
Cindy Kirtly

Neal Kohatsu, M.D.
Arthur S. Leon, M.D.
Henry S. Miller, Jr., M.D.
Nancy Houston Miller, R.N.
Ronald T. Mulder, Ed.D.
Kathleen Murphy
Francis J. Nagle, Ph.D.
Neil Oldridge, Ph.D.
David M. Orenstein, M.D.
Kenneth E. Powell, M.D., M.P.H.
John Rutigliano, M.S.
James Skinner, Ph.D.
Everett Smith, Ph.D.
Janet P. Wallace, Ph.D.
Arthur Weltman, Ph.D.
Phillip K. Wilson, Ed.D.
Marilyn Winkleby, Ph.D.

CONTRIBUTORS

Steven N. Blair, P.E.D.
Director, Epidemiology
Institute for Aerobics Research
Dallas, TX

Tommy Boone, Ph.D.
Professor and Director, Anatomy Laboratory
Department of Physical Education
School of HPER
University of Southern Mississippi
Hattiesburg, MS

Lawrence M. Borysyk, M.S.
Exercise Physiologist
Cardiac Rehabilitation Program
William Beaumont Hospital
Royal Oak, MI

Kelly D. Brownell, Ph.D.
Professor
Department of Psychiatry
University of Pennsylvania
School of Medicine
Philadelphia, PA

Carl J. Caspersen Ph.D., M.P.H.
Exercise Physiologist/Epidemiologist
Behavioral Epidemiology and Evaluation
   Branch
Center for Health Promotion and Education
Department of Health and Human Services
Centers for Disease Control

Division of Health Education
Atlanta, GA

Joe V. Chandler, Ed.D.
Chair, Division of Physical Education and
   Exercise Studies
Lander College
Greenwood, SC

Edward F. Coyle, Ph.D.
Director, Human Performance Laboratory
College of Education
The University of Texas at Austin
Department of Physical and Health Education
Austin, TX

J. Larry Durstine, Ph.D.
Associate Professor
Department of Physical Education
University of South Carolina
Columbia, SC

Robert H. Fitts, Ph.D.
Professor of Biology
Department of Biology
Marquette University
Milwaukee, WI

June Flora, Ph.D.
Assistant Professor
Department of Communications
Stanford University Medical Center
Stanford, CA

Barry A. Franklin, Ph.D.
Director, Cardiac Rehabilitation and Exercise
  Laboratories
William Beaumont Hospital
Division of Cardiovascular Diseases, Cardiac
  Rehabilitation
Royal Oak, MI

Larry R. Gettman, Ph.D.
Director, Research and Development
National Health Enhancement Systems
Phoenix, AZ

Michael D. Giese, M.S.
Program Director, Take Control
Health Enhancement Program
Milwaukee, WI

Andrew M. Gottlieb, Ph.D.
Clinical Psychologist
Stanford University Medical Center
Stanford, CA

Peter Hanson, M.S., M.D.
Professor of Medicine
Co-Director, Preventive Cardiology Program
University of Wisconsin
Clinical Science Center
Madison, WI

William L. Haskell, Ph.D.
Associate Professor of Medicine
Division of Cardiology
Stanford University
Palo Alto, CA

Jerald D. Hawkins, Ed.D.
Chairman, Department of Sport Studies
Guilford College
Greensboro, NC

Gregory W. Heath, D.H.Sc., M.P.H.
Behavioral Epidemiology and Evaluation
  Branch
Center for Health Promotion and Education
Department of Health and Human Services
Centers for Disease Control
Division of Health Education
Atlanta, GA

David L. Herbert, J.D.
Professional Reports Corporation
Canton, OH

William G. Herbert, Ph.D.
Professor, and Director, Cardiac Intervention
  Center

Virginia Tech University
Division of HPER
Blacksburg, VA

Victoria Hollingsworth, M.S.
Exercise Physiologist
Cardiac Rehabilitation Program
William Beaumont Hospital
Royal Oak, MI

Robert G. Holly, Ph.D.
Assistant Professor
Department of Physical Education
University of California — Davis
Davis, CA

Nancy Houston Miller, R.N.
Nurse Coordinator
Department of Cardiology
Stanford University Medical Center
Stanford, CA

Edward T. Howley, Ph.D.
Professor of Physical Education
University of Tennessee
Knoxville, TN

Bruce H. Jones, M.D., M.P.H., M.A.
Research Medical Officer
Investigator Unit 2
Major, U.S. Army Medical Corps
U.S. Army Research Institute of
  Environmental Medicine
Exercise Physiology Division
Natick, MA

David A. Kaufmann, Ph.D.
Professor
Department of Exercise and Sport Sciences
College of Health and Human Performance
University of Florida
Gainesville, FL

Abby C. King, Ph.D.
Stanford Center for Research in Disease
  Prevention
Stanford University School of Medicine
Palo Alto, CA

Diane Panton-Lapsley, R.N., M.S., C.S.
Cardiovascular Clinical Specialist
West Roxbury V.A. Medical Center
West Roxbury, MA

Julia M. Lash, Ph.D.
N.I.H. Postdoctoral Trainee
Exercise Physiology Laboratory
The Ohio State University
Columbus, OH

Maria Lonnett, M.S.
Department of Physical Education
University of South Carolina
Columbia, SC

John E. Martin, Ph.D.
Professor
Department of Psychology
San Diego State University
San Diego, CA

Kevin M. McIntyre, M.D., J.D.
Associate Clinical Professor
Harvard Medical School
Brockton — West Roxbury V.A. Medical Center
West Roxbury, MA

Mark E. McKinney, Ph.D.
Department of Family Practice
University of Nebraska Medical Center
Omaha, NE

Stephen P. Messier, Ph.D.
Associate Professor
Department of Health and Sport Science
Wake Forest University
Winston-Salem, NC

G. Curt Meyers, M.S.
Director of Wellness Programs
Lee Memorial Hospital
Fort Meyers, FL

Brenda S. Mitchell, Ph.D.
Director of Planning and Development
Institute for Aerobics Research
Dallas, TX

Jere H. Mitchell, M.D.
Harry S. Moss Heart Center
Departments of Internal Medicine and
    Physiology
University of Texas Health Science Center
Dallas, TX

Robert J. Moffatt, Ph.D.
Department of Movement Science and
    Physical Education

The Florida State University
Tallahassee, FL

Michael P. Moore, M.D., B.S.
Captain, U.S. Army Medical Corps
Visiting Research Scholar
Department of Human Kinetics
Walter Reed Army Medical Center
Washington, D.C.

Josephine Will Musser, B.S.N., M.S., M.B.A.
President
J.W. Musser, Consulting
Madison, WI

Neil B. Oldridge, Ph.D.
Professor, Department of Medicine
Cardiovascular Disease Section
University of Wisconsin Medical School
Milwaukee, WI

Patricia Painter, Ph.D.
Exercise Program Director
Satellite Dialysis Centers, Inc.
Redwood City, CA

Russell R. Pate, Ph.D.
Director, Human Performance Laboratory
Department of Physical Education
Professor, College of Health
University of South Carolina
Columbia, SC

Glen H. Porter, Ph.D.
Director, Rehabilitation Services
Seton Medical Center
Daly City, CA

Scott K. Powers, Ph.D., Ed.D.
Director, Applied Physiology Laboratory
Louisiana State University
School of HPERD
Baton Rouge, LA

Paul B. Rock, D.O., Ph.D.
Major, U.S. Army Medical Corps
Flight Surgeon, Altitude Research Division
U.S. Army Research, Institute of
    Environmental Medicine
Natick, MA

David P.L. Sachs, M.D.
Clinical Assistant Professor of Medicine
Division of Respiratory Medicine
Stanford University School of Medicine

Director, Center for Pulmonary Disease
Prevention
Director, Smoking Cessation Research Institute
Stanford, CA

J.P. Schaman, M.D.
Medical Director
Rehabilitation and Sports Medicine
Ontario Aerobics Centre
Breslau , Ontario, Canada

Michael S. Scaramuzzi, M.Ed., C.C.T., C.E.T.
Brockton-West Roxbury V.A. Medical Center
West Roxbury, MA

Brian J. Sharkey, Ph.D.
Dean, College of Human Performance and
Leisure Studies
University of Northern Colorado
Greeley, CO

Javaid Sheikh, M.D.
Coordinator, Geriatric Psychiatry Training
Department of Psychiatry
Stanford University Medical Center
Stanford, CA

Roy J. Shephard, M.D., Ph.D.
Director, School of Physical and Health
Education
Department of Preventive Medicine and
Biostatistics
Faculty of Medicine
University of Toronto
Toronto, Ontario, Canada

W. Mike Sherman, Ph.D.
Assistant Professor
Exercise Physiology Laboratory
The Ohio State University
Columbus, OH

Wesley E. Sime, Ph.D., M.P.H.
Associate Professor
Stress Physiology Laboratory
University of Nebraska-Lincoln
Lincoln, NE

L. Kent Smith, M.D., M.P.H.
Medical Director, Cardiac Rehabilitation and
Preventive Medicine Programs
Arizona Heart Institute
Phoenix, AZ

Michael L. Smith, Ph.D.
Cardiovascular Physiology

Research Division
Hunter Holmes McGuire V.A. Medical Center
Richmond, VA

Suzanne Nelson Steen, M.S., R.D.
Sports Nutritionist
Weight Cycling Project
University of Pennsylvania
School of Medicine
Philadelphia, PA

William E. Strauss, M.D.
Director, Heart Station
Brockton-West Roxbury V.A. Medical Center
West Roxbury, MA

H. Robert Superko, M.D.
Stanford Center for Research in Disease
Prevention
Clinical Assistant Professor of Medicine
Stanford University School of Medicine
Stanford, CA

C. Barr Taylor, M.D.
Associate Professor of Psychiatry
Department of Psychiatry and Behavioral
Medicine
Stanford University School of Medicine
Stanford, CA

Paul D. Thompson, M.D.
Associate Professor of Medicine
Brown University Program in Medicine
The Miriam Hospital
Providence, RI

Steven P. Van Camp, M.D.
Professor, College of Professional Studies
San Diego State University
Alvarado Medical Group, Inc.
Internal Medicine
San Diego, CA

James A. Vogel, Ph.D.
Director, Exercise Physiology Division
U.S. Army Research Institute of
Environmental Medicine
Natick, MA

Linda D. Zwiren, Ed.D.
Associate Professor Health, Physical
Education, and Recreation
Departments of HPER and Biology
Hofstra University
Hempstead, NY

CONTENTS

SECTION I. APPLIED ANATOMY

Russell R. Pate, Section Editor

SECTION II. EXERCISE PHYSIOLOGY

Russell R. Pate, Section Editor

SECTION III. PATHOPHYSIOLOGY

Steven N. Blair, Section Editor

SECTION IV. HEALTH APPRAISAL AND EXERCISE TESTING

L. Kent Smith, Section Editor

SECTION V. EXERCISE PROGRAMMING

Patricia Painter, Section Editor

SECTION VI. SAFETY, INJURIES, AND EMERGENCY PROCEDURES

Steven N. Blair, Section Editor

SECTION VII. HUMAN DEVELOPMENT AND AGING

C. Barr Taylor, Section Editor

SECTION VIII. HUMAN BEHAVIOR/PSYCHOLOGY

C. Barr Taylor, Section Editor

SECTION IX. ADMINISTRATIVE CONCERNS

Patricia Painter, Section Editor

I

APPLIED ANATOMY

CHAPTER 1

SURFACE ANATOMY FOR EXERCISE PROGRAMMING

TOMMY BOONE

ANATOMIC SITES FOR THE LIMB AND CHEST LEADS

Impulse formation and conduction throughout the heart produce electric currents, which are conveyed through tissues to the surface of the skin by salts dissolved in the body fluids.[1] The electrocardiogram (ECG) is a graphic record of the electric currents of the heart and the heart rate. The usefulness of the ECG depends on a knowledge of the anatomic landmarks and the various ECG lead configurations. The most common exercise ECG recording system is the modified 10-electrode combination that permits recording of the 12-lead ECG.[2] Of six frontal plane (limb) leads in the 12-lead ECG, three are bipolar (I, II, and III) and three are unipolar (aVR, aVL, and aVF). The remaining six leads are unipolar precordial (chest) leads (V_{1-6}). The frontal plane is represented by the anterior surface of the thorax. The precordial leads form a roughly horizontal plane through the thorax and perpendicular to the frontal plane.

Bipolar leads represent a difference of electric potential between two sites, whereas unipolar leads measure the electric potential at a specific site. Electrodes may be placed in a standard or modified placement. Standard placement is most appropriate for recording resting ECGs in the supine patient before exercise testing. Because standard conditions exist, this ECG is a point of comparison for all other preceding and succeeding standard ECGs obtained in this or any other setting. Modified electrode placement is most appropriate in the exercise setting because the focus is on obtaining a quality ECG tracing during exercise and not on standardizing the ECG across different laboratories and different times.

The axis of lead I extends from the right shoulder (RA), which is the negative electrode, to the left shoulder (LA), which is the positive electrode. Electrode I is positioned in the right infraclavicular fossa. This anatomic site is located on the upper right aspect of the chest-shoulder region just below the distal end of the right clavicle. Anatomically, the location is described as the anterior surface of the thorax between the superior margin of the right fan-shaped pectoralis major muscle and the medial border of the right anterior deltoid muscle. The axis of lead II extends from the right shoulder, which is the negative electrode, to the left leg (LL), which is the positive electrode. The positive electrode of lead II is positioned on the lower left anterolateral surface of the external oblique muscle. This site is typically addressed as just above the iliac crest at the level of the navel on the anterior surface of the abdomen in the outer one third of a line running from the navel to the anterior superior iliac crest. The placement of the right leg (RL) electrode, which is the ground electrode, is consistent with the procedures outlined for the LL electrode except that it is placed on the anterolateral surface of the right external oblique muscle. The axis of lead III is the difference of potential between the LL and the LA electrodes. The negative electrode is on the LA and the positive electrode is on the LL. The negative electrode of lead III is placed in the left infraclavicular fossa, which is located on the upper left aspect of the chest-shoulder region just inferior to the distal end of the left clavicle (Fig. 1–1). Anatomically, this site is located on the anterior surface of the thorax between the superior border of the left

pectoralis major muscle and the medial border of the left anterior deltoid.

The three unipolar limb leads are aVR, aVL, and aVF. The "a" and "V" indicate augmented and increased vector, respectively. The "R," "L," and "F" indicate the location of the positive electrode — R indicates the RA position, L indicates the LA position, and F denotes the LL position.[3] The anatomic landmarks for the three augmented unipolar limb electrodes are the same as the electrode positions for the three bipolar standard leads.

Although the precordial ("V") electrodes are positioned predominantly on the left side of the anterior chest wall, the precordial electrode site for V_1 is the fourth intercostal space just to the right border of the sternum.[4] The fourth intercostal space (space between the fourth and fifth

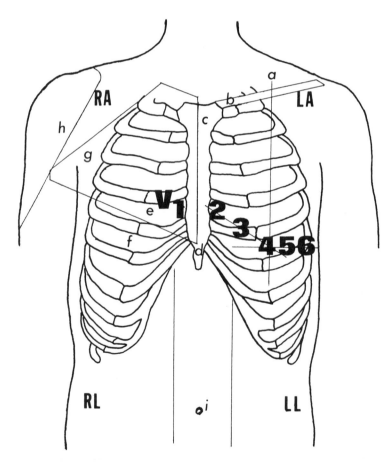

FIGURE 1–1. Anatomic sites for limb and chest electrodes. Note location of midclavicular line (a), clavicle (b), sternum (c), xiphoid process (d), fourth intercostal space (e), fifth intercostal space (f), line drawing for pectoralis major muscle (g), approximate position of anterior deltoid muscle (h), and umbilicus (i). RA, right arm; LA, left arm; RL, right leg; LL, left leg.

ribs) is identified by locating the proximal end of the clavicle and sliding the fingers caudad along the side of the sternum. V_2 is also positioned in the fourth intercostal space, but to the left side of the sternal border. V_4 is located in the fifth intercostal space at about the midpoint of the clavicle. Electrode placement for V_3 is equidistant (midway) between V_2 and V_4. The electrode site for V_5 is lateral to and at the same level as V_4 in the anterior axillary line. V_6 is lateral to and at the same level as V_5 in the midaxillary line.[5] Note that V_4, V_5, and V_6 are on the same level and do *not* curve upward to follow the fifth intercostal space.

In some instances, particularly in obese individuals with large breasts and when testing women with large breasts, moving a precordial lead to another position may be necessary, such as positioning V_4 or V_5 in the sixth intercostal space. In female subjects, the wearing of an undergarment to support the breasts during exercise might help to reduce motion artifacts leading to extremely poor quality ECG recordings.

Proper preparation of the anatomic skin-electrode sites is especially important. The overall quality of the site for electrode placement is improved first by shaving hair, if necessary, and second by removing the superficial layer of the skin. The oil should be removed with a fat solvent such as isopropyl alcohol and acetone. The electrode sites should then be abraded with fine-grain emery paper, dental burr, gauze, or other appropriate material. The end result is a further reduction in skin resistance and excellent electrode contact with body fluids.[6,7]

Excessive motion artifacts resulting from movement of the chest electrode during exercise can be minimized or even avoided in individuals with oily skin or who sweat excessively by using an additional adhesive (such as tincture of bezoin) to increase the stickiness of the electrodes.

ANATOMIC SITES FOR MEASUREMENT OF BLOOD PRESSURE

A stethoscope and a sphygmomanometer are used in the indirect measurement of systemic arterial blood pressure, which is that force exerted by the blood against the walls of blood vessels. A sphygmomanometer consists of an inflatable cuff connected by rubber tubes to a manometer (either mercury or anaeroid) and a rubber bulb to regulate air during inflation and deflation of the cuff (Fig. 1–2).

The deflated cuff is wrapped snugly around the arm. The lower margin of the cuff should be 2.5 cm above the antecubital fossa.[8] The boundaries of the fossa can be seen and felt. The pronator teres muscle (arising from the medial epicondyle of the humerus) forms the medial boundary and the brachioradialis muscle (arising from the lateral supracondylar ridge of the humerus) forms the lateral boundary. The tendon of the biceps brachii muscle, which inserts on the radial tuberosity of the radius, can

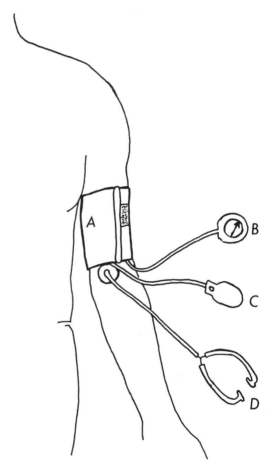

FIGURE 1–2. Anatomic site for measurement of blood pressure. Sphygmomanometer consists of inflatable cuff (A) connected by rubber tubes to manometer (B) and rubber bulb (C) to regulate air during measurement of blood pressure by a stethoscope (D).

be palpated as it passes downward into the fossa. The bicipital aponeurosis can be felt as it leaves the tendon to join the deep fascia on the medial side of the forearm.

After the cuff is in place, the brachial artery is located about 1 cm below the elbow joint beneath the bicipital aponeurosis. Given the variation in the point of origin of the radial and ulnar divisions from the brachial artery, locating the brachial artery may require first palpating its pulse in the antecubital fossa. The diaphragm of the stethoscope is then applied firmly over the artery during cuff inflation.[9]

To obtain accurate blood pressure measurements, the cuff must fit the limb properly. Cuffs that are too narrow result in a reading that is incorrectly high. If the cuff is too wide, a falsely low reading is obtained. The selection of the proper size of blood pressure cuff must be based on limb circumference. Normal-sized adults generally use a cuff of 12 to 14 cm in width and 30 cm in length.

ANATOMIC SITES IN DETERMINING THE PERIPHERAL PULSES

The purpose of the flow of blood from the left ventricle to the body is to carry oxygen and nutrients to body tissues and to remove carbon dioxide and other wastes from the tissues. The aorta emerges from the left ventricle as the main trunk of the systemic circulation (Fig. 1–3). Near its origin (i.e., the ascending aorta), it gives rise to the right and left coronary arteries, which supply the heart muscle. The arch of the aorta follows the ascending aorta and gives rise to the brachiocephalic, the left common carotid, and the left subclavian arteries.[10] The brachiocephalic artery is the first branch off the aortic arch. This major artery divides to form the right common carotid artery, which ascends to supply the neck and head, and the right subclavian artery, which passes laterally into the axilla (armpit) and downward into the arm, forearm, and hand.

The common carotid arteries on both sides of the neck have similar anatomic landmarks. Both arteries bifurcate into the internal and external carotid arteries at the level of the upper border of the thyroid cartilage, which is located in the anterior triangle of the neck. This triangle is bounded by the body of the mandible, the sternocleidomastoid muscle, and the midline. The carotid arterial pulses are palpated bilater-ally by pressing inward and backward along the anterior border of the sternocleidomastoid muscle at the level of the thyroid cartilage.[11] The carotid pulses are palpated singly to avoid excessive carotid sinus massage. In this regard, even though the carotid arteries are the best arteries in which to assess exercise heart rate, recent data suggest pressure on one carotid sinus resulted in increased parasympathetic activity and thus a lowered heart rate.[12] As might be expected, the determination of heart rate from post-exercise carotid palpation may misrepresent the actual (exercise) heart rate.

The subclavian artery is an excellent example of how the same vessel is given different names as it passes through different regions of the body.[13] Continuation of the right subclavian branch from the brachiocephalic trunk laterally behind the clavicle gives rise to the name subclavian artery. The pulsation of this artery can often be felt on pressure downwards, posteriorly, and medially behind the midpoint of the clavicle as the artery is pressed against the first rib.[14] The subclavian artery continues into the axilla, where it becomes the axillary artery. This artery extends from the outer border of the first rib to the lower border of the teres major muscle. The vessel then continues into the brachium (i.e., arm) as the brachial artery. Although its pulsation can often be felt along its length on the medial side of the biceps brachii muscle, a more direct and reliable site is directly medial to the biceps brachii tendon. The brachial artery ends in the antecubital fossa by dividing to form the radial and ulnar arteries, which pass toward the wrist (one on each side).

The radial artery descends on the lateral (thumb) side of the forearm to become quite superficial at the distal or lower end of the radius. It is at this point that the pulse is usually taken by gently compressing the artery against the anterior surface of the distal end of the radius. The pulse (i.e., the pressure wave that expands the arterial walls) is felt in the radial artery at the wrist about 0.1 second after the peak of systolic ejection into the aorta.[15] Although the ulnar artery is the larger terminal branch of the brachial artery, it is not palpated easily because its downward and medial descent into the forearm is deep to the mass of the superficial flexor muscles arising from the medial epicondyle of the humerus.[16] With practice, the ulnar pulse is palpable proximal to the pisiform (wrist) bone on the medial side of the wrist.[17]

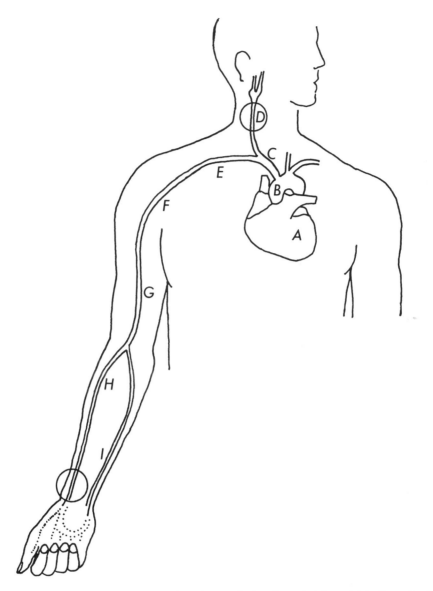

FIGURE 1–3. Anatomic sites in determining neck and upper limb pulses. A, left ventricle, B, aorta, C, brachiocephalic trunk, D, common carotid artery, E, right subclavian artery, F, axillary artery, G, brachial artery, H, radial artery, I, ulnar artery. *Upper circle,* anatomic site for right common carotid palpation for determining heart rate. *Lower circle,* anatomic site for palpation of radial artery.

All systemic arteries derive from the aorta. Thus, the descending aorta is a logical extension of the aorta from which blood and oxygen are made available to the thoracic, abdominal, and lower regions of the body. Dilatations of the aorta (aneurysms) or the abdominal part of the aorta usually result from atherosclerosis and occur most often in elderly men. Arteriosclerosis obliterans is a slow, progressive occlusion of the bifurcation of the abdominal aorta and/or

its terminal branches (i.e., within the lower limbs) resulting in the characteristic clinical symptoms of pain in the legs during exercise. This type of ischemic pain induced by exercise but relieved with rest is intermittent claudication.

Although less information concerning cardiac function is revealed from assessment of the peripheral pulses than that of the carotid (central) pulse, the information is valuable, particularly with respect to peripheral perfusion. In the cardiac subject, palpation of the dorsalis pedis and posterior tibial pulses must be gentle to avoid further marked reduction in arterial flow. In that the pulses may be difficult to palpate or are congenitally absent, bilateral comparison is frequently necessary.

The inguinal ligament is attached laterally to the anterior superior iliac spine and medially to the symphysis pubis. The femoral artery enters the anterior thigh posterior to the inguinal ligament approximately midway between the anterior superior iliac spine (i.e., the uppermost and largest anatomic landmark of the ilium) and the symphysis pubis. This location is the point at which the femoral artery is readily palpated,

because it can be pressed posteriorly against the pectineus muscle and the superior ramus of the pubic bone (Fig. 1–4). The popliteal artery lies deep within the posterior aspect of the knee (i.e., the popliteal fossa). The knee should be flexed to relax the deep fascia and related muscle. Then, the pulse may be determined as the fingertips press deeply into the popliteal fossa. To locate the posterior tibial artery, the fingers should be placed about halfway between the medial malleolus and the medial aspect of the tendo calcaneus. The artery is palpated by positioning the fingers between the tendons of the flexor hallucis longus and flexor digitorum longus muscles. With the foot in dorsiflexion to obviate tension on the artery, the pulsations of the dorsalis pedis artery can be felt between the tendons of the extensor hallucis longus and extensor digitorum longus muscles. Although this artery is typically located on the dorsum (front) of the foot between the two malleoli, clinically insignificant congenital variation in the arteries to the foot may result in only one pedal pulse or no dorsal pedal pulses.[18–20]

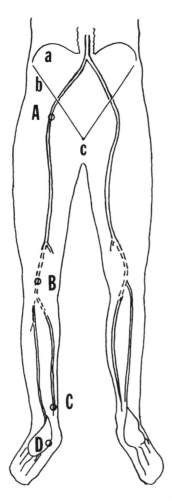

FIGURE 1–4. Anatomic sites for palpating peripheral arteries of lower limb. a, ilium, b, inguinal ligament, c, symphsis pubis, A, femoral pulse, B, popliteal pulse posterior to knee, C, posterior tibial pulse, D, dorsalis pedis pulse.

ANATOMIC SITES FOR SELECTED ANTHROPOMETRY

Basic human anthropometry includes standing height, body weight, girths, widths, and skinfolds. These measurements can be used to estimate percentage of body fat and the general external morphologic structure of the body.[21]

The standing height measurement should be measured from the top of the head to the bottom of the feet (no shoes). Duplicate measurements should be made to the nearest 0.2 cm. Body weight should be ascertained to the nearest 0.5 kg. All body girths should be measured in the standing position to the nearest 0.5 cm. The measurement for left- and right-arm circumferences should be taken at the midpoint of the biceps brachii muscle with the individual in the anatomic reference position (i.e., with the arms hanging to the sides of the body). Measure the girth of the chest (no shirt) at nipple level at the end of a normal expiration. The abdomen should be measured at the level of the umbilicus. The buttock measurement should be made at the protrusion of the gluteals and at the level of the symphysis pubis. Measure both thighs (unclothed) just inferior to the gluteal furrow at the maximal thigh circumference (Fig. 1–5). Either a nonstretch measuring tape or the Gulick

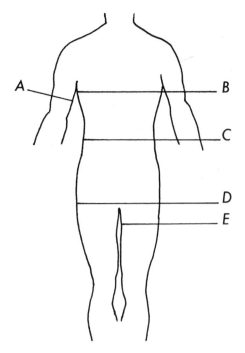

FIGURE 1-5. Anatomic sites for circumferences. A, left and right arm, B, chest at nipple level, C, abdomen at level of umbilicus, D, buttocks at protrusion of gluteals, E, left and right thigh just below gluteal furrow.

measuring tape is appropriate for body dimension measurements. Shoulder and hip widths should be measured to the nearest 0.5 cm by using a sliding meter-stick caliper. Shoulder width should be ascertained by measuring the distance between the two acromial processes. The distance between the iliac crests is the hip width (Fig. 1-6).

Anatomic landmarks for eight skinfold sites are considered: anterior chest, midaxilla, waist, suprailiac, anterior abdomen (umbilicus), anterior thigh, triceps, and scapula (Figs. 1-7 and 1-8). Note that all measurements are taken on the right side of the body with the subject standing. The anatomic landmark for the anterior chest skinfold is midway between the nipple and the acromial process. The skin should be lifted away from the underlying pectoralis major muscle such that the skinfold approxi-

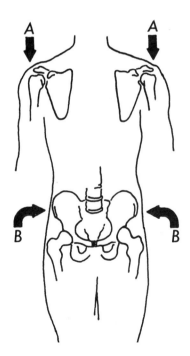

FIGURE 1-6. Anatomic sites for measurement of shoulder (A) and hip (B) widths when using sliding meter-stick caliper.

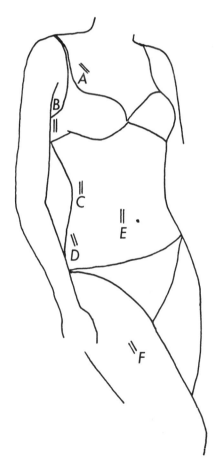

FIGURE 1-7. Anatomic landmarks for skinfold sites. A, anterior chest, B, midaxilla, C, waist, D, suprailiac, E, anterior abdomen (umbilicus), F, anterior thigh. *Parallel lines,* orientation of folds.

mates an angle of 45° from the xiphoid process (Fig. 1–7). Measure the midaxillary site by grasping a vertical fold on the midaxillary line at about the level of the fifth rib. A vertical fold should be taken at the waist site, which is located on the lateral side of the waist at the level at which the ribs can be felt at their lowest point. The suprailiac skinfold site is located about 3 cm above the anterior superior iliac crest. The fold runs either parallel to the sternum or about 45° to the pubic bone. The anterior abdominal or umbilical skinfold site runs vertically about 5 cm lateral to and just inferior to the umbilicus. The umbilical crease should be avoided.[22] The anterior thigh skinfold site is located on the anterior surface of the unclothed thigh midway between the hip joint and the knee joint (subject is standing). The fold runs parallel (vertical) to the long axis of the thigh. The triceps skinfold site is located posteriorly midway between the acromion and the olecranon. While the arm hangs relaxed, grasp the site vertically (Fig. 1–8). The scapula skinfold site is measured about 1 cm inferior to the inferior angle of the scapula. Lift the skinfold so that its crease follows the natural fold of the skin.[23,24]

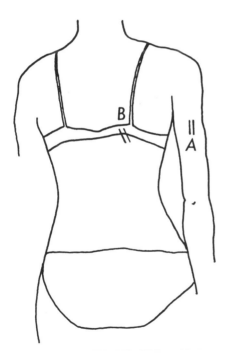

FIGURE 1–8. Anatomic landmarks for skinfold sites. A, triceps, B, scapula. *Parallel lines*, orientation of folds.

ANATOMIC SITES USED DURING CARDIOPULMONARY RESUSCITATION AND EMERGENCY PROCEDURES

Cardiopulmonary resuscitation (CPR) is the application of artificial ventilation and external cardiac compression to the individual in cardiopulmonary arrest. Establishing and maintaining an airway are the first steps in treatment. Because the tongue is the most common cause of airway obstruction, either the head-tilt method (i.e., tilting the head back) or the chin-lift method (lifting the jaw forward) helps to ensure adequate ventilation. In individuals with a neck (cervical spine) injury, the head-tilt method should not be used. Instead, the mandible should be displaced forward without moving the head. To clear a completely obstructed airway, when the individual is standing or sitting, place the thumb side of your fist on the subject's sternum. Be sure not to place the hand on the xiphoid process (i.e., the most inferior part of the sternum) or the costal cartilages of the rib cage. Then, from a position behind the individual, grasp your fist and deliver four quick compressions and then four sharp blows to the back to produce the necessary increase in pressure in the respiratory passages to dislodge the foreign body.

Artificial ventilation must begin immediately if the individual does not begin to breathe spontaneously. Pinch the nostrils with the thumb and index finger of one hand with the other hand placed under the neck to maintain the backward tilt of the head. With the establishment of effective ventilation of the lungs, determination of systemic circulation is required. The person is pulseless if cardiac arrest occurs. The carotid or femoral arteries are sufficiently large and of central position to determine if a pulse exists. Palpating, for example, the radial artery or the dorsalis pedis artery often results in error because of their distal sites.[25] The precordial thump should be used if the cardiac arrest is witnessed (i.e., within 1 min of the arrest). The technique dictates use of a sharp blow with the fist to the midsternum from 20 to 30 cm. Otherwise, external cardiac compressions over the inferior one half of the sternum should be initiated. The rhythmic applications of pressure compresses the ventricles between the sternum and the vertebral column (Fig. 1–9). Although artificial circulation is about 35% as efficient as normal carotid circulation, blood flow to the

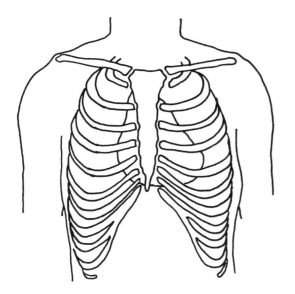

FIGURE 1–9. Bony thorax (ribs and sternum) in relation to heart.

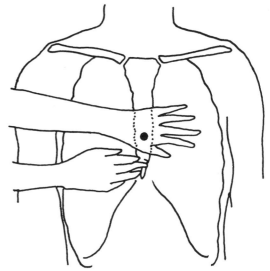

FIGURE 1–10. Placement of hands to locate correct hand position for external cardiac compression.

head does occur given the pressure gradient between the carotid artery and the compressible jugular vein.[22-27] Cardiac compression performed correctly results in an arterial blood pressure of over 100 mm Hg during the 80 to 120 lb of pressure over the sternum.

The anatomy of external cardiac compression is best understood when the heart is viewed in relation to the sternum, the costal cartilages, and the xiphoid process. The heart is located between two bony masses, the sternum anteriorly and the vertebral column posteriorly. Because the sternum can usually be depressed posteriorly about 5 cm, the movement results in blood ejected from the ventricles into the pulmonary artery and the aorta. Thus, cardiac compressions of the inferior one half of the sternum about 2.5 cm superior to the xiphoid process result in blood flow to the myocardium (by way of the coronary arteries) and the brain (by way of the vessels to the neck).[28] Note that the exact location of the sternum is important in that the xiphoid process overlies the liver. Compression of that organ increases the risk of perforating the liver, with resultant intra-abdominal bleeding.[29]

The xiphoid process should be palpated with the index and middle fingers to locate its junction with the sternum, which is usually 2.5 to 3.75 cm superior to the tip of the xiphoid process. Often, a necessary first step is to palpate the margin of the rib cage to the midline of the

body. The heel of the other hand is then placed next to the fingers overlying the xiphisternal junction. The hand used to palpate the anatomic landmarks is then placed over the hand on the sternum (Fig. 1–10). The cardiac compressions should be regular and smooth. The sternum should be allowed to assume its original position after compression to ensure filling of the ventricles.[30,31]

REFERENCES

1. Previte JJ: *Human Physiology.* New York: McGraw-Hill, 1983.
2. Hanson P: Clinical exercise testing. In *Sports Medicine.* Edited by RH Strauss. Philadelphia: W.B. Saunders, 1984.
3. Conover MH, Zalis EG: *Understanding Electrocardiography: Physiological and Interpretive Concepts.* 2nd Ed. St. Louis: C.V. Mosby, 1976.
4. Woods SL: Electrocardiography, vectorcardiography, and polarcardiography. In *Cardiac Nursing.* Edited by SL Underhill, SL Woods, ES Sivarajan, and CJ Halpenny. Philadelphia: J.B. Lippincott, 1982.
5. Adamovich DR: *The Heart.* New York: Sports Medicine Books, 1984.
6. Ellestad MH: *Stress Testing: Principles and Practice.* Philadelphia: F.A. Davis, 1986.
7. Froelicher VF: *Exercise Testing and Training.* Chicago: Year Book, 1983.
8. Underhill SL: History-taking and physical examination of the patient with cardiovascular disease. In *Cardiac Nursing.* Edited by SL Underhill, SL Woods, ES Sivara-

jan, and CJ Halpenny. Philadelphia: J.B. Lippincott, 1982.

9. Malasanos L, Barkauskas V, Moss M, Stoltenberg-Allen K: *Health Assessment*. St. Louis: C.V. Mosby, 1977.

10. Hamilton WJ: *Textbook of Human Anatomy*. 2nd Ed. St. Louis: C.V. Mosby, 1976.

11. Snell RS: *Atlas of Clinical Anatomy*. Boston: Little, Brown and Co., 1978.

12. Boone T, Frentz KL, Boyd NR: Carotid palpation at two exercise intensities. *Med Sci Sports Exerc*, 17:705, 1985.

13. Tortora GJ, Anagnostakos NP: *Principles of Anatomy and Physiology*. 3rd Ed. New York: Harper & Row, 1981.

14. Spence AP: *Basic Human Anatomy*. Reading, MA: The Benjamin/Cummings Publishing Co., 1982.

15. Ganong WF: *Review of Medical Physiology*. 11th Ed. Los Altos, CA: Lange, 1983.

16. Silverstein A: *Human Anatomy and Physiology*. New York: John Wiley & Sons, 1980.

17. Hoppenfeld S: *Physical Examination of the Spine and Extremities*. New York: Appleton-Century-Crofts, 1976.

18. Snell RS: *Atlas of Clinical Anatomy*. Boston: Little, Brown and Co., 1978.

19. Craven RF: Disorders of the peripheral vascular system. In *Cardiac Nursing*. Edited by SL Underhill, SL Woods, ES Sivarajan, and CJ Halpenny. Philadelphia: J.B. Lippincott, 1982.

20. Malasanos L, Barkauskas V, Moss M, Stoltenberg-Allen K: *Health Assessment*. St. Louis, C.V. Mosby, 1977.

21. Reid JG, Thomson JM: *Exercise Prescription for Fitness*. Englewood Cliffs, NJ: Prentice-Hall, 1985.

22. Roy S, Irvin R: *Sports Medicine: Prevention, Evaluation, Management, and Rehabilitation*. Englewood Cliffs, NJ: Prentice-Hall, 1983.

23. Wilmore JH: *Training for Sport and Activity: The Physiological Basis of the Conditioning Process*. 2nd Ed. Boston: Allyn and Bacon, 1982.

24. McArdle WD, Katch FI, Katch VL: *Exercise Physiology*. 2nd Ed. Philadelphia: Lea & Febiger, 1986.

25. Mustalish AC, Quash ET: Sports injuries to the chest and abdomen. In *Principles of Sports Medicine*. Edited by WN Scott, B Nisonson, and JA Nicholas. Baltimore: Williams & Wilkins, 1984.

26. Huszar RJ: *Emergency Cardiac Care*. Bowie, MD: Robert J. Brady Company, 1974.

27. Luce JM, et al.: New developments in cardiopulmonary resuscitation. *JAMA*, 244:1366, 1980.

28. American Heart Association Subcommittee on Emergency Cardiac Care: Standards for Cardiopulmonary Resuscitation (CRP) and Emergency Cardiac Care (ECC). *JAMA*, 227(Suppl):833, 1974.

29. National Committee for Emergency Coronary Care: Cardiopulmonary Resuscitation: Basic Life Support. *Clin Symp*, 26:17, 1974.

30. American Heart Association: Standards and Guidelines for Cardiopulmonary Resuscitation (CRP) and Emergency Cardiac Care (ECC). *JAMA, 244*:453, 1980.

31. American Heart Association: *Textbook of Advanced Cardiac Life Support*. Dallas: American Heart Association, 1982.

CHAPTER 2

FUNDAMENTALS OF CARDIORESPIRATORY ANATOMY

JOE V. CHANDLER AND
JERALD D. HAWKINS

CARDIOVASCULAR ANATOMY

The cardiovascular system consists of the heart, blood vessels, and blood. The heart, a muscular pump, forces blood through vessels called arteries to the capillaries, which are tiny vessels that collectively constitute the "functional level" of the system. The capillaries coalesce to form veins that are conduits for the transport of blood back to the heart. This section is primarily a description of the anatomy of the central organ in the cardiovascular system, the heart.

THE HEART

Figure 2–1 shows the structures that are visible on the anterior aspect of the surface of the heart. The heart is a four-chambered, conical muscular organ that is situated in the thoracic cavity such that approximately two thirds of its mass is located to the left of the midline. Much of the heart lies posterior to the sternum in a space known as the mediastinum. Its apex rests on the diaphragm at the level of the fifth intercostal space.

Although the heart is a single organ, the left and right sides of the heart can be viewed as two separate pumps. The right heart receives blood from the veins of the body and pumps it to the pulmonary circulation. The left heart receives blood from the lungs and pumps it into the systemic circulation. Under resting conditions, the entire blood volume (approximately 5 L) circulates each minute. This tremendous workload is accomplished by an organ about the size of the human fist, approximately 12 cm in length, 9 cm in width, 6 cm in depth, and weighing approximately 310 g.[1]

Tissue Layers of the Heart

The heart is composed of three specific tissue layers: the outer epicardium, the middle myocardium, and the inner endocardium. It is surrounded by a loose-fitting nonextensible sac called the pericardium. The epicardium, also referred to as the visceral pericardium, is a thin transparent membrane adhering to the outer surface of the heart. Between the pericardium and the epicardium is the pericardial space containing pericardial fluid. This fluid lubricates the surface of the heart, reducing friction during the heart's contractions. The myocardium is the contractile tissue of the heart and accounts for 75% of the heart's mass.[2] The endocardium lines the inner surface of the heart chambers and forms the valves of the heart.

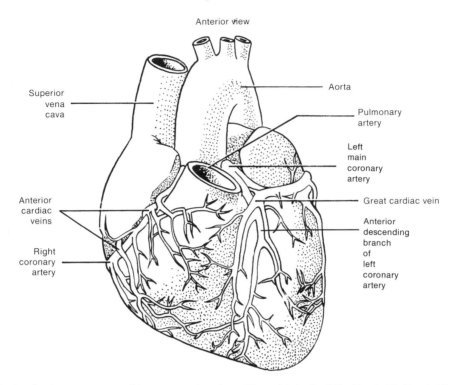

FIGURE 2-1. Surface anatomy of heart, anterior view. (From McArdle WD, Katch FI, Katch VL: *Exercise Physiology: Energy, Nutrition, and Human Performance.* 2nd Ed. Philadelphia: Lea & Febiger, 1986.)

Internal Structure of the Heart

Figure 2-2 presents the internal structure of the heart, demonstrating its four chambers. The two smaller superior chambers are the atria and the two larger inferior chambers are the ventricles. The major structural components of the heart are attached to an internal framework called the fibrous skeleton. This framework consists of four rings of dense connective tissue that enclose the openings between the atria and ventricles and also the openings between the ventricles and great arteries (aorta and pulmonary artery).[3] The heart is divided into left and right units by a septum. As compared with the atria, the ventricles have a considerably thicker layer of myocardial tissue that is needed to overcome the greater resistance against which the ventricles contract. For the same reason, the walls of the left ventricle are noticeably thicker than those of the right ventricle.

Four valves control the movement of blood through the heart. The two atrioventricular (AV) valves regulate flow between the atria and the ventricles. The tricuspid valve is located on the right side and the mitral (bicuspid) valve is

on the left side. The AV valves consist of triangular flaps, or cusps, that are attached superiorly to the fibrous skeleton and inferiorly to the papillary muscles by the chordae tendineae. These valves prevent the backflow of blood into the atria when the ventricles contract, but allow blood to pass freely from the atria to the ventricles during diastole. The major difference between the tricuspid valve and the mitral valve is the number of closure complexes (flap, chordae tendineae, and papillary muscle). The tricuspid valve has three and the mitral valve has only two such complexes.

The two semilunar valves control blood flow between the ventricles and the great arteries. They prevent backflow of blood from the arteries into the ventricles during diastole, but allow blood to flow into the arteries during systole. The pulmonary valve regulates blood flow between the right ventricle and the pulmonary artery, and the aortic valve regulates flow between the left ventricle and the aorta. The semilunar valves have no system of muscles and tendons; their closing apparatus consists of three half-moon cusps. During systole, the cusps are forced against the arterial walls, which allows movement of blood out of the heart. During diastole, blood fills the spaces between the cusps and the arterial wall, collapsing the cusps across the arterial lumen and preventing backflow. The pattern of blood flow is depicted in Figure 2–2.

Although the chambers of the heart are filled with blood, only the endocardium is directly nourished by that blood. Myocardial tissue is supplied by blood that flows through the coronary arteries (see Fig. 2–2). The two major coronary arteries are the left and right main coronary arteries, which branch extensively to supply the various cardiac tissues. The two main coronary arteries are the first vessels to branch from the aorta. The openings for the main coronary arteries are positioned immediately superior to the aortic fibrous skeleton, and therefore lie posterior to the cusps of the aortic valve. Consequently, blood cannot enter the coronary circulation during systole as the cusps of the aortic valve obstruct the entrance. Hence, the myocardium is perfused during the resting phase of the cardiac cycle (diastole).

Conduction System

The conduction system of the heart is responsible for initiating an action potential (electric

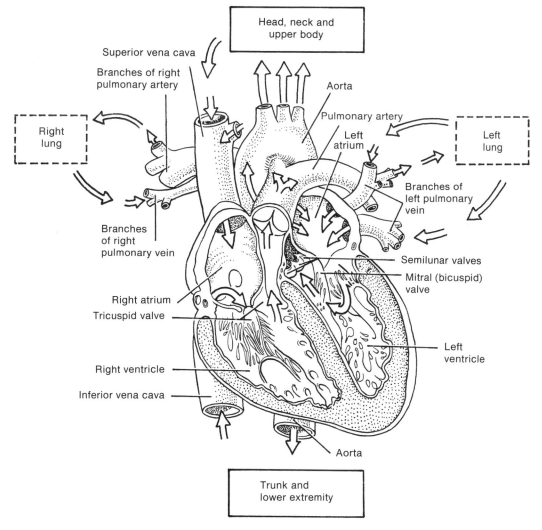

FIGURE 2–2. Internal structure of heart. *Arrows,* direction of blood flow. (From McArdle WD, Katch FI, Katch VL: *Exercise Physiology: Energy, Nutrition, and Human Performance.* 2nd Ed. Philadelphia: Lea & Febiger, 1986.)

depolarization leading to contraction) and transporting it throughout the myocardium. The heart is said to be "autorhythmic," indicating that its tissues tend to depolarize spontaneously at a regular rate.[4] The heart's conduction system is composed of specialized cardiac cells that are capable of only weak contraction, but are well adapted for spontaneous excitation and rapid conduction of impulses.[3] In addition, the myocardial fibers are interwoven, and at junctions between fibers, specialized structures called intercalated discs facilitate the rapid fiber-to-fiber passage of electric activity through the muscle tissue.

Figure 2–3 depicts the normal pathways for movement of electric impulses through the heart. The heart's conduction system consists of the sinoatrial node (S-A node), the atrioventricular node (A-V node), the bundle of His, bundle branches, and Purkinje fibers. The S-A node is located in the posterior wall of the right atrium near the opening of the superior vena cava. The S-A node depolarizes spontaneously and rhythmically and, because it tends to do so more rapidly than other tissues in the heart, it dictates the frequency of the contractions of the heart. Consequently, the S-A node is often labeled the pacemaker of the heart. During normal sinus rhythm, the resting heart rate ranges from 60 to 90 beats/min. The wave of depolarization initiated in the S-A node quickly traverses the two atria, resulting in atrial contraction. The fibrous skeleton and septum consist of nonconductive tissue, and the electric stimuli associated with atrial contraction therefore, do not pass directly into the ventricular tissues. Instead, the impulse is picked up by the A-V node,

which delays the impulse before transferring it to the bundle of His in the ventricular septum. The bundle of His carries the stimuli to the left and right bundle branches. The bundle branches are the major electric pathways for their respective ventricles and ultimately deliver the impulse to the Purkinje fibers. The Purkinje fibers constitute an extensive conductive network within the ventricular tissues and transmit impulses at a velocity approximately six times greater than that found in normal cardiac tissue.[4] The result is the rapid stimulation of the ventricular tissues and a coordinated, powerful contraction of the two ventricles.

RESPIRATORY ANATOMY

The major structures of the respiratory system include the nasal passages, pharynx, larynx, trachea, bronchi, and lungs (Fig. 2–4). The function of the respiratory system is to exchange air between the atmosphere and the alveoli of the lungs. This exchange facilitates oxygenation of and carbon dioxide removal from blood circulating through the lungs.

NASAL PASSAGES

The nasal passages are the primary entry site for air into the respiratory system. The mucous

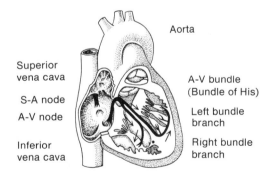

FIGURE 2–3. Excitation and conduction system of heart. (From McArdle, WD, Katch, FI, Katch, VL: *Exercise Physiology: Energy, Nutrition, and Human Performance.* 2nd Ed. Philadelphia: Lea & Febiger, 1986.)

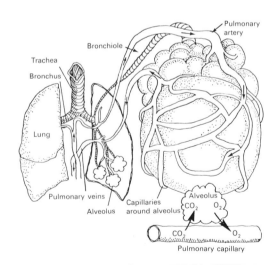

FIGURE 2–4. Pulmonary system. (From McArdle WD, Katch FI, Katch KL: *Exercise Physiology: Energy, Nutrition, and Human Performance.* 2nd Ed. Philadelphia, Lea & Febiger, 1986.)

membranes and tiny hairs (cilia) that line the nasal cavities help to moisturize and filter inhaled air. Blood flowing through the nasal tissues warms the air before its entry into the deeper respiratory passages.

PHARYNX AND LARYNX

The pharynx or throat cavity is the common pathway through which food enters the digestive tract and air enters the lower respiratory tract. The pharynx is subdivided into three portions. The most superior portion, the nasopharynx, lies posterior to the nasal cavity. The often troublesome tonsils and adenoids are located in this part of the tract. The oropharynx is the middle portion and it lies posterior to the oral cavity and extends to the hyoid bone. The most inferior portion, the laryngopharynx, extends inferiorly to the larynx or voice box. The larynx is a short passageway that connects the pharynx with the trachea. The larynx comprises nine sections of cartilage, the largest being the thyroid cartilage or "Adams apple." The larynx functions primarily in the production of sound by allowing air to pass across its vocal cords. The epiglottis is a leaf-shaped piece of cartilage that blocks the opening to the larynx during swallowing.

TRACHEOBRONCHIAL TREE

The trachea (windpipe) is a tubular passageway for air that extends from the larynx to the level of the fifth thoracic vertebra. It is approximately 12.5 cm in length and 2.5 cm in diameter. Its most prominent features are the 16 to 20 C-shaped cartilage rings that prevent the trachea from collapsing and obstructing the airway. The open section of these rings is composed of smooth muscle and elastic connective tissue. The trachea is lined with pseudostratified, ciliated columnal epithelium, which provides protection against dust and other particles.[5,6] The trachea branches into two primary bronchi, one bronchus serving each lung. The primary bronchi are structurally similar to the trachea, with the right primary bronchus being somewhat shorter, wider, and more vertical than the left primary bronchus.

Upon entry into the lungs, each primary bronchus branches into smaller structures, known as secondary bronchi. Because each sec-ondary bronchus serves a single lung lobe, these bronchi are often called lobar bronchi. This systematic pattern continues, with the secondary bronchi branching into tertiary bronchi, which subdivide into smaller bronchioles, and finally into very small, thin tubules called alveolar ducts.[7]

Like the trachea, the primary bronchi are surrounded by supportive cartilaginous rings. Smooth muscle tissue is the primary structural component of the secondary and tertiary bronchi and the bronchioles.

LUNGS

The most prominent structures in the respiratory system are the lungs. Located in the thoracic cavity, the lungs are a pair of conical organs that extend from the superior surface of the diaphragm (base) to just superior to the clavicles (apex). The lungs are separated by a space called the mediastinum, within which is located the heart and other thoracic structures. The right lung has three distinct lobes. It is wider and thicker than the left lung, which has two lobes. A secondary bronchus in turn serves each lobe.

The lungs are enclosed in two layers of membranous tissue known as pleura. The outer layer or parietal pleura is attached to the pleural cavity and the inner layer or visceral pleura directly overlays the lungs. The two layers are separated by a narrow space filled with a lubricating fluid.

The most intricate of all respiratory structures are the alveolar sacs. The lungs contain approximately 150 million alveoli with a total surface area of approximately 70 to 80 m^2.[6] Alveoli are epithelial structures and, like the capillaries that surround them, their walls are only one cell thick. These thin walls facilitate diffusion of respiratory gases.

Alveoli are clustered into functional units known as lobules, each consisting of 50 to 100 individual air sacs. Each cluster of alveoli are associated with a bronchiole, alveolar duct, capillary bed, and nerve fibers. Collectively, these structures form a pulmonary lobule, the primary functional unit of the lung.[8]

REFERENCES

1. Anthony CP, Thibodeau GA: *Textbook of Anatomy and Physiology.* 11 Ed. St. Louis: C.V. Mosby, 1983.

2. Creager JG: *Human Anatomy and Physiology*. Belmont, CA: Wadsworth, 1983.

3. Weinreb EL: *Anatomy and Physiology*. Reading, MA: Addison-Wesley, 1984.

4. Guyton AG: *Physiology of the Human Body*. 5th Ed. Philadelphia: W.B. Saunders, 1979.

5. Basmajian JV: *Primary Anatomy*. 7th Ed. Baltimore: Williams & Wilkins, 1976.

6. Hole JW, Jr: *Human Anatomy and Physiology*. 2nd Ed. Dubuque: William C. Brown, 1981.

7. Tortora GJ: *Principles of Human Anatomy*. San Francisco: Canfield Press, 1977.

8. Francis CC, Martin AH: *Introduction to Human Anatomy*. 7th Ed. St. Louis: C.V. Mosby, 1975.

3

FUNDAMENTALS OF MUSCULOSKELETAL ANATOMY

DAVID A. KAUFMANN

This discussion centers on the fundamental facts concerning musculoskeletal anatomy — the bones of the human skeleton, the major muscles of the upper and lower limbs, free-moving joints, the properties and functions of bone and muscle tissue, important connective tissue structures, joint movements, and certain musculoskeletal disorders.

OSTEOLOGY IN A NUTSHELL

The normal human skeleton contains 206 bones. Figure 3–1 depicts the human skeleton in anterior and posterior views. Table 3–1 presents the enumeration of the bones of the human skeleton. The skeletal system provides the framework for the body. The bones and their parts are landmarks to students of anatomy and to sports medicine professionals. The lumbar vertebrae and joints are susceptible to injury because they take the brunt of the weight of the trunk and upper extremities during movements. Rib fractures, usually the result of direct blows (steering wheel impact, falls, or crushing injuries) occur less often in ribs 1 and 2 (protected by the clavicle and pectoralis major) and the last two ribs (because they are immo-

bile) than in the middle ribs. Ribs tend to break at the point of greatest curvature. The thorax protects the heart and lung and provides for the movements of inspiration and expiration. The bones of the upper extremities provide the lever system for throwing, striking, catching, and skills of manual dexterity. The bones of the lower extremities provide for the movements of walking, running, jumping, and kicking.

MAJOR MUSCLES

An overview of the major muscles is provided. For a detailed analysis we refer the student to References 2 and 3.

MUSCLES OF THE UPPER LIMB

Muscles whose task it is to secure the scapula are the trapezius, serratus anterior, rhomboids, levator scapulae, and pectoralis minor. The rotator cuff muscles are the subscapularis, supraspinatus, infraspinatus, and teres minor. These muscles collectively hold the head of the humerus in the glenoid fossa of the scapula, preventing shoulder dislocation during vigorous movement. Muscles associated with movement

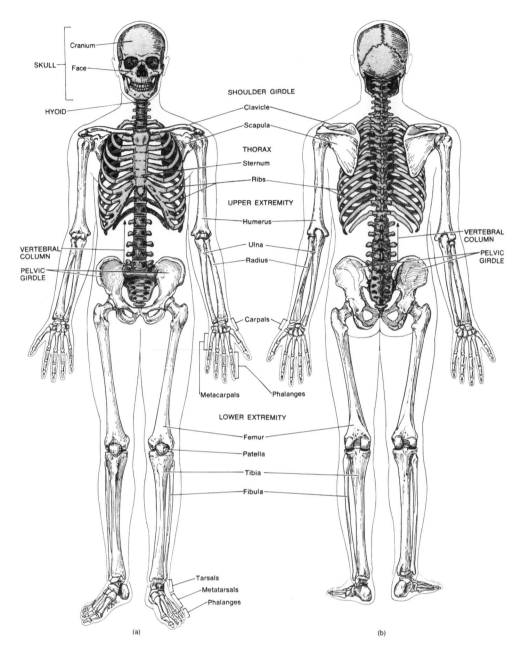

FIGURE 3-1. Divisions of the skeletal system. a, anterior view; b, posterior view. (Courtesy of Tortora GJ: *Principles of Human Anatomy.* 2nd Ed. New York: Harper & Row, 1986.)

of the upper arm are the pectoralis major, deltoid, latissimus dorsi, and teres major. Those involved in moving the forearm are the triceps brachii, biceps brachii, brachialis, brachioradialis, supinator, pronator teres, and pronator quadratus. The functions of the last three muscles are well known.

The flexor carpi radialis, flexor carpi ulnaris, extensor carpi radialis longus and brevis, and extensor carpi ulnaris move the wrist. Extensors occupy the posterior compartment of the forearm; flexors occupy the anterior compartment. The extrinsic muscles associated with movement of the fingers are the flexor digitorum su-

Table 3–1. Bones in the Human Skeleton

Skull:	6 single bones and 8 paired bones (16) **Subtotal: 22**
Vertebral column:	7 cervical (neck) vertebrae 12 thoracic (chest) vertebrae—one for each pair of ribs attached in back 5 lumbar (lower back) vertebrae 1 sacrum and 1 coccyx **Subtotal: 26**
Thorax:	12 pairs of ribs and 1 sternum **Subtotal: 25**
Upper extremity:	2 clavicles (collarbones) 2 scapulae (shoulder blades) 2 humeri (upper arms) 2 radii (lateral forearm) 2 ulnas (medial forearms) 16 carpals (wrist bones) 10 metacarpals (palm bones) 28 phalanges (finger bones) **Subtotal: 64**
Lower extremity:	2 hip bones (fusion of ilium, ischium, and pubis) 2 femurs (thigh bones) 2 patellae (knee caps) 2 tibias (stronger, medial calf bone) 2 fibulas (weaker, lateral calf bone) 14 tarsals (bones of rear foot) 10 metatarsals (bones of forefoot) 28 phalanges (toe bones) **Subtotal: 62**
Miscellaneous:	No ear bones, 1 hyoid (see reference 1) **Subtotal: 7**
TOTAL:	206 bones

perficialis, flexor digitorum profundus, extensor digitorum communis, flexor pollicis longus, extensor pollicis longus and brevis, and abductor pollicis longus. The actions of these muscles are made clear by their names.

MUSCLES OF THE LOWER LIMB

Muscles of the buttocks are the gluteus maximus, gluteus medius, gluteus minimus, tensor fasciae latae, and six lateral rotators. The lateral rotators are analogous to the upper limb rotator cuff. Those muscles of the posterior thigh (hamstrings) are the biceps femoris long and short, semitendinosus, and semimembranosus. The adductor magnus, adductor longus, adductor brevis, pectineus, and gracilis muscles are located in the medial thigh, and the iliopsoas, sartorius, and the quadriceps (rectus femoris, vastus lateralis, vastus medialis, and vastus intermedius) are the muscles of the anterior thigh.

The muscles of the calf are the gastrocnemius and soleus (triceps surae), popliteus, flexor digitorum longus, flexor hallucis longus, and tibialis posterior posteriorly; the peroneus longus and brevis laterally; and the tibialis anterior, extensor digitorum longus, and extensor hallucis longus anteriorly. The intrinsic muscles that move the foot are the muscles of the hallux, those of the digiti minimi, and the flexors and extensors of the toes and interossei (toe abductors and adductors). Important muscles of the trunk are the rectus abdominis, quadratus lumborum, external oblique, internal oblique, transversus abdominis, and the erector spinae (a column of nine muscles on the back).

DIARTHRODIAL (FREE MOVING) JOINTS

The term articulation or joint means a point of contact between bones, between cartilages, or between bones and cartilages. The structure of the joint determines its function. Some joints allow no movement, others some movement, and still others much movement. The extent of movement at joints is determined by the extensibility of the connective tissue that holds the bones together and by the position of ligaments, tendons, and muscles. The six types of diarthrodial joints are listed in Table 3–2.

Table 3–2. Diarthrodial Joints

Type of joint	Structure and movement
Hinge	Elbow and knee. Motion is limited to flexion and extension.
Gliding	Intercarpal joints.
Pivot	Head of radius and humerus. Motion limited to rotation.
Ellipsoidal	Wrist joint (radius and carpals). Circumduction can be accomplished by combinations of flexion, abduction, extension, and adduction.
Saddle	Trapezium and first metacarpal joint. All movements including some rotation are possible.
Ball and socket	Shoulder and hip. Provides widest range of motion in all planes, especially rotations.

PROPERTIES OF MUSCULOSKELETAL ANATOMY

BONE

Bone tissue consists of mature bone cells (osteocytes) and mineral salts (calcium phosphate, $Ca_3 (PO_4)_2 (OH)_2$ and calcium carbonate, $CaCo_3$). The functions of bone are to support soft tissues to maintain posture; to protect delicate structures, such as the brain, spinal cord, heart, lungs, and blood vessels; to be a lever for joint movement; to store mineral salts (calcium and phosphorus) and fat; and to perform blood cell production (hematopoiesis).

Movement occurs when muscles contract and lengthen, pulling on the bony levers. Muscle tissue constitutes about 40 to 50% of the total body weight and is composed of highly specialized cells with four fundamental properties.[4] These properties are: *excitability* — the ability of tissue to receive and react to stimuli; *contractility* — the ability of tissue to shorten and thicken; *extensibility* — the ability of tissue to be stretched; and *elasticity* — the ability of tissue to return to its original shape after being deformed. The three functions of muscle are movement of bones around their joints, maintenance of posture (held positions), and production of heat in maintaining body temperature.

ASSOCIATED CONNECTIVE TISSUE STRUCTURES

Seven types of connective tissue are associated with muscles and joints. These structures include:

- *Fascia* — a sheet or broad band of fibrous connective tissue beneath the skin or around muscles or certain organs.
- *Tendon* — a cord of connective tissue that attaches muscle to the periosteum of bone.
- *Aponeurosis* — a broad, flat tendon.
- *Tendinous sheaths* — coverings of fibrous connective tissue around tendons. Synovial fluid is between its visceral (inner) and parietal (outer) layers. These structures are prevalent sites of inflammation (tendinitis).
- *Ligaments* — dense, regularly arranged connective tissue bands connecting bone to bone.
- *Cartilage* — a layer of chondrocytes (cartilage cells) in spaces (lacunae) embedded in a dense network of collagenous and elastic fibers and a matrix of chondroitin sulfate. (Because of poor circulation, damaged cartilage heals poorly and slowly.)
- *Bursae* (G. wineskin) — a closed sac of synovial (G. egg white) fluid between tendons, ligaments, bones, and skin.

FUNCTIONS OF MUSCULOSKELETAL ANATOMY

The primary actions and applications of the major muscles are listed in Table 3–3. In addition to an understanding of these muscles and how they function, a familiarity with basic joint movement is necessary so to analyze movement and to diagnose, treat, and assess the prognosis for athletic injuries. The basic joint movements are:

- *Flexion (bending)* — decreasing the angle between two bones in the sagittal plane.
- *Extension (straightening)* — increasing the angle between two bones in the sagittal plane.
- *Hyperextension* — extension of the joint past its normal starting position.
- *Abduction (leading away)* — moving the bone away from midline in a frontal plane.
- *Adduction (leading toward)* — moving the bone toward midline in a frontal plane.
- *Pronation (palms up to palms down)* — rotation of the radius around the ulna so that the palm turns backward or downward or *abduction* — eversion of the talonavicular (subtalar) joint.
- *Supination (palms down to palms up)* — rotation of the radius around the ulna so that the palm turns forward or upward or *adduction* — inversion of the talonavicular (subtalar) joint.

MUSCULOSKELETAL DISORDERS

Some musculoskeletal disorders are common among athletes, including bursitis, which is the inflammation of the synovial fluid-filled sacs situated where friction develops; shin splints (tibial stress syndrome), which causes soreness or pain along the tibia or in the soft tissues of the anterior calf; stress fracture, a partial break in a

Table 3–3. Actions and Application of Major Muscle Groups

Muscle	Primary actions	Application
Trapezius	Elevates clavicle; adducts scapula; elevates or depresses scapula; extends head.	Fixation of scapula for; deltoid action.
Pectoralis major	Flexes, adducts, rotates medially, extends, and horizontally adducts humerus.	Used powerfully in pushups, pullups, throwing, and serving in tennis.
Latissimus dorsi	Extension, adduction, and medial rotation of humerus.	Used in pullups, rope climb, dips, and pullover exercise.
Biceps brachii	Flexion and supination of forearm; flexes humerus.	Flexes forearm primarily in supinated grasp.
Triceps brachii	Extension of forearm; helps extend humerus.	Used in pushups, dips, and all pressing movements.
Rectus abdominis	Flexion and lateral flexion of trunk.	Controls tilt of pelvis; used in situps and trunk curls.
Erector spinae	Extension of vertebral column and head.	Used in position of attention and layout position.
Gluteus maximus	Extension and lateral rotation of femur.	Used in running, jumping, and step climbing and only slightly in walking.
Quadriceps	Extends tibia; rectus femoris flexes femur.	When femur is flexed at hip, rectus femoris is ineffective in extending the tibia.
Hamstrings	Flexes tibia; extends femur.	Antagonists of quadriceps, hence can be injured during violent tibial extension.
Gastrocnemius	Flexes tibia; plantar flexes foot.	Stretched by doing straight-knee wall push-aways.
Tibialis anterior	Dorsiflexion; inversion of foot.	Sometimes involved in shin splints.

bone resulting from inability to withstand the repeated forces of increased intensity of training or running on hard surfaces; tendinitis (tenosynovitis), which is the inflammation of tendinous sheaths or synovial membranes of any joint structure; and tennis elbow which results in pain at or near the lateral epicondyle of the humerus. The condition is usually associated with an improper backhand technique, and frequently involves a strain of the extensor carpi radialis brevis.

The basic concepts of musculoskeletal anatomy, including the bones of the skeleton, major muscles of the upper and lower limbs, freemoving joints, properties and functions of bone and muscle tissue, connective tissue structures, joint movements, and certain musculoskeletal disorders have been presented.

REFERENCES

1. Kaufmann D: *Laboratory Manual for Applied Human Anatomy.* Minneapolis: Burgess Publishing, 1987.
2. Jacob S, Francone C, Lassow W: *Structure and Function in Man.* Philadelphia: W.B. Saunders, 1982.
3. Thompson C: *Manual of Structural Kinesiology.* 8th Ed. St. Louis: C.V. Mosby, 1977.
4. Tortora G: *Principles of Human Anatomy.* New York: Harper and Row, 1986.
5. Roy S, Irvin R: *Sports Medicine: Prevention, Evaluation, Management and Rehabilitation.* Englewood Cliffs, NJ: Prentice-Hall, 1983.

4

BIOMECHANICS OF FITNESS EXERCISE MODALITIES

STEPHEN P. MESSIER

One aspect of health enhancement programs that is often overlooked is the utilization of proper mechanics and equipment during the performance of aerobic and strength training exercises. Improper mechanics and/or the use of inappropriate equipment may lead to injury and subsequent noncompliance. In this chapter, we examine the biomechanics of selected fitness exercise modalities, including walking, running, bending, lifting and carrying objects, and resistance training.

WALKING

The most fundamental type of aerobic exercise is walking. Walking may be the first step leading to a more strenuous exercise regimen, or it may be the basic component of a fitness program.

The basic walking or gait cycle is divided into two phases, the stance and the swing (Fig. 4–1).[1] At a normal walking pace of 1.56 m · sec^{-1} (3.5 mph), the stance phase encompasses approximately 60% of the gait cycle. Three critical periods occur within the stance phase — heel strike, midstance, and push off. Heel strike encompasses the initial 15% of the gait cycle and

is characterized by the heel making initial contact with the ground (Fig. 4–1). During the midstance phase (15 to 30% of gait cycle), the foot assumes a relatively flat position. Subsequently, during the final 30% of the stance phase (termed push off), the walker accelerates in preparation for toe off.

Newton's third law of motion states that for every action there is an equal and opposite reaction. During walking, the walker applies a force to the ground and the ground applies an equal and opposite force to the walker. This latter force is termed the ground reaction force. Analysis of the ground reaction forces is important because it provides insight into what causes the walker to move. Additionally, the etiologic factors relative to injuries and abnormal gait patterns may be understood more fully by studying the input conditions experienced by the lower extremity each time the foot strikes the ground.[2]

The vertical ground reaction force pattern is bimodal (Fig. 4–2).[3] The first peak reaches a relative magnitude of 120% of the walker's body weight (1.2 BW) shortly after heel strike.[4] A second peak of approximately equivalent magnitude occurs during push off. Ground reaction forces are affected by the body's acceleration, hence the greater the velocity of walking the greater the magnitude of these forces.

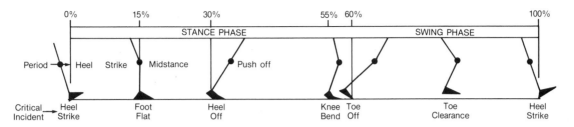

FIGURE 4 – 1. Phases, periods, and critical incidents of gait or walking cycle. (Adapted from Bowker JH, Hall CB: Normal walking gait. In *Atlas of Orthotics: Biomechanical Principles and Applications.* Edited by the American Academy of Orthopedic Surgeons. St. Louis: C.V. Mosby, 1975.)

Anteroposterior ground reaction forces produce a curve with two peaks that are opposite in direction. The first peak occurs after heel strike and retards the forward motion of the walker. The second peak occurs just before push off and accelerates or propels the walker forward. These braking and propulsive forces each reach maximal values of approximately 0.15 BW (Fig. 4 – 2).

The magnitude of the forces exerted during walking is far less than those exerted while running. Proper footwear, nevertheless, is essential. A walker's shoes should fit properly and have good shock absorption, adequate breathability, flexibility, and rearfoot support.

RUNNING

The basic running pattern is divided into two phases: support and flight. The critical periods during the support phase are heel strike, midstance, and toe off. One factor that distin-

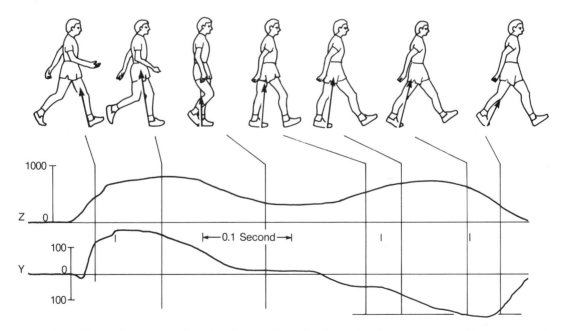

FIGURE 4 – 2. Force-time record of one foot in normal walking. Z, vertical force component; Y, anteroposterior force component. Forces are in newtons (N). Force produced by subject's body weight (60 Kg) was equal to 588 N. (Courtesy of Payne AH: A comparison of the ground reaction forces in race walking with those in normal walking. In *Biomechanics VI-A.* Edited by E Asmussen and K Jorgensen. Baltimore: University Park Press, 1978.)

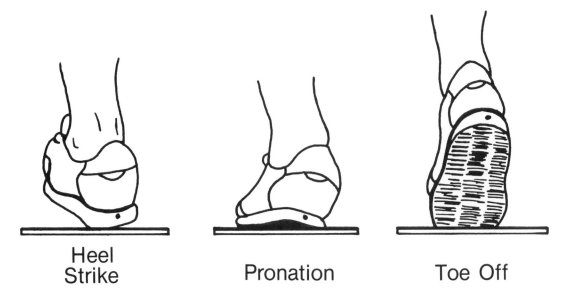

Heel Strike   Pronation   Toe Off

FIGURE 4-3. Depiction of rear foot movement during running. (Adapted from Nigg BM, et al.: Factors influencing kinetic and kinematic variables in running. In *Biomechanics of Running Shoes.* Edited by B Nigg. Champaign: Human Kinetics Publishers, 1986.)

guishes running from walking is the inclusion, during running, of a period of nonsupport or flight.

At completion of the flight phase, the runner strikes the ground with the rear, lateral border of the foot. The position of the rear foot (commonly referred to as the subtalar joint) at heel strike is approximately 6° supinated (Fig. 4-3).[5] As the runner's weight shifts forward, the rear foot is pronated. Much has been written concerning pronation and its effect on a runner's mechanics. By pronating after heel strike, the runner is able to dissipate the forces encountered at heel strike and facilitate the transfer of weight to the mid and forefoot. The problem arises when pronation does not stop within a normal range (approximately 9.4°). Excessive pronation is associated with running injuries that include shin splints, chondromalacia, plantar fasciitis, and Achilles tendinitis.

Runners generally exhibit one of two types of foot strike patterns; the most common pattern is shown in Figure 4-4a. Runners who exhibit this pattern are termed rearfoot strikers. They make contact with the rear, lateral border of the foot and rotate toward the midline. The second, less common pattern is exhibited by the midfoot striker (Fig. 4-4b). The midfoot striker contacts the ground at midfoot and, after a brief backward movement, moves forward in preparation for toe off.

Although running has long been established as an effective aerobic conditioning exercise, the relationship between running injuries and the forces generated during running remains an important topic of investigation for biomechanists. Peak vertical ground reaction forces reach magnitudes of 2 to 3 BW approximately 0.05 sec after heel strike, and again just before toe off. Peak forces before toe off are generally greater than those at heel strike (Fig. 4-5a). Because both feet strike the ground approximately 1500 times per mile, the stress exerted on the musculoskeletal system is considerable, and may result in abnormal biomechanical and orthopedic conditions. Correct running mechanics and sensible training methods are important factors in attenuating the potentially negative effects of running.

Furthermore, the use of proper footwear is essential to minimize the incidence of injury. Good rear and forefoot cushioning; a stiff heel counter and multidensity midsole to control rearfoot movement; a flexible forefoot; and an outsole that has good traction and wear are among the qualities that should be considered when selecting a running shoe.[6] Of special concern to the midfoot striker is that the mid and forefoot must absorb the shock that occurs at touchdown *and* at toe off. Therefore, the midfoot striker should select a running shoe that has excellent forefoot shock absorption.

A

Rearfoot Strikers
n = 12

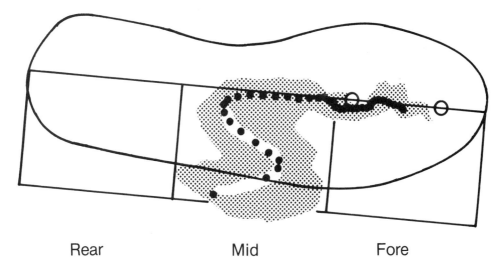

Rear   Mid   Fore

B

Midfoot Strikers
n = 5

Rear   Mid   Fore

FIGURE 4–4. Mean center of pressure locations under shoe outline at 2-msec intervals during contact. Shoe is divided into three equal regions for purpose of classifying running patterns. **A,** rearfoot striker. **B,** midfoot striker. (Courtesy of Cavanagh PR, LaFortune MA: Ground reaction forces in distance running. *J Biomech, 13:*397, 1980.)

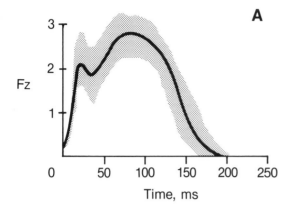

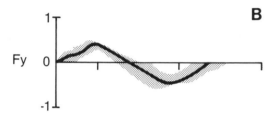

FIGURE 4–5. Mean force-time curves *(in units of body weight)* and range *(shaded area)* for contact phase of rearfoot striker. **A,** vertical component; **B,** anteroposterior component. (Courtesy of Cavanagh PR, LaFortune MA: Ground reaction forces in distance running. *J Biomech, 13:*397, 1980.)

The double-peaked anteroposterior ground reaction force pattern is similar to that exhibited during walking in that the peak forces act in opposite directions (Fig. 4–5). The first peak force decelerates the runner upon heel strike, and the second or propulsive peak causes the runner to accelerate forward. The magnitude of these forces reaches a maximum of between 0.4 and 0.5 BW. The alternating negative and positive accelerations within each footfall make it appear unlikely that a runner is able to run at a truly constant velocity.

Horizontal running velocity (HV) is the product of a runner's stride length (SL) and stride frequency (SF): [HV (m $\cdot$ sec^{-1}) = SL (m) $\cdot$ SF (strides $\cdot$ sec^{-1})]. At jogging and moderate running speeds, increases in running velocity primarily are accomplished by increasing stride length. At higher speeds, approximately 5.5 m $\cdot$ sec^{-1} (12 mph) for untrained runners, further increases in velocity are accomplished by increasing stride frequency.[7]

Increased running speed also affects the magnitude of the ground reaction forces. Re-

sults of studies show that, as running speed increases from 8 min $\cdot$ mile^{-1} to 6 min $\cdot$ mile^{-1}, vertical peak impact forces increase from approximately 2 BW to near 3 BW. Therefore, faster runners exert proportionately more stress on their lower extremities than do slower runners.

BENDING, LIFTING, AND CARRYING

Simple, everyday activities, such as sitting, bending, lifting, carrying, and moving objects can, if done improperly, exact a great toll on the lower back. The vast amount of research on lower back pain attests to this fact. An understanding of two important concepts, center of gravity and levers, is necessary before discussing the mechanics involved in the aforementioned activities.

Important to any analysis of bodies at rest or in motion is the principle of center of gravity

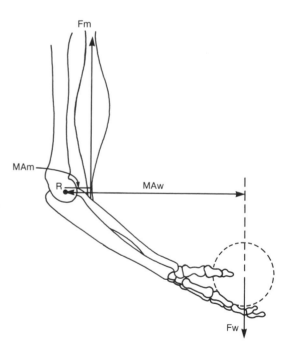

FIGURE 4–6. Depiction of lever system in human body. MAm and Fm as well as MAw and Fw are moment arms and forces for muscle (m) and weight (w), respectively. (Adapted from LeVeau B: *Biomechanics of Human Motion.* 2nd Ed. Philadelphia: W.B. Saunders, 1977.)

(COG) and its relationship to stability. The COG is the mass center or balance point of a body. In a uniform, geometrically shaped object, the COG is in the geometric center. In a solid object, the COG remains constantly located. In the human body, however, the location of the COG is dependent on the distribution of the mass. The movement of body segments causes a redistribution of mass and a subsequent shifting of the COG. To maintain balance (static equilibrium), a line that passes vertically through the COG must fall within the base of support. The base of support is the area in contact with the supporting surface plus the area between the supports when there is more than one support. For example, in a free standing position, the base of support would be the area under the feet plus the area between the feet.

The bones and joints of the body constitute a system of levers. The joints act as the axes about which the levers—the bones—rotate. The lever system is operated either internally by the muscles or externally by gravity, other objects, or persons. The result of the operation of the lever system is movement. Several distances are associated with the forces involved in the lever system; the most important is the moment arm. The moment arm is the perpendicular distance from the line of force (either internal or external force) to the axis of rotation (Fig. 4–6).[8] The product of a force (F) and its moment arm (MA) is called torque (τ) [τ (Newton-meters) = F (Newtons) $\cdot$ MA (meters)]. The torques created to operate the lever system are associated with either internal forces exerted by the muscles (termed effort torque) or external forces created by gravity or other objects (termed resistance

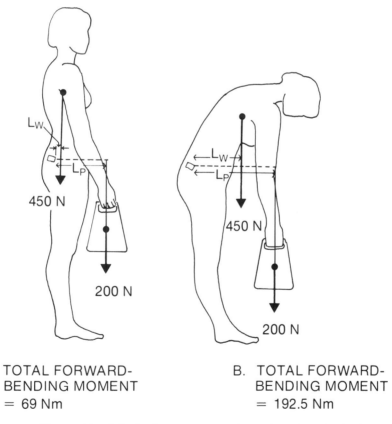

A. TOTAL FORWARD-
    BENDING MOMENT
    = 69 Nm

B. TOTAL FORWARD-
    BENDING MOMENT
    = 192.5 Nm

FIGURE 4–7. Influence of forward trunk inclination on moment (torque) produced at lumbar spine. **A,** erect trunk shortens length of moment arms for upper body (Lw) and weight (Lp), thereby attenuating forward bending torque. **B,** increasing forward trunk inclination increases Lw and Lp, placing greater load (torque) on spine. (Courtesy of Frankel VH, Nordin M: *Basic Biomechanics of the Skeletal System.* Philadelphia: Lea & Febiger, 1980.)

torque). To balance a lever, the effort and resistance torques must be equal in magnitude and opposite in direction.

Factors that influence the magnitude of the load on the lumbar spine while lifting and carrying objects include: (1) the position of the object relative to the COG of the spine; (2) the degree of flexion of the spine; and (3) the size, shape, and weight of the object.[9] In general, holding objects close to your body shortens the moment arm of the object, thereby decreasing the torque acting on the lumbar spine. When an object is held with the body in a forward bending position, the torque on the spine is created by the weight of the object and the force produced by the weight of the upper body. As forward inclination increases, the moment arms for the object and upper body weight lengthen. The result is increased torque on the spine (Fig. 4–7).

The size and shape of an object also influence the load placed on the spine. For two objects of similar weight, the COG of the larger object will be farther from the lumbar spine, resulting in a longer moment arm and a greater load (torque) placed on the spine (Fig. 4–8).

An acknowledged fact is that when lifting an object, flexing the knees reduces the load on the spine, particularly if the proper technique is utilized. Flexing the knees and minimizing forward trunk inclination while lifting an object may bring the object closer to the body, thus shortening the moment arm and minimizing the load placed on the spine. An object held in front of the knees, however, increases forward trunk inclination and lengthens the moment arm, resulting in an increased load placed on the spine (Fig. 4–9).[9] A comprehensive discussion of the effects of standing, sitting, lifting, and carrying objects on the lumbar spine, is provided in a text by Frankel and Nordin.[9]

The fundamental principles discussed rela-

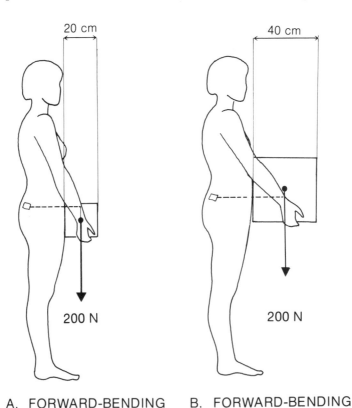

A. FORWARD-BENDING
MOMENT = 60 Nm

B. FORWARD-BENDING
MOMENT = 80 Nm

FIGURE 4–8. Size of object carried influences loads on lumbar spine. Although both objects have same weight, object B is larger and thus has longer moment arm, resulting in increased torque acting on lumbar spine. (Courtesy of Frankel VH, Nordin M: *Basic Biomechanics of the Skeletal System.* Philadelphia: Lea & Febiger, 1980.)

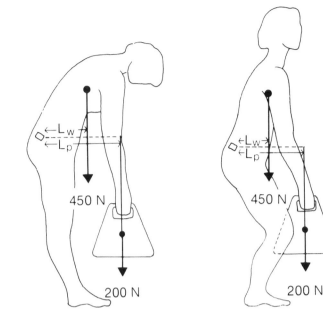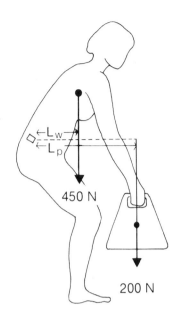

A. TOTAL
FORWARD-BENDING
MOMENT = 192.5 Nm

B. TOTAL
FORWARD-BENDING
MOMENT = 151 Nm

C. TOTAL
FORWARD-BENDING
MOMENT = 212.5 Nm

FIGURE 4–9. Technique employed during lifting influences loads on lumbar spine. **Case A,** lifting with trunk flexed forward. **Case B,** lifting with knees flexed and trunk erect. **Case C,** lifting with knees flexed but object is held out in front of knees, thereby increasing forward trunk inclination and forward bending moment (torque). L_w and L_p, moment arms for upper body and weight, respectively. (Courtesy of Frankel VH, Nordin M: *Basic Biomechanics of the Skeletal System.* Philadelphia: Lea & Febiger, 1980.)

tive to lifting objects also apply to the specialized case of weight training. Some weight-training exercises are conducive to lifting extremely heavy loads, hence injury prevention necessitates adherence to proper lifting mechanics. The military press and squat are two controversial weight-training exercises (Fig. 4–10).[10] Because a relatively heavy weight is lifted over the head during the military press, any anteroposterior or lateral sway will lengthen the moment arm of the weight about the lumbar spine; extremely large torques are thereby created, which could result in lower back injury. The lifter should strive to keep the COG of the lifter-weight system directly over the center of his base of support.

One of the more controversial weight-lifting exercises is the squat. Researchers have shown that improper mechanics during a squat drastically increase the torques at the trunk and knees.[11,12] The mechanical flaws found in less skilled lifters include increased forward trunk

lean and greater downward velocity of the weight. Conversely, a skilled lifter maintains a more vertical trunk position and lowers the weight in a slow, more controlled manner, thereby attenuating trunk and knee torques. Additionally, some authors suggest that, when a lifter reaches the full squat position, potentially damaging tensile and shear forces are placed on the ligaments and menisci of the knee. Consequently, the half squat as an alternate exercise is frequently recommended (Fig. 4–10).

RESISTANCE TRAINING EXERCISES

To increase the size and strength of a muscle, it must be subjected to a greater than normal load. Resistance training exercises are often used to achieve these objectives. The number

FIGURE 4-10. Common free weight exercises and major target muscle groups for each. (Adapted from Arnheim DD: Modern Principles of Athletic Training. St. Louis: Times Mirror/Mosby College Publishing, 1985.)

and variety of resistance-training regimens, however, is enough to confuse even the most enthusiastic novice lifter. Moreover, researchers do not concur as to the most effective method of increasing muscular strength. The intent of this section is to provide a technique for determining the muscles that are being used during a given exercise, and to describe some common weight-training exercises for major muscle groups.

The process of determining what muscles operate during an exercise, movement, or sport skill is anatomic analysis. The prerequisite skills necessary for performing an anatomic analysis include: (1) identifying the movement or position of a joint during the performance of an exercise; (2) identifying the cause of the movement; (3) understanding the different movement roles a muscle may play (e.g., agonist, antagonist); and (4) understanding the types of muscular tension (concentric, eccentric, and isometric).

If a weight moves against the force of gravity (which acts vertically downward), the muscles used are agonists for the movement taking place. For example, during a two-arm curl (Fig. 4–10), the weight is being lifted against gravity by flexing the elbows. The muscles utilized are the agonists for elbow flexion — the biceps, brachialis, and brachioradialis. Physiologically, these muscles cause movement by producing tension concentrically.

If a weight moves by the force of gravity, the muscles used are the antagonists to the movement taking place. Using the aforementioned example, the elbows are extended as the lifter lowers the weight to the original position. The muscles used to control the lowering of the weight are the antagonists to elbow extension, or the elbow flexors. Physiologically, the elbow flexors are lengthening (eccentric tension), controlling the downward movement of the weight. The external forces of gravity, the weight of the barbell, and the weight of the lifter's arms cause this movement. An exception to this rule occurs during very fast movements. In this situation, the agonist may be activated to accelerate the limb. Parenthetically, note that the only way a muscle can cause movement is by concentric tension. Given the preceding information, a determination of the muscles used in a variety of exercises should be possible.

Two common modes of resistance training are "constant resistance" (e.g., free weights and Universal) and "variable resistance" (e.g., Nautilus and Polaris) exercises. Although both modes of exercise involve the use of constant loads and variable resistance torques, "variable resistance" exercises attempt to alter the resistance torques to coincide with the muscle's capability of producing force (effort torque) throughout the range of motion. Theoretically, in the joint position at which the muscle is capable of producing its greatest torque, the resistance torque is maximized. Conversely, when the joint is in less advantageous positions (reduced effort torque), the resistance torque is attenuated.

Although each weight-training method and modality has its proponents, published comparisons of constant and variable resistance methods show no overall superiority in strength development for either technique.[13] Figure 4–10 depicts some common free weight exercises and the primary muscle groups used for each exercise.

SUMMARY

The forces exerted during walking are not as strong as those exerted during running. Vertical ground reaction forces reach a relative magnitude of 1.2 BW during walking, whereas peak forces during running range between 2 BW and 3 BW. To attenuate these forces and to decrease the risk of injury, good shock absorption should be an important element of any walking or running shoe. Other important qualities in walking and running shoes include proper fit, excellent rearfoot support, and good flexibility and breathability.

Everyday activities such as bending, lifting, and carrying and moving objects can, if done improperly, cause abnormally high loads to be exerted on the lumbar spine. Repeated trauma to the lumbar spine may lead to chronic back pain. Mechanical factors that attenuate the magnitude of the load placed on the lumbar spine while lifting objects include holding objects close to the body, flexing the knees, and minimizing forward trunk inclination. These fundamental principles also apply to the specialized case of weight training.

REFERENCES

1. Bowker JH, Hall CB: Normal walking gait. In *Atlas of Orthotics: Biomechanical Principles and Applications.* Edited by the American Academy of Orthopaedic Surgeons. St. Louis: C.V. Mosby, 1975.

2. Cavanagh PR, LaFortune MA: Ground reaction forces in distance running. *J Biomech, 13:*397, 1980.

3. Payne AH: A comparison of the ground reaction forces in race walking with those in normal walking and running. In *Biomechanics VI-A.* Edited by E Asmussen and K Jorgensen. Baltimore: University Park Press, 1978.

4. Perry J: The mechanics of walking: A clinical interpretation. *Phys Ther, 47:*778, 1967.

5. Nigg, BM, et al.: Factors influencing kinetic and kinematic variables in running. In *Biomechanics of Running Shoes.* Edited by B. Nigg. Champaign: Human Kinetics, 1986.

6. Ellis J: The Match Game. *Runner's World, October 20:*66, 1985.

7. Saito M, Kobayashi K, Miyashita M, Hoshikawa T: Temporal patterns in running. In *Biomechanics IV.* Edited by RC Nelson and CA Morehouse. London: Macmillan, 1974.

8. LeVeau B: Biomechanics of Human Motion. 2nd Ed. Philadelphia: W.B. Saunders, 1977.

9. Frankel VH, Nordin M: *Basic Biomechanics of the Skeletal System.* Philadelphia: Lea & Febiger, 1980.

10. Arnheim DD: Modern Principles of Athletic Training. St. Louis: Times Mirror/Mosby College Publishing, 1985.

11. Ariel GB: Biomechanical analysis of the knee joint during deep knee bends with heavy load. In *Biomechanics IV.* Edited by RC Nelson and CA Morehouse. London: Macmillan, 1974.

12. McLaughlin TM, Lardner TJ, Dillman CJ: Kinetics of the parallel squat. *Res Q, 49:*175, 1978.

13. Atha J: Strengthening muscle. In *Exercise and Sport Science Reviews.* Edited by D.I. Miller. Philadelphia: Franklin Institute, 1982.

EXERCISE PHYSIOLOGY

CHAPTER 5

TERMINOLOGY IN EXERCISE PHYSIOLOGY

RUSSELL R. PATE AND
MARIA LONNETT

The following glossary provides definitions of terms that are used frequently in the field of exercise physiology. Included in this list are terms that appear in the exercise physiology sections of the behavioral objectives that must be met by candidates for Preventive and Rehabilitative Exercise Program Certification at levels ranging from health fitness leader to program director.

1. **aerobic metabolism:** catabolism of energy substrates with the utilization of oxygen; energy transfer resulting from involvement of electron transport and the accompanying oxidative phosphorylation

2. **action potential:** the momentary change in electrical potential across the cell membrane of a nerve or muscle fiber that occurs with fiber stimulation.

3. **anaerobic metabolism:** catabolism of energy substrates without the utilization of oxygen; energy transfer that does not require oxygen.

4. **anaerobic threshold:** the work rate at which blood lactate concentration starts to increase during graded exercise (i.e., onset of blood lactate accumulation, OBLA); the work rate at which metabolic acidosis and associated changes in respiratory gas exchange occur during graded exercise.

5. **anemia:** a condition marked by an abnormally low number of circulating red blood cells and/or hemoglobin concentration.

6. **angina pectoris:** the pain associated with myocardial ischemia; usually manifested in the left side of the chest and/or in the left arm, but is sometimes in the right arm, back, and neck.

7. **anorexia nervosa:** loss of appetite for food not explainable by local disease; an eating disorder diagnosed as an intense fear of becoming obese.

8. **apnea:** a temporary cessation of breathing.

9. **atrophy, muscular:** decrease in size of muscle tissue, especially due to disease.

10. **arteriovenous oxygen difference** $(a - \bar{v}O_2)$: the difference in oxygen content between the blood entering and that leaving the pulmonary capillaries.

11. **blood pressure:** the pressure exerted by the blood against the walls of blood vessels.

12. **bradycardia:** slow heart action; usually defined as a heart rate under 60 beats $\cdot$ min^{-1}.

13. **breathing frequency:** the rate of breathing cycles (inhalation and exhalation); usually expressed as breaths per minute.

14. **bulimia:** a neurotic disorder characterized by bouts of overeating followed by voluntary vomiting, fasting, or induced diarrhea.

15. **calorimetry:** determination of heat loss or

gain; a means of determining energy expenditure of an animal by direct measurement of its heat production or indirect measurement of respiratory gas exchange.

16. cardiac output: volume of blood pumped from the heart each minute; the product of heart rate and stroke volume.

17. concentric muscle contraction: shortening of the muscle as it develops tension; sometimes referred to as "positive exercise."

18. diastolic blood pressure: arterial pressure during the diastolic phase of the heart's cycle (i.e., ventricular filling).

19. dynamic exercise: alternate contraction and relaxation of a skeletal muscle or group of muscles causing partial or complete movement through a joint's range of motion.

20. dyspnea: difficult or labored breathing.

21. eccentric muscle contraction: lengthening of a muscle as it develops tension; sometimes referred to as "negative exercise."

22. electrocardiogram (ECG): a record of the electrical activity of the heart; shows certain waves called P-, Q-, R-, S- and T-waves. (The P-wave is caused by depolarization and contraction of the atrial muscle tissues. The remaining waves are related to depolarization and contraction of the ventricles.)

23. ergometer: an instrument used to measure work and power output.

24. ergometry: measurement of work and power; utilizing standardized equipment to measure work and power output during exercise.

25. flexibility: range of motion possible in a joint or series of joints.

26. heart rate: number of contractions (beats) of the heart per unit of time; expressed as beats per minute.

27. hemodynamic: relating to the forces involved in circulating blood through the body.

28. hyperemia: increased amount of blood in a body part; caused by increased inflow or decreased outflow of blood.

29. hyperplasia: proliferation of cells.

30. hyperpnea: an increase in depth and rate of breathing as with exercise.

31. hypertension: higher than normal arterial blood pressure; often defined as a resting blood pressure greater than 140/90 mm Hg.

32. hypertrophy: increased size of an organ or tissue, usually due to increased size of cells or tissue elements.

33. hyperventilation: increased inspiration and expiration of air due to either or both increased rate or depth of respiration; can lead to respiratory alkalosis due to depletion of carbon dioxide in the blood.

34. hypoventilation: decreased inspiration and expiration of air due to reduced rate and/or depth of breathing.

35. hypoxia: low oxygen content; lack of adequate oxygen in inspired air as occurs at high altitude.

36. ischemia: local deficiency of blood, usually due to the constriction or partial occlusion of arterial blood vessels.

37. isokinetic: referring to contraction of a muscle or muscle group such that joint movement occurs at a constant angular velocity.

38. isometric: referring to contraction of a muscle in which shortening or lengthening is prevented; tension is developed but no mechanical work is performed, with all energy being liberated as heat.

39. isotonic: referring to muscle contraction in which constant tension is maintained by the muscle while the length of the muscle is increased or decreased.

40. kilocalorie (kcal): a unit of measure for heat; the amount of heat required to change the temperature of 1 kg of water from 14.5°C to 15.5°C.

41. lactic acid: an acidic metabolite that is the end product of anaerobic glycolysis.

42. maximal oxygen consumption ($\dot{V}O_{2\,max}$): the greatest rate of oxygen consumption attained during exercise at sea level; usually expressed in liters per minute ($1 \cdot min^{-1}$) or milliliters per kilogram body weight per minute ($ml \cdot kg^{-1} \cdot min^{-1}$).

43. MET: a metabolic equivalent unit; a unit used to estimate the metabolic cost of physical activity; one MET = 3.5 ml of oxygen consumed per kilogram of body weight per minute.

44. minute ventilation: the volume of air breathed per minute; the product of tidal volume and breathing frequency.

45. muscular endurance: the ability of a muscle or group of muscles to contract at a submaximal force level over a period of time; usually measured as the number of repeti-

tions completed against 50 to 60% of the maximal resistance.

46. muscular strength: the maximal force or tension generated by a muscle or muscle group.

47. myocardial; concerning the myocardium, the heart muscle.

48. myocardial infarction: an area of cardiac muscle tissue that undergoes necrosis after cessation of blood supply through a segment of the coronary arterial system.

49. orthostatic hypotension: lower than normal arterial blood pressure occurring when subject assumes an erect posture.

50. oxygen consumption: the rate at which oxygen is utilized by the body in aerobic metabolism; usually expressed as liters of oxygen consumed per minute ($L \cdot min^{-1}$) or millimeters of oxygen consumed per kilogram body weight per minute ($mL \cdot kg^{-1} \cdot min^{-1}$)

51. premature atrial contraction (PAC): early contraction of the atria originating at some ectopic site outside of the sinoatrial node.

52. premature ventricular contraction (PVC): early contraction of the ventricle resulting from initiation of an impulse either within or at some ectopic site outside of the conduction system.

53. reciprocal innervation: simultaneous activation of an agonist muscle group and inhibition of the antagonist muscle group.

54. respiratory exchange ratio: the ratio of carbon dioxide produced to oxygen consumed; computed as $\dot{V}CO_2/\dot{V}O_2$.

55. respiratory acidosis: lower than normal blood pH secondary to pulmonary insufficiency resulting in retention of carbon dioxide; can be caused by hypoventilation.

56. respiratory alkalosis: higher than normal pH of blood and other body fluids in association with reduced blood carbon dioxide level; can be caused by hyperventilation.

57. static exercise: the contraction of a skeletal muscle or group of muscles without movement of a joint.

58. stroke volume: the volume of blood pumped from the heart with each beat.

59. systolic blood pressure: arterial pressure during the systolic phase of the heart's cycle (i.e., ventricular contraction).

60. tachycardia: abnormal rapidity of heart action, usually defined as a heart rate over 100 beats $\cdot min^{-1}$.

61. tidal volume: the volume of air moved during a single respiratory cycle (inhalation or expiration).

62. Valsalva maneuver: an attempt to exhale forcibly with the glottis closed; causes increased intrathoracic pressure, slowed pulse rate, decreased venous return, and increased venous pressure.

6

FUNDAMENTALS OF EXERCISE METABOLISM

SCOTT K. POWERS

Almost all changes that occur in the body during exercise are related to the increase in energy metabolism that occurs within the contracting skeletal muscle. For example, cardiac output and heart rate increase as a linear function of metabolic rate. At rest, a 70-kg human has an energy expenditure of about 1.2 kcal/min; less than 20% of this resting energy expenditure is estimated to be used by skeletal muscle, which is a surprisingly low value given that skeletal muscle constitutes almost 50% of total body weight.

During intense exercise total energy expenditure may be 15 to 25 times that of the resting value, resulting in a caloric expenditure of approximately 18 to 30 kcal/min. Most of this increase is used to provide energy for the exercising muscles that may increase their energy utilization by a factor of 200 over resting levels.[1] The focus of this chapter is on a brief discussion of those concepts associated with exercise metabolism. By necessity, this section is concise, and the treatment of each topic is therefore brief and superficial. A detailed review of bioenergetics and exercise metabolism is provided in several sources.[2-6]

ENERGY FOR MUSCULAR CONTRACTION

Contraction of skeletal muscle is powered by the energy released through hydrolysis of the high-energy compound adenosine triphosphate (ATP) to form adenosine diphosphate (ADP) and inorganic phosphate (Pi). This reaction is catalyzed by the enzyme actomyosin ATPase as follows:

$$ATP \xrightarrow[\text{actomyosin ATPase}]{} ADP + Pi + energy$$

The amount of ATP in muscle at any time is small, and thus it must be resynthesized continuously if exercise continues for more than a few seconds. Each cell contains the metabolic machinery to produce ATP by three pathways: (1) creatine phosphate (CP) system; (2) glycolysis; and (3) aerobic oxidation of nutrients to produce CO_2 and H_2O. A brief discussion of each of these pathways follows.

The CP system involves the transfer of high-energy phosphate from CP to rephosphorylate ADP to ATP as follows:

$$ADP + CP \xrightarrow[\text{creatine kinase}]{} ATP + C$$

This reaction is rapid because it involves only one enzymatic step; however, CP exists in finite quantities in cells and thus the total amount of ATP that can be produced through this mechanism is limited. Note that oxygen (O_2) is not involved in the rephosphorylation of ADP to ATP in this reaction, and thus the CP system is considered anaerobic metabolism (without O_2).

A second metabolic pathway capable of producing ATP without the involvement of O_2 exists in the sarcoplasm of the muscle cell—this is called glycolysis. Glycolysis is the degradation of carbohydrate (glycogen or glucose) to pyruvate or lactate and involves a series of 10 enzymatically catalyzed steps (Fig. 6–1). The net energy yield of glycolysis is 2 ATP through substrate level phosphorylation. Of importance is the fact that although the process of glycoly-

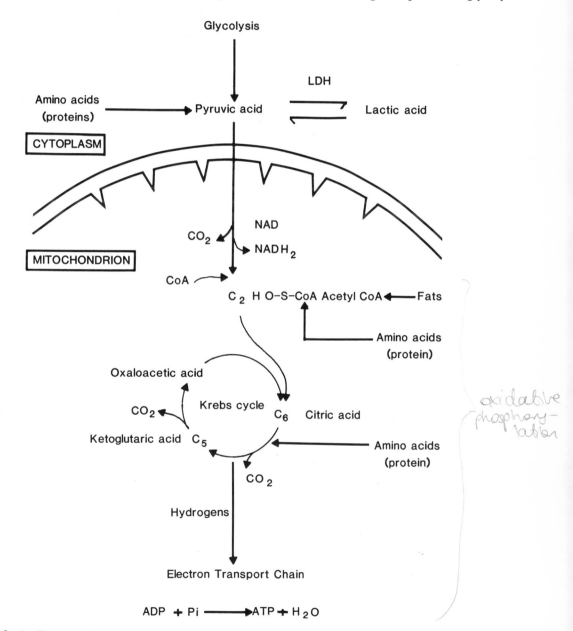

FIGURE 6–1. Relationship between glycolysis, the Krebs cycle, and the electron transport chain.

sis does not involve the use of O_2 and is thus considered an anaerobic pathway, pyruvate can participate in aerobic production of ATP when O_2 is available in the cell. Thus, in addition to being an anaerobic pathway capable of producing ATP without O_2, glycolysis can be considered the first step in the aerobic degradation of carbohydrate.

Historically, rising blood lactate levels during exercise have been considered an indication of increased anaerobic metabolism within the contracting muscle. Furthermore, several investigators believe the increase in muscle lactate production is related to tissue hypoxia. Whether the end product of glycolysis is pyruvate or lactate, however, depends on a variety of factors. First, if O_2 is not available in the mitochondria to accept the hydrogens released as a result of glycolysis, pyruvate must accept the hydrogens so glycolysis can proceed. Second, if glycolytic flux is extremely rapid, hydrogen production may then exceed the transport capability of those shuttle mechanisms required to move hydrogens from the sarcoplasm into the mitochondria where oxidative phosphorylation occurs. Again, pyruvate must accept the hydrogens to form lactate so glycolysis may continue. Finally, conversion of pyruvate to lactate (and vice versa) is catalyzed by the enzyme lactate dehydrogenase (LDH), which exists in several forms (isozymes). Fast-twitch muscle fibers contain an LDH isozyme that favors the formation of lactate; slow-twitch fibers contain an LDH form that promotes the conversion of lactate to pyruvate. Therefore, lactate formation might occur in fast-twitch fibers during work simply because of the type of LDH isozyme present, independent of O_2 availability in the muscle. A detailed discussion of this topic is available in a review by Graham.[7]

The final metabolic pathway found in cells to produce ATP is a combination of two complex metabolic processes (i.e., Krebs cycle and electron transport chain) and is located inside the mitochondria. As the name implies, oxidative phosphorylation involves the use of O_2 as the final hydrogen acceptor to form H_2O and ATP. Unlike glycolysis, aerobic metabolism can use fat, protein, and carbohydrate as substrate to produce ATP. The interaction of these nutrients is illustrated in Figure 6–1. Conceptually, a metabolic process called the Krebs cycle can be considered a ''primer'' for oxidative phosphorylation. Entry into the Krebs cycle begins with the combination of acetyl-CoA and oxaloacetic acid to form citric acid. In brief, the primary purpose of the Krebs cycle is to remove hydrogens from four of the reactants involved in the cycle. The electrons from these hydrogens then follow a chain of cytochromes (electron transport chain) in the mitochondria, and the energy released from this process is used to rephosphorylate ADP to form ATP. Oxygen is the final acceptor of these hydrogens to form H_2O (Fig. 6–1). Note that glycolysis can interact with the Krebs cycle in the presence of O_2 by the conversion of pyruvate to form acetyl-CoA.

METABOLIC RESPONSES TO EXERCISE

The importance of the interaction of the aforementioned metabolic pathways in the production of ATP during exercise should be emphasized. Although often we speak of aerobic versus anaerobic exercise, in reality the energy to perform most types of exercise comes from a combination of anaerobic/aerobic sources (see Fig. 6–2). The contribution of anaerobic sources (PC system and glycolysis) to exercise energy metabolism is inversely related to the duration and intensity of the activity. That is, the shorter the activity, the greater the contribution of anaerobic energy production; the longer the activity, the greater the contribution of aerobic energy production. Although proteins can be used as a fuel for aerobic exercise, carbohydrates and fats are believed to be the primary energy substrates during work in a healthy, well-fed individual. In general, carbohydrates are used as the primary fuel at the onset of exercise and during high intensity work.[8,9] During prolonged exercise (i.e., >30 min), however, a gradual shift occurs, from carbohydrate metabolism toward an increasing reliance on fat as a substrate (Fig. 6–3).[10,11] A detailed discussion outlining the interplay of substrates during exercise is available from several sources.[5,9,10,12,13] A brief discussion of the metabolic response to various types of exercise follows.

REST TO LIGHT EXERCISE

In the transition from rest to light exercise, oxygen uptake kinetics follow a monoexponential pattern, reaching a steady state generally

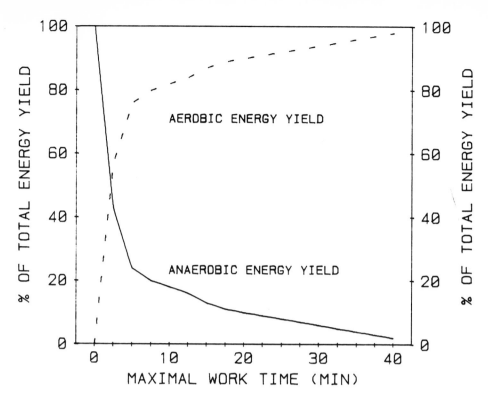

FIGURE 6–2. Interaction between anaerobic and aerobic metabolism during exercise. Note energy to perform short-term high-intensity exercise comes primarily from anaerobic sources whereas energy for muscular contraction during prolonged work comes from aerobic metabolism. (Redrawn from McArdle W, Katch F, Katch V: *Exercise Physiology*. Philadelphia: Lea & Febiger, 1981.)

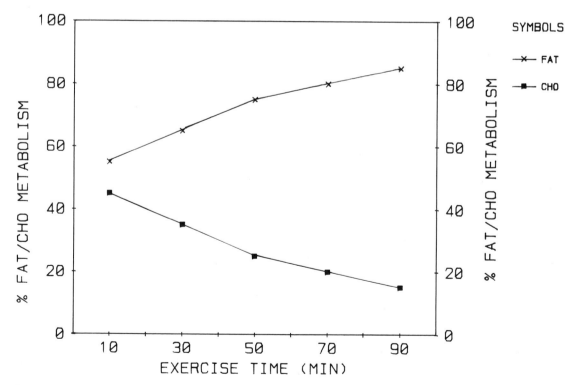

FIGURE 6–3. Alterations in substrate utilization during prolonged submaximal exercise. CHO, carbohydrate. (Data from Powers S, Riley W, Howley E: Comparison of fat metabolism between trained men and women during prolonged aerobic work. *Res Q Exerc Sport, 51*:427, 1980.)

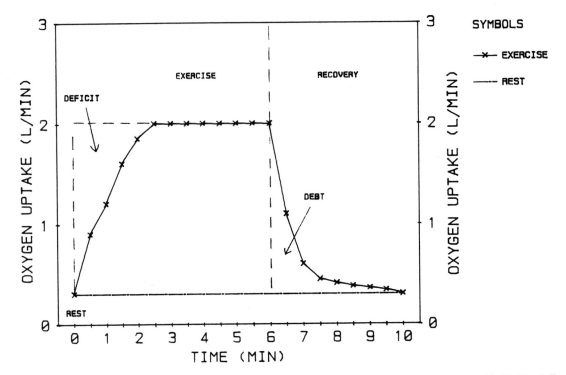

FIGURE 6–4. Oxygen uptake dynamics at onset and offset of exercise. (Redrawn from McArdle W, Katch F, Katch V: *Exercise Physiology.* Philadelphia: Lea & Febiger, 1981.)

within 1 to 4 minutes (Fig. 6–4).[14] The time required to reach a steady state increases at higher work rates and is longer in untrained subjects when compared to aerobically trained individuals. The fact that oxygen uptake does not increase instantaneously to a steady state at the onset of exercise implies that anaerobic energy sources contribute to the required $\dot{V}O_2$ at the beginning of exercise. Indeed, evidence exists that both the CP system and glycolysis contribute to the overall production of ATP at the onset of muscular work.[3,15] Once a steady state is obtained, however, the body's ATP requirements are met by aerobic metabolism. The term O_2 deficit has been used to describe the inadequate O_2 consumption at the onset of exercise (Fig. 6–4).

DURING PROLONGED EXERCISE

A steady-state $\dot{V}O_2$ can usually be maintained during 10 to 30 minutes of submaximal continuous exercise. Two exceptions to this rule exist. First, prolonged exercise in a hot and humid environment results in a steady "drift upward" of $\dot{V}O_2$ during the course of exercise

(Fig. 6–5).[16] Second, continuous exercise at a high relative work load results in a slow rise in $\dot{V}O_2$ across time similar to that in Figure 6–5. In both cases, this drift in $\dot{V}O_2$ probably occurs because of a variety of factors (i.e., rising body temperature and increasing blood catecholamines).[17,18]

INCREMENTAL EXERCISE

Oxygen uptake increases as a linear function to work rate until $\dot{V}O_{2\,max}$ is reached (Fig. 6–6). Most researchers believe that after reaching a steady state, most of the ATP production used for muscular contraction during the early stages of an incremental exercise test comes from aerobic metabolism. As the exercise intensity increases, however, blood levels of lactate rise (Fig. 6–6). Although much controversy surrounds this issue, many investigators believe that this lactate "inflection" point represents a point of increasing reliance upon anaerobic metabolism. Some reasons for lactate production in muscle were discussed previously. Although the precise terminology is controversial, this sudden increase in blood lactate levels—

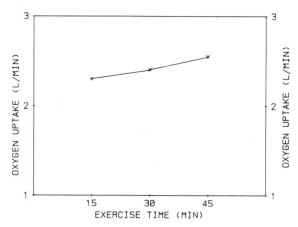

FIGURE 6–5. Changes in oxygen uptake during constant load exercise in the heat. Note V̇O₂ "drifts" upward across time during this type of work. (Redrawn from Powers S, Howley E, Cox R: Ventilatory and metabolic reactions to heat stress during prolonged exercise. *J Sports Med, 22:*32, 1982.)

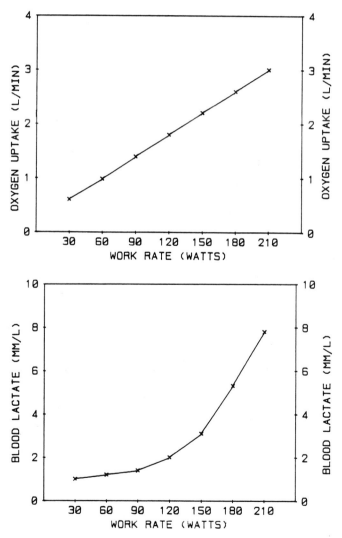

FIGURE 6–6. Changes in oxygen uptake and blood lactate concentrations as a function of work rate during incremental exercise. (Redrawn from Powers S, Byrd R, Tulley R, Callender T: Effects of caffeine ingestion on metabolism and performance during graded exercise. *Eur J Appl Physiol, 50:*301, 1983.)

termed the "anaerobic threshold"—has important implications for the prediction of performance and perhaps exercise prescription. For example, several investigators showed that the anaerobic threshold used in combination with other physiologic variables (i.e., $\dot{V}o_{2\,max}$) is a useful predictor of success in distance running.[19,20] The anaerobic threshold might also prove to be a useful marker of the transition from moderate to heavy exercise for subjects, and thus could be useful in exercise prescription.

RECOVERY FROM EXERCISE

An established fact is that $\dot{V}o_2$ values remain elevated above resting levels for several minutes during recovery from exercise (Fig. 6–4). This elevated post-exercise O_2 consumption has traditionally been termed the "oxygen debt." In general, post-exercise metabolism is higher after high-intensity exercise when compared to light to moderate work. Furthermore, post-exercise $\dot{V}o_2$ values remain elevated longer after prolonged exercise when compared to values associated with short-term exertion. The mechanisms to explain these observations are probably linked to the fact that both high-intensity and prolonged exercise result in higher body temperatures and higher plasma catecholamine levels than those values related to light or moderate short-term exercise.[17]

ENERGY COST OF ACTIVITIES

The energy cost of most types of physical activities has been established. Table 6–1 is a list of physical activities and their associated energy expenditures expressed in kilocalories per minute. Activities that are vigorous and involve large muscle groups usually result in more energy expended than those activities that use small muscle mass or require limited exertion. The estimates of energy expenditure listed in Table 6–1 were obtained by measuring the oxygen cost of these activities in an adult population. Although not precise, energy expenditure (kcal/min) can be estimated by multiplying the measured $\dot{V}o_2$ (L/min) and the coefficient 5 kcal/L. (Each liter of O_2 consumed represents an energy expenditure of 5 kcal.)

Clinicians often use the term "MET" to describe exercise intensity. One MET is equivalent

Table 6–1. Energy Expenditure During Activities

Activity	Energy expenditure (kcal/min/kg BW)
Badminton	0.06
Basketball	0.14
Boxing	0.22
Canoeing	
Leisure	0.04
Racing	0.10
Dancing	
Ballroom	0.05
Choreographed (vigorous)	0.17
Football	0.13
Golf (walking + carrying bag)	0.09
Running (horizontally)	
9 min/mile	0.19
8 min/mile	0.22
7 min/mile	0.24
6 min/mile	0.28
Swimming	
Backstroke	0.17
Breast stroke	0.16
Crawl, fast	0.16
Crawl, slow	0.13
Tennis (singles)	0.11
Volleyball	0.05
Walking (horizontal)	
16 min/mile	0.08
20 min/mile	0.07

to the amount of energy expended during 1 min of rest. For example, an individual exercising at a metabolic rate that is 5 times their resting $\dot{V}o_2$ is working at a 5 MET work rate. In a strict sense, the absolute energy expenditure during exercise at a 5-MET intensity would depend on the body size of the individual (i.e., a large individual would likely have a larger resting $\dot{V}o_2$ when compared to a smaller individual). For simplicity, individual differences in resting energy expenditures are often overlooked, and 1 MET is considered equivalent to a $\dot{V}o_2$ of 3.5 mL $\cdot$ kg^{-1} $\cdot$ min^{-1}. Hence, 1 MET represents an energy expenditure of approximately 1.5 kcal/min.

REFERENCES

1. Armstrong R: Biochemistry: Energy liberation and use. In *Sports Medicine and Physiology.* Edited by RS Strauss. Philadelphia: W.B. Saunders, 1979.
2. Brooks G, Fahey T: *Exercise Physiology: Human Bioenergetics and its Applications.* New York: John Wiley & Sons, 1984.
3. Cerretelli P, Rennie D, Pendergast D: Kinetics of metabolic transients during exercise. *Int J Sports Med,* 1:171, 1980.

4. McArdle W, Katch F, Katch V: *Exercise Physiology.* Philadelphia: Lea & Febiger, 1981.
5. Holloszy J: Muscle metabolism during exercise. *Arch Phys Med Rehabil, 63:*231, 1982.
6. Stryer L: *Biochemistry.* San Francisco: W.H. Freeman, 1981.
7. Graham T: Mechanisms of blood lactate increase during exercise. *Physiologist, 27:*299, 1984.
8. Gollnick P, Riedy M, Quintinskie J, Bertocci L: Differences in metabolic potential of skeletal muscle fibres and their significance for metabolic control. *J Exp Biol, 115:*191, 1985.
9. Gollnick P: Metabolism of substrates: Energy substrate metabolism during exercise and as modified by training. *Fed Proc, 44:*353, 1985.
10. Newsholme E: The control of fuel utilization by muscle during exercise and starvation. *Diabetes, 28 (Suppl. 1):*1, 1979.
11. Powers S, Riley W, Howley E: Comparison of fat metabolism between trained men and women during prolonged aerobic work. *Res Q Exerc Sport, 51:*427, 1980.
12. Holloszy J, Coyle E: Adaptations of skeletal muscle to endurance exercise and their metabolic consequences. *J Appl Physiol, 56:*831, 1984.
13. Powers S, Byrd R, Tulley R, Callender T: Effects of caffeine ingestion on metabolism and performance during graded exercise. *Eur J Appl Physiol, 50:*301, 1983.
14. Powers S, Dodd S, Beadle R: Oxygen uptake kinetics in trained athletes differing in $\dot{V}O_{2\,max}$. *Eur J Appl Physiol, 54:*306, 1985.
15. diPrampero P, Boutellier U, Pietsch P: Oxygen deficit and stores at onset of muscular exercise in humans. *J Appl Physiol, 55:*146, 1983.
16. Powers S, Howley E, Cox R: Ventilatory and metabolic reactions to heat stress during prolonged exercise. *J Sports Med, 22:*32, 1982.
17. Gaesser G, Brooks G: Metabolic bases of excess post-exercise oxygen consumption: A review. *Med Sci Sports Exerc, 16:*29, 1984.
18. Powers S, Howley E, Cox R: A differential catecholamine response during prolonged exercise and passive heating. *Med Sci Sports Exerc, 14:*435, 1982.
19. Farrell PA, et al.: Plasma lactate accumulation and distance running performance. *Med Sci Sports Exerc, 11:*338, 1979.
20. Powers S, et al.: Ventilatory threshold, running economy and distance running performance of trained athletes. *Res Q Exerc Sport, 51:*179, 1983.

7

CARDIORESPIRATORY RESPONSES TO ACUTE EXERCISE

J. LARRY DURSTINE AND
RUSSELL R. PATE

The cardiorespiratory system is the body's transportation network. The system functions by circulating blood through a closed network of blood vessels that infiltrate virtually all body tissues. The major components of the cardiorespiratory system (heart, blood, blood vessels, and pulmonary tract) are subject to an integrated set of control processes that enable it to respond effectively to many physiologic perturbations.

A long-recognized fact is that the cardiorespiratory system plays a critical role in the physiologic response to exercise. Vigorous exercise is associated with a marked increase in energy metabolism in the active skeletal muscles. This increased metabolic activity can be sustained only if the muscles are provided with metabolic substrates (e.g., oxygen, glucose, and free fatty acids) and are cleared of metabolic end products (e.g., carbon dioxide and lactic acid) at rates that match their rates of utilization and production, respectively. Because the cardiorespiratory system is the only supply line for muscle tissue, sustained, vigorous exercise clearly necessitates marked alterations in cardiorespiratory function.

The major functions of the cardiorespiratory system during exercise are: (1) to deliver oxygen to the active muscles at a rate that matches the rate at which it is used in aerobic metabolism; (2) to clear carbon dioxide and other metabolic end products from the active muscles at rates that match production; (3) to facilitate dissipation of metabolically produced heat to the environment by increasing blood flow to the skin; and (4) to support a properly integrated physiologic response to exercise by carrying regulatory substances such as hormones from sites of production to target tissues.

This chapter is a concise summary of the cardiorespiratory response to acute exercise. Major sections are dedicated to cardiovascular and respiratory responses. Within each of these major sections, the responses of key functional variables and their physiologic regulation are briefly discussed.

CARDIOVASCULAR RESPONSES

CARDIAC OUTPUT

The primary function of the heart is to pump blood through the pulmonary and systemic arterial circulations of the body. Cardiac output ($\dot{Q}$), quantified as liters of blood pumped per minute, is a reflection of the overall functional activity of the heart and is a principal determinant of the rate of oxygen delivery to peripheral tissues such as active skeletal muscles. Cardiac output is determined by heart rate (HR), the frequency of the heart's contractions (beats · min^{-1}), and stroke volume (SV), the volume of blood pumped by the heart with each contraction (ml of blood · contraction^{-1}). Thus, cardiac output ($\dot{Q}$) is equal to the product of heart rate (HR) and stroke volume (SV). ($\dot{Q}$ = HR · SV). At the onset of constant intensity exercise, $\dot{Q}$ increases rapidly at first and then more gradually until a plateau or "steady state" is attained. Subsequent increases in work rate and oxygen demand elicit similar responses in $\dot{Q}$ until a maximum is reached (Fig. 7–1). An average value for resting $\dot{Q}$ in normal healthy

men is 5 L · min.$^{-1}$ During exercise, $\dot{Q}$ may increase to 4 to 5 times the resting level (20 to 25 L · min^{-1}) in young, healthy men.[1] Somewhat lower maximal $\dot{Q}$ levels are observed in sedentary women (15 to 20 L · min^{-1}).[2] Maximal $\dot{Q}$ values as high as 35 to 40 L · min^{-1} have been observed in endurance athletes.[3]

Upright resting $\dot{Q}$ values are approximately 1 L · min^{-1} less than those observed in a supine position.[4,5] The mechanism underlying this difference is not fully understood, but SV values for supine subjects at rest are known to be higher than those reported for individuals while in the upright position.[4,5] Many individuals believe that, in the upright position, gravity impedes venous return of blood to the heart, causing a diminished SV and a lower $\dot{Q}$ value.

HEART RATE

Heart rate (HR), a major determinant of $\dot{Q}$, is controlled by factors intrinsic to the heart as well as by extrinsic neural and hormonal factors. The inherent rhythmicity of the heart, as established by its sinoatrial node, is regulated primarily by sympathetic and parasympathetic neurons emanating from the cardioregulatory center in the medulla. The sympathetic cardioaccelerator nerves release norepinephrine at their endings and cause the HR to increase during exercise.[6] The parasympathetic vagus nerve releases acetylcholine, which tends to reduce HR. Under resting conditions, the vagal influences are dominant over sympathetic influences. During exercise, this relationship is reversed, and HR consequently increases over its resting level. Also, circulating hormones such as epinephrine and norepinephrine, released by the adrenal glands into the blood, can increase the rate of contraction. In addition, factors such as increased temperature and stretch of the sinoatrial node (Bainbridge reflex) tend to increase HR.

The average resting HR for a sedentary individual is approximately 72 contractions per minute. The average resting HR for a trained person is somewhat lower, depending on the state of training. Maximal HR is relatively constant across various conditions, but tends to be slightly lower with the subject in the supine position than in the upright position.[5] Also, maximal HR decreases with aging.[7] A reasonably accurate estimate of average maximal HR for persons of a given age is obtained by using

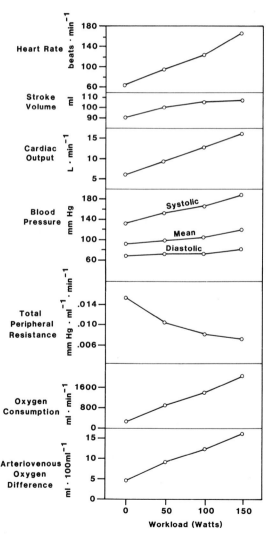

FIGURE 7–1. Cardiovascular responses to graded exercise.

the equation:

Average maximal HR (beats $\cdot$ min^{-1})
$$= 220 - \text{Age (years)}$$

This equation provides an indication of the *age group average* maximal HR; considerable variability in maximal HR exists among persons of a certain age (standard deviation of the mean is 10 to 12 beats $\cdot$ min^{-1}).[8]

HR often rises in anticipation of exercise. This pre-exercise increase is controlled by the limbic system, a regulatory center situated in the basal area of the brain surrounding the hypothalamus. Nerve fibers originating from this center and ending in the medulla result in activation of the cardioaccelerator nerves and inhibition of the vagus nerve. At the beginning of exercise, HR increases almost instantaneously.[9] The mechanism for this rapid response is not well understood, but a neural reflex with origins in joint receptors and muscle spindles may be involved.[9,10]

A strong positive correlation exists between HR and oxygen consumption (Fig. 7–1).[8,11] Both parameters increase linearly with increasing intensity of exercise.[11] As shown in Figure 7–1, HR increases with increasing workload until a maximal rate is reached.

STROKE VOLUME

Stroke volume (SV), the amount of blood pumped by the heart with each contraction, is regulated primarily by factors that are intrinsic to the heart. Principal among these factors is the Frank-Starling mechanism, which, stated simply, indicates that SV is determined by the rate at which blood is returned to the heart from the venous circulation (i.e., venous return). Increased venous return creates an increase in left ventricular end-diastolic volume, which increases the force of contraction of the myocardium through a mechanism that is similar to the length-tension relationship observed in skeletal muscle.[8] Factors extrinsic to the heart can also influence SV. Sympathetic neural stimulation of the myocardium, as well as epinephrine and norephinephrine released from the adrenal glands, can increase the contractile force of the heart.[8]

Stroke volume, unlike HR and $\dot{Q}$, does not increase linearly with workload and oxygen consumption (see Fig. 7–1). During graded exercise, SV increases progressively only until a workload that elicits 40 to 50% of $\dot{V}o_{2\,max}$ is attained. After this intensity level is reached, only small increases in SV occur with increasing oxygen demand.[6] Stroke volume increases with both upright and supine exercise as a consequence of increased venous return and sympathetic stimulation.[5] Greater increases in SV during exercise are observed when the subject is in the upright position.[4,5] This greater SV is probably accomplished by a decrease in left ventricular end-systolic volume resulting in a greater ejection fraction. Ejection fraction is the ratio of the volume of blood ejected from the left ventricle with each contraction to the volume of blood in the left ventricle at the end of diastole.[5]

Normal resting values for SV approximate 70 ml of blood per contraction in sedentary individuals. Highly trained persons may have values as high as 100 ml per contraction.[3,12] During exercise, SV increases to approximately twice its resting value.[3]

TOTAL PERIPHERAL RESISTANCE

Total peripheral resistance (TPR) is the sum of all forces that oppose blood flow in the systemic vascular bed. Factors that affect TPR include length of the arterial vasculature, blood viscosity, hydrostatic pressure, and vessel radius. Of these factors, vessel radius is the most important and, consequently, the balance between vasodilator and vasoconstrictor effects is a key determinant of TPR. Vessel radius is subject to neural control by the sympathetic nervous system; when activated, vasoconstriction results. Also, local control of vessels is exerted by chemical factors such as pH, Pco_2, and lactic acid concentration. Increased rates of muscle metabolism bring about local arterial vasodilation by decreasing pH and increasing Pco_2 and lactic acid concentration.

Total peripheral resistance decreases during exercise (Fig. 7–1).[13] This decrease occurs primarily through vasodilation of the arterial vascular beds in the active muscle tissues. The byproducts from energy metabolism, released in the exercising tissue, override the sympathetic vasoconstrictor effect of the nervous system. The outcome is a diversion of blood flow to the working tissue and away from the inactive muscles and viscera.[13]

MEAN ARTERIAL PRESSURE

The cardiac cycle has two major phases: (1) diastole, during which the ventricles are at rest, and (2) systole, a contractile period during which blood is forced by the ventricles into the pulmonary and systemic arterial systems. Fluid pressure in the systemic arteries fluctuates between systolic (higher) and diastolic (lower) pressures. The average pressure exerted by the blood against the inner walls of the arteries is a function of systolic and diastolic pressures and is termed the mean arterial pressure (MAP). The following equation includes the two major determinants of MAP, $\dot{Q}$ and TPR, and represents the mathematic model used to calculate MAP.

MAP = Cardiac output
$\qquad$ · Total peripheral resistance

An estimate of MAP is obtained easily by using the equation:

MAP = ⅓ (Systolic pressure
$\qquad$ − Diastolic pressure) + Diastolic pressure

Because the period of diastole is longer than the period of systole, MAP is less than the average of systolic and diastolic pressures.

Normal resting MAP is in the range of 90 to 100 mm Hg. Exercise MAP rises steadily with increasing workload (see Fig. 7–1). Maximal exercise MAP values approximate 130 mm Hg.[5] Data presented by Poliner et al. indicate that resting and exercise MAP are not affected by body position.[5]

SYSTOLIC BLOOD PRESSURE

The pressure in the arterial vessels is highest during ventricular systole. Systolic blood pressure (SBP) is indicative of the force generated by the heart during ventricular contraction. Normal resting systolic pressure is about 120 mm Hg. Systolic blood pressure increases with exercise but the magnitude of this response is specific to the type of exercise performed.

During dynamic, low-resistance exercise (e.g., jogging, swimming, and cycling), systolic blood pressure increases in proportion to exercise intensity (Fig. 7–1).[14] This overall response is the result of two countervailing effects of acute, dynamic exercise. Dilation of arterial blood vessels in active muscles reduces peripheral resistance, and this response tends to decrease blood pressure.[13] This effect, however, is more than offset by increased $\dot{Q}$, which as previously discussed, increases linearly with workload. Thus, the exercise-induced increase in SBP reflects an increase in $\dot{Q}$, the effect of which is partially offset by reduced peripheral resistance.

The magnitude of the response of SBP to dynamic exercise varies with body position and active muscle group. Somewhat lower pressure values are recorded when the subject exercises while supine than when the erect position is maintained.[5]

Researchers comparing leg and arm work have reported consistently higher SBP values (approximately 15%) associated with arm work.[14] This response is probably related to the smaller muscle mass of the arms, which offers greater resistance to blood flow than does the larger muscle mass of the legs.[14,15]

High-resistance exercise activities that involve forceful isometric, isotonic, or isokinetic muscle contractions cause marked increases in SBP.[16,17] In addition, the data presented by Seals et al. show that the SBP response to high-resistance exercise is directly related to the muscle mass activated.[18] These responses indicate that high-resistance exercise causes a substantial increase in myocardial work (and oxygen demand). As such, these activities should be used cautiously for persons with cardiovascular diseases.

DIASTOLIC BLOOD PRESSURE

Diastolic blood pressure, the pressure in the arterial system during ventricular diastole, provides an indication of peripheral resistance. High diastolic pressure values indicate elevated peripheral resistance. Normal resting diastolic blood pressure is approximately 80 mm Hg. Dynamic, low-resistance exercise usually causes little or no change in diastolic blood pressure (Fig. 7–1).[19–21] Investigators, comparing arm and leg work at the same relative percent $\dot{V}O_{2max}$ reported somewhat higher diastolic blood pressures for arm work.[14] Results of studies by Freedson et al. indicate that high-resistance exercise may result in large elevations in diastolic pressure.[16,17]

ARTERIOVENOUS OXYGEN DIFFERENCE

The oxygen-carrying capacity of blood is approximately 20 ml of oxygen per 100 ml of blood. Arteriovenous oxygen difference (a-$\bar{v}O_2$) is the difference between the oxygen contents of the arterial blood and mixed venous blood. The a-$\bar{v}O_2$ is a reflection of the extraction of oxygen from the blood by the peripheral tissues. The average value at rest is 5 ml of oxygen per 100 ml of blood (i.e., 5 ml of oxygen are extracted from each 100 ml of blood circulated). During dynamic exercise, a-$\bar{v}O_2$ increases linearly with workload to maximal values approximating 16 ml of oxygen per 100 ml of blood (Fig. 7–1).[12] Thus, about 85% of the oxygen in the blood is removed during maximal exercise. Even during maximal exercise, some oxygen in the mixed venous blood always returns to the heart; some blood continues to flow through less active tissues and not all of the oxygen is removed from this blood.

VENTILATORY RESPONSES

MINUTE VENTILATION

Minute ventilation is the volume of air passing through the pulmonary system in 1 min. Minute ventilation is often measured as the volume of air expired ($\dot{V}_E$) and is expressed as liters of air expired per minute (L · min^{-1}). Because the volume of a given amount of gas varies with environmental conditions, ventilatory volumes such as minute ventilation must be "corrected" to indicate the volume of the air under designated conditions. Ventilatory volumes are usually connected to either BTPS (body temperature and pressure, saturated with water vapor) or STPD (standard temperature (0°C) and pressure (760 mm Hg), dry). The latter convention is employed when minute ventilation is used with respiratory gas analysis in the measurement of oxygen consumption.

As shown in Figure 7–2, minute ventilation increases with increasing exercise intensity. Below approximately 50% $\dot{V}O_{2\,max}$, the relationship between ventilation and workload is linear. At higher intensities, however, the relationship is curvilinear, with ventilation increasing at a rate greater than the rates of work output and oxygen consumption. Minute ventilation is equal to the product of tidal vol-

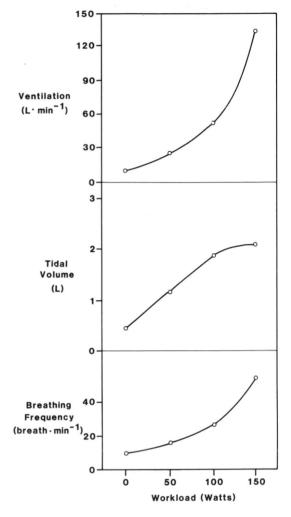

FIGURE 7–2. Ventilatory responses to graded exercise.

ume (volume expired per breath) and respiratory rate (breathing frequency). Across the lower range of exercise intensities, ventilation increases with increases in both tidal volume and respiratory rate.[22] At higher intensities, increases in ventilation are generated primarily by an increased respiratory rate.

The ventilatory response to exercise is controlled by a complex physiologic control process that is not fully understood.[8,23,24] The rate and depth of breathing are known to be controlled by nerve pathways that extend from the respiratory center in the medulla to the ventilatory musculature (i.e., diaphragm and intercostal and other muscles). Sensory input to the respiratory center comes from both neural and humoral sources. Central chemoreceptors, located on the ventral surface of the medulla, are sensitive to changes in the pH of cerebrospinal and medullary interstitial fluids, which are in turn affected by the pH and Pco_2 of arterial blood. Peripheral chemoreceptors, situated in the walls of the aorta and the carotid and brachiocephalic arteries, are sensitive to fluctuation in partial pressure of Po_2 in arterial blood. Both central and peripheral chemoreceptors function to alter ventilation in such a manner as to maintain normal pH, Pco_2, and Po_2 in arterial blood. For example, decreases in pH and Po_2 and increases in Pco_2 tend to cause increased ventilation.

Neural input to the respiratory center comes from other sites in the brain. For example, nerve pathways from the motor cortex provide a "feed forward" control in which ventilation increases as the skeletal muscles are activated in exercise. Also, afferent nerve pathways that arise from the skeletal muscles and joints likely play an important role in causing the rapid increase in ventilation that occurs at the onset of exercise.

VENTILATORY ANAEROBIC THRESHOLD (VANT)

As noted previously (and see Fig. 7–2) ventilation at higher intensities of exercise increases curvilinearly with increasing work rate. The work rate (or rate of oxygen consumption) at which the ventilatory response to graded exercise first departs from linearity is the ventilatory anaerobic threshold (VANT). Although the physiologic mechanism that underlies VANT is not fully understood, VANT usually occurs at a work rate that corresponds closely to that at which lactic acid begins to accumulate in the blood. The rapid increase in ventilation that occurs at exercise intensities above VANT may reflect activation of the bicarbonate buffer system that helps maintain blood pH by "blowing off" nonmetabolically produced carbon dioxide.

Most individuals who exercise regularly are able to perceive VANT as the exercise intensity at which breathing becomes somewhat labored and talking becomes difficult. Because VANT and blood lactic acid accumulation occur at similar exercise intensities in most persons, VANT provides a convenient marker for the upper end of the exercise intensity range usually applied in "aerobic" training programs. At exercise intensities above VANT, rapid accumulation of lactic acid in muscle and blood may preclude prolonged activity. Thus, participants in aerobic exercise programs are often advised to maintain exercise intensities below VANT.

SUMMARY

The cardiorespiratory system responds to acute exercise in such a manner as to increase blood flow and oxygen delivery to the active skeletal muscles. Certain major functional adjustments contribute to this overall response: (1) increased cardiac output ($\dot{Q}$) owing to increased heart rate (HR) and stroke volume (SV); (2) increased arteriovenous oxygen difference ($a\text{-}\bar{v}O_2$); (3) decreased total peripheral resistance (TPR) to blood flow owing to dilation of the arterial vasculature in active muscles; and (4) increased ventilation. The magnitude of these cardiorespiratory responses is graded to the intensity of the exercise. The responses are regulated by a complex and well-integrated set of neural and humoral control processes.

REFERENCES

1. Hossack KF, et al.: Maximal cardiac output during upright exercise: Approximate normal standards and variations with coronary heart disease. *Am J Cardiol*, 46:204, 1980.
2. Hossack KF, Kusumi F, Bruce RA: Approximate normal standards of maximal cardiac output during upright exercise in women. *Am J Cardiol*, 47:1080, 1981.
3. Ekblom B, Hermansen L: Cardiac output in athletes. *J Appl Physiol*, 25:619, 1968.
4. Bevegard S, Holmgren A, Jonsson B: Circulatory studies in well-trained athletes at rest and during heavy exercise with special reference to stroke volume and the influence of body position. *Acta Physiol Scand*, 57:26, 1963.
5. Poliner LR, et al.: Left ventricular performance in normal subjects: A comparison of the responses to exercise in the upright and supine positions. *Circulation*, 62:528, 1980.
6. Astrand P-O, Cuddy TE, Saltin B, Stenberg J: Cardiac output during submaximal and maximal work. *J Appl Physiol*, 19:268, 1964.
7. Londeree BR, Moeschberger ML: Effect of age and other factors on maximal heart rate. *Res Q Exerc Sports*, 53:297, 1982.
8. Martin BJ, Sparks KE, Zwillich CW, Weil JV: Low exercise ventilation in endurance athletes. *Med Sci Sports Exerc*, 11:181, 1979.
9. Petro JK, Hollandee AP, Bouman LN: Instantaneous cardiac acceleration in man induced by a voluntary contraction. *J Appl Physiol*, 29:794, 1970.

10. Rowell LB: What signals govern the cardiovascular responses to exercise? *Med Sci Sports Exerc, 12*:307, 1980.

11. Ekblom B, Goldberg AN, Kilbom A, Astrand P-O: Effects of atropine and propranolol on the oxygen transport system during exercise in man. *Scand J Clin Lab Invest, 30*:35, 1972.

12. Saltin B: Physiological effects of physical conditioning. *Med Sci Sports Exerc* 1:50, 1969.

13. Clausen JP: Effect of physical training on cardiovascular adjustments to exercise in man. *Physiol Rev, 57*:779, 1977.

14. Astrand P-O, et al.: Intra-arterial blood pressure during exercise with different muscle groups. *J Appl Physiol, 20*:253, 1965.

15. Blomqvist CG, Lewis SF, Taylor WF, Graham RM: Similarity of the hemodynamic responses to static and dynamic exercise of small muscle groups. *Circ Res, 48 (Suppl. 1)*:87, 1982.

16. Freedson PF, et al.: Intra-arterial blood pressure during free weight and hydraulic resistive exercise. *Med Sci Sports Exerc, 16*:131, 1984.

17. McArdle WP, Katch FI, Katch VL: *Exercise Physiology: Energy, Nutrition, and Human Performance.* 2nd Ed. Philadelphia: Lea & Febiger, 1986.

18. Seals DR, et al.: Increased cardiovascular response to static contraction of larger muscle groups. *J Appl Physiol, 54*:434, 1983.

19. Ekelund LG, Holmgren A: Central hemodynamics during exercise. *Circ Res, 21 (Suppl. 1)*:33, 1967.

20. Sheps DS: Exercise-induced increase in diastolic pressure: Indicator of severe coronary artery disease. *Am J Cardiol, 43*:708, 1979.

21. Hollmann W, Hettinger T: *Sportmedizin-Arbeits-und Trainingsgrundlagen.* 2nd Ed. Stuttgart: F.K. Schattauer, 1980.

22. Koyal SN, et al.: Ventilatory responses to the metabolic acidosis of treadmill and cycle ergometry. *J Appl Physiol, 40*:864, 1976.

23. Grimby G: Respiration in exercise. *Med Sci Sports Exerc, 1*:9, 1969.

24. Folinsbee LJ, et al: Exercise respiratory pattern in elite cyclists and sedentary subjects. *Med Sci Sports Exerc, 15*:503, 1983.

CHAPTER 8

SPECIFICITY OF EXERCISE

BRIAN J. SHARKEY

The responses and adaptations to exercise have been studied for more than a century. Not until 1967, however, when Holloszy reported the effect of endurance training on oxidative enzymes, did a coherent theory of specificity take shape.[1] Subsequent research has contributed to the principle that guides the development and conduct of exercise and training programs, the principle of specificity. The focus of this chapter is on the specificity of exercise and training, outlining responses and adaptations at both the peripheral and central levels, and showing how specificity applies to all types of training and modes of exercise. Because exercise and training are specific, it follows that tests should also be specific to the manner or mode of exercise if they are to reflect the effects of exercise and training.

SPECIFICITY OF EXERCISE

A particular exercise recruits individual motor units and their muscle fibers in a manner related to the exercise. Slow oxidative fibers are recruited for slow contractions, fast fibers are activated for fast contractions, and both types are engaged to lift heavy loads. The metabolic response within the individual fibers is also determined by the nature of the exercise. Anaerobic pathways provide energy for short-intense contractions, and aerobic pathways are used during extended contractions. Because the supply and support systems (respiratory, cardiovascular, and hormonal) supply these contracting muscle fibers, the systemic response to a particular exercise understandably is related to the fibers and energy systems employed, as well as the muscle mass involved. Submaximal contractions of a small muscle group elicit moderate changes in respiration, blood flow, and hormonal response; maximal effort with a large muscle mass requires major adjustments in these systems. Heart rate and blood pressure responses are exaggerated when strenuous work is performed by smaller muscle groups such as the arms.

STATIC VERSUS DYNAMIC EXERCISE

Dynamic muscular contractions, as in running, cycling, swimming, and other rhythmic aerobic activities, are characterized by periods of relaxation between contractions, allowing blood flow in the working muscles and assisting venous return (muscle pump). The constricting action of static or isometric contractions, or exercises with a static component (shoveling snow), restrict flow in blood vessels that serve the contracted muscle. When the contraction exceeds 60% of the maximal force of the muscle, the blood flow to the working fibers is severely reduced. These differences are reflected in the heart rate and blood pressure values during the exercise.

Dynamic exercise is characterized by moderate increases in heart rate and systolic blood pressure (rate-pressure product) and minimal change or a slight decrease in diastolic pressure. Static contractions provoke a pronounced rise in heart rate and systolic blood pressure along with an increase in diastolic and mean arterial pressure. The increases typically are proportional to the percent of the maximal force developed as well as the muscle mass involved.[2] Hence, static contractions elevate the rate-pressure product, an indicator of myocardial oxygen needs. The constricting or squeezing effect of static contractions on blood vessels increases peripheral resistance and the afterload on the heart. At the same time, because blood and oxygen are unable to reach the working muscles, the heart rate increases in an effort to meet the metabolic demands. The rise in heart rate exceeds the increase to be expected for a comparable level of oxygen intake during dynamic work.

A further complication is the possibility of a Valsalva maneuver during the static contraction. This forced expiratory effort against a closed glottis is common in weight lifting and exercises with a pronounced "static component," such as shoveling snow. Of concern is the possibility that the increased thoracic pressure caused by the Valsalva could impede venous return as well as blood flow in the coronary arteries. Proper breathing (exhale during lift) does minimize this problem. The exaggerated effects of static contractions (intra-arterial pressures approached 300 mm Hg) call for care in the use of heavy lifting exercises, especially in untrained, older, or coronary disease-prone populations. The cardiovascular responses can also be exaggerated when work is performed by the arms.

ARMS VERSUS LEGS

At a given submaximal workload (watts), arm work is performed at a greater physiologic cost than is leg work. Heart rate, systolic and dia-

stolic blood pressure, oxygen intake, and blood lactate values are increased, whereas stroke volume is decreased.[3] The involvement of a smaller muscle mass and the static component of arm work lead to increased peripheral vascular resistance, increased heart rate and blood pressure (rate-pressure product), and elevated myocardial oxygen needs. Heart rate and blood pressure levels climb even higher when the work is performed above the head, as in hammering nails.[4] The risks associated with shoveling snow, a situation in which blood pressure may be further exaggerated by peripheral vasoconstriction in cold air, can be reduced by warming up, selecting a smaller shovel to minimize the static component, using the legs to help push the shovel, and avoiding breath holding when the load is lifted.

The elevated heart rate during lifting exercises has led some researchers to believe that circuit weight training could be used to increase aerobic fitness. Hempel and Wells showed, however, that the heart rate overestimates the energy cost of circuit training.[5] Moreover, because each muscle group is only used for 20- to 30-sec intervals, how that amount of time could result in the overloading of the oxidative pathways and lead to an adaptive change is hard to imagine. Therefore, that circuit training falls short of other forms of aerobic training is not surprising. The elevated heart rate is useful as an indicator of metabolism in continuous dynamic work, but not when different muscle groups are used for short periods, as in circuit weight training. Training must be specific to the intended purpose.

SPECIFICITY OF TRAINING

When the tension-generating or metabolic properties of a muscle fiber are loaded beyond their usual range (overload), the fiber attempts to adapt to the new demand. Repeated and progressive overload of a fiber constitutes training, and the adaptations are specific to the manner and mode of exercise used in training. High-resistance strength training leads to increased synthesis of contractal proteins actin and myosin, whereas high-repetition endurance training brings about an increase in enzyme protein, specifically the energy-producing aerobic enzymes found in the mitochondria. The overload of a training bout triggers specific protein synthesis, but how the message is transmitted is not yet clear. A likely explanation is that messenger RNA carries the message from the nucleus, and that transfer RNA escorts individual amino acids to the ribosome where protein synthesis occurs.

These and other adaptations take place in the hours and days after a bout of training. Some adaptations occur in or around the muscle fiber (peripheral changes) and other adaptations occur in the cardiovascular, respiratory, and neuroendocrine systems (central changes).[6,7] Peripheral adaptations are usually specific to the manner and mode of exercise. Some of the central changes are specific and some are general, allowing for some transfer of training.

PERIPHERAL EFFECTS

Aerobic Training

As noted previously, aerobic or endurance training leads to increased concentrations of aerobic enzymes from the citric acid, electron transport, and β-oxidation pathways.[8] Endurance training also increases the size and number of the mitochondria in which these pathways are located. Pette suggests that prolonged exercise can even lead to a transformation from fast- to slow-twitch fiber properties.[9] Studies of rabbit and rat muscle show that fast fibers first take on the metabolic properties of the slow fibers, and eventually assume the contractile properties and myosin ATPase characteristic of slow oxidative muscle fibers. The hypothesis that higher intensity aerobic training may improve the oxidative capabilities of fast fibers while retaining the fast-twitch characteristics with fast contractions has yet to be supported.

Other peripheral changes include increased concentrations of muscle myoglobin, elevated stores of triglyceride, and, when training is accompanied by a high-carbohydrate diet, increased storage of muscle glycogen. All of these changes are specific to the fibers used in training. The capillary to fiber ratio is higher in endurance-trained muscle. These changes combine to make endurance-trained fibers more efficient through the effective use of oxygen and fat and the relative conservation of muscle glycogen. In addition, Gordon showed that endurance training is sometimes associated with the loss of contractile protein.[12]

Anaerobic Training

The effects of high-intensity anaerobic training are not as well documented. Some researchers note increases in the short-term energy source creatine phosphate; other investigators have not. A small change may take place at the start of training with little or no change thereafter. The effects of training on anaerobic glycolysis are equally uncertain. Gollnick and Hermansen reported changes in the rate-limiting enzyme phosphofructokinase, whereas other researchers have noted no such change.[10] Muscle does seem to have a greater capacity for pyruvate production through glycolysis than the mitochondria have for pyruvate utilization, and therefore aerobic training would seem more productive than anaerobic training to increase pyruvate utilization. For high-intensity sport contests, however, anaerobic training may provide a small but important edge. In addition, some anaerobic work may be necessary to help athletes become accustomed to the acidotic environment and to achieve efficiency in high-speed movement patterns.

Muscular Fitness Training

Strength Training. High-resistance strength training increases muscle size through the synthesis of contractile protein and thickening of connective tissue. The potential for creating additional fibers from fiber splitting or satellite cells in human muscle is still a matter for debate.[11] Some authors noted a modest rise in creatine phosphate levels with strength training, but this change may have resulted from the increased muscle mass (hypertrophy). Although strength training is sometimes associated with the loss of enzyme protein, Hickson showed that simultaneous strength and endurance training interferes with the development of strength.[12,13]

The effects of training may be viewed as occurring within the muscle (myogenic) or within the nervous system (neurogenic). Strength training seems to lead to decreased inhibitions and more effective application of force, examples of neurogenic training.

Endurance Training. Individual muscle groups may be trained for endurance. The peripheral effects of long-term endurance training are similar to those mentioned in *Aerobic Training*. The effects of short-term endurance training, accomplished with a maximum of 15 to 25 repetitions, fall between those found in strength training and those in long-term endurance training. From recent studies, researchers suggest that short-term endurance training leads to some increase in strength and work output, with no change in oxidative capability.[14] Incidentally, strength training does not seem to interfere with the development of endurance.[13]

Power Training. Power, defined as the rate of doing work, is a composite of strength (force) and speed (distance/time). The peripheral effects of power training, although not well studied, seem to combine some of the effects of strength and anaerobic training.

CENTRAL EFFECTS

Aerobic Training

Aerobic fitness is defined as the capacity to take in, transport, and utilize oxygen. Oxygen utilization, which takes place in the muscle fiber, is a peripheral effect of training; the ability to take in and to transport oxygen are central effects. Athletes often have larger lung volumes than nonathletes, yet lung capacity is not highly correlated to performance. Changes in lung capacity may be the result of peripheral training of specific respiratory muscles. Respiration does become more efficient with endurance training, leading to larger tidal volumes and slower respiratory rates for a given level of oxygen intake. Training also elevates the ventilatory threshold to a higher percentage of the maximal oxygen intake ($\dot{V}o_{2\,max}$).

Oxygen transport is accomplished by the heart, blood vessels, blood, red cells, and hemoglobin, as well as redistribution of blood through vasomotor regulation. Endurance training improves stroke volume while lowering the heart rate at submaximal exercise levels, and increases the maximal cardiac output. A characteristic of the endurance-trained heart is an elevated end-diastolic volume of the left ventricle.[17] This type of cardiac hypertrophy allows a greater stroke volume and slower heart rate for a given level of cardiac output. Surprisingly, studies of animal hearts reveal a minimal change in cardiac muscle enzymes. Authors suggest, however, that training might lead to enlargement of the coronary arteries.

Other effects of training include an increase in blood volume and total hemoglobin, important contributors to oxygen, carbon dioxide, and heat transport. One of the more important outcomes of endurance training is a rapidly acquired ability to redistribute blood from the skin, viscera, and unused muscles to the working muscles.[2] From recent research efforts, scientists suggest a possible peripheral effect of training that may have central implications. If trained muscle fibers are better able to take up lactate at rest, trained leg muscles could remove lactate produced during arm work, allowing improved arm performance after leg training.[15]

The temptation is great to suggest that while peripheral effects of training are specific, the central effects are general; to an extent this statement is true. Certainly blood volume, hemoglobin, and redistribution effects would seem to transfer to any endurance activity. But the effects of training on the heart may not transfer as well as was once thought. (See Modes of Training in this chapter.)

Finally, endurance training influences the neuroendocrine systems. Skill and efficiency improve with training and practice, leading to a lower energy cost for a given speed of movement. Training also reduces the levels of some hormones, such as epinephrine.[16] Training also increases the sensitivity to some hormones, such as insulin. These peripheral and central changes lead to impressive improvements in endurance performance. Significant predictors of performance in an event such as a 10,000-m run include the $\dot{V}o_{2\,max}$, the ventilatory threshold, and efficiency.

Anaerobic Training

Central effects of anaerobic training are poorly documented, probably because anaerobic effort is too short to overload the heart and other components of the oxygen transport system. Anaerobic training leads to greater accumulation of lactic acid in the blood after maximal effort, which may reflect improvements in peripheral muscle glycolysis. Increased blood lactate levels could also be due, however, to reduced uptake by skeletal or cardiac muscle. Anaerobic training is arduous and often unpleasant. When anaerobic work is a component of the sport, however, it may be important to include it in training to help the athlete to relax and become more efficient at high speed and, possibly, to gain peripheral or central benefits.

Muscular Fitness Training

Strength, short-term endurance, and power training have nominal effects on the components of the oxygen transport system. Some echocardiographic studies reveal, however, that resistance athletes exhibit cardiac hypertrophy characterized by increased ventricular wall thickness, which may result from the afterload caused by vascular constriction and elevated blood pressure during lifting. This adaptation, with a normal end-diastolic volume, is the opposite of that found in endurance athletes (greater end-diastolic volume with normal wall thickness).[17] Other investigators suggest that the wall thickness is not exceptional when it is adjusted for body size.

The effects of strength training on the central nervous system include reduced central inhibitions and an enhanced ability to recruit muscle fibers. Although these adjustments may occur in the central nervous system, they are probably specific to the muscles and movements used in training. How these peripheral and central changes influence the specificity of some common modes of training is discussed subsequently.

MODES OF TRAINING

Aerobic Training

The effects of training are highly task specific. Because most peripheral and some central effects are specific, that one form of training has little transfer to another is not surprising. For example, after 12 weeks of incline (uphill) training, the post-training $\dot{V}O_{2\,max}$ values on an inclined protocol were significantly greater than horizontal test values.[18] The effects of bicycle training do not transfer well to running, or vice versa. The same fact is true for swimming, cross-country skiing, rowing, or aerobic dance. When a cyclist shows improvement on a treadmill test, some of the increase can be attributed to generalizable central effects, such as increased blood volume, total hemoglobin and redistribution. Many persons believe that transfer is also due to the effects of training on the heart, which may be true only in part.

Saltin had subjects train one leg on a bicycle ergometer, with the other leg serving as a control.[19] Maximal oxygen intake and tissue enzyme levels were only improved in the trained leg, as you might expect. Even more interesting was the fact that the heart rate during exercise was lowered only when the trained leg was tested. Saltin and co-workers attribute the heart rate response to small nerve endings located in the muscle fibers.[20] The nerves sense the metabolic environment and influence the heart rate response through afferent nervous connection to the cardiac control center in the brain. The slower heart rate provides more filling time and allows a greater end-diastolic volume and stroke volume. Hence, some of the so-called central responses to training are apparently still subject to peripheral control. This conclusion presents another argument for the specificity of training.

Results of many studies show the specificity of either arm or leg training. Athletes with well-trained legs, such as runners, often have poorly trained arms. If they take up rowing or cross-country skiing, they dramatically increase the endurance capacity of the arms. Studies of arm cranking show that the initial limits to performance in previously untrained subjects are peripheral. As training continues, oxygen transport becomes the limiting factor.[21] In another study of arm cranking, arm work was added to leg work or vice versa. In fit but not highly trained subjects, the addition of arm to leg work caused a decrease in blood flow to the leg muscles. The demands of combined arm and leg work limit blood flow to both muscle groups, which adjust by increasing oxygen extraction from each unit of blood. When the muscles are not sufficiently trained to utilize oxygen or when blood flow becomes inadequate, however, the muscles work anaerobically and fatigue.[22] Therefore, arms and legs must both be trained to perform combined arm and leg activities such as rowing, swimming, and cross-country skiing.

Muscular Fitness Training

Strength, muscular endurance, and power are only improved in the muscles used in training. Upper body muscles may be highly trained while the legs are not, or vice versa. The quadricep group can be trained while ignoring the hamstrings. And one arm can be trained while the other is in a cast. Studies that demonstrate a cross-training effect (improvement in the untrained limb) probably involve neurogenic effects, such as learning, reduced inhibitions, and low levels of nervous stimulation in the control limb.

SPECIFICITY OF TESTING

Because exercise and training are specific, the tests used to evaluate training should also be specific, with respect to both the mode of exercise and the purpose of the test.

MODE

Aerobic Training

Runners achieve best results when tested on a treadmill, cyclists on a bicycle ergometer, swimmers in a swimming test, and rowers on a rowing ergometer. The effect of cross-country arm training is best evaluated in a test that simulates the sport. Unfortunately, no testing procedures are available to assess the effects of aerobic dance or circuit training. Yet even the most specific tests fail to account fully for all the effects and benefits of training. Davies et al. studied the effects of treadmill training on the $\dot{V}O_{2\,max}$ and muscle enzyme levels of rats.[23] They found that the max treadmill test was a relatively poor predictor of endurance, accounting for 49% of the variance in performance; muscle oxidase levels accounted for 85%. Endurance improved 500% and muscle oxidase increased 400% whereas the $\dot{V}O_{2\,max}$ increased 14%. deVries speculates that mitochondrial (peripheral) factors determine the duration of an endurance activity, and the $\dot{V}O_{2\,max}$ (including central factors) determines the intensity or maximal rate at which the activity can be performed.[24] Future tests may differentiate between the peripheral and central effects of training.

Anaerobic Training

Task-specific anaerobic tests are necessary to reflect the effects of training. Again, athletes should be tested as they train in their particular sport. Fortunately, equipment such as the Biokinetic swim bench is becoming available to provide sport-specific testing and training.

Muscular Fitness Training

Isometric training effects are best shown on an isometric test. Isometric training is also specific in regard to the angle used in training. Isotonic training is best assessed by an isotonic test that is specific to the manner of training (constant versus variable resistance). Isokinetic training effects are best revealed through an isokinetic test that is specific in regard to the speed of training. Tests should also reflect the component trained, using strength tests for strength training, endurance tests for endurance training, and so forth. Use of the wrong test can mask the benefits of training.

PURPOSE

Finally, consider the purpose of the test by using two common examples: testing for aerobic fitness versus testing for cardiovascular health. Tests for aerobic fitness or $\dot{V}O_{2\,max}$ are used on asymptomatic, low-risk subjects and athletes to assess the effects of training. Best results are achieved when the test is completed in 8 to 12 minutes. Tests should be specific to the mode of training, using increases in speed for track runners and increases in grade for hill runners. During the final stages, the subject can have the option of increasing rate or grade, thereby avoiding termination of the test because of test protocol rather than because of fatigue. This option is especially valid on the bicycle ergometer on which a slow cadence frequently causes the test to be terminated due to lack of muscle strength.

Tests of cardiovascular health, such as the treadmill stress test, are properly used to screen clients, to search for undiagnosed disease, or to assess progress in cardiac rehabilitation. Popular tests such as the Bruce or Balke protocols start slowly and progress at a moderate rate to higher work loads. When used to test the $\dot{V}O_{2\,max}$ of an endurance-trained runner, the Bruce test may require more than 18 min to complete, and the subject will not begin running until the grade reaches 20%. Similarly, the Balke test may last 30 min, causing the subject to stop because of leg cramps. Walking protocols are appropriate for untrained individuals and walkers, but not for trained runners seeking information concerning the effects of training on the $\dot{V}O_{2\,max}$. Use protocols appropriate to the activity and the purpose of the test.

The effects of exercise and training are specific. Although some effects of training are generalized to similar types of activity, all peripheral and some central effects are specific. Therefore, concentrate training on the fibers, pathways, support systems, and movements that are utilized in the sport or activity. Individuals should not ignore other exercises and muscle groups, however. Some additional training is necessary to avoid injury, to achieve muscular balance, and to provide backup for prime movers when they become fatigued. More detailed discussions concerning the peripheral and central effects of training, along with guidelines for the conduct of training and testing programs, are provided in subsequent chapters.

REFERENCES

1. Holloszy J: Biochemical adaptations in muscle. *J Biol Chem, 242:*2278, 1967.
2. Shephard RJ: *Physiology and Biochemistry of Exercise.* New York: Praeger, 1982.
3. Franklin B: Exercise testing, training and arm ergometry. *Sports Med, 2:*100, 1985.
4. Astrand P-O, Rodahl K: *Textbook of Work Physiology.* New York: McGraw-Hill, 1977.
5. Hempel L, Wells, CL: Cardiorespiratory cost of the Nautilus express circuit. *Phys Sportsmed, 13:*82, 1985.
6. Fox E: Physiological effects of training. In *Encyclopaedia of Physical Education, Fitness and Sports: Training, Environment, Nutrition and Fitness.* Edited by GA Stull and TK Cureton. Salt Lake City: Brighton Publishing, 1980.
7. McCafferty W, Horvath SM: Specificity of exercise and specificity of training: A subcellular review. *Res Q, 48:*358, 1977.
8. Knuttgen H, Vogel J, Poortmans J: *Biochemistry of Exercise.* Champaign; Human Kinetics, 1983.
9. Pette D: Activity-induced fast to slow transitions in mammalian muscle. *Med Sci Sports Exerc, 16:*517, 1984.
10. Gollnick PD, Hermansen L: Biochemical adaptations to exercise: Anaerobic metabolism. In *Exercise and Sports Science Reviews.* Vol. 1. Edited by JH Wilmore. New York: Academic Press, 1973.
11. Gonyea W: Skeletal muscle growth induced by strength training. In *Frontiers of Exercise Biology.* Edited by K Borer, DW Edington, and T White. Champaign: Human Kinetics, 1983.
12. Gordon E: Anatomical and biochemical adaptations of muscle to different exercises. *JAMA, 201:*755, 1967.
13. Hickson R: Interference of strength development by simultaneously training for strength and endurance. *Eur J Appl Physiol, 45:*255, 1980.
14. Sharkey BJ: *Training for Cross-country Ski Racing.* Champaign: Human Kinetics, 1984.
15. Rosler K, et al.: Transfer effects in endurance exercise. *Eur J Appl Physiol, 54:*355, 1985.
16. Doctor R, Sharkey BJ: Note on some physiological and subjective reactions to exercise and training. *Percept Mot Skills, 32:*233, 1971.
17. Morganroth J, Maron B: The athlete's heart syndrome: A new perspective. In *The Marathon.* Edited by P Milvey. New York: New York Academy of Sciences, 1977.
18. Freund BJ, Allen D, Wilmore JH: Interaction of test protocol and inclined run training on maximal oxygen uptake. *Med Sci Sports Exerc, 18:*588, 1986.
19. Saltin B: The interplay between peripheral and central factors in the adaptive response to exercise and training. In *The Marathon.* Edited by P Milvey. New York: New York Academy of Sciences, 1977.
20. Mitchell JH, Reardon W, McCloskey D, Wildnethal K: Possible roles of muscle receptors in the cardiovascular response to exercise. In *The Marathon.* Edited by P. Milvey. New York: New York Academy of Sciences, 1977.
21. Boileau R, McKeown B, Riner W: The influence of cardiovascular and metabolic parameters on arm and leg $Vo_{2\,max}$. Presented at the annual meeting of the American College of Sports Medicine, Miami, 1981.
22. Secher N, Ruberg-Larsen N, Brinkhorst R, Bonde-Petersen F: Maximal oxygen uptake during arm cranking and combined arm plus leg exercise. *J Appl Physiol, 36:*515, 1974.
23. Davies K, Packer L, Brooks G: Biochemical adaptation of mitochondria, muscle and whole-animal respiration to endurance training. *Arch Biochem Biophys, 209:*539, 1981.
24. deVries HA: *Physiology of Exercise.* Dubuque: William C. Brown, 1986.

CHAPTER 9

CARDIORESPIRATORY ADAPTATIONS TO TRAINING

MICHAEL L. SMITH AND
JERE H. MITCHELL

Exercise training-induced improvement in fitness is achieved primarily by enhanced maximal work capacity and reduced myocardial oxygen demand for any given level of total body oxygen consumption. The most accepted index of work capacity is maximal oxygen consumption ($\dot{V}O_{2\,max}$), which represents the maximal rate of delivery of oxygen from the lung to the working tissues. Defined physiologically, $\dot{V}O_{2\,max}$ is the product of maximal cardiac output and maximal arteriovenous oxygen difference, which is determined by oxygen extraction in active muscles and by shunting of blood flow away from inactive tissue. Exercise training can significantly improve the oxygen transport system and increase $\dot{V}O_{2\,max}$ by increasing both the maximal cardiac output and the maximal arteriovenous oxygen difference. This change could possibly occur by improvements in respiration, central circulation and cardiac function, peripheral circulation, or skeletal muscle metabolism.

RESPIRATION

At sea level, arterial oxygen tension is maintained at maximal workloads, demonstrating that pulmonary factors, ventilatory or diffusive, do not limit oxygen transport in normal individuals. Furthermore, maximal oxygen transport by the respiratory system is not significantly improved by endurance training. Thus, the limitation of oxygen transport appears to be imposed by maximal cardiac output and maximal arteriovenous oxygen difference. In the untrained individual, the capacity for oxygen transport by respiration is greater than that by circulation. This mismatch is dramatically reduced as the level of exercise training improves the cardiovascular capacity for oxygen transport.[1] Dempsey et al. demonstrated that oxygen saturation and content may begin to decrease near maximal work in elite endurance athletes.[2] Therefore, in some elite athletes, the respiratory system may contribute to the limitation of $\dot{V}O_{2\,max}$ by reducing maximal arteriovenous oxygen difference.

CARDIAC FUNCTION AND CENTRAL CIRCULATION

Resting cardiac output is not remarkably altered by exercise training, whereas maximal cardiac output can be twice as large in a well-trained endurance athlete as compared to an untrained subject of the same body size (Table 9–1; Fig. 9–1). The ability of an individual to have a high maximal cardiac output is probably related both to genetic factors and to a long

Table 9–1. Endurance Training-Induced Changes in Some Cardiovascular Variables

Variables	Resting	Maximal exercise
Oxgen consumption	No change	Increase
Heart rate	Decrease	No change
Stroke volume	Increase	Increase
Cardiac output	No change	Increase
Contractility	No change	No change
Muscle blood flow	No change	Increase
Splanchnic blood flow	No change	Decrease
Oxygen extraction	No change	Increase
Ventilation	No change	No change

period of endurance training. By definition, maximal cardiac output is the product of maximal heart rate and maximal stroke volume. Maximal heart rate is not affected by endurance training and is usually the same in highly trained athletes and in untrained subjects (Table 9–1; Fig. 9–1). Therefore, higher maximal cardiac outputs are attributed exclusively to the ability to eject a larger maximal stroke volume (Table 9–1; Fig. 9–1). Several factors are responsible for an increased maximal stroke volume. First, cardiac dimensions are increased. Left ventricular chamber size is greater in endurance-trained subjects as indicated by greater

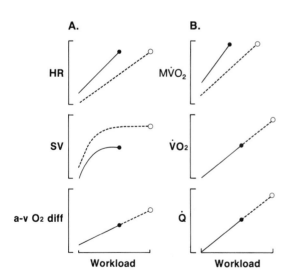

FIGURE 9–1. Cardiovascular responses to increasing workloads to a maximum. (●), untrained subject. (○), endurance trained subject. *Solid line,* submaximal responses in untrained subject. Dashed line, submaximal responses in trained subject. Q̇, cardiac output. HR, heart rate. SV, stroke volume. a-v O₂ diff, tissue oxygen extraction. V̇O₂, total body oxygen consumption. MV̇O₂, myocardial oxygen consumption.

end-diastolic volumes at rest and during exercise.[3,4] Also, endurance-trained athletes have a significantly greater absolute left ventricular mass (eccentric hypertrophy) and left ventricular mass normalized to lean body mass than sedentary subjects.[5,6] Results of short-term longitudinal training studies (less than 20 weeks) demonstrate smaller changes in wall thickness and chamber size.[7] Therefore, the increased left ventricular mass and increased chamber size that develops with endurance training must occur gradually over months or years of training. The enhanced maximal stroke volume is attributable primarily to the increased chamber size and an increased preload (as discussed later).

That endurance training can alter autonomic function, preload, and afterload is important. A change in the status of any of these variables at maximal exercise could affect cardiac output. An augmented preload independently could produce an increase in stroke volume by the Starling effect. Evidence exists to suggest that preload is increased after endurance training. This effect of training is related, in part, to an increase in total blood volume consequent to an increase in plasma volume.[8] In addition, the effective left ventricular diastolic compliance (or the ability of the chamber to accept blood) may be increased after endurance training, which also would enhance submaximal or maximal preload.[9–11]

Endurance-trained individuals often have a reduced heart rate at rest and at any level of submaximal exercise (Fig. 9–1). The resting bradycardia is attributable to a shift of autonomic balance in favor of the parasympathetic nervous system and a decrease in intrinsic heart rate, which is the rate obtained with complete ablation of the autonomic nervous system.[12,13] Cardiac output is not significantly changed at submaximal workloads by endurance training (see Fig. 9–1).[14] Hence, stroke volume is elevated at all levels of submaximal work in the trained state (Fig. 9–1). The result is improved "efficiency" of the heart at submaximal workloads (i.e., the myocardium does not use as much oxygen at a given workload) as illustrated by a decreased double product (heart rate · arterial pressure) at submaximal workloads. Myocardial oxygen consumption is strongly correlated with double product; therefore, an important benefit of endurance training is a reduced myocardial oxygen consumption at any submaximal workload (Fig. 9–1).

The effect of endurance training on ventricular performance or contractility is far less certain. Several authors suggest that contractility is enhanced by training, whereas other investigators find no training effect on ventricular performance.[10] Studies have yielded results to show that during maximal exercise in humans, the ejection fraction is high and the end-systolic volume is low irrespective of the training status.[4,11] Therefore, at maximal exercise, little is gained from enhanced contractility. The enhanced preload, decreased afterload (which is discussed in a subsequent section), and unaltered or slightly augmented contractility result in a dramatically increased maximal stroke volume.

PERIPHERAL CIRCULATION

Endurance training is associated with a reduction in total peripheral resistance, or afterload, during exercise. This reduction in peripheral resistance enables the endurance athlete to achieve levels of cardiac output that are double that of a sedentary subject at similar arterial pressures during maximal exercise. Although the mechanisms responsible for the augmented fall in peripheral resistance are not fully understood, an important factor is certainly the increase in vascularity associated with endurance training.[10,15,16] The increased vascular space augments the fall in peripheral resistance as maximal vasodilatation in skeletal muscle is approached during maximal exercise. Alterations in metabolic function at maximal work levels also may affect the maximal level of vasodilatation that is achieved. Together, these training effects reduce peripheral resistance at maximal workloads, thereby augmenting maximal cardiac output. The ability to vasodilate (and increase blood flow) in the active tissue does not reach a maximum, however, even at maximal workloads, as shown by Stray-Gundersen et al.[17] When the pericardium was removed in untrained dogs, a greater rise in cardiac output and a greater fall in peripheral vascular resistance occurred at maximal exercise. In fact, the vasculature of the contracting skeletal muscle appears to maintain some degree of tonic vasoconstriction such that if cardiac output is augmented further, the active muscle can receive a further increase in blood flow.[18] Saltin postulated that if most of the skeletal muscle of the body was engaged in maximal dynamic exercise, a cardiac output of more than 60 L/min would be required to prevent a measurable fall in blood pressure.[18] These findings strongly support the hypothesis that the pump capacity of the heart is the primary limitation to $Vo_{2\,max}$ in man.

The maximal total body oxygen extraction (arteriovenous oxygen difference) increases after endurance training (Table 9–1; Fig. 9–1). This effect is brought about, in part, by an increase in the diffusion gradient for oxygen between the capillaries and the active skeletal muscle cells. The total myoglobin (the oxygen-carrying protein complex in skeletal muscle) content of trained muscle also increases.[19,20] These changes within the skeletal muscle tissue enhance the diffusion capacity of oxygen. Also, tissue oxygen extraction within the active muscle is enhanced by the increased capillary density that occurs with endurance training. The total number and the density (total number per gram of tissue) of capillaries increases.[15,16,21] The increased capillary density results in an increased capillary diffusion surface area, which is advantageous for nutrient and metabolic by-product exchange. The arterial tree also may increase as a result of the opening of dormant collateral vessels. This change may contribute to improved extraction by improved blood flow to the working tissue. Recently, Musch et al. demonstrated that endurance training increases the degree of shunting of blood away from the splanchnic and renal circulations at maximal exercise.[22] This increase is associated with an increase in blood flow to the active skeletal muscle. This improved redistribution of blood flow during exercise acts in concert with the increased tissue extraction to augment total body arteriovenous oxygen difference. Hence, several training-induced adaptations within the skeletal muscle contribute to an augmented maximal arteriovenous oxygen difference.

MUSCLE METABOLISM

Although the metabolism of skeletal muscle is discussed in subsequent chapters, a few pertinent points are worth mentioning. Endurance training increases the capacity for aerobic metabolism. This effect is accomplished by an increase in the total number of mitochondria and in mitochondrial enzyme activity.[19] These biochemical alterations result in an increase in the preferential use of free fatty acids released from adipose tissue as an energy substrate during dynamic exercise. Skeletal muscle with an enhanced oxidative capacity is able to function at a lower oxygen tension, thereby delaying the onset of accelerated glycogenolysis and depletion of glycogen stores.[23] Hence, the individual demonstrates enhanced endurance and is able to sustain longer periods of work at a given percentage of $\dot{V}O_{2\,max}$.[24]

SUMMARY

Endurance training elicits several cardiovascular adaptations evident both at rest and during exercise. At rest, the only changes that occur are a decrease in heart rate and a concomitant increase in stroke volume. As a result, myocardial oxygen demand is moderately reduced at rest and at any given absolute submaximal workload. When the workload is considered as a percent of maximal capacity, however, the heart rate at any submaximal percent of capacity is the same, and stroke volume and cardiac output increase. At maximal exercise, the oxygen consumption, stroke volume, cardiac output, and tissue oxygen extraction achieved increase significantly, which translates into a significant improvement in performance. Maximal heart rate shows no change, and maximal ventilation or maximal diffusion capacity is not dramatically improved. Therefore, the oxygen delivery system is changed significantly for the better by improvements in cardiac function, the shunting of blood to the active tissue, and tissue extraction of oxygen. Cardiac pump function appears to be the primary limitation to maximal performance. Only in very elite athletes does respiratory function become a potential limitation. Lastly, improvements in aerobic metabolism in the skeletal muscle significantly improve the ability to sustain work at a given percent of $\dot{V}O_{2\,max}$.

REFERENCES

1. Johnson RL: Oxygen transport. In *Clinical Cardiology.* Edited by JT Willerson and CA Sanders. New York: Grune & Stratton, 1977.
2. Dempsey JA, Hanson P, Henderson K: Exercise-induced arterial hypoxemia in healthy humans at sea-level. *J Physiol (Lond), 355:*161, 1984.
3. Morganroth J, Maron BJ, Henry WL, Epstein SE: Comparative left ventricular dimensions in trained athletes. *Ann Intern Med, 82:*521, 1975.
4. Rerych SK, Scholz PM, Sabiston DC, Jones RH: Effects of exercise training on left ventricular function in normal subjects: A longitudinal study by radionuclide angiography. *Am J Cardiol, 45:*244, 1980.
5. Keul J, Dickhuth HH, Simon G, Lehmann M: Effect of status and dynamic exercise on heart volume, contractility, and left ventricular dimensions. *Circ Res, 48:*I162, 1981.
6. Longhurst JC, Kelly AR, Gonyea WJ, Mitchell JH: Chronic training with static and dynamic exercise: Cardiovascular adaptation and response to exercise. *Circ Res, 48:*I171, 1981.
7. Peronnet F, et al.: Echocardiography and the athlete's heart. *Phys Sports Med, 9:*102, 1981.
8. Oscai LB, Williams BT, Hertig BA: Effect of exercise on blood volume. *J Appl Physiol, 26:*622, 1968.
9. LeWinter MM, Pavelec R: Influence of the pericardium on left ventricular end-diastolic pressure-segment relations during early and late stages of experimental chronic volume overload in dogs. *Circ Res, 50:*501, 1982.
10. Blomqvist CG, Saltin B: Cardiovascular adaptations to physical training. *Annu Rev Physiol, 45:*169, 1983.
11. Poliner LR, et al.: Left ventricular performance in normal subjects. A comparison of the responses to exercise in the upright and supine position. *Circulation, 62:*528, 1980.
12. Ekblom B, Kilbom A, Soltysiak J: Physical training, bradycardia, and autonomic nervous system. *Scand J Clin Lab Invest, 32:*251, 1973.
13. Lewis SF, Nylander E, Gad P, Areskog NH: Nonautonomic component in bradycardia of endurance trained men at rest and during exercise. *Acta Physiol Scand, 109:*297, 1979.
14. Rowell LB: Human cardiovascular adjustments to exercise and thermal stress. *Physiol Rev, 54:*75, 1974.
15. Hudlicka O: Growth of capillaries in skeletal and cardiac muscle. *Circ Res, 50:*451, 1982.
16. Ingjer F, Brodal P: Capillary supply of skeletal muscle fibers in untrained and endurance-trained women. *Eur J Appl Physiol, 38:*291, 1978.
17. Stray-Gundersen J, et al.: The effect of pericardiectomy on maximal oxygen consumption and maximal cardiac output in untrained dogs. *Circ Res, 58:*523, 1986.
18. Saltin B: Physiological adaptation to physical conditioning: Old problems revisited. *Acta Med Scand [Suppl], 71:*11, 1986.
19. Holloszy JO: Adaptation of skeletal muscle to endurance exercise. *Med Sci Sports Exerc, 7:*155, 1975.
20. Meldon JH: Theoretical role of myoglobin in steady-state oxygen transport to tissue and its impact upon cardiac output requirements. *Acta Physiol Scand, 440:*S93, 1976.
21. Saltin B, Henrikson J, Nygaard E, Andersen P: Fiber types and metabolic potentials of skeletal muscles in sedentary man and endurance runners. *Ann NY Acad Sci, 301:*3, 1977.
22. Musch TI, et al.: Training effects on regional blood flow response to maximal exercise in foxhounds. *J Appl Physiol, 62:*1724, 1987.
23. Gollnick PD, Saltin B: Significance of skeletal muscle oxidative enzyme enhancement with endurance training. *Clin Physiol, 2:*1, 1982.
24. Snell PG, Mitchell JH: The role of maximal oxygen uptake in exercise performance. In *Clinics in Chest Medicine.* Vol. 5. Edited by J Loke. Philadelphia: W.B. Saunders, 1984.

10

ADAPTATIONS OF SKELETAL MUSCLE TO TRAINING

JULIA M. LASH AND
W. MIKE SHERMAN

Skeletal muscle produces the force required for movement of the skeletal system in the performance of work and exercise. Therefore, a basic understanding of the structure, function, and adaptability of skeletal muscle is essential for individuals involved in fitness evaluation and exercise prescription.

STRUCTURE

Skeletal muscle is composed of parallel multinucleated cells attached to the skeletal system by three structured layers of connective tissue (Fig. 10–1). Each skeletal muscle cell, or myofiber, is surrounded by adjacent fibers to which they are attached through a thin connective tissue layer, the endomysium. Groups of myofibers (fasciculi) are enclosed by the perimysium, and the entire muscle is covered by the epimysium. These connective tissue sheaths are interconnected, fuse at each end of the muscle, and form the muscle tendon that connects to bone.

Underlying the endomysium is the myofiber cell membrane, the sarcolemma. Regularly spaced invaginations of the sarcolemma form the T-tubules and place the extracellular fluid near the inner portions of the cell (Fig. 10–2).

The specialized endoplasmic reticulum of skeletal muscle, the sarcoplasmic reticulum (SR), consists of longitudinally oriented vesicles that store, release, and resequester calcium ions from the sarcoplasm. The terminal cisternae are enlargements of the SR vesicles and abut the T-tubules. A T-tubule and its two adjacent terminal cisternae form the triad.

Skeletal muscle is described as striated because of the appearance of alternating dark and light bands along the length of the muscle (Fig. 10–1). The banded appearance results from the overlap of myosin and actin myofilaments, the basic contractile proteins of skeletal muscle. The dark A-band contains thick myosin filaments, which are composed of a long, light meromyosin strand and a globular heavy meromyosin head projecting perpendicularly from the filament. The H-band, located in the center of the A-band, contains only the myosin filament; the remainder of the A-band contains overlapping myosin and actin filaments. The thin filament is a double helical strand of the globular protein actin. Double strands of tropomyosin lie in the grooves of the actin filament (Fig. 10–3), covering the actin "active sites" that have a high affinity for the myosin heads. Troponin, a three subunit globular protein, is found at regular intervals along the thin filament. Troponin T attaches to tropomyosin, tro-

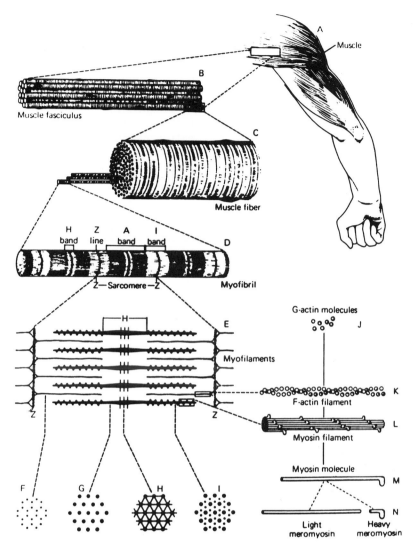

FIGURE 10–1. Macroscopic and microscopic structure of human skeletal muscle. Individual muscle cells (myofibers) are mechanically linked through endomysium (encompasses individual myofibers), perimysium (surrounds groups of myofibers or fasciculi), and epimysium (encapsulates entire muscle). Striated appearance of skeletal muscle is due to overlapping of myofilaments of actin and myosin within basic contractile unit, the sarcomere. (Drawing by Sylvia Colard Keene. From *Bloom's A Textbook of Histology.* Edited by DW Fawcett. Philadelphia: W.B. Saunders, 1975.)

ponin C binds calcium ions, and troponin I is attached to actin.

The smallest functional skeletal muscle subunit capable of contraction is the sarcomere, which extends from Z-disc to Z-disc (Fig. 10–1). Of the protein in the contractile subunit, 84% is actin and myosin, and 8% is tropomyosin. The remaining 6% of the sarcomere protein includes: α-actinin, which is in the Z-disc region; β-actinin, which is in the thin filaments;

M-protein, which is near the center of the A-band (the M-line); and C-protein, which is a structural protein.[1]

CONTRACTION

Skeletal muscle shortening is currently described by the sliding filament and crossbridge

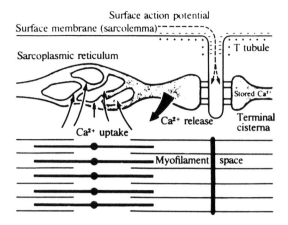

FIGURE 10-2. Skeletal muscle subcellular structure. Depolarization of sarcolemma in T-tubule region induces Ca²⁺ release from sarcoplasmic reticulum (SR), which causes muscle shortening. Ca²⁺ is resequestered by SR during relaxation. (From Selkurt EE: *Basic Physiology for the Health Sciences.* Boston: Little, Brown and Co. 1982.)

theories of contraction.[2] Interdigitation of the actin and myosin filaments allows, under appropriate conditions, binding of the heavy protein chains on the myosin heads (crossbridges) to the actin "active sites." This binding induces rotation of the myosin head, which pulls the actin filaments toward the center of the sarcomere. The amount of filament overlap increases and the overall muscle length is reduced. When sufficient ATP is available, the actin-myosin bond is broken and a new bond is formed at an adjacent "active site" to produce additional muscle shortening (see Fig. 10-3).

As in most cells of the human body, an unequal distribution of ions exists across the skeletal muscle sarcolemma. Potassium is the principal cation within the cell, and sodium is predominant in the extracellular fluid. Selective permeability of the cell membrane and an active electrogenic sodium-potassium pump maintain the unequal distribution of ions that produces a net charge across the sarcolemma. The resulting resting membrane potential

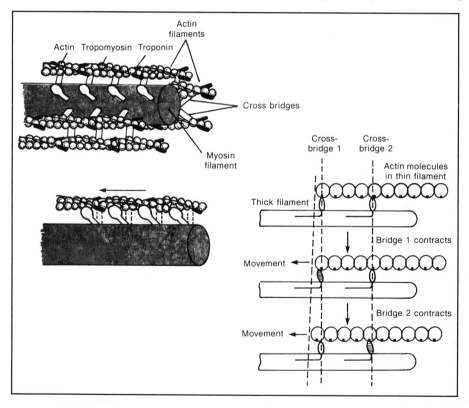

FIGURE 10-3. Molecular components of skeletal muscle thick (myosin) and thin (actin) filaments. Interaction of myofilaments and conformational changes in crossbridge formation increases myofilament overlap and results in muscle shortening. (From McArdle WD, Katch F, Katch V: *Exercise Physiology.* Philadelphia: Lea & Febiger, 1981.)

across the skeletal muscle cell membrane is approximately 90 mv, inside negative. Changes in membrane permeability or in the extracellular fluid ionic composition can alter the resting membrane potential.[3]

Muscle contraction is initiated by depolarization of the sarcolemma, which can be elicited by stimulation of the acetylcholine receptors at the myoneural junction.[3] Stimulation of these receptors produces local alterations in membrane permeability and the development of end-plate potentials (EPPs). Individual EPPs summate until a "threshold" level of depolarization is attained and an action potential (AP) develops. The AP is a progressive movement of membrane depolarization produced by changes in sarcolemma permeability to sodium and potassium ions. Once elicited, the AP propagates along the *entire* length of the cell membrane, and is therefore referred to as an "all-or-none" phenomenon.

As the AP is propagated along the sarcolemma, it spreads into the T-tubules (Fig. 10–2). Depolarization of the T-tubule membrane causes release of calcium ions from the SR. As the cytosolic concentration of calcium increases, calcium ions bind to troponin C and a conformational change in protein structure displaces troponin I and tropomyosin, exposing the actin "active sites." The actin-myosin crossbridge is formed, the myosin head rotates, and muscle shortening occurs by using the energy released by the hydrolysis of myosin-bound ATP. The cycling of crossbridge release and reattachment to the "active sites" produces additional muscle shortening that continues as long as calcium and ATP are available for binding to troponin and myosin, respectively. When the myoneural stimulus for contraction is removed, calcium is resequestered from the cytosol by an ATP-dependent calcium pump in the SR membrane. As a result, the number of calcium ions available for binding to troponin C decreases and tropomyosin again covers the actin "active sites." Crossbridge formation is inhibited, and the muscle returns to its relaxed length.

FUNCTIONAL PROPERTIES

Skeletal muscle performance, i.e., the force and velocity of contraction, is determined voluntarily by selective motor unit recruitment and involuntarily by the intrinsic properties of the muscle and the extrinsic properties of the load opposing muscle shortening.

GRADED CONTRACTIONS

Contraction of a single muscle fiber is an "all-or-none" phenomenon. Therefore, the force produced by a myofiber in response to a single AP is predetermined by the number of crossbridge interactions.[4] The total force produced by the muscle can be regulated, however, to meet the requirements of the movement by varying the number of fibers contracting and the frequency of contractions, or a combination of both.

A myofiber is innervated by only one motor neuron, but a single motor neuron innervates several myofibers (Fig. 10–4). A motor unit is a single motor neuron and the muscle fibers that it innervates.[4,5] The fibers of a motor unit are stimulated and contract simultaneously. The number of muscle fibers contained in a motor unit may vary from two or three, as in the laryngeal muscles or ocular muscles, to thousands, as in the gastrocnemius muscle. Motor unit size (fiber number) varies within a given muscle; force production is proportional to the cross-sectional area of the active muscle. An increase in force generation may be obtained by the simultaneous contraction of several motor units, which is referred to as spatial summation.

A single AP produces a distinct contraction and relaxation pattern known as a twitch (Fig. 10–5). A temporal summation of force and shortening occurs when a second AP develops before the muscle fiber completely relaxes. As the frequency of stimulation increases and the time for relaxation shortens, subsequent contractions fuse together because of the viscous nature of the muscle (i.e., resistance to change in length). As a result, force production is increased, and no relaxation (or decrement in force) is observed, producing a tetanic contraction. Tetanic contractions tend to be more efficient than twitch contractions in terms of energy used per unit of force developed, because relaxation lengthening is prevented, enhancing force production.

LENGTH-TENSION RELATIONSHIP

The ability of the myofiber to generate force is dependent upon the number of myosin-actin

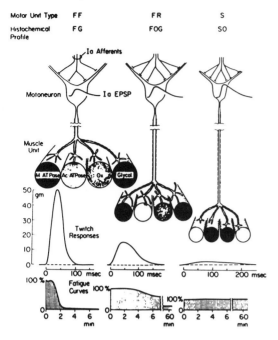

FIGURE 10–4. Important features of organization of motor units in medial gastrocnemius muscle of cat. Diameters of muscle fibers and unit mechanical responses are scaled appropriately for respective groups, representing typical observations. Shading in muscle fiber outlines denotes relative staining intensities found for each histochemical reaction (identified in the FF unit fibers). Motor unit type nomenclature: FF, fast twitch, fatiguable. FR, fast twitch, fatigue resistant. S, slow twitch. Histochemical profiles: FG, fast twitch, glycolytic. FOG, fast twitch, oxidative, glycolytic. SO, slow twitch, oxidative. These two systems are essentially interchangeable. (From Saltin B, Gollnick PD: Skeletal muscle adaptability: Significance for metabolism and performance. In *Handbook of Physiology*. Edited by LD Peachey. Baltimore: Williams & Wilkins, 1983. Adapted from Burke RE, Edgerton VR: Motor unit properties and selective involvement in movement. *Exerc Sport Sci Rev*, 3:31, 1975.)

crossbridge interactions. When the myofiber is stretched beyond resting length, the overlap of the myofilaments within the sarcomere and the potential number of crossbridge interactions are reduced, as is the capacity for force production (Fig. 10–6, point D). When the myofiber is compressed, the opposing actin filaments overlap and interfere with crossbridge formation near the center of the sarcomere, again reducing force generation (Fig. 10–6, point A). The

length of the sarcomere that is optimal for crossbridge formation and force production is 2.0 to 2.2 (μm).[2]

Under most in vivo conditions, the length-tension curve is of little consequence in muscle force production because sarcomere length is maintained within the optimal range by the muscle attachments to the skeletal system.[6] The angle of muscle attachment (and joint angle), however, determines the fraction of total muscle force available for movement of the limb through its range of motion (Fig. 10–7). The optimal amount of force is available for actual

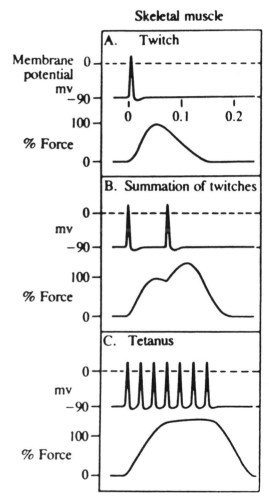

FIGURE 10–5. Skeletal muscle force generation resulting from single **(A)** and repetitive **(B)** stimulation. Second stimulus generated before complete relaxation enhances force generation. (From Selkurt EE: *Basic Physiology for the Health Sciences*. Boston: Little, Brown and Co., 1982.)

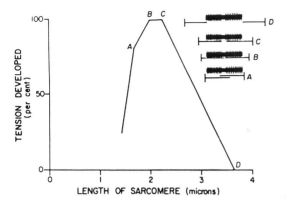

FIGURE 10–6. Length-tension relationship of skeletal muscle. Excessive overlap (A) or extension (D) of myofilaments decreases number of effective cross-bridge interactions and ability of myofiber to generate force. (From Guyton: *Textbook of Medical Physiology.* 6th Ed., Philadelphia: W.B. Saunders, 1981, p. 128.)

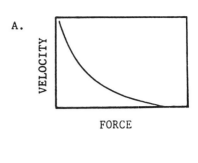

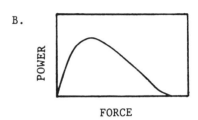

FIGURE 10–8. Force-velocity **(A)** and force-power **(B)** relationships of skeletal muscle. Maximal velocity of contraction is inversely related to resisting force. Optimal power output (force · velocity) is achieved at about 30% of maximal force generation. (Adapted from Selkurt EE: *Basic Physiology for the Health Sciences.* Boston, Little, Brown Co., and 1982.)

limb movement when the long axis of the muscle is perpendicular to the attached bone. At other joint angles, some of the force generated is transferred to compression and stabilization of the joint. As an example, during contraction of the biceps, force development is maximal for lifting a weight held in the hand when the long axis of the bicep and radius are at a 90° angle and the elbow is at approximately 60° flexion.

FORCE-VELOCITY RELATIONSHIP

The maximal velocity of muscle shortening is partially dependent upon the load that must be moved (Fig. 10–8). The greater the load, the slower muscle shortening occurs during maximal effort. This relationship is evident during a maximal isometric contraction when force production is maximal and velocity of shortening is zero. In contrast, unloaded muscles can shorten very rapidly, at near maximal velocities.

Power, by definition, is work produced per unit time, but it can also be calculated as the

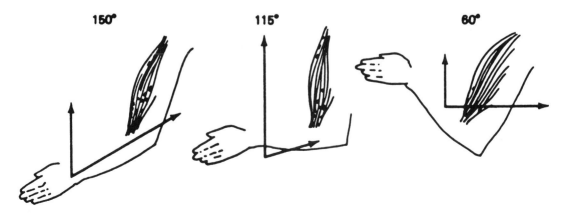

FIGURE 10–7. Relationship between joint angle and fraction of total muscular force available for limb movement. (From Lamb DR: *Physiology of Exercise — Responses and Adaptations.* New York: Macmillan, 1978.)

product of force and velocity. As a consequence of the aforementioned force-velocity relationship, there exists a range of force production over which power output is optimized. Optimal power is achieved at approximately 30% of maximal force (Fig. 10–8), which corresponds to approximately 40% of the maximal velocity of contraction.

MUSCLE FIBER TYPES

Although the structural and functional components of skeletal muscle cells are similar, basic biochemical and contractile differences exist.

CLASSIFICATION SYSTEMS

Muscle fibers are most often classified by their shortening velocity, which is determined by the intracellular myosin-ATPase activity, or by the metabolic pathway primarily responsible for ATP production.[4,5,7,8] Human skeletal muscle is commonly divided into three basic fiber types, but individual fibers may lie anywhere along the continuum, and the division between fiber types is often unclear.[4,9] In addition, the characteristics of a fiber are related to the functions for which it is most often recruited.

FIBER TYPE CHARACTERISTICS

Slow-twitch fibers (also called type I) are predominantly oxidative fibers and have a low glycolytic capacity (Fig. 10–4). Type I fibers have a rich capillary supply, small diameters (25 to 40 μm), and high myoglobin content, which facilitate the delivery of oxygen to the muscle cells. These fibers contain numerous and large mitochondria, which contribute to the characteristically high activity levels of mitochondrial enzymes such as succinate dehydrogenase (SDH) and NAD dehydrogenase. Slow-twitch fibers have low myosin-ATPase activities, slow contraction velocities, and prolonged twitch durations (Fig. 10–4). Therefore, temporal summation and tetanization occur at relatively low stimulation frequencies. The high oxidative capacity and low threshold for tetanization make the type I fibers well suited for prolonged tonic contractions, such as those required of the pos-

tural muscles. These fibers, because of their high oxidative capacity and oxygen delivery as well as their heavy reliance on fat oxidation, are also fatigue resistant.

Fast-twitch, or type II, fibers have short twitch durations (Fig. 10–4), high myosin ATPase activities, and are further subdivided into type IIa and type IIb fibers on the basis of their relative oxidative capacities. Type IIa fibers, or fast oxidative (FO) fibers, have moderate glycolytic and high oxidative capacities, a relatively high mitochondrial content, a rich capillary supply, and small diameters (25 to 40 μm), factors that facilitate oxygen delivery and utilization. Type IIa fibers are best suited for sustained phasic activities such as running and cycling. Type IIb fibers, fast glycolytic (FG) fibers, have a high glycolytic capacity, reflected by high phosphorylase (PHOS) activities, but few mitochondria and a low oxidative capacity. Type IIb fibers are large (30 to 60 μm in diameter) and are well suited for brief powerful contractions that can be sustained by anaerobic metabolism, such as jumping and throwing. Type IIc fibers have intermediate contractile and metabolic characteristics, are difficult to distinguish, and are thought to appear during fiber type transition.[10,11]

MOTOR UNITS

Motor units are composed of one fiber type (Fig. 10–4). Units containing type I or type IIa fibers are small and are recruited during sustained phasic contractions that require minimal to moderate force development. Motor units containing type IIb fibers are usually large. Simultaneous contraction of several large type IIb fibers produces the high level of force required for powerful movements. During an intense contraction, small motor units are recruited first, and recruitment of progressively larger units occurs until the desired force production is attained. This orderly pattern of motor unit recruitment, small to large, is described as the size principle.[12]

ADAPTATIONS TO TRAINING

Skeletal muscle adapts to increased activity. The specific adaptations that occur depend upon the frequency, duration, and intensity of

Table 10–1. Skeletal Muscle Adaptations to Training

Properties of muscle	Type of training		
	Endurance	Sprint	Strength
Fiber composition	+?*	+?	O?
Fiber area	O	+,−,O	+
Enzyme activities			
Krebs cycle	+++	++	+,−,O
Fatty acids	++	+	O
Glycolytic	+,−,O	+	+,O
		(Type I)	
Myosin ATPase	+?	+?	O
Substrate storage			
ATP/CP	+	+	O
Glycogen	+	+,O	O
Myoglobin content	+?	+?	O
Mitochondrial number	++	+	O
Capillary density	+	O?	O

* Symbols indicate relative changes: +,++,+++ = small, medium, and large increases; − = decrease; O = no change; ? = unknown.

the contractions. The muscles used during training become better equipped to perform the types of contractions encountered in the training program.[11] Skeletal muscle adaptations to endurance, sprint, and weight training are subsequently considered (Table 10–1).

ENDURANCE TRAINING

The capacity of skeletal muscle to perform prolonged work of moderate intensity is dependent upon its oxidative capacity. Endurance training regimens that produce increases in aerobic capacity ($\dot{V}o_{2\,max}$) also result in increased skeletal muscle oxidative enzyme activities.[8,9,11] Mitochondrial size and number increase in the trained state, and mitochondrial enzyme activities, such as cytochrome oxidase (CYTOX) and SDH, are similarly elevated.[7,8,13] The aerobic capacities of all muscle fiber types increase with endurance training, with the greatest increases observed in type I fibers after continuous training and in type IIa fibers after interval training.[8,9,11,14]

The various segments of the skeletal muscle oxidative system respond similarly to endurance training.[4] The capacities for oxidation of pyruvate, fatty acids, and ketone bodies appear to increase in parallel fashion.[8] Increases are observed in Krebs cycle enzyme activities (e.g., SDH); electron transport chain components (such as CYTOX and cytochrome c), and the capacities to transport and oxidize NADH (malate-aspartate shuttle), transport glucose

(hexokinase activity), and activate, transport, and oxidize fatty acids (e.g., carnitine palmitoyl transferase activity).[4] No changes have been noted in creatine kinase (CK) or adenosine kinase (AK) activity.[7,8] The increases in oxidative enzyme activities are probably the result of enhanced protein synthesis, which may be stimulated by the increased flux of substrate through the oxidative pathways.[4,7] Rarely is the maximal velocity of substrate utilization achieved under physiologic conditions.[4] Therefore, the functional significance of the increased oxidative potential after endurance training cannot be fully appreciated. Enhanced enzyme activities, however, allow increased flux through the metabolic pathways at relatively low substrate concentrations, such as those that may occur during prolonged exercise, and may provide more precise control of oxidative phosphorylation.[4,7,8,11]

Minor alterations in the activities of glycolytic enzymes are observed after endurance training.[7–9,13] Slight increases in PHOS, phosphofructokinase (PFK), and other glycolytic enzymes in ST fibers, and slight decreases in these enzyme activities in FT fibers, have been reported.[4] Therefore, the change in the overall glycolytic capacity of mixed muscle is minimal after endurance training.

Increases in substrate storage may occur with endurance training. Minimal increases in ATP and creatine phosphate (CP) contents have been reported.[4] These small increases are most likely functionally insignificant, however, because the total muscle stores of ATP and CP can sustain only 10 to 15 sec of muscle contraction. Therefore, the ability of the muscle metabolic machinery to replenish ATP and CP stores, rather than their absolute concentrations, is of primary importance in endurance activities. Glycogen stores may increase by approximately twofold with training, presumably owing to enhanced glycogen synthase (GS) and hexokinase (HK) activities.[4] Dietary factors, however, play the dominant role in determining muscle glycogen concentrations.[4] Combined diet and exercise manipulations that enhance muscle glycogen storage by approximately three-fold can improve endurance performance and delay the onset of fatigue during prolonged submaximal exercise.[4]

The general effects of enhanced skeletal muscle oxidative capacity in response to endurance training are improvements in endurance performance, increased fatty acid utilization, and decreased glycogen utilization during prolonged exercise. Presumably, with an increased oxidative potential, less of a disturbance in homeostasis occurs for a given level of work, minimizing the accumulation of ADP and activation of glycolysis, thereby sparing glycogen and enhancing fat utilization.[7,8] Furthermore, the enhanced oxidative capacity of type I and type IIa fibers allows more work to be done before anaerobic glycolysis and type IIb fiber recruitment are required, minimizing or delaying the onset of lactic acid accumulation.[14]

In addition to the enzymatic alterations that improve the ability of endurance-trained skeletal muscle to utilize oxygen, training can enhance the delivery of oxygen to muscle tissues. The number of capillaries per muscle fiber and per square millimeter of tissue increases in proportion to the total body aerobic capacity ($\dot{V}_{O_2\,max}$).[4,11,15] Increases in capillary number and diameter result in increased capillary surface area and decreased diffusion distances, thereby facilitating the diffusion and transport of oxygen and other metabolic substrates, such as fatty acids, to the metabolic machinery of the active fibers. Myoglobin concentrations may also increase concomitantly with $\dot{V}_{O_2\,max}$ to enhance even further the transport of oxygen in trained muscle.[8,11]

The oxidative capacities of type I and type IIa fibers become more similar after a period of aerobic training. The evidence for a true conversion of fiber type contractile properties with endurance training, however, has not been reported.[4] Endurance athletes tend to have a relatively high proportion of type I fibers which is probably the consequence of genetic predisposition and activity selection rather than an adaptive response to training.[4,7] Both increases and decreases in type I fiber cross-sectional areas have been reported, but overall muscle hypertrophy is *not* a consequence of endurance training.[4,15] Although a few investigators have reported an increase in myosin ATPase activity with aerobic training, and chronic stimulation has been shown to decrease twitch time in type II fibers in the rat, a training-induced transformation of type II to type I fibers has not been demonstrated clearly in humans.[8,11] A shift in the distribution of type II fibers is observed, however, with endurance training as the oxidative capacity of type IIb fibers increases and they become histologically indistinguishable from the type IIa fibers.[7,15]

SPRINT TRAINING

Sprint training induces changes in enzymatic activities in skeletal muscle similar to those observed with endurance training. Mitochondrial size and number increase, CYTOX activity increases, and an increase or no change is observed in SDH and CK activities.[4] Beta-oxidation of long-chain fatty acids increases with sprint training if the regimen is of appropriate intensity and duration to elicit fatty acid mobilization.[4] An increased oxidative capacity is primarily evident in type II fibers after sprint/interval training.[4]

Glycolytic enzyme activities increase in type I fibers in response to sprint training.[8] Glycolytic enzyme activities, including PHOS and PFK, increase, and LDH activity decreases or shows no change. Glycogen storage as well as GS and HK activities may be enhanced in response to sprint training.[4,8] Increased glycogen storage and substrate availability, however, enhances sprint performance only during repeated bouts of maximal exercise. Little or no change is observed in the glycolytic capacity of type II fibers after sprint training.[4]

A change in fiber type contractile properties can occur with sprint training. Repeated bouts of exercise at 90 to 100% of $\dot{V}_{O_2\,max}$ can produce a decrease in the proportion of type I fibers and an increase in the proportion of type IIc fibers.[16] Similar results were reported when endurance athletes were placed on an ''anaerobic'' training program, and a decrease in type I myofiber twitch time was observed after high-intensity training.[17,18] Whether a true conversion of type I to type II fibers occurs as a result of sprint training, however, remains uncertain.[4,11]

STRENGTH TRAINING

The primary adaptation of skeletal muscle to strength training is an increase in muscle bulk that results from hypertrophy of existing fibers. The cross-sectional area of the trained fibers, primarily the type IIa fibers, increases to accommodate additional sarcomeres formed in parallel with the existing myofibrils. Fiber type conversion does not appear to occur.[4] The contractility of the fibers, i.e., the maximal tension produced per square millimeter of muscle tissue and per crossbridge interaction, is not altered by strength training.[4] In general, the overall gain in strength is proportional to the increase in cross-sectional area of the muscle. In the early stages of training, however, strength may increase more rapidly than muscle bulk because of increased motor unit recruitment and coordination. In addition, muscle bulk may increase more than strength if hypertrophy alters the attachment angle to bone and reduces the mechanical advantage of the lever arm. The cross-sectional area and strength of connective tissue also increase in response to muscle overload and strength training.[4]

Little or no change in muscle enzyme activities occurs with strength training. Traditional high-resistance isotonic training regimens do not appear to enhance oxidative or glycolytic enzyme activities.[4] Mitochondrial enzyme activities may, in fact, be reduced because of the dilution effect of muscle hypertrophy in the absence of a compensatory increase in mitochondrial mass. In contrast, isometric contractions can increase CYTOX and SDH production.[19] Isokinetic training consisting of 30-second bouts of maximal contractions was shown to increase PHOS, PFK, CK, malate dehydrogenase, and SDH activities; conversely, 6-sec bouts of isokinetic contractions resulting in similar gains in strength produced an increase only in PFK activity.[20]

Optimal work and athletic performance are, at least in part, dependent upon skeletal muscle characteristics. Human skeletal muscle has the capability to adapt to chronic use. These adaptations, which include enhanced enzyme activities, protein synthesis, and capillary growth, enable the skeletal muscle and the overall human body to function more efficiently in frequently encountered activities.[11]

REFERENCES

1. McArdle WD, Katch FI, Katch VL: *Exercise Physiology.* Philadelphia: Lea & Febiger, 1981.
2. Huxley AF: Muscular contraction. *J Physiol (Lond)* 243:1, 1974.
3. Meiss RA: Muscle: Striated, smooth, cardiac. In *Basic Physiology for the Health Sciences.* Edited by EE Selkurt. Boston: Little, Brown, and Co., 1982.
4. Saltin B, Gollnick PD: Skeletal muscle adaptability: Significance for metabolism and performance. In *Handbook of Physiology.* Edited by LD Peachey. Baltimore: Williams & Wilkins, 1983.
5. Burke RE, Edgerton VR: Motor unit properties and selective involvement in movement. *Exerc Sport Sci Rev,* 3:31, 1975.
6. Lamb DR: *Exercise Physiology — Responses and Adaptations.* New York: Macmillan, 1978.
7. Holloszy JO, Coyle EF: Adaptations of skeletal muscle to endurance exercise and their metabolic consequences. *J Appl Physiol,* 56:831, 1984.
8. Holloszy JO, Booth FW: Biochemical adaptations to endurance exercise in muscle. *Annu Rev Physiol,* 38:273, 1976.
9. Essen-Gustavsson B, Henriksson J: Enzyme levels in pools of microdissected human muscle fibers of identified type. *Acta Physiol Scand,* 120:505, 1984.
10. Larsson L, Ansved T: Effects of long-term physical training and detraining on enzyme histochemical and functional skeletal muscle characteristics in man. *Muscle Nerve,* 8:714, 1985.
11. Salmons S, Henriksson J: The adaptive response of skeletal muscle to increased use. *Muscle Nerve,* 4:94, 1981.
12. Henneman E, Clamann JD, Gillies JD, Skinner RD: Rank order of motorneurons within a pool: Law of combination. *J Neurophysiol,* 37:1338, 1974.
13. Soar PK, Davies CTM, Fentem PH, Newsholme EA: The effect of endurance-training on the maximum activities of hexokinase, 6-phosphofructokinase, citrate synthase, and oxoglutarate dehydrogenase in red and white muscles of the rat. *Biosc Rep,* 3:831, 1983.
14. Baldwin KM, Winder WW: Adaptive responses in different types of muscle fibers to endurance exercise. *Ann NY Acad Sci,* 301:411, 1976.
15. Inger F: Effects of endurance training on fiber ATP-ase activity, capillary supply and mitochondrial content in man. *J Physiol (Lond),* 294:419, 1979.
16. Jansson E, Kaijser L: Muscle adaptation to extreme endurance training in man. *Acta Physiol Scand,* 100:315, 1977.
17. Henriksson J, Jansson E, Schantz P: Increase in myofibrillar ATPase intermediate skeletal muscle fibers with endurance training of extreme duration in man. *Muscle Nerve,* 3:274, 1980 (Abstract).
18. Staudte HW, Exner GU, Pette D: Effects of short-term, high-intensity (sprint) training on some contractile and metabolic characteristics of fast and slow muscle of the rat. *Pflugers Arch,* 344:159, 1973.
19. Grimby G, et al.: Metabolic effects of isometric training. *Scand J Clin Lab Invest,* 31:301, 1973.
20. Costill DL, et al.: Adaptations in skeletal muscle following strength training. *J Appl Physiol,* 46:96, 1979.

11

MECHANISMS OF MUSCULAR FATIGUE

ROBERT H. FITTS

The etiology of muscle fatigue is an important question that has interested exercise scientists for more than a century. A definitive fatigue agent(s) has yet to be identified, although progress has been made and theories have been developed that, for the most part, explain the experimental findings. The problem is complex because muscle fatigue might result from deleterious alterations in the muscle itself (peripheral fatigue) and/or from changes in the neural input to the muscle. The latter factor could itself be mediated by changes of central and/or peripheral origin. Furthermore, the nature and extent of muscle fatigue clearly depends on the type, duration, and intensity of exercise, the fiber type composition of the muscle, individual level of fitness, and numerous environmental factors. For example, fatigue experienced in high-intensity, short-duration exercise is surely dependent on factors that differ from those precipitating fatigue in endurance activity. Similarly, fatigue during tasks involving heavily loaded contractions (e.g., weight lifting) likely differs from that produced during relatively unloaded movement (running and swimming).

In this review, we discuss muscle fatigue resulting from two general types of activity: short-duration, high-intensity, and endurance exercise. The current theories and important supportive experimental results are presented.

Because of space limitations, this review cannot be complete. Detailed discussions are found in earlier reviews.[1,2]

SHORT-DURATION, HIGH-INTENSITY EXERCISE

SITES OF MUSCULAR FATIGUE

Muscle fatigue is defined, for the purposes of this review, as a loss of force output leading to reduced performance of a given task. Fatigue during short-duration, high-intensity exercise could result from an impairment of the central nervous system (CNS), such that the optimal frequency of motor nerve activation is not maintained. Bigland-Ritchie and co-workers clearly showed that the frequency of motor nerve firing decreases during continuous contractile activity.[3] The question is whether this change precipitates muscle fatigue or results from neuronal feedback (muscle afferents) in an attempt to maintain an optimal activation frequency as fatigue develops. The preponderance of evidence suggests the latter. The fatiguing muscle generally shows a prolonged force transient (primarily due to a slower relaxation time) in response to a single stimulus. Consequently, a lower frequency of activation is required to elicit peak tension (force-frequency curve shifts to the left). The primary sites of fatigue are apparently located within the muscle, and do not generally involve the CNS, peripheral nerves, or the neural-muscular (N-M) junction. The observation that fatigued muscles generate the same tension whether stimulated directly or by way of the motor nerve argues against N-M junction fatigue.

The major components of a muscle cell involved in excitation-contraction (E-C) coupling are shown in Figure 11–1. The numbers indicate possible sites within the cell where alteration during heavy exercise could induce fatigue. With fatigue, the shape of the sarcolemma action potential (AP) changes, with decreased amplitude and prolonged duration. These alterations probably do not induce fa-

tigue directly, however, because after contractile activity, the AP shows complete recovery long before peak tension returns to baseline.[4] Edwards and other authors suggest that fatigue during high-frequency stimulation results from alterations in the AP, mediated by increases in extracellular potassium.[1,3] The recent observation that the resting membrane potential is unchanged during fatiguing stimulation argues against this hypothesis.[4]

The primary sites of muscular fatigue apparently involve processes that occur after depolarization of the sarcolemmal and T-tubular membranes. The general process known as E-C coupling is likely disrupted. In nonfatigued muscle, the T-tubular AP produces a charge movement within the T-tubular membrane (see no. 2, Fig. 11–1), which subsequently, by an unknown process, leads to Ca^{2+} release from the sarcoplasmic reticulum (SR). Recently, Vergara et al. suggested that the T-tubular charge movement activates a second messenger system, which in turn triggers Ca^{2+} release.[5] The elevated level of intracellular Ca^{2+} binds to troponin C (see no. 6, Fig. 11–1), a regulatory protein, producing a molecular change in the troponin-tropomyosin complex that in turn allows the contractile proteins actin and myosin to bind and to generate force.[6]

Fatigued muscle frequently shows prolonged twitch duration and reduced peak rate of tension development.[7] With activation, intracellular Ca^{2+} levels rise, triggering crossbridge activation and force development. Prolonged twitch duration reflects a similar prolongation in the time course of the increase in intracellular levels of Ca^{2+} (Ca^{2+} transient). The lengthened Ca^{2+} transient is suggestive of either a reduced rate of release and/or re-uptake of Ca^{2+} by the SR. Such changes could take place for any number of reasons, from alterations in T-tubular charge movement (see no. 2, Fig. 11–1) to changes in the intrinsic ability of the SR to release or remove Ca^{2+}. Clearly, the answer to this question awaits a better understanding of the basic steps in E-C coupling as well as how such steps are altered during high-frequency contractile activity. Additionally, fatigue could result from a direct effect on the contractile proteins.

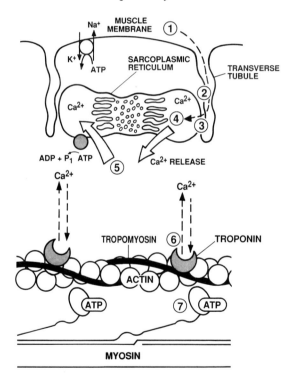

FIGURE 11–1. Major components of muscle cell involved in excitation-contraction (E-C) coupling. Possible sites of muscular fatigue during heavy exercise include: ① surface membrane; ② T-tubular charge movement; ③ unknown mechanism coupling T-tubular charge movement with sarcoplasmic reticulum (SR) Ca^{2+} release; ④ SR Ca^{2+} release; ⑤ SR Ca^{2+} re-uptake; ⑥ Ca^{2+} binding to troponin; ⑦ actomyosin hydrolysis of ATP and crossbridge force development and cycling rate.

MAJOR FATIGUE AGENTS

High-intensity exercise involves an energy demand that exceeds the individual's maximal aerobic power, and thus requires a high level of anaerobic metabolism. Consequently, the levels of high-energy phosphates, ATP, and phosphocreatine (PC) decrease, and levels of inorganic phosphate (Pi), ADP, lactate, and the H^+ ion increase as fatigue develops. All of these changes are possible fatigue-inducing agents, and since the development of the needle biopsy technique, each has been studied extensively.[2,8,9]

To avoid fatigue, adequate tissue ATP levels must be maintained because this substrate supplies the immediate source of energy for force generation by the myosin crossbridges. ATP is also needed in the functioning of the sodium-potassium (Na/K) pump, which is in turn essential in the maintenance of a normal sarcolemma and T-tubular AP. Additionally ATP is a substrate of the SR ATPase and thus is required in the process of Ca^{2+} re-uptake by the SR. As discussed previously, a disturbance in any of these processes could lead to muscle fatigue. Although the tissue ATP concentration decreases during intense muscular contraction, this reduction does not appear to limit force output or to cause muscular fatigue directly. The classic experiments of Karlsson and Saltin perhaps best illustrate the absence of correlated changes of ATP and performance.[10] In this work, the needle biopsy technique was used to evaluate substrate changes after exercise to exhaustion at three different work loads. After 2 minutes of work, ATP and PC were depleted to the same extent at all loads; however, fatigue occurred only with the highest work load. These results are equivocal, however, because the biopsy was acquired some seconds after work ceased, and the sample represented an average tissue ATP that might not reflect the concentration existing at the crossbridges. We also observed, however, a lack of a correlation between ATP and force in isolated muscles studied in vitro.[11,12] In these experiments, ATP showed complete recovery in the first 15 sec after a fatiguing stimulation bout, whereas peak tetanic tension (Po) remained depressed.

PC levels decline with contractile activity, and some authors suggest that low muscle PC levels could induce fatigue.[8,12] The decline in PC level and in tension during contractile activity, however, follow different time courses, making a causal relationship unlikely.[12] PC participates in the movement of ATP from the mitochondria to the crossbridges, a process called the PC-ATP shuttle.[13] The possibility exists that a critically low PC concentration may disrupt this shuttle system and slow the rate of ADP rephosphorylation to ATP. This interference could lead to a critically low ATP at the crossbridges, thus producing muscle fatigue. The exact role of PC (if any) in the etiology of muscular fatigue awaits further study of the PC-ATP shuttle mechanism.

Muscular contraction involves the hydrolysis of ATP by the actomyosin ATPase-producing energy and yielding ADP, Pi, and the H^+ ion as end products. All three of these products increase during intense contractile activity and could cause fatigue by direct inhibition of hydrolysis.[14,15] Results of recent studies that involved the use of the single-skinned fiber preparation have shown reduced peak tension in response to elevated values of both ADP and Pi.[14,15] The importance of ADP and Pi relative to other potential fatigue agents (particularly the H^+ ion) is unknown. The H^+ ion is a particularly interesting potential fatigue agent because it could produce fatigue at numerous sites. In addition to a direct inhibition of the actomyosin ATPase and ATP hydrolysis, a build-up in the intracellular H^+ ion (decreased intracellular pH, abbreviated pHi) could induce fatigue by: (1) inhibiting phosphofructokinase and thus the glycolytic rate; (2) competitive inhibition of Ca^{2+} binding to troponin C, reducing crossbridge activation; and (3) inhibiting the SR-ATPase-reducing Ca^{2+} re-uptake and subsequently Ca^{2+} release.[16–18]

A major source of H^+ ion production during intense muscular activity is the anaerobic production of lactic acid, the majority of which dissociates into lactate and H^+ ions. As early as

Table 11–1. Skeletal Muscle pH

Method	Rest value*	Fatigue value	Reference
Muscle homogenate	6.92 ± 0.03	6.41 ± 0.04	Hermansen and Osnes[21]
Calculated from $HCO_{3-} + PCO_2$	7.04 ± 0.05	6.37 ± 0.11	Sahlin et al.[22]
Microelectrode	7.07 ± 0.007		Aickin and Thomas[23]
DMO method	7.06 ± 0.02		Roos and Boron[24]

* Values are means $\pm$ SE except for findings of Sahlin et al., for which $\pm$ SD are listed.

1907, lactic acid was implicated as a possible fatigue agent.[19] This hypothesis gained popularity after publication of the work of A.V. Hill in the late 1920s.[20] The general consensus now is that fatigue results from the elevated number of H^+ ions rather than lactate or the undissociated lactic acid. Resting skeletal muscle pH, determined by a variety of techniques, is approximately 7.00, and declines with intense muscular contraction to values below 6.5 (Table 11–1).[2]

At least two observations lend support to the concept that an elevated H^+ ion concentration inhibits glycolysis. Hill found that lactate formation during muscle stimulation stopped when the intracellular pH dropped to 6.3.[20] Secondly, Hermansen and Osnes measured the pH of muscle homogenates and observed no change during a 60-second measurement period for the most acidic homogenates of fatigued muscle; the pH values of the homogenates from resting muscle fell markedly owing to significant glycolysis during the measurement period. Sahlin et al. suggest that this inhibition of glycolysis by the H^+ ion may be the limiting factor for performance of intense exercise, yet this conclusion is not supported by the aforementioned results in which the change in ATP and force were not significantly correlated.[11,12] If the inhibition of glycolysis was causative in fatigue, the decline in tissue ATP would likely reach limiting levels. Consequently, a significant correlation between force and ATP would exist during the development of and recovery from fatigue.

Results of studies on skinned fibers definitively showed acidosis depressed the force output of skeletal as well as cardiac muscle.[25] Decreasing pH from 7.4 to 6.2 not only reduced the maximal tension generated in the presence of optimal free Ca^{2+}, but also it increased the threshold of free Ca^{2+} required for contraction; the force-PCa curve shifted to the right such that higher free Ca^{2+} was required to reach a given tension.[25] Fast-twitch fibers were more sensitive to the acidotic depression of maximal tension than were the slow muscle fibers.[26] These effects may be mediated by a H^+ ion interference with Ca^{2+} binding to troponin.[17] The results reported by Bolitho-Donaldson and Hermansen as well as Fabiato and Fabiato indicate that the effect is not entirely a simple competitive inhibition of Ca^{2+} binding to troponin.[25,26] The observed depression of maximal tension was completely reversible when pH returned to a neutral value, but the depression could not be overcome by increasing free Ca^{2+}.[25] Fabiato and Fabiato suggest that the H^+ ion effect may act at some step in addition to the Ca^{2+} interaction with troponin, perhaps by directly affecting the myosin molecule. A direct effect on myosin is supported by the observation that a 33% reduction in maximal rigor tension occurs when pH changes from 7.00 to 6.2.

The rate of ATP hydrolysis by actomyosin is thought to limit the maximal speed of muscle shortening (V_{max}). Consequently, an elevated H^+ ion concentration, which inhibits the ATPase, should decrease V_{max} as well as P_o. Edman and Mattiazzi showed that V_{max} indeed decreases with fatigue, but not until peak tension falls by at least 10%.[27]

We recently observed a high negative correlation between free H^+ ion content and P_o during recovery, a result fully consistent with the H^+ ion theory of muscular fatigue. This and previously published work, however, clearly show force to recover in two phases—a short (~ 30 sec) rapid phase followed by a slower relatively prolonged (~ 15 min) phase of recovery.[11,28] The immediate, rapid phase of recovery cannot be explained by the H^+ ion theory because cell pHi actually decreases during this time (probably due to the rapid resynthesis of PC, a H^+ ion-generating reaction). This rapid phase of force recovery is likely explained by the reversal of a non-H^+ ion-mediated alteration in E-C coupling. The second, slower phase of recovery shows a high negative correlation with the H^+, which probably results in part from the removal of the excess intracellular H^+ ion.

Changes in pH may affect Ca^{2+} regulation by disturbing E-C coupling (see previous discussion) and/or Ca^{2+} re-uptake. Nakamura and Schwartz noted decreased pH increased the Ca^{2+}-binding capacity of isolated SR membranes, and suggested that a drop in pH might reduce the amount of Ca^{2+} released from the SR during excitation. Changes in free H^+ ion may also affect the Ca^{2+} binding properties of the Ca^{2+} binding protein parvalbumin (a protein found in relatively high concentrations in fast-twitch fibers), which by itself would alter the Ca^{2+} transient and force output.

A major challenge to the field of exercise science is to establish which (if any) of the abovementioned H^+ ion effects actually occurs in vivo, and to determine the relative importance of each in the fatigue process.

ENDURANCE EXERCISE

Numerous factors have been linked to fatigue resulting from prolonged endurance activity, including depletion of muscle and liver glycogen, decreases in blood glucose, dehydration, and increases in body temperature.[2] Undoubtedly, each of these factors contributes to fatigue to a varying degree, their relative importance depending on the environmental conditions and the nature of the activity. This section is a review of some of these potential fatigue factors, particularly carbohydrate depletion, as well as of evidence linking an alteration in SR function to the development of fatigue during prolonged exercise.

GLYCOGEN DEPLETION

In 1896, Chauveau suggested that the rate of carbohydrate utilization was dependent on the intensity of work.[2] This belief was based on the observation that the respiratory exchange ratio (RQ) increased from 0.75 during rest to 0.95 during exercise. With the development of the needle biopsy technique, these early theories based on RQ were proven correct by direct measurements of glycogen utilization at different work intensities.[9,29] Glycogen utilization was found to increase from 0.3 to 3.4 glucose units $\cdot$ kg^{-1} $\cdot$ min^{-1} as the relative work load increased from 25 to 100% of the maximal oxygen uptake ($\dot{V}_{O_2max}$).[29] Muscle glycogen depletion coincided with exhaustion during prolonged work bouts that required approximately 75% of $\dot{V}_{O_2max}$. With work loads below 50 or above 90% of $\dot{V}_{O_2max}$, ample muscle glycogen remained at exhaustion.[29] The rate of body carbohydrate usage is dependent not only on the intensity of the work but also on the state of fitness of the individual.[29] At a given work load, trained individuals have a lower RQ and deplete glycogen at a slower rate than untrained men.[29] The observation that the trained individual can work longer supports the hypothesis that depletion of body carbohydrate stores is not only correlated with, but is causative of, muscular fatigue during endurance activity. The exact mechanism of this protective effect is unknown. Although muscle glycogen represents an important fuel source, adequate levels of free fatty acids (FFA) and, in most cases, blood glucose are available at exhaustion. One possibility is that a certain level of muscle gly-

cogen metabolism is required for either the optimal production of NADH and electron transport or the maintenance of fat oxidation, perhaps intermediates of the Krebs cycle become limiting without adequate glycogen metabolism. Alternatively, the translocation of FFA into mitochondria may be rate limiting and/or a high concentration of long-chain FFA might inhibit ATP translocation across the mitochondria membrane. It seems apparent that future efforts should focus on the mechanisms by which glycogen depletion alters muscle function.

OTHER FACTORS

Glycogen depletion is probably not an exclusive fatigue factor during endurance exercise. Other potential candidates include disruption of important intracellular organelles, such as the mitochondria, the SR, or the myofilaments. Significant mitochondrial damage is an unlikely fatigue factor as the capacity of the mitochondria to oxidize substrate and generate ATP is unchanged by exercise to exhaustion.

The contractile proteins and in particular the myofibril ATPase (turnover measured by V_{max}) appear relatively resistant to fatigue. After a prolonged swim, the myofibril Mg^{2+} ATPase of fast and slow rat hind limb muscles was unaltered (Table 11–2). The V_{max} of the slow soleus muscle showed no significant change despite a 26% decline in peak tension. The fast-twitch extensor digitorum longus did undergo a significant 34% decline in V_{max}, but this muscle exhibited extreme fatigue, with a decrease in P_o of more than 70% (Table 11–2).[7] The fatigued (inactive) fibers might have provided a significant internal drag during the unloaded and lightly loaded contractions. These results imply that the activity of the myofibril ATPase and its functional correlate V_{max} are relatively resistant to alteration during prolonged exercise.

In the same study, we evaluated the functional capacity of isolated SR membranes.[7] The SR is an intracellular membrane system primarily involved in the regulation of intracellular Ca^{2+}. Alteration in the force transient of contraction (a reflection of an altered Ca^{2+} transient) is a common observation with fatigue, and thus the SR may be involved in the etiology of muscular fatigue. Our results showed that the prolonged swim had no effect on the amount of SR isolated (mg/g time) from any of

Table 11–2. Effect of Endurance Swim to Exhaustion on Myofibril ATPase, V_{max}, and P_o

Muscle	Myofibril ATPase (μmol/mg/min)	V_{max} (fiber lengths/sec)	P_o (g/cm^2)
Slow soleus			
Control	0.128 ± 0.008*	2.9 ± 0.2	2482 ± 208
Fatigued	0.104 ± 0.011	2.7 ± 0.2	1844 ± 203†
Fast extensor digitorum longus			
Control	0.204 ± 0.031	7.6 ± 0.8	2397 ± 171
Fatigued	0.309 ± 0.030	5.2 ± 0.7†	633 ± 190†
Fast SVL‡			
Control	0.301 ± 0.021	9.5 ± 1.2	1757 ± 88
Fatigued	0.343 ± 0.021	9.8 ± 0.8	1713 ± 86

* Values represent means $\pm$ SE.
† Significantly different ($p < 0.05$).
‡ Abbreviation SVL = superficial type IIb region of the vastus lateralis.

the fast muscles, but a significant decrease in SR protein isolated from the slow soleus did result (0.81 ± 0.05 versus 0.57 ± 0.05, mg/g, control versus fatigued). This decrease is unexplained, but it could reflect an elevated proteolytic enzyme activity shown to exist in fatigued muscle.[2] None of the muscles studied exhibited any change in the SR Ca^{2+}-stimulated ATPase activity. The uptake of Ca^{2+} by the SR vesicles (μmol $\cdot$ mg^{-1} SR), however, was depressed in the slow soleus and fast-twitch red region of the vastus lateralis. A decreased degree of Ca^{2+} uptake with no change in the SR ATPase activity is suggestive of either an uncoupling of the transport or a "leaky" membrane allowing Ca^{2+} flux back into the intracellular fluid. Although our results clearly show a major change in the SR, more experiments designed for studying the effects of prolonged activity on the kinetic properties of Ca^{2+} uptake and release during excitation are required before the exact nature of this change and its effect on muscle function can be elucidated.

The prolonged swim produced a significant decrease in glycogen concentration in muscles representative of the slow type I, fast type IIa, and fast type IIb fiber. Interestingly, the type IIb muscle showed no fatigue as reflected by an unaltered P_o value. Furthermore, despite significant glycogen depletion, the fast type IIb muscle showed no change in any of the contractile or biochemical properties measured.[7] The apparent explanation is that the type IIb (fast white glycolytic) fiber was recruited less frequently during the endurance activity and that the heavy reliance of this fiber on glycolysis produced levels of muscle glycogen usage similar to those of other fiber types despite fewer total contractions. It is apparent from these re-

sults that muscle fatigue during endurance activity is related in some way to the degree of muscle usage, and is not entirely dependent on the extent of glycogen depletion. An important unanswered question is whether glycogen depletion somehow mediates (and hence is a prerequisite for) the disruption of intracellular organelles such as the SR.

The observed disruption in protein systems, such as the SR, coupled with an increased concentration of intracellular metabolites would be expected to increase the intracellular solute concentration and quantity of tissue water. An elevated level of tissue water would produce swelling and thus could lead to muscle soreness. This possibility is supported by results of structural studies in which muscle soreness was related to changes in various intracellular organelles.[2] The time course of recovery from muscle soreness (days) exceeds that observed with fatigue (minutes), and reflects the time required to synthesize new muscle protein.

SUMMARY

The studies and findings described in this chapter illustrate the complex nature of muscle fatigue. After short duration, high-intensity exercise, recovery in force production usually shows two components that are probably caused by separate mechanisms: (1) a rapidly reversible non-H^+ ion-mediated perturbation in Ca^{2+} regulation, and (2) a slower change in E-C coupling that is likely mediated by the H^+ ion. The potential mechanisms of the deleterious effects of the H^+ ion are described. In prolonged endurance exercise, the depletion of body carbohydrate stores frequently occurs, and muscle glycogen depletion is probably an important fatigue agent. Undoubtedly, other factors are involved, however, because muscle glycogen depletion can exist without fatigue. Muscle organelles, particularly the SR, are probably also involved in the fatigue process.

REFERENCES

1. Edwards RHT: Human muscle function and fatigue. In *Human Muscle Fatigue: Physiological Mechanisms.* Edited by R Porter and J Whelan. London: Pitman Medical, 1981.
2. Fitts RH, Kim DH, Witzmann FA: The development of fatigue during high intensity and endurance exercise. In *Exercise in Health and Disease.* Edited by FJ Nagel and HJ Montoye. Springfield: Charles C Thomas, 1981.
3. Bigland-Ritchie B, Jones DA, Woods JJ: Excitation frequency and muscle fatigue: Electrical responses during human voluntary and stimulated contractions. *Exp Neurol, 64:*414, 1979.
4. Metzger JM, Fitts RH: Fatigue from high- and low-frequency muscle stimulation: Role of sarcolemma action potentials. *Exp Neurol, 93:*320, 1986.
5. Vergara J, Tsien RY, Delay M: Inositol 1,4,5-triphosphate: A possible chemical link in excitation-contraction coupling in muscle. *Proc Natl Acad Sci USA, 82:*6352, 1985.
6. Vander AJ, Sherman JH, Luciano DS: Muscle (CH.10). In *Human Physiology: The Mechanisms of Body Function.* 3rd. Ed. New York: McGraw-Hill, 1980.
7. Fitts RH, Courtright JB, Kim DH, Witzmann FA: Muscle fatigue with prolonged exercise: Contractile and biochemical alterations. *Am J Physiol, 242:*C65, 1982.
8. Simonson E: Accumulation of metabolites. In *Physiology of Work Capacity and Fatigue.* Edited by E Simonson. Springfield: Charles C Thomas, 1971.
9. Bergstrom J: Muscle electrolytes in man. *Scand J Clin Lab Invest [Suppl, 68]* 14:1962.
10. Karlsson J, Saltin B: Lactate, ATP, and CP in working muscles during exhaustive exercise in man. *J Appl Physiol, 29:*598, 1970.
11. Fitts RH, Holloszy JO: Effects of fatigue and recovery on contractile properties of frog muscle. *J Appl Physiol, 45:*899, 1978.
12. Fitts RH, Holloszy JO: Lactate and contractile force in frog muscle during development of fatigue and recovery. *Am J Physiol, 231:*430, 1976.
13. Savabi F, Geiger FJ, Bessman SP: Myofibrillar end of the creatine phosphate energy shuttle. *Am J Physiol, 247:*424, 1984.
14. Kawai M, Guth K: ATP hydrolysis rate and crossbridge kinetics as function of ionic strength and phosphate ion concentration in chemically skinned rabbit Psoas fibers. *Biophys J, 49:*9a, 1986.
15. Tuney DJE, Godt RE: Fatigue and maximal velocity of shortening in skinned fibers from rabbit soleus muscle: Effects of pH, ADP, and inorganic phosphate. *Biophys J, 49:*85a, 1986.
16. Danforth WH: Activation of glycolytic pathway in muscle. In *Control of Energy Metabolites.* Edited by B Chance, et al. New York: Academic Press, 1965.
17. Fuchs F, Reddy Y, Briggs FN: The interaction of cations with the calcium-binding site of troponin. *Biochim Biophys Acta, 221:*407, 1970.
18. Nakamura Y, Schwartz A: The influence of hydrogen ion concentration on calcium binding and release by skeletal muscle sarcoplasmic reticulum. *J Gen Physiol, 59:*22, 1972.
19. Fletcher WW, Hopkins FG: Lactic acid in mammalian muscle. *J Physiol, 35:*247, 1907.
20. Hill AV: The absolute value of the isometric heat coefficient T1/H in a muscle twitch, and the effect of stimulation and fatigue. *Proc R Soc Lond [B], 103:*163, 1928.
21. Hermansen L, Osnes J: Blood and muscle pH after maximal exercise in man. *J Appl Physiol, 32:*302, 1972.
22. Sahlin K, Harris RC, Nylind B, Hultman E: Lactate content and pH in muscle samples obtained after dynamic exercise. *Pflugers Arch, 367:*143, 1976.
23. Aickin CC, Thomas RC: Microelectrode measurement of the intracellular pH and buffering power of mouse soleus muscle fibers. *J. Physiol, 267:*791, 1977.
24. Roos A, Boron WF: Intracellular pH transients in rat diaphragm muscle measured with DMO. *Am J Physiol, 235:*C49, 1978.
25. Fabiato A, Fabiato F: Effects of pH on the myofilaments and the sarcoplasmic reticulum of skinned cells from cardiac and skeletal muscles. *J. Physiol, 276:*233, 1978.
26. Donaldson SKB, Hermansen L: Differential, direct effects of H^+ on Ca^{2+}-activated force of skinned fibers from the soleus, cardiac and adductor magnus muscles of rabbits. *Pflugers Arch, 376:*55, 1978.
27. Edman KAP, Mattiazzi AR: Effects of fatigue and altered pH on isometric force and velocity of shortening at zero load in frog muscle fibers. *J Muscle Res Cell Motil, 2:*321, 1981
28. Metzger JM, Fitts RH: Role of intracellular pH in muscle fatigue. *J Appl Physiol, 62*(4):1392, 1987.
29. Hikida RS, et al.: Muscle fiber necrosis associated with human marathon runners. *J Neurol Sci, 59:*185, 1983.

CHAPTER 12

DETRAINING AND RETENTION OF TRAINING-INDUCED ADAPTATIONS

EDWARD F. COYLE

REVERSIBILITY OF ADAPTATIONS INDUCED BY TRAINING

Physical training exposes the various systems of the body to potent physiologic stimuli. These stimuli induce specific adaptations that enhance an individual's tolerance for the type of exercise encountered in training. The level of adaptation and the magnitude of improvement in exercise tolerance is proportional to the potency of the physical training stimuli.

Inherent to these observations is the concept of the reversibility of the adaptations induced by training. The "reversibility concept" holds that when physical training is stopped (i.e., detraining) or reduced, the bodily systems readjust in accordance with the diminished physiologic stimuli. The focus of this chapter is on the time course of loss of the adaptations to endurance training as well as on the possibility that certain adaptations persist, to some extent, when training is stopped. Because endurance exercise training generally improves cardiovascular function and promotes metabolic adaptations within the exercising skeletal musculature, the reversibility of these specific adaptations is considered. Another approach to the study of the effects of reduced activity is to examine the exercise responses of people before and after prolonged bedrest. The idea that postural fluid shifts rather than inactivity account for the loss of cardiovascular function after bedrest is discussed.

CARDIOVASCULAR DETRAINING

MAXIMAL OXYGEN UPTAKE

Endurance training induces increases in maximal oxygen uptake (i.e., $\dot{V}O_{2\,max}$), cardiac output, and stroke volume.[1,2] When sedentary men participate in a 7-week, low-intensity training program (20 min/day^{-1}; 3 days/week^{-1}), $\dot{V}O_{2\,max}$ levels increase by 6%, with a return of $\dot{V}O_{2\,max}$ values to pretraining levels with 8 weeks of detraining.[3] Moderate endurance training increases $\dot{V}O_{2\,max}$ by 10 to 20%, yet again $\dot{V}O_{2\,max}$ may decline to pretraining levels when training is stopped.[4-6] Values of $\dot{V}O_{2\,max}$ decline rapidly during the first month of inactivity, whereas a slower decline to untrained levels occurs during the second and third months of detraining.[4-6] Therefore, the available evidence suggests that the increases in $\dot{V}O_{2\,max}$ produced by endurance training involving exercise of low to moderate intensities and durations are totally reversed after several months of detraining.

Investigators have not yet examined and then exposed untrained individuals to several years of intense endurance training and subsequent inactivity to determine if extreme training results in a persistent elevation of $\dot{V}o_{2\,max}$ above untrained levels. Our present knowledge is limited to findings of studies involving already trained endurance athletes who agreed to cease training so that reversibility of their physiologic

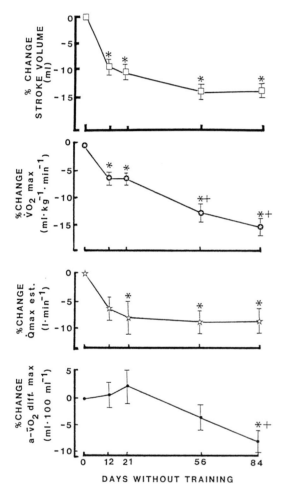

FIGURE 12-1. Effects of detraining upon percent changes in stroke volume during exercise, maximal O_2 uptake ($\dot{V}o_{2\,max}$), maximal cardiac output ($\dot{Q}_{max\,est.}$), and maximal arteriovenous O_2 difference (a-$\bar{v}\ O_{2\,diff.\,max}$). *, significantly lower than trained (day 0). +, significantly lower than 21 days. (Modified from Coyle EF, et al.: Time course of loss of adaptations after stopping prolonged intense endurance training. *J Appl Physiol*, 57:1857–1864, 1984.)

adaptations could be studied periodically.[7] Figure 12-1 is a display of the time course of the decline in $\dot{V}o_{2\,max}$ (and its components of maximal stroke volume, cardiac output, and arteriovenous O_2 difference) when people become sedentary after training intensely for approximately 10 years.

The $\dot{V}o_{2\,max}$ value was relatively high in trained subjects (i.e., 62 ml/min^{-1} at 0 days without training) and it declined a total of 16% after 84 days of detraining. A rapid decline of 7% occurred in the first 12 to 21 days with a further decline of 9% during the period from 21 to 84 days.[7] The rapid, early decline in $\dot{V}o_{2\,max}$ was related to a reduction in maximal stroke volume measured during exercise in the upright position. Most of the decline in stroke volume occurred during the first 12 days of inactivity. Adaptive increases in maximal heart rate compensated somewhat for this loss of stroke volume. The decline in $\dot{V}o_{2\,max}$ during the 21- to 84-day period was associated with a decline in maximal arteriovenous O_2 difference.

The 84-day period of detraining resulted in a stabilization of $\dot{V}o_{2\,max}$ and maximal stroke volume. Thus, the subjects appeared to have detrained for a sufficient length of time to display a complete readjustment of cardiovascular response in accordance with their sedentary lifestyle. Note that maximal stroke volume during upright exercise in the detrained subjects was virtually the same as that observed in people who had never engaged in endurance training (Table 12-1). The idea that this finding does not necessarily imply a loss of heart function is subsequently discussed. Although maximal cardiac output and stroke volume declined to untrained levels, $\dot{V}o_{2\,max}$ levels in the detrained subjects remained 17% above that of untrained individuals, primarily because of an elevation of maximal arteriovenous O_2 difference. The persistent elevation of $\dot{V}o_{2\,max}$ values in the detrained subjects, the result of an augmented ability of the exercising musculature to extract oxygen, may be related to the observation that these subjects displayed no loss of the increased capillary density derived from the training and only a partial loss of the increase in muscle mitochondria (see *Detraining and Muscle Metabolism*).

STROKE VOLUME AND HEART SIZE

Prolonged and intense endurance training is thought to promote an increase in heart mass,

Table 12–1. Comparison of Untrained People and Detrained Subjects after 84 Days of Detraining

Population	$\dot{V}O_{2\,max}$ (ml · kg^{-1} · min^{-1})	SV$_{max}$ (ml)	HR$_{max}$ (beats · min^{-1})	a-$\bar{v}$O$_2$ Difference (ml · 100 ml^{-1})
Untrained people	43.3	128	192	12.6
Detrained subjects	50.8*	129	197	14.1*
Percent difference from untrained	+17*	+1	+3	+12*

* Values for detrained subjects are significantly (p < 0.05) higher than untrained subjects. (Modified from Coyle EF, et al.: Time course of loss of adaptations after stopping prolonged intense endurance training. *J Appl Physiol 57*:1857–1864, 1984.)

and researchers believe detraining results in a decline in heart mass.[1,8,9] What is not clear, however, is whether the training-induced increases in ventricular volume and myocardial wall thickness regress totally with inactivity. Athletes who become sedentary have enlarged hearts and an elevated $\dot{V}O_{2\,max}$ level in contrast to people who have never trained.[10]

One of the most striking effects of detraining in endurance-trained individuals is the rapid decline in stroke volume. To gain information regarding the cause of this large and rapid decline, Martin et al. measured stroke volume during exercise in trained subjects in both the upright and supine positions and again after 21 and 56 days of inactivity (Figure 12–2).

Simultaneous measurements of the diameter of the left ventricle were obtained echocardiographically. The large decline in stroke volume during upright cycling was associated with parallel reductions in the diameter of the left ventricle at end-diastole (i.e., LVEDD). When the subjects were evaluated during exercise in the supine position, a condition that usually augments ventricular filling because of the drainage of blood from the elevated legs, reduction in LVEDD was minimal. As a result, stroke volume during exercise in the supine position was maintained within a few percent of trained levels during the 56-day detraining period.

ROLE OF BLOOD VOLUME

Along the same lines, results of recent studies indicate that the rapid reduction with detraining of stroke volume during exercise in the upright position is related to a decline in blood volume (Fig. 12–3).[12] Intense exercise training usually results in an increase in blood volume by approximately 500 ml through the expansion of plasma volume.[13,14] This adaptation is gained after only a few bouts of exercise, and it is quickly reversed when training ceases.[13,14] The decline in stroke volume and the increase in heart rate during submaximal exercise, which normally accompanies several weeks of de-

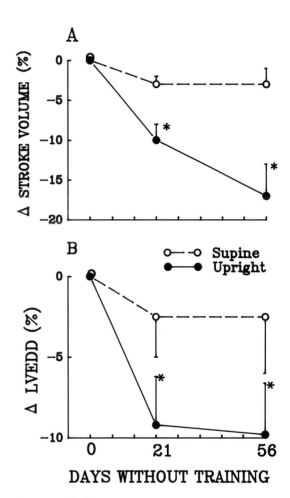

FIGURE 12–2. Percentage decline in exercise stroke volume **(A)** and left ventricular end diastolic diameter (LVEDD) (measured using echocardiography) **(B)** during exercise in upright and supine postures when trained and after 21 and 56 days of inactivity. *, responses in upright position are significantly (p < 0.05) lower than in supine position and lower than when trained (i.e., day 0). (From Martin WH, Coyle EF, Bloomfield SA, Ehsani AA: Effects of physical deconditioning after intense training on left ventricular dimensions and stroke volume. *J Am Coll Cardiol, 7*:982–989, 1986.)

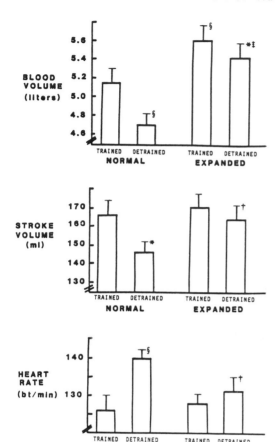

FIGURE 12-3. Responses to upright exercise with normal and expanded blood volume when trained and detrained. Significantly different from trained normal (*, p < 0.05; §, p < 0.01). Detrained with expanded blood volume significantly different from detrained with normal blood volume (†, p < 0.05; ‡, p < 0.01). (From Coyle EF, Hemmert MK, Coggan AR: Effects of detraining on cardiovascular responses to exercise: Role of blood volume. *J Appl Physiol*, 60:95–99, 1986.)

training, can be essentially reversed, and values return to near trained levels when the blood volume of detrained men expands to a level similar to that when the subjects were trained (Fig. 12-3).[12]

The observation that stroke volume during exercise is maintained at near trained levels when blood volume is high suggests that the ability of the heart to fill with blood is not significantly altered by detraining. If ventricular mass does indeed decline, a thinning of the ventricular walls and not a reduction in LVEDD is probably involved.[11] Thus, the reduction in intrinsic

cardiovascular function is apparently minimal after several weeks of inactivity in men who had been training intensely for several years.[12] The large reduction in stroke volume during exercise in the upright position is largely a result of reduced blood volume and not of a deterioration of heart function.[12]

DETRAINING AND MUSCLE METABOLISM

ENZYMES OF ENERGY METABOLISM

Endurance exercise training induces enzymatic adaptations in the exercising musculature that result in slower rates of glycogen utilization and lactate production and improved endurance during submaximal exercise.[15] One of the more important alterations is an increase in the activity of mitochondrial enzymes, which results in an increased ability to metabolize fuels in the presence of oxygen. Moderate endurance training (2 to 4 months duration) increases mitochondrial enzyme activity by 20 to 40% from untrained levels.[5,16] When moderate training ceases, however, and the stimuli for adaptation are removed, the increases in mitochondrial activity are quickly and totally reversed. Mitochondrial activity returns to pretraining levels within 28 to 56 days after the cessation of training.[5,16]

The pattern of change in enzyme activity observed when individuals who trained intensely for 10 years stopped training for 84 days is provided in Figure 12-4.[17] Mitochondrial enzyme activity in trained subjects (i.e., citrate synthase, succinate dehydrogenase, malate dehydrogenase, and β-hydroxyacyl-CoA dehydrogenase), which is initially twofold higher than those in untrained persons, declines progressively during the first 56 days of detraining and stabilizes at levels that are 50% higher than the values obtained from sedentary control subjects. The half-time of decline is approximately 12 days (i.e., declines one half the distance between trained and detrained in 12 days). Therefore, prolonged and intense training, in contrast to training programs that last only a few months, appears to result in only a partial loss of mitochondrial enzyme activity and thus a persistent elevation of activity above untrained levels. This elevation occurred almost entirely because of a persistent 80% elevation above untrained

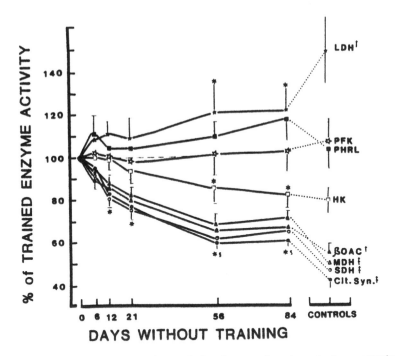

FIGURE 12–4. Enzyme activity during detraining period and comparison to sedentary control subjects. Values expressed as percentage of trained values. Cit. Syn., citrate synthase. SDH, succinate dehydrogenase. MDH, malate dehydrogenase. BOAC, B–hydroxyacyl-CoA dehydrogenase. HK, hexokinase. LDH, total lactate dehydrogenase. PHRL, phosphorylase. PFK, phosphofructokinase. *, significantly different from trained ($p < 0.05$); significantly different from 21 days ($p < 0.01$); ‡, control significantly different from 84 days ($p < 0.05$); †, control significantly different from 84 days ($p < 0.001$). (From Coyle EF, et al.: Effects of detraining on responses to submaximal exercise. *J Appl Physiol, 59:*853–859, 1985.)

levels in the mitochondrial enzyme activity in fast-twitch muscle fibers.[18]

MUSCLE CAPILLARIZATION

Endurance training promotes increased capillarization of the exercising musculature, which theoretically both prolongs the transit time of blood flow through the muscle and reduces diffusion distances, thus improving the availability of oxygen and nutrients to the muscle while also allowing for better removal of metabolic waste products. Moderate endurance training of several months' duration increases muscle capillarization by 20 to 30% above pretraining levels.[5,19] Results of preliminary studies indicate that certain indices of muscle capillarization remain somewhat higher than pretraining levels 8 weeks after the cessation of moderate training.[5]

More prolonged and intense training increases muscle capillary density by 40 to 50% from untrained levels.[7,19] No indication exists

that increases in muscle capillary density in highly trained people are reversed during 3 months of detraining.[7]

MUSCULAR ADAPTATIONS THAT PERSIST WITH DETRAINING

The detraining responses in the skeletal musculature of highly trained people who regularly engaged in intense exercise for several years apparently differ from those in individuals who have trained for only a few months. No loss of the increase in muscle capillarization occurs with the cessation of prolonged intense training, although such a loss does occur when moderate training is stopped. The cessation of moderate training results in a complete reversal of the training-induced increases in mitochondrial enzyme activity, whereas only a partial decline and therefore a persistent elevation of mitochondrial activity above untrained levels occurs with the cessation of exercise after prolonged intense endurance training.[3,5,16,17]

EXERCISE RESPONSES OF DETRAINED SUBJECTS

Currently, scant evidence is available to imply that the cardiovascular or skeletal musculature adaptations derived from mild and moderate endurance training are maintained above pretraining levels with cessation of training for more than approximately 8 weeks. Therefore, a person should be stressed to the same degree during exercise of a given intensity whether untrained or after a prolonged detraining period. This hypothesis has yet to be fully evaluated, however, and one factor to consider is the possibility that people may perceive exercise to be more comfortable when they are in the detrained state having already experienced physical training, as compared to the untrained condition.

In agreement with the findings that individuals who exercised intensely on a regular basis for several years remain superior in the detrained state with respect to their muscle metabolism and intrinsic heart function (i.e., stroke volume when ventricular filling is high) compared with untrained people, it appears that these detrained people can exercise more intensely before becoming inordinately stressed. One indication of this ability is the observation that detrained persons not only possess a $\dot{V}_{O_{2\,max}}$ level that is well above untrained values, but also they maintain the ability to exercise at a high percentage of $\dot{V}_{O_{2\,max}}$ before lactic acid begins to accumulate in the blood.[17]

BEDREST DECONDITIONING

Prolonged bedrest causes severe cardiovascular deconditioning, manifested by orthostatic intolerance and large reductions in maximal O_2 uptake and stroke volume during exercise.[20-22] This loss of cardiovascular function after bedrest results more from fluid shifts induced by a reclining posture than from inactivity. This reasoning is supported by the observation that the deterioration in cardiovascular function that results from 2 to 3 weeks of bedrest can be elicited after only 20 hours of bedrest with head-down tilt.[23] The primary cause of the cardiovascular dysfunction, especially during exercise in the upright position, appears to involve an altered distribution of body fluids and changes in intra-

vascular pressures. The factors responsible for the altered distribution of fluids may include autonomic nervous system dysfunction, a moderate reduction in blood volume (i.e., 500 ml), and altered venous compliance.[20]

Several methods can be used in an attempt to counteract the deterioration of cardiovascular function, which is most severe during exercise in the upright position after bedrest.[20] Blood volume expansion significantly improves cardiovascular status but it does not restore normal function. Treatments designed to induce venous pooling (i.e., lower body negative pressure and reverse gradient garments) during bedrest to stimulate conditions experienced in the upright position significantly reduce the deterioration in cardiovascular dysfunction.[20,24] Exercise in the supine position during bedrest, involving either dynamic or isometric contractions, tends to reduce cardiovascular deterioration; it is not capable, however, of preventing dysfunction.[20,25] Perhaps the best countermeasure for minimizing deconditioning of the cardiovascular system with bedrest is the mere exposure to the orthostatic stress encountered in the upright position.

SUMMARY

When physical training ceases (i.e., detraining), the bodily systems readjust in accordance with the diminished physiologic stimuli, and many training-induced adaptations are reversed to varying extents. The available evidence to date suggests that the increases in $\dot{V}_{O_{2\,max}}$ produced by endurance training of low to moderate intensities and durations are totally reversed after several months of detraining. When people detrain after several years of intense training, they display large reductions (i.e., 5 to 15%) in stroke volume and $\dot{V}_{O_{2\,max}}$ during the first 12 to 21 days of inactivity. These declines do not indicate a deterioration of heart function, but instead are largely a result of reduced blood volume and the ability to return venous blood to the heart. The $\dot{V}_{O_{2\,max}}$ of endurance athletes continues to decline during the 21 to 56 days of detraining because of reductions in maximal arteriovenous O_2 difference. These reductions are associated with a loss of mitochondrial enzyme activity within the trained musculature, which declines with a half-time of approximately 12 days. Endurance athletes, however, do not regress to levels displayed by individuals who never participated in exercise training. Levels of mitochondrial enzyme activity remain 50% higher than those of sedentary subjects, skeletal muscle capillarization is maintained at high levels, and $\dot{V}o_{2\,max}$ and the maximal arteriovenous O_2 difference stabilize at a point that is 12 to 17% higher than untrained levels after 84 days of detraining. The aims of future studies should be to determine if these superior physiologic abilities of people who cease prolonged and intense training are maintained for longer than 84 days and if these abilities relate to persistent effects of physical training or to inherent genetic predispositions.

REFERENCES

1. Blomqvist CG, Saltin B: Cardiovascular adaptations to physical training. *Annu Rev Physiol, 45*:169–189, 1983.
2. Rowell LB: Human cardiovascular adjustments to exercise and thermal stress. *Physiol Rev, 54*:75–159, 1974.
3. Orlander J, Kiessling KH, Karlsson J, Ekblom B: Low intensity training, inactivity and resumed training in sedentary men. *Acta Physiol Scand, 101*:351–362, 1977.
4. Fox EL, et al.: Frequency and duration of interval training programs and changes in aerobic power. *J Appl Physiol, 38*:481–484, 1975.
5. Klausen K, Andersen LB, Pelle I: Adaptive changes in work capacity, skeletal muscle capillarization and enzyme levels during training and detraining. *Acta Physiol Scand, 113*:9–16, 1981.
6. Drinkwater BL, Horvath SM: Detraining effects on young women. *Med Sci Sports Exerc, 4*:91–95, 1972.
7. Coyle EF, et al.: Time course of loss of adaptations after stopping prolonged intense endurance training. *J Appl Physiol, 57*:1857–1864, 1984.
8. Ehsani AA, Hagberg JM, Hickson RC: Rapid changes in left ventricular dimensions and mass in response to physical conditioning and deconditioning. *Am J Cardiol, 42*:52–56, 1978.
9. Hickson RC, Hammons GT, Holloszy JO: Development and regression of exercise-induced cardiac hypertrophy in rats. *Am J Physiol, 236*:H268–H272, 1979.
10. Saltin B, Grimby GG: Physiological analysis of middle-aged and old former athletes: Comparison with still active athletes of the same ages. *Circulation, 38*:1104–1115, 1968.
11. Martin WH, Coyle EF, Bloomfield SA, Ehsani AA: Effects of physical deconditioning after intense training on left ventricular dimensions and stroke volume. *J Am Coll Cardiol, 7*:982–989, 1986.
12. Coyle EF, Hemmert MK, Coggan AR: Effects of detraining on cardiovascular responses to exercise: Role of blood volume. *J Appl Physiol, 60*:95–99, 1986.
13. Convertino VA, et al.: Exercise training-induced hypervolemia: Role of plasma albumin, renin, and vasopressin. *J Appl Physiol, 48*:665–669, 1980.
14. Green HJ, et al.: Alterations in blood volume following short-term supramaximal exercise. *J Appl Physiol, 56*:145–149, 1984.
15. Holloszy JO, Coyle EF: Adaptations of skeletal muscle to endurance exercise and their metabolic consequences. *J Appl Physiol, 56*:831–838, 1984.
16. Henriksson J, Reitman JS: Time course of changes in human skeletal muscle succinate dehydrogenase and cytochrome oxidase activities and maximal oxygen uptake with physical activity and inactivity. *Acta Physiol Scand, 99*:91–97, 1977.
17. Coyle EF, et al.: Effects of detraining on responses to submaximal exercise. *J Appl Physiol, 59*:853–859, 1985.
18. Chi MM-Y, et al.: Effects of detraining on enzymes of energy metabolism in individual human muscle fibers. *Am J Physiol, 244*:C276–C287, 1983.
19. Ingjer F: Capillary supply and mitochondrial content of different skeletal muscle fiber types in untrained and endurance-trained men: A histochemical and ultrastructural study. *Eur J Appl Physiol, 40*:197–209, 1979.
20. Blomqvist CG, Stone HL: Cardiovascular adjustments to gravitational stress. In *The Handbook of Physiology. The Cardiovascular System.* Edited by JT Shepherd, FM Abboud, and SR Geiger. Bethesda, MD: American Physiology Society, 1982.
21. Convertino V, Hung J, Goldwater D, DeBusk R: Cardiovascular responses to exercise in middle-aged men after 10 days of bedrest. *Circulation, 65*:134–140, 1982.
22. Saltin B, et al.: Response to exercise after bed rest and after training: A longitudinal study of adaptive changes in oxygen transport and body composition. *Circulation, 7*:1–78, 1968.
23. Gaffney FA, et al.: Cardiovascular deconditioning produced by 20 hours of bedrest with head down tilt in middle-aged healthy men. *Am J Cardiol, 56*:634:638, 1985.
24. Convertino VA, Sandler H, Webb P, Annis JF: Induced venous pooling and the cardiorespiratory responses to exercise after bed rest. *J Appl Physiol, 52*:1343–1348, 1982.
25. Stremel RW, Convertino VA, Bernauer EM, Greenleaf JE: Cardiorespiratory deconditioning with static and dynamic leg exercise during bed rest. *J Appl Physiol, 41*:905–909, 1976.

CHAPTER 13

ENVIRONMENTAL CONSIDERATIONS IN EXERCISE TESTING AND TRAINING

JAMES A. VOGEL,
BRUCE H. JONES, AND
PAUL B. ROCK

For exercise testing and training prescription, health professionals must take into account the environment in which the tests are conducted. First, the three prominent environmental hazards—heat, cold, and high altitude—compete with the oxygen transport processes or thermoregulatory processes that are crucial to the ability to exercise. Secondly, exercising in these harsh environments places the individual at increased risk for injury or illness. An understanding of the body's responses to these environmental conditions and how to adjust for performance decrements and to avoid injury are important for those persons who conduct testing and training.

HIGH AMBIENT TEMPERATURE

Of the potential environmental hazards of concern to individuals who supervise exercise testing and training, heat stress is the greatest concern. High environmental temperature can diminish exercise capacity and is a frequent cause of potentially serious illness.

PHYSIOLOGIC RESPONSES

Heat is a byproduct of muscular activity. Even at moderate exercise intensities, this heat production is sufficient to raise the body's core temperature to lethal levels in 15 to 30 minutes; processes that dissipate this heat and maintain a near constant internal temperature prevent this occurrence. The excess heat is lost through radiation, convection, and conduction from the skin surface and, particularly during exercise, by the production and evaporation of sweat.

Heat produced metabolically is brought to the surface for dissipation by increasing skin blood flow. The body monitors both deep central and skin temperature through the thermoregulatory center in the hypothalamus, which in turn makes circulatory adjustments. As exercise occurs, blood flow increases to the active muscle to support metabolic demands and, at the same time, increases flow to the skin to dissipate the enhanced heat production. This increased flow is made possible both by increasing total blood flow (cardiac output) and by a redistribution of regional blood flow, i.e., reducing flow to the visceral organs.

The body's ability to balance these competing demands can be overwhelmed by exercise at high ambient temperatures (high external heat load). A high ambient temperature reduces the gradient between the air and skin, reducing effective convection and sweat evaporation. The body attempts to compensate by enhancing skin blood flow and cutaneous blood volume. This peripheral shunting of blood leads to a decline in central venous pressure, cardiac filling, and stroke volume. Heart rate must therefore increase to maintain the same cardiac output at a fixed exercise intensity. If the exercise and thermal load is sufficiently severe, heart rate reaches its maximum and cardiac output is insufficient to meet the competing demands. The need to decrease the level of exercise heightens so to prevent heat illness or because of the inability to maintain metabolic support of the exercising muscle.

ACCLIMATIZATION

The ability to tolerate and exercise in the heat can be improved by repeated exposures to heat, referred to as heat acclimatization. The primary physiologic adaptations of this process include an expansion of plasma volume, increased sweat rate, and improved circulatory control. These adaptations result in a reduced core temperature and heart rate response for a given heat exposure and exercise intensity. This process is achieved most effectively by exercising moderately during repeated heat exposures, producing an elevated core temperature that is a necessary stimulus for the acclimatization process. A high level of aerobic fitness increases heat tolerance but does not replace repeated heat exposures to achieve acclimatization. No apparent difference exists in the process between men and women.

HEAT STRESS INDEX

The assessment of the safety and effect of exercising at high temperatures necessitates quantification of the external heat load, i.e., an index of heat stress. The ordinary thermometer (dry bulb thermometer, Tdb) is not adequate because it does not take into account the ambient humidity, which has a direct bearing on the ability to evaporate sweat. The addition of the wet bulb thermometer (Twb) adds a mea-

surement of humidity, but this instrument still omits the factor of solar radiant energy and air movement. The solar radiant energy factor can be quantitated by the additional use of a black globe thermometer (Tg). Thus, the "wet bulb globe temperature (WBGT) index" was developed. WBGT is computed as: (outdoors) WBGT = (0.7 Twb) + (0.2 Tg) + 0.1 Tdb); (indoors) WBGT = (0.7 Twb) + (0.3 Tg). (Use of this index is explained in a subsequent section.)

TESTING AND TRAINING ADJUSTMENTS

Exercise capacity is adversely affected if the heat index is sufficiently high and the exposure is prolonged to the degree that it prevents the thermoregulatory system from coping with the combined environmental and metabolic heat loads. Heart rate is a valid and useful indicator of the additional stress imposed by environmental heat load. Thus, heart rate can be used as an indicator of heat placing an additional load on the circulatory system, and as a guide when reducing training intensity to achieve a constant load on the cardiovascular system.

For laboratory exercise testing application, a cool or neutral room temperature (22°C or less) is desirable for comfort and to minimize the possibility of compromising cardiac output to meet competing demands. Because electrocardiographic exercise testing and maximal oxygen uptake determinations are relatively brief, however, room temperatures of as much as 26°C can be used if air movement is increased.

Prolonged exercise for aerobic training is a different problem. Prolonged exercise allows for the body heat load to increase when a high heat-stress index is present. Training prescriptions must be adjusted downward for intensity and possibly duration to achieve the same cardiovascular load, again using heart rate as an indicator. Very high heat-stress indices necessitate reduction of intensity/duration by a further increment to provide some safety margin. Special precautions are needed when assessing cardiac rehabilitation patients who already have a narrowed tolerance limit.

HEAT ILLNESS

Heat illness (or injury) is a category of symptoms that occur as thermoregulatory mechanisms fail to cope with the competing loads of external heat load and metabolically produced heat so that core temperature continues to rise. Heat illness exhibits a spectrum of symptom severity, ranging from heat cramps and heat-induced dehydration to heat exhaustion and heat stroke.

Description

Heat Cramp. Heat cramps are benign heat injuries, which can be painful. They are typified by involuntary, sometimes painful, cramping of the muscles, usually in the calves or abdomen. They probably result from an imbalance of sodium and potassium across muscle cell membranes as a result of heavy sweating. Fluid replacement is the treatment of choice. Salting of food and a balanced diet are adequate to restore appropriate electrolyte levels.

Dehydration. Dehydration as a result of sweating accompanies and complicates other heat injuries. A 5% weight loss (3.5 kg) is common for an average sized man in the course of a 16-km (10 mile) run in 27 to 32°C (80 to 90°F) heat. Such sweat loss must be replaced by drinking cool water or dilute electrolyte solutions. Early signs of dehydration are lethargy, anxiety, and irritability. Severe dehydration may be manifest by uncoordinated, spastic gait, and altered consciousness. Individuals with symptoms of dehydration should be treated in the same manner as those with heat exhaustion and heat stroke.

Heat Exhaustion. Heat exhaustion is a potentially serious condition. It occurs in the exercise setting as a result of two events, increased "internal heat load" from physical activity and dehydration secondary to sweating. With heat exhaustion, body temperature (rectal) is elevated but is usually less than 39.5°C (103°F). Common symptoms included gooseflesh, headache, dizziness, shortness of breath, pallor, nausea, vomiting, and uncoordinated gait. Treatment is similar to that for heat stroke.

Heat Stroke. Heat stroke and heat exhaustion may be difficult to distinguish on clinical grounds. Although heat stroke casualties tend to have higher rectal temperatures (4°C (106°F) or higher), some individuals spontaneously recover from temperatures as high as 41.5°C

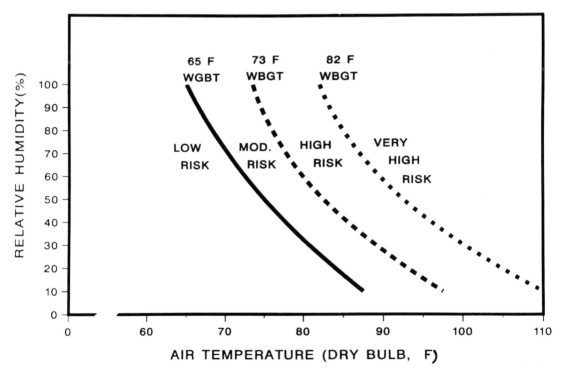

FIGURE 13–1. Risk of injury during exercise in high environmental temperature and humidity. (Adapted from Armstrong LE, Hubbard RW: High and dry. *Runners World*, June, 1985, p. 38.)

(107°F) without sequelae. Heat stroke victims, contrary to popular belief, may sweat profusely. Symptoms of both conditions are similar, but heat stroke casualties are more likely to manifest central nervous system disturbances such as unsteady gait, disorientation, confusion, bizarre or combative behavior, and unconsciousness. Individuals who are delirious, convulsive, or comatose are more likely to have suffered heat stroke and need prompt medical attention.

Prevention

Key to the prevention of heat injuries is the avoidance of testing and training in harsh ambient conditions that place the individual at increased risk. The WBGT index integrates the primary extrinsic risk factors—absolute temperature, humidity, and solar radiant energy—into a practical indication of the relative risk for injury. Moderate risk exists at WGBT between 65°F and 73°F, high risk between 73°F and 82°F, and very high risk above 82°F. Figure 13–1 provides a means of translating known dry bulb temperature and relative humidity into WBGT readings and risk levels. The *ACSM Position Statement: Prevention of Thermal Injuries During Distance Running* gives further information concerning these risks levels. A summary of the recommended strategies for minimizing the risks of exercising in the heat follows.

1. Allow time for acclimatization to the heat, usually 10 to 14 days.
2. Exercise during cooler parts of day.
3. Limit or defer exercise if WBGT is in high-risk zone (Fig. 13–1).
4. Plan to drink before, during, and after exercise in the heat, even during training runs (see *ACSM Guidelines*). Recommended quantities are 400 to 500 ml before and 300 ml every 20 min during the activity.
5. Modulate training intensity (by heart rate monitoring).
6. Monitor daily body weight closely. Acute losses are water. If losses are greater than 3% of weight, they need to be replaced by drinking before the next training session.
7. Salt replacement is essential. Adequate electrolyte replacement is provided by liberal salting of food and a balanced diet. Use of salt tablets is not advised.

Treatment

Individuals who exhibit signs and symptoms of heat injury should be removed to a shaded area immediately. They should be laid down with their feet elevated above the level of the heart. Excess clothing should be opened or removed. If rectal temperatures are above 39.5°C (103°F), cooling of the victims should begin immediately. Sprinkling with water and fanning to increase evaporative cooling or rubbing ice packs over major blood vessels in the arm pits, groin, and neck areas are effective means of cooling. Cooling should proceed until rectal temperatures are 39°C (102°F). Victims should be given cool fluids to *sip* if they are conscious, but only if they are not nauseated or vomiting. If they cannot take fluids by mouth, intravenous fluids should be administered if medical personnel are available or they should be rapidly evacuated to the nearest hospital. All individuals who have exhibited serious disturbances of behavior or neurologic function should receive medical attention from a physician, especially if they fail to recover after the cessation of exercise and onset of cooling.

LOW AMBIENT TEMPERATURE

Performance decrements and injuries from cold exposure are reported less frequently than those from heat in the exercising adult. This difference results in part because exercise itself generates enough heat to warm the body and because protective clothing can readily be added for heat retention. Nevertheless, cold weather can pose a significant threat to the exercising individual.

PHYSIOLOGIC RESPONSES

Heat is lost from the body through radiation, conduction, and convection, or through sweat evaporation. Although these processes are desirable and necessary when activity occurs in hot environments, they can be deleterious in cold weather conditions. Unwanted heat loss is normally avoided by adding layers of clothing (reducing losses through radiation and convection) and keeping the skin dry. If these measures are insufficient and skin temperature falls, cutaneous vasoconstriction occurs, drawing blood away from the body surface and extremities and thereby reducing heat loss and maintaining core temperature. If the cold stress is sufficiently severe and core temperature continues to fall, shivering results in an effort to produce additional metabolic heat. Exercising in a cold environment can be helpful in most situations by producing additional heat, as with shivering.

ACCLIMATIZATION

Man apparently does not exhibit the pronounced physiologic acclimatization responses that he does in the heat. Some evidence exist, however, that people who habitually function in cold temperatures develop the ability to burn more calories per unit of exercise than the unhabituated person.

PERFORMANCE DECREMENTS AND TRAINING ADJUSTMENTS

Acute cold exposure, at least to $-20°C$, does not affect maximal oxygen uptake because the oxygen transport system to active muscles is not compromised. Significant cold exposure can reduce submaximal endurance performance, although the mechanism for this occurrence is not established. This reduction is not a major concern in training prescription during cold periods, and training adjustments are not necessary for the nonathlete on the basis of performance capacity concerns.

COLD EXPOSURE INDEX

The severity of cold exposure on the body, like heat, depends on air movement, humidity, and precipitation as well as absolute temperature. Humidity is less of a factor as temperatures drop below freezing. Wind velocity, however, is a major factor in the severity of cold stress by markedly increasing heat loss by radiation, convection, and evaporation. The extent of the air velocity factor (or wind chill effect) is shown in Table 13–1. The equivalent temperature depicted on the wind chill chart relates to the cooling effect on exposed skin.

COLD INJURY

The cold injuries of concern during outdoor training are hypothermia and frostbite.

Description

Hypothermia is a depression in core temperature sufficient to affect body functions, usually below 95°F. Frostbite is the process of tissue water crystallization and subsequent cell dehydration and destruction.

Breathing cold air does not cause injury to the trachea and lung tissue, although it may be uncomfortable. The inhalation of very cold air by cardiac patients can cause angina, and precautions should be taken for rehabilitation training of these individuals.

Table 13–1. Wind Chill Index

Wind speed (mph)	Thermometer reading (°F)										
	50	40	30	20	10	0	−10	−20	−30	−40	−50
	(Equivalent temperature [°F])										
5	48	37	27	16	6	−5	−15	−26	−36	−47	−57
10	40	28	16	4	−9	−24	−33	−46	−58	−70	−83
15	36	22	9	−5	−18	−32	−45	−58	−72	−85	−99
20	32	18	4	−10	−25	−39	−53	−67	−82	−96	−110
25	30	16	0	−15	−29	−44	−59	−74	−88	−104	−118
30	28	13	−2	−18	−33	−48	−63	−79	−94	−109	−125
35	27	11	−4	−20	−35	−51	−67	−82	−98	−113	−129
40	26	10	−6	−21	−37	−53	−69	−85	−100	−115	−132
	Minimal Risk			*Increasing Risk*				*Great Risk*			

Prevention

The primary extrinsic risk factors other than cold air temperature are wind speed, humidity or wetness, immersion in cold water, and inadequate protective clothing. Perhaps the most significant is wind, as illustrated by the wind chill information in Table 13–1. The important intrinsic risk factors are primarily those that affect energy metabolism and/or circulation, such as fatigue, hunger, low percent body fat (less insulation), use of tobacco or caffeine (vasoconstriction), and use of alcohol (vasodilatation).

Most important in the prevention of cold injury during training is adequate clothing. If the wind chill temperature is −15°F to −20°F or lower, exposed peripheral areas such as the face, nose, ears, hands, and feet should be adequately protected with masks or scarfs, caps, mittens, and dry insulated shoes, respectively. Several layers of loose fitting clothing should be worn under a windproof, water-repellent (not water tight) outer layer. Clothing should be kept dry from both inside (sweat) and outside (rain, mist) because water conducts cold more rapidly than air. Thus, both exercise intensity and clothing should be adjusted to maintain body heat but to prevent the accumulation of excessive amounts of sweat.

During extended training periods, the pace should be set to avoid a significant decrease toward the end and therefore loss of adequate heat production. Running, walking, or skiing into the wind may also be helpful so that the wind chill is less during the later phases of the activity. Additional clothing or protection from the wind may be desirable during the cool-down phase of exercise to avoid excessive cooling.

Treatment

Frostbite injuries can be serious, leading to gangrene and loss of the body part if the trauma is not recognized early and/or treated properly. The key is to leave the affected part until it can be thawed without risk of refreezing, preferably in a hospital. Injured parts can be thawed in warm water (38°C to 43°C or 100°F to 110°F); the temperature of the water should be measured with a thermometer.

Mild hypothermia can be managed by removing the victim to a sheltered warm location and providing dry garments and warm beverages (if alert). Moderate to severe cases should be transported gently to a hospital for rewarming. Gentle handling is crucial so as to avoid precipitating dangerous, cardiac arrhythmias. These victims should also be kept still to avoid recirculation of cold blood from the extremities to the central circulation.

HIGH TERRESTRIAL ALTITUDE

Testing and training at high elevations are unavoidable for those who reside there; other individuals choose to train under the conditions of reduced oxygen pressure. The reduced oxygen availability has profound effects on physical performance and can lead to illness in unacclimated individuals.

PHYSIOLOGIC RESPONSES

The partial pressure of oxygen in the air decreases as barometric pressure declines with increasing altitudes above sea level. Thus, in Denver (5280 ft), ambient O_2 pressure declines to 132 from 159 mm Hg at sea level and is as low as 94 mm Hg at Pikes Peak, CO (14,110 ft). With the decline in inspired O_2 tension is a concomitant fall in arterial oxygen saturation, which triggers compensatory mechanisms in an attempt by the body to maintain oxygen transport.

On initial exposure to altitude, stimulation of pulmonary ventilation and a consequent respiratory alkalosis occur. The alkalosis, in turn, causes a left shift in the oxygen-hemoglobin dissociation curve, which allows oxygen to be more available to the tissue at a given O_2 pressure. Additional physiologic adjustments include a temporary increase in submaximal exercise heart rate and cardiac output. The sum of these adjustments supports the transport of oxygen to the tissues despite the diminished O_2 availability.

ACCLIMATIZATION

As altitude exposure continues, the acclimatization process occurs. The initial alkalosis precipitates a change in red blood cell enzymes, which supports the shift in the oxygen-hemoglobin curve. At the same time, red cell production increases, leading to increased hematocrit and hemoglobin volume. Prolonged high-altitude exposure leads to further adaptation at the level of the mitochondria and in exercise muscle-capillary density. These adaptive mechanisms are readily demonstrated by comparing the decreased physical performance of newly arrived lowlanders with that of persons who have lived for extended periods at altitude and who can perform heavy physical activity, such as mining or mountain climbing. Despite the significant physiologic and acclimatization responses, levels of physical performance remain decreased at altitude, even in well-acclimatized individuals.

TESTING AND TRAINING ADJUSTMENTS

The persistent decrement in physical performance at high altitudes should be considered in testing and training. The magnitude of the effect of altitude on any activity is a function of its dependence on oxygen transport. Aerobic events are greatly affected whereas anaerobic events are not. Thus, maximal oxygen uptake and submaximal endurance times are decreased at altitude, whereas sprinting may be actually improved because of decreased air resistance. The decrease in maximal oxygen uptake as a function of altitude is illustrated in Figure 13-2.

HIGH ALTITUDE ILLNESS

Pathologic conditions related to exposure to high altitude are not prominent until an elevation of about 8000 ft. Individuals may then experience acute mountain sickness or the more severe conditions, such as high-altitude pulmonary and cerebral edema.

Description

Acute mountain sickness is a complex of symptoms that results from rapid ascent of an unacclimatized individual. Principal symptoms include severe headache, lassitude, nausea,

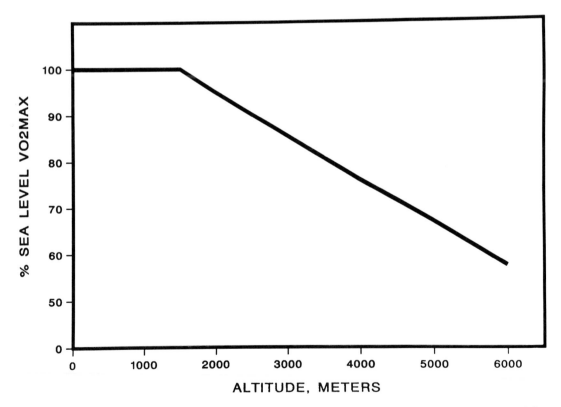

FIGURE 13-2. Approximate reduction in maximal oxygen uptake with increasing altitude. (Adapted from Hartley LH: Effects of high-altitude environment on the cardiovascular system of man. *JAMA, 215:*241, 1971.)

vomiting, anorexia, indigestion, and sleep disturbances. Symptoms begin after 6 hours, peak between 24 and 48 hours, and resolve after 3 to 4 days.

High-altitude pulmonary edema is characterized by fluid accumulation in the lungs that is not associated with heart failure. Characteristic signs include increased breathing and heart rate, cyanosis, and pulmonary rales along with coughing. The condition can be confirmed radiographically, with evidence of multiple patchy infiltrates throughout the lungs. Young active individuals seem especially susceptible to this condition. Heavy exercise and cold exposure are predisposing factors. High-altitude cerebral edema is a rare form of severe acute mountain sickness in which an individual exhibits certain abnormal neurologic signs and symptoms.

Prevention

Acute mountain sickness and high altitude pulmonary and cerebral edema result from failure to acclimatize properly to altitude. These conditions essentially can be prevented by using a gradual ascent, thus allowing sufficient time to acclimatize. An ascent rate of no more than 1000 to 2000 ft per day at altitudes greater than 8000 ft is recommended. Additionally, sleep should occur at as low an altitude as possible. Acetazolamide, a carbonic anhydrase inhibitor, can be prescribed to prevent acute mountain sickness in people who cannot take time to acclimate properly.

Treatment

Any pre-existing medical condition in which oxygen delivery is compromised, such as anemia or heart and lung disease, is made worse by altitude exposure. Evaluation to determine whether a person with these conditions can be exposed to altitude safely should be made by a physician.

REFERENCES AND SUGGESTED READING

1. ACSM Position Statement: Prevention of thermal injuries during distance running. *Med Sci Sports Exerc, 16*:ii, 1984.
2. Armstrong LE, Dziados JE: Effects of heat exposure on the exercising adult. In *Sports Physical Therapy.* Edited by DB Bernhardt. New York: Churchill Livingstone, 1986.
3. Armstrong LE, Hubbard RW: High and dry. *Runners World, June:* 38, 1985.
4. Brown CF, Oldridge NB: Exercise-induced angina in the cold. *Med Sci Sports Exerc, 17*:607, 1985.
5. Burton AC, Edholm OG: *Man in a Cold Environment.* London: Arnold, 1955.
6. Hackett P: *Mountain Sickness: Prevention, Recognition and Treatment.* New York: American Alpine Club, 1980.
7. Hartley LH: Effects of high-altitude environment on the cardiovascular system of man. *JAMA, 215*:241, 1971.
8. Heath D, Williams D: *Man at High Altitude.* Edinburgh: Churchill Livingstone, 1977.
9. Houston C: *Going High.* New York: American Alpine Club, 1980.
10. Horvath SM: Exercise in a cold environment. In *Exercise and Sport Sciences Reviews.* Vol. 9. Edited by DI Miller. Philadelphia: Franklin Institute, 1981.
11. Pandolf KB: Effects of physical training and cardiorespiratory physical fitness on exercise-heat tolerance: Recent observations. *Med Sci Sports Exerc, 11*:60, 1979.
12. Patton JF, Vogel JA: Effects of acute cold exposure on submaximal endurance performance. *Med Sci Sports Exerc, 16*:494, 1984.
13. Nadel ER (ed): *Problems with Temperature Regulation during Exercise.* New York: Academic Press, 1977.

PATHOPHYSIOLOGY

14

THE ATHEROSCLEROTIC PROCESS

H. ROBERT SUPERKO

Atherosclerosis is the pathologic process responsible for coronary artery disease (CAD). This process is the underlying cause that led to 703,500 deaths from heart attack or stroke in 1983.[1] An understanding of the process of atherosclerosis provides an appreciation for the importance of lifestyle modifications that may affect this disease process. The formal definition of atherosclerosis is brief and is easy to understand: "A lesion of large and medium-sized arteries, with deposits in the intima of yellowish plaques containing cholesterol, lipoid material, and lipophages."[2]

The development of atherosclerosis is more complex than is the definition. The process continues to be investigated actively, and current pathophysiologic descriptions inevitably will change as research findings enhance our understanding. Excellent review articles are available and we encourage the student to refer to these additional sources of information.[3,4]

Although this chapter is subdivided to help concentrate attention on a single topic, in reality all factors are integrated and the atherosclerotic process is continuously in a dynamic state of flux.

ANATOMY

An understanding of basic vascular anatomy is fundamental to the understanding of the pathophysiologic process of atherosclerosis. Factors that disrupt the integrity of the vessel wall can promote the atherosclerotic process. The general anatomic structure of a small artery is provided in Figure 14–1.

The walls of small arteries have three layers; the tunica intima, the tunica media, and the tunica adventitia. The tunica intima is composed of endothelial cells adherent to an internal elastic membrane, which is a network of elastic fibers. The tunica media is composed of smooth muscle cells; the number of layers of smooth muscle cells tends to increase as the caliber of vessels increases. External to this layer of smooth muscle cells is the external elastic membrane. The third layer, the tunica adventitia, is composed of connective tissue as well as elastic and collagenous fibers, which often merge with the surrounding connective tissue. The integrity of this system can be disrupted by physical action, such as high blood

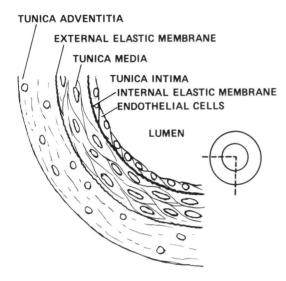

FIGURE 14–1. Anatomic cross-section of small artery.

pressure, or trauma, such as balloon angioplasty; by invasive actions of lipoproteins; by toxic metabolic factors, such as carbon monoxide; by immunologic activity; and probably by as yet undiscovered mechanisms. Disruption of the integrity of this system often results in some physical obstruction of the vessel lumen, such as from chronic accumulation of connective tissue, blood cells, and material transported by lipoproteins, and more acutely, by thrombus formation and smooth muscle spasm.

ETIOLOGY AND PATHOPHYSIOLOGY

Atherosclerosis is a multifactorial process. The specific factors associated with the development and progression of atherosclerosis have been clarified by the findings of numerous investigations. During the early 20th century, investigators hypothesized that either dietary protein or fat was the primary cause of atherosclerosis.[5] In part because of the availability of laboratory techniques, the fat hypothesis gained favor over the protein hypothesis. Abnormalities in fat metabolism are now considered to be among the primary causes of atherosclerosis.

The recurrent injury hypothesis, as developed by Russell Ross, is a comprehensive pathophysiologic description of atherosclerosis.[3]

This hypothesis has several major steps, all of which are continuously interactive. The recurrent injury hypothesis is based on substantial evidence gathered from animal and cellular physiologic studies. Direct confirmation of how some established CAD risk factors interact on the cellular level to result in atherosclerotic plaque in humans, however, is unavailable. The classic CAD risk factors interact with these developmental steps in multiple ways; their effect on plasma lipoproteins is illustrated in Table 14–1. The classic CAD risk factor, high blood pressure, exerts its effect on plasma lipids primarily because of the metabolic effects of certain antihypertensive medications.[6]

The pathophysiologic steps in the recurrent injury hypothesis include recurrent injury, endothelial disruption, monocyte adherence and activation, smooth muscle cell proliferation, accumulation of lipids, and organization of the mature plaque. The process involves four major cell types; endothelium, smooth muscle, platelet, and the macrophage/monocyte. Initial INJURY occurs from a variety of mechanisms that may include physical trauma, carbon monoxide toxicity, inflammation, and immune-mediated and metabolic factors, such as hyperlipidemia.

As a part of the response to injury, the white blood cell monocyte ATTACHES to the endothelium and eventually migrates between and beneath the endothelial layer. DISRUPTION of the endothelial integrity results, which enhances further migration. These subendothelial macrophages become ACTIVATED, which causes secretion of substances (chemoattractants) that further attract cells, and promote CELL DIVISION (mitogens). Smooth muscle cells begin to accumulate in the intima and, as a result of the disruption of the normal cellular milieu, platelets in the vascular compartment are activated. From this process, growth factor

Table 14–1. Classic CAD Risk Factors and Potential Effect on Lipid Profile

Risk factor	TG*	LDLC	HDLC
Hypercholesterolemia	±†	I	±D
Smoking	±D	±I	D
Diabetes (noninsulin-dependent)	I	±	D
Sedentary lifestyle	I	±	D
High fat diet	±I	I	±
High blood pressure‡	±	±	±

* TG, triglycerides; LDLC, low-density lipoprotein-cholesterol; HDLC, high-density lipoprotein-cholesterol.
† I, increase; D, decrease; ±, variable effect.
‡ Dependent on anti-hypertensive drug interaction with lipoproteins.

is derived and is released from three sources: endothelium, macrophage, and platelet.

Consequent to growth factor release, smooth muscle cell PROLIFERATION occurs, and the maturing atherosclerotic plaque becomes a complex matrix of smooth muscle cells, macrophages, fibrous and collagenous material, and cellular debris. The smooth muscle cells and macrophages may both ACCUMULATE LIPID material and, along with intercellular lipid accumulation, contribute to the mass of material that protrudes into the luminal space. The MATURE plaque develops a fibrous smooth muscle cell cap, whereas the base of the plaque may necrose, resulting in deposition of cholesterol crystals and accumulation of calcium complexes.

The updated version of the response to injury hypothesis is suggestive of the existence of two pathways that would result in the atherosclerotic lesion. The monocyte pathway involves the interaction of monocytes and platelets to stimulate growth factor release and the consequent smooth muscle cell proliferation. An example of this pathway is thought to be the pathologic response to hypercholesterolemia. The updated pathway involves a direct role for the endothelial cell to release growth factors in response to stimuli associated with cigarette smoking, hypertension, or diabetes. Similar to the first pathway, the result is smooth muscle cell proliferation and ultimately the atherosclerotic plaque.

The old and updated versions are dominated by two major blood components, platelets and lipoproteins. A basic understanding of these two groups is necessary to comprehend the metabolic approach to the management of atherosclerosis.

PLATELETS

Platelets are blood products that have various functions, including stimulating contraction of injured vessels, formation of adhesive plugs, and a role in the initiation of the blood clotting mechanism. Platelets are small blood products with an average diameter of 3 μm. By comparison, the average diameter of a red blood cell is 7.7 μm; that for a white blood cell is 7 to 12 μm. The platelet is a storehouse of factors that can modulate cell division, cell migration, adhesion, and coagulation. Intracellular

granules package and store these factors, which can be released in response to specific stimuli.

Several mitogens (growth factors) have been identified in platelets and are responsible for smooth muscle cell proliferation.[7] In addition to its mitogenic properties, platelet-derived growth factor (PDGF) also has chemotactic properties. These chemotactic attributes permit the stimulation of the migration of smooth-muscle cells and monocyte/macrophage cells toward and into the atherosclerotic lesion.

Another metabolic role of platelets involves a balance between thromboxane (TX) A_2 and prostaglandin (PGI$_2$). TXA$_2$ has powerful platelet-aggregating and vasoconstricting properties that under normal conditions are balanced by the antiaggregating and vasodilating properties of PGI$_2$. Factors that alter this balance may promote or retard the pathophysiologic actions of platelets.[8]

LIPOPROTEINS AND CHOLESTEROL

The role of lipoproteins in fat metabolism is both simple and complex. The lipoproteins can be simply a means of cholesterol and triglyceride transport; the control and modulation of this transport system is more complex. To address the influence of a variety of factors on plasma lipids and lipoproteins clearly, a discussion of definition, composition, and function is necessary.

LIPIDS

Lipids are water-soluble macromolecules that have three major biologic functions: (1) a transportable metabolic energy pool; (2) a structural component for cell membranes, cell walls, and large molecules; and (3) a stationary energy supply. The major groups of lipids relating to our discussion are triglycerides (TG), phospholipids (PL), and steroids (Fig. 14–2).

The TG are an important storage and transport mode for fatty acids (FA). They are composed of three FA esterified to the hydroxyl groups of glycerol, creating a structure with a three-carbon backbone and three FA dangling from each carbon atom.

Phospholipids (PL) (or phosphoglycerides) are similar to TG, with the exception that one hydroxyl group is esterified to phosphoric acid as opposed to a FA. The structure appears as a

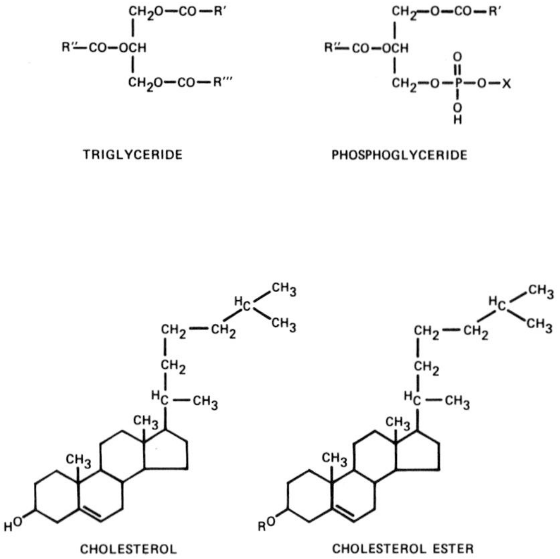

FIGURE 14–2. Major plasma lipids.

three-carbon backbone with one phosphoric acid and two FA attached. The PL are important components of cell membranes and are the most polar of the lipids. The relative type of PL composition in lipoproteins appears to affect the ability to bind apoproteins that regulate biochemical reactions. For example, apoprotein (Apo) CII is removed more rapidly than Apo CIII from chylomicrons during TG hydrolysis apparently because of a reduced remnant affinity for Apo CII that results from a relative increase in two phospholipids, lysophosphatidylcholine and sphingomyelin.[9] This alteration in the ability to bind to receptor sites and to regulate biochemical reactions owing to changes in PL composition may eventually explain part of the effect of dietary FA content on lipid metabolism.

Steroids are a group of lipids that are biologically quite diverse, and include sex hormones, bile acids, and adrenocortical hormones. The steroids include the biologically abundant sterols, among which is cholesterol. The cholesterol structure is somewhat more complex than the other lipids, and occurs as a "free" alcohol or in an "esterified" form.

LIPOPROTEINS

Lipids are usually transported through the plasma as a variety of particles composed of protein, PL, TG, and cholesterol. This conglomeration is termed a lipoprotein, and allows hydrophobic lipids to disperse in the blood system. The lipoproteins are a diverse group of particles that are separated into various categories on the basis of their density or composition characteristics. The density range of the major lipoprotein classes is illustrated in Figure 14–3.

Work summarized by Pownall and Gotto indicates a spherical structure of lipoproteins.[10] Polar PL, proteins, and nonesterified cholesterol form a structure that is a monolayer shell surrounding a core of cholesterol esters.[11] Various proteins located on the surface (apoproteins) allow interaction with other biologic systems.

Lipoproteins appear to have two major functions: the transport of TG and cholesterol, and the regulation of lipid metabolism. The transport role follows a path of large particles, rich in TG and relatively poor in cholesterol, that undergo a series of metabolic interactions resulting in more dense particles that are relatively rich in cholesterol and poor in TG. The large transport particles of intestinal origin are termed chylomicrons; somewhat smaller particles of hepatic origin are termed very low-density lipoproteins (VLDL). After a series of interactions with lipase enzymes, the particles are more dense and are relatively cholesterol-rich. An intermediate-density lipoprotein (IDL) precedes the appearance of low-density lipoprotein (LDL), which is the greatest source of cholesterol transport among the lipoproteins. The cycle of metabolic events is illustrated in Figure 14–4.

The high-density lipoprotein (HDL) is derived from both an intestinal and a hepatic source. The hepatic HDL is described as nascent, or new HDL, and is discoid. Intestinally derived HDL is more spherical, and varies in its protein composition. Both HDL particles are relatively cholesterol-poor; after interaction with lecithin-cholesterol acyltransferase (LCAT) and lipoprotein lipase (LPL) in both adipose and muscle tissue, the cholesterol ester content increases and the particle becomes less dense. On the basis of the relative density obtained in the analytic ultracentrifuge, the more dense, relatively cholesterol-poor form is termed HDL_3 (1.125 to 1.21 g/ml) and the less dense, relatively cholesterol-rich form is termed HDL_2 (1.062 to 1.125 g/ml).[12] The function and result of this change in cholesterol content may be to play a role in what has been termed "reverse cholesterol transport."[13,14] After interaction with the enzyme hepatic lipase (HL), HDL

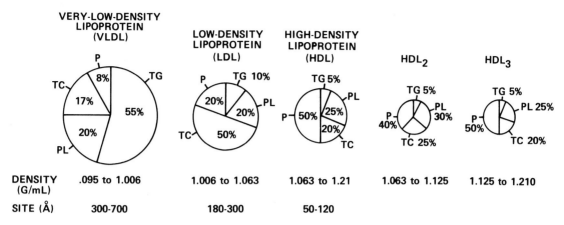

FIGURE 14–3. Composition, density range, and size of plasma lipoproteins. (Schlieren pattern obtained with analytic ultracentrifuge. Mass seen as distribution of lipoproteins according to flotation rates.)

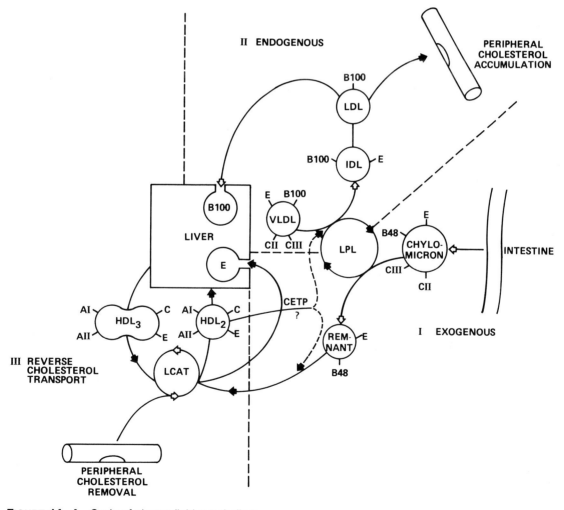

FIGURE 14–4. Cycle of plasma lipid metabolism.

reappears as the relatively cholesterol-poor form HDL_3.[15]

The measurement of plasma cholesterol can vary considerably depending upon a variety of physiologic and pathologic variables.[16] The problem is even more critical when considering the issue of precision for HDLC measurement.[17] This topic has important clinical implications that include the need to obtain multiple samples before the determination of an accurate baseline, and the need to be familiar with the quality control aspects of the laboratory in which the blood analysis occurs.

PROTEINS

Proteins play a prominent role in lipoprotein metabolism that includes identification of receptor sites on the surface of cells, enzyme activation, and lipoprotein structure.[18-20] Each apoprotein probably has more than one function, and is in a continuous spectrum of activity. Table 14-2 is a list of the major apoproteins, associated lipoproteins, and their physiologic function. These lipid-associated proteins are termed apoproteins, and are given alphabetical names.[21] They tend to be associated with lipoprotein groups, and are identified on the basis of specific antibody-binding characteristics. A variety of methods are available for use to identify apoproteins, including radial immunodiffusion, radioimmunoassay, and nephelometry.[22-24] The use of apoprotein measurements as a clinical tool is rapidly becoming more popular, and different methods can result in substantial differences in apoprotein values. The function of apoproteins is often elucidated by the study of patients who genetically lack a specific protein.

The apoproteins are produced primarily in the intestinal mucosa and liver. Use of radiolabeled precursor amino acids fed to rats have implicated the intestine as the primary source of Apo AI, Apo AIV, and Apo B.[25,26] Some Apo CII is produced in the rat intestine, but the liver remains the major source of Apo C.[27] Thus, it appears that Apo A and some amount of B and C are produced in the intestine, whereas the liver is the major source of Apo B, C, and E. Similar evidence is available from investigations involving human subjects.[20,29] In human beings, Apo B100 is secreted by the liver and Apo B48 by the small intestine. The site of apoprotein production is important for selection of proper means of therapy and to clarify the effect of other, noncardiovascular diseases. In elegant work, Brown and Goldstein elucidated the molecular role played by protein conformation in receptor site identification and function.[30]

Apoprotein A is identified as AI and AII. It is principally associated with HDL, and values may change acutely in the postprandial state.[31] Apo AI, along with CI, is an activator of LCAT.[32] LCAT activity is associated with the HDL particle, and is the major enzyme involved in the formulation of cholesterol ester in blood. Plasma AI content may be a better predictor of future cardiovascular events than HDL values, and a ratio of TG, Apo B, and Apo AI appears to be a better discriminator than simple lipid values between myocardial infarction survivors and control subjects.[33-35]

Apo B is an identifying protein for specific cell receptors.[35] Apo B has been identified as two apoproteins. Apo B100 is produced mainly in the liver; Apo B48 is derived from the intestines and is approximately one half the molecu-

Table 14-2. Approximate Percent Association of Apoproteins with Lipoprotein Classes and Major Physiologic Functions*

| Apoproteins | Lipoprotein class | | | | Major function |
	VLDL	IDL	LDL	HDL	
AI	———	———	———	100	LCAT activation
AII	———	———	———	100	LCAT inhibition (?) and/or activation of heparin releasable hepatic triglyceride hydrolase
B	2	8	82	———	
B48					Required for synthesis of chylomicrons
B100					LDL receptor binding
CI	2	1	———	97	LCAT activator
CII	30	10	———	60	LPL activation
CIII	20	10	10	60	LPL inhibition
D	———	———	———	100	Core lipid transfer protein
E	20	20	10	50	Remnant receptor binding

* Based on data from Pownall HJ, Gotto AM: Plasma apoproteins: Composition, structure and function. In *Atherosclerosis: Mechanisms and Approaches to Therapy*. Edited by NE Miller. New York: Raven Press, 1983. VLDL, very low-density lipoprotein; IDL, intermediate-density lipoprotein; LDL, low-density lipoprotein; HDL, high density lipoprotein; LCAT, lecithin-cholesterol acyltransferase; LPL, lipoprotein lipase.

lar weight of Apo B100. The B apoproteins appear to be necessary for dietary fat absorption and cell receptor site identification.

Apo CI, along with Apo AI, is an activator of LCAT.[32] The hydrolysis of TG by LPL associated with fat and muscle cells is dependent upon Apo CII.[36] This relationship is reflected in the substantial elevation in chylomicrons and VLDL noted in patients that lack this apoprotein.[37] Homozygote patients lacking Apo CII have markedly decreased LDL and HDL values, a finding that supports its role as a co-factor in the conversion of chylomicrons and VLDL to denser lipoproteins.[38]

Comparatively few facts are known about the function of Apo D. It is primarily found in HDL and may assist in the transfer of cholesterol ester between VLDL, LDL, and HDL.[39]

Apo E plays an important role in hepatic clearance of VLDL remnants and HDL recognition, as well as a recognition site of IDL for specific receptors in the liver. Patients that lack normal function of Apo E demonstrate a characteristic familial dysbetalipoproteinemia, which results from a structural abnormality of Apo E.[40,41] With the use of isoelectric focusing, Apo E can be identified as a number of isoforms that are distinguished on the basis of cysteine and arginine content.[42,43] This method is used to classify patients with Apo E of abnormal structure.

PATHWAYS

Lipoprotein metabolism involves an exogenous and endogenous pathway that involves all of the aforementioned components (see Fig. 14–4).[30] The EXOGENOUS pathway involves the packaging of cholesterol into large TG-rich chylomicron particles that are derived from a gastrointestinal source. After TG hydrolysis by LPL, remnant particles are cleared by the liver with the aid of receptor-mediated endocytosis, which is enhanced by the presence of Apo B48 and Apo E.

The ENDOGENOUS pathway involves the production of VLDL in the liver. This particle is relatively TG-rich and cholesterol-poor. Its major apoproteins include B100, E, and C. During its journey through tissue capillaries, LPL helps in the removal of a portion of the TG component, thus reversing the initial TG/cholesterol balance. This conversion results in a particle of intermediate density that is choles-

terol-rich and TG-poor, the intermediate-density lipopoprotein (IDL). Many of these particles are cleared by the liver; other particles lose their Apo E component and become more dense. This modified particle is now termed LDL, on the basis of its density and flotation rate in analytic ultracentrifugation. The primary apoprotein of LDL is B100, which is the key to its cellular binding and endocytosis. A third pathway that involves HDL, the reverse cholesterol transport pathway, was previously described. It may be a counterbalance to the exogenous and endogenous pathways.

IMMUNOLOGY

The immune system can participate in the initiation of atherosclerotic plaque. Severe premature atherosclerosis occurs in patients with CAD associated with autoimmune diseases.[44] The combination of elevated LDL and immune dysfunction, as defined by the presence of cytotoxic B-cell antibodies, is associated with a particularly aggressive form of atherosclerosis in cardiac transplant patients.[45,46] Although less well defined than that of the lipoprotein system, the role of the immune system in initiating and maintaining the atherosclerotic process appears to be significant and cannot be ignored.

CLINICAL MANIFESTATIONS OF CORONARY ATHEROSCLEROSIS

In 1628, William Harvey described the circulation of blood through the heart and blood vessels.[47] He demonstrated the path in which blood circulates and the potential harm resulting from obstruction of the normal flow of blood. When the supply of nutrients required for proper end-organ function is diminished to a critical level, a mismatch in the supply and demand of these nutrients results. When the demand for myocardial oxygen exceeds the supply, an oxygen-poor state results, which is termed *myocardial ischemia*. This situation is reversible if the demand decreases or the supply increases.

The importance of this clinical consequence

of coronary atherosclerosis is the astounding fact that approximately 50% of all deaths in the United States in 1983 were classified as cardio-vascular in nature; atherosclerosis was a con-tributing factor to many of the 737,300 deaths from heart attack and stroke in 1980.[48] Results of international autopsy studies indicate that atherosclerotic plaque is evident in the coronary arteries of individuals in their second decade of life.[49-51] The plaque covers approximately 2% more of the arterial surface each year. When the obstruction compromises 60 to 75% of the ves-sel diameter, it becomes hemodynamically sig-nificant.

The pathophysiologic process that results in myocardial ischemia may be the result of a fixed obstruction, a dynamic process, or a combina-tion of the two. *Coronary artery spasm* is a dy-namic process that can produce reversible nar-rowing of the coronary lumen.[52] The factors that contribute to spasm remain unclear, but they may include the autonomic nervous sys-tem, prostaglandins, endoperoxides, throm-boxanes, and calcium availability.[53,54] Spasm is the pathogenetic mechanism of chest pain often described as variant, or Prinzmetal's angina.[55] The spasm often occurs at the site of an athero-sclerotic plaque and is sensitive to ergonovine, possibly because of the amplification of normal vasoconstriction at the atherosclerotic site.[56] This unpredictable hyper-reactive state is not limited to rest or ergonovine stimulation. The variable threshold of angina during exercise in some patients may be related to vasospastic an-gina resulting from a difference in coronary ar-tery tone at the onset of exercise.[57] After acute myocardial ischemia, coronary artery tone may change, making it susceptible to coronary vaso-spasm.[58]

Thrombosis at the site of a partial obstruction can result in a relatively rapid reduction in oxy-gen availability. Part of this process involves platelet activity, as discussed previously. Some authors suggest that this process may play a significant role in as many as 25% of sudden coronary deaths.[59] The use of anticoagulant medication in the postmyocardial infarction pa-tient is the subject of debate, but practitioners currently reserve anticoagulation therapy for specific indications, such as prolonged bedrest, artificial valves, documented emboli, and thrombi within the heart chambers.[60] The use of thrombolytic therapy is gaining popularity as a productive means to treat the acute infarction

patient. Initially, streptokinase was used in the lysis of coronary artery thrombosis, but tissue plasminogen activator appears to be a more ef-fective agent.[61] In recent large clinical trials, re-searchers noted a reduction in the mortality rate after initiation of thrombolytic therapy.[62]

Silent ischemia is currently reported more fre-quently in individuals who were considered healthy as well as in patients with known coro-nary atherosclerosis.[63] The importance of this entity is demonstrated by the finding that al-most 25% of individuals who experience sud-den cardiac death and in whom autopsy shows severe coronary atherosclerosis never indicated clinical symptoms of coronary heart disease.[64] Therefore, an important fact that warrants at-tention is that significant myocardial ischemia can exist without angina pectoris.

The death of myocardial tissue resulting from myocardial ischemia is termed *myocardial in-farction*. Unlike ischemia, infarction is an irre-versible process. As soon as 12 hours after in-farction, the myocardium shows histologic changes. By 18 hours after infarction, neutro-phil infiltration is evident, and 24 hours later infiltration is well established. During the sec-ond and third days, the infarcted muscle cells disappear; most of the necrotic tissue is re-moved by the third day. Surviving muscle fibers can persist in the area of infarction and may provide the site of origin for ventricular arrhythmias resulting from residual ischemia or metabolic imbalances. Scar formation is evident by the third week and is well established by the fourth week.

The atherosclerotic process is multifactorial and involves a response to chronic injury. The process involves disruption of the endothelial lining, monocyte adherence and activation, smooth muscle cell proliferation, accumulation of lipids, and organization of the mature plaque. Platelets play a role in the modulation of cell division, cell migration, cell adhesion, and the coagulation process. Platelets are a source of vasoactive thromboxane A_2 and pros-taglandin I_2. Lipoproteins, cholesterol, and fat metabolism are active in the pathologic process and HDL may play a role in what is termed the reverse cholesterol process. Immunologic ab-normalities are associated with aggressive ath-erosclerosis. Appreciation of the interaction of all these factors is necessary to comprehend the potential for altering the atherosclerotic pro-cess.

REFERENCES

1. American Heart Association: *1968 Heart Facts*. Dallas, TX: American Heart Association, 1986.
2. *Dorland's Medical Dictionary*. 24th Ed. Philadelphia: W.B. Saunders, 1965.
3. Ross R: The pathogenesis of atherosclerosis—an update. *N Engl J Med*, 314:488–500, 1986.
4. Camejo G: The interaction of lipids and lipoproteins with the intercellular matrix of arterial tissue: Its possible role in atherogenesis. *Adv Lipid Res*, 19:1–49, 1982.
5. Ignatowsky IA: Influence de la nourriture animale sur l'organisme des lapins. *Arch Med Exp Anat Pathol*, 20:1–20, 1908.
6. Rohlfing JJ, Brunzell JD: The effects of diuretics and adrenergic-blocking agents on plasma lipids. *West J Med*, 145:210–218, 1986.
7. Ross R, Glomset JA: Atherosclerosis and the arterial smooth muscle. *Science*, 180:1332–1339, 1973.
8. Bertele HV, Salzman EW: Antithrombotic therapy in coronary artery disease. *Arteriosclerosis*, 5:119–134, 1985.
9. Windler E, Preyer S, Greten H: Change in affinity of triglyceride-rich lipoproteins to apolipoprotein C-II during lipolysis. In *Treatment of Hyperlipoproteinemia*. Edited by LA Carlson and AG Olsson. New York: Raven Press, 1984.
10. Pownall HJ, Gotto AM: Plasma apolipoproteins: Composition, structure and function. In *Atherosclerosis: Mechanisms and Approaches to Therapy*. Edited by NE Miller. New York, Raven Press, 1983.
11. Shen BW, Scanu AM, Kezdy FJ: Structure of human serum lipoproteins inferred from compositional analysis. *Proc Natl Acad Sci USA*, 74:837–841, 1977.
12. Nikkila EA, Kusi T, Taskinen MJ, Tikkanen MJ: Regulation of lipoprotein metabolism by endothelial lipolytic enzymes. In *Treatment of Hyperlipoproteinemia*. Edited by LA Carlson and AG Olsson. New York: Raven Press, 1984.
13. Grundy SM: Hyperlipoproteinemia: Metabolic basis and rationale for therapy. *Am J Cardiol*, 54:20C–26C, 1984.
14. Norum KR: Role of lecithin: Cholesterol acyltransferase in the metabolism of plasma lipoproteins. In *Treatment of* New York: *Hyperlipoproteinemia*. Edited by LA Carlson and AG Olsson. New York: Raven Press, 1984.
15. Kusi T, Saarinen P, Nikkila E: Evidence for the role of hepatic endothelial lipase in the metabolism of plasma high density lipoprotein 2 in man. *Atherosclerosis*, 36:589–593, 1980.
16. Blank DW, Hoeg JM, Kroll MH, Ruddel ME: The method of determination must be considered in interpreting blood cholesterol levels. *JAMA*, 256:2767–2770, 1986.
17. Superko HR, Bachorik PS, Wood PD: High-density lipoprotein cholesterol measurements. A help or hindrance in practical clinical medicine? *JAMA*, 256:2714–2717, 1986.
18. Brown MS, Goldstein JL: Receptor-mediated endocytosis: Insights from the lipoprotein receptor system. *Proc Natl Acad Sci USA*, 76:3330–3337, 1979.
19. Ekman R, Nilsson-Ehle P: Effects of apolipoproteins on lipoprotein lipase activity of human adipose tissue. *Clin Chim Acta*, 63:29–35, 1975.
20. Osborne JC, Brewer HB: The plasma lipoproteins. *Adv Protein Chem*, 31:253–337, 1977.
21. Alaupovic P, Lee DM, McConathy WJ: Studies on the composition and structure of plasma lipoproteins. Distribution of lipoprotein families in major density classes of normal human plasma lipoproteins. *Biochim Biophys Acta*, 260:689–787, 1972.
22. Mancini G, Carbonara AO, Heremans JF: Immunochemical quantitation of antigens by single radial immunodiffusion. *Immunochemistry*, 2:235–254, 1965.
23. Karlin JB, et al.: Measurement of human high density lipoprotein apolipoprotein A-I in serum by radioimmunoassay. *J Lipid Res*, 17:30–37, 1976.
24. Heuck CC, Schlierf G: Nephelometry of apolipoprotein B in human serum. *Clin Chem*, 25:221–226, 1979.
25. Schonfeld G, Bell E, Alpers DH: Intestinal apoproteins during fat absorption. *J Clin Invest*, 61:1539–1550, 1978.
26. Wu AL, Windmuller HG: Relative contributions by liver and intestine to individual plasma apolipoproteins in the rat. *J Biol Chem*, 254:7316–7322, 1979.
27. Holt PR, Wu AL, Clark SB: Apoprotein composition and turnover in rat intestinal lymph during steady-state triglyceride absorption. *J Lipid Res*, 20:494–502, 1979.
28. Anderson DW, et al.: Evidence for recirculation of apolipoproteins A-I and A-II between plasma and human thoracic duct lymph. *Clin Res*, 27:362, 1979.
29. Green PHR, et al.: Human intestinal lipoproteins—studies in chyluric subjects. *J Clin Invest*, 64:233–242, 1979.
30. Brown MS, Goldstein JL: How LDL receptors influence cholesterol and atherosclerosis. *Sci Am*, November: 58–66, 1984.
31. Baggio G, et al.: Postprandial metabolism of lipoproteins: An overview. In *Lipoprotein Metabolism and Therapy of Lipid Disorders*. Amsterdam: Excerpta Medica, 1982.
32. Felding CJ, Shore VG, Felding PE: A protein cofactor of lecithin:cholesterol acyltransferase. *Biochem Biophys Res Commun*, 46:1493–1498, 1972.
33. Maciejko JJ, et al.: Apolipoprotein A-I as a marker of angiographically assessed coronary-artery disease. *N Engl J Med*, 309:385–389, 1983.
34. Avogaro P, Bittolo G, Cazzolato G, Quinci GB: Are apolipoproteins better discriminators than lipids for atherosclerosis? *Lancet*, April 28:901–904, 1979.
35. Goldstein JL, Brown MS: Atherosclerosis—The low density lipoprotein receptor hypothesis. *Metabolism*, 26:1257–1275, 1977.
36. Tan MH, Sata T, Havel RJ: The significance of lipoprotein lipase in rat skeletal muscles. *J Lipid Res*, 18:363–370, 1977.
37. Gotto AM: High-density lipoproteins: Biochemical and metabolic factors. *Am J Cardiol*, 52:2B–4B, 1983.
38. Breckenridge WC, Alaupovic P, Cox DW, Little JA: Apolipoprotein and lipoprotein concentrations in familial apolipoprotein C-II deficiency. *Atherosclerosis*, 44:223–235, 1982.
39. Felding PE, Fielding CJ: A cholesterol transfer complex in human plasma. *Proc Natl Acad Sci USA*, 77:3327–3330, 1980.
40. Fainaru M, Mahley RW, Hamilton RL, Innerarity TG: Structural and metabolic heterogeneity of B-very low density lipoprotein from cholesterol-fed dogs and from

humans with type III hyperlipoproteinemia. *J Lipid Res,* 23:702–714, 1982.

41. Kane JP, et al.: Remnants of lipoproteins of intestinal and hepatic origin in familial dysbetalipoproteinemia. *Arteriosclerosis,* 3:47–56, 1983.

42. Zannis WI, Breslow JL: Human very low density lipoprotein apolipoprotein E isoprotein polymorphism is explained by genetic variation and posttranslational modification. *Biochemistry,* 20:1033–1041, 1981.

43. Weisgraber KH, Rall SC, Mahley RW: Human E apoprotein heterogeneity. Cysteine-arginine interchanges in the amino acid sequence of the apo-E isoforms. *J Biol Chem,* 256:9077–9083, 1981.

44. Tsakraklides UG, Blieden LC, Edwards JE: Coronary atherosclerosis and myocardial infarction associated with systemic lupus erythematosus. *Am Heart J,* 87:637–641, 1974.

45. Caplan M, Hastillo A, Mohanakumar T, Hess ML: Immunologic mechanisms in the atherosclerotic process. *Cardiovasc Rev Rep,* 5:713–721, 1984.

46. Hess ML, et al.: Accelerated atherosclerosis in cardiac transplantation: Role of cytotoxic B-cell antibodies and hyperlipidemia. *Circulation,* 68:94–101, 1983.

47. Harvey W: Anatomical studies on the motion of the heart and blood—1628. The Leake Translation. Springfield, IL: Charles C Thomas, 1928.

48. American Heart Association: *Heart Facts 1983.* Dallas, TX: American Heart Association, 1983.

49. McGill HC, et al.: The geographic pathology of atherosclerosis. *Lab Invest,* 18:465–640, 1968.

50. Solberg LA, Strong JP: Risk factors and atherosclerotic lesions. A review of autopsy studies. *Arteriosclerosis,* 3:187–198, 1983.

51. Kagan AR, et al.: Atherosclerosis of the aorta and coronary arteries in five towns. *Bull WHO,* 53:485–645, 1976.

52. Marx JL: Coronary artery spasms and heart disease. *Science,* 208:1127–1130, 1980.

53. Luchi RJ, Chahine RA, Raizner AE: Coronary artery spasm. *Ann Intern Med,* 91:441–449, 1979.

54. Rubenstein MD, Wall RT, Baim DS, Harrison DC: Platelet activation in clinical coronary artery disease and spasm. *Am Heart J,* 102:363–367, 1981.

55. Oliva PB, Potts DE, Pluss RG: Coronary arterial spasm in Prinzmetal angina: Documentation by coronary arteriography. *N Engl J Med,* 288:745–751, 1973.

56. Freedman B, Richmond DR, Kelly DT: Pathophysiology of coronary artery spasm. *Circulation,* 66:705–709, 1982.

57. Servi SD, et al.: Variable threshold of angina during exercise. *Am J Cardiol,* 48:189–192, 1981.

58. Ku DD: Coronary vascular reactivity after acute myocardial ischemia. *Science,* 218:576–578, 1982.

59. Schwartz CJ, Walsh WJ: The pathologic basis of sudden death. *Prog Cardiovasc Dis,* 13:465–481, 1971.

60. Chalmers TC, et al.: Evidence favoring the use of anticoagulants in the hospital phase of acute myocardial infarction. *N Engl J Med,* 297:1091–1096, 1977.

61. Verstraete M, et al.: Randomized trial of intravenous recombinant tissue-type plasminogen activator versus intravenous streptokinase in acute myocardial infarction. *Lancet* 2:965–971, 1985.

62. Yusuf S, et al.: Intravenous and intracoronary fibrinolytic therapy in acute myocardial infarction: Overview or results on mortality, reinfarction and side-effects from 33 randomized controlled trials. *Eur Heart J,* 6:556–566, 1985.

63. Weisfeldt ML (ed): Exploring myocardial ischemia: Silent and symptomatic. *Am J Med,* 80:1–55, 1986.

64. Lown B: Sudden cardiac death: The major challenge confronting contemporary cardiology. *Am J Cardiol,* 43:313–328, 1979.

CHAPTER 15

THE RISK FACTOR CONCEPT OF CORONARY HEART DISEASE

CARL J. CASPERSEN AND
GREGORY W. HEATH

Since the middle to the late 1960s the number of deaths related to coronary heart disease (CHD), stroke, and associated cardiovascular problems has continued to decline.[1] Still, the overall economic impact and the number of people afflicted with diseases in these three categories make cardiovascular disease (CVD) a major national health problem. Education of both health professionals and lay persons in identifying and implementing effective ways to reduce risk factors associated with the development of CHD remains paramount.

Multiple factors are responsible for the development of CHD in an individual. Therefore, the estimation of risk and management of intervention measures are important considerations in the control of this disease. The optimal time to begin preventative steps to combat CHD is not firmly established. Evidence exists to indicate, however, that the longer potentially reversible risk factors are allowed to operate in a person, the greater is the impact on that individual, especially when multiple factors coexist. The rise in serum lipid levels, blood pressure, weight, and blood glucose concentration often observed in the transition from childhood to adulthood is not necessarily inevitable, desirable, or part of normal physiologic growth. Although no absolute proof exists that all recommended interventions eliminate CHD risk, the magnitude of the problem does not permit indefinite temporizing while awaiting such proof. Similarly, the logic for secondary prevention in patients with documented CHD is also reasonable and is based on knowledge of the natural history of CHD and the control of risk factors. The following hygienic proposals should therefore be appropriate additions to a total cardiovascular health program.

1. Identify and control blood lipid levels.
2. Promote cessation and prevention of cigarette smoking.
3. Enhance hypertension control (drug and nondrug).
4. Encourage (prescribe) regular physical activity and exercise training.
5. Facilitate weight control.
6. Identify and control diabetes.
7. Identify and modify type A behavior.

Our discussion of these proposals follows the same order, highlighting the importance of each risk factor and the current management strategies.

RISK FACTORS

BLOOD LIPIDS

Cholesterol is the predominant lipid constituent of the atherosclerotic lesion. Serum cholesterol levels are consistently correlated with CHD in retrospective comparisons of populations with large differences in CHD mortality. For example, the Seven Countries study revealed very low CHD and very low serum cholesterol levels in Japan and very high levels of both parameters in Finland (Fig. 15–1)[2,3] Similar findings are also noted in prospective studies of population samples (Fig. 15–2). In the American population under age 50 years, the difference in risk that is related to the differences in serum cholesterol levels is more than fivefold. Hypercholesterolemia is sometimes a familial trait, but rarely is this condition the result of a demonstrable monogenetic disorder. In a recent study, researchers revealed that even persons possessing specific lethal genes for hypercholesterolemia can reduce their risk of CHD

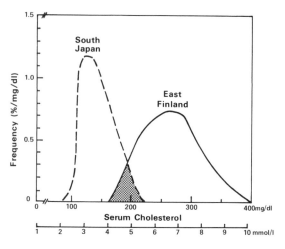

FIGURE 15–2. Cultural differences in serum cholesterol levels. (From Blackburn H: Diet and mass hyperlipidemia: A public health view. In *Nutrition, Lipids, and Coronary Heart Disease.* Edited by RI Levy, et al. New York: Raven Press, 1976, with permission.)

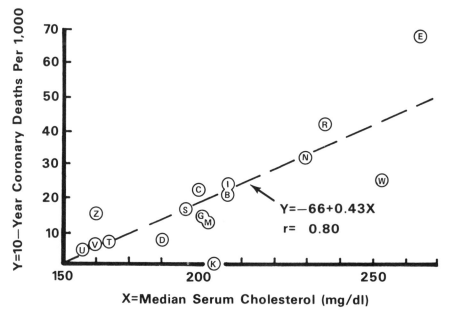

FIGURE 15–1. Coronary heart disease age-standardized 10-year death rates versus median serum cholesterol levels (mg/dl) for 16 cohorts. All men judged free of coronary heart disease at entry. Correlation coefficient (r) = 0.80. Ⓑ, Belgrade, Ⓒ, Crevalcore, Ⓓ, Dalmatia, Ⓔ, East Finland, Ⓖ, Corfu, Ⓘ, Italian railroad, Ⓚ, Crete, Ⓜ, Montegiorgio, Ⓝ, Zutphen, Ⓡ, American railroad, Ⓢ, Slavonia, Ⓣ, Tanushimaru, Ⓤ, Ushibuka, Ⓥ, Velika Krsna, Ⓦ, West Finland, Ⓩ, Zrenianin. (From Keys A: *Seven Countries: A Multivariate Analysis of Death and Coronary Heart Disease.* Cambridge: Harvard University Press, 1980, with permission.)

through lifestyle alterations.[4] Hence, although the range of cholesterol levels in the general population is broad and is influenced by genetic factors, the high average level is considered of dietary origin. Results of dietary studies show that the serum cholesterol level can be predictably raised by increasing saturated fat and cholesterol in the diet, and can be lowered substantially by reducing the intake of these nutrients.[5]

The association between elevated serum total cholesterol levels and an increased risk of CHD is principally derived from the low-density lipoprotein (LDL) cholesterol fraction, the principal carrier of cholesterol in the serum. An elevated LDL level consistently correlates with a higher incidence of CHD.[6] In a recent experiment, the reduction of LDL cholesterol levels with the drug cholestyramine convincingly demonstrated a decreased incidence of CHD.[7] In addition, the National Heart, Lung, and Blood Institute Type II Study showed that the lowering of LDL and raising of high-density lipoprotein (HDL) cholesterol levels in persons with documented CHD retards the progression of atherosclerosis.[8,9]

Other recent findings are indicative of an inverse relationship between an elevated HDL cholesterol fraction and CHD.[10] Increases in HDL cholesterol blood levels were noted in some persons by weight reduction, physical exercise, avoidance of cigarettes, and moderate ingestion of alcohol, although the last association is as yet imperfectly defined.[11-13] Because HDL cholesterol serves to transport cholesterol out of the system, higher levels are desirable so as to reduce the risk of CHD. Therefore, the partitioning of the serum total cholesterol value into the LDL and HDL fractions is apparently important in determining risk, particularly in persons older than age 50 years.[4,15]

The National Institutes of Health recently convened a consensus development conference in which the conclusion was drawn that lowering blood cholesterol levels reduces the incidence of CHD.[16] The panel also determined cholesterol levels that would aid in the identification of individuals at risk of developing CHD and in need of treatment. Table 15-1 provides the values set forth by the panel for those persons from age 2 to 40 or more years.[16] Recommendations of dietary and drug therapy were made so as to reduce cholesterol in persons determined to be at moderate or high risk.

Results of international dietary comparisons, human metabolic studies, and feeding experiments in animals clearly implicate the ingestion of large amounts of saturated fat and cholesterol in the hypercholesterolemia regularly noted in populations in which CHD is highly prevalent.[2] This condition is exacerbated when the diet also includes an intake of calories in excess of need. Although conclusive demonstration of this relationship is difficult in typical American populations, because of a high consumption of foods considered atherogenic, vegetarians in the United States were found to have lower than average levels of blood lipids and a lower incidence of CHD.[5,17]

Serum lipid values in humans and animals can be effectively altered by dietary modification.[18] A high intake of complex carbohydrate is generally associated with low CHD mortality rates, particularly when it replaces saturated fat in the diet. Some recent reports are aimed at assisting health professionals in implementing dietary therapy. A synopsis of effective methods of dietary counseling was recently presented by the U.S. Department of Health and Human Services.[19] In addition, the American Heart Association recommends a three-phase approach to dietary therapy for high levels of serum cholesterol (Table 15-2).[20] In each phase, weight control is emphasized. Phase 1 is considered a moderately low-fat, low-cholesterol plan for persons with safe cho-

Table 15-1. Cholesterol Values for Persons at Moderate and High Risk

Age (yr)	Cholesterol level (mg/dl)	
	Moderate risk	High risk
2-19	170-185	>185
20-29	201-220	>220
30-39	221-240	>240
40 and over	240-260	>260

(From the Consensus conference: Lowering blood cholesterol to prevent heart disease. *JAMA, 251*:365, 1984.)

Table 15-2. Goals of Three Phases for Lowering Cholesterol with Dietary Modifications

Nutrient	Phase		
	1	2	3
Fat (% calories)	30	25	20
Carbohydrate (% calories)	55	60	65
Protein (% calories)	15	15	15
Cholesterol (mg)	300	200-250	100-150
Polyunsaturated: saturated fat	1	1	1-2

(From the American Heart Association Special Report: Recommendations for treatment of hyperlipidemia in adults. *Circulation,* 69:1065A, 1984, with permission.)

lesterol levels; it is offered as a "prudent diet." Phase 1, however, is also the first step in attempting to modify the diet of those with moderate or high-risk cholesterol levels, and phases 2 and 3 are for those persons who fail to respond to phase 1 efforts. Drug therapy is reserved for individuals who fail to respond to rigorous dietary modification, weight control, and exercise; even with drug therapy, however, dietary therapy should still continue. In such cases, effective forms of drug therapy are available.[21] In a recent multicenter, double-blind, placebo-controlled study, investigators revealed that Lovastatin, a 3-hydroxy-3-methylglutaryl coenzyme A reductase inhibitor, can effectively lower total and low-density lipoprotein cholesterol levels by about 33% in patients with diagnosed type IIa or IIb hypercholesterolemia. This drug is an important pharmacologic agent for persons unable to respond to nonpharmacologic approaches to lowering cholesterol levels.[21]

SMOKING

Evidence incriminating cigarette smoking in CHD is substantial. Overall, smokers have a 70% greater level of CHD risk than nonsmokers; individuals who smoke two or more packs of cigarettes per day have a two- to threefold greater risk of CHD (Table 15–3).[22] The CHD risk also increases with the depth of inhalation and with the total number of years as a smoker, although persons who give up the habit reduce their risk level to one that is close to that of nonsmokers.[22,23] Findings of laboratory studies suggest smoking can accelerate atherogenesis and provoke myocardial infarction. Smoking increases platelet adhesiveness, damage to arterial endothelium, susceptibility to ventricular dysrhythmias, oxygen transport and utilization, heart rate, and blood pressure.[24,25] Cigarette smoking has an independent effect on CHD risk and acts synergistically with other well-established CHD risk factors. A variety of behavioral approaches can be successful in promoting smoking cessation.[26] Nicotine gum has also been proposed as a pharmacologic measure to assist smoking cessation efforts.[27]

HYPERTENSION

The role of high blood pressure as a major risk factor for CHD and stroke is beyond serious doubt.[28–30] Blood pressure-related risks appear to increase continuously from lowest to highest

Table 15–3. Standardized CHD Incidence Ratio and Risk Ratios by Smoking Behavior in Five Cohort Studies (Individual and Pooled Results)

Smoking behavior	Standardized incidence ratio by study group					
	Pooling Project Research Group	Albany Cardiovascular Health Study	Chicago Peoples Gas Company Study	Chicago Western Electric Company Study	Framingham Heart Disease Epidemiology Study	Tecumseh Health Study
All	100	100	100	100	100	100
Nonsmokers	58	55	48	59	67	53*
Never smoked	54	45	53*	44	77*	60*
Past smoker	63	67	56	89	46*	50*
< ½ pack/day	55	67*	43*	78	43*	*
Cigar and pipe only	71	78	58*	98	57	61*
Cigarette smokers						
About ½ pack/day	104	52*	64*	139	106	151*
About 1 pack/day	120	108	125	128	119	117
> 1 pack/day	183	200	190	162	174	151
Risk ratio						
≥ 1 Pack/day : nonsmokers	2.5	2.7	3.3	2.4	2.2	*
95% Confidence interval	(2.1, 3.1)	(1.8, 4.3)	(2.1, 6.2)	(1.6, 3.7)	(1.5, 3.4)	
Risk ratio						
> 1 Pack/day : nonsmokers	3.2	3.7	4.0	2.8	2.6	*
95% Confidence interval	(2.6, 4.2)	(2.4, 6.1)	(2.5, 8.4)	(1.2, 5.5)	(1.8, 4.5)	
Number of men at risk	8,282	1,796	1,258	1,926	2,162	1,140
Person-years of experience	70,970	17,240	11,017	16,072	19,756	6,885
Number of first events	644	154	123	140	178	49

* Based on fewer than 10 first events.
(From the Pooling Project Research Group. Relationship of blood pressure, serum cholesterol, smoking habit, relative weight and ECG abnormalities to incidence of major coronary events: Final report of the Pooling Project. *J Chronic Dis*, 31:202–306, 1978, with permission.)

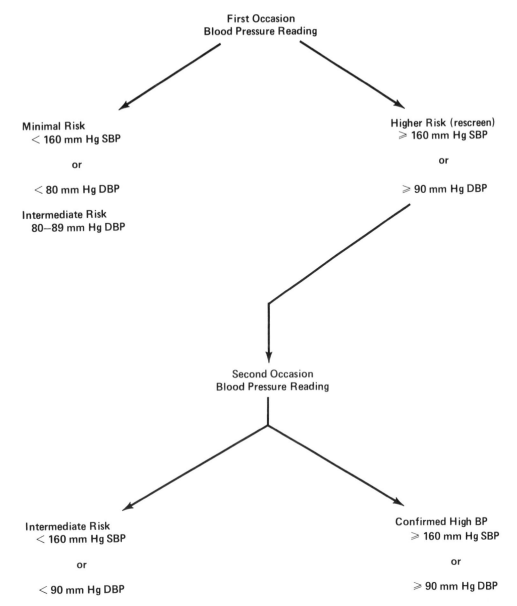

FIGURE 15 – 3. Classification of persons according to systolic (SBP) and diastolic (DBP) blood pressure value on two occasions (BP = blood pressure). (From the Joint National Committee on Detection, Evaluation, and Treatment of High Blood Pressure: The 1984 Report of the Joint National Committee on Detection, Evaluation, and Treatment of High Blood Pressure. *Arch Intern Med, 144*:1045, 1984.)

values. Thus, although no "ideal" blood pressure value truly exists, evidence indicates that with each increment in both systolic and diastolic pressure, the risk for adverse cardiovascular effects increases with time. Elevated blood pressure seldom works alone but more often in concert with other well-identified risk factors, including dietary intake, elevated lipids, obesity, smoking, diabetes mellitus, and lack of exercise.

The approach to the treatment of the patient with elevated blood pressure includes adequate documentation that the blood pressure values are elevated and of the degree of elevation of the blood pressure when discovered. Figure 15 – 3 outlines the appropriate classification of persons according to their measured levels of diastolic and systolic blood pressure.[31] When hypertension is confirmed, an appropriate history, a physical examination, and a pathologic assessment are undertaken. The primary goal of treating these patients is to prevent premature morbidity and mortality. Therefore, the intent of treatment is to reduce the elevation in blood pressure to the extent that excessive cardiovascular risks are eliminated.

Therapeutic approaches include nonpharmacologic therapy, particularly weight reduction and reduced dietary sodium intake. Although other ions, including potassium, calcium, and magnesium, are suspected of influencing blood pressure, fewer data are available for specific therapeutic recommendations.[32] Exercise is a recommended form of therapy; recent reports cite evidence that regular physical activity that emphasizes rhythmic, sustained, and regular muscular movement substantially lowers elevated blood pressure.[33] Epidemiologists, too, have identified a lower prevalence of hypertension in individuals who are more physically active.[34] Other therapeutic approaches include the assessment of alcohol consumption; heavy consumption of alcohol (five drinks or more per day) is often associated with elevated blood pressure and cardiovascular damage. A dietary history relating to fat ingestion, particularly the polyunsaturated to saturated ratio, appears critical. Appropriate intervention for tobacco use is also an integral part of this process.[35,36]

Pharmacologic intervention to treat hypertension revolves around several available drugs. Their applicability is often related to the level of blood pressure but even more to the presence of target organ damage, the presence of diabetes mellitus, or other major risk factors for CHD and stroke. An ultimate goal of therapy is to maximize blood pressure control to as

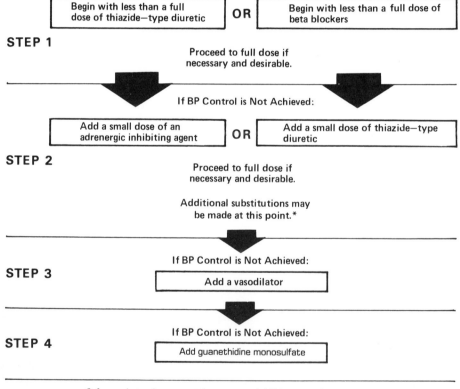

FIGURE 15–4. Stepped-care approach to antihypertensive drug therapy. (From the Joint National Committee on Detection, Evaluation, and Treatment of High Blood Pressure: The 1984 Report of the Joint National Committee on Detection, Evaluation, and Treatment of High Blood Pressure. *Arch Intern Med, 144*:1045, 1984.)

normal or near normal a level as can be achieved with a minimum of side effects. Figure 15–4 outlines the stepped-care approach to treatment of hypertension as adopted by the Joint National Committee on Detection, Evaluation, and Treatment of High Blood Pressure.[31] A particular and peculiar set of hypertension-related problems that are still incompletely resolved relates to the wisdom in treating patients with "mild" hypertension with drugs as well as to what is the "best" form of therapy for the elderly with so-called isolated systolic hypertension.[37-39]

PHYSICAL INACTIVITY

Powell and co-workers undertook an extensive review of 43 epidemiologic studies and concluded that physical activity has a protective effect on CHD.[40] Figure 15–5 represents the type of decline often noted in CHD risk with increasing physical activity.[41] Although only two thirds of the 43 studies reviewed showed a significant inverse relationship, an important additional finding was that the methodologically superior studies were more likely to report a significant inverse association. As the quality of the measure of physical activity, the measure of CHD outcome, and the epidemiologic methods improved, the results were more pronounced. Additional evidence reveals that physical activity may improve the likelihood of survival from a myocardial infarction.[42] In several studies, investigators show that endurance exercise training is associated with reduced morbidity and mortality among patients with documented CHD.[43-45]

A variety of mechanisms may account for the protective effect of physical activity in reducing the risk of CHD and its progression. For example, physical activity may be a useful adjunct in eliminating or controlling other risk factors, such as obesity, glucose intolerance, insulin insensitivity, and mild hypertension.[46,47] Exercise training can alter blood lipid levels in a desirable manner in normal men.[48] In addition, higher levels of HDL cholesterol were noted in cross-sections of populations ranging from low to high on the physical activity continuum; in men who simply report some regular strenuous activity; and in endurance-trained athletes.[49-51] The level of HDL cholesterol was shown to increase in previously inactive men after physical training.[52] Vigorous physical activity also reduces fasting triglyceride concentrations and enhances intravenous fat clearance, thereby reducing the number of potentially atherogenic, triglyceride-rich lipoproteins.[53,54]

Studies of physical activity in animals have produced encouraging results relative to the reduction of CHD factors, but these studies have not been successfully applied to man. A physical training program applied to monkeys resulted in higher HDL and lower LDL and VLDL cholesterol and triglyceride levels with a concomitant lower incidence of coronary atherosclerosis.[55] Similar studies of coronary atherosclerosis in man are not conclusive.[56] Also, physical training was shown to increase the diameter of coronary arteries in various animal models and to induce proliferation of coronary collateral development.[55, 57, 58] Angiographic investigations have failed to demonstrate collateral development in CHD patients after an extended period of physical training.[59,60]

Other effects of physical activity are acute increases in fibrinolysis and enhanced fibrinolytic capacity in response to venous occlusion, which may combat coronary thrombosis.[61,62] Physical activity can enhance myocardial electrical stability and decrease coronary vasospasm in response to adrenergic stimulation.[63,64] Physical training in man increases cardiac parasympathetic tone, reducing the risk of ventricular fibrillation during cardiac ischemia.[65-67] These sources of evidence demonstrate that physical activity may reduce the risk of CHD through risk factor modification,

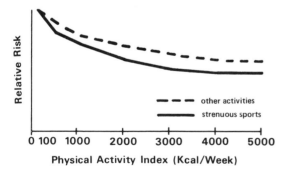

FIGURE 15–5. Relative risks of first heart attack by physical activity index for strenuous sports and other activities in 6- to 10-year follow-up study of Harvard male alumni (first-order multiple logistic model). (From Paffenbarger RS Jr, Wing AL, Hyde RT: Physical activity as an index of heart attack risk in college alumni. *Am J Epidemiol, 108*:161, 1978.)

enhancement of myocardial perfusion, or off-setting the likelihood of acute coronary events.

No randomized, controlled clinical trials demonstrating the role of physical activity in CHD prevention are currently underway. Such a trial will not likely be forthcoming because of the expense, the required sample size to demonstrate a statistically significant effect, and adherence problems.[68,69] An identical situation exists relative to conducting definitive dietary studies designed to lower CHD risk.

The review by Powell and co-workers also revealed that the calculated relative risk for CHD with reduced physical activity was about 1.9. This value was essentially similar to the relative risks associated with increased systolic blood pressure (2.1), cigarette smoking (2.5), and serum cholesterol (2.4) as found in the Pooling Project.[22] Because the number of individuals who are inactive is substantially greater than the number of persons who smoke cigarettes, have high levels of serum cholesterol, or have hypertension, the overall impact of stimulating Americans to be more physically active could effectively lower the country's CHD rates even further.

OBESITY

With rare exceptions, obesity evolves from eating too much and exercising too little. Obesity is associated with an excessive number of CHD deaths, especially sudden death in men and congestive heart failure in women. This high death rate appears to occur largely as a consequence of the influence of obesity on blood pressure, blood lipid levels, and the risk of precipitating the onset of diabetes; recent reports from the Framingham Study, however, indicate the independence of obesity as a risk factor for CHD (Figs. 15–6 and 15–7).[70-72] An eating pattern low in saturated fat and cholesterol often leads to weight reduction, which in time improves the level of all major atherogenic risk factors with the exception of cigarette smoking.[73] Obesity is also associated with depressed HDL cholesterol levels. Weight control is a logical first step in the control of mild hypertension, hyperlipidemia, and impaired glucose tolerance, and may eliminate the necessity of life-long drug therapy. Therapeutic efforts for weight control have been rather disappointing, although researchers recently demonstrated the effectiveness of combined programs of behavior modification and exercise.[46] Therapeutic approaches that emphasize increased levels of physical activity have the advantage of not only enhancing caloric expenditure but also drawing on the beneficial effects of exercise in influencing blood lipids, blood pressure, mood, and attitude.[74-76] A more comprehensive intervention strategy was recently suggested.[46] Table 15–4 is an outline of a broad-based public health approach to weight control, whereby

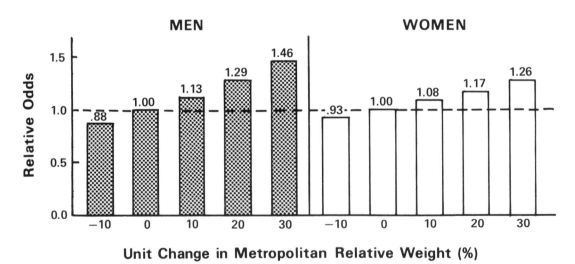

FIGURE 15–6. Relative odds of developing cardiovascular disease corresponding to degrees of change in Metropolitan Relative Weight between age 25 years and entry into Framingham Study. Odds ratios reflect adjustments for effects of relative weight at age 25 years and risk factor levels at exam 1. (From Hubert HB, et al.: Obesity as an independent risk factor for cardiovascular disease: A 26-year follow-up of participants in the Framingham Heart Study. *Circulation,* 67:968, 1983, with permission.)

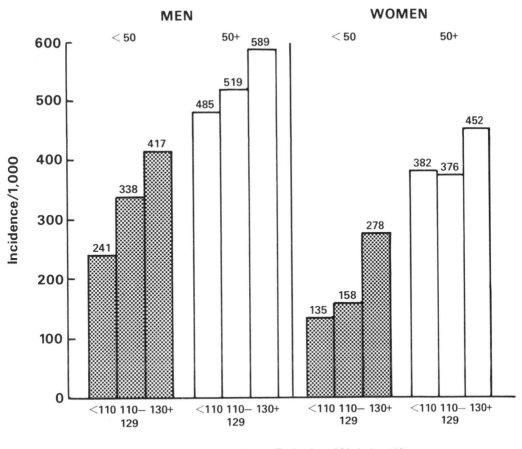

FIGURE 15–7. Twenty-six year incidence of cardiovascular disease by Metropolitan Relative Weight at entry among Framingham men and women ages <50 years and ≥50 years. Numbers above bars are incidence rate per 1000. (From Hubert HB, et al.: Obesity as an independent risk factor for cardiovascular disease: A 26-year follow-up of participants in the Framingham Heart Study. *Circulation, 67*:968, 1983, with permission.)

the individual approach integrates well into a stepped-care approach to weight reduction.

DIABETES AND GLUCOSE INTOLERANCE

Glucose intolerance is a direct effect of obesity and is often associated with hypertriglycer-idemia, hypertension, elevated LDL cholesterol values, and depressed HDL values. All of these findings are associated with an increased risk of CHD. Diabetes mellitus appears to have a vasculotoxic effect, which is greatest for occlusive peripheral vascular disease, but CHD is still its most common manifestation (Fig. 15–8).[77] The

Table 15–4. Stepped-care Model for the Management of Obesity

	Step			
	1	2	3	4
Action	Media programs Competitions Popular books Brochures Self-diet	Commercial programs Self-help groups	Clinical groups Aggressive diets	Individual programs Residential programs Surgery

(From Brownell KD: Public health approaches to obesity and its management. *Annu Rev Public Health, 7*:521, 1986, with permission.)

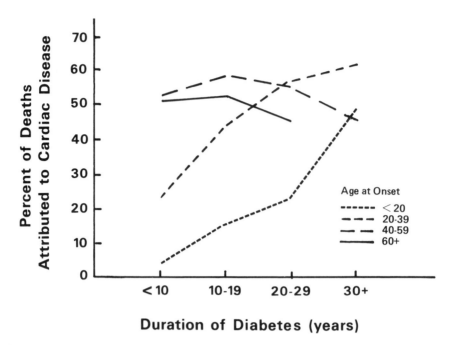

FIGURE 15–8. Percent of deaths during 1956–1968 attributed to cardiac disease among diabetic patients, by age at onset and duration of diabetes, Joslin Clinic. (From Barrett-Connor E, Orchard T: Diabetes and heart disease. In *Diabetes in America.* Chapter XVI. Edited by MI Harris and RF Hamman. Washington, DC, NIH publication number 85–1468, 1985.

risk of CHD is twice as great in diabetic men and three times as great in diabetic women as in persons free of clinical diabetes.

The mortality rate from CHD for diabetic women appears to be as great as the rate for nondiabetic men of the same age. The control of hyperglycemia alone does not appear to reduce the risk of the macrovascular sequelae of diabetes mellitus. The excess risk is also not clearly related to the duration of diabetes. Because individuals with diabetes are more likely than those without diabetes to have characteristics associated with an increased risk of CHD, direct, aggressive attention toward the management of these risk factors is essential. Special attention should be paid to effective weight control, adequate treatment of hypertension, smoking cessation, and increased levels of physical activity. Although a diet high in fiber, rich in complex carbohydrate, and low in fat may be helpful, definitive evidence of its effectiveness is forthcoming.

PSYCHOSOCIAL STRESS

According to several prospective studies, persons with an overdeveloped sense of time-urgency, drive, and competitiveness (type A behavior) develop an excess of CHD (Fig. 15–9).[78–80] The mechanism is obscure but appears to be associated with the sympathetic nervous system and the secretion of catecholamines.[81] The established major risk factors seem to have a greater impact on type A persons. These relationships have been described primarily in white middle-aged men, but few data exist associating type A behavior and CHD in women, blacks, Hispanics, and young adults. In addition, the relationship between type A behavior and CHD outcomes appears to be influenced by other behavioral responses, such as hostility, because type As with this pattern of response are more likely to develop CHD.[82]

Difficulty in assessing the behavior pattern has contributed to the discrepancies noted in studies investigating type A persons and CHD. Structured interviews tend to be the most reliable and valid forms of assessing the behavior pattern; pencil and paper methods are less effective.[83] Because authors of current reports emphasize results from studies employing various assessment tools, a consensus regarding the role of type A behavior and CHD is difficult to develop. Matthews and Haynes attempted to evaluate these discrepancies.[83]

Various methods can be effective in controlling the physiologic variables of type A behavior (i.e., heart rate, blood pressure, and catecholamine response). These methods include biofeedback, behavior modification, meditation, and exercise.[84] Currently, no researchers of intervention measures have documented a reduction in morbidity or mortality, although implications that these measures enhance quality of life have been drawn.

FAMILY HISTORY

A history of premature fatal or nonfatal stroke, fatal or nonfatal myocardial infarction, or sudden coronary death in siblings or parents is suggestive of increased susceptibility to CHD. Familial history of diabetes, hypertension, or hyperlipidemia also increases the likelihood for the development of CHD. Often this familial aggregation of diseases can be accounted for by the familial aggregation of CHD risk factors. In a recent review, authors showed that when considering the effects of CHD risk factors, the effect of family history on CHD risk appears to

be minimal.[85] This finding was most recently proven with regard to a true family history of heart attack.[86] Therefore, the most prudent approach to CHD prevention and control is to direct efforts toward the control of hyperlipidemia and hypertension, prevention and cessation of smoking, weight control, and increased physical activity. Researchers place special emphasis on interventions in individuals who demonstrate a familial tendency toward the presence of such risk factors and their premature disease outcomes.

CLUSTERING OF CHD RISK FACTORS

Many CHD risk factors are associated with each other as well as with CHD itself (Fig. 15–10).[70,87,88] Therefore, individuals with combinations of risk factors are at an increased risk for CHD. Obesity is an example of a risk factor for CHD that influences other potent risk factors, including hyperlipidemia, hypertension, and diabetes mellitus. Physical inactivity has been

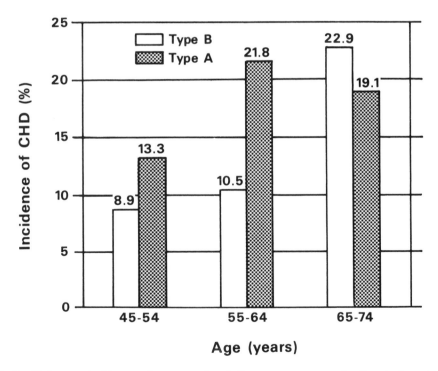

FIGURE 15-9. Eight-year incidence of coronary heart disease among men by Framingham type A and B behavior patterns. (From Haynes SG, Feinleib M, Kannel WB: The relationship of psychosocial factors to coronary heart disease in the Framingham Study. III. Eight-year incidence of coronary heart disease. *Am J Epidemiol, 111*:37, 1980.)

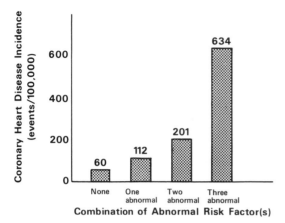

FIGURE 15 – 10. Relationship between a combination of abnormal risk factors (cholesterol ≥ 250 mg/dl; systolic blood pressure ≥ 160 mm Hg; smoking ≥ 1 pack of cigarettes/day) and incidence of coronary heart disease. (From Kannel WB, Gordon T: The Framingham Study: An Epidemiological Investigation of Cardiovascular Disease, Section 30. Washington DC, Public Health Service, NIH, DHEW Publication No. (NIH) 74-599, Feb. 1974.)

related to obesity, lipid abnormalities, hypertension, and diabetes mellitus.

Many risk factors evolve from similar health behavior patterns and therefore can be influenced by similar, and in some instances identical, intervention approaches. Thus, individuals with one risk factor for CHD should be carefully evaluated for other risk factors. Intervention strategies should focus on the specific health behavior patterns known to influence the greatest number of risk factors. Careful attention could then be paid to these particular health behaviors in hopes of simultaneously lowering the levels of multiple risk factors and thus substantially reducing overall CHD risk.

INTERVENTION MEASURES

HIGH-RISK VERSUS POPULATION-BASED INTERVENTIONS

Substantially different rates of reduction in cardiovascular disease (including CHD) deaths may result when interventions target only persons with the highest risk factor levels rather than the entire population. Using actual data from the North Karelia Study, Kottke and co-workers applied a logistic risk function to a

group at the top 10% of serum cholesterol and diastolic blood pressure risk distributions, as well as to the general North Karelia population.[89] They examined three types of intervention results. Specific criteria for the attainment of "achieved," "goal," and "ideal" intervention results were formulated for both approaches (Fig. 15 – 11). Achieved, goal, and ideal results in the high-risk approach would decrease individual serum cholesterol levels (only for persons with levels higher than 325 mg/dl) by 10%, by 20%, and to 190 mg/dl, and would decrease individual diastolic blood pressure (only for those people with levels higher than 105 mm Hg) to 95, 90, and 85 mm Hg, respectively. Achieved, goal, and ideal results in the population-based approach would decrease the population mean of serum cholesterol levels by 10%, by 20%, and to 190 mg/dl, and would decrease the population mean diastolic blood pressure by 5%, by 10%, and to 80 mm Hg, respectively. As revealed in Figure 15 – 11, the population-based intervention strategy would yield a cardiovascular disease death rate in the entire population that was nearly two times lower for each of the three intervention results. In fact, lowering the risk factor levels to the ideal level for the high-risk group would not yield death rates that were substantially lower than the achieved results of the population-based approach. Findings from this study support the use of the population-based intervention approach, because so many persons have greater than optimal levels of risk factors. In addition, an approach that includes a focused strategy for persons known to be at high risk appears warranted.

Many practical problems arise when treating a patient with several risk factors. The question of which intervention measures to use and in what order they should be applied becomes crucial. Because of the many ways in which cigarette smoking can affect the cardiorespiratory system, smoking is probably the most important risk factor to attack. A group of researchers in Oslo demonstrated the utility of both smoking and dietary interventions in high-risk patients.[90] Hypertension control can also bring about immediate reductions in risk. On the other hand, patients may find that making changes in their physical activity pattern is less imposing and more enjoyable than giving up cigarettes and high-fat foods. After a stable physical activity pattern is established by the patient, integration of steps to promote smok-

Strategy:	High Risk Approach			Population Based Approach		
Focus:	Top 10% of Distribution			Entire Population		
Intervention Goals:	Achieved	Goal	Ideal	Achieved	Goal	Ideal
Serum Cholesterol	10% ↓	20% ↓	190 mg/dl	10% ↓	20% ↓	190 mg/dl
Diastolic BP	95 mm Hg	90 mm Hg	85 mm Hg	5% ↓	10% ↓	80 mm Hg

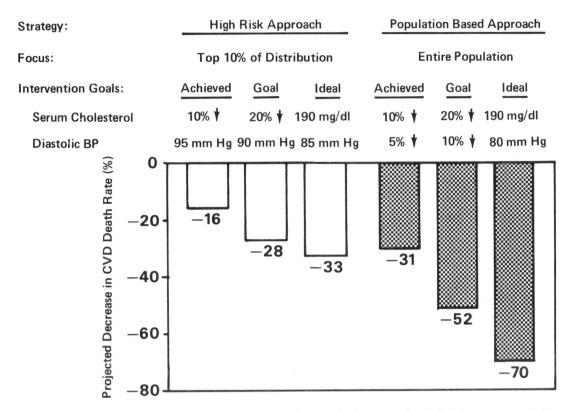

FIGURE 15–11. Projected decrease in cardiovascular disease death rates using high-risk versus population-based approaches for three types of intervention goals. (From Kottke, TE, et al.: Projected effects of high-risk versus population-based prevention strategies in coronary heart disease. *Am J Epidemiol, 121*:697, 1985.)

ing cessation and dietary modification may be feasible. A reasonable approach involves emphasizing the importance of oxygen delivery to enhance or maintain work capacity and the importance of an appropriate nutrient mix for both fuel and weight control. Changes in physical activity should not be used as an excuse to avoid making changes in the other high-risk factors. Use of health education techniques is also important to provide information on all the important risk factors and to establish the patient's perceived ability and willingness to make changes.

REFERENCES

1. Goldman L, Cook EF: The decline in ischemic heart disease mortality rates. *Ann Intern Med, 101*:825, 1984.
2. Keys A: *Seven Countries: A Multivariate Analysis of Death and Coronary Heart Disease.* Cambridge: Harvard University Press, 1980.
3. Blackburn H: Diet and mass hyperlipidemia: A public health view. In *Nutrition, Lipids, and Coronary Heart Disease.* Edited by RI Levy, et al. Raven Press; New York, 1976.
4. Williams RR, et al.: Evidence that men with familial hypercholesterolemia can avoid early coronary death. *JAMA, 255*:219, 1986.
5. Glueck CJ, Connor WE: Diet-coronary heart disease relationships reconnoitered. *Am J Clin Nutr, 31*:727, 1978.
6. Tyroler HA: Total serum cholesterol and ischemic heart disease in clinical and observational studies. *Am J Prev Med, 1*:18, 1984.
7. Lipid Research Clinics Program: The Lipid Research Clinics Coronary Primary Prevention Trial results. I & II. *JAMA, 251*:351, 1984.
8. Brensike JF, et al.: Effects of therapy with cholestyramine on progression of coronary arteriosclerosis: Results of the NHLBI Type II coronary intervention study. *Circulation, 69*:313, 1984.
9. Levy RI, et al.: The influence of changes in lipid values induced by cholestyramine and diet on progression of coronary artery disease: Results of the NHLBI Type II coronary intervention study. *Circulation, 69*:325, 1984.
10. Castelli WP, et al.: HDL cholesterol and other lipids in coronary heart disease. The cooperative lipoprotein phenotyping study. *Circulation, 55*:767, 1977.
11. Olefsky T, Reaven GM, Farquhar JW: Effects of weight reduction on obesity: Studies of lipid and carbohydrate metabolism in normal and hyperlipidemic subjects. *J Clin Invest, 64*, 1974.

12. Wood PC, et al.: Increased exercise level and plasma lipoprotein concentrations: A one year randomized, controlled study in sedentary middle aged men. *Metabolism*, 32:31, 1983.

13. Hartung GH, et al.: Effect of alcohol intake and exercise on plasma high-density lipoprotein cholesterol subfractions and apoliproprotein A-1 in women. *Am J Cardiol*, 58:148, 1986.

14. Miller GJ, Miller NE: Plasma HDL concentration and development of ischemic heart disease. *Lancet*, 1:16, 1975.

15. Gordon T, et al.: The prediction of coronary heart disease by high-density and other lipoproteins: An historical perspective. In *Hyperlipidemia: Diagnosis and Therapy*. Edited by BM Rifkind and RI Levy. New York: Grune and Stratton, 1977.

16. Consensus Conference: Lowering blood cholesterol to prevent heart disease. *JAMA*, 251:365, 1984.

17. Sacks FM, et al.: Plasma lipids and lipoproteins in vegetarians and controls. *N Engl J Med*, 292:1148, 1975.

18. Vesselinovitch D, et al.: Reversal of advanced atherosclerosis in rhesus monkeys. I. Light microscopic studies. *Atherosclerosis*, 23:155, 1976.

19. *Heart to Heart: A Manual on Nutrition Counseling for the Reduction of Cardiovascular Disease Risk Factors*. U.S. Department of Health and Human Services, Public Health Service, NIH publication No. 83-1528, 1983.

20. American Heart Association Special Report: Recommendations for treatment of hyperlipidemia in adults. *Circulation*, 69:1065A, 1984.

21. The Lovastatin Study Group II: Therapeutic response to Lovastatin (mevinolin) in nonfamilial hypercholesterolemia. A multicenter study. *JAMA*, 256:2829, 1986.

22. Pooling Project Research Group. Relationship of blood pressure, serum cholesterol, smoking habit, relative weight and ECG abnormalities to incidence of major coronary events: Final report of the Pooling Project. *J Chronic Dis*, 31:202–306, 1978.

23. Gordon T, Kannel WB, McGee D: Death and coronary attacks in men after giving up cigarette smoking. *Lancet*, 2:1348, 1974.

24. Kannel WB, Castelli WP, McNamara PM: Cigarette smoking and risk of CHD: Epidemiologic clues to pathogenesis. *The Framingham Study: N.C.I. Monograph*, 28:9–20, 1968.

25. U.S. Department of Health and Human Services: *Smoking and Health: A report of the Surgeon General*. Washington DC: DHHS Publication No. (PHS) 79-50066, 1979.

26. Health and Public Policy Committee, American College of Physicians: Methods for stopping cigarette smoking. *Ann Intern Med*, 105:281, 1986.

27. Hughes JR, Miller SA: Nicotine gum to help stop smoking. *JAMA*, 252:2855, 1984.

28. Gordon T, Sorlie P, Kannel WB: Problems in the assessment of blood pressure. The Framingham Study. *Int J Epidemiol*, 5:327, 1976.

29. Freis E: Salt volume and the prevention of hypertension. *Circulation*, 53:589, 1976.

30. Berglund G, et al.: Coronary heart disease after treatment of hypertension. *Lancet*, 1:1, 1978.

31. The Joint National Committee on Detection, Evaluation, and Treatment of High Blood Pressure: The 1984 Report of the Joint National Committee on Detection, Evaluation, and Treatment of High Blood Pressure. *Arch Intern Med*, 144:1045, 1984.

32. An epidemiological approach to describing risk associated with blood pressure levels: Final report of the Working Group on Risk and High Blood Pressure. *Hypertension*, 7:641, 1985.

33. Levine DM, et al.: Health education for hypertensive patients. *JAMA*, 241:1700, 1979.

34. Paffenbarger RS Jr, et al.: Physical activity and incidence of hypertension. *Am J Epidemiol*, 117:245, 1983.

35. Stamler R, et al.: Primary prevention of hypertension. *Circulation*, 68:362, 1983.

36. Boyer JL, Kasch FW: Exercise therapy in hypertensive men. *JAMA*, 211:1668, 1970.

37. Toth PJ, Horwitz RI: Conflicting clinical trials and the uncertainty of treating mild hypertension. *Am J Med*, 75:482, 1983.

38. Hypertension Detection and Follow-up Program Cooperative Group: Results of the Hypertension Detection and Follow-up Program. *N Engl J Med*, 307:976, 1982.

39. Gross F, et al.: Guidelines for the treatment of mild hypertension: Memorandum from a W.H.O./I.S.H. Meeting. *Lancet*, 1:457, 1983.

40. Powell KE, et al.: Physical activity and the incidence of coronary heart disease. *Annu Rev Public Health*, 8:253, 1987.

41. Paffenbarger RS Jr, Wing AL, Hyde RT: Physical activity as an index of heart attack risk in college alumni. *Am J Epidemiol*, 108:161, 1978.

42. Morris JN, et al.: Coronary heart disease and physical activity of work. *Lancet*, 2:1053, 1953.

43. May GS, et al.: Secondary prevention after myocardial infarction: A review of long term trials. *Prog Cardiovasc Dis*, 24:331, 1982.

44. Barnard RJ: Effects of an intensive exercise and nutrition program in patients with coronary artery disease: Five year follow-up. *J Cardiac Rehab*, 3:183, 1983.

45. Kavanagh T, et al.: Prognostic indexes for patients with ischemic heart disease enrolled in an exercise-centered rehabilitation program. *Am J Cardiol*, 44:1230, 1979.

46. Brownell KD: Public health approaches to obesity and its management. *Annu Rev Public Health*, 7:521, 1986.

47. Kemmer FW, Berger M: Exercise and diabetes mellitus: Physical activity as part of daily life and its role in the treatment of diabetic patients. *Int J Sports Med*, 4:77, 1983.

48. Farrell PA, Barboriak J: Time course in alterations in plasma lipid and lipoprotein concentrations during eight weeks of endurance training. *Atherosclerosis*, 27:231, 1980.

49. LaPorte RE, et al.: The spectrum of physical activity, cardiovascular disease and health: An epidemiologic perspective. *Am J Epidemiol*, 120:507, 1984.

50. Haskell WL, et al.: Strenuous physical activity, treadmill exercise test performance and plasma high-density lipoprotein cholesterol. The Lipid Research Clinics Program Prevalence Study. *Circulation*, 62:53, 1980.

51. Wood PD, et al.: The distribution of plasma lipoproteins in middle aged male runners. *Metabolism*, 25:1249, 1976.

52. Kiens B, et al.: Increased plasma HDL-cholesterol and apo A-1 in sedentary middle age men after physical conditioning. *Eur J Clin Invest*, 10:203, 1980.

53. Sady SP, et al.: Prolonged exercise augments plasma triglyceride clearance. *JAMA*, 256:2552, 1986.

54. Zilversmit DB: Atherogenesis: A postprandial phenomenon. *Circulation*, 60:473, 1979.

55. Kramsch DM, et al.: Reduction of coronary atherosclerosis by moderate conditioning exercise in monkeys on an atherogenic diet. *N Engl J Med, 305*:1483, 1981.

56. Stamler J, et al.: Prevalence and incidence of coronary heart disease in strata of the labor force of a Chicago industrial corporation. *J Chronic Dis, 11*:405, 1960.

57. Wyatt HL, Mitchell J: Influences of physical conditioning and deconditioning on coronary vasculature of dogs. *J Appl Physiol, 45*:619, 1978.

58. Neill WA, Oxendine JM: Exercise can promote coronary collateral development without improving perfusion of ischemic myocardium. *Circulation, 60*:1513, 1979.

59. Nolewajka AJ, et al.: Exercise and human collateralization: An angiographic and scintigraphic assessment. *Circulation, 60*:114, 1979.

60. Kennedy CC, et al.: One-year graduated exercise program for men with angina pectoris. Evaluation by physiologic studies and coronary arteriography. *Mayo Clin Proc, 51*:231, 1976.

61. Rosing DR, et al.: Blood fibrinolytic activity in man. Diurnal variation and the response to varying intensities of exercise. *Circ Res, 27*:171, 1970.

62. Williams RS, et al.: Physical conditioning augments the fibrinolytic response to venous occlusion in healthy adults. *N Engl J Med, 302*:987, 1980.

63. Bove AA, Dewey JD: Proximal coronary vasomotor reactivity after exercise training in dogs. *Circulation, 71*:620, 1985.

64. Maseri A, et al.: Coronary vasospasm as a possible cause of myocardial infarction. A conclusion derived from the study of "preinfarction" angina. *N Engl J Med, 299*:1271, 1978.

65. Kenney WL: Parasympathetic control of resting heart rate: Relationship to aerobic power. *Med Sci Sports Exerc, 17*:451, 1985.

66. Billman GE, Schwartz PJ, Stone HL: The effects of daily exercise on susceptibility to sudden cardiac death. *Circulation, 69*:1182, 1984.

67. Noakes TD, Higginson L, Opie LH: Physical training increases ventricular fibrillation thresholds of isolated rat hearts during normoxia, hypoxia, and regional ischemia. *Circulation, 67*:24, 1983.

68. Friedewald WT: Physical activity research and coronary heart disease. *Public Health Rep, 100*:115, 1985.

69. Taylor HL, Buskirk ER, Remington, RD: Exercise in controlled trials of the prevention of coronary heart disease. *Fed Proc, 32*:1623, 1973.

70. Kannel WB, Gordon T: *The Framingham Study: An Epidemiological Investigation of Cardiovascular Disease.* Section 30. Washington, DC, Public Health Service, NIH, DHEW Publication No. (NIH) 74-599, Feb. 1974.

71. Hubert HB, et al.: Obesity as an independent risk factor for cardiovascular disease: A 26 year follow-up of participants in the Framingham Heart Study. *Circulation, 67*:968, 1983.

72. Hubert HB: The importance of obesity in the development of coronary risk factors and disease: The epidemiological evidence. *Annu Rev Public Health, 7*:493, 1986.

73. Ashley FW Jr, Kannel WB: Relation of weight change to changes in atherogenic traits. The Framingham Study. *J Chronic Dis, 27*:103, 1974.

74. Seals DR, Hagberg JM: The effect of exercise training on human hypertension: A review. *Med Sci Sports Exerc, 16*:207, 1984.

75. Blair SN, Jacobs DR Jr, Powell KE: Relationships between exercise or physical activity and other health behaviors. *Public Health Rep., 100*:172, 1985.

76. Taylor CB, Sallis JF, Needle R: The relation of physical activity and exercise to mental health. *Public Health Rep., 100*:195, 1985.

77. Barrett-Connor E, Orchard T: Diabetes and heart disease. In *Diabetes in America.* Edited by MI Harris and RF Hamman. NIH Publication No. 85-1468, 1985.

78. Jenkins CD, Rosenman RH, Zyzanski SJ: Prediction of clinical coronary heart disease by a test for the coronary-prone behavior pattern. *N Engl J Med, 290*:1271, 1974.

79. Haynes SG, Feinleib M, Kannel WB: The relationship of psychosocial factors to coronary heart disease in the Framingham Study. III. Eight-year incidence of coronary heart disease. *Am J Epidemiol, 111*:37, 1980.

80. Jenkins CD: Psychological and social precursors of coronary disease. *N Engl J Med, 244*:207, 1971.

81. Von Eulen US: Quantitation of stress by catecholamine analysis. *Clin Pharmacol Ther, 5*:398, 1964.

82. Shekelle RB, et al.: The MRFIT Behavior Pattern Study. II: Type A behavior and the incidence of coronary heart disease. *Am J Epidemiol, 123*:923, 1985.

83. Matthews KA, Haynes SG: Type A behavior pattern and coronary disease risk: Update and critical evaluation. *Am J Epidemiol, 123*:923, 1986.

84. Eliot RS, Forker AD, Robertson RJ: Aerobic exercise as a therapeutic modality in the relief of stress. *Adv Cardiol, 18*:231, 1976.

85. Perkins KA: Family history of coronary heart disease: Is it still an independent risk factor? *Am J Epidemiol, 124*:182, 1986.

86. Khaw KT, Barrett-Connor E: Family history of heart attack: A modifiable risk factor? *Circulation, 74*:239, 1986.

87. Criqui MH, et al.: Clustering of cardiovascular disease risk factors. *Prev Med, 9*:525, 1980.

88. Gotto A: Interactions of the major risk factors for coronary heart disease. *Am J Med, 80* (Suppl):48, 1986.

89. Kottke TE, et al.: Projected effects of high-risk versus population-based prevention strategies in coronary heart disease. *Am J Epidemiol, 121*:697, 1985.

90. Hjermann I, et al.: Effect of diet and smoking intervention on the incidence of coronary heart disease: Report of the Oslo Study Group of a randomised trial in healthy men. *Lancet, 2*:1303, 1981.

CHAPTER 16

PATHOPHYSIOLOGY OF CHRONIC DISEASES AND EXERCISE TRAINING

PETER HANSON

Exercise training is currently recommended as an adjunct treatment for coronary heart disease. Prescribed exercise training may also be useful in the management of other chronic cardiovascular and metabolic disorders. This chapter summarizes the role of exercise training in hypertension, diabetes mellitus, renal failure, pulmonary disease, and peripheral vascular disease.

HYPERTENSION

Hypertension is the most common cardiovascular disease in human populations. Blood pressure values are deemed "hypertensive" on the basis of epidemiologic criteria that show increasing risk of morbidity and mortality with increasing systolic and diastolic pressures. The World Health Organization defines normal resting blood pressure as less than 140/90 and hypertension as greater than 160/95. Intermediate blood pressure values are defined as borderline or mild hypertension. Results of recent studies led authors to suggest that hypertension be designated as systolic or diastolic pressures exceeding 140/90.

The prevalence of hypertension in persons from most Western industrialized countries is 15 to 20%. The prevalence of hypertension in the black population is substantially higher (25 to 30%). Hypertension is a major risk factor for coronary artery disease, stroke, and congestive heart failure. Hypertension may contribute to 2,000,000 excess deaths every 10 years. In several recent blood pressure intervention trials, however, mortality and morbidity were substantially reduced when adequate antihypertensive treatment was maintained.

PATHOPHYSIOLOGY

For clinical purposes, hypertension is divided into two subgroups: primary hypertension and secondary hypertension. Primary hypertension (essential hypertension) accounts for sustained high blood pressure in over 95% of patients. Multiple regulatory mechanisms contribute to the evolution of primary hypertension, including abnormal central and sympathetic mediation of increased peripheral resistance; renal and metabolic control of increased vascular volume; and decreased compliance and possibly unidentified circulating hypertensive mediators. In a variety of studies of primary hypertension, authors reported increased numbers of circulating catecholamines, increased (or normal) renin levels, and evidence of abnormally high sodium transport across cell membranes in hypertensive patients.

These neurohumoral and metabolic disturbances all contribute to the gradual increase in systemic vascular resistance that is characteristic of primary hypertension. In addition, an alteration of arterial baroreceptor function occurs, leading to a "re-setting" of baroreflexes to accommodate higher systemic pressure levels. In hemodynamic studies involving subjects with primary hypertension, systemic vascular resistance was increased at rest and throughout exercise. During the early phases of primary hypertension, cardiac output may be increased, whereas in the later stages, cardiac output is normal or reduced as systemic vascular resistance continues to increase.

Secondary hypertension is caused by specific endocrine or renal abnormalities. Examples include tumors of the adrenal medulla, which release catecholamines (epinephrine and norepinephrine), and tumors of the adrenal cortex, which release hypertension-mediating steroid hormones (cortisol and aldosterone). Renal vascular disease causes increased production of renin, which stimulates the conversion of plasma angiotensin and the release of aldosterone. Angiotensin is a potent mediator of peripheral vasoconstriction, and aldosterone stimulates renal retention of sodium and water. Most of these unusual causes of hypertension, which account for less than 2% of all sustained hypertension, are treatable by surgical intervention or medical management.

Regardless of cause, increasing blood pressure levels produce a predictable pattern of end-organ pathologic processes. Echocardiographic studies in borderline hypertension patients show early left ventricular hypertrophy. With sustained hypertension, concentric left ventricular hypertrophy increases. In addition, a progressive hypertensive thickening and degeneration of medium and small arterial vessels (arteriosclerosis) occurs, which is particularly evident in the retina and renal glomerular arterioles, leading to hypertensive retinopathy and nephropathy. Hypertensive cerebral vascular disease and rupture produce catastrophic stroke.

We emphasize that the end-organ damage from hypertension evolves over many years. Rapid increases in blood pressure, which usually occur in secondary hypertension, may be poorly tolerated whereas gradual increases in blood pressure and sustained systolic hypertension in older patients may be well tolerated for long periods without morbid events.

RESPONSES TO EXERCISE

The normal pattern of blood pressure response to exercise is characterized by a near-linear increase in systolic pressure combined with a gradual decline in diastolic pressure. Peak blood pressure values at maximal work intensity are in the range of 180–210/60–80. These values may vary considerably, depending on age, weight, and gender. For example, young, adult women may show normal peak blood pressure values of 140/60.

Patients with hypertension usually show systolic and diastolic pressure values that are maintained above the expected normal range. The magnitude of added increase in systolic and diastolic pressure during exercise is usually proportional to the elevation in systolic and diastolic pressure measured at rest. This indicates that blood pressure is "reset" and is maintained at higher levels throughout the spectrum of activity from rest to peak exercise; yet some patients with mild hypertension may demonstrate a normalization of blood pressure during exercise relative to resting values. This normalization is attributed to metabolic vasodilation, which temporarily corrects the elevated resting peripheral resistance.

Results of recent studies lead researchers to suggest that blood pressure responses to exercise provide additional criteria for diagnosis and management of hypertension. Maximal blood pressure values during submaximal and maximal exercise have been reported for a variety of patient groups. Recent reports reveal that blood pressure values exceeding 180/90 at 50% maximal exercise capacity and maximal blood pressure values exceeding 225/90 are common in patients with mild primary hypertension. A subset of patients with mild hypertension may show an early rise in systolic pressure to levels of 180 to 200 during submaximal exercise, followed by maximal values in the normal range of 200 to 210. These patients may generate excessively high systolic blood pressures with activities of daily living, although the resting blood pressure and maximal blood pressure values are at the upper limits of normal. Results of studies involving a comparison of blood pressure values during exercise and ambulatory blood pressure monitoring indicate that patients with this pattern of blood pressure response also show evidence of early left ventricular hypertrophy and are at greater risk for the development of fixed hypertension.

The evaluation of blood pressure responses to exercise should involve the use of protocols permitting accurate measurement of blood pressure. A Balke format treadmill protocol is superior to the Bruce protocol, which is commonly used for diagnostic exercise testing. The Balke treadmill protocol is conducted at a constant walking speed and does not require jogging or running at high work intensities that interfere with measurement of blood pressure. Blood pressure criteria for discontinuation of exercise testing are controversial. In most laboratories, researchers set an arbitrary value of more than 250/110 as a termination point, yet no evidence exists to support these criteria, and in no case reports have hypertensive emergencies been reported to result when subjects exceed these levels.

TREATMENT

An abundance of antihypertensive agents are currently available, including: (1) diuretics, (2) adrenergic blocking agents, (3) vasodilators, and (4) converting enzyme inhibitors. The major classes of antihypertensive agents and their mechanism of action is summarized in Table 16–1. Selection of a form of antihypertensive therapy should be directed at the underlying pathophysiologic process. Patients with increased plasma volume and high salt intake may benefit from salt restriction and diuretic agents. Patients with evidence of high sympathetic activity characterized by increasing resting heart rate and rapid increases in heart rate during exercise would benefit from β-adrenergic blocking agents. Persons with hypertension associated with high renin-angiotensin levels are ideally treated with converting enzyme-inhibiting agents.

Other adrenergic blocking agents include peripheral α-receptor-blocking agents such as prazosin, which reduce peripheral vasoconstriction mediated by increased sympathetic α-stimulation. Centrally acting adrenergic blocking agents, such as clonidine, attenuate sympathetic outflow at the level of medullary vasomotor centers. The peripheral and central-acting α-adrenergic blocking agents appear to have minimal adverse effects on heart rate, cardiac output, and metabolic responses to exercise.

Direct-acting vasodilators are also used in the treatment of patients with hypertension. These agents include hydralazine and the calcium channel-inhibiting agents. The vasodilating agents tend to produce tachycardia secondary to baroreflex responses to lowered blood pressure. They are frequently used in combination with β-adrenergic blocking agents to control the secondary increases in heart rates.

Antihypertensive agents may interact adversely with exercise. Excessive use of most diuretic agents produces hypokalemia, the result of increased loss of urinary potassium. Hypokalemia is associated with skeletal muscle weakness and may aggravate ventricular arrhythmias or ventricular fibrillation. Beta-adrenergic blocking agents restrict heart rate, cardiac output, and maximal oxygen consumption. The combined use of beta-blocking agents and vasodilators may cause post-exercise hypotension.

The treatment of athletes or active adults with sustained hypertension is frequently complicated by the side effects of standard antihypertensive therapy. A recent trend in the treatment of hypertension emphasizes the initial use of converting enzyme-inhibiting agents (captopril and enalapril), which have no effect on the sympathetic nervous system and do not produce hypokalemia. The converting enzyme inhibitors are well tolerated and have no adverse effect on exercise performance. Finally, the use of a long-acting transcutaneous form of cloni-

Table 16–1. Major Classes of Antihypertensive Drugs

Drugs	Major action	Exercise side effects
Diuretics	Renal salt and water loss	Hypokalemia
β-blocking	Reduced cardiac output	Reduced $\dot{V}O_{2\,max}$, fatigue
α-blocking	Vasodilation, reduced vascular resistance	Hypotension
Ca^{2+} blocking	Vasodilation, reduced vascular resistance	Tachycardia, cramps
Vasodilators	Vasodilation, reduced vascular resistance	Reflex tachycardia
Converting enzyme inhibitors	Inhibition of renin-angiotensin, aldosterone, vasodilation, reduced water and salt retention.	Excessive hypotension

dine may also be a viable alternative. The transcutaneous patches provide 7 days of antihypertensive therapy, which optimizes compliance. In addition, the side effects associated with oral clonidine are minimal.

EXERCISE TRAINING AND HYPERTENSION

Exercise training may be useful in the management of mild hypertension. In recent studies a significant decrease in blood pressure level was shown to occur after 6 to 8 weeks of aerobic exercise conditioning prescribed by the usual criteria. The decrease in blood pressure is attributed to a decrease in systemic vascular resistance and is associated with a decrease in plasma norepinephrine levels.

Although these results are encouraging, the clinical efficacy of exercise training for the management of hypertension requires further study. Results of most acute studies of exercise training show a return of the hypertensive blood pressure patterns after 3 to 6 weeks of detraining.

DIABETES MELLITUS

Diabetes is a serious metabolic disorder with wide-ranging complications; the high levels of plasma glucose and secondary microvascular degeneration can affect the eye, kidneys, and peripheral circulation. Diabetes is classified as insulin dependent (type I) or noninsulin dependent (type II). The clinical characteristics of patients with insulin- and noninsulin-dependent diabetes are summarized in Table 16–2. Type I diabetes typically occurs in children and young adults under the age of 30 years. Of all patients with diabetes mellitus, about 5% are insulin-

dependent diabetics. The prevalence of diabetes in the United States is estimated to be 1 in every 300 to 400 persons under age 20 years.

PATHOPHYSIOLOGY

Insulin-dependent diabetes is caused by destruction of the insulin-producing beta cells in the pancreas. This process may involve genetic, viral, and/or autoimmune factors, either separately or in combination.

Patients with type I diabetes maintain high levels of plasma glucose and are subject to ketoacidosis resulting from the increased metabolism of fat and production of ketone bodies. High levels of plasma glucose cause increased loss of water and sugar through the urine, which leads to secondary thirst, weight loss, and increased appetite.

Insulin-dependent diabetics have multiple systemic complications, including characteristic degeneration of the small arterial vessels within the eye, kidneys, and peripheral arterioles of the lower extremities. Retinal hemorrhage and a high frequency of blindness and progressive renal failure result. Degeneration of peripheral and autonomic nerve function also occurs. The heart and peripheral blood vessels are affected; diabetes accelerates coronary atherosclerosis and symptomatic coronary disease may develop between the ages of 20 and 40 years. In addition, cardiac function is affected directly, with loss of contractile performance of the ventricles, as is the peripheral circulation which is compromised by degenerative changes in distal arterioles. Perfusion of the lower extremities is therefore poor and frequent complications ensue, including infections of the feet and poor healing of cuts and wounds, which often require amputation because of gangrene.

Type II diabetes typically occurs in overweight adults over the age of 40 years. These patients show high levels of circulating plasma glucose but they do not respond with excess fat metabolism and ketosis. The cause of type II diabetes is apparently correlated with diminished sensitivity of peripheral insulin receptors, which may result from a combination of obesity, genetic susceptibility, and age. Plasma insulin levels are actually increased because of the excessive release of insulin that results from the stimulatory effect of high circulating glucose levels. Eventually, insulin levels fall to subnormal levels because of failure of beta cell function.

Table 16–2. Comparison of Insulin-dependent (type I) and Noninsulin-dependent (type II) Diabetes

Characteristics	Type I	Type II
Age of onset	< 20 yr	> 40 yr
Family history	Probable	Frequent
Weight	Usually underweight	Overweight
Serum insulin level (late)	Low or zero	High or low
Insulin therapy	Always	20 to 30%
Complications	Frequent	Variable
Lifespan	Maximum of 40 yr	

Type II diabetics have fewer complications than their type I counterparts, and may live a relatively normal life span. The incidence of coronary artery disease is increased, however, and hypertension and other complications of obesity frequently accompany type II diabetes.

TREATMENT

Patients with insulin-dependent diabetes are treated with subcutaneous injections of insulin. A typical prescription consists of a mixture of short-acting (crystalline) insulin and longer-acting insulin preparations. Precise control of insulin levels frequently requires morning and evening doses, which are adjusted according to self-monitored blood glucose determinations. Strict dietary regulation is also mandatory so that total carbohydrate and calorie intake are maintained to match insulin therapy.

Noninsulin-dependent diabetic patients are treated with a combination of weight loss and oral hypoglycemic agents, which increase the sensitivity of peripheral insulin receptors and stimulate the release of insulin from beta cells.

EXERCISE TRAINING AND DIABETES

Exercise may be beneficial in the control of diabetes. Submaximal aerobic exercise produces an increase in glucose uptake in skeletal muscle, which is independent of insulin. In a number of studies, exercise training produced an increase in peripheral sensitivity to insulin in type I diabetics. These changes may permit a reduction in the dosage of insulin required to control glucose levels. In other reports, improvement of several markers of diabetic control are suggested, including lower hemoglobin A-1c levels, which reflect the overall regulation of plasma glucose. The long-term effects of aerobic exercise training in the management of patients with type I diabetes, however, requires further evaluation.

Individuals with type II diabetes also benefit from exercise training. As shown in available studies, exercise can also produce an increase in insulin sensitivity in these patients, although this effect may be mediated by weight loss that occurs with exercise training. The combination of dietary and exercise management of patients with type II diabetes is attractive and certainly should be utilized whenever possible as an initial step.

Complications of exercise training in type I diabetics should be anticipated. The cardiovascular responses to graded exercise may be substantially impaired in type I diabetics. For example, maximal oxygen consumption and maximal attainable heart rate may be as much as 15 to 20% less than those values in age-matched control subjects. In addition, diabetic patients frequently have hypertensive blood pressure responses during exercise as well as post-exertional hypotension. Abnormal cardiovascular responses are attributed to altered autonomic and baroreflex control of heart rate and blood pressure. The incidence of asymptomatic coronary disease is also increased in type I and type II diabetics. Exercise testing is recommended for these patients before an exercise program is prescribed.

Insulin therapy in persons with type I diabetes must be adjusted to compensate for anticipated exercise. This step may require a reduction in the longer-acting insulin dosage, which typically has its peak effect in early to late afternoon. Intake of carbohydrate may also be used to compensate for hypoglycemia that may occur with exercise.

The uptake of insulin from subcutaneous injection sites may be influenced by exercise. Several researchers report an increase in insulin uptake from injection in sites that overlie active muscle, such as in the thigh. The increased insulin levels could aggravate hypoglycemia in patients who have an otherwise satisfactory balance of carbohydrate intake and insulin therapy. Most authorities recommend an alternate injection site over the abdomen or in muscle groups that are not involved in vigorous exercise.

END-STAGE RENAL DISEASE

End-stage renal disease (ESRD) affects approximately 100,000 persons in the United States. The causes of ESRD include diabetes, hypertension, kidney infections, and a variety of autoimmune and inherited disorders.

PATHOPHYSIOLOGY

ESRD is characterized by a gradual loss of glomerular filtration capacity in the kidney. The result is an accumulation of a variety of circu-

Table 16–3. Signs and Symptoms of Uremia

System	Corrected by dialysis	Not corrected by dialysis
Musculoskeletal		Renal osteodystrophy; metastatic calcifications; decreased growth; muscle weakness
Neurologic	Encephalopathy Peripheral neuropathy (early)	Peripheral neuropathy (late)
Cardiopulmonary	Volume-dependent hypertension; pericarditis; pleuritis; pulmonary edema; heart murmur	Hyper-reninemic hypertension; accelerated atherogenesis; calcifications
Hematologic	Platelet and white cell dysfunction	Anemia
Immunologic	Decreased immune responsiveness (?)	
Gastrointestinal	Anorexia, nausea, vomiting; colitis; uremic breath	Peptic ulcer disease
Cutaneous	Pruritus due to uremia; uremic frost	Pruritus due to calcium deposition; pallor
Electrolytes	Hyperkalemia; hyponatremia	Hyperphosphatemia; hypocalcemia; hyperuricemia; metabolic acidosis
Endocrine-metabolic	Carbohydrate intolerance; malnutrition; sexual dysfunction; amenorrhea	Hyperlipidemia; thyroid dysfunction; infertility (women); hyperparathyroidism; vitamin D deficiency

lating waste products, including urea, non-urea nitrogen, and creatinine, which is collectively referred to as "uremia." The accumulation of these waste products leads to multisystem dysfunction, including muscle weakness, osteodystrophy, cardiac dysfunction, severe anemia, and endocrine and metabolic imbalance. The composite effects of these systemic disorders result in marked reduction in functional capacity.

TREATMENT

Three forms of treatment are currently available for chronic renal failure: hemodialysis, peritoneal dialysis, and kidney transplantation. ESRD patients do not survive without treatment, and with therapy they may be sustained for a prolonged period. Not all signs and symptoms are corrected by dialysis, however (Table 16–3). Therefore, life function and activities are severely curtailed by the time required to undergo these procedures. In addition, frequent infections and adverse reactions are associated with dialysis. Renal transplantation, with use of a kidney of a living, related donor or from a properly matched cadaver, usually results in normalization of renal function and lifestyle, although many transplant patients experience side effects from immunosuppressive medications.

EXERCISE TRAINING AND ESRD

As previously mentioned, ESRD patients show marked impairment of functional capacity in addition to impairment of heart rate and ventricular responses to exercise. This impairment has been attributed to the combined effects of anemia, the effects of circulating uremic products on ventricular function, and autonomic function. The exercise capacity of younger patients with ESRD may be 50% of anticipated normal levels. In addition, the maximal heart rate and cardiac output are attenuated.

Researchers from several institutions have reported experience with moderate exercise training of ESRD patients. In all of these studies, increase in functional capacity was noted as measured by oxygen consumption and an improvement in subjective tolerance to activities of daily living. Whether routine exercise training affects the uremic state or the secondary complications of uremia is not clear. Some investigators describe an increase in hematocrit and hemoglobin levels in ESRD patients undergoing hemodialysis. These results are difficult to interpret because of the variable effects of hemodialysis on blood volume.

Researchers from some institutions now recommend routine exercise training before and after renal transplantation. Such training may result in improved functional status before and an optimal ability to restore the functional capacity after kidney transplantation. In recent studies, investigators noted that functional capacity may increase by 25%, without exercise training, after successful renal transplantation. This increase in exercise capacity is at least partially attributed to restoration of cardiac output and maximal heart rate as well as normalization of hematocrit determination.

CHRONIC OBSTRUCTIVE PULMONARY DISEASE

Chronic obstructive pulmonary disease (COPD) includes a spectrum of airways disorders ranging from asthma and simple bronchitis to chronic obstructive bronchitis and emphysema. The hallmark of COPD is obstruction to airway flow as shown by a variety of timed expiratory volume measurements. These parameters include: vital capacity, forced expiratory volume achieved in 1 sec, and the forced expiratory flow rate measured at 25% of forced expiratory volume and at 75% of forced expiratory flow rate. Additional measurements of airway function include pressure-volume loops, which are measured by a simultaneous recording of instantaneous pressure and volume during maximal inspiration and expiration. In addition, measurements of pulmonary diffusing capacity are determined by the rate of inhaled carbon monoxide uptake. These measurements permit accurate classification of lung disease on the basis of alterations in volume, flow rates, compliance, and capacity for diffusion.

PATHOPHYSIOLOGY

Asthma is a common form of reversible bronchospasm elicited by allergy, exercise, infections, or other environmental irritants. The bronchial airways respond with increased secretion of mucus and constriction. This response results in the typical combination of nonproductive cough and wheezing, which is reversible with bronchodilator therapy. Symptoms of asthma may be controlled by the prophylactic administration of oral bronchodilator medication in addition to inhaled bronchodilator preparations as needed. In patients with severe asthma, the use of oral and inhaled steroid preparations is required to control persistent bronchospasm.

Bronchitis is an inflammatory disorder of small airways in the lung (less than 2 mm in diameter). Bronchitis is typically seen in smokers and is characterized by coughing, wheezing, and sputum production. During the initial phases of bronchitis, evidence of impaired lung function as measured by standard spirometry may be minimal. Alterations in "small airways" function is detectable with more sensitive tests. In chronic obstructive bronchitis, forced vital capacity and expiratory flow rates are depressed because of obstruction and dynamic compression of airways at high intrapulmonic pressures. Patients with chronic bronchitis have reduced arterial oxygen saturation and increased arterial CO_2 levels as a result of hypoventilation. Physically they appear congested and plethoric and are nicknamed "blue bloaters."

Emphysema involves the gradual destruction of lung alveolar units and connective tissue in addition to airway inflammation. Most patients with emphysema are longstanding smokers; however, a subgroup of the patients have a genetic insufficiency of α_1-antitrypsin, which is important in controlling the production of endogenous proteolytic enzymes. Lack of α_1-antitrypsin permits these proteolytic enzymes to destroy lung tissue, leading to enlargement of alveolar units and formation of large (bullous) spaces within the lung. The loss of supporting lung tissue leads to early collapse of airways during expiration and also requires high inspiratory lung volumes to maintain airway patency during inspiration. Accordingly, the total lung volume increases and tidal volume changes are achieved at the peak of inspiratory capacity.

Emphysema also produces arterial desaturation because of the marked disturbance in the matching of ventilation to perfusion within the lung. Arterial CO_2 levels are mildly elevated or are normal. Some investigators suggest the use of supplementary oxygen to permit a higher intensity and duration of exercise training for COPD patients. Symptom-limited exercise tests during which supplementary oxygen is used are usually performed for a longer duration with reduced ventilation and heart rates at submaximal efforts.

EXERCISE TRAINING AND COPD

Most patients with asthma benefit from aerobic exercise training, although the mechanism of this improvement is not clear. In studies of adolescent patients with asthma, exercise tolerance increased and some improvement in airway function with regular exercise training was noted. Exercise training complements the use of bronchodilator agents and may decrease the need for these agents in a few patients.

Some individuals do suffer from a form of "exercise-induced" asthma. In these patients, the onset of asthma is related to water loss and cooling of the airways. The development of exercise-induced asthma may be prevented by the use of various inhaled bronchodilating agents (β_2-agonists) and other substances (cromolyn sodium) before anticipated exercise.

Patients with chronic bronchitis and emphysema may benefit from mild exercise training. Results of most available studies show an increase in exercise tolerance with minimal or no increase in measured oxygen uptake, possibly related to increased efficiency of movement or increased tolerance to dyspnea. In studies of airway function and arterial blood gases, patients showed no improvement of airway conductance measurements or significant changes in arterial oxygen or carbon dioxide levels after exercise training.

Patients with COPD should be evaluated with symptom-limited exercise testing and measurement of ventilation, electrocardiography, and arterial saturation by ear oximetry. Patients who show marked decreases in saturation may be poor candidates for any form of exercise training. Some of these patients may be able to perform limited exercise with supplementary oxygen. Supraventricular and ventricular arrhythmias are common in patients with COPD who use theophylline-based bronchodilator agents.

Patients with asthma and early bronchitis may benefit from exercise training in addition to prescribed bronchodilator therapy. Patients with late-stage chronic bronchitis or emphysema may show some improvement in exercise tolerance with no evidence of improvement in pulmonary function or arterial blood gas transport.

PERIPHERAL VASCULAR DISEASE

Obstructive peripheral vascular disease is commonly seen in patients over 50 years of age. The usual cause of peripheral vascular disease is atherosclerotic obstruction of the iliac, femoral, and popliteal arteries. Peripheral vascular disease is also a frequent complication of diabetes.

The hallmark symptom of peripheral vascular disease is muscular pain (claudication) during exercise that is relieved by rest. Claudication involves muscular units that are distal to the region of vascular obstruction. Typically, the calf and foot are affected, with obstruction of the femoral and popliteal arteries. Obstruction in a more superior part of the iliac arteries may produce claudication of the buttock and quadriceps groups in addition to the gastrocnemius muscles.

DIAGNOSIS

The initial diagnosis of peripheral vascular disease is made on the basis of clinical history and the findings on physical examination. Auscultation of the femoral arteries may reveal bruits and reduced pulse volume on palpation. Measurement of popliteal and ankle systolic pressures are also helpful. The popliteal or posterior tibial systolic pressure is usually 15 to 25 mm Hg higher than the simultaneous brachial artery pressure. A ratio of the posterior tibial to the brachial pressure index of 1 or less is suggestive of peripheral vascular disease. Values of less than 80% are suggestive of moderate peripheral vascular disease, and ratios of less than 50% indicate severe peripheral vascular disease. Exercise testing may be used to amplify these findings. Immediately after exercise, the systolic pressure index may fall to 50% or less in patients with moderate to peripheral vascular disease and less than 15% in persons with severe peripheral vascular disease. The anatomic location and severity of peripheral vascular disease is determined by using arteriography. The arteriogram is useful for determining possible sites for surgical bypass of obstructive lesions.

TREATMENT

Medical management of patients with peripheral vascular disease is marginally effective. A variety of vasodilating agents have achieved variable results. One problem with this approach is the phenomenon of arterial "steal," in which vasodilation of normally perfused segments may shunt blood away from already underperfused areas. Some symptoms of peripheral vascular disease may result from periodic platelet obstruction in the narrowed vascular lumen. The use of antiplatelet agents such as aspirin may be beneficial in these patients. Most patients with peripheral vascular disease are chronic smokers and have other risk factors for coronary artery disease. Discontinuation of smoking and modification of these risk factors is mandatory.

EXERCISE TRAINING AND PERIPHERAL VASCULAR DISEASE

Exercise training has been used to improve functional tolerance to exercise and to diminish symptoms of claudication. Some patients show an improvement in walking distance and a delay in onset of claudication symptoms. In a number of studies, researchers showed that this increase in exercise tolerance is not accompanied by improvement in peripheral blood flow, although they noted an increased oxidative enzyme capacity within skeletal muscle after exercise training. Therefore, an improvement in the efficiency of energy production for muscle contraction may be the basis for symptomatic improvement after exercise training.

Cardiovascular exercise training may be achieved in patients with claudication through the use of combined arm and leg exercise ergometers. Many of these patients achieve a typical training effect with improved oxygen consumption and reduction in heart rate response to standard exercise testing. The incidence of coronary artery disease in patients with established peripheral vascular disease varies from 50 to 80%. Patients with peripheral vascular disease must be evaluated with an arm exercise test before beginning an exercise training program.

SUGGESTED READING

1. Kaplan N: *Clinical Hypertension.* 3rd Ed. Baltimore: Williams & Wilkins, 1985.
2. Lund-Johanson P: Hemodynamic in essential hypertension. *Clin Sci, 59:*343, 1980.
3. Seals D, Hagberg J: The effect of exercise training on human hypertension. *Med Sci Sports Exerc, 16:*207, 1984.
4. Lowenthal DT, et al.: The clinical pharmacology of cardiovascular drugs during exercise. *J Cardiac Rehab, 3:*829, 1983.
5. Zinman B, Vranic M: Diabetes and exercise. *Med Clin North Am, 69:*145, 1985.
6. Painter P, et al.: Exercise capacity in hemodialysis CAPD, and renal transplant patients. *Nephron, 42:*47, 1986.
7. Harter HR, Goldberg AP: Endurance exercise training: An effective modality for hemodialysis patients. *Med Clin North Am, 69:*159, 1985.
8. Blecker ER: Exercise-induced asthma. *Clin Chest Med, 5:*109, 1984.
9. Loke J, et al.: Exercise impairment in chronic obstructive pulmonary disease. *Clin Chest Med, 5:*121, 1984.

CHAPTER 17

PHARMACOLOGIC FACTORS IN EXERCISE AND EXERCISE TESTING

STEVEN P. VAN CAMP

Medications that affect the exercise response or exercise test are taken by many people who exercise regularly, want to begin an exercise program, or undergo exercise tests. These medications may be administered for noncardiovascular as well as cardiovascular conditions. To understand the exercise response and the exercise electrocardiogram of a patient receiving such medications, the actions of these medications must be clearly understood.

Medications may directly affect the exercise response, such as the effects of β-adrenergic blocking agents (beta blockers) on heart rate, blood pressure, and thus myocardial oxygen consumption. Other medications may affect exercise indirectly; an example is the potential for certain diuretics to produce hypokalemia, which may result in the development of cardiac arrhythmias or false-positive results of an exercise electrocardiogram. In this chapter, we address the importance of medications, their actions, side effects, and considerations relevant to exercise and exercise testing.

The acute and chronic physiologic responses to exercise involve changes in sympathetic and parasympathetic tone, heart rate, blood pressure, myocardial contractility, venous return, arterial resistance, fluid loss, and exercise capacity. Any medication that alters, either inhibiting or exaggerating, these responses or the electrocardiogram (which is monitored during an exercise test) may affect the exercise response and exercise test of the patient receiving that medication.

As the effects of medications upon heart rate, blood pressure, myocardial contractility, cardiac rhythm, electrocardiographic findings, and exercise capacity are considered, the physiologic and pathophysiologic status of the patient must also be considered and understood. An important fact to remember is that medications are usually administered because of pathophysiologic abnormalities such as angina pectoris, congestive heart failure, or arrhythmias rather than for the pathologic conditions alone (coronary heart disease, valvular heart disease, or congenital heart disease). Patients should not be considered as homogeneous groups of either "normal," "diseased," or cardiac patients. "Normal" and "diseased" patients vary greatly with respect to exercise capacity, autonomic tone, body size, and general medical status, including orthopedic disorders as well as kidney and liver function. Patients with cardiovascular and pulmonary diseases, diabetes mellitus, and renal failure also have a wide range of pathophysiologic responses to exercise. Among these responses are variations in blood pressure, resting and maximal heart rates, left ventricular function, and exercise-limiting pathophysiologic factors (such as myocardial ischemia, poor left ventricular function, arrhythmias, intermittent claudication, bronchospasm, and pulmonary insufficiency). Another important factor is the individual variation in response to medication (interpatient variability). These variations may result from metabolic or other unknown factors. All of these individual factors must be considered to understand the role of medications in exercise and exercise testing.

In addition to individual patient responses, pharmacologic factors require consideration. Most medications have effects that are dose related. Medications administered in dosages that result in subtherapeutic levels usually have no effects. Within therapeutic ranges, greater effects may occur with larger doses. An adverse response may occur as toxic levels are reached. Many medications interact positively (synergistically) or negatively with other medications. Medications may also induce clinical problems, including arrhythmias, bronchospasm, abnormal ST-T wave responses (the so-called "false-positive" test for myocardial ischemia), hypokalemia, hypovolemia, and depression. Hypokalemia may, in turn, increase the likelihood of cardiac arrhythmias and abnormal ST-T wave changes. Hypovolemia increases the tendency toward orthostatic hypotension, especially in the post-exercise period. Depression affects the desire to exercise rather than the hemodynamic elements of exercise or any parameter measured during an exercise test.

The best approach therefore to understanding the role of medications in exercise and exercise testing is to: (1) understand the physiologic and pathophysiologic responses of the individual patient to exercise and exercise testing; (2) understand the mechanism of action and general actions of the medications, appreciating the individual dose-response factors. To understand the general characteristics of medications within a therapeutic class is important, remembering that sometimes medications within these classes may have variable properties (see sections concerning beta blockers and calcium channel blockers); (3) understand that individual variability occurs in patient responses; (4) apply the generalities of the properties of the medication and the specifics of a patient's circumstances to the exercise test or exercise prescription. Remember that the hemodynamic effects of a medication usually occur only if the medication is administered in therapeutic doses. Finally, observation of a response while the patient is receiving medication can confirm

suspected responses or identify any individual or idiosyncratic responses.

Medications that can be administered to ambulatory (nonhospitalized) patients are discussed. To consider all medications specifically is impossible, and thus the major categories of medications are discussed, along with relevant examples of specific medications. Understanding of most of those medications not included is possible by considering the class to which they belong. Effects of the medications on heart rate, blood pressure, the electrocardiogram, and exercise capacity are indicated when clinically important. Naturally, if a medication results in an increase or decrease in myocardial ischemia, it may have corresponding effects on the symptom of angina pectoris and the electrocardiographic findings.

Generic rather than brand names of medications are used, although it is important to know both terms. For some generic medications, more than one brand name may be available (e.g., Procardia and Adalat are brand names of nifedipine). Brand names of the generic medications discussed in the chapter are listed in Table 17–1.

Not all side effects are discussed, but an attempt has been made to include those related to exercise testing and prescription.

Medications are often used in combination, so consideration of the pharmacologic actions of all drugs is important when predicting the net effect of simultaneously administered medications.

The effects of medications on heart rate, blood pressure, electrocardiographic findings, and exercise capacity are detailed in Table 17–2. These effects are those typically observed, but the factors mentioned previously must, of course, be considered as well.

Medications that are not administered specifically for cardiovascular conditions may still have effects on resting or exercise heart rate, blood pressure, electrocardiographic findings, or exercise capacity. Therefore, they also merit consideration.

THE β-ADRENERGIC BLOCKING AGENTS

The β-adrenergic blocking agents, or beta blockers, are used in the treatment of patients with a variety of cardiovascular and other med-

Table 17–1. Medications Discussed Relative to Exercise and Exercise Testing

Generic name	Brand name	Generic name	Brand name
Beta blockers		*α-Adrenergic blocker*	
Acebutolol	Sectral	Prazosin	Minipress
Atenolol	Tenormin	*Antiadrenergic agents without selective blockade of*	
Metoprolol	Lopressor	*peripheral receptors*	
Nadolol	Corgard	Clonidine	Catapres
Pindolol	Visken	Guanabenz	Wytensin
Propranolol	Inderal	Guanethidine	Ismelin
Timolol	Blocadren	Guanfacine	Tenex
		Methyldopa	Aldomet
Alpha and beta blockers		Reserpine	Serapasil
Labetalol	Trandate, Normodyne	*Antiarrhythmic agents*	
Nitrates and nitroglycerin		Class I	
Isosorbide dinitrate	Isordil	Quinidine	Quinidex, Quinaglute
Nitroglycerin	Nitrostat	Procainamide	Pronestyl, Procan SR
Nitroglycerin ointment	Nitrol ointment	Disopyramide	Norpace
Nitroglycerin patches	Transderm Nitro,	Phenytoin	Dilantin
	Nitro-Dur II, Nitrodisc	Tocainide	Tonocard
		Mexiletine	Mexitil
Calcium channel blockers		Encainide	Enkaid
Diltiazem	Cardizem	Flecainide	Tambocor
Nifedipine	Procardia, Adalat		
Verapamil	Calan, Isoptin	Class II	
		Amiodarone	Cordarone
Digitalis			
Digoxin	Lanoxin	*Bronchodilators*	
		Methylxanthines	
Diuretics		Aminophylline	Theo-Dur
Thiazides		*Sympathomimetic agents*	
Hydrochlorothiazide (HCTZ)	Esidrix	Ephedrine	
"Loop" Furosemide	Lasix	Epinephrine	Adrenalin
Ethacrynic acid	Edecrin	Metaproterenol	Alupent
Potassium-sparing		Albuterol	Proventil, Ventolin
Spironolactone	Aldactone	Isoetharine	Bronkosol
Triamterene	Dyrenium	Terbutaline	Brethine
Amiloride	Midamor		
Combinations		Cromolyn sodium	Intal
Triamterene and		*Hyperlipidemic agents*	
hydrochlorothiazide	Dyazide, Maxzide	Cholestyramine	Questran
Amiloride and		Colestipol	Colestid
hydrochlorothiazide	Moduretic	Clofibrate	Atromid-S
Others		Dextrothyroxine	Choloxin
Metolazone	Zaroxolyn	Gemfibrozil	Lopid
		Lovastatin	Mevacor
Peripheral vasodilators		Nicotinic acid (niacin)	Nicobid
Nonadrendergic		Probucol	Lorelco
Hydralazine	Apresoline		
Minoxidil	Loniten	*Other*	
Angiotensin-converting enzyme (ACE) inhibitors		Dipyridamole	Persantin
Captopril	Capoten	Warfarin	Coumadin
Enalapril	Vasotec	Pentoxifylline	Trental

ical conditions, including angina pectoris, hypertension, previous myocardial infarction, cardiac arrhythmias, essential (familial) tremors, and migraine headaches.

ACTIONS

These drugs exert their effects by competitively blocking β-adrenergic receptors, thereby limiting their stimulation at rest and during periods of exercise and emotional excitement. The β_1 receptors mediate cardiac stimulation, whereas β_2-receptors mediate relaxation of vascular and bronchial smooth muscle. Beta blockers act on both of these types of receptors, although "cardioselective" beta blockers exert a greater effect on β_1 receptors than on β_2-receptors.

Table 17–2. Effects of Medications on Heart Rate, Blood Pressure, Electrocardiographic Findings (ECG), and Exercise Capacity

Medications	Heart rate		Blood pressure [Rest(R) and Exercise (E)]	ECG		Exercise capacity
	Rest	Exercise		Rest	Exercise	
Beta blockers (including labetalol)	↓*	↓	↓	↓ HR*	↓ ischemia†	↑ in patients with angina; ↓ or ↔ in patients without angina
Nitrates	↑	↑ or ↔	↓ (R) ↓ or ↔ (E)	↑ HR	↑ or ↔ HR ↓ ischemia†	↑ in patients with angina; ↔ in patients without angina; ↑ or ↔ in patients with congestive heart failure (CHF)
Calcium channel blockers						
Nifedipine	↑	↑	↓	↑ HR	↑ Hr ↓ ischemia†	↑ in patients with angina; ↔ in patients without angina
Diltiazem	↓	↓	↓	↓ HR	↓ HR ↓ ischemia†	↑ in patients with angina; ↔ in patients without angina
Verapamil	↓	↓	↓	↓ HR	↓ HR ↓ ischemia†	↑ in patients with angina; ↔ in patients without angina
Digitalis	↓ in patients w̄ atrial fibrillation and possibly CHF. Not significantly altered in patients w̄ sinus rhythm	↔	↔	May produce nonspecific ST-T wave changes	May produce ST segment depression	Improved only in patients with atrial fibrillation or in patients with CHF
Diuretics	↔	↔	↔ or ↓	↔	May cause PVCs and "false-positive" test results if hypokalemia occurs	↔, except possibly in patients with CHF (see text)
Vasodilators						
Nonadrenergic vasodilators	↑ or ↔	↑ or ↔	↓	↑ or ↔ HR	↑ or ↔ HR	↔, except ↑ or ↔ in patients with CHF
α-Adrenergic blockers	↔	↔	↓	↔	↔	↔
Antiadrenergic agents without selective blockade of peripheral receptors	↓ or ↔	↓ or ↔	↓	↓ or ↔ HR	↓ or ↔ HR	↔
Antiarrhythmic agents Class I Quinidine Disopyramide	↑ or ↔	↑ or ↔	↑ or ↔ (R) ↔ (E)	May prolong QRS and QT intervals	Quinidine may cause "false-negative" test results	↔
Procainamide Phenytoin Tocainide	↔	↔	↔	May prolong QRS and QT intervals	Procainamide may cause "false positive" test results	↔

Medications	Rest (HR / BP)	Exercise (HR / BP)	ECG (Rest)	ECG (Exercise)	Exercise Capacity
Mexiletine					
Encainide					
Flecainide					
Class II Beta blockers	(see previous entry)				
Class III Amiodarone	↓	→	↕	↕	↕
Class IV Calcium channel blockers	(see previous entry)				↕
Bronchodilators Methylxanthines	↑ or ↔	↑ or ↔	↑ or ↔ HR; may produce PVCs	↑ or ↔ HR; may produce PVCs	Bronchodilators ↑ exercise capacity in patients limited by bronchospasm
Sympathomimetic agents	↑ or ↔	↑, ↔, or ↓	↑ or ↔ HR	↑ or ↔ HR	
Cromolyn sodium	↕	↕	↕	↕	
Corticosteriods	↕	↕	↕		
Hyperlipidemic agents	Clofibrate may provoke arrhythmias, angina in patients with prior myocardial infarction. Dextrothyroxine may ↑ HR and BP at rest and during exercise, provoke arrhythmias, and worsen myocardial ischemia and angina. Nicotinic acid may ↓ BP. Probucol may cause QT interval prolongation. All other hyperlipidemic agents have no effect on HR, BP, and ECG.				↕
Psychotropic medications: Minor tranquilizers Antidepressants	↑ or ↔	↑ or ↔	May ↓ HR and BP by controlling anxiety. No other effects. ↓ or ↔	(see text)	May cause "false-positive" test results
Major tranquilizers	↑ or ↔		↓ or ↔	(see text)	May cause "false-positive" or "false-negative" test results / ↕
Lithium	↕		May cause T-wave changes and arrhythmias	May cause T-wave changes and arrhythmias	
Nicotine	↑ or ↔	↑	↑ or ↔ HR; may provoke ischemia, arrhythmias	↑ or ↔ HR; may provoke ischemia, arrhythmias	↕
Antihistamines	↕		↕	↕	↕
Cold medications with sympathomimetic agents	Effects similar to those described in Sympathomimetic agents, although magnitude of effects is usually diminished.			↕	↔, except ↓ or ↔ in patients with angina / ↕

Table 17–2. Effects of Medications on Heart Rate, Blood Pressure, Electrocardiographic Findings (ECG), and Exercise Capacity (*Continued*)

Medications	Heart rate		Blood pressure [Rest(R) and Exercise (E)]	ECG		Exercise capacity
	Rest	Exercise		Rest	Exercise	
Thyroid medications Only levothyroxine	↑	↑	↑	↑ HR; provoke arrhythmias; ↑ ischemia	↑ HR; provoke arrhythmias; ↑ ischemia	↔, unless angina worsened
Alcohol	↔	↔	Chronic use may have role in ↑ BP	May provoke arrhythmias	May provoke arrhythmias	↔
Hypoglycemic agents Insulin and oral agents	↔	↔	↔	↔	↔	↔
Dipyridamole	↔	↔	↔	↔	↔	↔
Anticoagulants	↔	↔	↔	↔	↔	↔
Antigout medications	↔	↔	↔	↔	↔	↔
Antiplatelet medications	↔	↔	↔	↔	↔	↔
Pentoxifylline	↔	↔	↔	↔	↔	↑ or ↔ in patients limited by intermittent claudication

* Beta blockers with ISA lower resting HR only slightly. ↑, increase; ↔, no effect; ↓, decrease.
† May prevent or delay myocardial ischemia (see text).

The specific effects of beta blockers on heart rate, blood pressure, and the electrocardiogram are detailed in Table 17–2. Heart rate, blood pressure, and myocardial contractility are decreased at rest and with submaximal or maximal exercise. Therefore, myocardial oxygen consumption is decreased. Additionally, as heart rate decreases, diastolic filling time of coronary arteries increases, thus allowing for increased myocardial oxygen supply in comparison to the "unblocked" state. These changes are responsible for the beneficial effects of beta blockers observed in patients with angina pectoris.

Use of beta blockers results in a lower blood pressure, probably by suppressing renin release from the kidneys, decreasing cardiac output, and, possibly, by decreasing central nervous system sympathetic discharge. Other actions include inhibition of platelet aggregation and inhibition of synthesis of thromboxane, a potent vasoconstrictor. Beta blockers are also useful in the management of certain cardiac arrhythmias by virtue of their direct beta blocking actions or by a quinidine-like membrane-stabilizing effect. Beta blockers also appear to improve the prognosis in selected patients after myocardial infarction. The mechanism by which this occurs is unknown, but the antiarrhythmic effects of the beta blockers are probably instrumental.

Patients for whom exercise capacity is limited by angina pectoris experience improved exercise tolerance while being treated with beta blockers. These patients are able to perform more exercise before reaching their myocardial ischemic threshold, with its accompanying angina pectoris and electrocardiographic changes of ischemia. For patients who are not limited by angina pectoris, beta blocker therapy may decrease exercise capacity if significant fatigue is a side effect of this form of therapy. Patients with significant left ventricular dysfunction with or without angina pectoris may experience a decrease in maximal exercise capacity as a result of the adverse effect of the drugs on myocardial contractility (i.e., negative inotropic effect).

Because beta blockers are competitive, reversible antagonists of β-adrenergic stimulation, their effects are dose related, temporary, and dependent upon the endogenous catecholamine concentration of the individual. The general responses are uniform among individuals, but the magnitude of the response varies markedly from patient to patient.

SIDE EFFECTS

Beta blockade may produce peripheral arteriolar constriction by blocking β_2-mediated vasodilation, allowing unopposed α-adrenergically mediated vasoconstriction. Worsening of claudication in people with peripheral vascular disease and complaints of cold extremities thus may result. Other possible side effects include coronary artery vasoconstriction and worsening of coronary artery spasm, also resulting from unopposed vasoconstriction; precipitation or worsening of bronchospasm secondary to inhibition of β_2-receptor-mediated relaxation of bronchial smooth muscle; and possible congestive heart failure because of depression of myocardial contractility. Because of their effects on heart rate and atrioventricular (AV) nodal conduction, beta blockers may result in bradycardia or AV block. Beta blocker therapy may prove hazardous to patients with diabetes who receive insulin therapy because beta blockers depress the sympathetic nervous system-mediated response to, and warning signs of, hypoglycemia. These agents inhibit catecholamine-induced glycogenolysis and the signs of hypoglycemia, including nervousness and tachycardia.

Therefore, beta blocker therapy is generally contraindicated in patients with peripheral vascular disease and claudication, coronary artery spasm, congestive heart failure (or poor left ventricular function), sinus node disease, and who receive insulin therapy for diabetes mellitus.

Adverse lipid effects of increased triglycerides and decreased HDL cholesterol have been reported, although these effects are apparently less prominent with cardioselective beta blockers. Abrupt withdrawal of beta blocker therapy may result in acceleration of angina pectoris, tachycardia, myocardial infarction, sudden death, and hypertension (the propranolol withdrawal rebound phenomenon). These effects appear related to increased sensitivity to β-adrenergic stimulation after chronic beta blocker administration. Bothersome side effects of beta blockers that affect the central nervous system are fatigue, depression, and vivid or bizarre dreams.

VARIABLE CHARACTERISTICS

Cardioselectivity is a relative property by which certain beta blockers exert greater effects on β_1-receptors than on β_2-receptors. Theoretically, this property results in fewer side effects and also allows persons with peripheral vascular disease and bronchospasm to use beta blockers. Atenolol and metoprolol are cardioselective beta blockers. This property is *relative* in that it is lost at higher doses and does not occur to an absolute extent (see Table 17–3).

Beta blockers with *intrinsic sympathomimetic activity (ISA)* retain their beta blocking action, but do exert some sympathetic stimulation, primarily at rest. This property results in only a slight decline in resting heart rate and is helpful in treating patients in whom bradycardia would otherwise limit the use of beta blockers. Acebutolol and pindolol are beta blockers that possess ISA.

The *lipid solubility* of a beta blocker determines its duration of action. Beta blockers with low lipid solubility are metabolized by the liver at slow rates and are excreted primarily by the renal route. Additionally, they do not cross the blood-brain barrier. These beta blockers, such as atenolol and nadolol, have the longest duration of action (approximately 24 hours) and theoretically are less likely to cause central nervous system side effects (depression, nightmares, and possibly fatigue) than other beta blockers.

Labetalol is a medication that exerts both alpha and beta blocking effects. Thus, its actions are a combination of both of these effects, although the beta blocker effects predominate.

EXERCISE AND EXERCISE TESTING CONSIDERATIONS

Researchers have shown that although the heart rate and blood pressure response to exercise is blunted in the beta-blocked state, the acute administration of beta blockers does not affect maximal oxygen consumption ($\dot{V}O_{2\,max}$) or maximal exercise capacity. The ability of patients receiving beta blocker therapy to train is controversial, but it appears that a training effect (an increase in $\dot{V}O_{2\,max}$ or exercise capacity after periods of training) can be achieved despite long-term therapy. Beta blocker therapy also apparently does not change the relationship between percent $\dot{V}O_{2\,max}$ and percent of maximal heart rate. Therefore, the usual methods to calculate target heart rate for exercise prescriptions can still be used with reasonable accuracy, with consideration, of course, that the maximal heart rate and thus also the training heart rate will be lower in persons receiving beta blockers. It is the maximal heart rate with beta blocker therapy that must be used for prescription purposes. (See the discussion of exercise prescription at the end of this chapter for target heart rate calculation for patients receiving beta blockers.)

Beta blockers are said to cause false-negative results on electrocardiographic tests for myocardial ischemia. A more appropriate way to look at the situation follows. If the level of myocardial oxygen consumption at which a patient develops ischemia is exceeded, he will still develop ischemia, even while receiving beta blocker therapy. Signs of ischemia would be present on the exercise electrocardiogram as would be true in the untreated situation. If beta blocker therapy prevents the rate pressure product from reaching the point at which myocardial ischemia occurs, neither myocardial ischemia nor electrocardiograpic signs of myocardial ischemia will occur. Often the maximal exercise heart rate in patients receiving beta blocker therapy is blunted to the degree that the tests should be considered *suboptimal* for the purposes of diagnosis rather than negative for the presence of myocardial ischemia. In certain

Table 17–3. Characteristics of Beta Blockers

Specific beta blockers	Cardioselectivity	Intrinsic sympathomimetic activity	Lipid solubility
cebutolol (Sectral)	—*	+	Moderate
Atenolol (Tenormin)	+	—	Low
Metoprolol (Lopressor)	+	—	Moderate
Nadolol (Corgard)	—	—	Low
Pindolol (Visken)	—	+	Moderate
Propranolol (Inderal)	—	—	High
Timolol (Blocadren)	—	—	Low

* +, presence of characteristic; —, absence of characteristic.

situations, therefore, it may be appropriate to discontinue medication before a diagnostic exercise test is performed.

NITRATES

Nitrates are the oldest and most commonly used medications for angina pectoris.

ACTIONS

Nitrates directly relax vascular smooth muscle by an unknown mechanism, exerting their primary effects on the *venous* system and a lesser effect on the arterial system. The resulting venodilation decreases ventricular volume and end-diastolic pressure (preload), and the arteriolar vasodilation decreases systemic vascular resistance and arterial blood pressure (afterload). These specific effects on heart rate, blood pressure, and the electrocardiographic findings are detailed in Table 17–2. An increase in resting heart rate, and to a lesser extent the heart rate during exercise, occurs through a baroreceptor-mediated reflex tachycardia that occurs in response to the arterial vasodilation. Blood pressure declines with the subject at rest and may decline during exercise. At rest, a reflex tachycardia may be noted electrocardiographically. During exercise, ischemic electrocardiographic changes may be prevented, decreased, or delayed. They occur to a lesser extent at similar submaximal workloads when compared with the untreated state; in other words, greater amounts of exercise may be performed before the development of ischemia.

Nitrates are administered in multiple forms and dosages by numerous routes. The hemodynamic effects to be described, as is true for all medications, are seen only if nitrates are administered in therapeutic doses. Nitrates especially may be taken at subtherapeutic doses. This information regarding dosage must be considered when evaluating or anticipating hemodynamic effects.

Patients in whom exercise capacity is limited by angina pectoris show improvement with nitrate administration because of prevention, reduction, or delay in ischemia, and hence angina pectoris. In patients with congestive heart failure, nitrates may improve exercise capacity through a reduction in pulmonary venous pressure and aortic impedance. Nitrates have no effect on the exercise capacity of patients without myocardial ischemia, angina pectoris, or congestive heart failure.

The hemodynamic effects of nitrates, in concert, lower myocardial oxygen consumption, an effect of primary clinical importance in the treatment of angina pectoris. Additionally, coronary blood flow to ischemic areas of myocardium may improve because of increased collateral flow or decreased ventricular diastolic pressure with reduced subendocardial vessel compression. Thus, nitrates may increase myocardial supply as well as decrease myocardial oxygen demand in patients with coronary heart disease, although the latter effect is of greater clinical importance. Another hemodynamic effect of nitrates, resulting from their vasodilatory capacity, is the reduction of impedance to ventricular systolic emptying. Although nitrates have no direct effect upon myocardial contractility, they may indirectly improve it by reducing ischemia and impedance to systolic emptying.

By the aforementioned actions, angina pectoris is prevented, reduced, or relieved in patients receiving therapeutic doses of nitrates. Nitrates improve exercise capacity before angina pectoris occurs, and decrease or eliminate electrocardiographic findings of ischemia at submaximal work loads when compared with the untreated state.

The prevention and relief of coronary artery spasm occur with nitrates, but otherwise the net effect on the coronary vasculature is of questionable significance. High-grade coronary artery stenoses are unlikely to be significantly improved with nitroglycerin. Eccentric coronary artery narrowings, however, may be improved by dilation of the uninvolved portion of the vessel. Improvement in congestive heart failure symptoms occurs because of the decrease in preload and decrease in impedance to ventricular systolic emptying.

FORMS AND ROUTES OF ADMINISTRATION

Nitrates can be administered in multiple forms and by multiple routes: (1) sublingual, (2) oral (long acting), (3) aerosol oral spray, (4) intravenous, and (5) transdermal (ointments and patches).

Larger doses are necessary when nitrates are

administered orally because much of the drug is removed from the blood by the liver before reaching the systemic circulation. These medications may be used for the treatment of angina pectoris on an as-needed basis or may be administered prophylactically to prevent or to reduce the likelihood of angina. Typically, medication doses are adjusted until the desired effects are achieved or bothersome side effects occur. Note that marked differences occur between patients with regard to the amount of nitrates that may be required for therapeutic effect or before side effects occur. Additionally, patients receiving nitrates on a chronic basis may develop tolerance, with decreasing effect noted with chronic use.

SIDE EFFECTS

Postural hypotension that results from a decrease in systemic blood pressure, headaches related to cerebral blood vessel dilatation, and flushing sensations resulting from peripheral vasodilation are the most bothersome side effects of nitrate usage. These side effects often decrease or disappear in time with continued administration, or a decrease in dosage may be required.

EXERCISE AND EXERCISE TESTING CONSIDERATIONS

Prophylactic use of sublingual nitroglycerin is often effective in preventing angina pectoris. Thus, before an activity that the patient knows might provoke angina, sublingual nitroglycerin may be used to prevent or reduce its occurrence. The possible occurrence of postural hypotension resulting from peripheral vasodilation merits consideration, especially in the post-exercise period. Exercise prescriptions involving target heart rates need no alteration if nitrates are administered to a patient because these agents do not significantly affect heart rate response.

CALCIUM CHANNEL BLOCKERS

The most recently available category of potent cardiovascular medications is the calcium channel blockers, also known as calcium antagonists or calcium blockers.

ACTIONS

Calcium channel blockers act by blocking a variety of calcium-dependent processes in vascular smooth muscle and myocardial cells. This action occurs through selective blockade of transmembrane calcium flow and the resulting slow inward calcium current. Thus, calcium entry into cardiac and smooth muscle cells is limited.

Although the three currently available calcium channel blockers have a similar mechanism of action, they have variable vasodilatory, negative inotropic, and electrophysiologic effects. Nifedipine results in the greatest reduction of coronary and peripheral vascular resistance without significant inotropic or electrophysiologic effects. Verapamil and diltiazem have lesser but significant coronary and peripheral vasodilatory effects, with modest negative inotropic and electrophysiologic effects. The resultant effects on heart rate, blood pressure, electrocardiographic findings, and exercise capacity are detailed in Table 17–2.

All three calcium channel blockers are useful in the treatment of angina pectoris, coronary artery spasm, and hypertension. The beneficial action in angina pectoris results primarily from a decrease in myocardial oxygen consumption by way of the effects on blood pressure (reduction) and heart rate (reduction). These medications additionally may increase myocardial oxygen supply when coronary artery spasm plays a role in the myocardial ischemia. The relief or prevention of coronary artery spasm occurs because of direct coronary artery vasodilation. Peripheral vasodilation causes a reduction in blood pressure levels with nifedipine having the greatest and diltiazem the least effects. Whereas diltiazim and verapamil decrease heart rate, nifedipine does not.

Verapamil is the only calcium channel blocker with significantly useful antiarrhythmic properties. It is used primarily in the treatment and prevention of paroxysmal supraventricular tachycardia. Verapamil has also been used in the treatment of patients with hypertrophic cardiomyopathy.

Because these medications may be administered with other types of medication, including nitrates and beta blockers, the net effects are related to the sum of the hemodynamic and electrophysiologic effects.

SIDE EFFECTS

Although no adverse effects result from the coronary vasodilation of calcium channel blockers, the resulting peripheral vasodilation may produce symptoms of headache, flushing, orthostatic hypotension, dizziness, or syncope. Nifedipine is the most troublesome in terms of these side effects and is usually contraindicated in patients with low blood pressure.

The negative inotropic effects of verapamil and diltiazem are generally counterbalanced by the peripheral vasodilatory effects; thus congestive heart failure is rarely a problem. Verapamil and diltiazem may produce heart block through depression of AV conduction, although this adverse effect is usually limited to patients with conduction system disease.

Thus, the administration of verapamil and diltiazem to patients with poor left ventricular functions, bradycardia, sick sinus syndrome, and high-grade AV block is usually contraindicated.

Constipation may be a bothersome side effect of verapamil, which inhibits intestinal smooth muscle contraction. Peripheral edema may occur with nifedipine use, and less frequently with verapamil, because of their venodilating effects. This edema is usually treated effectively with diuretic therapy. In contrast to beta blockers, none of the calcium channel blockers result in bronchospasm. Increases in serum digitalis levels are noted in patients receiving verapamil, principally because this drug can cause a decrease in the renal excretion of digitalis.

Verapamil and diltiazem should be used with beta blockers only with caution because all of these medications have negative inotropic and electrophysiologic effects, increasing the likelihood of congestive heart failure, heart block, and bradycardia with combined administration.

EXERCISE AND EXERCISE TRAINING CONSIDERATIONS

The calcium channel blockers do not limit the ability of an individual to achieve a training effect. Because of their effects on the heart rate and blood pressure response to exercise, an ex-

ercise prescription should be calculated ideally by using data from an exercise test performed with the patient following the usual medical regimen.

DIGITALIS

Since its discovery, more than 200 years ago, by William Withering, digitalis has been used for the treatment of congestive heart failure.

ACTIONS

All digitalis glycosides possess similar positive inotropic and electrophysiologic effects. Digitalis preparations inhibit the magnesium and ATP-dependent, sodium and potassium-activated transport enzyme complex known as Na^+, K^+-ATPase. In so doing, digitalis preparations limit the movement of sodium and potassium across the myocardial cell membrane. Subsequently, as the sodium concentration increases intracellularly, the sodium-calcium exchange increases, resulting in increased intracellular calcium concentration. This increase may be responsible for the enhancement of myocardial contractility (positive inotropic action). The electrophysiologic effects of digitalis may also be related to the inhibition of Na^+, K^+-ATPase. Digitalis does not directly affect heart rate or blood pressure at rest or with exercise. Parasympathomimetic (vagal) effects may produce a decrease in heart rate, although typically no significant change in heart rate occurs. Exceptions are the slowing of the ventricular response in patients with atrial fibrillation receiving digitalis as well as patients with congestive heart failure who experience a decrease in heart rate as the congestive heart failure state improves. The effects of digitalis on heart rate, blood pressure, the electrocardiographic findings, and exercise capacity are outlined in Table 17–2.

Digitalis has beneficial effects in the treatment of congestive heart failure and atrial arrhythmias. Both the control of the ventricular response in chronic atrial fibrillation or atrial flutter and the prevention of recurrences of paroxysmal atrial fibrillation, atrial flutter, and paroxysmal supraventricular tachycardia occur with digitalis therapy. Multiple forms of digitalis glycosides are available. Digoxin (Lanoxin) is the most commonly used form of digitalis.

SIDE EFFECTS

The side effects associated with digitalis are almost nonexistent unless serum digitalis levels reach the toxic range. Signs and symptoms of digitalis toxicity include variable neurologic and visual symptoms and, most prominently, cardiac arrhythmias. Almost any cardiac arrhythmia may occur, but classic digitalis toxic arrhythmias include premature ventricular complexes (PVCs), AV junctional escape rhythms, and AV block.

EXERCISE AND EXERCISE TESTING CONSIDERATIONS

Because digitalis preparations do not significantly affect heart rate, blood pressure, or exercise capacity, except as previously indicated, the most important aspect of its use in exercise testing and training is the possible development of false-positive results on the exercise electrocardiogram. Digitalis therapy may produce exercise-induced ST-segment depression in patients without coronary artery disease or myocardial ischemia. So that digitalis is not a factor in the exercise test, its use should be stopped 10 to 14 days before the exercise test, if clinically feasible.

DIURETICS

Diuretics increase renal excretion of salt and water and are used primarily for the treatment of hypertension, congestive heart failure, and peripheral edema.

ACTIONS

Diuretics prevent sodium reabsorption at different sites of the nephron, including the proximal and distal tubules and along the loop of Henle. Additionally, some diuretics increase urinary potassium excretion. A reduction of arteriolar sodium content results in decreased peripheral vascular resistance and, subsequently, blood pressure elevation to a mild degree. In congestive heart failure and edematous states, intravascular volume and edema decrease.

The major diuretics include the thiazide diuretics, metolazone, the "loop" diuretics (furosemide and ethacrynic acid), and the potassium-sparing diuretics (spironolactone, triamterene, and amiloride). These diuretics vary in chemical structure, site of action, and potassium-sparing ability. Additionally, combinations of a thiazide (hydrochlorothiazide) and a potassium-sparing diuretic (triamterene) are marketed as Dyazide and Maxzide; the combination of hydrochlorothiazide and amiloride is available as Moduretic.

Diuretics have no effect on heart rate at rest or with exercise, although they may lower blood pressure. If hypokalemia (low serum potassium) results, PVCs and repolarization changes simulating ischemia may occur, resulting in false-positive results of a test for ischemia using the exercise electrocardiogram. Diuretics have no effect on exercise capacity, except as they act to control congestive heart failure. A summary of these effects is provided in Table 17–2.

SIDE EFFECTS

Multiple fluid and electrolyte abnormalities may occur, including decreases in serum levels of potassium, sodium, and magnesium and increases in serum levels of uric acid and glucose. Hypokalemic, hypochloremic alkalosis may also occur. Adverse serum lipid effects of increased cholesterol, low-density lipoprotein (LDL)-cholesterol, and triglycerides have also been reported. Another potential problem is intravascular volume depletion (hypovolemia), resulting in decreases in cardiac output, renal perfusion, and blood pressure.

EXERCISE TESTING AND TRAINING CONSIDERATIONS

Because diuretics do not affect heart rate or exercise capacity, no alteration in exercise prescription is necessary. The potential to produce hypokalemia and hypovolemia are the most important characteristics of these drugs in exercise testing and training. As noted previously, PVCs and false-positive test results for ischemia may occur if the patient is hypokalemic at the time of an exercise electrocardiogram. Hypokalemia may occur even with the administration or prescription of potassium supplements or the use of potassium-sparing diuretics.

Therefore, checking for hypokalemia in patients receiving diuretics, especially before stress tests, is important.

Diuretic-induced hypovolemia may occur, increasing the vulnerability of a patient to hypotension in the post-exercise period when peripheral vasodilatation occurs. This side effect is of even greater concern after prolonged periods of exercise when dehydration may compound the problem.

PERIPHERAL VASODILATORS

Peripheral vasodilators are used in the treatment of congestive heart failure and hypertension. These agents are subsequently discussed according to their mechanism of action.

NONADRENERGIC VASODILATORS

Nonadrenergic vasodilators include hydralazine, minoxidil, captopril, and enalapril. Each of these produces peripheral vasodilatation. Hydralazine and minoxidil produce direct vascular smooth muscle dilatation, whereas captopril and enalapril produce vasodilation through angiotensin-converting enzyme inhibition. The resulting vasodilation lowers blood pressure and may improve left ventricular function in patients with depressed left ventricular function. Thus, these drugs are used to treat individuals with hypertension and congestive heart failure. The effects of vasodilators on heart rate, blood pressure, the electrocardiographic findings, and exercise capacity are described in Table 17–2.

Side Effects

Each of these drugs may have multiple side effects. In relation to exercise testing and training, however, the reflex tachycardia that may occur, especially with hydralazine and minoxidil use, is the most important. This tachycardia may cause a worsening of angina pectoris as a result of increased myocardial oxygen demand. The concurrent use of beta blockers is useful in preventing this side effect from occurring. Post-exercise hypotension may be accentuated by any of these medications, which lower blood pressure.

THE α-ADRENERGIC BLOCKERS

Prazosin, an α-adrenergic blocking agent, results in peripheral vasodilation and subsequent lowering of blood pressure. Its effects on heart rate, blood pressure, electrocardiographic findings, and exercise capacity are summarized in Table 17–2. Prazosin lowers blood pressure at rest and during exercise but has no effect on heart rate, the results of the electrocardiogram, or exercise capacity.

ANTIADRENERGIC AGENTS WITHOUT SELECTIVE BLOCKADE OF PERIPHERAL RECEPTORS

Medications in this class include methyldopa, clonidine, guanabenz, guanfacine, reserpine, and guanethidine. The first four medications suppress central nervous sympathetic outflow through central α-adrenergic stimulation. Reserpine depletes norepinephrine stored in peripheral nerve endings, and guanethedine directly inhibits norepinephrine release. The effects of these medications on heart rate, blood pressure, electrocardiographic findings, and exercise capacity are summarized in Table 17–2. These medications may decrease resting and exercise heart rate, although the effects are usually slight. Resting and exercise blood pressure levels are diminished. No effect is noted electrocardiographically or in regard to exercise capacity.

Side Effects

Methyldopa, reserpine, and guanethidine have the potential to produce orthostatic hypotension, which may be more serious immediately after exercise. Clonidine typically does not produce orthostatic or exercise-induced hypotension. Reserpine may cause depression, increased fatigue, and decreased desire for exercise.

EXERCISE AND EXERCISE TESTING CONSIDERATIONS

Although a gradual "cool down" is often helpful in preventing hypotension after exercise, patients receiving medications known to cause hypotension should be monitored closely. The effects of the medications on the exercise prescription are related to their effects on heart rate (see Table 17-2). Ideally, the exercise prescription for patients receiving those medications that affect heart rate should be based on their exercise test results while medicated.

ANTIARRHYTHMIC AGENTS

Antiarrhythmic medications used in the treatment of patients with cardiac arrhythmias are classified by their electrophysiologic effects. Most of these agents do not have significant effects on heart rate, blood pressure, exercise capacity, or exercise training, but they may have effects on the exercise electrocardiogram. Exceptions to this statement include β-adrenergic blocking agents and calcium channel blockers, which were discussed previously. These medications may be used for a variety of arrhythmias. As noted previously, digitalis also may be used in the management of cardiac arrhythmias.

Many antiarrhythmic agents do not have significant direct effects on hemodynamic and exercise parameters; however, indirect effects may occur through medication-induced autonomic nervous system effects. By improving or preventing significant arrhythmia, these drugs may improve a patient's physiologic status and exercise capacity.

Class I antiarrhythmic medications include quinidine, procainamide, disopyramide, phenytoin, tocainide, mexiletine, encainide, and flecainide. These medications have the electrophysiologic effects of decreasing conduction velocity, excitability, and automaticity. They are myocardial depressants, some of which have peripheral vasodilatation effects. These drugs have no significant effects on heart rate, with the exception of quinidine and disopyramide, which may elevate heart rates at rest and at low exercise work loads through their parasympathomimetic effects. These medications may lower resting blood pressure, but typically they have no effect on exercising blood pressure. These agents may produce prolongation of QRS complex and/or QT interval because of their effects on impulse conduction velocity. Quinidine use can produce false-negative results on exercise electrocardiograms; procainamide has been reported to cause false-positive results on exercise electrocardiograms. Little other information exists concerning the effects

of these medications, especially with regard to the newer drugs—flecainide, mexiletine, encainide, and tocainide—on the exercise electrocardiograms.

Class II and IV antiarrhythmic agents, β-adrenergic blockers, and calcium channel blockers, respectively, were previously discussed. Class III antiarrhythmic agents include amiodarone. This drug slows the heart rate at rest and during exercise through noncompetitive adrenergic inhibition. Amiodarone does not exert significant effects on blood pressure, and no significant effects on the resting or exercise electrocardiogram or the exercise capacity are known.

SIDE EFFECTS

These medications have multiple individual side effects. The possibility of myocardial depression and precipitation of congestive heart failure by disopyramide is the side effect of greatest clinical importance with regard to exercise testing and training. Any of these drugs, however, may have proarrhythmic effects (the capacity to worsen the arrhythmias for which they are administered).

EXERCISE AND EXERCISE TESTING CONSIDERATIONS

Exercise tests for the purpose of exercise prescription need not be performed while the patient is receiving medications, because these antiarrhythmic agents do not significantly affect heart rates, with the possible exception of amiodarone and quinidine. Because of their effect on cardiac rhythm, however, it would be ideal if the patient were receiving these medications at the time of the test.

BRONCHODILATORS

Bronchodilators include theophylline preparations and sympathomimetic medications. Bronchodilators are administered to correct or prevent bronchial smooth muscle constriction in patients with asthma or other forms of pulmonary disease in which bronchospasm occurs. They may be administered by a variety of routes, on a continuous or intermittent basis. By preventing or reversing bronchospasm, these

PATHOPHYSIOLOGY **149**

medications increase exercise capacity in patients who are otherwise limited by bronchospasm. They have no effect, however, on exercise capacity of people who are not so limited.

Methylxanthines, including aminophylline and theophylline, produce bronchodilatation by increasing intracellular quantities of cyclic AMP through inhibition of the enzyme phosphodiesterase. Methylxanthine use may result in increased heart rates and the appearance of cardiac arrhythmias, including PVCs as well as nausea and vomiting.

Sympathomimetic agents may also be prescribed for patients with bronchospasm. These medications have variable cardiovascular effects depending on their preferential stimulatory effects on β_1 (cardiac) or β_2 (bronchial smooth muscle) receptors. Drugs with primary or significant β_1 effects are likely to produce elevated heart rates and, possibly, hypertension and PVCs. These drugs include ephedrine, epinephrine, and metaproterenol. Drugs with primarily β_2 effects are less likely to cause these changes, but may produce systemic vasodilation and compensatory tachycardia. These agents include albuterol, isoetharine, and terbutaline. None of these medications, however, have pure β_1 or β_2 effects.

Cromolyn sodium (a mast cell stabilizer taken by inhalation) and corticosteroids (taken orally or by inhalation) have no effects on heart rate, blood pressure, or electrocardiographic findings, with one exception. Corticosteroids administered in moderate to high oral doses may result in hypertension.

HYPERLIPIDEMIC AGENTS

Hyperlipidemic agents may be administered to patients with and without cardiovascular disease in the treatment of abnormal elevations of serum lipids. Hyperlipidemic medications include cholestyramine, clofibrate, colestipol, dextrothyroxine, gemfibrozil, lovastatin, nicotinic acid, and probucol. They act by a variety of mechanisms, but few have significant hemodynamic or electrocardiographic effects. An exception is dextrothyroxine, which may produce elevations of heart rate and blood pressure; cardiac arrhythmias; and in patients with coronary heart disease, increases in myocardial ischemia and angina. The side effects of nicotinic acid

include flushing, decrease in blood pressure, and headaches. Clofibrate has been associated with an increase in arrhythmias, angina, and claudication in patients with previous myocardial infarction. Probucol may cause QT-interval prolongation.

PSYCHOTROPIC MEDICATIONS

Psychotropic medications are used in the treatment of a variety of emotional and psychiatric disorders. They may be categorized as: (1) minor tranquilizers or antianxiety agents, (2) antidepressants, (3) antipsychotic agents, and (4) lithium carbonate.

MINOR TRANQUILIZERS

Minor tranquilizers, including diazepam, do not have significant effects on hemodynamics, exercise capacity, or electrocardiographic findings, with the exception of possibly lowering heart rate and blood pressure as they control anxiety.

ANTIDEPRESSANTS

Antidepressants include tricyclic antidepressants and monoamine oxidase (MAO) inhibitors. Tricyclic antidepressants appear to act by blocking the uptake of norepinephrine in central nervous system synapses. Their effects include an anticholinergic effect and a quinidine-like effect, which may result in an elevation of heart rate and an increase or decrease in atrial and ventricular arrhythmias; a lower blood pressure, and multiple potential electrocardiographic changes, including an increase in the PR interval and the QT interval and ST-T wave changes. These medications potentially may produce false-positive results in exercise electrocardiograms. MAO inhibitors act by blocking the breakdown of norepinephrine in the central nervous system. They may produce orthostatic hypotension, but the most serious side effect is a hypertensive crisis, which may occur if these medications interact with certain drugs, including sympathomimetic agents and related compounds or foods with high concentrations of tyramine.

ANTIPSYCHOTIC MEDICATIONS, MAJOR TRANQUILIZERS

Phenothiazines are the major category of antipsychotic agents or major tranquilizers. These drugs have anticholinergic and direct myocardial depressant effects in addition to producing α-adrenergic blockade. These properties may result in elevated heart rate; decreased blood pressure, especially orthostatic hypotension; and electrocardiographic changes including increased PR and QT intervals, QRS widening, and ST-T wave changes. Various arrhythmias may also occur. These drugs may also have the potential to produce false-positive and false-negative results on exercise electrocardiograms.

LITHIUM CARBONATE

Lithium carbonate is used primarily to treat manic-depressive illnesses. It has a minimal effect on hemodynamic variables. Possible electrocardiographic changes include T-wave changes and arrhythmias. Whether this medication may effect changes on the exercise electrocardiogram is not clear.

NICOTINE

Nicotine from cigarette smoking as well as smokeless tobacco results in the release of epinephrine and norepinephrine. In addition, structures activated by the release of acetylcholine are stimulated by nicotine. The resulting effects include increases in heart rate as well as systolic, diastolic, and pulse pressures. Angina and myocardial ischemia may be exacerbated, with resultant changes evident on the exercise electrocardiogram. No evidence exists that nicotine causes false-positive results on the exercise electrocardiograms. Additionally, nicotine may produce atrial or ventricular arrhythmias.

ANTIHISTAMINES AND COLD MEDICATIONS

Antihistamines have no effects on hemodynamic variables, the findings of resting or exercise electrocardiograms, or exercise capacity. These medications may, however, be combined with sympathomimetics, such as pseudoephedrine, in some cold remedies. Thus any effects, including elevated heart rates and possibly elevated blood pressure, are related to the sympathomimetic agent. Sympathomimetic agents do not affect electrocardiographic findings or exercise capacity (see *Bronchodilators*).

THYROID MEDICATIONS

The only thyroid medications that might have an effect on exercise or exercise testing are natural and synthetic forms of levothyroxine. These agents may produce elevations of heart rate and blood pressure; cardiac arrhythmias; and, in patients with coronary heart disease, increases in myocardial ischemia and angina.

ALCOHOL

Alcohol may act primarily as a myocardial depressant when ingested on a chronic basis. Chronic alcohol intake may be a contributing factor in the development of hypertension. It may also provoke arrhythmias. Alcohol does not change the results of resting or exercise electrocardiograms, although its use may blunt the appreciation of the symptom of angina on the part of the patient despite the presence of myocardial ischemia.

HYPOGLYCEMIC AGENTS

Hypoglycemic agents, including oral agents and insulin, have no effect on heart rate, blood pressure, electrocardiographic findings, or exercise capacity.

OTHER MEDICATIONS

Dipyridamole is currently used for its antiplatelet effects. It does dilate small (resistance) vessels, but has little value in the treatment of myocardial ischemia. These vessels are also acted on by adenosine, an endogenous vasodilator. Dipyridamole has no significant hemodynamic, electrocardiographic, or exercise effects. Other medications that have no effect on hemodynamic variables or electrocardiographic findings include anticoagulants (heparin or warfarin), antigout medications, and antiplatelet medications.

Pentoxifylline has no effect on hemodynamic variables or the electrocardiogram, but reportedly increases exercise capacity in patients limited by intermittent claudication. This effect apparently occurs through improved blood flow and oxygenation of ischemic tissue by lowering blood viscosity and improving red blood cell flexibility.

APPLICATION TO EXERCISE TESTS

When exercise testing is performed, numerous factors must be remembered and considered. First, remember the indication for the exercise test. Is it being performed for diagnostic or prognostic reasons, for the evaluation of treatment, or for exercise prescription purposes? Tests performed for diagnostic or prognostic reasons are often best performed while patients are not taking medications. To understand an individual's response, however, having patients continue their medications at full dose is often best.

Secondly, the dosage and time of administration of any medication taken before a test should be recorded when that medication is known to affect heart rate, blood pressure, myocardial contractility, and cardiac rhythm. This information is necessary for proper test interpretation and comparison with subsequent tests. Also remember that exercise tests for diagnostic purposes are not 100% accurate, i.e., they are neither 100% sensitive nor specific. Because medications may further alter the sensitivity or specificity of the exercise test, discontinuation of medications before an exercise test merits consideration to enhance specificity or sensitivity. Ideally, exercise tests conducted for prescriptive purposes should be performed while patients are taking the medications that they will receive while training.

A significant change in the medication dosage or schedule may indicate a need for repeat exercise testing for prescription purposes. This need is especially great when the medication

has significant effects on the heart rate and blood pressure response to exercise. If it is not feasible to retest a patient after changes in the medical regimen, knowledge of the pharmacologic effects of medications and the clinical status of the patient usually allows appropriate adjustments in target heart rate and exercise prescriptions.

EXERCISE PRESCRIPTION

Modifications of the exercise prescription are not based solely on medication administration, although they may be appropriate for any pathophysiologic state that is incompletely treated, such as reduction in target heart rate to avoid myocardial ischemia. Medications that affect determinants of myocardial oxygen consumption (heart rate, blood pressure, and myocardial contractility) may have significant effects on the exercise prescription. Because most of these effects are dose related, the exercise prescription can often be calculated by using maximal and resting heart rates obtained from the subject while receiving medications at the time of the exercise test. The exercise prescription is usually not affected if medications do not alter the heart rate or blood pressure response to exercise.

No medications are known to limit the ability to train. Regarding the issue of whether medications enhance exercise capacity and performance, authorities state that exercise capacity is improved only insofar as exercise-limiting, pathophysiologic abnormalities, such as myocardial ischemia, arrhythmias, and bronchospasm, can be eliminated or reduced. Medications do not otherwise improve exercise capacity.

Calculation of target heart rates for patients receiving beta blockers can be performed in the following manner. Because the relationship between exercise intensity and the percent of maximal heart rate is essentially preserved when a person is receiving beta blocker therapy, the target heart rate range can be calculated by using resting and maximal exercise heart rates (if the latter is known) during medical therapy. For example, with the use of the Karvonen formula, if the desired target heart rate range is 70 to 85% of the maximal heart rate reserve for a person receiving beta blocker therapy, who has a resting heart rate of 55 and a maximal exercising heart rate of 135, the calculation is:

Maximal HR	135
Resting HR (RHR)	− 55
HR Reserve	80
70% × 80 = 56	56 + 55 (RHR) = 111
85% × 80 = 68	68 + 55 (RHR) = 123

Thus, 70 to 85% of maximal HR reserve during beta blocker therapy is 111 to 123 (target heart rate range). If the percent of maximal HR is used to calculate the target heart rate range, the following calculation is appropriate:

For 75% of max HR (135), 75% × 135 = 101

The target heart rate ranges are thus lower for persons receiving beta blockers, but the new ranges are appropriate because they represent the correct percent of maximal capacity for the exerciser.

REFERENCES

1. American College of Sports Medicine: *Guidelines for Exercise Testing and Prescription.* Philadelphia: Lea & Febiger, 1986.
2. Braunwald E: *Heart Disease—A Textbook of Cardiovascular Medicine.* Philadelphia: W.B. Saunders, 1984.
3. Ellestad MH: *Stress Testing—Principles and Practice.* Philadelphia: F.A. Davis, 1986.
4. Wenger NK: Cardiovascular drugs: Effects on exercise testing and exercise training of the coronary patient. In *Exercise and the Heart.* Edited by NK Wenger. Philadelphia: F.A. Davis, 1985.

HEALTH APPRAISAL
AND EXERCISE TESTING

18

HEALTH APPRAISAL

L. KENT SMITH

The quest for fitness attracts an increasing number of men and women in the population. The role of the health care professional in guiding this quest, therefore, assumes increasing importance. As more individuals seek guidance and professional counsel in the achievement of their fitness goals, the responsibility of the health care professional in providing an appropriate and thorough appraisal of their state of health and fitness is essential. The appraisal of an individual's true level of fitness encompasses a broad measurement of their health status. This measurement includes the appropriate documentation of behaviors as they affect health status, the health history of an individual, and essential physiologic measurements, with appropriate comparison to well-established parameters that define the optimal health status of an individual.

HEALTH BEHAVIORS

DIET

Food choices affect various parameters of health. The clear linkage between dietary habits and the development of several disease states in the American population has been unequivo-

cally established. Most clear cut is a linkage between saturated fat and cholesterol content of a diet and the development of narrowed arteries —the atherosclerotic process. The mediator in this process is the elevation of specific cholesterol-containing elements in the blood. Most specifically, elevation of either total cholesterol or low-density lipoprotein cholesterol, particularly if combined with low levels of high-density lipoprotein cholesterol, are strongly associated with the development and progression of narrowing in vital arteries. This progressive process leads to coronary artery disease, manifested by angina pectoris, heart attack, or sudden death. In later decades, the process often precipitates stroke. Diets high in sodium can lead to persistent elevation of systemic blood pressure values and the ravages of hypertension, namely heart attack, heart failure, stroke, or kidney failure. Diets deficient in complex carbohydrates and low in fiber have been linked with excessive rates of development of cancers of the gastrointestinal tract. The appraisal of dietary fitness, therefore, should include documentation of usual dietary choices as they pertain to saturated fat, cholesterol, sodium, and types of carbohydrate.

Methods of appraising a diet history are readily available and can range from a simple evaluation of dietary preferences to computer-scored

155

instruments that analyze 24-hour dietary patterns, 3-day food records, or even 7-day food records. Generally speaking, the more thorough and complex the dietary appraisal, the more valid the results. When assessing dietary patterns, an important step is to determine a linkage between the reported dietary pattern and objective measures of health that relate in part to nutritional factors (for example, excessive calories in an overweight individual, excessive sodium intake as well as overweight in a hypertensive individual, and the role of saturated fat and cholesterol content of the diet in subjects with elevated blood lipid levels). A review of a subject's self-reported dietary pattern, particularly in a subject who is overweight, hypertensive, or has elevated blood lipid levels, can be an excellent starting point for changing dietary patterns to improve health status.

EXERCISE

Exercise, when regarded as therapy, is like any other means of treatment. For most individuals, it provides a clearly established benefit. For certain individuals, however, exercise may in fact be inappropriate and dangerous. The identification of individuals who may be at risk when exercising is provided elsewhere in this volume. In appraising exercise habits, however, the assessment must include the past history of vigorous physical activity performance, current physical activity habits, both in leisure time and on the job, and the important documentation of any physical symptoms associated with activity, particularly any discomfort in the chest and/or disproportionate development of shortness of breath related to physical activity. Information pertaining to previous biomechanical injuries related to exercise should be elicited.

SMOKING

Cigarette smoking is one of the most well-established risks to maintaining optimal health. The toll extracted by cigarette smoking is most dramatic in the areas of cardiovascular disease and lung cancer. In fully 90% of persons with carcinoma of the lung, the disease is attributable to cigarette smoking. Furthermore, the increasing numbers of cigarette smokers especially young women, are associated with the recent increase in the number of deaths from lung carcinoma in American women. With regard to cardiovascular disease, cigarette smoking is clearly associated with incremental risk of developing coronary artery disease. A dose-response relationship exists, with a steadily rising increase in the risk of suffering a heart attack with increasing cigarette usage. For each pack of cigarettes smoked on average per day, the risk of developing coronary artery disease doubles in population studies. The risk of sudden death, defined as death within 1 hour in an apparently healthy individual, occurs five times more commonly among a pack-per-day or greater cigarette smokers when compared to noncigarette smokers. Such bleak statistics are counterbalanced by the encouraging and well-documented benefits of smoking cessation. Within 2 years of stopping cigarette smoking, the excess risk of cardiovascular disease drops dramatically. This decline in cardiovascular risk is also a dose-response phenomenon; the heavier the prior habit, the more dramatic the benefit.

The rationale for these observed facts is well understood. Cigarette smoke has dozens of components that are demonstrated as carcinogenic to laboratory animals. A lifetime of exposure to these carcinogenic compounds induces subtle and then more dramatic changes in pulmonary tissue, which eventually lead to carcinoma. In most instances, when radiographic examination of the lung demonstrates a carcinoma, the patient is beyond cure.

The cardiovascular risk associated with cigarette smoking relates principally to the carbon monoxide and nicotine components of cigarette smoke. In an experimental setting, carbon monoxide accelerated the atherosclerotic process in arteries. Furthermore, carbon monoxide competes with oxygen for saturation on the hemoglobin molecule. The other major component of cigarette smoke, nicotine, is a cardiovascular stimulant. It increases heart rate and blood pressure, thereby increasing oxygen demand by heart muscle. As oxygen demand increases, the ability of the blood to deliver oxygen has been blunted by the effects of carbon monoxide. Over decades of smoking, the atherosclerotic process is more likely to be further advanced in the cigarette smoker. This state establishes a dangerous supply-to-demand imbalance within heart muscle, leading to angina pectoris, heart attack, or, most dramatically, sudden cardiac death. Cessation of cigarette smoking quickly clears the acute effects of nicotine and carbon monoxide from the system. The rate of progression of atherosclerosis is likely to decline in the ex-smoker as well. Furthermore, cigarette smoking is associated with an unfavorable and significant reduction in HDL-cholesterol levels. Identification of current smoking habits, therefore, is of major importance in overall appraisal of fitness. The health care professional must provide clear and persuasive information regarding the risks associated with continued smoking and the benefits of cessation.

STRESS/TYPE A

The type A behavior pattern is a well-established contributor to the overall risk of developing coronary artery disease. The original description and identification of type A behavior required a difficult and elaborate technique known as a structured interview. Subsequent means of evaluating type A behavior are more objective and streamlined. One of these methods should be an essential component of a health behaviors appraisal. Furthermore, at least in the postmyocardial infarction setting, strategies designed to lessen the type A behavior pattern appear to lessen the development of subsequent coronary artery disease events. Therefore, it is imperative to identify a subject whose behavior pattern places them at high risk for heart attack and to provide counseling to lower that risk.

HEALTH HISTORY

FAMILY HISTORY

Heart disease runs in families. The independent contribution of a positive family history for heart disease development is well established. This history goes beyond the measured risk factors that also tend to run in families (cigarette smoking, excess overweight, nutritional factors, and lack of physical exercise). Therefore, a genetic predisposition to the development of coronary artery disease seems to be at play. An important step, therefore, is to elicit a history of cardiovascular disease in first-degree relatives (parents, siblings, and children). The risk of developing a heart attack is particularly high when the family history documents heart attack in a first-degree relative with its onset

under age 60 years. In these instances, the identification of the pattern of blood fats (especially lipoprotein levels) is particularly important. Blood fat levels are more likely to be elevated in the offspring of patients whose first event related to coronary artery disease occurred under age 60 years.

Although less carefully documented, a familial tendency for developing certain types of carcinoma has been suggested. Additionally, a positive family history for the development of diabetes mellitus should be noted. Such knowledge will guide the health care provider in making optimal recommendations regarding dietary practices.

PERSONAL HISTORY

A personal health history can be quite extensive. As part of an overall health risk appraisal, the personal history should be tailored to emphasize specific features that will help to categorize an individual in regard to several broad areas. The most important area is that of manifestation of symptoms (symptomatic or asymptomatic). Beyond this stratification is the documentation as to whether a symptom-free individual is at high risk for the future development of disease or for participation in an exercise program.

Evidence of known cardiovascular disease or of symptoms of cardiovascular disease must be documented. In seeking to establish symptoms compatible with angina pectoris, the questions must be kept deliberately broad. The word discomfort is preferred to more specific terms such as pain or heaviness. Additional characteristics of the discomfort should also be elicited, including precipitating factors, duration, frequency, and location within the upper half of the body. Obviously, a history of known findings of diagnostic measures related to cardiovascular disease should be documented, including hypertension as well as any known heart murmurs or arrhythmias. Symptoms of peripheral vascular disease, particularly discomfort in one or both legs with walking, should also be recorded.

A respiratory disease history should be determined as well. Seasonal difficulties with breathing or breathing discomfort brought on by physical or emotional stress warrant particular attention. Respiratory symptoms may be a manifestation of cardiovascular disease or of pulmonary pathologic processes. The subject should also be queried regarding any of the other known cardiovascular risk factors (diabetes or abnormal blood fat levels). The history of current and past use of medication, both prescription and over-the-counter, requires documentation. Allergies to drugs or other substances must also be documented.

PHYSIOLOGIC APPRAISAL

BLOOD PRESSURE

Elevated blood pressure levels are common in the adult American population. The occurrence is more common among blacks and is most prevalent in black men (28 %). Hypertension is documented in more than 24% of black women, 14% of white men, and 8% of white women. If left uncontrolled, hypertension leads to an increased risk of heart attack, heart failure, stroke, and kidney failure. Because elevations in blood pressure usually do not produce symptoms, the measurement of blood pressure levels is essential to detect the hypertensive individual. The standard method of measuring blood pressure is to use the right arm and to obtain the pressure in the antecubital space. The patient should be seated, with the arm resting comfortably on a solid surface. Systolic blood pressure is recorded at the moment the first sounds are heard (phase I) with the clear and rhythmic tapping of two consecutive beats. Diastolic pressures are measured when these sounds disappear (phase V). No less than two consecutive readings should be taken approximately 1 minute apart.

Blood pressure measurement and categorization of blood pressure elevations have been standardized. The publication in which this information is described also provides national guidelines for the follow-up and management of persons with elevated blood pressure levels. The importance of adequate control of blood pressure is well established. Lessening of the incidence of stroke, heart failure, and heart attack has been documented in well-designed large clinical trials. With hypertension so prevalent and management so effective, the determination of blood pressure levels is a cornerstone of health appraisal.

DIABETES MELLITUS

Individuals with diabetes, like those persons with hypertension, may be symptom-free in the earliest stages of the disease. Screening for diabetes is best undertaken by using a standardized method for measuring fasting blood sugar levels. Although standards for the upper limit of normal vary, fasting blood sugar readings greater than 120 should be cause for concern and the need for further testing is indicated. Glucose tolerance testing, in which a standard amount of ingested glucose is used, permits more specific documentation and quantification of the diabetic state. Diabetes is an independent contributor to the risk of cardiovascular disease development. For reasons that are not clear, diabetes tends to play a greater role in increasing the risk of cardiovascular disease in women than in men. This excessive risk includes coronary artery disease, peripheral vascular disease, and congestive heart failure. Diabetes is, of course, its own metabolic disease and requires specific therapy with diet alone or in combination with prescribed medication.

BLOOD FATS

Abnormalities in blood lipid levels appear to be at the basis of the atherosclerotic process. Certain populations or individuals within populations appear to be free of the atherosclerotic disease process. This freedom from atherosclerosis appears to be correlated with a total blood cholesterol level that is consistently below 150 mg/dl. As total blood cholesterol levels rise, a parallel rise in the development of atherosclerotic disease end-points occurs. For every 1% increase in the cholesterol level, a 2% increase occurs in the risk of heart attack. Newly established guidelines provide definition of low-moderate and high-risk total cholesterol levels. These determinations are age specific and are summarized as follows:

	Cholesterol level (mg/dl)		
Age group	Normal	Moderate risk	High risk
20–29 yr	<200	200–219	220 and above
30–39 yr	<220	220–239	240 and above
40– above	<240	240–259	260 and above

The establishment of this new assessment scheme for identifying subjects at moderate or high risk for the development of atherosclerosis on the basis of their total cholesterol levels is linked to a plan of action for lowering cholesterol levels. The focus of this action plan is dietary intervention. Both nationally and internationally, several research groups have documented the beneficial effects of a low-saturated fat, low-cholesterol diet. The three-phase dietary plan of the American Heart Association should be the first step in the management of subjects with moderate- or high-risk cholesterol levels. Should dietary management fail to achieve adequate control of cholesterol levels, a wide array of medications also hold promise for improving the cholesterol profile.

BODY WEIGHT

Overweight or, more appropriately, overfatness continues to be a common problem in the American population. Furthermore, overweight or obesity is an independent risk factor for the development of cardiovascular disease. In addition, obesity is frequently a predecessor of adult-onset diabetes. Weight gain beyond ideal levels in adult populations is usually the result of a combination of insufficient physical activity and excessive caloric intake. This imbalance leads to increases in the percent body fat in men and women above the recommended ranges. (See Chapter 18 for standard ranges.)

The health professional must be fully acquainted with the dynamic relationship between exercise and caloric intake. Fueling this dynamic relationship is a series of behavioral and motivational dynamics that must be understood by both the health professional and the individual participant. These behavioral dynamics are addressed elsewhere in this text. Simply stated, 1 lb of excess body weight represents an intake of 3500 calories beyond the ideal to maintain normal body weight. To bring about reduction of excess body fat to the ideal level, 3500 calories must be expended and/or not consumed to result in the loss of 1 lb of body weight. Centers that have established effective weight loss and weight maintenance programs generally combine diet with exercise. This step not only allows for modification of behaviors in two areas simultaneously, but also provides motivation to the exercising subject to maintain a modestly calorie-restricted diet plan. Additionally, if an adequate exercise stress is provided within the program, physiologic enhancement of fitness levels also takes place. The composition of the diet should be determined with consideration of the wisdom of restricting saturated fat and cholesterol calories to continue to improve the blood fat profile. In addition, results of studies reveal that inclusion of complex carbohydrates in the daily diet improves the blood fat profile and may play a role in reducing the risk of developing cancer of the gastrointestinal tract.

The exercise component of an effective weight loss program may improve modestly elevated blood pressure levels, enhance the effect of antihypertensive medications, or bring about adequate control of elevated blood pressure without medication usage. Furthermore, modestly elevated blood sugar levels may decrease as a result of weight loss combined with physical activity.

SELECTED REFERENCES

1. Reardon, MF, Nestel, PJ, Craig, IH, and Harper, RW: Lipoprotein predictors of the severity of coronary artery disease in men and women. *Circulation, 71*:881–888, 1985.
2. Lewis, B et al.: Towards an improved lipid-lowering diet: Additive effects of changes in nutrient intake. *Lancet, 2 (8259)*:1310–1313, 1981.
3. Paffenbarger, RS, Jr., Wing, AL, and Hyde, RT: Physical activity as an index of heart attack risk in college alumni. *Am J Epidemiol, 108*:161–175, 1978.
4. Thompson, PD, Funk, EJ, Carleton, RA, and Sturner, WQ: Incidence of death during jogging in Rhode Island from 1975 through 1980. *JAMA, 247*:25, 35–38, 1982.
5. Siscovick, DS, Weiss, NS, Fletcher, RH, and Lasky, T: The incidence of primary cardiac arrest during vigorous exercise. *N Engl J Med, 311*:874–877, 1984.
6. Fielding, JE: Smoking: Health effects and control. *N Engl J Med, 313*:491–498, 555–561, 1985.
7. Holbrook, JH, et al.: Cigarette smoking and cardiovascular disease. *Circulation, 70*:1114A–1117A, 1984.
8. Rosenberg, L, Kaufman, DW, Helmrich, SP, and Shapiro, S: The risk of myocardial infarction after quitting smoking in men under 55 years of age. *N Engl J Med, 313*:1511–1514, 1985.
9. Brand, RJ, Rosenman, RH, Sholtz, RI, and Friedman, M: Multivariant prediction of coronary heart disease in the Western Collaborative Group Study compared to the findings in the Framingham study. *Circulation, 53*:348–355, 1976.
10. Haynes, SG, Feinleib, M, and Kannel, WB: The relationship of psychosocial factors to coronary heart disease in the Framingham study III. *Am J Epidemiol, 111*:37–58, 1980.
11. Friedman, M et al.: Feasibility of altering type A behavior pattern after myocardial infarction. *Circulation, 66*:83–92, 1982.
12. Snowden, CB et al.: Predicting coronary disease in siblings—a multivariate assessment: the Framingham Heart Study. *Am J Epidemiol, 115*:217–222, 1982.
13. The 1984 Report of the Joint National Committee on the Detection, Evaluation and Treatment of High Blood Pressure. *Arch Intern Med, 144*:1045–1056, 1984.
14. The Australian Therapeutic Trial of Mild Hypertension: Report by the management committee. *Lancet 1*:1261–1267, 1980.
15. Hypertension and Follow-up Program Cooperative Group: The effect of treatment on mortality in mild hypertension. *N Engl J Med, 307*:976–980, 1983.

16. Kannel, WB, and McGee, DL: Diabetes and cardiovascular disease: The Framingham study. *JAMA* 241:2035–2038, 1979.

17. Lowering blood cholesterol to prevent heart disease. National Institutes of Health consensus development conference statement. *JAMA* 253:2080–2086, 1985.

18. Kannel, WB et al.: Obesity as an independent risk factor for cardiovascular disease: A 26-year follow-up of participants in the Framingham Heart Study. *Circulation,* 67:968–976, 1983.

19. Duncan, JJ et al.: The effects of aerobic exercise on plasma catecholamines and blood pressure in patients with mild essential hypertension. *JAMA,* 254:2609–2613, 1985.

CHAPTER 19

FITNESS TESTING

LARRY R. GETTMAN

HEALTH-RELATED FITNESS TESTING

The term "fitness testing" in this manual refers to evaluating the four main health-related areas of physical fitness: (1) cardiovascular-respiratory function, (2) body composition, (3) flexibility, and (4) muscular strength and muscular endurance. The evaluation of cardiovascular-respiratory function is explained in Chapters 7, 20, and 22. Testing to evaluate body composition, flexibility, and muscular strength and endurance is described in this chapter.

A principal reason for health-related fitness is to move efficiently in work, play, and sports performance. Considerable amounts of time and effort are spent by school physical educators in helping young people learn how to engage successfully in sports. Yet many youths grow into adulthood without a solid foundation of knowledge and practices in the health-related fitness areas. Maladies such as obesity, heart disease, and low back pain are significant problems in the adult population. Thus, a need to improve fitness has arisen, and to do so, one must assess present levels and the changes that take place with exercise programs.

Periodic testing of health-related fitness shows the participants how they stand relative to normal fitness levels. The results can then be used to emphasize the importance of having an active lifestyle to achieve and maintain high levels of cardiovascular and respiratory function, low amounts of body fat, sufficient muscular strength and endurance, and flexibility, especially in the lower trunk and posterior thigh areas for a healthy back. Results from fitness tests should be viewed as the means to an end and not as an end in themselves. The results from fitness tests should be used in the exercise prescription. They give a picture (snapshot) of present health and fitness status and can be motivators for improvement and reinforcers for fitness maintenance. Several ways in which test results can be effectively utilized include:

Diagnosis. Scores of the fitness tests can be used to identify strengths and weaknesses within the individual. Appropriate counseling can aid those individuals who need to improve identified weaknesses.

Achievement of Individual Goals. Periodic fitness tests can be used to verify the degree of achievement of individually established goals.

Educational Purposes. Test results can be used to stimulate further interest in health-related topics. For example, body composition tests can be used to teach concepts in nutrition and weight control, flexibility tests for control of low-back pain, and muscular strength and endurance tests for accomplishing work tasks with ease and efficiency.

Motivation. Most individuals are inherently curious about their physical capabilities and how their fitness test scores compare with other individuals. By becoming aware of how they compare with criterion standards and with other individuals, participants may become motivated to improve their scores or at least maintain a desired level.

Program Evaluation. Test results can also be used to determine if a fitness program is achieving desired goals. The average score of a group can be compared to a determined normal value or the changes in average scores can reflect the amount of fitness change in the group as a result of the program.

MEASUREMENT OF BODY COMPOSITION

The term body composition refers to the lean body weight (LBW) and the fat weight of the body, which together equal the total body weight. Body composition is measured in many ways.

1. Chemical analysis of cadavers.
2. Hydrostatic weighing: weighing an individual underwater to determine body density by using Archimedes' principle.
3. Volumetry: determining body density by using water displacement to measure body volume.
4. Helium dilution: determining body density by using a helium dilution chamber to measure body volume.
5. Radiographic analysis: using radiography to differentiate thicknesses of skin, fat, muscle, and bone.
6. K-40 counting: determining LBW by counting γ-radiation emission from muscle tissue.
7. Total body water: determining LBW from isotopic or bioimpedance methods that estimate total body water.
8. Ultrasound: determining the thickness of the subcutaneous fat layer by using high-frequency sound waves.
9. Anthropometry: estimating body density or

LBW by measuring skeletal diameters, body girths, or skinfolds.

In addition to the direct chemical analysis of cadavers, underwater weighing is the most accurate method of estimating body composition. The most practical method of assessing body composition is anthropometry, and, in particular, the skinfold technique. Skinfold measurements are used in most clinical settings for determining body composition; however, the American College of Sports Medicine does not accept the skinfold technique as a "measure" of body composition. Therefore, for our purposes, underwater weighing is described briefly.

UNDERWATER WEIGHING

In the underwater weighing technique, body density is calculated from the relationship of body weight and body volume:

$$\left[\text{Density} = \frac{\text{Body weight}}{\text{Body volume}} \right]$$

Body weight determination is easily made on a scale; the volume of the body is determined by weighing a person underwater and is equal to the loss of weight in the water (Archimedes' principle). The density of bone and muscle tissue (LBW) is higher than the density of water and will therefore sink. The density of fat tissue is less than the density of water and will float. A person with a large amount of body fat will weigh less underwater than a person with a high LBW.

The underwater weighing technique requires that the residual volume (RV) of air in the lungs be measured to account for its buoyancy effect upon the underwater weight. Ideally, the RV is measured while the person is being weighed underwater. If this timing is not feasible, the next best procedure is to measure RV outside the water and then calculate underwater body weight on the assumption that this RV is the same as that when weighed underwater. Some error may occur in making this assumption.

The underwater weighing technique requires the use of special equipment, such as a large tank of water with a secured weighing scale suspended over the tank or a load-cell system built into the underwater chair used for weight measurement. The water in the tank must be constantly filtered, heated, and chemically controlled for health safety. This technique is expensive, complicated, and time consuming, and if not conducted properly, is subject to great error.

After body density is determined by underwater weighing, this value may be converted to percentage of body fat by using either the formula of Brozek et al. (%Fat = (457/D) − 414.2) or the Siri formula (%Fat = (495/D = 450).

IDEAL BODY WEIGHT

After the percentage of body fat is calculated for an individual, it may be compared to standard values (Table 19–1). These norms are based on the average fat percentage levels of 308 men and 249 women from studies conducted by Jackson Pollock, and Ward. The norms cited in Table 19–1 were calculated by using multiple units of the standard error of estimate from the mean in each age decade.

The recommended body fat levels for men and women in the various age groups could be defined as the best value in the average range of scores for each sex and age group. On the basis of norms detailed in Table 19–1 the recommended body fat levels for men and women are:

	Age in years				
	20–29	*30–39*	*40–49*	*50–59*	*60+*
Men	14	15	17	18	19
Women	20	21	22	23	24

The establishment of one recommended body fat level for all men or for all women is difficult because of the aging effect. The "ideal

body weight" for each person should be derived by using the assumption that body composition will change normally with age.

The ideal body weight may be defined as the weight at which the body fat percentage is equal to or lower than the recommended fat level for the sex and age of the individual. For competitive athletes, the "ideal body weight" may be synonymous with "playing weight," which is equivalent to the average fat level for a sport or the playing position in that sport. As an example, the calculation of ideal body weight for a 42-year-old man weighing 210 lbs with a current body fat level of 29.0% follows.

Step 1. Calculate current fat weight in pounds.

Current body weight (lbs) · current body fat (%) = current fat weight (lbs)
Example: 210 lbs · 0.290 = 61 lbs of current fat weight.

Step 2. Calculate current LBW in pounds.

Current body weight (lbs) − current fat weight (lbs) = current LBW (lbs)
Example: 210 lbs − 61 lbs = 149 lbs of current LBW (or 71% of the total body weight).

On the assumption that LBW can be at least maintained in a program of regular exercise and a calorically restricted diet, the "ideal weight" is calculated by adding 17.0% fat to the LBW (the value 17.0% is the best value of the average range of scores for men aged 40 to 49 years, see Table 19–1). The logic of this procedure is subsequently illustrated.

Step 3. Calculate ideal body weight by using a constant LBW.

Ideal body weight (100%) = ideal fat

Table 19–1. Standard Values for Percent Body Fat

		Age (yr)				
	Rating	*20–29*	*30–39*	*40–49*	*50–59*	*60+*
Men*						
	Excellent	<10	<11	<13	<14	<15
	Good	11–13	12–14	14–16	15–17	16–18
	Average	14–20	15–21	17–23	18–24	19–25
	Fair	21–23	22–24	24–26	25–27	26–28
	Poor	>24	>25	>27	>28	>29
Women†						
	Excellent	<15	<16	<17	<18	<19
	Good	16–19	17–20	18–21	19–22	20–23
	Average	20–28	21–29	22–30	23–31	24–32
	Fair	29–31	30–32	31–33	32–34	33–35
	Poor	>32	>33	>34	>35	>36

* From Jackson AS, Pollock ML: Generalized equations for predicting body density of men. *Br J Nutr*, 40:497–504, 1978.
† From Jackson AS, Pollock ML, and Ward A: Generalized equations for predicting body density of women. *Med Sci Sports Exerc*, 12:175–182, 1980.

weight (17.0%) + LBW (83.0%)

Example: LBW (lbs) = 83.0% of ideal body weight

149   lbs = 0.83 × ideal body weight

Ideal body weight (lbs) = 149 lbs/0.83

Ideal body weight = 180 lbs

Therefore, this man should lose 30 pounds (from 210 to 180 lbs) to achieve his ideal weight. Any percent fat level can be selected as the recommended level for "ideal" within any individual. The main consideration is to be realistic when selecting a recommended fat level and to consider the individual's age and physical activity level of the individual.

Some clinicians recommend that all men should attain 15 or 16% body fat and all women should attain 19 or 22% as the ideal level. Following this procedure may not be appropriate because the norms listed in Table 19–1 indicate that body fat increases normally with age and no "fixed" average fat level exists. Another problem with using a fixed value involves those individuals who are already under those values. The 15 or 16% fat goal for men would necessitate a gain in weight for individuals who are already below these levels. For men to be lower than 15 or 16% fat is not necessarily unhealthy. In fact, most men below those levels are probably at a desirable body weight and may not need to change.

Athletes are prime examples of individuals with low body fat levels associated with high fitness levels. The concept of recommending an "ideal weight" or "playing weight" for an athlete can follow the same logic as the previous example. For instance, a football player weighing 280 lb with 15% fat may want to play at the 13% fat level. If his LBW is maintained at 238 lb, his playing weight would be 273 lb (playing weight = 238 lb/0.87). Thus, an ideal body weight can be calculated for any individual when sex, age, and fitness level are considered.

OVERWEIGHT VERSUS OBESITY

Overweight is defined as exceeding the normal or standard weight for a specific height and skeletal frame size, when grouped by sex. As an example, if the recommended weight range for a man 5 feet 10 in. tall is 136 to 170 lb, any weight in excess of this range is considered overweight. Any weight under this range would be considered underweight. No consideration is given to the levels of body fat or LBW in these definitions. Individuals who are overweight might be carrying too much fat or they might have above average LBW development. Most football players could be considered overweight by the aforementioned definition because they have such high LBW. The term overweight is not necessarily undesirable, especially when the LBW development is high.

Obesity may be defined as exceeding 1 standard deviation above the mean body fat levels of men and women relative to the age categories. The obesity values would be the body fat percentages in the "poor" categories listed in Table 19–1. Generally, body fat levels greater than 25% in men and 30% in women are considered levels of "obesity."

FLEXIBILITY MEASUREMENT

Flexibility refers to the ability to move the body parts through a wide range of motion without undue strain to the articulations and muscle attachments. Flexibility measurements include flexion and extension movements. No general test is available that provides representative values of total body flexibility; tests are specific to each joint and muscle group and connective tissue area.

The most accurate tests of flexibility are those in which a goniometer is used to measure the actual degrees of rotation of the various joints. A goniometer is a protractor type of instrument that is used to measure the joint angle at both extremes in the total range of movement. The goniometer has two arms that attach to two body parts with the center of the instrument over the center of the joint tested. The center of the goniometer must be placed carefully over the exact center of the joint tested. The arms of the goniometer should be taped over each midline of the bones emanating from the joint center. The difference between the joint angles recorded at both extremes in the total range of movement of the joint indicates the number of degrees of movement possible.

An electrogoniometer has a potentiometer that replaces the protractor of the goniometer. The potentiometer provides an electric signal proportional to the angle of the joint. This device can give continuous recordings of the degrees of rotation of the joint tested. Because continuous recordings of joint movement are possible with the electrogoniometer, it is used to assess flexibility during physical activity; the assessment of functional flexibility is much more accurate and realistic. The goniometer and electrogoniometer techniques, however, can be time consuming and expensive. More practical tests have been developed to estimate general flexibility of joints, such as the trunk flexion, shoulder elevation, trunk extension, and ankle flexibility tests.

Before flexibility tests are administered, the person should warm up with a series of general flexibility exercises, such as arm circles, trunk twists, side bends, toe touches, and back, calf, and ankle stretches. These exercises can also be used in a general exercise program for warm up, cool down, and flexibility training.

Because lower back problems are prevalent in the adult population, the sit-and-reach test (trunk flexion) is used to assess lower back flexibility. It is easily administered and requires minimal equipment. Actually, the sit-and-reach test also involves the extensibility (or tightness) of the hamstring musculature, buttocks, lower back, upper back, and shoulders.

In the sit-and-reach test, the subject sits on the floor with legs extended straight in front and against a 12-in. high box with a yardstick secured on top. The 15-in. mark of the yardstick should be at the edge of the box. The person then places the index fingers of both hands together and slowly reaches forward as far as possible on the yardstick, holding the position for 1 sec. The score is the most distant point reached by the fingertips in the best of three trials. The knees must be straight and in contact with the floor at all times. Bouncing into the stretch position is not allowed and the movement must be slow and gradual. Normal values for adults are listed in Table 19–2.

Shoulder elevation, trunk extension, and ankle flexibility tests are also used in general flexibility assessment. The shoulder elevation test measures the ability to elevate the shoulders. From a prone position with the arms straight and shoulder width apart, the subject raises a stick upward as high as possible while keeping the chin on the floor and the elbows and wrists straight. The examiner measures the distance from the bottom of the stick to the floor, and the best measurement from three trials is recorded. The best measurement in inches is then multiplied by 100, and the product is divided by arm length measured in inches. The arm length is defined as the distance between the acromion process and the upper surface of the stick, which is held with the arms hanging downward. The shoulder elevation measurement should be taken at the highest vertical point at which the stick is held momentarily. Normal values for men and women are provided in Table 19–3.

In the trunk extension test, the subject lies on a mat with the feet and hips secured by the examiner. With the hands resting on the lower back, the subject raises the trunk as far upward and backward as possible. The vertical distance between the mat and the suprasternal notch is measured to the nearest ¼ in. This measurement is multiplied by 100 and the product is divided by trunk length measured in inches. Trunk length is defined as the vertical distance between the suprasternal notch and the floor

Table 19–2. Standard Values for Trunk Flexion in Inches

	Age (yr)				
Rating	20–29	30–39	40–49	50–59	60+
Men					
Excellent	>22	>21	>20	>19	>18
Good	19–21	18–20	17–19	16–18	15–17
Average	13–18	12–17	11–16	10–15	9–14
Fair	10–12	9–11	8–10	7–9	6–8
Poor	<9	<8	<7	<6	<5
Women					
Excellent	>24	>23	>22	>21	>20
Good	22–23	21–22	20–21	19–20	18–19
Average	16–21	15–20	14–19	13–18	12–17
Fair	13–15	12–14	11–13	10–12	9–11
Poor	<12	<11	<10	<9	<8

(Adapted from Golding LA, Myers CR, Sinning WE (eds): *The Y's Way to Physical Fitness*. Rosemont, IL: YMCA of the USA, 1982.)

Table 19-3. Standard Values for Shoulder Elevation

Rating	Shoulder elevation score (inches)
Men	
Excellent	106–123
Good	88–105
Average	70–87
Fair	53–69
Poor	35–52
Women	
Excellent	105–123
Good	86–104
Average	68–85
Fair	50–67
Poor	31–49

(From Johnson BL, Nelson JK: *Practical Measurements for Evaluation in Physical Education.* Minneapolis: Burgess Publishing, 1969.)

Table 19-5. Standard Values for Ankle Flexibility

Rating	Ankle flexibility score (degrees of movement)
Men	
Excellent	77–99
Good	63–76
Average	48–62
Fair	34–47
Poor	15–33
Women	
Excellent	81–89
Good	68–80
Average	56–67
Fair	43–55
Poor	32–42

(From Johnson BL, Nelson JK: *Practical Measurements for Evaluation in Physical Education.* Minneapolis: Burgess Publishing, 1969.)

while the subject is seated with the back against a wall. Standard values for men and women are provided in Table 19-4.

Extreme caution is required when administering the trunk extension test, because pressure is exerted on the posterior areas of the lumbar vertebrae. Individuals with existing or suspected back problems should not attempt this test.

The average ankle flexibility test measures the ability to flex and extend the ankle. The subject sits on the floor or a table with the back of the knee touching the surface. Keeping the heel stationary, the foot is dorsiflexed as much as possible. The angle of this foot position is recorded on a protractor placed at the side of the foot. The subject then extends (plantar flexes) the foot as far as possible, and the angle of the foot position is noted. The difference between the positions in dorsiflexion and plantarflexion is the average ankle flexibility score in degrees

of movement. Normal values for average ankle flexibility are provided in Table 19-5.

The flexibility warm-up exercises and tests could be administered before starting a cardiovascular-respiratory function test, because they are beneficial ways to stretch the muscles in preparation for the test. If the stretching is too vigorous, however, it may increase heart rate and blood pressure and cause spurious results on the "resting" measurements taken before the graded exercise test. The slow, gradual movements in the flexibility warm-up exercises are emphasized not only for safety in the flexibility tests, but also to minimize any rise in heart rate and blood pressure before starting an exercise test.

MUSCULAR STRENGTH AND MUSCULAR ENDURANCE ASSESSMENT

Possession of superior muscular strength enables the individual to perform any task involving strength with greater ease and control. Superior muscle endurance allows an individual to perform muscular tasks for a long period without undue fatigue. The measurement of total body strength and total muscle endurance is difficult because different muscles and muscle groups to assess are numerous. The tests that we recommend were selected on the basis of their practicality and appropriateness for use in adult fitness programs. Muscular strength and muscular endurance tests should be given after completion of the graded exercise test or on another day, if appropriate, because their vigor-

Table 19-4. Standard Values for Trunk Extension

Rating	Trunk extension score (inches)
Men	
Excellent	50–64
Good	43–49
Average	37–42
Fair	31–36
Poor	28–30
Women	
Excellent	48–63
Good	42–47
Average	35–41
Fair	29–34
Poor	23–28

(From Johnson BL, Nelson JK: *Practical Measurements for Evaluation in Physical Education.* Minneapolis: Burgess Publishing, 1969.)

ous nature could influence the "resting" measures of the graded exercise test.

MUSCULAR STRENGTH ASSESSMENT

Strength is defined as the muscular force exerted against movable and immovable objects. Strength is best measured by tests that require one maximal effort on a given movement or position. The two types of muscular contraction most frequently measured are isotonic (dynamic) and isometric (static) contractions. Isotonic contraction takes place when muscular force moves an object of resistance, such as a weight, so that muscle contraction takes place over a range of movement. Isometric contraction takes place when muscular force is exerted briefly (usually a few seconds) without movement of the object or body joints. Pushing against a wall and gripping a hand dynamometer are examples of isometric contractions. A third type of contraction, called isokinetic, has been described in recent years. Isokinetic contraction requires a special device that offers accomodating resistance to a muscle group going through a range of motion at a constant speed.

Isotonic test items include just about any calisthenic or weightlifting type of exercise. Isometric strength is usually measured by using dynamometers or cable tensiometers. Isokinetic machines that offer accomodating resistance can be used to record the force exerted throughout an entire range of motion in a muscle group. Isokinetic devices involve electronic recording mechanisms that typically are expensive. In addition, the testing procedures and interpretation of results can be time consuming.

The principle of specificity must be considered when administering strength tests. If participants are training isotonically with calisthenics and weight training, isotonic strength tests should be given to assess isotonic strength changes. Isometric or isokinetic strength tests may not be sufficiently specific to assess isotonic strength changes during an isotonic exercise program. Although some transfer of isotonic strength to isometric or isokinetic testing occurs, the isometric or isokinetic tests are not as specific in evaluating isotonic strength.

Isotonic strength can be easily assessed by the one-repetition maximum (1RM) weightlifting test. Weight training machines are usually used for isotonic strength tests because the weights are easily and quickly changed in the testing protocol and the weights are safely secured in the weight apparatus. Because no additional spotters are required with machine weights, the test is efficient in terms of time and manpower.

In the 1RM testing protocol, the subject has a series of trials to determine the greatest weight that can be lifted just once for that particular movement. The procedure starts with a low weight that can be easily and safely lifted. Weight is added gradually until the lift can be performed correctly just one time. The subjects should be encouraged to breathe freely with each lift and discouraged from holding their breath or performing a Valsalva maneuver.

A 1RM isotonic strength measure can be obtained for any weight training exercise. For practical purposes, the 1RM bench press and leg press tests described by Jackson, Watkins, and Patton are recommended for assessment of upper and lower body strength. These authors reported that the 1RM bench press and military press tests are the most valid measures of upper body strength and that the upper leg press and lower leg press tests are the most valid measures of lower body strength with use of Universal Gym equipment.

The 1RM bench press test is recommended for the assessment of upper body strength because the procedure is safe, easy to administer, and not too time consuming. The participant's back is supported by the bench apparatus, making it a safe test. The 1RM seated leg press test (upper leg press with the seat in the middle position for all participants) is also a safe test because the back is supported by the seat apparatus.

After the 1RM is obtained for the bench press test, the 1RM weight in pounds is divided by the participant's body weight in pounds to obtain strength represented per pound of body weight (1RM lb/body weight lb). This value is then compared to the bench press norms listed in Table 19–6. The same procedure is used for calculating the leg press results; normal values for this test are presented in Table 19–7.

In the past, the hand grip strength test was used to assess isometric muscular strength. The results of these tests were quite variable and not reliable, however, because of inconsistent testing protocols.

MUSCULAR ENDURANCE ASSESSMENT

Muscular endurance involves the ability of a muscle or muscle group to repeat identical movements (dynamic) or to maintain a certain

Table 19-6. Standard Values for Bench Press Strength in 1RM lb/lb Body Weight

Rating	Age (yr)				
	20-29	30-39	40-49	50-59	60+
Men					
Excellent	>1.26	>1.08	>0.97	>0.86	>0.78
Good	1.17-1.25	1.01-1.07	0.91-0.96	0.81-0.85	0.74-0.77
Average	0.97-1.16	0.86-1.00	0.78-0.90	0.70-0.80	0.64-0.73
Fair	0.88-0.96	0.79-0.85	0.72-0.77	0.65-0.69	0.60-0.63
Poor	<0.87	<0.78	<0.71	<0.64	<0.59
Women					
Excellent	>0.78	>0.66	>0.61	>0.54	>0.55
Good	0.72-0.77	0.62-0.65	0.57-0.60	0.51-0.53	0.51-0.54
Average	0.59-0.71	0.53-0.61	0.48-0.56	0.43-0.50	0.41-0.50
Fair	0.53-0.58	0.49-0.52	0.44-0.47	0.40-0.42	0.37-0.40
Poor	<0.52	<0.48	<0.43	<0.39	<0.36

(Adapted from The Institute for Aerobics Research. 1985 Physical Fitness Norms. [Unpublished Data.] Dallas, TX, 1985, with permission).

degree of tension over time (static). Muscular endurance tests may be relative or absolute. In a relative endurance test, the muscles work with a proportionate amount of the maximal strength load. An absolute endurance test requires a set load for all subjects without a definite relationship to the maximal strength of each individual. The three types of muscular endurance tests are:

1. *Dynamic:* identical repetitions of a movement are repeated over time, such as in the situp and pushup tests.
2. *Static repetitive:* the number of times a force equal to a certain percentage of maximal strength or body weight is registered against a static measuring device.
3. *Static timed:* the amount of time a muscle contraction is maintained, such as in the flexed arm hang test.

The situp and pushup tests are perhaps the easiest and most practical tests to use for evaluation of dynamic muscle endurance. Static repetitive and static timed tests require special equipment and may involve time-consuming procedures.

Muscular endurance tests primarily tax the skeletal muscles and differ from cardiovascular-respiratory endurance tests, which mainly tax the heart and lungs. As with muscular strength tests, muscular endurance tests are specific to the muscles and muscle groups tested. Because most muscular endurance tests involve a subjective end point that is dependent upon motivation and technique, the examiner should be consistent in offering any type of verbal motivation to subjects.

In the 1-min situp test, the subject lies on the back with hands interlocked behind the neck and the knees bent so that the heels are 18 in. from the buttocks. A partner or the tester holds the ankles to give support. Within a 1-min period, the subject performs as many correct situps as possible (elbows alternately touching opposite knee). The subject should not hold the

Table 19-7. Standard Values for Upper Leg Press Strength in 1RM lb/lb Body Weight

Rating	Age (yr)				
	20-29	30-39	40-49	50-59	60+
Men					
Excellent	>2.08	>1.88	>1.76	>1.66	>1.56
Good	2.00-2.07	1.80-1.87	1.70-1.75	1.60-1.65	1.50-1.55
Average	1.83-1.99	1.63-1.79	1.56-1.69	1.46-1.59	1.37-1.49
Fair	1.65-1.82	1.55-1.62	1.50-1.55	1.40-1.45	1.31-1.36
Poor	<1.64	<1.54	<1.49	<1.39	<1.30
Women					
Excellent	>1.63	>1.42	>1.32	>1.26	>1.15
Good	1.54-1.62	1.35-1.41	1.26-1.31	1.13-1.25	1.08-1.14
Average	1.35-1.53	1.20-1.34	1.12-1.25	0.99-1.12	0.92-1.07
Fair	1.26-1.34	1.13-1.19	1.06-1.11	0.86-0.98	0.85-0.91
Poor	<1.25	<1.12	<1.05	<0.85	<0.84

(Adapted from The Institute for Aerobics Research. 1985 Physical Fitness Norms. [Unpublished Data.] Dallas, TX, 1985, with permission).

Table 19-8. Standard Values for 1-min Situp Endurance

Rating	Age (yr)				
	20-29	30-39	40-49	50-59	60+
Men					
Excellent	>48	>40	>35	>30	>25
Good	43-47	35-39	30-34	25-29	20-24
Average	37-42	29-34	24-29	19-24	14-19
Fair	33-36	25-28	20-23	15-18	10-13
Poor	<32	<24	<19	<14	<9
Women					
Excellent	>44	>36	>31	>26	>21
Good	39-43	31-35	26-30	21-25	16-20
Average	33-38	25-30	19-25	15-20	10-15
Fair	29-32	21-24	16-18	11-14	6-9
Poor	<28	<20	<15	<10	<5

(From Pollock ML, Wilmore JH, Fox SM: *Health and Fitness through Physical Activity.* New York: John Wiley & Sons, 1978.)

Table 19-9. Standard Values for Pushup Endurance

Rating	Age (yr)				
	20-29	30-39	40-49	50-59	60+
Men					
Excellent	>55	>45	>40	>35	>30
Good	45-54	35-44	30-39	25-34	20-29
Average	35-44	25-34	20-29	15-24	10-19
Fair	20-34	15-24	12-19	8-14	5-9
Poor	<19	<14	<11	<7	<4
Women					
Excellent	>49	>40	>35	>30	>20
Good	34-48	25-39	20-34	15-29	5-19
Average	17-33	12-24	8-19	6-14	3-4
Fair	6-16	4-11	3-7	2-5	1-2
Poor	<5	<3	<2	<1	<0

(From Pollock ML, Wilmore JH, Fox SM: *Health and Fitness through Physical Activity.* New York: John Wiley & Sons, 1978.)

breath during this test, but rather should breathe freely with each repetition. Standard values for adults appear in Table 19-8.

The pushup test is administered with male subjects in the standard "up" position and female subjects in the modified "knee" position. When testing male subjects, the tester places a fist on the floor beneath the subject's chest and the subject must lower the body to the floor until the chest touches the tester's fist. The fist method is not used for female subjects and no criteria are established for determining how the chest must touch the floor for a proper pushup. For both men and women, however, the subject's back must be straight at all times and the subject must push up to a straight arm position. The maximal number of pushups performed consecutively without rest is counted as the score, and the result is compared to normal values detailed in Table 19-9.

Descriptions of static repetitive, static timed, and other dynamic muscle endurance tests

(e.g., chinups, squat thrusts, and dips) are provided in textbooks detailing physical education tests and measurements. Definite guidelines must be followed when scoring muscular endurance tests because correct (or incorrect) form influences final results. As mentioned previously, motivational factors greatly affect results, and motivation procedures must therefore be standardized. Because muscle endurance tests are specific, dynamic endurance tests should be used to evaluate dynamic muscle endurance, and static tests should be used to determine static muscle endurance.

SELECTED REFERENCES

1. American Alliance for Health, Physical Education, Recreation and Dance: Health-Related Physical Fitness Test Manual. Reston, VA: AAHPERD, 1980.
2. Brozek J, Grande F, Anderson JT, Keys A: Densiometric analysis of body composition: Revision of some quanti-

tative assumptions. *Ann NY Acad Sci,* 110:113–114, 1963.

3. Siri WE: Body composition from fluid spaces and density. *Univ Calif Donner Lab Med Phys Rep, March,* 1956.

4. Jackson AS, Pollock ML: Generalized equations for predicting body density of men. *Br J Nutr,* 40:497–504, 1978.

5. Jackson AS, Pollock ML, Ward A: Generalized equations for predicting body density of women. *Med Sci Sports Exerc,* 12:175–182, 1980.

6. Pollock ML, Wilmore JM, Fox SM: *Health and Fitness through Physical Activity.* New York: John Wiley & Sons, 1978.

7. Johnson BL, Nelson JK: *Practical Measurements for Evaluation in Physical Education.* Minneapolis: Burgess Publishing, 1969.

8. Gettman LR, Culter LA, Strathman TA: Physiologic changes after 20 weeks of isotonic vs isokinetic circuit training. *J Sports Med,* 20:265–274, 1980.

9. Jackson A, Watkins M, Patton R: A factor analysis of twelve selected maximal isotonic strength performances on the Universal Gym. *Med Sci Sports Exerc,* 12:274–277, 1980.

10. Golding LA, Myers CR, Sinning WE (eds): *The Y's Way to Physical Fitness.* Rosemont, IL: YMCA of the USA, 1982.

20

MEASUREMENT OF THE MAXIMAL RATE OF OXYGEN UPTAKE

ROBERT G. HOLLY

The maximal rate of oxygen uptake is the maximal rate at which oxygen can be taken up, distributed, and used by the body in the performance of work. As such, a high level depends upon the proper functioning of three important systems within the body: the respiratory system, which takes up oxygen from inspired air and transports it into the blood; the cardiovascular system, which pumps and distributes this oxygen-laden blood throughout body tissues; and the musculoskeletal system, which uses this oxygen to convert stored substrates into work and heat during physical activity.[1] The maximal rate of oxygen uptake is most often abbreviated: $\dot{V}O_{2\,max}$, in which $\dot{V}$ is the volume used per minute, O_2 is oxygen, and max represents maximal conditions. Thus, $\dot{V}O_{2\,max}$ is the maximal volume of oxygen used by the body per minute. It is the measure of the maximal aerobic (or oxygen-requiring) metabolism of the body, and therefore this determination is often referred to as the maximal aerobic capacity or maximal aerobic power. Although the former term is frequently used, the latter term is the more accurate. Because $\dot{V}O_{2\,max}$ is a measure of energy flow, it is a measure of power rather than a measure of volume or capacity. For this reason, we refer to $\dot{V}O_{2\,max}$ as maximal aerobic power or the maximal *rate* of oxygen uptake.

With the exception of steady-state exercise at light to moderate work rates, a significant and variable component to the total metabolism from anaerobic processes typically exists. At maximal exercise, the total metabolism or rate of energy transfer is the sum of maximal aerobic power ($\dot{V}O_{2\,max}$) and maximal anaerobic power. Various tests of anaerobic power have been described and are not considered further in this discussion.[2] Of importance, however, is the fact that aerobic metabolism is only one component of the total metabolic rate.

Maximal aerobic power is assessed for many reasons, ranging from an assessment of cardiovascular function in cardiac patients to the prediction of performance in world class athletes. Appendix D in the *Guidelines* presents an approach to estimating oxygen consumption under standardized conditions.[3] These equations have limited utility, however, in estimating maximal aerobic power in nonsteady-state conditions (such as those occurring at peak exercise). In a variety of situations, therefore, such as in scientific studies, in the assessment of athletes, and in clinical evaluations for which it is desirable to have an accurate measure of maximal aerobic power rather than an estimate, the measurement of $\dot{V}O_{2\,max}$ is preferred.

Historically, the measurement of $\dot{V}O_{2\,max}$ has been costly, laborious, and time-consuming, and was primarily attempted by research laboratory personnel.[4] With the advent of reasonably priced and rapidly responding gas analyzers, accurate volume flow meters, and associated computer technology, the measurement of $\dot{V}O_{2max}$ is now accessible to more scientists, clinicians, and fitness personnel.

THEORY

As work rate increases on an ergometric device (e.g., speed and grade on a treadmill or resistance and tempo on a bicycle ergometer), the rate of oxygen uptake ($\dot{V}O_2$) also increases.[1] If the subject is not limited by prior signs or symptoms of exertional intolerance, $\dot{V}O_2$ increases with increasing work rate until it plateaus. At that time, work rate may continue to increase with no further increase in $\dot{V}O_2$. This maximal rate of oxygen uptake is the $\dot{V}O_{2max}$ and represents a physiologic limit. Work rate may continue to increase past the plateau of $\dot{V}O_{2max}$, yet this increase is accomplished anaerobically. The magnitude of this increase in work rate in excess of $\dot{V}O_{2max}$ does not affect the measurement of $\dot{V}O_{2max}$, but instead relates to the subject's anaerobic power and motivation. The $\dot{V}O_{2max}$ is also a reliable marker of maximal aerobic power with a test-retest reliability of 0.95 and a percent error (standard error/mean $\times$ 100%) of 2.4%.[5]

From the early work of Taylor et al., a plateau in $\dot{V}O_{2max}$ was presumed to occur when less than a 150-ml $\cdot$ min^{-1} (2.1 ml $\cdot$ kg^{-1} $\cdot$ min^{-1}) increase in $\dot{V}O_2$ occurred with an increase in grade of 2.5% at a speed of 7 mph. Thus, an increase of less than 0.6 METs resulted when an increase of about 2.5 METs was expected. Other common presumptions of $\dot{V}O_{2max}$ include a respiratory exchange ratio (R) of greater than 1.1, and lactic acid levels greater than 10 mM.

In older, sedentary, and diseased individuals, a common finding is that $\dot{V}O_2$ never reaches a plateau, principally because the subject ceases exercise before reaching the plateau because of a limiting sign or symptom, such as angina, fatigue, blurred vision, or ST segment depression. In this instance, the peak $\dot{V}O_2$ measurement is more representative of a limiting disease or condition rather than of a physiologic limit. Thus, this determination is often referred to as a symptom-limited $\dot{V}O_{2max}$ or functional capacity,

to differentiate it from the true or physiologic $\dot{V}O_{2max}$.

CALCULATIONS

The determination of $\dot{V}O_2$ can be calculated from either cardiovascular or respiratory parameters. For example, a common relationship is:

$$\dot{V}O_2 = \dot{Q} \cdot (\text{a-}\bar{\text{v}}O_2 \text{ difference}) \qquad [1]$$

in which $\dot{Q}$ is cardiac output (in L/min) and a-$\bar{\text{v}}O_2$ difference is the difference in oxygen concentration between arterial blood (commonly written C_{aO_2}) and mixed venous blood ($C_{\bar{v}O_2}$). The result is expressed as a fraction (e.g., 5 ml O_2/100 ml blood = 0.05). Although this relationship is a good example of the interplay between the cardiovascular and respiratory systems, it does little to help in the calculation of $\dot{V}O_2$ because neither $\dot{Q}$ nor a-$\bar{\text{v}}O_2$ difference are readily measured noninvasively.

A more helpful relationship is:

$$\dot{V}O_2 = (\dot{V}_I \cdot F_{IO_2}) - (\dot{V}_E \cdot F_{EO_2}) \qquad [2]$$

in which $\dot{V}_I$ is the rate at which air is inspired, F_{IO_2} is the fraction of oxygen in the inspired air, $\dot{V}_E$ is the rate at which air is expired, and F_{EO_2} is the fraction of oxygen in the expired air.[4,6] Thus, $\dot{V}O_2$ or the rate of oxygen consumption simply represents the difference between the rate of oxygen inspiration and the rate of oxygen expiration. Recall that $\dot{V}_I$ only equals $\dot{V}_E$ when the respiratory exchange ratio, $R = \dot{V}_{CO_2}/\dot{V}_{O_2}$, equals 1.00 (i.e., when the rate of production of CO_2 is equal to the rate of consumption of O_2). In this simplified case and only in this case can equation 2 be rewritten

$$\dot{V}O_2 = \dot{V}_E \cdot (F_{IO_2} - F_{EO_2}). \qquad [3]$$

More generally, $\dot{V}O_2$ can be calculated from equation 2 by one of two methods. First, because the concentration or fraction of oxygen in inspired air (F_{IO_2} = 20.93% = 0.2093) is known, $\dot{V}O_2$ can be calculated using two volume flow meters to measure the inspired and expired volume flow rates and an oxygen analyzer to measure oxygen concentration in expired air. Thus, the four factors to the right of the equal sign in equation 2 would be known and $\dot{V}O_2$ could be calculated.

More typically, $\dot{V}O_2$ is calculated as follows.[6] $\dot{V}_E$ and F_{EO_2} are measured from expired air with a volume flow meter and an oxygen analyzer, respectively. F_{IO_2} is known and equals 20.93% or 0.2093. $\dot{V}_I$ is then calculated from the following relationship called the Haldane transform. Because nitrogen is neither produced nor consumed to any great extent during metabolism, $\dot{V}N_2$, the rate of nitrogen production or consumption, is equal to zero, or

$$\dot{V}N_2 = (\dot{V}_I \cdot F_{IN_2}) - (\dot{V}_E \cdot F_{EN_2}) = 0 \quad [4]$$

Therefore,

$$\dot{V}_I \cdot F_{IN_2} = \dot{V}_E \cdot F_{EN_2} \quad [5]$$

or

$$\dot{V}_I = (\dot{V}_E \cdot F_{EN_2})/F_{IN_2} \quad [6]$$

The fraction of N_2 in inspired air (F_{IN_2}) is known and is equal to 79.04% or 0.7904. The fraction of N_2 in the expired air (F_{EN_2}) can be calculated from the relationship,

$$F_{EN_2} = 1.0000 - F_{EO_2} - F_{ECO_2} \quad [7]$$

as long as dry gases are analyzed (see subsequent discussion). Note that the difference in concentration of nitrogen in inspired and expired air is a consequence of the differences in the inspiratory and expiratory volume flow rates and not of the production or consumption of nitrogen by the body. For example, if more oxygen is consumed than carbon dioxide is produced ($R < 1.00$), $\dot{V}_I$ will be greater than $\dot{V}_E$ and nitrogen will occupy a greater fraction of the expiratory volume than of the inspiratory volume ($F_{EN_2} > F_{IN_2}$). By using equation 7 and the value for F_{IN_2}, we can calculate $\dot{V}_I$ in equation 6:

$$\dot{V}_I = [\dot{V}_E \cdot (1.0000 - F_{EO_2} - F_{ECO_2})]/0.7904 \quad [8]$$

By recalling equation 2,

$$\dot{V}O_2 = (\dot{V}_I \cdot F_{IO_2}) - (\dot{V}_E \cdot F_{EO_2}) \quad [2]$$

we can solve for $\dot{V}O_2$ by substituting equation 8 and the value for F_{IO_2} (0.2093) into equation 2:

$$\dot{V}O_2 = \dot{V}_E$$
$$\cdot [0.265 \times (1.0000 - F_{EO_2} - F_{ECO_2}) - F_{EO_2}] \quad [9]$$

The value contained within the brackets in equation 9 is the True O_2 and is the fraction of oxygen consumed for any $\dot{V}_E$. By inspecting equation 9, we see that $\dot{V}O_2$ can be calculated by using a volume flow meter to measure $\dot{V}_E$ and by gas analyzers to measure the fractions of oxygen and carbon dioxide in expired air (F_{EO_2} and F_{ECO_2}, respectively).

Whereas $\dot{V}_E$ is measured under ambient conditions, i.e., at **A**mbient **T**emperature, **P**ressure, and **S**aturated with water vapor (ATPS), in metabolic calculations $\dot{V}_E$ must be expressed relative to **S**tandard conditions of **T**emperature (273°K), **P**ressure (760 mm Hg), and **D**ry (i.e., no water vapor) (STPD) so that these flow rates may be compared in environmental conditions that may vary relative to altitude, heat, and humidity. $\dot{V}_E$(ATPS) may be converted to $\dot{V}_E$(STPD) as follows:[6]

$$\dot{V}_E(STPD) = \dot{V}_E(ATPS)$$
$$\cdot [(P_B - WVP)/760 \text{ mm Hg}]$$
$$\cdot [273°K/(273°K + T_G)], \quad [10]$$

in which P_B is ambient barometric pressure and WVP is the water vapor pressure at the gas temperature (T_G) in the volume flow meter. T_G is presented in °C and WVP can be found in standard tables.[6]

MEASUREMENT

Properly calibrated and functioning equipment is required to obtain accurate, reproducible, and valid results.[7] Calibration gases must be of known concentration: the gas should be certified against a primary gravimetric standard, chemical gas analyzer, or read against a gas chromatograph, mass spectrometer, or other calibrating instrument that has, itself, been calibrated against a primary gravimetric standard or chemical gas analyzer. Calibrate gas analyzers immediately before each test with the calibration gas. Gas analyzers of unknown or questionable stability also require calibration immediately after the test is completed to correct for analyzer drift. Before each testing session, check all respiratory hoses and connections for air tightness. On a routine (monthly to quarterly) basis, calibrate ergometric devices, thermistors, and volume flow meters. Closely monitor respiratory valves for proper functioning and ensure the desiccant (used to dry gases) is fresh. If the subject uses a mouthpiece, ensure that a noseclip is placed securely on the nose and that the mouth seals well around the mouthpiece.

The measurement of $\dot{V}_{O_2}$ can be made manually, semiautomatically, or automatically with a microprocessed system.[4,8,9] The generality of the approach is illustrated by describing a system for manual or semiautomatic measurement of $\dot{V}_{O_2}$ (Fig. 20–1). A brief discussion of on-line (microprocessed) data collection follows (Fig. 20–2).

OPERATION OF THE MANUAL OR SEMIAUTOMATIC SYSTEM FOR $\dot{V}_{O_2}$ MEASUREMENT

General

1. Volume flow rates and gas compositions are measured.
2. Volume flow rates to be measured are:
    a. Portion of $\dot{V}_E$ through the volume flow meter.
    b. Additional ventilation or the portion of $\dot{V}_E$ drawn off by the gas sample (vacuum) pump that fills the gas sample bag.

3. The gas compositions to be measured are:
    a. $F_{E_{O_2}}$
    b. $F_{E_{CO_2}}$.
4. To measure gas composition of dry expired gases, the gases being sampled by the analyzers are passed through a desiccant.
5. To convert $\dot{V}_E$ in ATPS to STPD conditions, record gas temperature at the volume flow meter and barometric pressure.

System Configuration (Fig. 20–1)

1. Air is drawn in through the one-way mouthpiece valve (i.e., flapper valves are placed in the mouthpiece so air flows into the mouth only from the room and exhaled air flows only into the mixing chamber). Upon expiration, air is blown out through the mixing chamber, which mixes the expired gases, and travels past the thermometer or thermistor, and through the volume flow meter, which records $\dot{V}_E$ (minus additional ventilation) on a calibrated chart recorder.
2. The gas sample for analysis (i.e., additional ventilation) is drawn off through a sampling port on the mixing chamber by the vacuum pump and passes through a three-way spin-

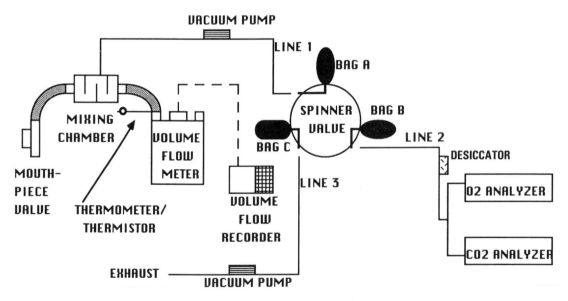

FIGURE 20–1. System configuration for manual or semi-automatic $\dot{V}_{O_2}$ measurement. *Solid lines*, gas sample lines. *Dashed lines*, electric lines. *Shaded areas*, respiratory hoses.

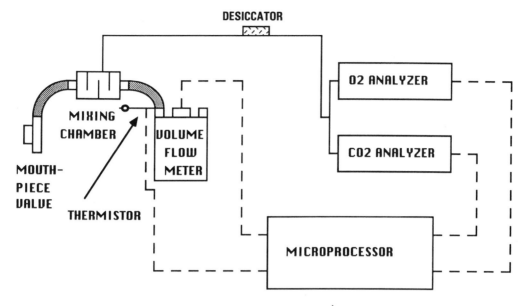

FIGURE 20–2. System configuration for on-line (microprocessed) $\dot{V}O_2$ measurement. Note that in breath-by-breath analysis, sampling gas line would connect directly to mouthpiece, obviating a mixing chamber.

ner valve and into a 2-L gas collecting bag (A). In the absence of the spinner valve, gases are measured in a similar fashion as that described subsequently with the use of the three hoses shown: line 1 to vacuum pump, line 2 to analyzers, and line 3 to gas bag being sampled.

3. Three bags are on the valve at any one time. Gas collects in one bag (bag A on line 1), the gas in a second bag is being analyzed (bag B on line 2), and a third bag is being evacuated (bag C on line 3) so that bag C can be filled again with a new gas sample when it is rotated onto line 1 in the next minute. Thus, the spinner valve is turned from line 1 to 2 to 3 to 1, and so forth, so that after 1 minute of sample collection, the sample is analyzed in the next minute, and the bag is evacuated in the following minute. Note that the two other bags are also being either filled, analyzed, or evacuated simultaneously so that all of these processes are essentially continuous, they just involve different bags.

Precollection Procedures

1. Determine barometric pressure.
2. Fill desiccant column with new desiccant.

3. Ensure all equipment is operating, warmed-up, and calibrated.
4. Measure additional ventilation by collecting a sample of room air for exactly 1 min from line 1 (Fig. 20–1). Limit flow through the vacuum pump to 1 to 1.5 L/min with a hose clamp. Using the gas sample port on the spirometer, empty this bag into the spirometer to measure the volume of gas that this system draws in 1 min. This quantity is additional ventilation.
5. Shortly before starting gas collection (within 1 to 3 min), calibrate the gas analyzers. Mark the time of the calibration so that later adjustment for analyzer drift is possible, if necessary.
6. To fill a bag with calibration gas, evacuate the flush bag with calibration gas twice. Then turn on the calibration gas, insert the tip of the gas bag firmly into the gas line, and open the valve on the gas bag. When the bag is full, close the valve first, then remove the bag from the gas line and turn off the calibration gas valve.

Collection Procedures

1. Have the subject place the mouthpiece se-

curely in their mouth and check the seal. Adjust for comfort and put on the noseclip.

2. At time $t = 0$
   a. Start the stopwatch.
   b. Mark the $\dot{V}_E$ recorder accurately.
   c. Switch a new bag to the gas collection port.

3. At each minute of exercise
   a. Mark $\dot{V}_E$ recorder accurately.
   b. Rotate or place the evacuated bag onto the gas collection port.
   c. Analyze the gas previously collected. Record this value after readings are stabilized.
   d. Read the gas temperature at the gas flow meter.
   e. Evacuate the bag for the gas collection during the next minute.

4. At end of exercise
   a. Accurately mark the $\dot{V}_E$ recorder. If less than one full minute of exercise is recorded, calculate what $\dot{V}_E$ would have been for that minute. For example, if the subject stopped at 8 min and 47 sec of exercise, the correction to your recorded ventilation volume in the last 47 sec is $\dot{V}_E = [(60 \text{ sec/min})/47 \text{ sec}] \cdot$ ventilation volume. The result provides $\dot{V}_E$ in units of L/min versus L/47 sec.
   b. Rotate the gas sample to the analyzer and record the values.
   c. Immediately after recording the final values, recalibrate the gas analyzers if of unknown or uncertain stability. Mark the time of recalibration and, if necessary, calculate the drift rates for both of your analyzers. (Drift rate = analyzer drift/Δ time). Assume a linear drift rate and correct all minute values of F_{EO_2} and F_{ECO_2}. For example, if data collection began 2 min after the analyzers were initially calibrated, data collection lasted 17 min, recalibration was complete 1 min after the end of exercise, and the drift in the O_2 analyzer was -0.20%, then the drift rate would be $-0.20\%/20 \text{ min} = -0.01\%/$ min. If the recorded F_{EO_2} after 6 min of exercise was 17.13%, then the corrected F_{EO_2} would be $17.13\% + (-0.01\%/\text{min})(6 \text{ min}) = 17.13\% - 0.06\% = 17.07\%$. With analyzers of established stability and minimal drift, drift rate correction is also minimal and may not be necessary if the gas analyzers are calibrated immediately before each test.

d. Upon completion of gas collection, evacuate bags, turn off the vacuum pumps, place analyzers in standby, turn off other equipment, and blow fresh air through the volume flow meter to dry the components. Wash and disinfect respiratory equipment (mouthpiece and hoses).

Calculate $\dot{V}O_2$ from Equation 9

1. Calculate total $\dot{V}_E(ATPS) = \dot{V}_E$ measured plus additional ventilation. (Note $\dot{V}_E$ measured may need to be adjusted by a calibration factor, according to the last calibration of the volume flow meter).
2. Convert $\dot{V}_E(ATPS)$ to $\dot{V}_E(STPD)$.
3. Correct F_{EO_2} and F_{ECO_2} for drift, if necessary.
4. Solve for $\dot{V}O_2$ by using equation 9:

$$\dot{V}O_2 = \dot{V}_E \cdot [0.265 \times (1.0000 - F_{EO_2} - F_{ECO_2}) - F_{EO_2}] \quad [9]$$

OPERATION OF AN ON-LINE (MICROPROCESSED) SYSTEM FOR $\dot{V}O_2$ MEASUREMENT

1. The theory and operation of $\dot{V}O_2$ measurement with computers is analogous to manual collection. A block diagram is shown in Figure 20–2. We direct the interested reader to an article by Wilmore, Davis, and Norton.[9]
2. On-line data collection and analysis greatly speed $\dot{V}O_2$ measurement; however, care is required to ensure the system operates correctly. An effective initial check of system operation is to observe that reasonable (physiologic) values are recorded for respiratory parameters.
3. On-line data collection and analysis also enable the investigator to make breath-by-breath $\dot{V}O_2$ measurements. Although such analysis is important in scientific metabolic studies and in clinical testing of cardiopulmonary patients, the greater initial expense perhaps argues against such measurement in general fitness testing in which the measurement of $\dot{V}O_{2\,max}$ is typically sufficient.

REFERENCES

1. Wasserman K, Whipp BJ: Exercise physiology in health and disease. *Am Rev Respir Dis*, 112:219, 1975.

2. Lamb DR: *Physiology of Exercise.* 2nd Ed. New York: MacMillan, 1984.

3. American College of Sports Medicine: *Guidelines for Exercise Testing and Prescription.* 3rd Ed. Philadelphia: Lea & Febiger, 1986.

4. Consolazio CF, Johnson RE, Pecora LJ: *Physiological Measurements of Metabolic Functions in Man.* New York: McGraw-Hill, 1963.

5. Taylor HL, Buskirk E, Henschel A: Maximal oxygen uptake as an objective measure of cardiorespiratory performance. *J Appl Physiol, 8:*73, 1955.

6. McArdle WD, Katch FI, Katch VL: *Exercise Physiology.* 2nd Ed. Philadelphia: Lea & Febiger, 1986.

7. Jones NL, Campbell EJM: *Clinical Exercise Testing.* 2nd Ed. Philadelphia: W.B. Saunders, 1982.

8. Wilmore JH, Costill DL: Semiautomated systems approach to the assessment of oxygen uptake during exercise. *J Appl Physiol, 36:*618, 1974.

9. Wilmore JH, Davis JA, Norton AC: An automated system for assessing metabolic and respiratory function during exercise. *J Appl Physiol, 40:*619, 1976.

21

BASIC ELECTROCARDIOGRAPHIC ANALYSIS

J. P. SCHAMAN

Electrocardiographic (ECG) interpretation can at times be simple and at other times be complex. The evaluation of ECG findings is always best in the light of clinical information, if available. For example, ST segment elevation in a patient with chest pain could very well indicate an acute myocardial infarction, whereas the same tracing in a young healthy asymptomatic man is most likely the normal variant, "early repolarization ST segment elevation." Our knowledge of the ECG has known limitations, and occasionally even experienced interpreters have differing opinions. Occasionally, tracings must be considered "borderline" or "nonspecific," and are therefore not helpful and are frankly dissatisfying. We must also realize that ECG findings do not necessarily provide the data to predict the ultimate outcome of the patient. A patient with a normal ECG may die suddenly of a heart attack, whereas a patient with grossly abnormal ECG findings may live many years without apparent difficulty.

Despite these shortcomings, ECG interpretation can be most rewarding and enjoyable, particularly if approached somewhat as a game rather than as an academic struggle. By following the rules and "game plan" presented in this chapter, most ECGs can be evaluated accurately with pleasure rather than with frustration.

BASIC ELECTROPHYSIOLOGY

The resting myocardial cell is in a "polarized" state, i.e., the resting potential is about −90 mV, when comparing the inside and the outside of the cell. This resting state is regularly interrupted by a jolt of electric activity that causes the cell membrane to become permeable. A rapid ionic shift and the development of a positive potential of approximately +30 mV result. This reaction is called phase 0 of the action potential (Fig. 21−1), or the depolarization phase. Phases 1 to 3 represent the three phases of repolarization, with phase 2 being the "plateau," which is usually slightly positive or close to 0 mV. Phase 4 is the period of electric diastole. In nonpacemaker cells, this phase is flat; in pacemaker cells, this phase is gradually upsloping until it reaches a threshold level, at which time phase 0 depolarization follows.

The cell interior usually has a preponderance of potassium ions and only a small number of sodium ions. Considerably more negative charge is inside the cell and more positive charge is outside the cell. The cell exterior has primarily sodium ions. During depolarization, the membrane becomes more permeable and sodium rushes into the cell, increasing the total intracellular amount of sodium. Sodium carries

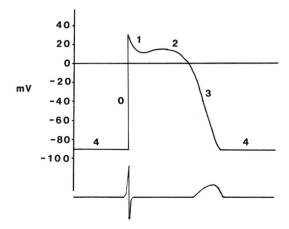

FIGURE 21–1. Action potential.

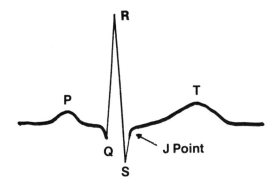

FIGURE 21–3. Major waves of normal electrocardiographic pathway.

positive charges and hence creates a positive environment intracellularly. During repolarization, sodium and potassium pumps return the ions to their previous resting locations, and the myocardium is prepared for the next depolarization and contraction.

WAVES, LEADS, AND AXIS

The ECG tracing is a plot of the electric activity of the heart in millivolts against time. The ECG graph paper is divided into small 1-mm squares and larger 5-mm squares (Fig. 21–2). Horizontally, each small square is equivalent to 0.04 sec (with standard paper speed of 25 mm/sec) and each large square is equivalent to 0.2 sec. Vertically, each small square is 0.1 mV (with a calibration of 10 mm/mV).

A normal, single heart beat consists of five major waves: P, Q, R, S, and T (Fig. 21–3). The P-wave is the electric impulse associated with contraction of the atria. The Q-, R-, and S-waves are considered as a unit, representing the depolarization of the ventricles. These waves are known as the QRS complex. The T-wave is produced by repolarization of the ventricles.

The 12-lead ECG comprises three groups of leads: (1) bipolar limb leads I, II, III; (2) unipolar limb leads aVR, aVL, aVF; and (3) precordial or chest leads V_{1-6}. Each bipolar limb lead has a negative or ground electrode and a positive exploring electrode. In lead I, the positive electrode is on the left arm and the negative electrode is on the right arm. In lead II, the positive electrode is on the left leg and the negative electrode is on the right arm. Lead III has the positive electrode on the left leg and the negative electrode on the left arm. These three leads form the sides of Einthoven's triangle (Fig. 21–4). By moving these three leads so they intersect at a common point, a useful axis system results (Fig. 21–5).

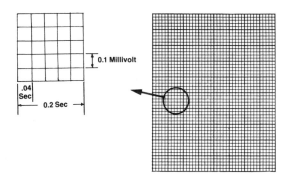

FIGURE 21–2. Electrocardiogram graph paper.

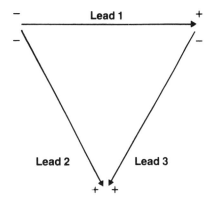

FIGURE 21–4. Einthoven's triangle.

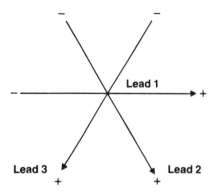

FIGURE 21–5. Axis system incorporating leads I, II, and III.

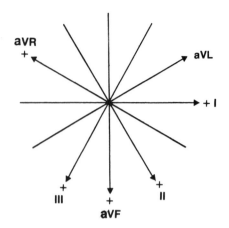

FIGURE 21–7. Total axis system.

One of the most important concepts in electrocardiography is the relationship between the direction of travel of the electric impulse and a given lead. If the impulse travels toward the positive pole (electrode), an upward deflection in the ECG tracing results. If the impulse travels toward the negative pole, a downward deflection results.

The unipolar or augmented leads have the positive electrode on one of the limbs: R-right arm, L-left arm, and F-left foot. The ground electrode consists of all of the remaining electrodes. The axis system formed by these leads differs from the bipolar limb leads (Fig. 21–6). By combining the two groups, however, a total axis system for the limb leads results (Fig. 21–7). This system can be used to determine the mean electric axis of ventricular depolarization. By plotting the mean QRS deflection, either negative or positive, of two perpendicular

leads, the interpreter can plot the axis of depolarization. By using this principle, a short-cut estimation of axis can be made, because the axis is perpendicular to the lead that has a zero mean QRS deflection (i.e., R = Q + S).

If, for example, the height of the R-wave equals the sum of the heights of the Q- and S-waves in lead I, then this lead has a zero mean QRS deflection. By plotting the axis on Figure 21–7, we see that the QRS axis is perpendicular to lead I, i.e., along lead aVF, either upward or downward. The next step is to inspect lead aVF to determine whether the QRS is primarily positive or negative. If positive, the axis will be +90° (Fig. 21–8); if negative, the axis will be −90°. The normal electric axis is thought to be

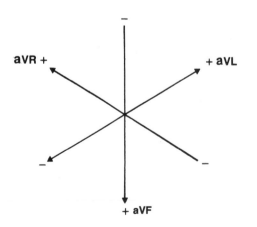

FIGURE 21–6. Axis system incorporating leads aVR, aVL, and aVF.

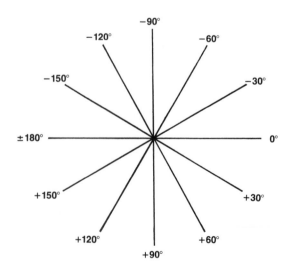

FIGURE 21–8. Axis frame.

from −30 to +120°. Left axis deviation refers to a mean QRS frontal axis between −30 and −120°, which may result from a horizontal position assumed by the heart, the upward displacement of the diaphragm (as occurs with pregnancy, tumors, ascites, and so forth), left bundle branch block, left anterior hemiblock, left ventricular hypertrophy, inferior myocardial infarction, cardiomyopathy, and other causes. Right axis deviation refers to a QRS axis between +120 and +180°, which may result from a vertical position assumed by the heart, downward displacement of the diaphragm (as occurs with inspiration or emphysema), right ventricular hypertrophy, right bundle branch block, and anterior myocardial infarction.

The limb leads, bipolar and unipolar, give information about the electric activity of the heart in only the frontal plane (Fig. 21–7). The precordial leads, V_{1-6}, give information in the precordial plane, which is perpendicular to the frontal plane. The appropriate positioning of the positive electrode in the precordial leads follows:

V_1: Right sternal border in the fourth intercostal space
V_2: Left sternal border in the fourth intercostal space
V_3: Equally spaced between V_2 and V_4
V_4: Midclavicular line in the fifth intercostal space

V_5: Anterior axillary line in the fifth intercostal space
V_6: Midaxillary line in the fifth intercostal space.

Correct lead placement in electrocardiography is critical. Any variation from correct lead placement results in tracings other than the "standard 12 ECG." For example, in exercise stress testing, patients are frequently prepared with a 12-lead ECG during exercise. Because standard limb lead placement results in considerable movement artifact, the limb leads are frequently placed at the anterior aspects of the shoulders and at the right and left lower costal margins. This adjustment allows useful and "readable" tracings to be obtained, yet it does not give a "standard 12-lead ECG." Therefore, recording a 12-lead ECG with standard limb lead placement before rewiring the leads to the exercise placement is important.

THE ELECTRIC CONDUCTION SYSTEM

The interpretation of an ECG tracing necessitates an understanding of the electric conduction system of the heart (Fig. 21–9). The impulse originates in the sino-atrial (SA) node and

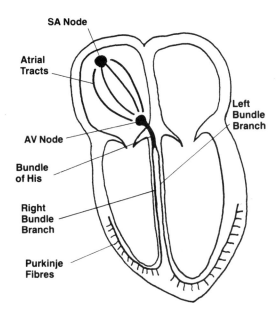

FIGURE 21–9. Electric conduction system.

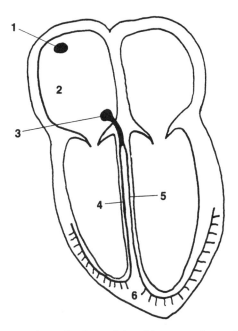

FIGURE 21–10. Potential problem areas in conduction system.

Table 21–1. Relationship of Potential ECG Problems to the Electric Conduction System

Problem area	Potential problem
Sinoatrial node	Sinus arrhythmia Sinus tachycardia Sinus bradycardia SA block—incomplete 　　　　—complete Sinus arrest Sick sinus syndrome
Atria	Atrial premature beats Paroxysmal atrial tachycardia Wandering atrial pacemaker Atrial flutter Atrial fibrillation Right or left atrial hypertrophy Intra-atrial block
Atrioventricular node	Nodal premature beats Nodal tachycardia Pre-excitation (Wolff-Parkinson-White syndrome) AV block—1st degree 　　　　—2nd degree—Mobitz Type I (Wenckebach) 　　　　　　　　　　—Mobitz Type II 　　　　—3rd degree AV dissociation
Right bundle branch	Right bundle branch block Aberrant conduction
Left bundle branch	Left bundle branch block Fascicular block—Left anterior hemiblock 　　　　　　　—Left posterior hemiblock Aberrant conduction
Ventricles	Premature ventricular contractions Ventricular tachycardia Ventricular flutter Ventricular fibrillation Myocardial ischemia Myocardial infarction Right or left ventricular hypertrophy

travels through the atrial tracts to the atrioventricular (AV) node. During this time, the atria are depolarized and a P-wave is inscribed on the ECG tracing (Fig. 21–3). After a brief pause at the AV node (PR interval), which allows time for the atria to contract and to eject their contents into the ventricles, the impulse travels down the bundle branches to depolarize the ventricles by way of the Purkinje fibers (QRS complex).

By referring to the electric conduction system of the heart, an electrophysiologic explanation for all ECG abnormalities is possible. Figure 21–10 illustrates the various locations of potential problems. In Table 21–1, these areas are correlated to most known ECG abnormalities. Before discussing many of these conditions, a game plan is needed that will facilitate almost

without fail the accurate interpretation of any ECG tracing.

PRACTICAL RULES IN ECG EVALUATION

Even an inexperienced electrocardiographer can interpret most ECG tracings by memorizing and systematically following, preferably in the order listed, nine points:

1. Rate
2. Rhythm
3. P-waves
4. PR interval

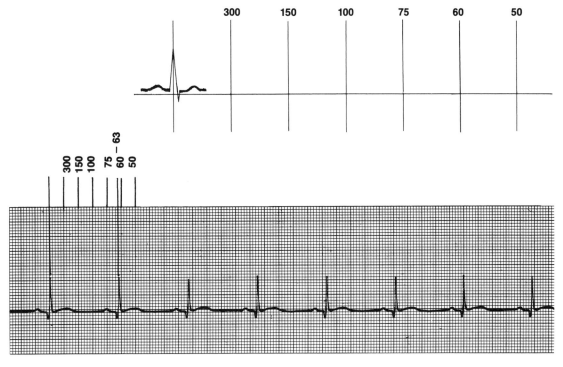

FIGURE 21-11. Rate determination.

5. QRS complex:
  a. Duration
  b. Configuration
  c. Axis
6. ST segment
7. T-waves
8. U-waves
9. QT interval

RATE

Rate can be determined by using an ECG Heart Rate ruler or several other techniques, such as

$$Rate = \frac{300}{\text{(Number of large squares between two R-waves)}}$$

or the $(300 - 150 - 100 - 75 - 60 - 50)$ technique (see Fig. 21-11).

RHYTHM

Regular rhythm usually refers to ventricular rhythm and implies equal R-R intervals. Such is the case in normal sinus rhythm (Fig. 21-12);

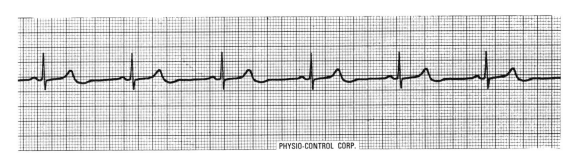

FIGURE 21-12. Normal sinus rhythm.

however, equal R-R intervals can also occur in such rhythms as paroxysmal atrial tachycardia or idioventricular rhythm (Figs. 21–13, 21–14).

An irregularity in rhythm is called an arrhythmia, but a better term would be dysrhythmia, because arrhythmia implies no rhythm at all. An arrhythmia can have a certain degree of system to the irregularity, as in respiratory sinus arrhythmia, bigeminy, or Wenckebach AV block (Figs. 21–15 to 21–17). The arrhythmia could also appear randomly, as in scattered extrasystoles or premature beats (Fig. 21–18), or with complete irregularity, as in atrial fibrillation or ventricular fibrillation (Figs. 21–19, 21–20).

P-WAVES

A necessary step in analysis is to note the shape, duration, and amplitude of P-waves, as well as to determine whether a QRS complex follows each P-wave and if a P-wave precedes each QRS complex. P-wave duration is usually less than 0.11 sec. In right atrial hypertrophy, the P-waves are tall and narrow (Fig. 21–21); in

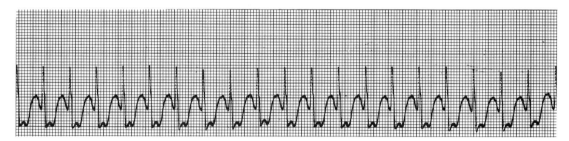

FIGURE 21–13. Paroxysmal atrial tachycardia (PAT).

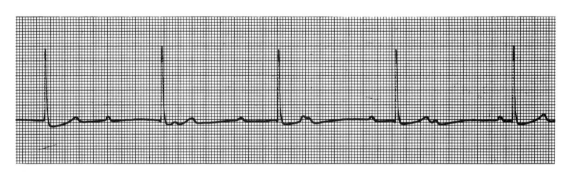

FIGURE 21–14. Idioventricular rhythm.

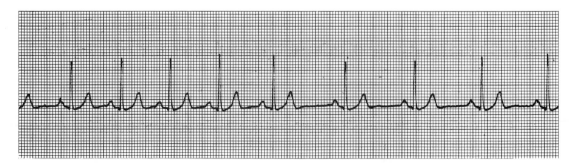

FIGURE 21–15. Sinus arrhythmia.

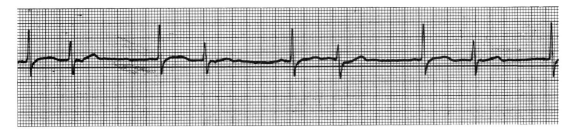

FIGURE 21 – 16. Bigeminy.

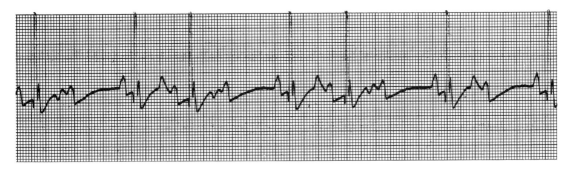

FIGURE 21 – 17. Wenckebach phenomenon.

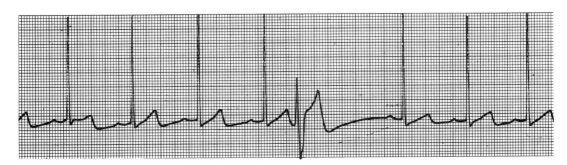

FIGURE 21 – 18. Premature ventricular contractions (PVCs).

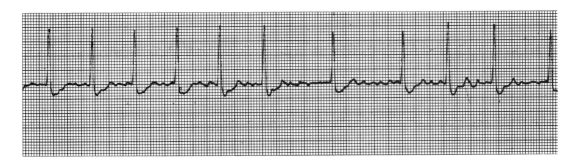

FIGURE 21 – 19. Atrial fibrillation.

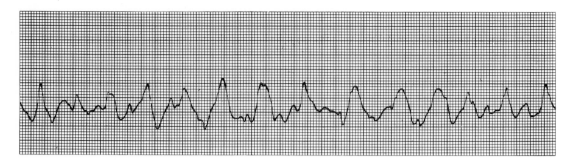

FIGURE 21–20. Ventricular fibrillation.

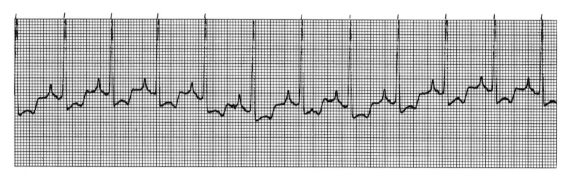

FIGURE 21–21. Tall and narrow P-waves suggestive of right atrial hypertrophy.

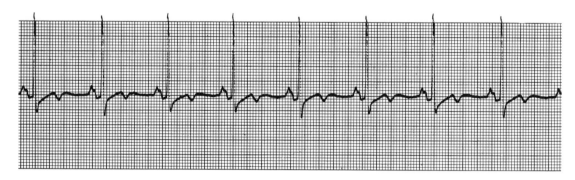

FIGURE 21–22. Wide and notched P-waves suggestive of left atrial hypertrophy.

left atrial hypertrophy, the P-waves are wide and often notched (Fig. 21–22). In atrial flutter, the P-waves take on a "sawtoothed pattern," which characterizes flutter waves (Fig. 21–23). In atrial fibrillation, no identifiable P-waves are seen, and the rhythm is said to be "irregularly irregular" (Fig. 21–24). In essence, the R-R intervals do not have pattern or regularity.

PR INTERVAL

The PR interval is measured from the beginning of the P-wave to the beginning of the QRS complex. It is normally not shorter than 0.12 sec and not longer than 0.20 sec. This amount of time is required to allow the atria to eject blood into the ventricles before ventricular contraction. A shortened PR interval is noted in Wolff-Parkinson-White (W-P-W) syndrome (pre-excitation), in which abnormal conduction pathways bypass the AV node, or occasionally in nodal rhythm, in which retrograde conduction through the atria occurs. The PR interval is prolonged in first-degree AV block (Fig. 21–26). An important step is to determine if the PR interval is constant and if the P-waves are re-

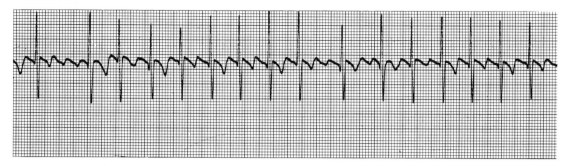

FIGURE 21–23. Atrial flutter.

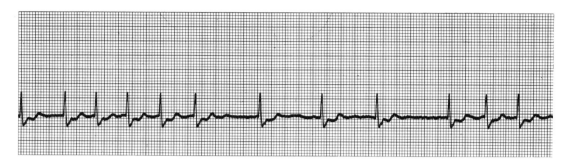

FIGURE 21–24. Atrial fibrillation.

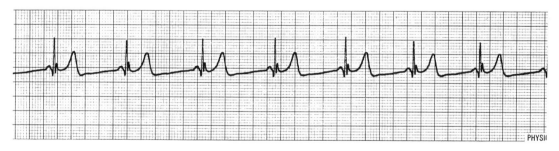

FIGURE 21–25. Short PR interval.

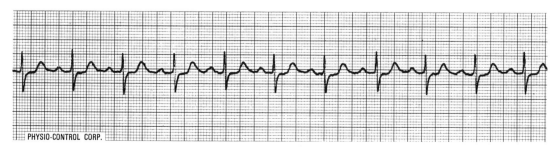

FIGURE 21–26. Prolonged PR interval (0.22 sec) in first-degree block.

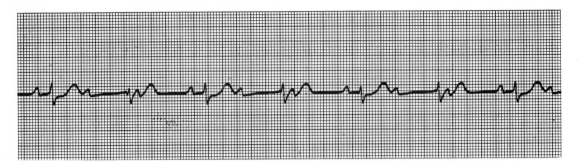

FIGURE 21–27. Third-degree atrioventricular block with two QRS complexes for every three P-waves.

lated to the QRS complexes. Occasionally, the atria and ventricles can beat independently (third-degree AV block), but appear to be related. In Figure 21–27, every second QRS complex is preceded by a P-wave with a constant PR interval. In actual fact, three P-waves occur for every two QRS complexes, and the atria beat independently of the ventricles. The atrial rate is 84 and regular and the ventricular rate is 56 and regular.

QRS COMPLEX

Duration

The duration of the normal QRS complex is less than 0.12 sec. A widened QRS complex can occur in right and left bundle branch block (Table 21–2, Fig. 21–28), pre-excitation syndrome (W-P-W), left ventricular hypertrophy, aberrant conduction, premature ventricular contractions, ventricular tachycardia, and hyperkalemia.

Configuration

When assessing the configuration of the QRS complex, its nature, constant or varying, should be noted. Slight changes in QRS amplitude can occur during respiration because of changes in the position of the heart (Fig. 21–29). During exercise, this change in amplitude can be significant. The presence of premature ventricular contractions (PVCs) with varying QRS configuration is indicative of multifocal extrasystoles, which are more significant findings than unifocal extra beats (Figs. 21–30, 21–31).

That the relative amplitudes of Q-, R-, and S-waves are helpful in diagnosing ventricular hypertrophy (Table 21–3) has become a matter

Table 21–2. Comparison of ECG Findings in Bundle Branch Block

ECG findings	
Right bundle branch block	Left bundle branch block
M-shaped QRS complex in V_{1-2} and broad S in lead I	M-shaped QRS complex in V_{5-6} and broad S in lead III
ST depression and T inversion in lead III, V_{1-2}	ST depression and T inversion in lead I, aVL, V_{5-6}

of controversy. The theory relating to ventricular hypertrophy is based on the premise that if the ventricular wall is thicker than normal, the impulse will take longer to traverse it and the voltage of the QRS complexes will increase in leads that overlook the hypertrophied ventricular muscle. The various criteria proposed for the diagnosis of ventricular hypertrophy are not reliable, with poor sensitivity but good specificity.

Axis

The determination of the frontal plane electric axis was previously discussed. Axis deviation can be important in the diagnosis of ventricular hypertrophy as well as left anterior and posterior hemiblocks (Tables 21–3, 21–4). The left bundle branch comprises the anterior and the posterior fascicles. Left anterior hemiblock is common and is not usually of major significance; left posterior hemiblock rarely occurs and is usually indicative of a significant disease process.

ST SEGMENT

Changes in the ST segment are important in the diagnosis of myocardial ischemia or infarction. The ST segment level is compared to the

Left   **Right**

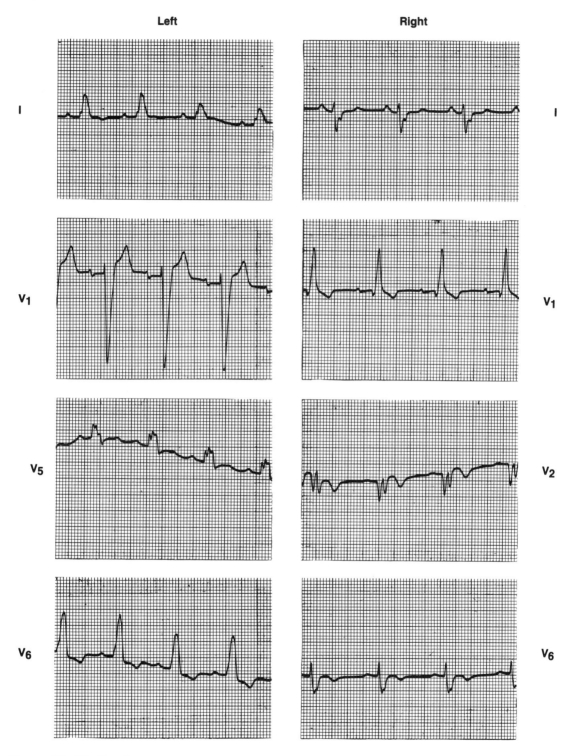

FIGURE 21-28. Bundle branch block.

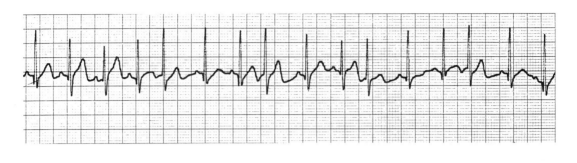

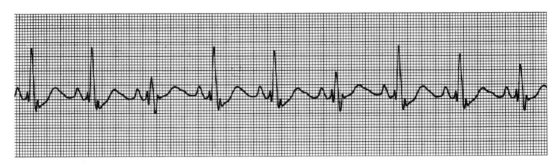

FIGURE 21–29. QRS amplitude variation.

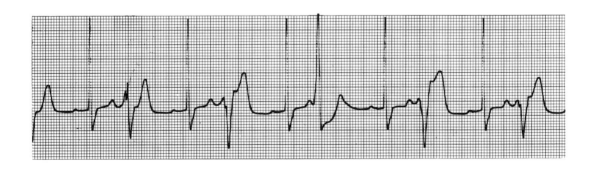

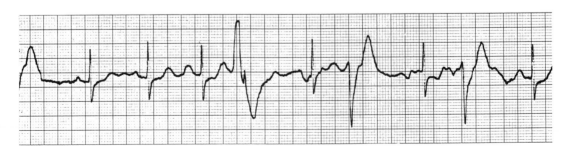

FIGURE 21–30. Multifocal PVCs.

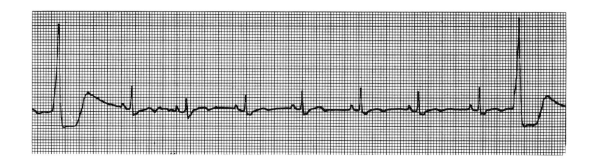

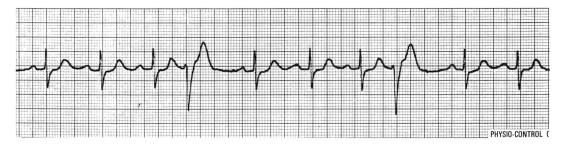

PHYSIO-CONTROL (

FIGURE 21–31. Unifocal PVCs.

Table 21–3. Comparison of ECG Findings in Ventricular Hypertrophy

ECG findings	
Right ventricle	Left ventricle
Tall R or R' in V_{1-2}; small S in V_{1-2}; deep S in V_{5-6}	Tall R in V_{5-6} (> 25 mm); deep S in V_{1-2} (> 25 mm)
ST depression and T-wave inversion in leads II, III, V_{1-3}	ST depression and T-wave inversion in lead I, aVL, V_{5-6}
Right axis deviation	Left axis deviation
QRS duration usually normal	QRS duration 0.09 sec or more

Table 21–4. Comparison of ECG Findings in Hemiblock

ECG findings	
Left anterior hemiblock	Left posterior hemiblock
Left axis deviation (−60°)	Right axis deviation (+120°)
Small Q in lead I; small R in lead III	Small R in lead I; small Q in lead III
Normal QRS duration	Normal QRS duration
	No evidence of right ventricular hypertrophy

isoelectric line, which is the level of the segment from the T-wave to the P-wave of the following beat. For instances in which this level is not well defined, especially during exercise, the isoelectric line is considered the level of the PR interval immediately preceding the QRS complex. The ST segment is discussed more fully in *Myocardial Infarction and Ischemia.*

T-WAVES

In assessing T-waves, an important step is to note their direction and amplitude. They can be upright (Fig. 21–32A), inverted (Fig. 21–32B), flattened (Fig. 21–32C), or diphasic (Fig. 21–32D). T-waves are usually upright in leads I, II, and V_{5-6}, and are inverted in aVR. Inverted or diphasic T-waves can be seen in normal subjects in leads III and V_{1-2}. T-wave changes, either alone or with ST segment changes, are frequent ECG abnormalities. These findings can often be normal variants or may result from a wide range of physiologic conditions (posture changes, respiration, drugs, mental factors, and so forth). Because of the high correlation of T-wave changes with coronary heart disease, however, they should be treated with respect.

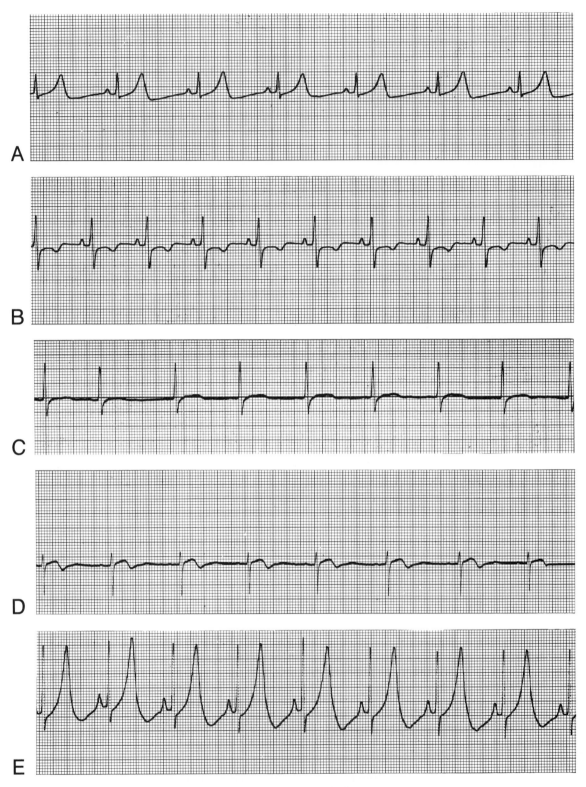

FIGURE 21–32. T-waves. **A,** upright; **B,** inverted; **C,** flattened; **D,** diphasic; **E,** tall tented, as in hyperkalemia.

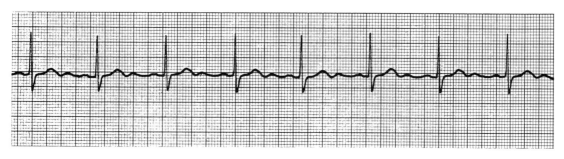

FIGURE 21-33. U-waves.

The amplitude of the T-wave is also extremely variable. Very tall, tented T-waves are a feature of hyperkalemia (Fig. 21-32E).

U-WAVES

The U-wave is usually of low amplitude, and immediately follows the T-wave. The U-wave is usually in the same direction as the T-wave. This wave is most easily seen in the middle precordial leads (V_{2-4}) and is more pronounced in patients with hypokalemia (Fig. 21-33).

QT INTERVAL

This segment is measured from the beginning of the QRS complex to the end of the T-wave. It correlates well with the ejection time of the heart (systole). The normal range is from 0.35 to 0.45 sec, although this segment varies greatly with heart rate (Table 21-5). Prolonged QT intervals occur in patients with myocardial ischemia, myocardial infarction, ventricular dysfunction, bundle branch block, left ventricular hypertrophy, hypokalemia, and hypocalcemia.

ARRHYTHMIAS (VENTRICULAR AND SUPRAVENTRICULAR)

PREMATURE CONTRACTIONS

A premature beat is one that comes before the expected normal sinus-node originating beat. In other words, the interval from the preceding normal beat to the abnormal beat is less than the normal RR interval. The premature contraction can be supraventricular, either atrial or junctional (previously called nodal), or it can be ventricular. Making the distinction between ventricular and supraventricular premature contractions is important. Table 21-6 is a list of various criteria that are often, but not always, helpful in distinguishing ventricular and supraventricular premature beats. Use of these cri-

Table 21-5. Normal QT Intervals at Various Heart Rates

Heart rate (beats/min)	QT interval (sec)
40	0.42-0.50
50	0.36-0.46
60	0.33-0.43
70	0.30-0.40
80	0.29-0.38
90	0.28-0.36
100	0.27-0.35
110	0.26-0.33
120	0.25-0.32
150	0.23-0.28

Table 21-6. Supraventricular versus Ventricular Premature Beats

ECG criteria	Premature beats	
	Supraventricular	Ventricular
QRS complex of beat in question	Normal duration (<0.12 sec); same configuration as normal beat	Increased duration (≥0.12 sec); bizarre configuration compared to normal beat
P-wave preceding beat in question	Usually present (sometimes difficult to see in nodal premature contractions)	Absent
Interval between two normal beats on either side of beat in question	Less than two normal RR intervals (i.e., <2/RR/)	Equal to two normal RR intervals (see Fig. 21-35)

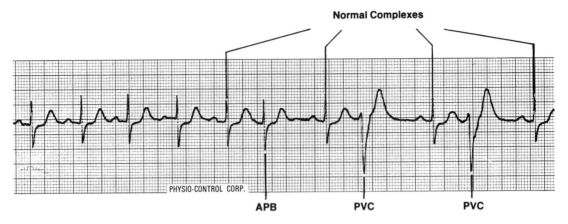

FIGURE 21-34. PVC versus atrial premature beats (APB).

teria is illustrated in Figure 21–34; examples of premature beats are illustrated in Figure 21–35 and 21–36. A particular challenge arises when premature beats of supraventricular origin are conducted with aberrant conduction. In aberrant conduction, the electric impulse takes a different route through the conduction system, which usually results in QRS complexes that are wide and different in configuration when compared to regular beats. In this instance, the QRS criteria are no longer helpful, however, the

other criteria can be useful in the diagnosis of this conduction disturbance.

Occasionally, premature beats are frequent and occur with a predictable regularity. If every second beat is premature, this rhythm is called bigeminy. Similarly, if the premature beat occurs every third beat, the rhythm is labeled trigeminy (Fig. 21–37). A premature ventricular contraction (PVC) that occurs at the same time as or close to the preceding T-wave is significantly more dangerous, because ventricular

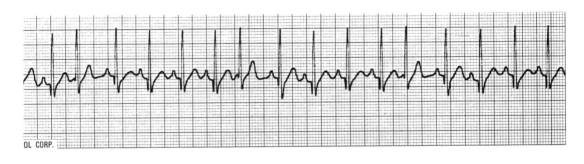

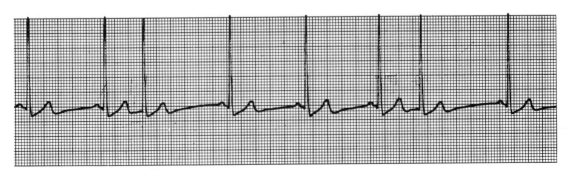

FIGURE 21-35. Supraventricular premature contractions.

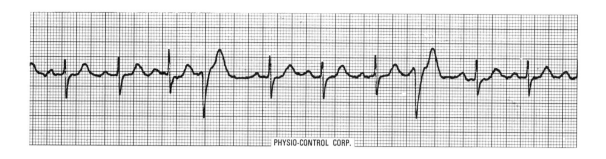

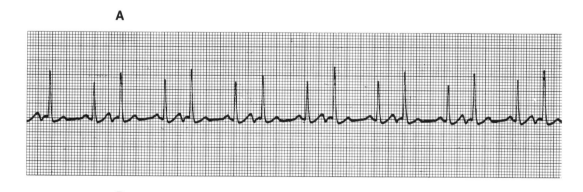

FIGURE 21-36. Premature ventricular contractions.

A

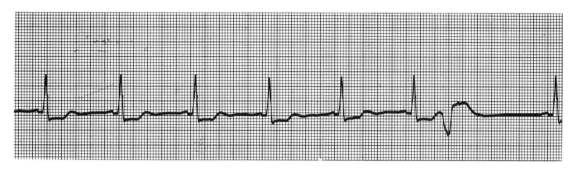

B

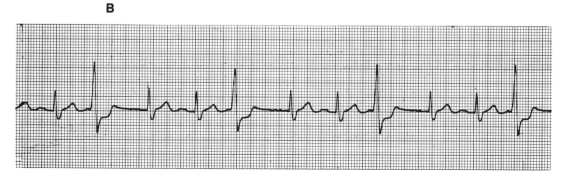

FIGURE 21-37. **A,** bigeminy; **B,** trigeminy.

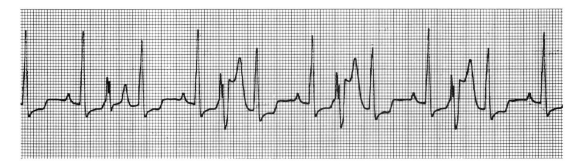

FIGURE 21–38. Interpolated PVCs.

tachycardia or fibrillation can develop. Similarly, multifocal PVCs are more ominous than unifocal PVCs (Figs. 21–30, 21–31). Interpolated PVCs are exceptions to the rules (Fig. 21–38). They are interposed between two normal sinus beats without disturbing the basic rhythm. They occur only in persons with a slow heart rate.

SUPRAVENTRICULAR TACHYCARDIAS

Paroxysmal supraventricular tachycardias are characterized by sudden onset and abrupt termination (Fig. 21–39). They are usually initiated by a premature beat and the rate is generally between 130 and 220 beats/min. This common dysrhythmia, frequently called PAT (paroxysmal atrial tachycardia, often occurs in people with structurally normal hearts.

Atrial Flutter and Fibrillation

People with atrial flutter usually exhibit a regular atrial rate of between 250 and 320 beats/min, with varying degrees of AV block. A characteristic "sawtoothed" pattern results

(Fig. 21–40). Atrial flutter can occur in individuals with normal hearts, in patients with chronic obstructive lung disease, pulmonary embolism, hyperthyroidism, alcoholism, mitral valve disease, myocardial infarction, and in association with thoracic and cardiac surgical procedures.

Atrial fibrillation is characterized by totally chaotic atrial activity, with no discernible P-waves, at a rate of 350 to 500 beats/min. The ventricular response is always "irregularly irregular" at a rate of 140 to 170 beats/min, if not treated (Fig. 21–41). Treatment is digitalization, and a ventricular rate of 70 to 90 beats/min is considered adequate control. The cause of atrial fibrillation is similar to that for atrial flutter.

Pre-excitation Syndromes

Pre-excitation is present when the ventricle is activated by atrial impulses earlier than if the impulses were to reach the ventricles by the normal conduction pathway. Several abnormal AV "bridges" have been described, the most common probably being that described by Wolff, Parkinson, and White (W-P-W). The

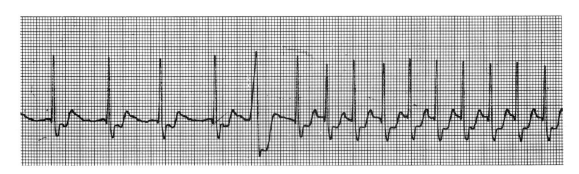

FIGURE 21–39. Development of paroxysmal supraventricular tachycardia.

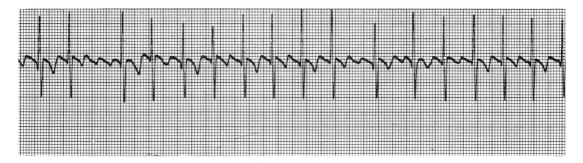

FIGURE 21–40. Atrial flutter.

ECG shows a short PR interval followed by a wide QRS complex with a delta wave. The delta wave is a slurred initial deflection of the QRS complex.

Ventricular Tachycardia, Flutter, and Fibrillation

Ventricular tachycardia is a rhythm of ventricular origin consisting of three or more consecutive premature beats at a rate of 120 to 200 beats/min (Fig. 21–42). Occasionally, if the tachycardia is slow, atrial fusion beats can be seen. Fusion beats occur when normally conducted sinus beats "fuse" or merge with ventricular ectopic beats. Ventricular tachycardia is common in patients with coronary artery disease, particularly with ischemia and acute infarction. The pattern of ventricular flutter is more rapid than normal ventricular tachycardia (Fig. 21–43). To distinguish between ventricular arrhythmias and supraventricular arrhythmias with aberrant interventricular conduction is difficult if not impossible. Because this distinction is important, clinicians sometimes need to perform electrophysiologic studies (EP stud-

ies), which involve intracardiac and His bundle electrocardiography.

Ventricular fibrillation is fatal unless it can be reverted by defibrillation (Fig. 21–44). Ventricular fibrillation frequently occurs with acute myocardial infarction, ischemia, and as the end stage in heart failure. Ventricular asystole has complete absence of ventricular activity and appears as a straight line on the ECG tracing (Fig. 21–45).

Myocardial Infarction and Ischemia

Acute myocardial infarction is caused by a sudden occlusion of a major branch of a coronary artery, usually the result of a thrombus forming at the site of an atheromatous plaque. Myocardial infarction is the death of heart muscle that results from a deficiency in the oxygen supply. Characteristic ECG changes are usually, but not always, seen. The ST segment is the most important component of the ECG when diagnosing acute myocardial infarction or myocardial ischemia. The three ECG changes that are indicative of myocardial infarction are: (1) pathologic Q-wave, which is

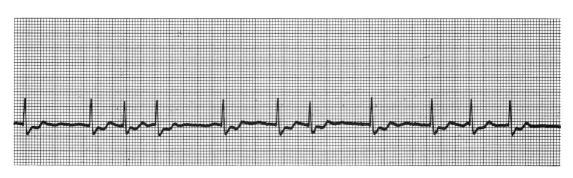

FIGURE 21–41. Atrial fibrillation.

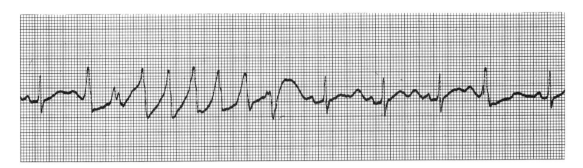

FIGURE 21-42. Paroxysmal ventricular tachycardia.

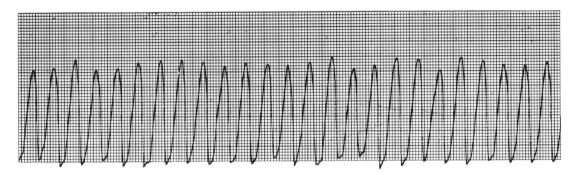

FIGURE 21-43. Ventricular flutter.

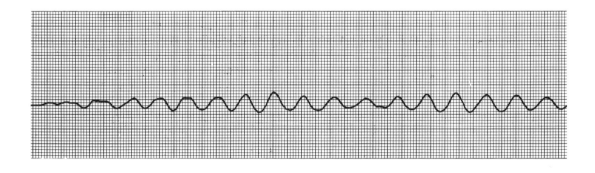

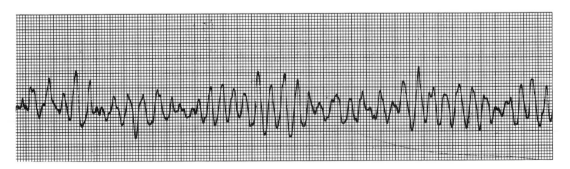

FIGURE 21-44. Ventricular fibrillation.

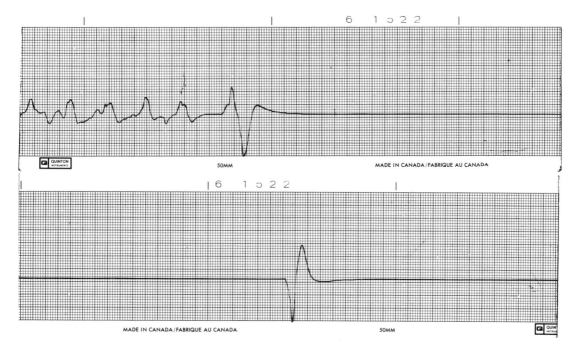

FIGURE 21–45. Ventricular asystole.

characterized by a width of 0.04 sec or more, a depth greater than 2 mm, or both; (2) ST segment elevation; and (3) T-wave inversion (Fig. 21–46). Only about 33% of persons with myocardial infarction develop pathologic Q-waves. These Q-waves are said to be a sign of a true transmural infarction. If only ST segment and T-wave changes are noted, the infarction is said to be nontransmural or subendocardial. This distinction is not always hard and fast.

These changes can help in the decision as to whether an infarction is acute, recent, or old (Table 21–7). Localization of a myocardial infarction is possible because the ECG changes occur in leads that point in the direction of the infarction (Table 21–8).

Myocardial ischemia occurs when the heart muscle starves for oxygen, usually because of insufficient blood flow that results from coronary atherosclerosis. During times of ischemia, the patient develops chest pain, or angina. Most patients with ischemic heart disease have normal ECG findings in the absence of chest pain. Signs of an old myocardial infarction and occasionally "nonspecific T-wave changes" might be evident. These changes consist of T-wave flattening and inversion, and are not diagnostic, only suggestive, of ischemia. ST depression is the usual ECG change noted in individuals with acute ischemia. An ECG obtained during exercise is helpful when assessing a patient for ischemic heart disease. Myocardial ischemia may be reflected in the exercise ECG by the following changes:

1. ST segment depression
2. T-wave inversion or flattening
3. Prolongation of the QT interval

Table 21–7. Staging of Myocardial Infarction

| Stage | ECG change | | |
	ST segment	T-wave	Q-wave
Acute	Elevated	Normal or inverted	Sometimes present
Recent	Normal	Usually inverted	Present
Old	Normal	Usually normal	Present

Table 21–8. Localization of Myocardial Infarction

Area of infarction	Leads showing changes
Inferior	II, III, aVf
Anterior	V_{1-3}
Lateral	I, aVL, V_{4-6}
Posterior	Look for reciprocal changes in V_{1-2}

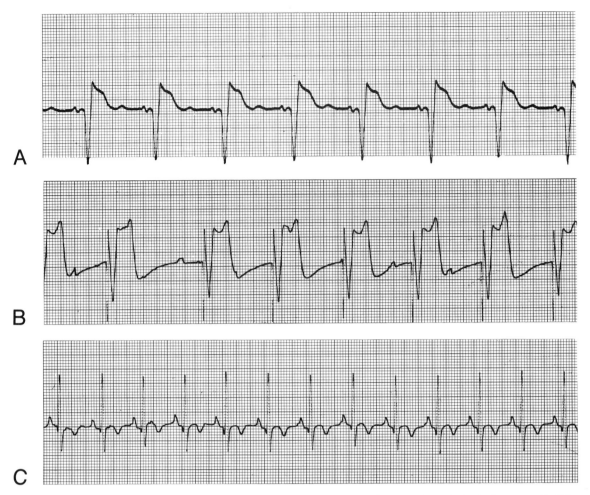

FIGURE 21-46. Characteristic changes associated with myocardial infarction. **A,** pathologic Q-waves. **B,** ST segment elevation. **C,** T-wave inversion.

4. Appearance of ventricular or supraventricular arrhythmias
5. Conduction disturbances (AV block, bundle branch block, etc.)
6. Inappropriate heart rate increase
7. Increase in R-wave amplitude

Not all ST segment depression is considered pathologic, rather it depends on the depth of depression and on the configuration of the ST segment, whether horizontal, upsloping, or downsloping (Fig. 21-47). The exercise ECG and the significance of the changes noted is discussed in Chapter 22.

OTHER CONDUCTION DISTURBANCES

SA Block, Sinus Arrest, and Sick Sinus Syndrome

Sinus arrest implies nonfunction of the SA node, an occurrence that usually cannot be distinguished from SA block, which implies exit block of the impulse from the SA node to the atria. SA block can be incomplete (Fig. 21-48A) or complete (Fig. 21-48B). In the former, an occasional absence of P-QRS-T sequence is noted. In the latter, P-waves are absent (depending on the site of the ectopic pacemaker);

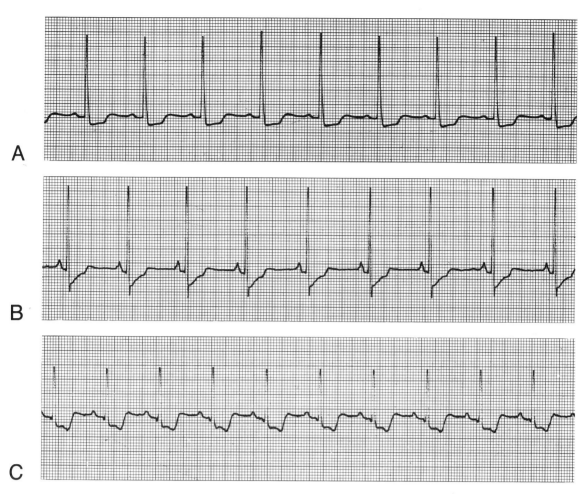

FIGURE 21–47. ST segment depression. **A,** horizontal; **B,** upsloping; **C,** downsloping.

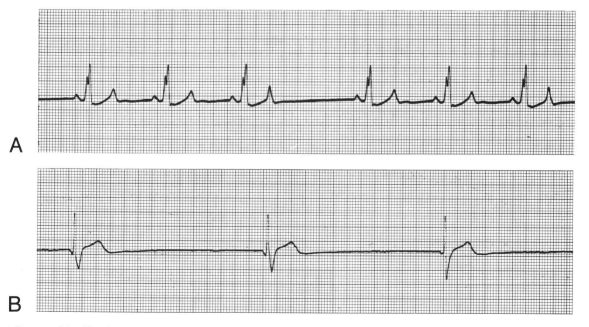

FIGURE 21–48. Sinoatrial block. **A,** incomplete; **B,** complete.

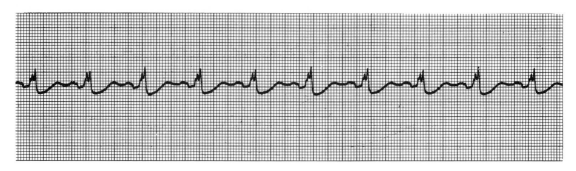

FIGURE 21–49. Intra-atrial block. Note wide (0.12 sec) notched P-wave.

the QRST sequence is slow; and the QRS interval is normal or prolonged, depending on the site of the ectopic pacemaker.

The designation sick sinus syndrome or "tachy-brady syndrome," is applied to rhythms characterized by severe bradycardia and irregular atrial tachycardia. The cause is a diseased sinus node, which is usually the result of ischemic heart disease. Patients with this condition often require a permanent pacemaker.

Intra-atrial Block

A P-wave duration of longer than 0.11 sec and notched P-waves are indicative of intra-atrial (IA) block (Fig. 21–49). This condition is common and is seen most often in individuals with coronary artery disease as well as in association with left ventricular hypertrophy. On occasion, IA block may actually represent left atrial enlargement, in which case it is not a true block.

AV Block

AV block is an abnormal delay or failure of conduction at the AV node, which must be kept distinct from normal delay or conduction failure that is the result of physiologic refractoriness. The three degrees of AV block are:

First degree: prolongation of the PR interval beyond 0.20 sec (Fig. 21–50A)
Second degree: dropped QRS complexes (Fig. 21–50B)
    Mobitz Type I: progressive lengthening of the PR intervals until a beat is dropped (Wenckebach phenomenon)
    Mobitz Type II: consecutively conducted

beats with constant PR intervals before the dropped beat
Third degree: complete AV block with a slower ventricular rhythm unrelated to the P-waves (Fig. 21–50C)

AV block can also result from conduction failure related to physiologic refractoriness, as is often seen in rapid supraventricular tachycardias (Fig. 21–50D). In this situation, the AV node is usually not diseased.

Aberrant Conduction

In aberrant ventricular conduction, a supraventricular impulse arrives so early that parts of the bundle of His are refractory after the preceding beat; a bundle branch block pattern then develops (Fig. 21–51). In 85% of individuals, the result is a right bundle branch block pattern. This finding is often overlooked, with the result that supraventricular arrhythmias are frequently misdiagnosed as ventricular. Such a misdiagnosis has important therapeutic implications. A tracing of lead V_1 with two aberrantly conducted beats of right bundle branch block configuration is illustrated in Figure 21–51.

Drug Effects on the ECG

Drugs can cause various alterations in the resting ECG. Digitalis has the most prominent effect, producing changes that mimic heart disease and causing many blocks and arrhythmias. Digitalis causes depression of the ST segment as well as flattening and inversion of T-waves. The ST segment develops a characteristic "sag" which is upwardly concave. The arrhythmias associated with digitalis toxicity can be life threatening.

The antiarrhythmic agent quinidine also affects the ECG, with ST-T wave changes as well as potentially life-threatening SA blocks. Many diuretics cause hypokalemia, which can cause arrhythmias as well as prolongation of the QT interval. Tricyclic antidepressant drugs increase the tendency to develop arrhythmias and also cause T-wave inversion. Beta blockers cause negative chronotropic effects and, in combination with nitrates and calcium channel blockers,

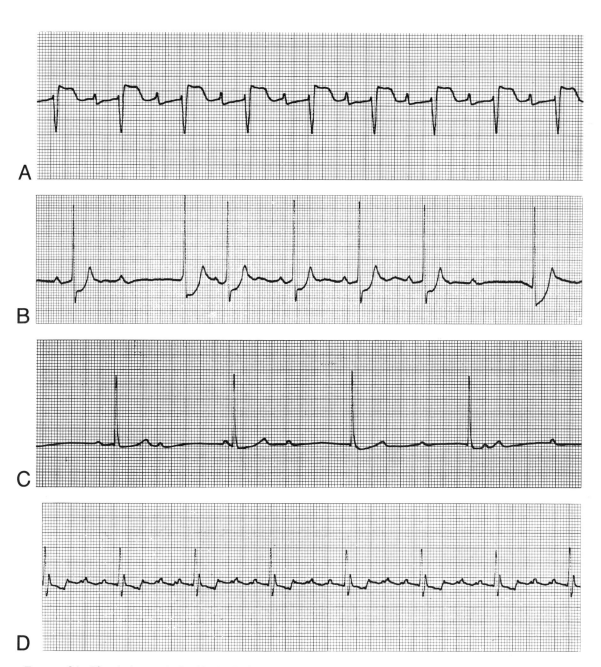

FIGURE 21–50. Atrioventricular block. **A,** first-degree; **B,** second-degree, Mobitz type I (Wenckebach); **C,** third-degree; **D,** atrial tachycardia with 4:1 block.

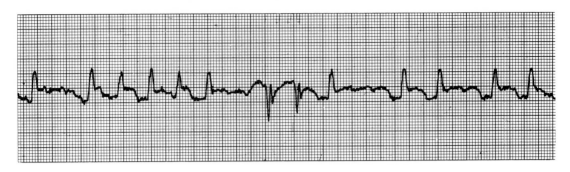

FIGURE 21–51. Aberrant ventricular conduction.

may delay the onset of ischemia and create a possible false-negative ECG response to exercise. The effects that drugs may have on the ECG are extensive and variable. Therefore, a review of the specific effects of those drugs taken by the individual patient is useful, particularly if ECG abnormalities are noted in that patient.

CHAPTER 22

CLINICAL EXERCISE TESTING

PETER HANSON

Clinical exercise testing is now used widely in the evaluation of cardiovascular disease. The indications and predictive capacity of standard exercise testing have been studied in detail. As a result, the appropriate uses of exercise testing are more thoroughly understood. This chapter is a summary of the physiologic principles, clinical applications, and methods of standard electrocardiographic (ECG) exercise testing. The detailed interpretation of exercise stress tests is discussed elsewhere in this book.

CLINICAL INDICATIONS AND USES OF EXERCISE TESTING

The purpose of exercise testing is to determine physiologic responses to controlled exercise stress. Clinical applications may include diagnostic, functional, and therapeutic objectives (Table 22–1). Diagnosis and evaluation of suspected or established cardiovascular disease is the most common clinical application of exercise testing. For this purpose, standard ECG stress testing and exercise testing with radionuclide perfusion or ventriculography are used. In addition, modified and submaximal exercise testing is used increasingly to evaluate and

modify medical management of patients after myocardial infarction and coronary bypass procedures, as well as of patients who have undergone coronary angioplasty, before discharge and during subsequent recovery. Routine exercise testing to screen for coronary artery disease in asymptomatic low-risk patients is more controversial because of the limited predictive capacity for detection of disease in this population.

Functional exercise testing is used in the determination of exercise capacity and cardiopulmonary responses in healthy individuals who require exercise prescription guidelines. Patients who have undergone repair of a congenital heart defect, valvular replacement, or cardiac transplant are also candidates for functional assessment, because many such individuals have been physically restricted before surgery and require guidelines for exercise. Other special groups evaluated for exercise capacity include patients with congestive heart failure, diabetes, chronic renal failure, and chronic pulmonary disease.

Exercise testing may also be used to optimize medical therapy with certain classes of drugs, such as antiarrhythmic agents, antianginal agents, and antihypertensive agents. Patients who appear to be well controlled while taking these drugs at rest may show surprising abnor-

Table 22–1. Uses of Clinical Exercise Testing

Diagnostic or prognostic
  Evaluation of suspected heart disease
  Evaluation of asymptomatic individuals with risk of coronary heart disease
  After myocardial infarction (predischarge)
  After coronary angioplasty
  Dysrhythmia provocation
  Peripheral vascular disease

Functional capacity
  Exercise prescription for healthy, sedentary individuals
  After myocardial infarction
  After coronary bypass
  After repair of valvular or congenital heart defect
  Chronic pulmonary disease
  Chronic renal failure

Therapeutic efficacy
  Antianginal agents (nitrates, beta blockers, and calcium channel blockers)
  Antidysrhythmic agents
  Antihypertensive agents
  Bronchodilators (exercise-induced asthma)
  Vasodilators (congestive heart failure)

Table 22–2. Contraindications to Exercise Testing

Major Contraindications
  1. Recent acute myocardial infarction
  2. Unstable angina
  3. Uncontrolled ventricular dysrhythmia
  4. Uncontrolled atrial dysrhythmia that compromises cardiac function
  5. Congestive heart failure
  6. Severe aortic stenosis
  7. Suspected or known dissecting aneurysm
  8. Active or suspected myocarditis
  9. Thrombophlebitis or intracardiac thrombi
  10. Recent systemic or pulmonary embolus
  11. Acute infection
  12. Third-degree heart block
  13. Significant emotional distress (psychosis)
  14. A recent significant change in the resting ECG
  15. Acute pericarditis

Relative Contraindications
  1. Resting diastolic blood pressure over 120 mm Hg or resting systolic blood pressure over 200 mm Hg
  2. Moderate valvular heart disease
  3. Digitalis or other drug effect
  4. Electrolyte abnormalities
  5. Fixed-rate artificial pacemaker
  6. Frequent or complex ventricular irritability
  7. Ventricular aneurysm
  8. Cardiomyopathy, including hypertrophic cardiomyopathy
  9. Uncontrolled metabolic disease (e.g., diabetes, thyrotoxicosis, or myxedema)
  10. Any serious systemic disorder (e.g., mononucleosis or hepatitis)
  11. Neuromuscular, musculoskeletal, or rheumatoid disorders that make exercise difficult

malities or therapeutic limitations with moderate exertion. Exercise testing is frequently utilized for objective evaluation of vasodilator or inotropic therapy in patients with congestive heart failure.

CONTRAINDICATIONS TO EXERCISE TESTING

Accepted contraindications to exercise testing are summarized in Table 22–2. Major contraindications include unstable cardiopulmonary or metabolic status, severe angina, or orthopedic limitations that clearly preclude exercise testing. Some of the relative contraindications include several conditions, such as dysrhythmias, mild to moderate cardiac failure, or hypertension, in which drug therapy may be optimized by knowledge of responses to submaximal or maximal exercise. Therefore, limited exercise testing may be indicated when therapeutic or prognostic information is required and when the potential benefit to the patient clearly exceeds the increased risk.

The morbidity and mortality rate from exercise testing appears to be low. Available surveys of exercise test facilities in the United States reveal a mortality rate of 0.5 per 10,000 individuals and a complication rate of 8.8 per 10,000 individuals. Similar reports from Europe show

a mortality rate of 0.2 per 10,000 persons and a complication rate of 9.6 per 10,000 persons. These values suggest good adherence to recommended guidelines for exercise test monitoring, end points, and management of emergencies.

PHYSIOLOGIC RESPONSES TO EXERCISE

DYNAMIC EXERCISE

Normal cardiopulmonary responses to dynamic, upright exercise are illustrated in Figure 22–1. During short-term dynamic exercise (10 to 15 min), a progressive increase in cardiac output ($\dot{Q}$) occurs, which is linearly related to the percent of maximal aerobic power ($\dot{V}O_{2\,max}$). Increased $\dot{Q}$ is mediated by combined increases in left ventricular stroke volume (SV) and heart rate (HR) ($\dot{Q} = HR \times SV$).

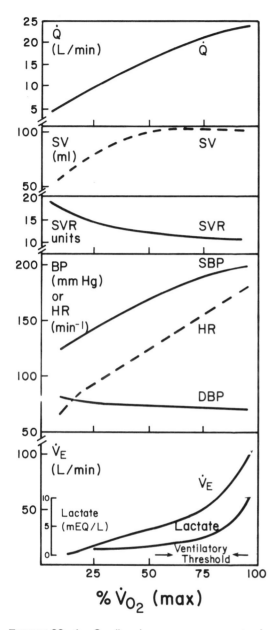

FIGURE 22–1. Cardiopulmonary responses to dynamic exercise in normal subject. Exercise intensity expressed as percent of $\dot{V}O_{2\,max}$.

sympathetic nerve activity. The relative contributions of SV and HR may vary with differences in position (upright and supine) and mode of activity (legs as opposed to arms or combined). The resultant increase in $\dot{Q}$, however, is consistently related to $\dot{V}O_2$ requirements.

Arterial blood pressure (BP) response to dynamic exercise is characterized by a progressive rise in systolic BP and a gradual fall in diastolic BP. This response produces a moderate increase in mean arterial pressure (MAP), which is necessary to provide additional perfusion pressure for muscle blood flow and to maintain regional blood flow in other organs.

Arterial pressure reflects the balance between increasing $\dot{Q}$ and decreasing systemic vascular resistance: $MAP = \dot{Q} \times SVR$. During dynamic exercise, SVR decreases because of the combined metabolic and neuroreflex vasodilatation of active muscle. Regional blood flow to nonactive muscle and the visceral circulation (kidney, liver, and gastrointestinal tract) decreases as a result of sympathetic vasoconstriction.

Peripheral oxygen transport ($\dot{V}O_2$) is a function of $\dot{Q}$ and arteriovenous O_2 extraction $(a - \bar{v})O_2$:

$$\dot{V}O_2 = \dot{Q} \times a - \bar{v}O_2$$

The $a - \bar{v}O_2$ difference increases as a linear response to increases in percent $\dot{V}O_{2\,max}$. Maximal $a - \bar{v}O_2$ (15 to 17 ml O_2/100 ml) is similar in healthy subjects and in most cardiovascularly impaired patients. Maximal $\dot{V}O_2$ ($\dot{V}O_{2\,max}$) is usually determined by available $\dot{Q}$. Accordingly, $\dot{V}O_{2\,max}$ in cardiac patients is limited in proportion to the impairment of maximal $\dot{Q}$.

Pulmonary ventilatory responses to exercise also reflect increased $\dot{V}O_2$ consumption and CO_2 production (V_{co_2}). A linear increase in ventilation (V_E) follows that $\dot{V}O_2$ and V_{co_2} to a point, 60 to 75% of $\dot{V}O_{2\,max}$. Above this level, V_E rises abruptly because of added stimulus of metabolic acidosis from increasing muscle lactate release and CO_2 production. This combined metabolic and ventilatory response pattern is designated the "lactate" or "ventilatory" threshold. Exercise performed at a level below the region of the lactate or ventilatory threshold is comfortably sustained for longer periods (30 to 60 min). Exercise intensity that exceeds this threshold produces rapid muscle fatigue and hyperpnea.

Left ventricular SV is determined by diastolic filling volume (preload), ventricular contractility, and aortic impedance (afterload). Maximal SV is usually achieved during the initial 40 to 60% $\dot{V}O_{2\,max}$. Further increases in $\dot{Q}$ are determined by HR. Augmentation of LV contractility and HR are primarily mediated by increased

ARM EXERCISE

Exercise performed with arms and shoulders involves a smaller total muscle mass. The linear relationship between $\dot{V}o_2$ and $\dot{Q}$ is maintained during arm exercise (such as cranking). The $\dot{V}o_{2\,max}$ of arm exercise is usually 60 to 70% of that measured for leg exercise. In addition, upright arm exercise is performed with higher HR and lower SV, as a result of reduced venous return from inactive lower body venous capacitance beds.

ISOMETRIC EXERCISE

A characteristic feature of isometric exercise is a "pressor" response, resulting in MAP that is significantly greater than that associated with typical dynamic exercise (see Fig. 22–2). A marked rise in BP occurs because of a combination of increased $\dot{Q}$ with little or no decrease in peripheral resistance. The reflex control of this response is in part due to peripheral feedback from afferent receptors in skeletal muscle that are sensitive to ischemia or local metabolic changes associated with reduction of blood flow in muscle during contraction.

The magnitude of the pressor response is also related to the size of muscle mass and degree of tension exerted (percent of maximal isometric tension). Therefore, isometric lifting (which involves the use of the legs, back, shoulders, and arms) produces a greater pressor response than that produced by isometric handgrip.

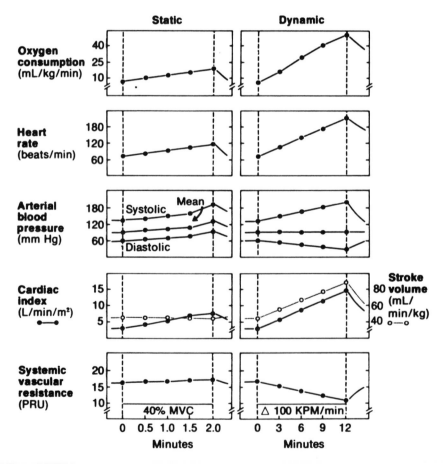

FIGURE 22–2. Comparison of hemodynamic responses to isometric (static) handgrip (40% max) and progressive dynamic cycle exercise (100 kpm/min increase). Note systolic, diastolic, and mean blood pressure increase throughout isometric exercise. Response associated with small increases in cardiac index and no significant change in systemic vascular resistance. (From Longhurst JC, Mitchell JH: *J Cardiovasc Med*, 8:227, 1983.)

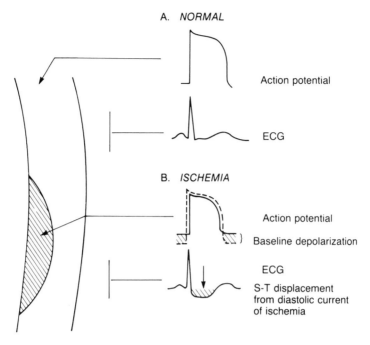

A. *NORMAL*

Action potential

ECG

B. *ISCHEMIA*

Action potential

Baseline depolarization

ECG

S-T displacement
from diastolic current
of ischemia

FIGURE 22–3. Electrocardiographic (ECG) changes in myocardial ischemia. **A,** normal cellular action potential and corresponding surface ECG. **B,** ischemic cellular action potential altered by baseline depolarization offset and shortened phase 3 compared with normal *(dashed overlay).* Surface ECG shows ST segment displacement due to ischemic diastolic depolarization shift of baseline. (Modified from Vincent G, et al.: *Circulation, 56:*559, 1977.)

EXERCISE AND MYOCARDIAL ISCHEMIA

The major determinants of myocardial oxygen demand ($M\dot{V}O_2$) are HR, ventricular wall tension, and contractility. During exercise, $M\dot{V}O_2$ increases, primarily as a result of increases in HR, afterload, and contractility. An indirect measure of $M\dot{V}O_2$ demand is the product of HR and systolic pressure (HR × SP).

The rate of myocardial blood flow usually increases in proportion to $M\dot{V}O_2$. Resting myocardial a $- \bar{v}O_2$ is high (70 to 80%), so that additional $M\dot{V}O_2$ during exercise must be supplied by increased coronary blood flow. Coronary blood flow and myocardial perfusion are determined by the interplay between aortic diastolic pressure and resistance of epicardial and intramyocardial vessels. The subendocardium is the most vulnerable region for ischemia when myocardial flow is compromised because of proximal coronary artery obstruction or other factors that alter normal subendocardial perfusion.

Myocardial contractile function is significantly altered by ischemia. Left ventricular SV decreases as a result of reduced force and velocity of contraction. Left ventricular wall tension and end-diastolic pressure values increase because of incomplete relaxation. Pulmonary capillary pressure values also increase because of higher left ventricular and atrial filling pressures. During exercise, $\dot{Q}$ is increasingly dependent on HR because SV cannot be augmented.

Myocardial transmembrane potentials are also altered by ischemia (Fig. 22–3). The ischemic cell population creates a region of abnormal diastolic current that is detected by conventional surface ECG electrodes. When ischemia is predominantly of subendocardial origin, the major ECG change is displacement or delay of the S-T segment below the isoelectric point. More extensive transmural ischemia, which extends to the epicardial surface, would produce S-T segment elevation.

Exercise-induced ischemia is usually confined to the subendocardium; recording electrodes positioned over ischemic regions detect alterations in ECG responses. The sensitivity of various ECG leads for detection of ischemic changes is discussed in subsequent sections.

We emphasize that many factors may limit subendocardial blood flow or oxygen transport independent of coronary artery obstruction. Ventricular hypertrophy, hypertension, and hypoxia are additional causes of ischemia that exist in the presence of apparently normal coronary arteries.

EXERCISE TESTING METHODS

TEST PROTOCOLS

A variety of graded exercise test protocols have been used successfully during the last decade. The basic principle of all graded exercise test protocols is a progressive increase in external work of large muscle groups (usually legs) to an end point of fatigue of $\dot{V}_{O_2 max}$ or termination because of abnormal responses. Several common treadmill test protocols are summarized in Figure 22–4.

The Balke and Naughton formats involve the use of constant walking speeds of 2.0 to 3.3 mph with increasing grade increments of 2 to 3% every 2 or 3 min to a point of maximal effort. These protocols are better suited for testing cardiac patients or subjects with limited exercise capacities.

The Bruce protocol involves a change in speed and grade every 3 min, so that the incremental increases of external work are greater for each stage (2 to 3 METs). The major advantage of the Bruce protocol is relative brevity. Most nonconditioned persons can complete only stage III (9 min). The Bruce protocol is suitable for younger patients who are capable of performing frequent changes in speed and grade. The Bruce protocol is not recommended for cardiac patients with low anginal thresholds or post-myocardial infarction predischarge exercise testing. In several recent studies, researchers have shown 10 to 20% error in estimating $\dot{V}_{O_2}$ from the Bruce protocol. This error is attributed to rapid increases in treadmill speed and grade that exceed the $\dot{V}_{O_2}$ uptake kinetics of most cardiac patients. In addition,

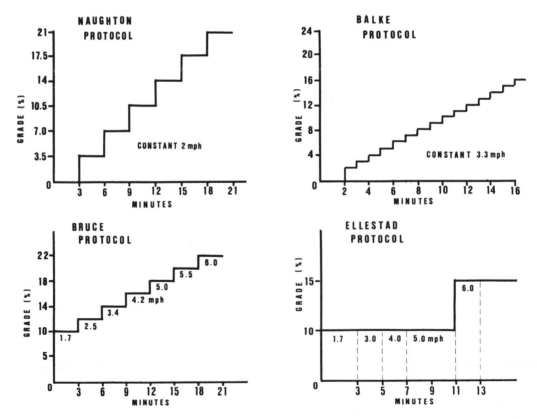

FIGURE 22–4. Commonly used treadmill protocols showing format of speed and grade and minutes of testing.

Table 22–3. University of Wisconsin Cardiac Rehabilitation Program Branching Treadmill Exercise Test Protocol

Exercise intensity (METS)	Treadmill speed (mph)						
	2.0	2.25	2.5	2.75	3.0	3.25	3.5
2	0	0*					
3	1.5	1.0	0	0	0	0	0
4	5.0	4.0	3.0	2.0	1.5	1.0	0.5
5	9.0	7.0	6.0	5.0	4.0	3.0	2.5
6	12.5	10.0	9.0	7.5	6.5	5.5	5.0
7	16.0	13.5	12.0	10.0	9.0	7.5	7.0
8	20.0	17.5	15.0	13.0	11.0	10.0	9.0
9		20.0	17.5	15.0	13.5	12.0	11.0
10			20.0	18.0	16.0	14.0	13.0
11				21.0	18.0	16.5	15.0
12					21.0	19.0	17.0

* Values are the percent grade required at a selected speed to achieve intensity. Treadmill speed is selected to provide a brisk walking pace compatible with the subject's gait and stride. Grade is then increased every 2 min at a constant treadmill speed to produce 1-MET increments.

the Bruce protocol usually requires extensive use of handrails for support, which also contributes to error in $\dot{V}o_2$ estimates.

The Balke-type protocol is more applicable to functional exercise testing in cardiac rehabilitation programs because the incremental increase in workload is more gradual and there is less chance for error when estimating $\dot{V}o_2$. Low-level predischarge exercise tests may also involve the use of a similar "branching" format, which can accommodate a variety of individual walking speeds. An example of a branching protocol developed at the University of Wisconsin Hospital Cardiac Rehabilitation Program is shown in Table 22–3. This protocol allows initial selection of an appropriate individual walking speed (2.0 to 3.5 mph; 0.25-mph increments). The work intensity is then increased by increasing the grade in 1-MET increments every 2 min. Correlation between estimated and measured $\dot{V}o_2$ is excellent (0.98) for normal and post-MI patients.

Bicycle exercise protocols are popular in Europe and in Canada. Bicycle ergometers are more easily operated by some patients who have difficulty with ambulation. The gradation of work intensity is easy to control, and the difficulty and body movement interference with ECG and blood pressure monitoring is diminished. The maximal $\dot{V}o_2$ determination is somewhat lower, however, when compared with treadmill exercise.

ARM EXERCISE TESTING

Patients with peripheral vascular disease or musculoskeletal disorders who are unable to perform treadmill or cycle ergometer exercise may be evaluated with arm exercise testing. Arm or upper extremity exercise is performed with an arm crank ergometer while the subject is seated or is standing. (Standing usually permits a greater use of torso and postural muscle groups to achieve higher peak cardiopulmonary stress.) Arm exercise protocols may be continuous, increasing in 150-kpm increments every 2 min, or in discontinuous stages of 150 kpm for 2 min separated by 1 or 2 min of rest. Discontinuous stages are not only better tolerated by most patients, but also permit more frequent measurement of immediate post-exercise BP.

Maximal arm exercise $\dot{V}o_2$ is usually 60 to 70% of that determined for leg exercise $\dot{V}o_{2\,max}$. Typical peak values of 600 kpm are achieved by men from age 50 to 65 years. Maximal HR attained during arm exercise are similar to those that are recorded during treadmill or cycle ergometer exercise. Periodic measurement of BP is possible in one arm while cranking at submaximal intensities or immediately after cessation of a 2-min stage. Maximal BP levels are difficult to obtain during exercise and the immediate post-exercise values are undoubtedly reduced from peak exercise.

Some patients with peripheral vascular disease or orthopedic limitations may perform combined arm and leg exercise test using an Airdyne ergometer (Schwinn, Inc.). This ergometer permits patients to utilize variable combinations of arm and leg exercise effort. Maximal exercise $\dot{V}o_2$ and HR are usually higher than those obtained from arm cranking exercise protocols.

The sensitivity of arm exercise testing for detection of coronary artery disease appears to be less than that associated with treadmill exercise. In recent reports, investigators cited a higher rate of false-negative arm exercise test results in patients with coronary artery disease who were also evaluated with treadmill exercise.

EXERCISE INTENSITY

Measurement of $\dot{V}o_2$ is usually impractical for routine exercise testing; however, the $\dot{V}o_2$ requirement may be estimated from speed and grade determinations from treadmill protocols and from cycle ergometer resistance load and speed values. These values are usually available in standard tables (see Figure 22–5). The calculations from basic data, however, are not difficult and may be used to determine work capacity when testing is performed under protocol nonstandard conditions.

A convenient unit of work intensity used in exercise testing is the MET (metabolic unit). One MET is equal to $\dot{V}o_2$ at rest and has a nominal value of 3.5 ml O_2/kg/min. Work intensities with various $\dot{V}o_2$ demands may be expressed in MET units by dividing by this constant.

The MET system provides a simple translation of exercise oxygen demand into multiples of resting $\dot{V}o_2$, which can be used to communicate work intensity from exercise testing results. Various physical activities are conveniently described in terms of MET requirements.

PATIENT MONITORING

Electrocardiography

Electrocardiographic monitoring is an essential component of diagnostic and functional exercise testing. In most exercise ECG recording systems, a modified 10-lead combination is used that permits continuous monitoring with an oscilloscope and recording of the 12 standard limb and precordial leads. Results of numerous studies show increased sensitivity for detection of ischemic ECG changes when multiple leads (12-lead or multiple bipolar) are employed in exercise testing. Bipolar leads in single or multiple combination (CM5, CC5) are less sensitive for diagnostic testing but are still useful and are less expensive for routine ECG monitoring in functional exercise tests (Fig. 22–6).

The most important determinant of satisfactory ECG monitoring is adequate preparation of skin sites for electrode placement. Skin sites must be abraded with fine sandpaper (or commercially available pads) and alcohol to remove surface epidermis and oil. After placement, each electrode should be tapped vigorously while the corresponding lead is monitored on the oscilloscope. Noisy leads should be readjusted or replaced.

Blood Pressure (BP)

Frequent measurements of BP must be obtained throughout the exercise test. Response patterns provide useful diagnostic and prognostic information that adds to interpretation of the test.

Auscultatory pressure is often difficult to determine because of improper technique. Most clinical stethoscopes held by hand against the brachial artery usually produce excessive noise. A standard binaural stethoscope, with extended length (60 to 80 cm), single Tygon tubing, and a flat anesthesia diaphragm (held in place by an adjustable Velcro strap), provides an inexpensive modification that obviates hold-

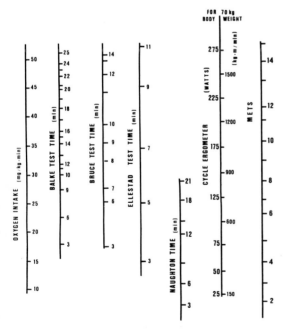

FIGURE 22–5. Estimate exercise intensity equivalents by drawing horizontal line from time on given treadmill or cycle ergometer protocol to oxygen uptake (left) or MET level (right). (Modified from Pollock ML, et al.: *Am Heart J*, 92:39–46, 1976.)

BIPOLAR

STANDARD

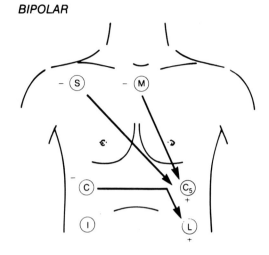

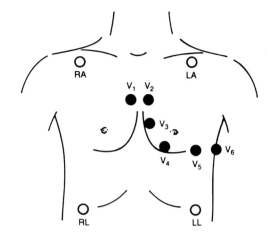

−M = Manubrium
−S = Right shoulder
−C = Right fifth interspace
+C₅ = Left fifth interspace
+L = Left leg (suprailiac)
I = Indifferent

FIGURE 22 – 6. Electrocardiographic (ECG) leads used in exercise testing. Bipolar single-lead systems usually less sensitive in detecting ischemic ECG changes than 10-lead system recording of standard 12-lead ECG complexes during exercise. (Modified from Chaitman B, Hanson T: *Am J Cardiol, 47:*1335, 1981.)

ing the stethoscope head during exercise. Unpublished data from the University of Wisconsin Biodynamics Laboratory show excellent correlation between auscultation and brachial intra-arterial systolic pressure ($r = 0.95$) during exercise.

Several models of automatic monitors are available for BP measurement during exercise. These monitors have surface transducers to detect onset of systolic pressure and diastolic cutoff pressure. Analysis of pressure recordings is facilitated by microcomputer circuits. Published data show reasonable correlation with simultaneous auscultatory and intra-arterial pressures.

Rated Exertion

Subjective exertion or effort level is a valuable parameter to monitor. The Borg scale of rated perceived exertion (RPE) has been studied in detail and is often used as an adjunct to exercise testing (Fig. 22 – 7).

The numeric scale correlates closely with several exercise variables, including HR, ventila-

RPE		New Rating Scale	
6		0	Nothing at all
7	Very, very light	0.5	Very, very weak
8		1	Very weak
9	Very light	2	Weak
10		3	Moderate
11	Fairly light	4	Somewhat strong
12		5	Strong
13	Somewhat hard	6	
14		7	Very strong
15	Hard	8	
16		9	
17	Very hard	10	Very, very strong
18		.	Maximal
19	Very, very hard		

FIGURE 22–7. Rated perceived exertion (RPE) scales. Original scale (6 to 19) on left and revised scale (1 to 10) on right. (From Borg GA: *Med Sci Sports Exerc, 14:*377–387, 1982.)

tion, lactate production, and percent $\dot{V}_{O_{2\,max}}$. In numerous clinical studies, researchers show the RPE scale to be a reproducible measure of effort within a wide variety of human subjects regardless of age, sex, or cultural origin. RPE is also unaffected by β-blockade.

During exercise testing, the RPE scale is a surprisingly accurate gauge of impending fatigue. Most patients rate the ventilatory threshold (75 to 85% $\dot{V}_{O_{2\,max}}$) as hard (RPE 15 to 16) and reach the subjective limit of fatigue at RPE 18 to 19 (very, very hard).

CONDUCTING THE TEST

Patient Instructions

The purpose and sequence of the test should be explained in detail. Many patients are highly anxious before exercise testing and may perform awkwardly, with rigid walking and tense gripping of support rails. Their anxiety can be relieved by careful explanation, which may include a demonstration of how to walk on a treadmill (including stepping on and off). Patients should be instructed to maintain a steady walking pace and to avoid turning their head or trunk, causing loss of balance. Excessive use of support rails for balance results in major errors in estimating exercise capacity from treadmill speed and grade.

Test Sequence and Measurements

A routine set of measurements should be obtained at rest, during exercise, and after exercise recovery. Before exercise, ECG tracings are taken with the patient supine and then while standing and after 30 sec of seated hyperventilation. Significant changes in S-T segment, T-waves, or mean frontal axis may occur while standing or after hyperventilation.

During exercise, the ECG is monitored continuously by oscilloscope and recordings are made at 1-min intervals. Measurements of BP must be taken every minute to allow early identification of abnormal trends. Rated exertion is a valuable guide to effort level and participants should be queried every 2 min (or at the end of each stage).

Recovery should include a 2- to 3-min period of walking (2.0 to 3.0 mph at 0% grade or at no-tension cycling) followed by seated rest for 2 to 3 min or until abnormal ECG or BP responses

resolve. The determined values for HR and BP should be stable, but not necessarily at pre-exercise levels, before discontinuation of monitoring. In some laboratories, a supine recovery protocol is used immediately after exercise. The increase in venous return in the supine position may produce additional left ventricular preload and increase the detection of ischemic ECG changes.

EXERCISE TEST RESPONSES

TEST END POINTS

Normal end points for termination of an exercise test include symptoms of muscle fatigue, hyperpnea, achievement of maximal predicted HR, and a rated exertion level of 17 (very hard). Because these responses may converge rapidly over a short period (60 to 90 sec), careful observation and monitoring are necessary to avoid excessive stress.

Abnormal responses to exercise may require discontinuation of stress testing before attaining maximal levels of effort (Table 22–4). Important clinical criteria for immediate termination of the test include angina, dyspnea, dizziness, falling systolic BP, or other indica-

---

Table 22–4. Indications for Stopping an Exercise Test

1. Subject requests to stop
2. Failure of the monitoring system
3. Progressive angina (stop at 3+ level or earlier on a scale of 1+ to 4+) (see Table 22–5)
4. Early onset deep (> 4 mm) horizontal or downsloping ST depression or elevation
5. Sustained supraventricular tachycardia
6. Ventricular tachycardia
7. Exercise-induced left or right bundle branch block
8. Any significant drop (10 mm Hg) of systolic blood pressure, or failure of the systolic blood pressure to rise with an increase in exercise load after the initial adjustment period
9. Lightheadedness, confusion, ataxia, pallor, cyanosis, nausea, or signs of severe peripheral circulatory insufficiency
10. Excessive rise in blood pressure: systolic pressure greater than 250 mm Hg; diastolic pressure greater than 120 mm Hg
11. R or T premature ventricular complexes
12. Unexplained inappropriate bradycardia: rise in pulse rate that is slower than 2 S.D. below age-adjusted normal values
13. Onset of second- or third-degree heart block
14. Multifocal PVCs
15. Increasing ventricular ectopy

tions of severe ischemia with left ventricular failure. Dangerous dysrhythmias (increasing or multiform premature ventricular contractions, ventricular tachycardia, supraventricular tachycardia, new atrial fibrillation, or heart block) demand immediate termination of the test.

Other nonemergent abnormal responses may be evaluated on an individual basis to determine the relative risk of continuing exercise. In some instances, the goal of the test may be to establish efficacy of treatment with antianginal or antiarrhythmic drugs so that continuation of the test may be warranted.

SYMPTOMATIC RESPONSES

Angina and dyspnea are the most common cardiac symptoms produced by exercise testing. Subjective ratings of the intensity of angina or dyspnea are graded on a scale of 1 to 4 (Table 22–5). The onset of typical angina during exercise is an accurate predictor of coronary heart disease; however, fewer than 50% of patients with coronary artery disease experience angina with maximal effort exercise. In addition, the degree of anginal symptoms is poorly correlated with the extent of disease. The onset of angina, dyspnea, or fatigue at low exercise loads (3 to 4 METs), however, is usually predictive of multiple vessel coronary artery disease, poor cardiac function, and low $\dot{Q}$.

Mild (grade 1) angina or atypical chest pain may be observed while continuing the exercise test for short periods if ECG findings and BP levels stabilize. A trial administration of sublingual nitroglycerin is a useful diagnostic challenge that may confirm the presence of angina in the absence of characteristic ECG findings.

Dyspnea may be the dominant exercise symptom in severe stenosis of the left coronary or anterior descending coronary artery. Dysp-

nea is usually accompanied by poor exercise capacity and impaired systolic BP responses or decreasing systolic BP values.

CARDIOVASCULAR RESPONSES (Fig. 22–8)

Increases in HR and BP usually occur in proportion to exercise intensity. The average age-predicted maximal HR value may be obtained from published tables or may be estimated from regression equations. One common estimate of predicted maximal HR is max HR = 220 − age. In a recent report, the use of max HR = 205 − 0.5 (age) for men was recommended.

Exercise tests that fail to elicit 85% of predicted maximal HR are usually considered submaximal and not a valid cardiovascular stress. Patients with cardiac disease, however, usually show a restricted HR increase in response to progressive exercise (chronotropic incompetence).

Maximal BP values usually occur at peak HR. Normal values for maximal BP may vary widely (160–220/50–90). Hypertensive BP responses are usually defined as systolic pressure is 225 and diastolic pressure is 90. Many professionals discontinue exercise when the systolic pressure reaches 250 or the diastolic pressure is 120.

Hypotensive or restricted BP response patterns are often noted in individuals with severe ischemic heart disease or heart failure. An inadequate rise in systolic pressure (less than +20 mm Hg from rest) or a decreasing systolic pressure (−15 to 20 mm Hg from previous level) are signs of poor ventricular function that require termination of exercise. An isolated increase in diastolic pressure (+25 mm Hg above rest) during exercise is also a predictor of coronary heart disease.

Exercise-induced BP changes are characteristically attenuated by β-blockade and vasodilator drug therapy. For patients receiving therapeutic β-blockade peak HR may be limited to 50 or 60% of the predicted maximal rate, with a corresponding rise in systolic pressure of only 20 to 30 mm Hg. The BP responses are also increased by excessive use of handgripping for support (treadmill rails or cycle ergometer handles).

ELECTROCARDIOGRAPHIC (ECG) RESPONSES

Normal and common abnormal ECG responses to exercise are illustrated in Figure 22–

Table 22–5. Rating of Intensity of Angina and Dyspnea

Angina scale
  1+ Light, barely noticeable
  2+ Moderate, bothersome
  3+ Severe, very uncomfortable
  4+ Most severe pain ever experienced in the past

Dyspnea scale
  1. Mild, noticeable to patient but not to observer
  2. Some difficulty, noticeable to observer
  3. Moderate difficulty, but can continue
  4. Severe difficulty, patient cannot continue

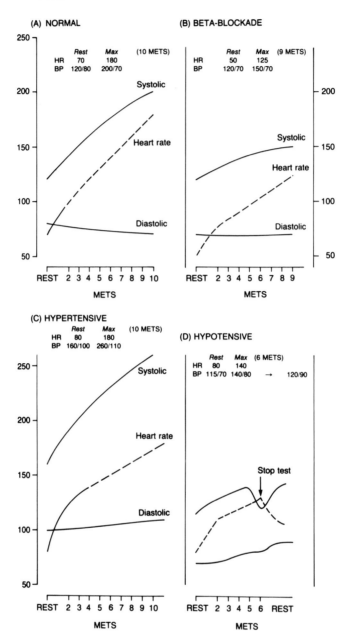

FIGURE 22–8. Common hemodynamic patterns in exercise tests. **A,** normal responses (age 40 to 50 years). **B,** normal responses with beta-blockade showing attenuation of heart rate and blood pressure and slight reduction in exercise capacity (compared with **A**). **C,** hypertensive response. Starting from hypertensive levels (160/100), peak pressures are 260/110. Hypertensive responses usually defined as >225 systolic and 100 diastolic. **D,** hypotensive response shows poor increase of pulse pressure and eventual fall in systolic pressure, suggesting ventricular dysfunction. Rising diastolic pressure and systolic pressure peak also common during recovery phase.

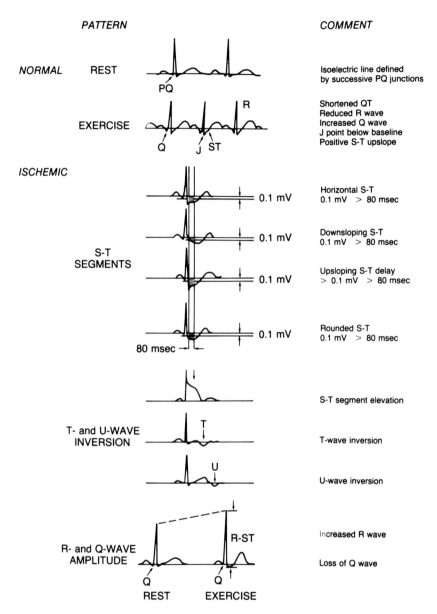

FIGURE 22–9. Common abnormal electrocardiographic (ECG) responses to exercise correlated with myocardial ischemia.

9. The normal pattern of exercise-induced ECG change includes rate-related shortening of the QT interval and superposition of the P- and T-waves. The amplitude of the R-wave decreases (from resting height), and the amplitudes of septal Q-waves and T-waves increase. The S-T segment shows a positive upslope, beginning from the J point (which is usually displaced below the isoelectric baseline) and returning to above the baseline within 60 to 80 msec. (Exercise ECG baseline is defined by successive PQ junctions.)

S-T Changes

S-T segment depression or delayed repolarization are widely accepted diagnostic criteria for myocardial ischemia. Most researchers consider S-T depression of -1.0 mm (0.1 mV) below the resting baseline for a duration of 80 msec or longer as significant evidence of myocardial ischemia. The pattern of S-T depression may vary from horizontal to downsloping. Rounded S-T depression and delayed upsloping patterns also correlate with ischemia that results from coronary heart disease. The depth of S-T depression may be affected by the pre-exercise ECG configuration (left ventricular hypertrophy) and pharmacologic agents (digoxin). When S-T depression is a baseline finding, an additional 0.1 mV decrease is usually required as evidence of ischemia.

The onset, duration, and magnitude of S-T depression usually correlates with the severity of myocardial ischemia. Early onset S-T depression of greater than −0.2 mV depth that lasts 5 min or more into the recovery stage is strongly predictive of three-vessel or left main coronary artery stenosis. No definitive criteria are established for discontinuing exercise on the basis of S-T depression. Some laboratories set −0.2 to −0.4 mV as an arbitrary value in the absence of other limiting factors.

S-T segment elevation during exercise may be caused by several mechanisms. Most commonly, S-T elevation is seen in leads overlying regional ventricular dyskinesis or aneurysm formation. Acute transmural ischemia may also produce S-T elevation during exercise, and it is frequently associated with severe left main stem or anterior descending coronary artery stenosis. Coronary spasm induced during exercise may produce variable patterns of S-T elevation or depression.

R-Wave Amplitude

Failure of the R-wave amplitude to decrease with exercise is an ancillary finding in myocardial ischemia. The combination of increases in R-wave amplitude and S-T depression may be an additional index of ischemic response. Although this finding is controversial, the assessment of R-wave amplitude may be useful in the interpretation of equivocal S-T depression, and is probably the only useful ECG indicator of ischemia in left bundle branch block.

T-Wave Changes

Changes in T-wave polarity and amplitude may be seen during exercise stress. Unfortunately, in most studies, wide variations in T-wave responses occur, even in healthy subjects.

Most healthy young men have increased T-wave responses during and immediately after exercise. Some patients may show flattening and inversion of T-waves as a result of hyperventilation, hypokalemia, and superimposed stress. T-wave inversion, which usually occurs in the post-exercise recovery period, must be interpreted in conjunction with other test responses. Normalization of inverted resting T-waves may occur during exercise and usually is associated with simultaneous ischemic S-T depression. The usefulness of T-wave changes as independent criteria for ischemia is controversial.

U-Wave Inversion

U-wave inversion during or after exercise has been correlated with myocardial ischemia and significant stenosis of the left anterior coronary artery. The inversion pattern is defined as a discrete negative deflection within the T-P segment and is best appreciated in the V_5 (or equivalent) precordial lead. The mechanism of the U-wave inversion is not known. In initial reports, researchers suggest U-wave inversion provides additional confirmation of severe or proximal left anterior descending coronary artery disease when seen in conjunction with S-T depression, and may be predictive of coronary artery disease in the absence of S-T depression.

DYSRHYTHMIAS

Exercise-associated dysrhythmias occur in healthy subjects as well as patients with cardiac disease. Increased sympathetic drive and changes in extracellular and intracellular electrolytes, pH, and oxygen tension contribute to disturbances in myocardial and conducting tissue automaticity and re-entry, which are major mechanisms of dysrhythmias.

Supraventricular Dysrhythmias

Isolated atrial premature contractions are common and require no special precautions. Chaotic atrial rhythm, atrial flutter, or fibrillation may occur in organic heart disease or secondary to endocrine, metabolic, or drug effects (hyperthyroidism, alcoholic cardiomyopathy, "holiday heart," and digoxin toxicity).

Sustained supraventricular tachycardia (SVT) occasionally induced by exercise may require treatment if discontinuation of exercise or vagal stimulation maneuvers fail to abolish the rhythm. Patients who experience exercise-induced SVT may be evaluated by repeated exercise testing after appropriate pharmacologic treatment.

Ventricular Dysrhythmias

Exercise-induced ventricular dysrhythmias are a more serious response. Isolated ventricular premature beats, or contractions (VPCs), may occur in 30 to 40% of healthy subjects and in 50 to 60% of patients with coronary artery disease during exercise. In follow-up studies, a higher rate of coronary events occurred in patients who exhibit VPCs and S-T segment depression. In addition, results of angiographic studies show a greater degree of coronary artery disease in patients who had exercise- and post-exercise-induced VPCs. VPCs may occur in association with a wide variety of underlying cardiac disorders, including mitral valve prolapse, hypertrophic cardiomyopathy, and valvular heart disease.

Induction or suppression of VPC activity by exercise is difficult to evaluate. VPCs in healthy young adults are usually suppressed with exercise. In older age groups, however, significant coronary artery disease may be found in patients who show suppression of VPCs during exercise. The daily variability of VPC activity is considerable. Sequential exercise tests on the same day may yield widely differing rates of VPCs.

Criteria for terminating exercise tests for ventricular ectopic beats usually include increasing frequency, multiform appearance, and coupling of ventricular tachycardia. The decision to stop exercise stress may also be influenced by simultaneous evidence of ischemia or symptoms of angina.

PREDICTIVE VALUE AND LIMITATIONS

During the past decade, the major focus of exercise stress testing was the diagnosis of coronary heart disease. Results of initial studies of exercise electrocardiography showed excellent correlation between ischemic S-T changes and angiographic findings of coronary stenosis. These studies were strongly influenced, however, by the high prevalence of symptomatic coronary artery disease in patients selected by evaluation. Subsequent studies of larger populations with variable prevalence of coronary artery disease have yielded findings to demonstrate the inherent limitations in using exercise electrocardiography in the diagnosis of coronary artery disease.

The diagnostic capacity of the predictive value of exercise testing is determined by the sensitivity and specificity of the test and the prevalence of coronary heart disease in the population tested. In the following discussion, the exercise ECG is the primary diagnostic criterion for ischemic heart disease. Other criteria that may be used to improve the diagnostic accuracy of exercise test results are emphasized.

SENSITIVITY

Sensitivity is the percent of patients tested with coronary heart disease who show positive test results. Exercise ECG sensitivity for the detection of coronary heart disease is usually based on subsequent angiographic findings of coronary stenosis of 50 to 70% in at least one vessel. A true-positive ECG exercise test (S-T depression of -0.1 mV for 80 msec) correctly identifies a patient with coronary artery disease. False-negative test results show nondiagnostic ECG changes and fail to identify patients with true coronary heart disease. Therefore, the sensitivity of ECG exercise testing is reduced from unity depending on the number of false-negative tests:

$$\text{Sensitivity} = \frac{\text{True-positive tests}}{\text{True-positive} + \text{false-negative tests}} \times 100\%$$

Common factors that contribute to false-negative results of exercise tests are summarized in Table 22–6. Test sensitivity is decreased by in-

Table 22–6. Causes of False-Negative Test Results

1. Failure to reach an adequate exercise workload
2. Insufficient number of leads to detect ECG changes
3. Failure to use other information such as systolic blood pressure drop, symptoms, dysrhythmias, or heart rate response, in test interpretation
4. Single vessel disease
5. Good collateral circulation
6. Musculoskeletal limitations before cardiac abnormalities occur
7. Technical or observer error

adequate or submaximal stress, insufficient ECG leads, and drugs that alter cardiac work responses to exercise or reduce ischemia (beta blockers, nitrates, and calcium channel-blocking agents). Pre-existing ECG changes, such as left bundle branch block or loss of precordial R-wave voltage from prior anterior infarction, limit test interpretation for ischemic ECG responses. If the criteria for a positive test are increased (from -0.1 to -0.2 MV S-T depression), overall sensitivity decreases because a significant number of true-positive tests (with less than -0.2 mV S-T depression) are excluded.

Sensitivity is increased by the use of maximal effort stress testing, multiple-lead ECG monitoring, computer analysis of ECG records, and additional criteria for abnormal test responses, such as low work capacity, poor BP response, and other ECG findings. If the criteria for a positive test are reduced (-0.5 mV S-T depression), the sensitivity increases, but the rate of false-positive tests also increases.

SPECIFICITY

The specificity of exercise tests is determined by the percent of normal subjects (without coronary artery disease) who show a negative or nondiagnostic stress test. A true-negative test correctly identifies a person without disease. Specificity is reduced by false-positive tests in persons without coronary heart disease.

Specificity =

$$\frac{\text{True-negative tests}}{\text{True-negative} + \text{false-positive tests}} \times 100\%$$

Many conditions may cause individuals to have false-positive exercise ECG responses (Table 22–7). Ischemic S-T changes may occur as a result of pathophysiologic states not related to coronary artery stenosis. Left ventricular hypertrophy, anemia, hypoxia, and coronary spasm are common underlying causes of false-positive responses to exercise. Abnormal S-T repolarization related to digoxin therapy, pre-excitation conduction patterns, type I antiarrhythmic drugs, phenothiazines, and lithium can produce apparent ischemic S-T changes in normal subjects. False-positive ECG responses occur more frequently in women (20 to 50 years of age) for undetermined reasons.

Specificity and sensitivity of exercise ECG responses have been studied in great detail. Most

Table 22–7. Causes of False-Positive Test Results

1. A pre-existing abnormal resting ECG (e.g., ST-T abnormalities)
2. Cardiac hypertrophy
3. Wolff-Parkinson-White syndrome and other conduction defects
4. Hypertension
5. Drugs (e.g., digitalis)
6. Cardiomyopathy
7. Hypokalemia
8. Vasoregulatory abnormalities
9. Sudden intense exercise
10. Mitral valve prolapse
11. Pericardial disorders
12. Pectus excavatum
13. Technical or observer error

data show sensitivity varies from 55 to 88% and specificity varies from 60 to 100%. The wide variation in these reported values has been attributed to significant differences in patient selection, test protocols, ECG criteria for a positive test, and angiographic definition of coronary artery disease.

PREDICTIVE VALUE

The predictive value of exercise testing is a measure of how accurately a test result (positive or negative) correctly identifies the patients tested. For a positive test:

$$\text{Predictive value} = \frac{\text{True-positive tests}}{\text{All positive tests}} \times 100\%$$

For a negative test:

Predictive value =

$$\frac{\text{True-negative tests}}{\text{All negative tests}} \times 100\%$$

The most important determinant of predictive value is the pretest likelihood of disease in the patient. For example, male patients over 50 years of age with typical angina have a 90 to 95% pretest likelihood of disease; therefore, the test approaches 100%. The pretest likelihood of disease in a 45-year-old man with atypical chest pain is reduced to between 40 and 50%. A positive test response would have a predictive value range of 75 to 85%. A female patient, 45 years of age, with atypical chest pain, however, would have a lower pretest likelihood of disease (10 to 15%), and a positive test would have a predictive value of only 35 to 45%. Finally, young patients in the range of 30 to 35 years with non-anginal chest pain also have a low pretest likelihood of disease (5%), and accordingly have only a 15% predictive value for a positive test.

Clinical data from a large series of patients evaluated in the coronary artery surgery study (CASS) show the general range of predictive values for exercise testing (both positive and negative) based on prevalence of coronary heart disease determined angiographically (Table 22–8). These data illustrate the efficacy and limitations of standard ECG stress testing in various subgroups of patients with chest pain that are frequently encountered by the clinical practitioner.

ENHANCEMENT OF PREDICTIVE VALUE

The diagnostic accuracy of exercise test results may be improved by using additional criteria for interpretation, including quantitative description of the onset, duration, depth, and location (leads) of S-T segment depression and other ECG changes (R-wave voltage and ventricular ectopic activity). Researchers suggest that computer analysis of exercise ECG records significantly increase the level of accuracy for S-T changes.

Other non-ECG criteria, such as duration of exercise or MET level attained, systolic blood pressure response pattern, maximal HR, HR × systolic pressure, and symptoms of angina or dyspnea, must be considered in the overall interpretation of exercise test results. Multivariate analysis of these variables in combination with ECG criteria show improved overall sensitivity for detection of coronary heart disease and higher specificity for the absence of multivessel coronary heart disease in patients with probable angina. Multiple exercise criteria, however, provide minimal added diagnostic value to the clinical assessment of patients with atypical angina or atypical chest pain.

COMPARISON WITH RADIONUCLIDE IMAGING

Advances in radionuclide myocardial perfusion and ventricular angiography have greatly improved the predictive value of exercise stress testing for coronary heart disease. The reported sensitivity and specificity for both radionuclide methods are 10 to 15% greater than those of the standard exercise ECG. The combined use of radionuclide and ECG stress testing usually provides a further increase in sensitivity with no loss in specificity.

Exercise radionuclide studies often reveal myocardial ischemic changes at submaximal workloads and HR before the onset of abnormal ECG responses. Therefore, adequate assessment of patients who are unable to perform near maximal exercise because of orthopedic or pulmonary limitations is possible. In addition, abnormal ECG patterns (resulting from left bundle branch block, prior MI, Wolff-Parkinson-White syndrome, and digoxin use) that preclude satisfactory interpretation of exercise ECG may be evaluated using radionuclide studies. Radionuclide techniques are especially useful in the evaluation of typical or atypical angina with apparently normal exercise ECG and for the evaluation of probable false-positive exercise ECG responses.

SUBMAXIMAL PREDISCHARGE EXERCISE TESTING

Exercise testing of patients soon after myocardial infarction or other cardiac events provides useful prognostic and therapeutic infor-

Table 22–8. Pretest Risk of Coronary Heart Disease (CHD) and Predictive Value of Positive and Negative Exercise Tests*

History	Sex	No. of Patients	% CHD Prevalence	% Predictive value†	
				+ET	−ET
Definite angina	M	620	89	96	35
	F	98	62	73	67
Probable angina	M	594	70	87	56
	F	240	40	54	78
Nonischemic chest pain	M	251	22	39	86
	F	242	5	6	95

* Adapted from Weiner DA: Exercise testing for the diagnosis and severity of coronary disease. *J Cardiac Rehab, 1:*438–444, 1981, with permission.

† +ET, predictive value of positive test defined by 1 mm horizontal or downsloping S-T depression; CHD prevalence based on 70% stenosis in at least one vessel: −ET, predictive value of a negative test.

mation. Results of multiple studies show patients who develop angina, additional S-T segment depression (> -0.1 mV from rest), or ventricular ectopic activity during submaximal exercise are at a high risk for future reinfarction or sudden death. Coronary angiography performed in these patients also reveals a high incidence of residual multivessel disease.

Low-level treadmill exercise tests usually involve use of a constant speed (2 to 2.5 mph) with 1-MET increases in grade every 2 to 3 min (see Branching protocol, Table 22–3). Modified end points include: 75% predicted maximal HR (60% with β-blockade); 4 to 6 METs of treadmill or equivalent cycle ergometer work and usual end points for abnormal ECG; dysrhythmias; and drop in systolic BP or symptoms.

The timing of low-level exercise testing after infarction varies widely. Predischarge exercise test studies are reported from 7 to 21 days after infarction. Findings of sequential exercise tests show that the S-T depression noted 2 to 3 weeks after myocardial infarction was also detected at 6 to 11 weeks. Abnormal BP levels, ventricular ectopic activity, and angina may improve with the second test.

EVALUATION OF MEDICAL THERAPY

Low-level and symptom-limited exercise testing is a useful method for evaluating the medical management of patients with cardiac disease. Isometric responses (S-T depression or angina) on predischarge testing favor early angiographic studies to define the extent of residual coronary disease.

Antianginal therapy may be optimized by serial exercise tests to determine the efficacy of symptom control with various agents. Nitrates, β-adrenoreceptor blocking agents, and calcium-blocking agents have been evaluated during exercise. Antiarrhythmic therapy may be improved by the use of ambulatory Holter monitoring and exercise testing to determine ectopic activity patterns.

Antihypertensive therapy can be evaluated to identify possible exercise-associated hypertension. Some patients show surprising degrees of hypertension with minimal exercise, and may require additional therapy for this pattern of response.

Exercise testing is an important clinical method for the evaluation of cardiopulmonary function. The diagnostic accuracy of exercise testing for coronary artery disease depends on the extent of the disease process and the sensitivity of the monitoring methods. Present methods of ECG recording provide a reasonable method of screening patients with probable ischemic heart disease. The addition of radionuclide perfusion or angiography to exercise testing increases sensitivity and specificity of exercise testing for coronary heart disease. Functional exercise testing provides quantitative assessment of work capacity in patients and in healthy subjects. Periodic testing is essential for achieving accuracy in exercise prescription training of cardiac patients, and of other individuals who require supervised exercise.

SELECTED REFERENCES

BOOKS

1. American College of Sports Medicine: *Guidelines for Exercise Testing and Prescription.* 3rd Ed. Philadelphia: Lea & Febiger, 1986.
2. Ellestad, MH: *Stress Testing: Principles and Practice.* 3rd Ed. Baltimore: Williams & Wilkins, 1986.

ARTICLES

1. American Heart Association: Guidelines for Exercise Testing. *Circulation, 75:*653A–667A, 1986.
2. Balady GJ, et al.: Value of arm exercise testing in detecting coronary artery disease. *Am J Cardiol, 55:*37–39, 1985.
3. Borg GV, Linderholm H: Perceived exertion and pulse rate during graded exercise in various age groups. *Acta Med Scand [Suppl], 472:*194, 1967.
4. Bruce RA: Exercise testing for ventricular function. *N Engl J Med, 296:*671, 1977.
5. Diamond GA, Forrester JS: Analysis of probability as an aid in the clinical diagnosis of coronary artery disease. *N Engl J Med, 300:*1350, 1979.
6. Ellestad MH, Savitz S, Bergdall D, Teske J: The false-positive stress test: Multivariate analysis of 215 subjects with hemodynamic, angiographic and clinical data. *Am J Cardiol, 40:*681, 1977.
7. Hamm LF, Stull GA, Crow RF: Exercise testing early after myocardial infarction: Historic perspective and current use. *Prog Cardiovasc Dis, 28:*463, 1986.
8. Weber KT, Janicki JS: Cardiopulmonary testing for the evaluation of chronic cardiac failure. *Am J Cardiol, 55:*224, 1985.
9. Weiner DA, McCabe CH, Ryan TJ: Identification of patients with left main and three vessel coronary disease with clinical and exercise test variable. *Am J Cardiol, 46:*21, 1980.
10. Weiner DA, et al.: Exercise stress testing: Correlations among history of angina. ST segment response and prevalence of coronary artery disease in the coronary artery surgery study (CASS). *N Engl J Med, 301:*230, 1979.

CHAPTER

23

ADDITIONAL DIAGNOSTIC TESTS: SPECIAL POPULATIONS

BARRY A. FRANKLIN,
VICTORIA HOLLINGSWORTH, AND
LAWRENCE M. BORYSYK

Over the past decade, several advances have been made in the diagnosis and treatment of coronary artery disease (CAD). Developments in nuclear cardiology, including myocardial perfusion imaging and ventricular function testing, have yielded greater accuracy in diagnosing the presence of CAD when compared with conventional exercise electrocardiography. Clinicians now recognize the value of serial noninvasive testing in predicting the likelihood of disease through the application of Bayesian analysis. Such information has markedly improved the objectivity of clinical decision-making regarding the need for coronary arteriography. Finally, new thrombolytic agents can reduce damage to the myocardium during acute infarction, and coronary angioplasty has sufficiently evolved to present a viable alternative to revascularization surgery in selected patients. This chapter is an overview of these additional diagnostic tests and treatment procedures, with specific reference to their clinical utility, risk, indications and contraindications, and advantages and limitations.

LIMITATIONS OF THE EXERCISE ELECTROCARDIOGRAM: DEVELOPMENT OF RADIONUCLIDE METHODS FOR CAD DETECTION

Exercise tolerance testing is one of the most common methods performed in the evaluation of the patient with suspected CAD. The test is based primarily on the electrocardiographic (ECG) response to exercise, with 1 mm or more ST-segment depression used as an indicator of myocardial ischemia (Fig. 23–1). The conventional exercise ECG, however, apparently has significant limitations in the diagnosis of hidden or latent CAD.[1] In some instances, exercise-induced ST-segment depression may be suggestive of underlying heart disease when, in fact, no disease is present. This situation occurs predominantly in populations with a low prevalence of CAD (e.g., young, asymptomatic women). Conversely, a lack of exercise-induced ST segment depression may imply that CAD is absent when disease may actually be present.

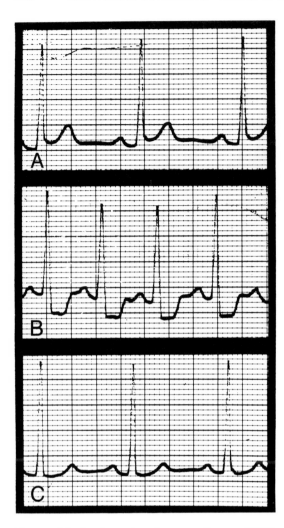

FIGURE 23–1. **A,** resting electrocardiogram (ECG) (V₅) before exercise testing. **B,** after several minutes of exercise test. Subject concurrently experienced mild angina pectoris. Myocardial ischemia verified further by significant ST-segment depression. **C,** resting ECG 6 minutes after exercise again representative of "normal" ECG.

Although the predictive accuracy of the exercise ECG appears reasonable, with an approximate 75% sensitivity and an 85% specificity, the 25% false-negative rate and 15% false-positive rate highlight its limitations in detecting latent CAD and its use as a screening procedure.[2] These limitations have led to the development of two noninvasive radionuclide methods for CAD detection: those that assess myocardial perfusion and those that assess ventricular function.

ASSESSING MYOCARDIAL PERFUSION WITH THALLIUM-201

Thallium-201 (^{201}Tl) has emerged as the radionuclide of choice for assessing regional perfusion in ischemic and nonischemic myocardium. It is distributed after intravenous injection according to myocardial blood flow, and is extracted by cells in a manner analogous to potassium. Normally perfused myocardium reaches a maximum ^{201}Tl uptake within minutes after its injection. In persons without obstructive CAD, the distribution of ^{201}Tl in the myocardium is relatively homogenous; however, myocardium supplied by a compromised coronary artery may be underperfused at peak exercise and ^{201}Tl accumulation may be attenuated and delayed. This scenario provides the clinical rationale for the injection of ^{201}Tl at near maximal exercise, with imaging scheduled as soon as possible in recovery (within approximately 10 min) and again several hours after exercise to assess for redistribution.

EXERCISE AND MYOCARDIAL PERFUSION IMAGING PROCEDURES

Myocardial perfusion imaging with ^{201}Tl has been used primarily in conjunction with exercise tolerance testing to detect areas of stress-induced ischemia or myocardial scar secondary to total coronary occlusion. Exercise testing is generally performed on a treadmill following standard protocols (e.g., Balke or Bruce) and using routine ECG and blood pressure monitoring. At near maximal exertion, however, the patient is injected with a small intravenous dose of ^{201}Tl (3 ml of saline containing 2 mCi of ^{201}Tl), and is instructed to continue to exercise for an additional 60 sec. Gamma camera imaging is performed within 10 min of ^{201}Tl injection, typically including the anterior and 45° left anterior oblique (LAO) views, and again 2 to 4 hr after exercise.

Differentiating Areas of Exercise-Induced Ischemia from Myocardial Scar Tissue

Images obtained shortly after exercise demonstrate the regional perfusion pattern at the time of stress. If the coronary arteries are normal, all portions of the myocardium receive approximately the same amount of isotope and

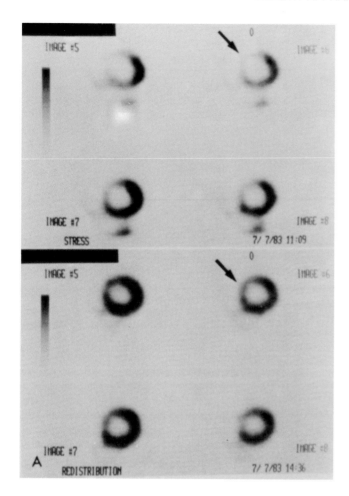

FIGURE 23-2. Thallium images immediately after exercise *(top)* and during redistribution phase 4 hours later *(bottom). Arrow,* anteroseptal defect during exercise stress that exhibits redistribution, signifying viable but transiently ischemic myocardium. (From Willens HJ: Advances in cardiac diagnosis: Nuclear Cardiology. In *Clinics in Sports Medicine.* Edited by B Franklin and M Rubenfire. Philadelphia: W.B. Saunders, 1984, with permission.)

the images have a uniform appearance. If, however, one or more of the coronary arteries is obstructed, the portions of myocardium supplied by these arteries show a relative lack of activity, called "cold spots," representing areas of stress-induced ischemia or myocardial scar tissue. The second set of images, taken several hours after exercise, helps to differentiate the regions of diminished isotopic activity as either exercise-induced ischemia in areas of viable myocardium, or areas of prior infarction with scar tissue. If the area is only transiently hypoperfused, the redistribution scan shows similar activity in the normal and ischemic segments and, therefore, a defect is no longer seen (Fig. 23-2).[3] Consequently, the second set of images appears normal. Old infarcts or injuries, however, are identified as persistent regions of diminished activity, or "fixed defects." Partial redistribution may occur in areas of infarction with adjacent or surrounding areas of ischemia.

Assessing Coronary Anatomy

The location of the perfusion defect can be used to predict the site of individual coronary stenoses. Septal and anterior defects are suggestive of left anterior descending CAD (sensitivity, 74%; specificity, 90%); inferior defects signify right coronary artery stenosis (sensitivity, 69%; specificity, 86%); and posterolateral defects imply left circumflex artery obstruction (sensitivity, 38%; specificity, 91%).[4] Predicting which vessel is involved when inferolateral ^{201}Tl defects occur, however, is difficult because of considerable interindividual variation in myocardium perfused by the right and left circumflex coronary arteries. Moreover, although simultaneous defects in the anterior, septal, and lateral vascular beds are highly sensitive (92%) for left main coronary artery stenosis, similar perfusion abnormalities may occur with double or triple vessel disease, a more common occur-

Table 23–1. Causes of "False-Positive" Exercise ECG Responses

1. Syndrome X in women
2. Left ventricular hypertrophy
3. Drugs (e.g., digitalis, antianxiety, and antidepressants)
4. ST segment abnormality at rest
5. Hypertension
6. Sudden intense exercise
7. Valvular heart disease—aortic stenosis, aortic insufficiency, and mitral valve prolapse syndrome
8. Left bundle branch block
9. Anemia
10. Hypoxia
11. Vasoregulatory abnormalities
12. Wolff-Parkinson-White syndrome and other conduction defects
13. Pectus excavatum
14. Hypokalemia
15. Cardiomyopathy
16. Pericardial disorders

rence. Consequently, many false-positive findings result (specificity, 15%) with this pattern.[5]

Accuracy in Comparison with Exercise ECG Findings

In numerous clinical studies, researchers have compared exercise ^{201}Tl myocardial perfusion imaging with conventional exercise ECG testing as a means of defining the presence or absence of CAD. In most studies, stress ^{201}Tl scintigraphy was superior to exercise electrocardiography in terms of sensitivity, specificity, and predictive accuracy, particularly when quantitative approaches (planar method or tomography) were employed for image interpretation.[6]

As a means of diagnosing CAD, the presence of a defect noted on exercise ^{201}Tl imaging has a sensitivity and specificity of approximately 85% and 90%, respectively.[2] The improved sensitivity in comparison with exercise stress electrocardiography is attributed to the fact that imaging may reveal regions of diminished radionuclide activity when the exercise ECG is

uninterpretable for ischemia or when suboptimal levels of exercise fail to elicit ischemic ST-segment depression. The improved specificity is a result of the fact that the primary cause of thallium perfusion defects is coronary artery stenosis, whereas there are numerous causes of ST segment displacement with exercise other than myocardial ischemia (Table 23–1). Although the results of radionuclide studies are uniformly better than those obtained with exercise electrocardiography alone, these studies do require the application of Bayesian analyses.[2,4,7] Accordingly, noninvasive tests have the greatest impact in patient groups with an intermediate pretest likelihood of disease.

Estimating Pretest Likelihood of Heart Disease

Clinicians now use three variables to estimate the risk of heart disease even *before* the exercise test is conducted. These variables, including age, sex, and symptoms, define a person's pretest risk or likelihood of disease (Table 23–2).[7]

In general, the risk of heart disease increases with advancing age. Moreover, at any given age, men are at a higher risk than women. Individuals who have anginal symptoms also have a greater pretest probability of disease than those who are free of symptoms. For example, an asymptomatic 45-year-old woman has only 1 chance in 100 of having significant CAD (see Table 23–2). A 55-year-old man with atypical angina has a 59% pretest probability of heart disease, whereas a 65-year-old man with typical angina has a very high (94%) pretest risk of heart disease.

Determining Post-test Likelihood of Disease

The results of the exercise test are considered along with the pretest risk to determine the post-test likelihood of disease. When the pretest

Table 23–2. Pre-test Likelihood of CAD (Percentage) in Patients by Age, Sex, and Symptoms*

Age (yr)	Asymptomatic		Nonanginal chest pain		Atypical angina		Typical angina	
	Men	Women	Men	Women	Men	Women	Men	Women
35	1.9	0.3	5.2	0.8	21.8	4.2	69.7	25.8
45	5.5	1.0	14.1	2.8	46.1	13.3	87.3	55.2
55	9.7	3.2	21.5	8.4	58.9	32.4	92.0	79.4
65	12.3	7.5	28.1	18.6	67.1	54.4	94.3	90.6

* Adapted from Diamond GA, Forrester JS: Analysis of probability as an aid in the clinical diagnosis of coronary artery disease. *N Engl J Med, 300:*1350, 1979.)

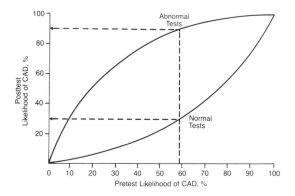

FIGURE 23–3. Impact of 59% pretest likelihood of CAD on post-test likelihood of disease when exercise ECG is normal, 30%, or abnormal, 90%. Sensitivity of exercise ECG is 75%; specificity 85%. (Adapted from Epstein SE: Implications of probability analysis on the strategy used for non-invasive detection of coronary artery disease. *Am J Cardiol,* 46:491, 1980.)

risk of CAD is either very high or very low, a normal or abnormal exercise ECG response has minimal impact on the post-test likelihood of disease. Thus, for the aforementioned 45-year-old woman or 65-year-old man, any findings from an exercise ECG would be of limited additional value in the diagnosis of CAD. On the other hand, when the pretest risk of heart disease is in the intermediate range (i.e., the 55-year-old man), the exercise test results may substantially alter the post-test likelihood of disease. For instance, the 55-year-old man with atypical angina has an approximate 59% likelihood of having significant CAD before any testing is done ("pretest likelihood of disease"). After an exercise ECG, his likelihood of having significant CAD ("post-test likelihood of disease") separates to about 90% if the test results are abnormal, demonstrating significant ST segment depression, and about 30% if the test yields normal findings (Fig. 23–3).[2]

Selection of Patients

The results of exercise ^{201}Tl testing have the greatest impact in patients with an intermediate likelihood of CAD, that is, in the 30 to 70% range of pretest probability. These patients demonstrate the greatest degree of change in the post-test probability of disease. Thus, the middle-aged or elderly patient with atypical angina receives the greatest benefit from [201]Tl

scintigraphy (see Table 23–2), because by considering the clinical history alone, the physician has already determined a moderate pretest likelihood of disease.

Rationale for Employing Multiple Noninvasive Studies

Most asymptomatic patients with exercise-induced ST-segment depression do not require exposure to the risk (albeit small) and expense of coronary arteriography, but further investigation of the possible presence of significant CAD is advisable. For these individuals, serial noninvasive testing appears warranted, because each test offers independent and additive data concerning the presence of disease.[1] Thus, an individual with a 10% pretest likelihood of CAD has a 30% likelihood after a "positive" exercise ECG. Figure 23–4 shows how this 30% likelihood becomes the pretest likelihood for the second test. When a ^{201}Tl exercise myocardial perfusion scan is used as the second test,

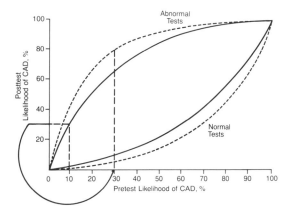

FIGURE 23–4. Use of two noninvasive tests in predicting existence of CAD. Pretest likelihood of coronary disease of 10% yields likelihood of 30% after abnormal exercise ECG. This 30% likelihood becomes pretest likelihood for second test—exercise thallium myocardial perfusion scintigram. Abnormal scintigraphic findings increase likelihood of disease to about 80%; normal findings reduce likelihood of disease to less than 5%. *Solid lines,* exercise ECG (sensitivity, 75%; specificity, 85%); *broken lines,* thallium exercise myocardial perfusion scan (sensitivity, 85%; specificity, 90%). (Adapted from Epstein SE: Implications of probability analysis on the strategy used for non-invasive detection of coronary artery disease. *Am J Cardiol,* 46:491, 1980.)

abnormal results increase the likelihood of disease to about 80%, whereas normal findings reduce the likelihood of disease to less than 5%.[2] In the first instance, cardiac catheterization may be advisable; in the second instance, it is not recommended. Thus, with the use of exercise ^{201}Tl scintigraphy in conjunction with the conventional exercise ECG, the need for coronary arteriography can be defined more intelligently.

Clinical Uses

In several clinical situations, a ^{201}Tl exercise myocardial perfusion scan may be particularly useful. Thallium-201 imaging should be considered for use in patients with chest pain who fail to achieve 85% of the age-predicted maximal heart rate because of dyspnea, fatigue, or β-blockade therapy, and in whom the exercise ECG shows no ischemic ST-segment depression.[6] Experience shows that ^{201}Tl scintigraphy maintains both sensitivity and specificity in this setting, approximating 80% and 90%, respectively.[8] Another group of patients in which ^{201}Tl imaging can be of value includes individuals who are asymptomatic but have "positive" exercise ECGs.

Thallium-201 exercise scintigraphy may also be of particular value in patients with ECG abnormalities that develop during exercise and are uninterpretable with respect to evidence of ischemia, e.g., in the presence of digitalis, significant ST-segment depression at rest, left ventricular hypertrophy, or left bundle branch block. Finally, ^{201}Tl scintigraphy may be used to assess coronary anatomy and severity of disease, to predict residual CAD after myocardial infarction, and to assess patients after percutaneous transluminal coronary angioplasty or coronary artery bypass graft surgery. Such information has important prognostic and therapeutic implications.[3]

Limitations

Despite the improved accuracy of stress ^{201}Tl scintigraphy over the conventional exercise ECG, radionuclide imaging techniques have certain problems. Major drawbacks include variability in imaging techniques and the qualitative visual interpretation of planar ^{201}Tl images. False-negative results of studies may occur in some patients with double or triple vessel CAD and severe left ventricular hypertrophy, or in patients unable to achieve at least 70% of age-predicted maximal heart rate.[6] Nonjeopardized coronary collateral vessels may also represent another important cause of false-negative ^{201}Tl studies, affording some protection during exercise to myocardium perfused by critically stenosed coronary arteries.[9] Finally, small defects, left circumflex arterial obstructions, and perfusion abnormalities in the distribution of vessels with a moderate (50 to 70%) stenosis, may at times not be detected.

Because the normal radionuclide scan is dependent on both adequate coronary perfusion and normal functioning myocardium, disorders other than CAD may elicit abnormal findings. False-positive defects may occur in the inferior wall, the septum (particularly in women), and in mitral valve prolapse. The septum may also be abnormal in patients with aortic stenosis and left bundle branch block because of localized calcification or fibrosis. Moreover, coronary spasm, myocardial bridge, and maldistribution of the coronary arteries have produced "abnormal" thallium scans, but false-positive results still occur in about 10% of patients without these anomalies.[3]

Use During Intravenous Dipyridamole Infusion: An Alternative to Exercise Stress

Thallium imaging undertaken during intravenous dipyridamole infusion can be used as a means of inducing regional myocardial flow heterogeneity in patients who are unable to perform sustained exercise, such as those with disabling arthritis, peripheral vascular disease, or other limitations.[6] This potent vasodilator markedly enhances blood flow to normally perfused myocardium, whereas myocardium fed by stenotic coronary arteries demonstrates relative hypoperfusion and diminished thallium activity. The approach assesses coronary flow reserve, in contrast to exercise-induced ischemia, and appears comparable to exercise ^{201}Tl imaging in sensitivity and specificity.

ASSESSING VENTRICULAR FUNCTION WITH RADIONUCLIDE ANGIOCARDIOGRAPHY

Cardiac blood-pool imaging facilitates the evaluation of cardiac function at rest and during exercise, including the rapid sequential assessment of the left vetricular ejection fraction, regional wall motion, ventricular volumes, and diastolic filling rates. The left and right ventricles can be visualized by the intravenous injection of the radioisotope technetium-99m so that it binds to the red blood cells and remains in the blood pool during scintigraphy. With the use of a computer, rapid serial images of the heart can be obtained.

EXERCISE AND RADIONUCLIDE ANGIOCARDIOGRAPHY

Radionuclide angiocardiography is an accurate and reproducible method that correlates well with cardiac catheterization for the determination of left ventricular ejection fraction. Because it is a noninvasive technique, it has the advantage of allowing low-risk serial studies of the effect of interventions such as exercise, medication, or coronary artery reperfusion, for example, after percutaneous transluminal coronary angioplasty or coronary artery bypass surgery.[3] Two approaches to exercise radionuclide angiocardiography have emerged: the "first-pass" method and the "gated equilibrium" method; in both, technetium-99m is used as the tracer.[6] In first-pass studies, the tracer is injected as a bolus and activity is recorded with a scintillation camera during the initial passage of the tracer through the heart. A time-activity curve is constructed, and the ejection fraction is calculated by determining the number of radioactive counts in the area of the left or right ventricle at end-diastole and end-systole. Regional wall motion can also be assessed by using this method, with end-diastolic and end-systolic silhouettes, cine-like movies, and functional images.

Equilibrium blood-pool imaging differs slightly in that the isotope is allowed to equilibrate within the vasculature. The cardiac cycle is divided into 12 to 28 frames, with the R-wave of the ECG used as a reference point. Images are obtained during several hundred cardiac cycles to generate a multigated radionuclide cineangiogram (MUGA). The left ventricular ejection fraction can be calculated in a manner similar to that with the first-pass technique.

Exercise Testing: Methods and Protocol

During exercise, the subject uses a cycle ergometer while in the supine, upright, or semi-upright position, and the camera is positioned to obtain a 45 to 50° left anterior oblique image. The initial workload (warmup) generally involves pedaling at power outputs of 300 kilopond-meters per minute (kpm/min) or less, thereafter, workload increments average 100 to 150 kpm/min every 3 min, to attainment of clinical signs, symptoms, or volitional fatigue. Measurements of the ejection fraction and regional wall motion at rest and during exercise are compared.

Interpretation of Results

The resting radionuclide angiocardiogram is evaluated for ejection fraction, regional wall motion, and end-diastolic and end-systolic volumes. Mean normal values ($\pm$ SD) for left and right ventricular ejection fraction at rest are 62.3% $\pm$ 6.1 and 52.3% $\pm$ 6.2, respectively.[10] Damage from a previous myocardial infarction is evident as either akinesis or hypokinesis of a segment of the myocardium in the distribution of the obstructed coronary artery.

The ejection fraction and wall motion response to exercise can be a sensitive indicator of left ventricular performance. In patients with ischemic CAD, ventricular function may be normal at rest; with the increased stress of exercise, however, a portion of the wall may become transiently ischemic and exhibit impaired contractility. Thus, abnormal exercise responses that are highly sensitive for the presence of CAD include the development of new regional wall motion abnormalities, an increase in end-systolic volume, and an inability to augment the ejection fraction by at least 5%.[11]

Clinical Uses

Exercise radionuclide angiocardiography may be used to diagnose the presence of CAD (sensitivity $\geq$ 85%), to assess the severity and extent of CAD, to evaluate prognosis after myocardial infarction, to clarify the risk of open heart surgery, and to identify viable but ischemic myocardium that may respond favorably to coronary artery bypass grafting.[11,12] Radionuclide angiocardiography can also be used to assess the effects of medication and exercise therapy in patients with CAD; however, in preliminary reports investigators indicate that ejection fraction and regional wall motion remain unchanged after physical conditioning programs.[13]

Comparison with Thallium-201 Myocardial Perfusion Imaging

Myocardial perfusion imaging and radionuclide angiocardiography offer the physician readily available and clinically valuable noninvasive techniques in the evaluation of CAD. These techniques provide information that complements and sometimes replaces that previously obtained through cardiac catheterization. Moreover, both methods appear to have comparable sensitivity and specificity for CAD detection, in the range of 85 to 90%.[12]

Limitations

Problems encountered with exercise radionuclide angiocardiography include patient difficulty in achieving prolonged (≥ 2 min) optimal stress levels to obtain statistically valid counts, observer variance in the qualitative evaluation of regional wall motion and the quantitation of left ventricular ejection fraction, and the lack of specificity for ejection fraction diminution with exercise stress.[6] Many patients with nonischemic-induced cardiac dysfunction, including those with hypertension, valvular heart disease, chronic obstructive pulmonary disease, and dilated cardiomyopathy, demonstrate an unchanged or decreased ejection fraction with exercise. Evidence exists also to suggest that abnormalities other than major coronary artery stenosis may be important in false-positive responses; for example, microvascular disease may play a role.[14]

PERCUTANEOUS TRANSLUMINAL CORONARY ANGIOPLASTY

Percutaneous transluminal coronary angioplasty (PTCA) was first presented to the American medical community in 1979 through a report by Dr. Andreas Gruntzig.[15] Although authors of an accompanying editorial from the National Institutes of Health raised the possibility that PTCA might eventually obviate coronary artery bypass grafting in a small number of patients, more than 100,000 PTCA procedures per year are currently performed in the United States.[16] The phenomenal growth in popularity of this technique is attributed in part to the development of a new catheter system that permits rapid, reliable access to the distal and branching coronary anatomy.[17]

EQUIPMENT AND PROCEDURES

The equipment for PTCA is, for the most part, the same as that for cardiac catheterization. The angiographer introduces a balloon or double-lumen dilation catheter into an artery and directs it, with a guidewire, to the site of a coronary lesion until it lies within the vascular stenosis (Fig. 23–5).[18] Inflation of the balloon with a solution of contrast medium and saline, to 5 to 15 atm, produces intimal disruption and splitting (rather than compression) of the atherosclerotic plaque (Fig. 23–6).[18] Successful PTCA increases lumen size and blood flow through the previously stenotic vascular segment, and promotes immediate decreases in the trans-stenotic pressure gradient. Other improvements include increased exercise ejection fraction and enhanced regional wall motion, reduced anginal symptoms, augmented exercise capacity, and normal thallium exercise myocardial perfusion scans.[19]

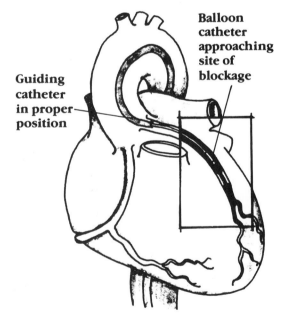

Balloon catheter approaching site of blockage

Guiding catheter in proper position

FIGURE 23–5. Guiding catheter directs balloon catheter used for percutaneous transluminal coronary angioplasty (PTCA). Balloon catheter ultimately advanced to middle of coronary artery stenosis. (From Department of Professional Clinical Education Services, USCI Division: *A Patient's Guide to PTCA.* Billerica, MA: C.R. Bard, 1985, with permission.)

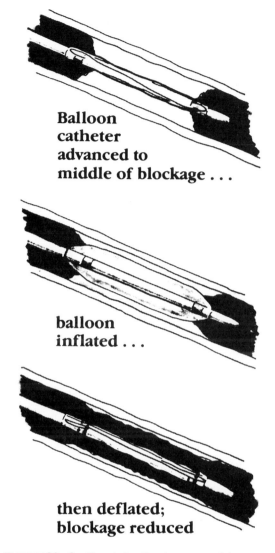

Balloon catheter advanced to middle of blockage . . .

balloon inflated . . .

then deflated; blockage reduced

FIGURE 23-6. Events leading to successful percutaneous transluminal coronary angioplasty (PTCA). (From Department of Professional Clinical Education Services, USCI Division: *A Patient's Guide to PTCA.* Billerica, MA: C.R. Bard, 1985, with permission.)

CANDIDATES FOR PTCA

Current estimates cite about 10% of candidates for coronary artery bypass graft surgery are candidates for PTCA. If patients with double lesions are included, the candidacy rate is greater. Minimal criteria for PTCA candidacy include angina, objective evidence of myocardial ischemia, a significant coronary artery lesion that is technically amenable to the procedure, and willingness of the patient to accept coronary artery bypass surgery if dilation fails or complications occur. Guidelines in selecting patients for PTCA have been proposed by the JAMA Council on Scientific Affairs (Table 23-3), although individual clinical circumstances may also be important when recommending the procedure.[20]

Clinicians can perform PTCA of bypass grafts with low complications and success rates comparable to those with native coronary arteries. Reasonable success rates (53%) have also been reported in patients with recent total occlusions, i.e., less than 20 weeks in duration, although PTCA on longstanding, totally occluded arteries is thought to be controversial in light of the high cost-benefit ratio.[21] Moreover, the prophylactic dilation of minor (<60% obstruction) lesions may be unjustified because of the dubious clinical and hemodynamic significance of these stenoses and the potential for complications and malignant restenosis.[16]

SUCCESS RATE AND RESTENOSIS OF CORONARY ARTERY PTCA

The National Heart, Lung, and Blood Institute (NHLBI) Registry cited an overall success rate of 66% in 2822 cases (single attempts). More recently, researchers performing a high volume of PTCA indicate that the rate of successful dilation may approach or even exceed 90%, with no significant difference between the major or branch vessels.[16,22] Restenosis occurred in 33% of the initial 665 NHLBI registry patients, and was highest within the first 5 months after angioplasty. Other individuals reported a comparable likelihood (29%) of early recurrence (within 6 months) of stenosis at the

Table 23-3. Guidelines in Selecting Patients for PTCA

Ideal factors
Single vessel disease
Lesions not longer than 1.5 cm
Proximal concentric lesion
Noncalcified lesion
Relative contraindications*
Left main artery stenosis†
Long stenotic segments
Multiple stenoses in one artery
Multivessel disease or calcified lesions
Contraindications
Lesions that occur at bifurcation of major vessel

* Procedure should be selectively applied.
† PTCA often performed only when patient is "protected" by saphenous vein or internal mammary grafts to the left anterior descending and/or the left circumflex coronary arteries.

site of PTCA.[23] For these patients, repeat PTCA has a high success rate, exceeding that of the initial PTCA. If restenosis occurs soon after a second successful PTCA procedure, however, treatment with a bypass graft procedure is preferable.[20]

COMPLICATIONS

In 6 to 8% of patients, abrupt closure occurs or blood flow in the area of vascular stenosis is significantly diminished. Pain continues and the potential for infarction remains.[20] Although sudden occlusion caused by arterial spasm can usually be relieved by the use of nitrates, calcium channel blockers, or repeat angioplasty, emergency bypass surgery may be necessary in some persons. The chance of myocardial infarction complicating the procedure is currently only 3%.[19] Furthermore, the mortality rate associated with PTCA is only about 1%, although the rate is somewhat higher in patients with multivessel disease or in those patients who have had previous coronary bypass surgery. Otherwise, complications inherent in PTCA appear to be similar to those associated with cardiac catheterization.

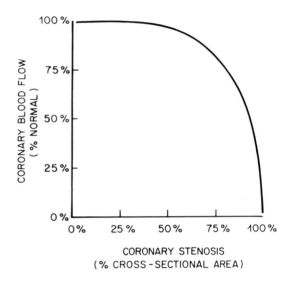

FIGURE 23-7. Relationship between myocardial perfusion and coronary artery stenosis. Coronary blood flow not significantly impaired until stenosis exceeds 75% of cross-sectional area of vessel. (From Dehn M, et al.: Clinical exercise performance. In *Clinics in Sports Medicine.* Edited by B Franklin and M Rubenfire. Philadelphia: W.B. Saunders, 1984, with permission.)

CORONARY ARTERY BYPASS GRAFTS

Coronary atherosclerosis involves a localized accumulation of lipid and fibrous tissue within the coronary artery, causing progressive narrowing of the vessel lumen. Fatty streaks progress to fibrous plaques, which usually develop in the proximal, epicardial segments of the coronary artery at sites of abrupt curvature or branching. Clinically significant lesions, producing either or both angina pectoris and ischemic ST segment depression usually exceed 75% of the vessel lumen (Fig. 23-7).[24] Atheroma or complex atherosclerotic plaques may then become complicated by hemorrhage, ulceration, calcification, or thrombosis, producing myocardial infarction with accompanying tissue necrosis.[25]

The objective of coronary artery bypass graft surgery (CABGS) is to increase blood flow and oxygen delivery to ischemic myocardium beyond an obstructive arterial lesion. The surgical technique involves bypassing the critically obstructed coronary artery with either a saphenous vein, removed from the patient's legs, or an internal mammary artery, one of the major arteries carrying blood to the chest wall (Fig. 23-8).[25] The internal mammary artery is not as versatile a conduit, however, and is technically more difficult to construct.

INDICATIONS

Recommendations for CABGS may include: (1) disabling or unstable angina that is refractory to pharmacologic treatment; (2) lesions threatening major portions of viable myocardium (i.e., left main coronary artery obstructions); (3) multivessel disease; (4) severe proximal left anterior descending coronary artery disease; and (5) ongoing ischemia after myocardial infarction.[19]

COMPLICATIONS

Major complications associated with CABGS occur in about 13% of revascularization patients.[26] Complications, including perioperative infarction in 2 to 8% of cases, occur more frequently in women, obese patients, patients with

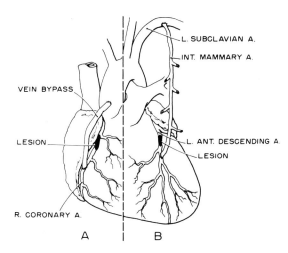

FIGURE 23–8. Coronary artery bypass graft procedures. **A,** saphenous vein bypass graft. Leg vein is sutured to ascending aorta and to right coronary artery beyond critical stenosis, creating vascular conduit to shunt blood around blockage to ischemic myocardium. **B,** mammary artery graft procedure. Mammary artery is anastomosed to anterior descending branch of left coronary artery distal to blockage so blood flow is re-established. (From Price SA, Wilson LM: *Pathophysiology: Clinical Concepts of Disease Processes.* New York: McGraw-Hill, 1978, with permission.)

impaired left ventricular function (ejection fraction of <30%), and persons undergoing emergency bypass surgery.[19] Overall operative mortality rate is currently 1 to 2% in many institutions; however, this figure varies somewhat depending on the patient's age, extent of disease, and degree of left ventricular dysfunction. Sex is another determinant of risk in that the operative mortality rate is slightly higher in women, probably because of greater severity of angina and smaller coronary arteries. Finally, for patients who require repeat bypass, the mortality rate is twice that for the initial procedure.

GRAFT PATENCY

Current patency rates for saphenous vein grafts are 90% after 1 year and 80% after 5 years.[19] A marked attrition of vein grafts occurs between postoperative years 6 and 11, however, which is related to the development of atherosclerosis. After 11 years, only 60% of vein grafts are patent and nearly one half of these grafts are severely atherosclerotic.[19] In

contrast, internal mammary grafts have a 93% 10-year graft patency and appear to be resistant to atherosclerosis.[27] This fact may partially explain the impressive 10-year actuarial survival advantage in patients undergoing CABGS who received internal mammary grafts when compared to patients who received saphenous vein grafts.[28]

RELIEF OF ANGINA

Total relief of angina typically occurs in 60 to 75% of patients during the first five postoperative years; an additional 20 to 25% of patients report a significant reduction in symptoms.[29] Angina recurs in about 15% of CABGS patients over this same time period, however, primarily because of incomplete bypass grafting, progression of disease in native vessels, or graft occlusion.

PROLONGATION OF LIFE

A recent review of three major randomized trials, in which researchers compared surgical intervention with medical management, concluded that: (1) CABGS improved survival in patients with left main disease; (2) CABGS improved survival in patients with three-vessel disease and impaired ventricular function; and (3) CABGS offered no survival advantage to mildly symptomatic or asymptomatic patients.[30]

THROMBOLYTIC THERAPY

Thrombolytic therapy for acute myocardial infarction is a promising new therapeutic approach that can re-establish vessel patency and achieve reperfusion in a high percentage of patients. Consideration of this strategy emerged when investigators showed that acute transmural myocardial infarction was associated with a high incidence of coronary thrombosis. Such findings rekindled interest in using thrombolytic enzymes to limit infarct size and to preserve ventricular function.

AGENTS AND MECHANISM OF ACTION

Streptokinase, urokinase, and tissue-plasminogen activator (tPA) are specific thrombolytic agents that may be used to activate the fibrinolytic process. Activation results in the conversion of plasminogen, the inactive enzyme precursor, to plasmin, the active fibrinolytic enzyme, which is then able to lyse (dissolve) the clot. Plasminogen activation with either streptokinase or urokinase, however, results in the production of circulating plasmins, systemic lysis, and frequent bleeding complications, regardless of the method of infusion (intravenous or intracoronary). In contrast, tPA dissolves thrombi but does not produce serious generalized bleeding.

EFFECTIVENESS

Reperfusion was achieved in about 75% of patients when streptokinase was infused directly into a thrombosed coronary artery *within the first 6 hours* after the onset of infarction. Intravenous infusion of streptokinase, which can be done more simply and more rapidly than intracoronary infusion, can restore perfusion in about 50% of patients with acute myocardial infarction.[31] In addition, successful thrombolytic therapy may provide sudden relief of angina and rapid resolution of ST-segment elevation. High-grade stenoses usually remain, however, with an attendant risk of reinfarction.

Several clot-selective plasminogen activators that do not induce systemic fibrinolysis are currently under investigation. Of these activators, tPA appears to have the greatest potential in that it produces in vivo clot dissolution without systemic effects. In the European Cooperative tPA Trial, patients treated with tPA demonstrated a 70% reperfusion rate as compared with a 55% rate in patients treated with intravenous streptokinase.[32] Successful thrombolysis was also accompanied by a lower incidence of systemic bleeding in the tPA-treated patients. In the Thrombolysis in Myocardial Infarction (TIMI) trial, reperfusion was achieved in 60 and 35% of the tPA and streptokinase-treated patients, respectively.[33] Results of these prospective clinical trials showed that tPA is significantly more effective in achieving coronary reperfusion and may be associated with fewer bleeding complications.

REFERENCES

1. Laslett LJ, Amsterdam EA: Management of the asymptomatic patient with an abnormal ECG. *JAMA*, 252:1744, 1984.
2. Epstein SE: Implications of probability analysis on the strategy used for non-invasive detection of coronary artery disease. *Am J Cardiol*, 46:491, 1980.
3. Willens HJ: Advances in cardiac diagnosis: Nuclear cardiology. In *Clinics in Sports Medicine* Edited by B Franklin and M Rubenfire. Philadelphia: W.B. Saunders, 1984.
4. Berman DS, Garcia EV, Maddahi J: Thallium-201 myocardial scintigraphy in the detection and evaluation of coronary artery disease. In *Clinical Nuclear Cardiology.* Edited by DS Berman and DT Mason. New York: Grune and Stratton, 1981.
5. Rigo P, et al.: Value and limitations of segmental analysis of stress thallium myocardial imaging for localization of coronary artery disease. *Circulation, 61*:973, 1980.
6. Beller GA: Radionuclide techniques in the evaluation of the patient with chest pain. *Mod Concepts Cardiovasc Dis, 50*:43, 1981.
7. Diamond GA, Forrester JS: Analysis of probability as an aid in the clinical diagnosis of coronary artery disease. *N Engl J Med*, 300:1350, 1979.
8. Iskandrian AS, Segal BL: Value of exercise thallium-201 imaging in patients with diagnostic and non-diagnostic electrocardiograms. *Am J Cardiol*, 48:233, 1981.
9. Rigo P, et al.: Influence of coronary collateral vessels on the results of thallium-201 myocardial stress imaging. *Am J Cardiol*, 44:452, 1979.
10. Pfisterer ME, Battler A, Zaret BL: Range of normal values for left and right ventricular ejection fraction at rest and during exercise assessed by radionuclide angiocardiography. *Eur Heart J*, 6:647, 1985.
11. Okada RD, et al.: Exercise radionuclide imaging approaches to coronary artery disease. *Am J Cardiol*, 46:1188, 1980.
12. Meizlish JL, Berger HJ, Zaret BL: Exercise nuclear imaging for the evaluation of coronary artery disease. In *Exercise and the Heart.* 2nd Ed. Edited by NK Wenger. Philadelphia: F.A. Davis, 1985.
13. Jensen D, et al.: Improvement in ventricular function during exercise studies with radionuclide ventriculography after cardiac rehabilitation. *Am J Cardiol*, 46:770, 1980.
14. Opherk D, et al.: Reduced coronary reserve and ultrastructural changes of the myocardium in patients with angina pectoris but normal coronary arteries. *Circulation, 59*:11–75, 1979.
15. Gruntzig AR, Senning A, Siegenthaler WE: Nonoperative dilation of coronary artery stenosis: Percutaneous transluminal coronary angioplasty. *N Engl J Med, 301*:61, 1979.
16. Oesterle SN: Controversies in coronary angioplasty. *Cardiology, 11*:37, 1986.
17. Simpson JB, et al.: A new catheter system for coronary angioplasty. *Am J Cardiol*, 49:216, 1982.
18. Department of Professional Clinical Education Services, USCI Division: A Patient's Guide to PTCA. Billerica, MA: C.R. Bard, 1985.
19. Timmis GC, et al.: *Cardiovascular Review.* 8th Ed. New York: Pergamon Press, 1987.
20. JAMA Council on Scientific Affairs: Percutaneous transluminal angioplasty. *JAMA*, 251:764, 1984.
21. Kereiakes DJ, et al.: Angioplasty in total coronary artery occlusion: Experience in 76 consecutive patients. *J Am Coll Cardiol*, 6:526, 1985.
22. Proceedings of the National Heart, Lung, and Blood Institute Workshop on the outcome of percutaneous coronary angioplasty. *Am J Cardiol*, 53:1c, 1984.

23. Rosing DR, et al.: Three year anatomic, functional and clinical follow-up after successful percutaneous transluminal coronary angioplasty. *J Am Coll Cardiol, 9*:1, 1987.

24. Dehn M, et al.: Clinical exercise performance. In *Clinics in Sports Medicine.* Edited by B Franklin and M Rubenfire. Philadelphia: W.B. Saunders, 1984.

25. Price SA, Wilson LM: *Pathophysiology: Clinical Concepts of Disease Processes.* New York: McGraw-Hill, 1978.

26. Kuan P, Bernstein SB, Ellestad MH: Coronary artery bypass surgery morbidity. *J Am Coll Cardiol, 3*:1391, 1984.

27. Lytle BW, et al.: Young adults with coronary atherosclerosis: 10 year results of surgical myocardial revascularization. *J Am Coll Cardiol, 4*:445, 1984.

28. Loop FD, et al.: Influence of the internal-mammary-artery graft on 10-year survival and other cardiac events. *N Engl J Med, 314*:1, 1986.

29. Loop FD: Coronary artery surgery—1982. *Coronary Club Bulletin, 11*:1, 1982.

30. Killip T, Ryan TJ: Randomized trials in coronary bypass surgery. *Circulation, 71*:418, 1985.

31. Laffel GL, Braunwald E: Thrombolytic therapy: A new strategy for the treatment of acute myocardial infarction. *N Engl J Med, 311*:770, 1984.

32. European Cooperative Study Group: Randomised trial of intravenous recombinant tissue-type plasminogen activator versus intravenous streptokinase in acute myocardial infarction. *Lancet, 1*:842, 1985.

33. TIMI Study Group: The thrombolysis in myocardial infarction (TIMI) trial: Phase I findings. *N Engl J Med, 312*:932, 1984.

V

EXERCISE PROGRAMMING

24

QUALITIES OF AN EXERCISE LEADER

NEIL B. OLDRIDGE

The dictionary definition of a leader is "guide, conductor" or "a person who has commanding authority or influence." Synonyms for leader, according to Roget's Thesaurus, are: "director, conductor, head, commander, chief." Two less restrictive descriptions of a leader are: (1) a person who succeeds in getting others to follow him or her, and (2) a person who creates the most effective change in group performance. Leadership, therefore, is the process of influencing behavior and motivating or stimulating other individuals to meet some goal or goals.

The goals in preventive and rehabilitative programs are to prevent disease or the further progression of disease, and to rehabilitate, which is best defined as the "sum of activity required to ensure cardiac patients the best possible physical, mental, and social conditions so that they may, by their own efforts, regain as normal as possible a place in the community and lead an active and productive life."[1] The responsibility of the exercise leader is to provide the participant with motivation and, when necessary, skills for regaining an active and productive life.

EXERCISE LEADER RESPONSIBILITIES

Successful prevention and rehabilitation of disease include appropriate progressive withdrawal of supervision and support, and in so doing, increasing participant self-responsibility with the goal of regaining an active and productive life. The effective exercise leader understands the barriers that often prevent the assumption of self-responsibility for health care. These barriers are (1) inadequate knowledge and lack of interest in factors that can be prevented and/or modified; (2) lack of knowledge of the strategies and skills needed to prevent and modify health behaviors; and (3) a culture that de-emphasizes individual responsibility, stressing instead individual rights and society's responsibility.[3] The responsibilities of an effective exercise leader are to reduce these barriers to health care self-responsibility and to educate and motivate individuals referred to preventive or rehabilitative exercise programs to assume some responsibility for changing health behaviors safely and realistically.

EFFECTIVE LEADERSHIP

An effective leader possesses task-related abilities or knowledge and competencies (Table 24–1), a keen sense of relationship-oriented abilities or social skills (Table 24–2), and the motivation to be a leader. Figure 24–1 illustrates how behavior can be described as having antecedents and consequences. Effective leadership behavior reinforces a high likelihood that the consequences of behavior change will be positive, which in turn increases the chances of goal attainment. This situation occurs when appropriate cooperation exists between the leader and the individual participants or groups of participants. The behavior of the leader is determined by several factors, including the characteristics and expectations of the participants, the situation at hand, and the individual characteristics of the leader. The likelihood of achieving goals is optimized when a leader has the knowledge, competencies, and skills to educate and motivate participants who are willing to take the appropriate steps to maintain or regain an active, productive life.

The ability to assess a given situation and to implement the appropriate balance between the task-related and relationship-oriented abilities in different situations with various patients determines the outcome of the program (Fig. 24–1).

Table 24–1. Task-Related Abilities Associated with Effective Leadership

Examples include appropriate:
  Interpretation of graded exercise tests
  Explanation of myocardial ischemia
  Explanation of physiologic response to exercise
  Design of appropriate exercise prescriptions
  Modification of intensity and type of exercise
  Explanation of precautions in different environmental situations
  Scheduling of program and personnel
  Record keeping and data storage
  Decision-making in an emergency
  Referral to others

Table 24–2. Relationship-Oriented Abilities Associated with Effective Leadership

Examples include:
  Listening skills
  Attention to individual needs
  Concern regarding integration of new participants
  Acceptance of individual differences
  Attention to group interaction
  Educational skills
  Motivational skills with participants and staff
  Rapport and empathy leading to sensitivity
  Consistency/honesty/tactfulness
  Avenues of communication between participants and staff

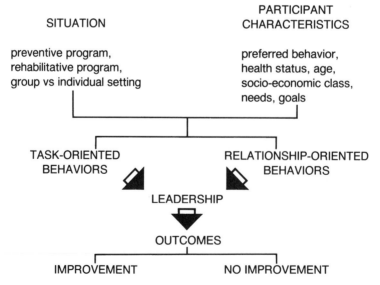

FIGURE 24–1. Antecedents and consequences of behavior and impact of effective leadership on outcome of program.

TASK-RELATED ABILITIES

Task-related behaviors require knowledge and competency, including exercise testing and prescription, supervising and leading physical activity, motivating and educating participants, program organization, and program administration. These behaviors relate specifically to the general objectives for exercise programming and leadership as described in the ACSM *Guidelines.* The leader must possess knowledge and skills as they relate to the group's task. In this particular case, the group's task is to become more familiar with various physical activities and more adept in defining the appropriate intensity of physical activity, with the goals of improving functional capacity, understanding more clearly the risk factor concept, as well as learning appropriate coping skills. The knowledge and competencies of the exercise leader, according to ACSM *Guidelines,* include the scientific principles of exercise and conditioning; the ability to design safe, appropriate, and enjoyable individualized exercise prescriptions; and the means to modify cardiovascular risks appropriately. Examples of some task-related abilities are listed in Table 24 – 1.

RELATIONSHIP-ORIENTED ABILITIES

Relationship-oriented abilities tend to promote an environment in which friction and disagreement are at a minimum. In this context, the activities of the effective leader are more difficult to learn and include the abilities to: (1) pay attention to participants so to develop an esprit de corps; (2) integrate new participants comfortably into the group; be aware of potential personality, cultural, or ideologic conflicts; (4) provide a means of communication between participants and staff; (5) encourage interaction and self-responsibility; and (6) make exercising enjoyable. Further examples of relationship-oriented abilities are given in Table 24 – 2.

LEADERSHIP STYLE

Personality traits certainly play an important part in effective leadership, as does the ability to act appropriately in any situation. "What you are" is not as important as "how you are" in determining leadership effectiveness. The most effective style of leadership is to generate actions with an appropriate balance between task-oriented and relationship-oriented behaviors. Principles of conducting programs have been put forth, but the actual style of leadership is unique to each individual.[2,4,6] Therefore, within any given situation and set of participant characteristics, an effective leader is able to manage the balance between task-related and relationship-oriented behaviors in any situation with any given set of participant personality traits, and succeeds in getting participants to create effective change in group performance.

SITUATION

Leadership style and the necessary balance in using task and relationship behaviors is determined by the situation at hand. Effective leadership style in a fitness program for healthy 20- to 25-year-old women interested in losing weight is obviously different than effective leadership style in a cardiac rehabilitation program in which most of the participants are men 55 years of age or older.

Leadership is essentially a continuum of styles from authoritarian through democratic to laissez-faire. In the military, the most appropriate leadership style is authoritarian. In other situations, i.e., a think tank, in which individuality is desired and structure is resisted, the most appropriate style of leadership may be laissez-faire. In other situations, often the most effective style is democratic, whereby the group, including the leader, defines the structure and objectives. Whichever style is chosen, a large group, for example, necessitates more structure than if the group size is small. Likewise, more structure is needed in a rehabilitative program than in an adult fitness class.

PARTICIPANTS

Characteristics and personalities of the participants also determine leadership style. In this determination, certain characteristics of the participant must be assessed: (1) health status, (2) age, (3) goals and needs, and (4) socioeconomic class and educational level.[4,5,7]

MOTIVATION

Established guidelines help a leader to be as effective as possible in motivating individuals to adopt and then maintain change over time.[2,4-6,8] These guidelines include knowing that reasons for adopting a new behavior are not the same as reasons for maintaining the new behavior over time, understanding theories of motivation, knowing whether certain characteristics are predictive of compliance, and knowing which of the behavioral management strategies are likely to be useful in motivating people to be active for extended periods. To optimize the probability of success in improving participant motivation, a variety of program strategies and activities must be considered by the effective leader.[2,5,6,9,10] Behavioral management strategies are discussed elsewhere in this book.

STRATEGIES

Participant motivation to change and maintain personal health behaviors depends on education, decision-making, and coping skills as well as self-evaluation of effort and performance.[9,10] Motivation is optimized when participants perceive that they have some control over goals and activities and are successful; and that their effort or performance has resulted in equitable rewards, which may be either intrinsic (increased self-esteem or self-confidence) or extrinsic (from some external source). The effective leader pays attention to the characteristics, needs, and expectations of the participant to optimize motivation, with the underlying assumption that an acceptance of self-responsibility is central to personal health behavior change.[3,11]

PROGRAM ACTIVITIES

The effective exercise leader attends to the needs and goals of individuals while maintaining sufficient interaction between participants to optimize group support. The effective leader incorporates fun and play elements into the program, exposing participants to alternative activities.[2,4-6] Useful program activity suggestions to increase motivation and compliance can be spelled out in the word VARIATION:[5]

V — variety
A — aerobic
R — relaxing and recreative
I — individualized
A — attitude
T — therapeutic

I — isotonic
O — objective testing
N — noncompetitive and fun

Too often, lack of motivation is identified as the central reason for participant dropout. The exercise leader also must take some responsibility for poor compliance in an exercise program. Providing strategies to increase motivation and using a variety of programs are integral components of effective leadership.

OUTCOME OF EFFECTIVE LEADERSHIP

The most important outcome of effective exercise leadership, both preventive and rehabilitative, is the development of a sense of self-responsibility for personal health by the participant.[3,11] The effective leader must therefore have the ability to assess the situation and the participant characteristics and needs, respond with appropriate balance between task-oriented skills and relationship-oriented skills, and have unique leadership style that is sufficiently effective to motivate the individuals involved to make changes.

"Exercise leadership and the program activities selected must recognize individual needs, set appropriate goals, permit opportunities for choice, provide feedback, and have a functioning reward system. The exercise specialist should be able to master the science of leading physical activity. Making those activities enjoyable and rewarding is an art form."[2] These skills can be learned, and therefore an interest in further education is an indispensable part of effective leadership.

REFERENCES

1. World Health Organization: *Rehabilitation of Patients with Cardiovascular Disease. Report of a W.H.O. Expert Committee*, Technical Report Series #270. Geneva: World Health Organization, 1964.
2. Stoedefalke KG: Principle of conducting exercise programs. In *Exercise Testing and Exercise Training in Coronary Heart Disease*. Edited by JP Naughton and HK Hellerstein. New York: Academic Press, 1973.
3. Knowles JH: The responsibility of the individual. *Daedelus, 106*:57–80, 1977.
4. Heinzelmann F: Social and psychological factors that influence the effectiveness of exercise programs. In *Ex-*

ercise Testing and Exercise Training in Coronary Heart Disease. Edited by JP Naughton and HK Hellerstein. New York: Academic Press, 1973.

5. Oldridge NB: What to look for in an exercise class leader. *Phys Sports Med,* 5:85–88, 1977.

6. Franklin BA: Motivating and educating adults to exercise. *J Health Phys Ed Rec,* 49:13–17, 1978.

7. Oldridge NB: Compliance with intervention and rehabilitation exercise programs—a review. *Prev Med,* 11:56–70, 1982.

8. Oldridge NB, Stoedefalke K: Compliance and motivation in cardiac exercise programs. *Clin Sports Med,* 3:443–454, 1984.

9. Martin JE, Dubbert PM: Behavioral management strategies for inforcing health and fitness. *J Cardiac Rehab,* 4:200–208, 1984.

10. Wankel LM: Decision making and social support strategies for increasing exercise involvement. *J Cardiac Rehab,* 4:124–135, 1984.

11. Oldridge NB: Cardiac rehabilitation, self-responsibility, and quality of life. *J Cardiopul Rehab,* 6:153–156, 1986.

25

ORGANIZATION OF AN EXERCISE SESSION

MICHAEL D. GIESE

A high level of organization within the health care provider community does not assure that each individual exercise session will be well organized. The exercise leader must assure that the most crucial part of the clinical exercise program — the actual exercise session — is organized in such a way that the overall objectives of the program are met. To meet these objectives, the adherence to lifelong exercise must improve. Studies of compliance in clinical exercise programs reveal dropout rates of no less than 12% at 3 months and as high as 87% at 12 months.[1,2]

The organizational format of a clinical exercise session must provide: (1) a pre-exercise assessment, (2) warmup and cool-down phases; and (3) a session that provides improvement in overall fitness, including cardiovascular fitness, muscular strength and endurance, and flexibility.

PRE-EXERCISE ASSESSMENT

The pre-exercise assessment is needed in any program that involves a population that is at risk during exercise. Screening of the individual at risk should include the measurement of pre-

exercise blood pressure and heart rate. While taking blood pressure, the exercise leader should ask questions that encourage the patient to share any prodromal signs or symptoms. Individual assessment of participants before each session is not indicated in fitness programs for apparently healthy adults. A reminder of symptoms or other concerns given by the exercise leader at the start of the session, however, is appropriate. A discussion of the selection and appropriate levels of screening is found in Chapters 26 and 27.

WARMUP AND COOL-DOWN PHASES

Warmup and cool-down activities are essential in all adult exercise programs, and are based on firm, physiologic considerations. The warmup period permits a gradual increase of metabolic requirement, which enables the organ systems involved with exercise to adapt gradually to the increasing level of activity. In the patient with a compromised circulatory system, a low degree of activity provides a powerful stimulus for dilation of peripheral and coronary arteries. With this dilation, the patient meets more easily the higher energy demands of the conditioning period of the exercise session. The length of the warmup depends on the type of activity involved in the conditioning period, the levels of intensity of those activities, as well as the level of fitness of the participants.

An appreciation of the physiologic importance of warmup can be gained by considering the anginal walk-through phenomenon. In the walk-through phenomenon, a patient may experience mild angina and accompanying ischemic ECG changes while initiating low-level walking (i.e., 2.5 mph). After 5 to 10 min of warmup, that same patient is able to exercise at three to four times the initial work requirement with no angina or ischemic ECG changes.[3]

The cool-down phase assures that venous return is maintained in the face of significant peripheral dilation. This post-exercise time is the period during which the individual is most vulnerable to arrhythmias and participants with cardiac disease require close monitoring. Lack of appropriate cool-down can result in dramatic venous pooling and hypotension. The warmup and cool-down periods provide the opportunity for both active and passive exercise. Passive activities, such as flexibility exercises, can be used as an integral part of warmup and cool-down. Remember that no single exercise can develop flexibility of all body parts. A planned approach to enhance flexibility in the major muscle groups is indicated. Resources are available that demonstrate flexibility exercises for various muscle groups and for various activities.[4] Active warmup and cool-down activities may include individual and dual stunts, games, contests, and relays, which require participants to challenge their range of motion and thereby increase their flexibility. An advantage to this "games approach" is the intrinsic enjoyment and peer interaction.

CONDITIONING PHASE

The training stimulus phase, or conditioning period, of the exercise program must impose a metabolic requirement unique to each participant to stimulate an adaptive response while assuring safety. Several methods can be used: (1) individualized exercise performed at home or on a treadmill or cycle ergometer in a supervised setting; (2) group activities, such as games; and (3) circuit training activities.

INDIVIDUAL EXERCISE

Simply describing an exercise regimen for each individual on the basis of metabolic requirements for treadmill walking or stationary cycling may be appropriate for some individuals. Other participants may require more attention, guidance, and interaction with the exercise leader and their peers to accomplish the goals of exercise training.

GROUP EXERCISE

Games with or without equipment, walking or jogging, swimming, stunts, and contests provide variety within group conditioning activities. Participation in well-organized games and group activities allows the exercise leader to observe individual participants in spontaneous activity. Group conditioning activity permits social interaction among the participants and contributes to improved adherence. Levels of supervision required for the group and the staff available to the session determine the types of activities possible.

A program of walking or jogging enables the individual to progress at their own pace while interacting with their peers. Such a program also provides a good balance between individual attention given by the exercise leader and the individual's responsibility for their exercise prescription. In this setting, the exercise leader is not primarily concerned with leading the group activity, and thus is able to circulate among the participants and to monitor and motivate them as needed.

Suggested group activities for use in adult exercise sessions are available from several sources, including (1) elementary physical education textbooks; (2) playgrounds, parks, and recreational manuals; (3) military physical training manuals (many ROTC supply sergeants provide these at no charge); and (4) general reference publications, usually described as new games or children's activity books. With experience, the exercise leader will have no difficulty in creating new and innovative plans.

The following activities, which focus on skills, can also be employed to provide a variety of activities. Any activity that is competitive may have to be adapted (i.e., changing rules or not keeping score) to reduce the degree of competition among the participants and so to minimize the possibility of exceeding the prescribed exercise intensity.

1. *Skills and games with balls of various sizes.* The size and type of ball can lead to innovative use, i.e., the cage ball can be used as a substitute for a basketball. Examples of other balls include tennis balls, volleyballs, playground balls, basketballs, medicine balls, handballs, softballs, mush balls, and nerf balls.
2. *Activities with apparatus.* Examples include hoola hoops, frisbees, paddle rackets, skip ropes, skittles, "quoits," surgical tubing, culverts, and play bouys.
3. *Chasing games.* Examples include tag, chain tag, fox and geese, and dodge ball.
4. *Relays with and without apparatus.* Examples such as running, hopping, rolling, crawling, and dribbling with hands and feet.
5. *Stunts and contests.* Including dual activities such as balancing stunts, forward rolls, backward rolls, strength moves, pushups, situps, and limited combatives such as rooster fights and partner sparring.
6. *Lead-up games for major sport games.* Examples are soccer, tennis, basketball, volleyball, handball, and football, often with rules adjusted to fit the level of skill and capacity of the participants.
7. *Children's games.* Activities such as skittle ball, four squares, and bounce ball.

One objective of exercise programming is to help the participant develop a strong concept of perceived exertion. Ideally, the exercise leader assists in relating the metabolic costs of various games and activities to the participant, so these requirements (and sense of perceived exertion) can be transfered to activities of daily living, such as tennis, swimming, and hunting. In group activities, the participant must self-regulate the intensity of exercise to the type of activity, and the exercise leader can assist in this regulation in this supervised setting; frequent checks of heart rate and rate of perceived exertion are helpful. More frequent checks are appropriate in beginning level sessions, decreasing the frequency as the participant gains an understanding of their responses to the exercise. This practice assists the participant in following a prudent, lifelong self-directed exercise program.

For group activities to be successful, a high degree of structure and autocratic leadership may be required. All participants need to understand exactly what is expected of them. Effective communication can only be achieved if everyone is able to hear and see the exercise leader. The physical formation in which the exercise leader places the participants is therefore critical. Formations of lines and complete circles make the leader less visible. Semi-circles are usually most effective. With careful planning, the usual gymnasium floor markings and apparatus can be used to advantage; semi-circles can be formed by using the free-throw circle, and lines can be formed by following the sidelines of the free-throw circle.

Of equal importance is the need for the leader to be able to monitor the participants throughout the exercise sessions. Monitoring of training heart rate can be achieved by temporarily interrupting the activity for heart rate checks by the participants. In the clinical setting, the exercise leader is responsible for observing any signs in the participants that indicate excessive intensity or effort. Thus, the organization of the activities must permit group leadership as well as individual monitoring when indicated.

The ratio of exercise leaders to participants is important. No set formula for determining this ratio exists; however, for those programs in which participants are at greater risk to exercise, as well as in a beginning program, a higher staffing ratio is indicated. This ratio helps the leaders to maximize contact with the participant and to facilitate education and monitoring. Gradual progression to less contact is appropriate as the participant gains knowledge of the exercise prescription and the motivation to continue on a more independent level increases.

Effective use of the exercise leaders within the exercise session also determines the success of the exercise program. In beginning classes, or those with participants at higher risk with exercise, a head leader responsible for the overall mechanics of the session should be assisted by other staff members, the number of which is determined by the size of the class and the health status of the participants. These assistant exercise leaders can circulate through the class to (1) enhance communication; (2) monitor exertion levels; (3) assure correct performance of activities; (4) educate individual participants; (5) individualize exercises; and (6) provide feedback to the head leader concerning the responses of the participants to the exercise session. In classes with participants of various fitness levels, several exercise leaders may be used to direct activities at the various intensity levels. Experienced exercise program participants can be used as assistant exercise leaders.

In a clinical exercise setting, a variety of individual patient needs are represented. Patients with chronic obstructive pulmonary disease, intermittent claudication, marked deconditioning, as well as elderly persons respond better to an interval approach to conditioning. This type of training allows the participant to exercise at variable work intervals of higher intensities (in the training heart rate/MET range) followed by an interval of rest or lower intensity activity. The varied tempo that is a basic part of the aforementioned group activities makes this approach well suited for these patient groups.

CIRCUIT TRAINING

To meet the overall program objectives of total body fitness, muscular strength and endurance exercises of both the upper and lower body should be incorporated into the exercise regimen. Circuit training is especially useful in accomplishing this goal. Circuit training involves the use of multiple exercise stations, which vary between activities that use upper and lower body exercise and between resistive and dynamic activities. The incorporation of resistance-type activity in the circuit training program prepares the patient for activities of daily living, such as shoveling snow or vocational tasks.

Cardiovascular disease patients traditionally have been advised to avoid isometric or static exercise because of well-documented pressor response that is characterized by an increase in mean arterial blood pressure resulting from an increase in systolic and diastolic pressure.[5] Thus, periodic evaluation of the patient's responses to resistive exercise is important. Isometric training is indicated for patients who demonstrate a stable hemodynamic response to isometric exercise with no indication of myocardial ischemia. Researchers report that when patients perform isometric exercise at a rate pressure product that induces angina or ischemic ECG changes during dynamic exercise, no ischemic ECG changes or angina results.[6-8] Reviews of the implications of isometric exercise for the cardiac patient are available elsewhere.[6-8]

The skills and organizational abilities of an exercise leader have a profound influence on motivation and compliance to clinical or adult exercise programs. The importance of the role of the exercise leader in improving participant motivation and adherence to exercise is well documented. Group activities and games can be used to improve compliance. Organization is of the utmost importance when considering games for conditioning programs. Simplicity — making sure rules are kept to a minimum — is important, and deviation from the expected skill level is accepted to accommodate participation of individuals with a variety of fitness levels. The successful exercise leader organizes the session so to project vocally and to be seen by all participants.

The exercise leader must consider the total learning situation, which includes the size of the group, the physical condition of each class member, the nature and extent of the facilities, the social maturity of group members, and the levels of skill present. Activities should be organized so that the chance of success and enjoyment is high, and the chance of failure is nonexistent. Activities that are enjoyed by all members of the group should be allowed to continue, without overusing favorites. A change in setting, such as moving out of doors, also offers variety.

Adherence to clinical and adult exercise programs is a significant problem. If we make the activity session intrinsically enjoyable for participants while assuring safety for the participants, we will improve adherence statistics. The exercise leader controls the exercise environment. An exercise session that is fun and well organized ensures that the adult participant will look forward to the next session and thus will adhere to the exercise program.

REFERENCES

1. Oldridge NB: Compliance and exercise in primary and secondary prevention of coronary heart disease: A review. *Prev Med*, 11:56, 1982.
2. Oldridge NB, Stoedefalke KG: Compliance and motivation in cardiac exercise programs. *Clin Sports Med*, 3:443, 1984.
3. MacAlpin RH, Kattus AA: Adaptation to exercise in angina pectoris. The electrocardiograms during treadmill walking and coronary angiographic findings. *Circulation*, 33:183, 1966.
4. Anderson R: *Stretching.* Fullerton, CA: Shelter Publications, 1980.
5. Bezucha GR, et al.: Comparison of hemodynamic responses to static and dynamic exercise. *J Appl Physiol*, 53:1589, 1982.
6. Painter P, Hanson P: Isometric exercise: Implications for the cardiac patient. *Cardiovasc Rev Rep*, 5:261, 1984.
7. DeBusk R, et al.: Comparison of cardiovascular responses to static-dynamic effort and dynamic effort alone in patients with ischemic heart disease. *Circulation*, 59:977, 1978.
8. Taylor JL, et al.: The effect of isometric exercise on the graded exercise test in patients with stable angina pectoris. *J Cardiac Rehab*, 1:450, 1981.

26

CASE STUDY EVALUATION FOR EXERCISE PRESCRIPTION

GLEN H. PORTER

Exercise training plays a significant role in developing and maintaining improved levels of physical fitness in most individuals, including persons who: (1) are apparently healthy, (2) are at increased risk of developing cardiac, pulmonary, or metabolic disease; and (3) already have documented disease states. Exercise training must be prescribed as carefully as any other form of preventive or therapeutic intervention. For one individual, exercise training may be strongly recommended, but for another person the initiation of an exercise program is contraindicated. In addition, optimal improvements in the health-related fitness components (cardiorespiratory endurance, body composition, flexibility, and muscular strength and endurance) are attained when an appropriate, individualized exercise prescription is developed on the basis of the individual's current medical condition, ability, and interest.

Thus, the development of an adequate and safe exercise prescription depends on the availability of the following information:

1. Sufficient medical information to assess the past and present health status of the individual, including patient demographics, a medical and surgical history, findings of physical examination, signs and symptoms, essential test results (blood chemistry, electrocardiography (ECG), echocardiography, and angi-

ography), and a risk factor assessment and profile.
2. Graded exercise test data (if advised, based on age and risk category; see *Guidelines for Exercise Testing and Prescription*) that quantify current physical work capacity. Documentation of current exercise habits should also be available.
3. The person's expression of interests, needs, and objectives for wanting to participate in an exercise training program.

Evaluation of this information may bring to light some important concerns, and this evaluation may establish the need for additional testing and assessment before an individual is given clearance for participation in your specific exercise program.

Having access to a participant's complete medical record is not always possible, and in most situations, extraction and abstraction of the essential information needed for exercise prescription, risk evaluation, and/or lifestyle intervention is preferable. Such a summary is called a *Case Study*.

THE CASE STUDY

The Case Study format is used extensively in the American College of Sports Medicine

(ACSM) certification process (see Appendix to this chapter). Candidates may be asked to submit a series of Case Studies based on individuals they have evaluated. These Case Studies are used to assess the candidate's experience with individuals at various risk levels, as well as the ability to extract and organize pertinent information. The candidate is also evaluated as to the ability to interpret and communicate effectively the essential patient or client information from Case Study reports as it pertains to exercise evaluation, exercise prescription, and/or risk stratification.

For purposes of the ACSM certification process, the case study information can be grouped into the following topic areas: (1) demographic data and characteristics, including any family history of coronary heart disease (CHD); (2) medical and surgical history, including past and present data and a description of medical problems of significance; (3) behavioral and risk factor assessment data; (4) findings of the most recent physical examination; (5) laboratory test results and procedures; and (6) results of any recent exercise evaluation and the interpreted findings.

DEMOGRAPHY

Important demographic information includes age, sex, race, ethnic group, occupation, marital status, height, weight, and any significant family history of disease. Each of these factors can be helpful in developing an overall risk factor profile and optimal activity prescription for the individual. Advanced age and the male gender place a person at a slightly higher risk of developing CHD. A particular race and/or ethnic group may be at increased risk for developing particular disease states, i.e., blacks have an increased prevalence of hypertension and postmenopausal women have an increased likelihood of developing osteoarthritis. Careful evaluation of the height and weight can provide a simple indication of the need for body weight/body fat reduction (although an actual determination of body composition is preferable). The family history is extremely important because several disease states, including CHD, have a strong familial component. Particularly important is the early development of CHD or other atherosclerotic disease in grandparents, parents, aunts, uncles, and siblings before 50 years of age. Thus, just on the basis of the demographic information discussed, we can already get a good feel for the risk factor status of the individual described.

MEDICAL AND SURGICAL HISTORY

The present medical history should include a brief, but informative, summary of the current health status of the individual. Does the person have complaints or symptoms of any kind? If so, what are these complaints? Does shortness of breath result with low-level exertion? Does the person complain of typical angina or chest discomfort with physical activity? Are leg cramps or claudication-type pains associated with walking or other physical activities? Evidence of shortness of breath, chest pains, and/or leg cramps is important singly and collectively, because they can be markers of significant atherosclerotic disease. In addition, a brief summary of the orthopedic evaluation should be included to identify any musculoskeletal problems or limitations. The present medical history should include a specific list of any and all medications currently used by the individual. The specific reason why each medication is used should also be noted. The drug information is of great importance because several agents can have a significant effect on exercise responses and interpretation, i.e., beta blockers, antianginal agents, or digitalis.

Often as important as the present medical history is a good summary of past medical problems. This review should include any diseases or injuries experienced by the participant. Individuals with current and/or past history of arthritis, chondromalacia, lower back discomfort, or any other general problems of the ankle, knee, hip, or shoulder necessitate consideration of each of these special problems when the components of the exercise prescription are developed. The well-planned exercise prescription must accomplish its training goals without leading to aggravation of the particular musculoskeletal problems. Another component of the past history should be the results of laboratory tests or procedures that may impact on the risk status or activity capacity of the individual. Elevated blood cholesterol levels, decreased pulmonary function, coronary angiographic findings, and previous exercise evaluation results contribute important information to the decision regarding testing or prescription protocols.

A surgical history should also include the type of and reason for any previous surgical procedures. This information may indicate the need for special testing or prescriptive considerations, i.e., spinal fusions or total hip replacements. The date of the operation should also be included in a Case Study. Recent interventions are more likely to impact the testing procedures or exercise prescription; a patient who only 2 weeks before has undergone coronary artery bypass surgery (CABG) is not ready for a vigorous, heavy resistance, upper extremity exercise program because of potential sternal instability. After 15 weeks, however, such a program may be extremely beneficial.

BEHAVIOR AND RISK FACTOR ASSESSMENT

Careful analysis and interpretation of the demographic and historical information have already allowed us to begin developing a good risk-factor profile. In addition, several individual behavior patterns can add important information to the overall risk-factor profile, including the following:

1. Smoking habit, if any, including the number of cigarettes or amount of tobacco smoked per day times the number of years (i.e., 1 pack/day × 10 years = 10 pack-year history).
2. Alcohol and caffeine intake per day or week.
3. Food intake and meal patterns, including the amount and analysis of the food groups and types.
4. Physical activity habits.
5. Sleep habits and patterns.
6. Occupation, including any excessive travel and significant job pressures or time-related urgencies that frequently occur.
7. Family lifestyle (i.e., single parent, happily married).

These factors can provide a good picture of the type of individual you are trying to motivate toward lifestyle modifications, including regular exercise training. The information not only helps to classify further risk-factor status but also provides input about the likelihood of the person being motivated to make a commitment and then comply with a lifestyle/behavior modification program. The busy executive who smokes too much, drinks and eats too much, has poor sleeping habits, and does not participate in physical activities, is the type of person who is most difficult to motivate. In this person's mind, the day is already overcrowded with important matters and little time or room is available for additional things like regular exercise training.

PHYSICAL EXAMINATION

At this point in the evaluation of the information provided or obtained for the development of a Case Study, you should know the potential exercise candidate quite well. The major (cigarette smoking, elevated blood cholesterol, history of hypertension, family history of CHD, abnormal ECG findings, and diabetes mellitus) and the secondary or predisposing (obesity, inactivity, and stress) risk factors should already be identified. The results of a recent physical examination should be included to exclude new changes in medical status and to ensure that no specific contraindications exist to beginning or continuing participation in an exercise program. Current blood pressure readings are significant as are any noted problems with heart or chest sounds. The recent onset of any orthopedic problems is also noteworthy. If the individual had a recent hospital stay for cardiac or pulmonary problems, this person is likely a candidate for a supervised and/or ECG-monitored rehabilitation program. The reader is referred to Chapter 4 of the *Guidelines for Exercise Testing and Prescription* for details concerning exercise training for this type of patient.

LABORATORY TESTS AND PROCEDURES

The results of previous laboratory tests or procedures should be documented in the medical and surgical history. Current tests or procedures, however, may be ordered as a result of the physical examination findings, medical or surgical history, or risk factor assessment. The results of these studies and how they impact the participant's risk profile or indications for exercise should be included in a developed Case Study.

The laboratory test values for triglycerides, total serum cholesterol, high-density lipoprotein (HDL) cholesterol, and blood glucose are of particular significance. The low-density lipoprotein (LDL) cholesterol can be calculated from the formula:

LDL cholesterol = Total serum cholesterol
    − HDL cholesterol − ⅕ triglycerides.

These determinations are helpful when developing a good lipid profile for the individual and also when assessing if any tendency exists toward diabetes mellitus in the individual. Significant findings that indicate a marked increase in the risk of developing CHD are a total serum cholesterol value greater than 240 mg/dl, a serum triglyceride value greater than 150 mg/dl, an HDL cholesterol value below 35 mg/dl, and/or a total serum cholesterol to HDL cholesterol ratio of greater than 5.0. A fasting blood glucose value above 115 mg/dl would be suggestive of blood sugar control problems. Ideal determinations would be a total serum cholesterol level below 200 mg/dl, a total serum cholesterol to HDL cholesterol ratio of less than 3.5, and a serum triglyceride value below 100 mg/dl. The fasting blood glucose value should be between 65 and 110 mg/dl.

Other common test values of importance, especially with respect to the exercise evaluation, include hemoglobin (13.5 to 17.5 g/dl), hematocrit (40 to 52%), potassium (3.5 to 5.0 mEq/dl), blood urea nitrogen (BUN) (10 to 21 mg/dl), and creatinine (0.7 to 1.4 mg/dl).

If a body composition analysis has been completed, the calculated percent body fat value is helpful in the evaluation of the current proportion of bone, muscle, and fat tissue. Male subjects in excess of 20% body fat and female subjects in excess of 27% body fat may need body fat reduction to decrease their risk status. Desired percent body fat values are 16 to 20% and 23 to 27% for men and women, respectively. On the basis of the current percent body fat and percent lean body weight, the ideal or desired body weight value is calculated according to the formula:

Ideal body weight = Lean body mass/% lean body weight desired/100

Any person with increased body weight and percentage of body fat may be at an increased risk for developing additional problems with the exercise prescription and exercise programming efforts. Modifications in the type, intensity, frequency, and duration of exercise may be necessary for the overweight or obese participant to maximize caloric expenditure while minimizing orthopedic trauma (see *Guidelines*).

The interpretation of any recent ECGs should be included in the Case Study. Again, this information is helpful in trying to classify the risk status of the individual. Recent, significant ECG abnormalities could be important in making a decision about the level of monitoring and/or level of supervision that may be prudent for the person during the initial phase of exercise programming. In addition, you may determine, on the basis of this interpretation, that further tests or studies are needed before the individual is a legitimate candidate for your particular exercise program. This decision depends in large part on the kind of program conducted in your facility, for example, fitness or cardiopulmonary rehabilitation.

Other procedures may also have been performed for the patient or client, and these results should be reported when they affect the exercise evaluation or prescription. These procedures include pulmonary function tests, echocardiograms, ambulatory (Holter) monitoring of ECG leads, and coronary angiograms.

GRADED EXERCISE EVALUATION

The graded exercise evaluation provides direct information about the functional capacity and current fitness level of the individual. On the basis of hemodynamic, ECG, and symptomatic responses to the increasing exercise intensities, inferences can be made with respect to the likelihood of significant underlying CHD problems. Of particular interest are the heart rate responses, systolic blood pressure changes, ratings of perceived exertion, MET levels attained, ECG ST-segment changes, arrhythmia provocation, and any anginal symptoms reported by the individual during the exercise test. Standard exercise ECG results can be augmented by the injection of thallium or other radionuclides to evaluate myocardial perfusion or cardiac function, respectively. The ACSM certification candidate should include these results in the Case Study and be prepared to evaluate their impact on exercise prescription. The assessment of gas exchange parameters during an exercise evaluation may also be beneficial in differentiating between cardiac, pulmonary, or deconditioning limitations to functional capacity. Candidates should also be prepared to evaluate and discuss oxygen uptake, respiratory exchange ratios, ventilatory (anaerobic) threshold, cardiac output, and other related gas exchange parameters as they relate to the interpretation of the exercise evaluation, activity prescription, and risk stratification.

Several parameters clearly can be evaluated

during an exercise evaluation. Each measurement should be interpreted individually and the meaning of each abnormality should be clearly identified. The overall impression of the graded exercise evaluation (normal or abnormal study) incorporates all of these individual findings.

An important fact to remember is that an exercise evaluation does not diagnose disease states, but rather adds to or subtracts from the overall likelihood of disease for each patient/client. Candidates should have a basic knowledge of Bayesian theory and the interactive role of disease prevalence in a given population as it relates to the sensitivity and specificity of the test. The significance of false-positive and false-negative test findings should be familiar to the candidate as well as the possible reasons for these findings (i.e., medications, baseline ECG abnormalities, conduction abnormalities, or mitral valve prolapse).

THE EXERCISE PRESCRIPTION

The exercise evaluation results, along with the other, aforementioned information help classify the patient or client into one of the following risk categories:

1. An apparently healthy, normal adult.
2. An individual at higher risk on the basis of having at least one of the six major risk factors (see *Guidelines*).
3. An individual with documented CHD, pulmonary disease, or other metabolic diseases based upon prior assessments and evaluations.

The individual should then be placed in either a low, moderate, or high-risk group for the purposes of exercise programming. This placement may then lead to the decision that further testing and evaluation is necessary before entrance into your particular exercise training program. Of particular importance is the need to make an appropriate selection of the level of supervision and monitoring needed for the person to participate safely in progressive exercise training. The goal is to provide safe and effective exercise programming for the individual while not making it overly difficult to enter the program that is most feasible in terms of work schedules and economic situation.

From an exercise prescription standpoint, a person should be considered at higher risk if they have at least one of the major risk factors for CHD and/or have symptoms of CHD, pulmonary disease, or other metabolic diseases. Important in this regard are the cigarette smokers, persons with a history of blood pressure readings greater than 145 mm Hg systolic and/or 95 mm Hg diastolic, and persons with a total serum cholesterol to HDL cholesterol ratio of greater than 5.0. In addition, a person with family members who developed CHD or other atherosclerotic disease before the age of 50 years are at increased risk. Resting ECG abnormalities and diabetes mellitus place a person at increased risk of developing or having significant underlying CHD.

The data obtained from the exercise evaluation become essential for the development of the individualized intensity component of the exercise prescription. The exercise intensity portion of the prescription is calculated and the target range is set on the basis of the peak heart rate attained, perceived exertion ratings, and/or the MET level attained during the exercise evaluation. Modifications to these calculations may be required, however, as a result of ECG abnormalities, inappropriate blood pressure responses, or symptoms uncovered during the exercise evaluation. Chapter 3 of the *Guidelines for Exercise Testing and Prescription,* as well as several references listed at the end of this chapter, detail the standard methods used to develop the individualized exercise prescription, which includes the type of exercise to be used for training, the frequency of training, the duration for an exercise session, and the appropriate exercise intensity for a given participant.

A reasonable rate of exercise progression based on individual ability, needs, and goals should be developed and discussed with the participant. Each participant should also be carefully instructed about signs or symptoms that would contraindicate continuation of the exercise training until these developing signs and/or symptoms are fully investigated. They should be aware of the common side effects that occur as a result of beginning and continuing a regular exercise training program so that each individual can learn to "listen" to their bodies and make adjustments in exercise sessions as the situation dictates. The most important point, however, is that each person should be able to separate carefully any significant warning signs and symptoms from the more common and normal feelings associated with participation in regular exercise training.

APPROPRIATE MODIFICATIONS OF THE EXERCISE PRESCRIPTION FOR PARTICULAR TYPES OF PARTICIPANTS

The exercise prescription process and its component parts are quite similar when considering any one of several types of participants. The major difference is that one or more of the component parts (type, frequency, duration, intensity, and rate of progression) may require specific modification or adjustment to meet the particular characteristics of a given participant. The largest group of participants that fall into this category are cardiac patients. Exercise prescription for these individuals is discussed in detail in Chapter 4 of the *Guidelines for Exercise Testing and Prescription.*

Other special populations that are of interest include those persons with: (1) pulmonary disease, (2) diabetes mellitus, (3) obesity, (4) hypertension, (5) peripheral vascular disease, (6) arthritis, (7) mental disease, (8) pregnancy, and (9) renal disease. A discussion of each of these special groups is included in Chapter 5 of the *Guidelines for Exercise Testing and Prescription.* (Some additional references are included at the end of this chapter.) A most important point is that these special types of participants and their specific problems are recognized through careful analysis and interpretation of the Case Study information, because the best possible individualized exercise prescription can then be developed to meet the needs and goals of each exercise participant.

In summary, the developed Case Study is a brief, concise report of the essential information pertaining to the risk status, exercise evaluation, and/or activity prescription of a given individual. The Case Study should assist the reader in knowing the individual for whom the exercise prescription is developed. This written information enables the reader to classify the individual into the appropriate risk category (i.e., healthy, at higher risk, or with documented disease). The risk categorization then leads to the placement of the individual into an exercise setting that meets their unique requirements in terms of a recommended level of supervision and monitoring. Most importantly

the Case Study information helps the reader make reasonable, common sense judgments about the development of a safe and effective exercise training program.

REFERENCES

1. American College of Sports Medicine: *Guidelines for Exercise Testing and Prescription.* 3rd. Ed. Philadelphia: Lea & Febiger, 1986.
2. American College of Sports Medicine: Position statement on the recommended quantity and quality of exercise for developing and maintaining fitness in healthy adults. *Med Sci Sports,* 10:vii–x, 1978.
3. Berman LB, Sutton JR: Exercise for the pulmonary patient. *J Cardiopul Rehab,* 6:52–61, 1986.
4. Foster C, Jacobson MM, Pollock ML: Exercise for the diabetic patient. In *Heart Disease and Rehabilitation.* 2nd Ed. Edited by ML Pollock and DH Schmidt. New York: John Wiley & Sons, 1986.
5. Franklin BA: Exercise testing, training and arm ergometry. *Sports Med,* 2:100–119, 1985.
6. Franklin BA, Hellerstein HK, Gordon S, Timmis GC: Exercise prescription for the myocardial infarction patient. *J Cardiopul Rehab,* 6:62–79, 1986.
7. Froelicher VF: *Exercise Testing & Training.* New York: Le Jacq Publishing, 1983.
8. Getchell LH: Exercise prescription for the healthy adult. *J Cardiopul Rehab,* 6:46–51, 1986.
9. Hanson P, Ward A, Painter P: Exercise training for special patient populations. *J Cardiopul Rehab,* 6:104–112, 1986.
10. Metier CP, Pollock ML, Graves JE: Exercise prescription for the coronary artery bypass graft surgery patient. *J Cardiopul Rehab,* 6:85–103, 1986.
11. Pollock ML, Wilmore JH, Fox SM: *Exercise in Health and Disease.* Philadelphia: W.B. Saunders, 1984.
12. Porter GH: General concepts and a specific approach to phase II exercise programming. In *Cardiac Rehabilitation: Exercise Testing and Prescription.* Edited by LK Hall, GC Meyer, and HK Hellerstein. New York: SP Medical & Scientific Books, 1984.

APPENDIX

Two case studies are presented that are examples of those used by ACSM for certification.

CASE STUDY A

A 39-year-old married woman with two teenage children came to our clinic 1 year ago because of fatigue, dyspnea on exertion, and palpitations. Her history reveals a 40-pack-year smoking habit, with a current consumption of 2 packs per day. Although she had scarlet fever as a child, the only remarkable finding on her physical examinations is a mid-systolic click. She has had no previous operations. She does experience some moderate low back pain from time to time, usually after lifting boxes at the jewelry shop that she owns. She reports no significant job-related or family stress. She drinks in moderation (a glass or two of wine with dinner in the evening). She reports that her father died of myocardial infarction at the age of 58 years.

Analysis of blood chemistry 1 year ago revealed a serum cholesterol value of 330 mg/dl, HDL of 65 mg/dl, and a triglyceride level of 110 mg/dl. The fasting blood glucose determination was 98 mg/dl. She has been physically inactive for the past 20 years. The results of her treadmill exercise evaluation 1 year ago are summarized as follows:

Protocol: Balke
Resting: HR = 100 beats/min;
            Bp = 160/100 mm Hg
End point: Stage 4 (3 mph, 10%) for 2 min
            HR = 180 beats/min;
            BP = 236/110 mm Hg
            Terminated because of fatigue
            No significant ST-segment
            changes
            No reported symptoms
            Short episode of paroxysmal
            atrial fibrillation

About 6 months ago, digitalis therapy was initiated after multiple episodes of atrial fibrillation and chlorthalidone (Hygroton) was prescribed for blood pressure control. She was instructed to get daily exercise, lose 20 lb, quit smoking, and reduce salt consumption.

At the most recent visit, she reveals that she has joined a health spa and enjoys using the vibrator belt and riding the stationary bike with no tension for 20 min. She purchased a rubber sweat suit for exercise "to help weight loss." She would like to begin a swimming program, which she can complete in her pool this summer as well as at the spa. Her weight remains unchanged from 6 months ago (152 lb; body fat of 30% from skinfold calipers). She continues to smoke although she says that she quit 3 times for 1 week during the past several months. Current blood chemistry analysis reveals values for potassium of 3.1 mEq/L, cholesterol of 318 mg/dl, HDL of 58 mg/dl, and a triglyceride of 122 mg/dl. The fasting blood glucose level was 102 mg/dl.

An exercise evaluation was performed with the following results:

Protocol: Bicycle
Resting: HR = 88 beats/min; BP = 130/
            90 mm Hg
End point: Stage 4 (600 kpm/min) for 3 min
            HR = 176 beats/min;
            BP = 186/96 mm Hg; RPE = 18
            Terminated because of fatigue
            with vague chest pain
            2 mm of horizontal ST-segment
            depression at peak load
            Occasional single PVCs, with
            one couplet in recovery
            ST segments returned to
            baseline by 3 min recovery

Because of the findings of this recent exercise evaluation, a thallium exercise study was completed the same week. No perfusion defects were observed at a similar heart rate and workload. We are referring this patient to the cardiac rehabilitation center for supervised exercise and risk-factor modification strategies.

CASE STUDY B

A 60-year-old corporate executive was first evaluated by members of our hospital-based cardiology group at the time of his acute myocardial infarction. Only 6 weeks earlier, he had stopped his two-pack-a-day cigarette habit through a smoking cessation program. Cardiac catheterization performed before his discharge from the hospital revealed complete occlusion of the right coronary artery and an 80% occlusive lesion of the left anterior descending (LAD) artery at the first septal branch. The left ventricular ejection fraction was 48%. He was discharged from the hospital on a regimen of nifedipine (Procardia) 10 mg TID, baby aspirin QD, and dipyridamole (Persantine) 50 mg TID. Six weeks later, the patient developed sharp chest pain, a pericardial friction rub, and diffuse ST-segment elevation (Dressler's syndrome) at which time indomethacin (Indocin) was prescribed. The performance of percutaneous transluminal coronary angioplasty (PTCA) on the LAD lesion was recommended.

Two weeks after PTCA, this patient underwent a treadmill evaluation. The results of this exercise study follow:

Protocol: Balke
Resting: HR = 72 beats/min; BP = 110/
            70 mm Hg

End point: Stage 6 (3 mph, 12 1/2%) for
3 min
HR = 135 beats/min;
BP = 180/90 mm Hg
Terminated because of fatigue
only
No significant ST-segment
depression or arrhythmias

Additional information obtained at the time of this test revealed that he was walking 2 miles in 40 min, 4 times a week. Body composition studies indicated a body weight of 179 lb with 26% body fat as determined by skinfold calipers. Analysis of blood chemistry indicated a total serum cholesterol level of 260 mg/dl, an HDL value of 22 mg/dl, and a triglyceride value of 200 mg/dl. The fasting blood glucose was 118 mg/dl. Psychologic testing indicated a "type A" personality with elevated clinical scores for depression, hysteria, and hypochondriasis. He does not drink alcohol, and he is making a good effort to adhere to a cardiovascularly prudent diet. Dietary restriction is hard for him because he lives alone and frequently eats out.

The patient returned 4 months later for re-evaluation. Follow-up studies revealed the following blood chemistry profile: total serum cholesterol value of 199 mg/dl, HDL level of 33 mg/dl, and a triglyceride value of 190 mg/dl. The fasting blood glucose was 96 mg/dl. Body fatness was 22% and the body weight was 169 lb. The patient had been exercising for 20 min, 3 times a week on the Nordic cross-country ski machine and 20 min on his Schwinn air-dyne ergometer at a setting of 2 (600 kpm/min). Because of a knee injury and subsequent orthopedic surgery 5 years ago, he finds these forms of exercise the most appropriate and comfortable.

Although he is now interested in cross-country skiing in Colorado this winter, he expresses some concern about the recent onset of mild chest discomfort during his exercise training program. The patient also questioned the staff about the merits of chelation therapy as a follow-up to the previous PTCA procedure performed on his LAD lesion. Finally, he inquired about the safety and effectiveness of a sauna and hot tub.

The results of the 4-month exercise re-evaluation follow:

Protocol: Bruce treadmill
Resting: HR = 56 beats/min; BP = 100/
60 mm Hg; RPE = 17
End point: Terminated because of chest
pain and 3-mm ST depression
2 mm of ST depression were
seen at stage 3, HR = 130
ST segments returned to
baseline by 4-min recovery
No arrhythmias

We anticipate that repeat PTCA will be attempted and the patient will then be referred to an outpatient cardiac rehabilitation program for supervised, monitored exercise.

The repeat PTCA was successful and the patient has been out of the hospital for 2 weeks. We now refer him to your program.

CHAPTER 27

DECISION MAKING IN PROGRAMMING EXERCISE

PATRICIA PAINTER AND
WILLIAM L. HASKELL

The accumulation of information, experience, and knowledge in the science of exercise physiology has resulted in the widespread incorporation of exercise training as adjunctive therapy for individuals with documented heart disease, those at high risk for its development, and those interested in prevention of disease. The rapid growth of preventive and rehabilitative programs may result in a haphazard or "cookbook" approach to exercise prescription in which exercise staff members use only minimal information when developing an exercise prescription according to a set of guidelines that may not, in all cases, be appropriate. Decision making in preventive and rehabilitative exercise programming should be a logically consistent and comprehensive approach to developing and implementing exercise programs and lifestyle modifications. Such an approach increases the chances of achieving the goals of (1) individualized exercise prescription, (2) assuring safety for participants, and (3) facilitating regular participation in lifelong activity.

We present a model for decision making in preventive and rehabilitative exercise programs. This model is developed from extensive clinical experience in cardiac rehabilitation, although it is applicable when developing and implementing exercise for any population. When using this model, we emphasize the use of the *Guidelines for Exercise Testing and Prescription* as a starting point, making modifications for individuals according to sound clinical judgment and common sense. The *Guidelines* are not intended to provide final answers for all situations encountered in exercise prescription or programming, because a vast amount of information on the optimal relationships between frequency, intensity, and duration for developing cardiovascular fitness, modifying risk factors, assisting in weight control, or affecting psychologic status remain unknown and are subject to further study.

DEVELOPING POLICY AND MAKING DECISIONS

To assure the safety of all who participate in exercise (participant, staff, and facility), program policy must be firmly established and followed. This policy must address all phases of the participant/program interactions shown in Table 27–1: (1) screening for exercise; (2) developing the exercise prescription; (3) implementing the exercise prescription; and (4) maintenance of appropriate exercise. Good policy development should be based on available sci-

Table 27–1. Phases of Program/Participant Interactions

Screening
    Exercise
    No exercise
    Further evaluation → no exercise
    Further evaluation → exercise

Exercise prescription development
    Type of activity
    Frequency
    Duration
    Intensity
    Progression

Implementation of the exercise prescription
    Exercise setting
    Time of exercise
    Level of monitoring
    Level of supervision
    Group or individual exercise
    Emergency plans

Maintenance
    Progression
    Periodic evaluation
    Supervision levels
    Motivational techniques

Each of these factors for consideration is actually a continuum of possibilities (Table 27–2); for example, the health status of individuals interested in exercise training will span from normal, healthy individuals with no risk factors for disease to persons with multisystem disease processes. Similarly, program settings can span from the community health club or recreation department to the medical center research exercise laboratory.

The focus of this discussion is the importance of each of these considerations in developing policy and making decisions concerning exercise programming. Whatever policy is developed for an exercise program, the program personnel must understand the reasons behind the policies and be comfortable with their implementation. Exceptions to any policy should be kept to a minimum and then only with documented rationale.

entific and clinical principles of exercise testing, prescription, and training; facilitate flexibility and guidance in decision making by exercise program staff members and participants; protect and provide for the safety of the participant; and protect the program and exercise personnel.

The development of program policy and the decision making on the part of the exercise staff require consideration of several factors at all levels of the participant/program interaction.

PHASES OF PROGRAM/PARTICIPANT INTERACTIONS (Table 27–1)

Screening is the process by which the determination is made whether a participant will exercise in a given exercise program. Screening results in a decision to (1) reject an individual for exercise; (2) refer the individual for further medical evaluation and/or treatment before acceptance for exercise; (3) refer the individual to a program with more appropriate levels of su-

Table 27–2. Factors to Consider at Every Level of Program/Participant Interaction

Health status				
Clinically healthy	High risk for CAD	Stable documented disease	Unstable documented disease	Exercise contraindicated
Exercise setting				
Community health club	Community-based clinical program	Hospital-based program		Medical center research-oriented program
Exercise program goals				
High-intensity training	Maintain stable patients/modify risks	Condition-post convalescence	Maintain functional status during recovery	Monitor for study/ therapy
Participant goals				
Competition	Increase functional capacity	Modify risk of CAD	Prevent disease progression	Rehabilitate from disease	Prevent deterioration of condition
Community standards				
Home exercise	Community-based non-medically supervised	Hospital-based medically supervised	Hospital-based program	Exercise not recommended

pervision; or (4) accept the individual for exercise. The *Development of an Exercise Prescription* is the process of integrating information obtained from the medical and/or health history and exercise assessment into an individualized exercise program, with specific prescription of the appropriate type, frequency, duration, and intensity of activity. The *Implementation of the Exercise Prescription* phase is the manner in which the participants follow their unique exercise prescription. The variable factors in successful implementation of exercise include the time of exercise, the physical setting, level of monitoring, levels of staff supervision and qualifications of staff, group or individual exercise, the use of resistance and upper body exercise, and emergency plans to assure safety for the participant and the program. Successful implementation of exercise facilitates regular participation, enjoyment, and safety for all participants. The *Maintenance or Continuation of the Exercise Program* phase is the process of keeping a participant involved in appropriate levels of physical activity for a lifetime. This process involves periodic evaluation of a participant's responses to exercise, modification of the exercise (increasing or decreasing duration or intensity), re-evaluation of the levels of supervision and/ or monitoring, and developing motivational techniques to increase adherence and enjoyability.

SCREENING

The *health status* of the individual participant is of major importance in all levels of exercise programming. An individual may become involved in an exercise program at any point on a continuum (see Table 27–2). Therefore, to know that for certain medical conditions there are definite contraindications to exercise is essential. For these patients, any benefits that may be derived from exercise training are outweighed by the potential risk of medical complications and possible death when exercise is applied (see page 13 in *Guidelines for Exercise Testing and Prescription.* 3rd Ed.). In addition, certain conditions exist in which the individual is at risk of medical complications and/or death with exercise, but in whom the benefits of exercise training (either physiologic or possibly psychologic) may outweigh the risks. Careful screening and subsequent placement into appropriate programs can reduce the risks to acceptable levels.

The *exercise setting* also determines whether an individual's participation in a given exercise program is appropriate. A hospital-based exercise program that is medically supervised with ECG monitoring capabilities and has rapid in-house emergency response time is most appropriate for individuals at high risk of medical complications with exercise (i.e., low ejection fraction, poorly controlled dysrythmias, and angina). For participants with documented disease who demonstrate stable responses to exercise, a program with less supervision and less of a "medical" environment may be most appropriate to decrease dependency on the clinical team, decrease costs, and encourage individual responsibility in the rehabilitation process. Interaction with normal, healthy individuals in a well-controlled environment may be beneficial for many of these patients.

Program goals and *participant goals* for exercise must also be considered in the screening process. If the goals of the program and the participant are compatible, then acceptance into the program is appropriate. For example, if a program is designed solely for maintaining cardiovascular fitness, and an individual's goal is to train for competition, a more appropriate gesture is to refer the individual to a program that can assist in meeting that goal (if that goal is appropriate considering their health status).

Community standards may also be considered in the screening process, although this factor should not dictate the criteria for entry into the program. Respecting community attitudes, even if somewhat conservative, is important, especially when starting a program. Experience and careful implementation and documentation assists in molding community standards as long as there is well-documented clinical data to support a more progressive approach to screening for exercise.

The screening process must assess the risk-benefit ratio of exercise not only for the individual participant, but also for the exercise program. Appropriate screening of individuals for entrance into a program is a major step in avoiding potential legal problems with the exercise, which can have serious financial and public relations consequences. Program staff-members should never hesitate to request further evaluation and/or treatment from the referring physician before accepting a participant into the exercise program. They also should not hesitate to refer individuals to another program if they believe the individual requires a higher level of medical monitoring and supervision than they are able to provide. Program personnel should also be willing to refer an individual to a program with lower levels of supervision in an attempt to decrease dependence on the clinical staff.

DEVELOPMENT OF THE EXERCISE PRESCRIPTION

The *health status* of the individual is a major consideration when developing an exercise prescription. Examples include special concern for the type of activity when a subject has orthopedic limitations and exclusion of patients with poor left ventricular function in strength training activities. As indicated in the *Guidelines*, the health status of the individual also determines the intensity and duration of exercise. The rate of progression of exercise is also affected by health status. For example, individuals at a higher risk stratification level are expected to progress more slowly because of a more conservative exercise prescription (i.e., lower intensity) and often as a result of the physiologic limitations imposed by the disease. Likewise, individuals who have been somewhat active should progress faster in their exercise program than sedentary individuals whose slower progression is primarily to avoid injuries and to assure appropriate adaptation in previously unused muscles.

The *exercise setting* clearly impacts the exercise prescription—activities depending on facilities, equipment, and emergency responses available. *Program goals* and *participant goals* must be assessed carefully when developing the exercise prescription. Ideally, an exercise program is established with the goals of improving health status, including exercise tolerance and reducing risk factors for heart disease. A program designed to develop strength with minimal cardiovascular training (i.e., high-intensity, short-duration cardiovascular training) is inappropriate for a participant who has a primary goal of losing weight. That participant should be referred to a program that offers aerobic exercise at lower intensity and longer duration as well as dietary counseling.

The *goals of the participant* are of paramount importance when developing an exercise prescription. Little is gained to develop an exercise prescription of aerobic exercise 3 times/week for 30 min at an intensity of 60 to 70% of maximal capacity if the individual's goal is to change

from a totally sedentary lifestyle and maybe get some social interaction as well. The closer the prescribed exercise is to meeting the goals of the individual, the more likely the individual is to adhere to the exercise and possibly become interested in more structured exercise at the frequency, intensity, and duration that result in positive health benefits in the future.

Epidemiologic evidence exists that only 15 to 20% of the general population exercises regularly, according to the recommended "ideal" exercise prescription. In most cases, getting the individual to initiate some form of acceptable activity is of benefit, as is spending time identifying barriers that may exist to incorporating regular activity into their lifestyle. Such barriers may include previous experiences with exercise that either were not enjoyable or were unsuccessful; time demands placed on the individual by job, family commitments, and the like; and cultural background and socioeconomic status, which dictate acceptable and feasible activity patterns. Identification of such "barriers" should assist program staff members and the participant to be creative in developing plans to overcome the barriers and to optimize the potential for success with the exercise program.

Community standards for exercise prescription may vary widely; often, any deviation from the typical 3 days per week for 30 min at 60 to 70% of maximal capacity may be questioned. It is well worth the efforts of the program staff to document compliance to exercise and physiologic responses to the exercise prescriptions to demonstrate safety and efficacy of variations in the typical exercise prescription.

IMPLEMENTATION OF THE EXERCISE PRESCRIPTION

The *health status* of the participants has significant bearing on how exercise is implemented; it determines the levels of monitoring, supervision (numbers of staff and qualifications necessary), as well as necessary emergency procedures. The organization of the actual exercise session also is affected by the health status of participants; for example, those persons requiring careful monitoring would not be involved in group activities.

Assessment of participants before the exercise session varies according to health status. At certain times, an individual should not exercise, and reasons for temporarily deferring physical activity on a given day are listed in Table 27-3.

Table 27–3. Reasons to Temporarily Defer Physical Activity*

Recurrent illness
Progression of cardiac disease
Abnormally elevated blood pressure
Recent changes in symptoms (see Table 27–4)
Orthopedic problem
Emotional turmoil
Severe sunburn
Alcoholic hangover
Cerebral dysfunction—dizziness or vertigo
Sodium retention—edema or weight gain
Dehydration
Environmental factors
Weather (excessive heat or humidity)
Air pollution (smog or carbon monoxide)
Overindulgence
Heavy, large meal within 2 hours
Coffee, tea, Coke (xanthines and other stimulating beverages)
Drugs
Decongestants
Bronchodilators
Atropine
Weight reduction agents

*Modified from the American Heart Association.

In some instances, the exercise staff may allow a participant to exercise—with a modified prescription (i.e., decreased intensity) and/or with increased levels of supervision or monitoring—depending on established policy as well as the personnel and resources available for the exercise session.

The regular assessment of the participant's response to exercise is an essential part of implementing the exercise prescription. Such an assessment may: (1) indicate the need to modify the exercise prescription (i.e., increase duration and/or intensity in an individual who may not be achieving an appropriate training stimulus);

Table 27–4. Signs and Symptoms of Excessive Effort

During and/or immediately after exercise:
Anginal discomfort
Ataxia, lightheadedness, or confusion
Nausea or vomiting
Leg claudication
Pallor or cyanosis
Dyspnea persisting for more than 10 min
Dysrhythmia
Inappropriate brachycardia
Decrease in systolic blood pressure
Delayed:
Prolonged fatigue (24 hr or more)
Insomnia
Weight gain due to fluid retention—salt and water overload; heart failure
Persistent tachycardia

Table 27–5. Indications to Discontinue Exercise Program

Orthopedic problems aggravated by activity
Progression of cardiac illness unresponsive to medical therapy
Development of new systemic disease aggravated by exercise
Major surgery
Psychiatric decompensation
Acute alcoholism

(2) reveal symptoms or signs of excessive effort (Table 27–4); and (3) reveal inappropriate responses to exercise, which may be indicative of a progression of disease and/or the appearance of symptoms that may in turn indicate the development of new medical problems. Levels of concern about such signs depends on the health status of the participant involved. Often a decrease in the intensity of exercise may alleviate the symptoms; however, persistence of such signs and/or symptoms should prompt discontinuation of exercise and referral to the physician for further evaluation (Table 27–5).

Remember that healthy individuals participating in an exercise program may also experience changes in their physiologic status with exercise and/or over time, which may be indicative of early signs and/or progression of subclinical disease. Examples of such signs and symptoms are listed in Table 27–6. All exercise staff members should be aware of these symptoms and should be prepared to refer the individual to a physician should they appear.

The *program goals* determine not only the equipment and staffing requirements, but also the actual structure of the exercise sessions. The implementation of the exercise prescription in programs designed to monitor medically high-risk individuals differs from implementation in those programs that provide a supervised setting for stable patients with documented disease. The level of responsibility placed on the

Table 27–6. Indications of a Change in Physiologic Status or Progression of Disease

Excessive fatigue
Shortness of breath
Angina (or change in typical angina patterns)
Change in cardiac rhythm
Dramatic increase in weight
Swelling of extremities
Unexplained restlessness or fatigue
Unexplained change in blood pressure at rest or during exercise
Reduction in physical working capacity

individual in an exercise program should be determined by the program goals. For example, a program designed to return the participant to an active job places emphasis on individual responsibility (with staff support and encouragement) to help promote a sense of independence and a healthy lifestyle, which includes a program of lifelong exercise. In contrast, the staff of a program designed to monitor high-risk patients need to observe ECG and blood pressure responses to exercise carefully and to document any signs or symptoms of "maladaptation" in the physiologic responses for further evaluation and treatment by the physician. This setting requires higher staffing ratios, and the participant's involvement in implementing the exercise prescription may be minimal.

Successful implementation of the exercise prescription also necessitates evaluation of the participant goals and needs. For most participants, convenient access to the exercise setting is important. Timing of the exercise sessions should meet the needs of the participants involved and not only those of the staff or facility. Participants who work full-time and/or odd shifts may be excluded from programs that are unable to offer flexible hours. To have participants feel rushed or stressed getting to the exercise session is undersirable especially for individuals who use the exercise as a part of a stress management program.

Patient expectations should also be considered when organizing exercise classes. For example, participants who are interested in efficient use of time may want to complete the exercise sessions with little social interaction; individual exercise on a treadmill or other exercise equipment may be appropriate for these individuals. People who are interested in a variety of activities and peer interaction may be most compliant to a program that provides group or game activities. Patients for whom the primary goal is to return to work and/or leisure time activities, such as gardening, hunting, and the like that require significant use of the upper body, benefit from the incorporation of resistance training and upper body activities as a part of their program. Circuit training involving the use of a variety of types of apparatus may be well suited for these individuals (Chapter 25).

Community standards may dictate some aspects of exercise implementation. Communities with a limited number of programs available have to accommodate a wide variety of participants (and therefore medical conditions) in the same setting. This spectrum complicates the organization of the sessions, staffing requirements, and possibly the monitoring procedures. Other factors affected by community standards include: (1) levels of monitoring required for various patient groups; (2) use of resistance exercise in clinical populations; (3) qualifications of the staff for various patient populations; (4) levels of physician involvement in the exercise program; and (5) emergency procedures. The variable expectations and attitudes of referring physicians in the community must be addressed when developing and implementing the exercise prescription.

MAINTENANCE

Once the exercise program is initiated, the challenge to the exercise staff is to motivate the participants to continue to try to keep physical activity as an integral part of the lifestyle. The health status of an individual may determine how this task is accomplished. We recommend some form of periodic evaluation of exercise responses in all participants. Participants at high risk for developing heart disease and those with documented disease should be evaluated for ECG and blood pressure responses, either during an exercise stress test or at their prescribed exercise intensity. As described in the previous section, such periodic evaluations may result in modification of the exercise prescription, decreased or increased levels of supervision, referral to the personal physician for further evaluation and/or treatment, discontinuation of the exercise program, or referral to a more appropriate exercise setting. In community-based adult fitness programs, field testing or submaximal exercise testing can be used to demonstrate progress. Periodic evaluations track progress with the exercise and may be used for motivational purposes.

Motivational techniques, such as distance records, noncompetitive games, low-level competitions, and predicted time runs, challenge the staff to be creative and keep participants involved and satisfied with their program.

The *exercise setting* often determines the long-term outcome of an exercise program. For example, a hospital-based, monitored exercise program often is not able to accommodate those individuals who "graduate" to nonmonitored exercise; these participants should be referred to a less-supervised exercise program. Another example is the participant in a jogging program who is injured and thus requires the use of facilities to perform other activities.

Similarly, the *exercise program goals* determine which participants continue to exercise in their program. As long as the exercise program goals and the *participant goals* are in accord and the health status does not change, the participant can continue to exercise. These goals must also be reassessed periodically to assure all parties involved remain satisfied with the current program.

The consideration of *community standards* in maintenance of the exercise program is similar to that discussed in *Implementation of the Exercise Prescription.* Because of the lack of third-party payments for some exercise programs, many physicians refer their patients to community-based programs, or advise home exercise. This practice is reasonable for normal healthy individuals or for persons with risk factors for development of coronary artery disease. Low-risk patients with stable exercise responses can maintain their exercise programs at home or in unmonitored and minimally supervised programs. The key factor in this approach is identification of patients who are at high risk for complications during exercise before advising continuation of exercise outside the monitored setting.

Exercise training is a valuable tool in the management of patients, as well as in improving the health and functional status of the healthy population. Exercise can, however, have deleterious effects if participants are inappropriately screened; if the exercise prescription is developed and implemented from inadequate information (medical and individual); or if the exercise staff members are unaware of changes in a participant's health status. Exercise is, in itself, a physiologic stress to the individual, which is only beneficial when applied to individuals who are in a stable medical and physiologic state. The benefits of exercise training are cumulative with time. Therefore, to defer exercise for evaluation (and possible follow-up treatment) is reasonable when a change in medical status is suspected, instead of continuing exercise when the individual is not stable and therefore is placed at undue risk.

Decisions must be made by the exercise program staff at each of the possible participant/program interactions. These decisions should be made based on sound clinical judgment with consideration of the factors discussed in this chapter. Program policy must support this decision-making process. The decisions made by the exercise program staff are actually risk and benefit evaluations. In decision making, the exercise staff should ask, "what are the risks to the participant," and "what would result in the greatest short- and long-term benefit to the participant?" A risk-benefit evaluation must also be made for the program. For example, in the screening process, the staff should ask, "what risks are associated with involving this individual in our exercise program," and "what short- and long-term benefits can we provide for this individual?" This framework of policy development and decision making aids the exercise staff in meeting the goals of providing a safe, beneficial, and enjoyable exercise program for all persons involved.

Acknowledgments

The authors thank Neil Oldridge, Steve Blair, and William Allen for their ideas, review, and support in preparing this chapter.

28

STRENGTH AND FLEXIBILITY CONSIDERATIONS FOR EXERCISE PRESCRIPTION

ROBERT J. MOFFATT

High-level musculoskeletal function is vital to optimal health. Without it, in fact, total fitness cannot truly be achieved. Its importance lies with the potential to maximize performance and to limit musculoskeletal injury. A concept that is widely accepted is that poor flexibility as well as inadequate muscular strength can contribute to musculoskeletal disorders; in more than 80% of individuals with low-back pain, pain is attributable to muscular deficiency.[1] Flexibility and muscle strengthening programs have been used to improve low back problems in more than 90% of patients studied.[1]

FLEXIBILITY

Flexibility is a highly important and often overlooked component of muscular performance. A simple definition of flexibility is the range of possible motion about a given joint or a combination of joints. Flexibility is identified as either static or dynamic. Static flexibility is the measure of the total range of motion (ROM) at the joint, whereas the torque or resistance to movement is used to assess dynamic flexibility.

The ROM about a joint is dependent on the joint structure and is highly specific to that joint. Limitations to ROM are usually dependent on the status of the soft tissues surrounding the joint. The relative contribution of soft tissue that may impose limitations on a joint during movement were determined by Johns and Wright: joint capsule (47%), muscle and its fascia (41%), tendons and ligaments (10%), and skin (2%).[2] The muscle and fascial sheath have more elastic tissue and the resistance to movement is primarily due to the fascia that covers the muscle.[3,4] Efforts to improve flexibility therefore should focus on modifying these structures.

EVALUATION OF FLEXIBILITY

Flexibility is typically measured from ROM data, either directly or indirectly. These measures may be more meaningful with regard to potential physical performance than to measures of dynamic flexibility, for which methods of assessment have not been developed.[5]

Direct measurements of static flexibility involve the use of a goniometer to determine the joint angle at both extremes of the ROM. A goniometer is a protractor-like device with two protruding arms (Fig. 28–1). One arm is stationary at the zero line of the protractor, and the other arm is movable. The goniometer is cen-

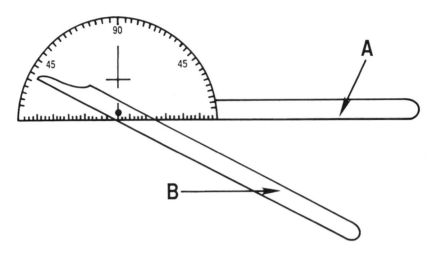

FIGURE 28–1. Goniometer. A, stationary arm; B, movable arm.

tered over the axis of the bony lever. The arms of the device are aligned with the longitudinal axis of each moving body segment. The ROM is the difference between the joint angles at the beginning and end of the movement. Particular care must be taken when determining the location of the axis of the bony lever as this may introduce error into the measurement.

A more commonly used device to measure static flexibility is the Leighton flexometer (Figure 28–2). This device consists of a pointer that is weighted at one end to keep it vertical and a weighted 360° dial that rotates with respect to the pointer with movement of the body part. The flexometer is strapped onto a body segment and records ROM with respect to the downward pull of gravity on the dial and pointer. Reliability coefficients greater than 0.90 have been reported for many joints when using the Leighton flexometer.[6,7]

Indirect methods for evaluating static flexibility often involve the use of a ruler, sliding

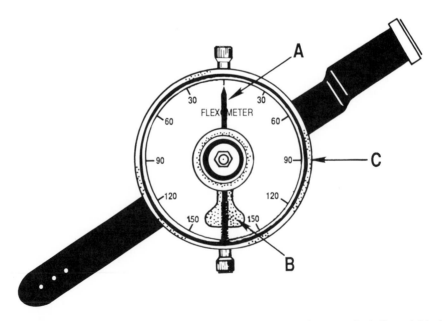

FIGURE 28–2. Leighton flexometer. A, pointer; B, weight to keep pointer vertical; C, weighted 360°, dial.

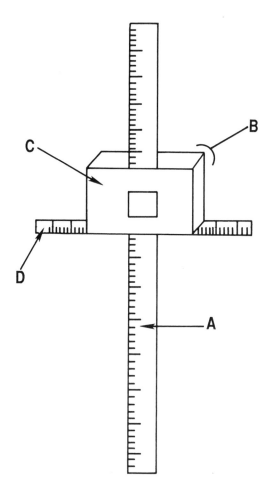

FIGURE 28–3. Flexomeasure. A, ruler; B, flexomeasure case; C, window side of flexomeasure; D, ruler guide stick.

caliper, or flexomeasure to obtain a linear measurement of ROM (Fig. 28–3). Indirect assessment of flexibility has been criticized because the outcome of such tests may be influenced by various lengths and widths of body segments.[8] Indirect tests of static flexibility with the use of a flexomeasure are described, along with test norms by Johnson.[9]

FACTORS THAT INFLUENCE FLEXIBILITY

Before interpreting data and prescribing a program for improving flexibility, consider those factors that influence stretch as well as factors that affect flexibility. Sapega et al. provide a comprehensive, well-written review on this topic.[10] When applying stretching exer-

cises, remember that connective tissue is a primary target. Factors that influence stretch are: (1) the amount and duration of applied force; and (2) the temperature of deep muscle tissue. The time required to stretch the tissue a specified amount is inversely related to the forces applied.[11,12] Although low-force stretching requires more time than a higher force method to produce a given tissue elongation, the proportion of lengthening remaining after stretching is greater for the low-force, long-duration stretch.[11,12] Warren et al. also showed that a high-force method of stretching produces more structural weakening than a slower, low-force method for the same amount of tissue elongation.[11]

Deep muscle temperature significantly influences the mechanical behavior of connective tissue under force. When stretching occurs at muscle temperatures within the range of 102 to 110°F, the amount of structural weakening produced by a given amount of tissue elongation varies inversely to the temperature.[13] Stretching cold muscles and tendons is not as effective; in fact, they may be more vulnerable to injury if over-eager methods are used. Wright and Johns report that local warming of a joint to 113°F may improve dynamic flexibility by 20% and cooling to 65°F produces a 10 to 20% decrease.[5] Stretching, therefore should most profitably be done at the end of an aerobic warmup when the tissue temperatures are higher. Mild progressive exercise, such as a brisk walk lasting a minimum of 5 min, should precede stretching.

Flexibility is also related to age, sex, and physical activity. Aging results in a progressive decline in flexibility.[14,15] This decline is most likely due to changes in the elasticity of the soft tissues as well as a less active lifestyle. Muscle disuse tends to allow connective tissues to shorten, thereby impairing joint mobility. Inactive individuals tend to be less flexible than active individuals.[16] Furthermore, exercise can improve flexibility.[17–19] Although data comparing the flexibility of men and women are not available, evidence exists to indicate that young girls are more flexible than boys.[15,20]

DESIGNING PROGRAMS TO IMPROVE ROM

To improve the ROM at a joint effectively, the overload principle should be applied by increasing the length of time the stretch position is held for each repetition. Because flexibility is joint specific, exercises that affect the appropriate muscle groups must be selected. Stretching techniques are commonly used to improve flexibility. Therefore, an important issue to address is the effectiveness of the most common methods used for improving ROM.

Ballistic Stretching. With this long-used technique, a bouncing or bobbing motion is used to stretch the muscles and connective tissue. With this technique, the muscle is rapidly stretched, an action that may increase intrafusal muscle spindle activity, which reflexively causes protective muscle contraction of the activated muscles. This process appears contradictory to the aim of increased muscle flexibility. Moore and Hutton, however, suggest that full muscle relaxation is not imperative for effective stretching of the muscle.[21]

Static Stretching. The static technique involves stretching the muscles and connective tissue of the joint passively at the extreme end of the ROM. At this point, torque is slowly applied to the muscle to produce further stretching. This technique allows rapid muscle spindle adaptation to the lengthened position, thereby decreasing spindle discharge that lessens the muscles reflexive contraction and thus allows the muscle to relax and to stretch further. Static techniques can be as effective as the traditional ballistic stretching and impose less risk of tissue injury and muscle soreness that often results from ballistic techniques.[19]

Proprioceptive Neuromuscular Facilitation. Proprioceptive neuromuscular facilitation (PNF) is another common stretching technique. By using a contract-relax sequence, muscle relaxation occurs through spinal reflex mechanisms. The PNF technique is based on the concept of reciprocal inhibition. An isometric contraction of the muscle group being stretched is followed by slow passive (static) stretching of the same muscles. In theory, a reflex facilitation is induced by the isometric contraction of the antagonist muscles being stretched. The induced reflex facilitation and contraction of the agonist suppresses contractile activity in the antagonist during the static phase. Recent experimental results indicate that PNF is no more effective than conventional techniques of stretching (static and ballistic).[17,21] Wallin et al. report, however, that a modified PNF procedure improved muscle flexibility more effectively than ballistic stretching.[22]

THE FLEXIBILITY PRESCRIPTION

Prescriptions of stretching programs are outlined in a publication by Anderson.[23] (This book also contains examples and illustrations of exercises for various body regions and for various activities.) A well-rounded general program includes at least one exercise for each of the major muscle groups, with particular emphasis on problem areas. Static stretching exercises should be maintained in the stretched position for about 8 to 12 sec, just below the threshold of pain. Progressive overload of the muscle group is required for continued improvement. Two to six repetitions of each exercise are performed daily until desired results are achieved. Maintenance programs may be conducted three or four times per week.

When using the PNF technique, the contraction phase is sustained for 4 to 6 sec, followed immediately by the static stretch for 6 to 10 sec. Each exercise is repeated four to six times each minute, with each 1-min bout repeated four or five times.

MUSCULAR FITNESS

Adequate levels of muscular strength and endurance are typically achieved through systematic programs of weight training. Such programs may be designed for a variety of athletic purposes, as well as for rehabilitation and general muscular conditioning. Before discussing the physiology of strength and endurance and basic weight training principles for the development of muscular fitness, we must first define muscular strength and muscular endurance.

Strength is the force a muscle group can apply against a given resistance. The force exerted is typically determined by one maximal effort, or one repetition maximum (RM). Muscular endurance is the ability of the muscle group to sustain repeated contractions of a given force for an extended period.

PRINCIPLES OF WEIGHT TRAINING

To develop the muscle effectively, we must overload the muscle by forcing it to perform against workloads greater than it normally encounters. The most rapid gains in strength are attained by exercising the muscle at 80 to 100% of maximum.[24] Exercise intensities of at least 60% of maximum, however, should be sufficient to develop strength.[25] To develop muscular endurance, muscle groups should be exercised at lower intensities and higher repetitions to the point of fatigue.

For continued muscular development during weight training programs, periodic adjustments to the work load must be made. The resistance against which the muscle trains must continue to overload the muscle as it gains in strength and endurance. In other words, as the muscle becomes stronger, more resistance is needed for gains to continue. This modification of the overload principle is referred to as progressive resistance exercise, and forms the basis for weight training programs.

Methods for developing muscular fitness should be selected on the basis of the specific needs of the individual — the principle of specificity. Muscular fitness development is not only specific to the muscle group exercised but also to the type of contraction, training intensity, training velocity, and pattern of movement. The scientific evidence to support the need for movement-specific exercises was reviewed by Sale and MacDougall.[26]

TRAINING MUSCLES

Several methods are available for use in developing muscular strength and endurance. Training procedures are classified according to the type of muscular contraction: isometric, isotonic (concentric and eccentric), and isokinetic (Table 28–1). A comprehensive list of exercises and illustrations is provided in a text by Stone and O'Bryant.[27]

Isometric Training. Isometric strength has been shown to improve at an average rate of 5% per week with the use of a single 1-sec isometric contraction held at two-thirds maximal voluntary contraction for 5 days per week.[28] By repeating this contraction 5 to 10 times per day, isometric strength improved greatly. Although isometric exercise is effective in providing overload and improving strength, its use may be limited because of the specific nature of the isometric process. Strength gains are specific to the joint angle at which the isometric contraction is performed.[29] To improve strength throughout the ROM, the exercise must be performed at

Table 28–1. Classification of Muscular Contraction

Type of contraction	Definition
Isometric or static	No change in muscle length with tension development
Isotonic or dynamic	
Concentric	Muscle shortens during contraction while it overcomes constant resistance
Eccentric	Muscle lengthens during contraction while resisting constant load
Isokinetic	Muscle shortens with maximal tension developed at constant speed over full ROM

various positions of the joint. Despite its limitations, isometric training does seem to be beneficial in rehabilitation as a counter measure to strength loss and atrophy associated with limb immobilization. Isometric training may cause dramatic elevations in blood pressure and large increases in intrathoracic pressure during the static contraction. Therefore, this type of training may be contraindicated for some hypertensive and certain coronary prone individuals.

Isotonic Training. Isotonic training consists of movements that contain both concentric and eccentric contractions performed against a constant or variable resistance. Delorme and Watkins are credited with the development of a systematic isotonic training program.[30] They determined that strength would increase if resistance was manipulated in three sets of 10 repetitions. The first set began with one half of a 10-RM load (the maximal amount of weight that can be lifted for 10 repetitions). The second set increased the resistance to three fourths of 10 RM followed by the full 10 RM load, which was designed to overload the muscle group being trained.

Research leading to the development of the optimal number of sets, repetitions, and resistance to maximize strength gains and muscular endurance was summarized by Atha.[31] In general, the stimulus for strength improvement when using isotonic training appears to require a three-set program with the use of 5 to 10 RM, 3 to 5 days per week. The weight used for each set should provide sufficient resistance to fatigue the muscle by the last repetition of the set. Work loads greater than 10 RM are more effective when attempting to improve muscular endurance.

Isotonic training involves both concentric

and eccentric components; however, training programs are usually designed with the concentric component in mind. By using eccentric contractions, it may be possible to train at heavier loads and yield greater gains because eccentric contractions use fewer fibers at the same work load.[32] Although eccentric training does not appear to be any more effective than concentric training for strength development, individuals perceive eccentric exercise as easier than concentric exercise. Eccentric exercise may also place less strain on the joints involved in the movement.[33] On the other hand, eccentric training produces more muscle soreness than does concentric training.[34,35]

Isokinetic Training. Isokinetic training involves the use of specialized equipment that permits the muscle to develop maximal tension as it shortens at a constant speed throughout the complete ROM. The speed of movement is mechanically controlled by the isokinetic exercise device such as the Cybex, Orthotron, and Mini-Gym. The advantage of isokinetic training is the ability to develop strength at different velocities. Isokinetic training is performed at speeds ranging from 24 to 180° per second. This type of training may be especially valuable for athletes who wish to develop strength at speeds that approximate the speeds at which they perform. Coyle et al. and Lesmes et al. suggest that fast-speed training may be more beneficial than slow-speed training, because gains in strength are limited to velocities at or below the velocity of training.[36,37] Isokinetic training appears to have an advantage over isometric and isotonic methods because of the opportunity to: (1) develop maximal force throughout the full ROM, and (2) develop strength at variable speeds.

The procedures for the development of strength and endurance in isokinetic training are similar to those used for isotonic training. Three sets are performed for each exercise, with 5 to 10 repetitions, 3 to 5 days per week at speeds varying between 24 and 180° per second for strength development. For muscular endurance training, maximal contractions should be performed at 180° until exhaustion.

Circuit Weight Training. Circuit weight training has been promoted as a method to develop strength as well as aerobic capacity. Use of this method has been shown to result in increased muscular strength, especially when low-repetition and high-resistance exercises are included.[38–40]

Circuit programs are usually devised to enable participants to perform as many repetitions

Table 28–2. Effects of Weight Training on Morphologic, Biochemical, Neural, and Anthropometric Factors

Factors	Effect		
	Increase	Decrease	No change
Morphologic factors			
Contractile proteins, number and size of myofibrils	X		
Muscle connective tissue	X		
Size of fast-twitch fibers	X		
Number of muscle fiber types			X
Size and strength of ligaments and tendons	X		
Biochemical factors			
ATP and CP	X		
Myokinase activity	X		
Mitochondrial volume density		X	
Neural factors			
Discharge frequency of motoneurons	X		
Motor unit recruitment	X		
Inhibitions		X	
Motor skill performance	X		
Anthropometric factors			
Body weight			X
Lean body weight	X		
Percent body fat		X	
Flexibility	X		
Speed and power	X		

as possible at 40 to 60% of 1 RM for 30 sec with 15- to 20-sec rest periods between exercise stations. Programs typically consist of 6 to 10 stations per circuit, which are repeated 2 to 3 times per training session.

COMPARISONS OF WEIGHT TRAINING PROGRAMS

Strength effectively increases when the exercised muscles are overloaded, regardless of which method of training is used. Fleck and Schutt published a comparative review of various weight training programs.[41] In summary, isokinetic training increases both isokinetic strength and isotonic strength and appears to cause less muscle soreness. Isotonic training is superior to isometric training for the development of strength and muscular endurance.

ADAPTATIONS TO STRENGTH TRAINING PROGRAMS

A variety of physiologic, morphologic, neural, anthropometric, and biochemical alterations occur in muscle tissue in response to a systematic weight training program. Table 28–2 is a summary of the effects of weight training.

MAINTENANCE OF STRENGTH AND ENDURANCE GAINS

Once the development of muscular strength and endurance is accomplished, its maintenance is relatively easy. Strength gains were reportedly retained for 6 weeks after stopping an isotonic program.[42] Furthermore, strength was improved by a subsequent 6-week program of training involving 1 RM performed each week.[42] In another study, subjects retained 45% of their strength gains after 1 year.[43] Muscular endurance, too, can be retained; muscular endurance was retained at 70% of training gains after 12 weeks of detraining.[44,45] Muscles will atrophy, however, as a result of disuse, such as immobilization. Disuse leads to a decrease in strength as well as in muscle mass.

REFERENCES

1. Kraus H, Raab W: *Hypokinetic Disease.* Springfield, IL: Charles C Thomas, 1961.
2. Johns R, Wright V: Relative importance of various tissue in joint stiffness. *J Appl Physiol*, 17:824, 1962.
3. Banus M, Zetlin A: The relation of isometric tension to length in skeletal muscle. *J Cell Physiol*, 12:403, 1938.
4. Ramsey R, Street S: The isometric length tension diagram of isolated skeletal muscle fibers of the frog. *J Cell Physiol*, 15:11, 1940.
5. Wright V, Johns R: Physical factors concerned with the stiffness of normal and diseased joints. *Bull Johns Hopkins Hosp*, 106:215, 1960.
6. Leighton J: An instrument and technic for the measurement of range of joint motion. *Arch Phys Med Rehabil*, 36:571, 1955.
7. Verducci F: *Measurement Concepts in Physical Education.* St. Louis: C.V. Mosby, 1980.
8. Wear C: Relationships of flexibility measurements to length of body segments. *Res Q Exerc Sport*, 34:234, 1963.
9. Johnson B: *Practical Flexibility Measurements With the Flexomeasure.* Portland, TX: Brown and Little, 1977.
10. Sapega A, Quedenfeld T, Moyer R, Butler R: Biophysical factors in range-of-motion exercise. *Phys Sports Med*, 9:57, 1981.
11. Warren C, Lehmann J, Koblanski J: Elongation of rat tail tendon: Effect of load and temperature. *Arch Phys Med Rehabil*, 52:465, 1971.
12. Warren C, Lehmann J, Koblanski, J.: Heat and stretch procedures: An evaluation using rat tail tendon. *Arch Phys Med Rehabil*, 57:122, 1976.
13. Lehmann J, Masock A, Warren C: Effect of therapeutic temperatures on tendon extensibility. *Arch Phys Med Rehabil*, 51:481, 1970.
14. Buxton D: Extension of the Kraus-Weber test. *Res Q Exerc Sport*, 29:210, 1957.
15. Phillips M: Analysis of results from the Kraus-Weber test of minimum muscular fitness in children. *Res Exerc Sport*, 26:314, 1955.
16. McCue B: Flexibility of college women. *Res Q Exerc Sport*, 24:316, 1953.
17. Hartley-O'Brien S: Six mobilization exercises for active range of hip flexion. *Res Q Exerc Sport*, 51:625, 1980.
18. Chapman E, deVries H, Swezey R: Joint stiffness: Effects of exercise on young and old men. *J Gerontol*, 27:218, 1972.
19. deVries H: Evaluation of static stretching procedures for improvement of flexibility. *Res Q Exerc Sport*, 33:222, 1962.
20. Kraus H, Hirschland R: Minimum muscular fitness tests in school children. *Res Q Exerc Sport*, 25:178, 1954.
21. Moore M, Hutton R: Electromyographic evaluation of muscle stretching techniques. *Med Sci Sports Exerc*, 12:322, 1980.
22. Wallin D, Ekblom B, Grahn R, Nordenborg T: Improvement of muscle flexibility. *Am J Sports Med*, 13:263, 1985.
23. Anderson R: *Stretching.* Fullerton, CA: Shelter Publications, 1980.
24. Stone W, Kroll W: *Sports Conditioning and Weight Training.* Boston: Allyn and Bacon, 1978.
25. McArdle W, Katch F, Katch V: *Exercise Physiology.* 2nd Ed. Philadelphia: Lea & Febiger. 1986.
26. Sale D, MacDougall D: Specificity in strength training, a review for the coach and athlete. Science Periodical on Research and Technology in Sport. Ottawa: The Coaching Association of Canada, March, 1981.
27. Stone M, O'Bryant H: *Weight Training: A Scientific Approach.* Minneapolis: Burgess Publishing, 1984.

28. Hettinger T, Muller E: Muskelleistung and muskeltraining. *Arbeitsphysiologie,* 5:11, 1953.

29. Gardner G: Specificity of strength changes of the exercised and nonexercised limb following isometric training. *Res Q Exerc Sport,* 34:98, 1963.

30. DeLorme T, Watkins A: Techniques of progressive resistance exercise. *Arch Phys Med Rehabil,* 29:263, 1948.

31. Atha J: Strengthening muscle. In *Exercise and Sport Sciences Reviews.* Vol. 9. Edited by D. Miller. Philadelphia: Franklin Institute Press, 1982.

32. Orlander J, Kiessling K-H, Karlsson J: Low intensity training, inactivity and resumed training in sedentary men. *Acta Physiol Scand,* 101:351, 1977.

33. Johnson B, et al: A comparison of concentric and eccentric muscle training. *Med Sci Sports Exerc,* 8:355, 1976.

34. Byrnes W: Muscle soreness following resistance exercise with and without eccentric contractions. *Res Q Exerc Sport,* 56:283, 1985.

35. Tulag T: Residual muscular soreness as influenced by concentric, eccentric and static contractions. *Res Q Exerc Sport,* 44:458, 1973.

36. Coyle E, et al.: Specificity of power improvements through slow and fast isokinetic training. *J Appl Physiol,* 51:1437, 1981.

37. Lesmes G, Costill D, Coyle E, Fink W: Muscle strength and power changes during maximal isokinetic training. *Med Sci Sports Exerc,* 10:266, 1978.

38. Gettman L, Pollock M: Circuit weight training: A critical review of its physiological benefits. *Phys Sports Med,* 9:44, 1981.

39. Allen T, Byrd R, Smith D: Hemo-dynamic consequences of circuit weight training. *Res Q Exerc Sport,* 47:299, 1976.

40. Wilmore J: Alterations in strength, body composition and anthropometric measurements consequent to a 10-week weight training program. *Med Sci Sports Exerc,* 6:133, 1974.

41. Fleck S, Schutt R: Types of strength training. *Orthop Clin North Am,* 4:449, 1983.

42. Berger R: Comparison of the effect of various weight training loads on health. *Res Q Exerc Sport,* 36:141, 1965.

43. McMorris J, Elkins E: A study of prediction and evaluation of muscular hypertrophy. *Arch Phys Med Rehabil,* 35:420, 1954.

44. Syster B, Stull G: Muscular endurance retention as a function of length of detraining. *Res Q Exerc Sport,* 41:105, 1970.

45. Waldman R, Stull G: Effects of various periods of inactivity on retention of newly acquired levels of muscular endurance. *Res Q Exerc Sport,* 40:393, 1969.

SAFETY, INJURIES, AND EMERGENCY PROCEDURES

CHAPTER 29

THE SAFETY OF EXERCISE TESTING AND PARTICIPATION

PAUL D. THOMPSON

The design of this chapter is: (1) to present the cardiovascular complications that occur during exercise and the pathologic conditions underlying these complications; and (2) to quantify the incidence of exercise-related cardiovascular events. Our ultimate purpose is to enable the exercise leader to recognize potentially dangerous situations and to inform exercise participants of the risks of exercise.

The cardiovascular complications occurring during exercise are cardiac arrhythmias, myocardial infarction, and sudden cardiac death.[1]

CARDIAC ARRHYTHMIAS

Cardiac arrhythmias are a frequent complication of exercise. The participant and exercise leader are usually unaware of the arrhythmia, except when the individual is exercising in an electrocardiographically (ECG) monitored situation. Some patients do feel palpitations during the arrhythmia, however, or they may detect changes in the heart beat when monitoring their pulse. Therefore, the exercise leader should have a general understanding of cardiac arrhythmias during exercise and their significance.

Changes in cardiac control that occur during exercise increase the frequency of cardiac arrhythmias.[1] The decrease in parasympathetic tone and the increase in sympathetic activity with exercise increase cardiac automaticity. Furthermore, exercise may induce myocardial ischemia, which increases cardiac ectopic beats. Cardiac arrhythmias can occur in otherwise healthy people, but are more frequent and more dangerous in patients with heart disease.

Cardiac arrhythmias during exercise may be either supraventricular or ventricular in origin. Supraventricular arrhythmias include paroxysmal atrial tachycardia (PAT), atrial fibrillation, and atrial flutter. These arrhythmias usually produce a rapid ventricular rate of 150 beats/min or greater. Exercising subjects may complain of a "fluttering" in their chest or use another expression for palpitations. Differentiation from the normal increased heart rate of exercise may be difficult. Whereas the normal exercise heart rate decreases gradually with exercise cessation, the tachycardia of an arrhythmia often persists or suddenly decreases to a much slower rate when the arrhythmia "breaks."

Ventricular arrhythmias during exercise include premature ventricular impulses (PVIs), ventricular tachycardia, and ventricular fibrillation. PVIs occur frequently in the general population and usually are noted as a skipped beat or as a pulse drop when subjects monitor their heart rate. As many as 44% of apparently healthy men may demonstrate PVIs during maximal exercise testing.[2] Ventricular tachycardia may be felt only as palpitations, but is often associated with dizziness, weakness, or loss of consciousness. Ventricular tachycardia may precede ventricular fibrillation, which is the probable mediator of most sudden cardiac deaths and requires immediate cardiopulmonary resuscitation.

The exercise leader's response to a subject with a cardiac arrhythmia other than ventricular fibrillation depends on the clinical situation. Arrhythmias causing significant symptoms, such as prolonged palpitations, dizziness, or loss of consciousness, require immediate medical attention. The only exception is with individuals who have an episodic arrhythmia and have been instructed in self-treatment. These patients often have mild PAT. Arrhythmias detected as skipped beats during pulse monitoring but without other symptoms are frequently benign. The subject should discuss the problem with a physician, but it is not of immediate concern, especially in healthy young people. All cardiac arrhythmias are more dangerous in subjects with known cardiac disease and should be brought to the attention of the patient's physician.

EXERCISE-RELATED MYOCARDIAL INFARCTIONS AND SUDDEN CARDIAC DEATH

Myocardial infarctions and sudden cardiac deaths in adults during exercise are usually caused by atherosclerotic coronary artery disease (CAD). This correlation is not surprising in that CAD is the major cause of sudden death in the general adult population.[1] Exercise increases myocardial oxygen demand. CAD limits myocardial oxygen supply with resultant myocardial ischemia. Myocardial ischemia predisposes the myocardium to ventricular arrhythmias and the final event in most sudden cardiac deaths is almost certainly ventricular fibrillation.[1]

Occasionally, sudden death in adults occurs without pathologic findings of CAD. Muscular contraction of the coronary artery wall or "coronary spasm" may be operative in these instances. A runner in the 1975 Boston Marathon developed ventricular fibrillation and subsequent ECG evidence of a myocardial infarction. He died 2 months later of complications. Autopsy confirmed the myocardial infarction, but the coronary arteries were widely patent.[3] An alternate possibility is that coronary artery thrombosis with subsequent clot lysis may cause exercise-related cardiac events. A 34-year-old participant in the 1982 Montreal Marathon sustained an acute myocardial infarction immediately after the race. Arteriography demonstrated a coronary artery thrombus.[4] Coronary spasm cannot be excluded, even in this instance, however, because coronary spasm can reduce blood flow and may result in clot formation.[5]

CAD is a rare cause of exercise-related sudden death in individuals under age 30 years.[6] In this group, a variety of congenital or other abnormalities are associated with exercise-related deaths, including hypertrophic cardiomyopathy, anomalous origin of the coronary arteries, aortic rupture, aortic valve stenosis, cerebrovascular accidents, conducting system abnormalities, and myocarditis.[1] An insufficient amount of information is available to rank-order these diagnoses as to the frequency with which they cause cardiac death.

Hypertrophic cardiomyopathy is a condition in which the left ventricular septum is markedly enlarged and may obstruct blood flow during ventricular contraction. The catecholamine stimulation of exercise increases cardiac contractility and may further compromise left ventricular outflow. Sudden death during exercise with anomalous coronary artery origin most frequently involves the left coronary artery arising from the anterior aortic cusp. Flow in the left coronary artery can be restricted during exercise, leading to myocardial ischemia. Sudden death from aortic rupture recently received national attention with the death of volleyball player Flo Hyman.[7] Certain very tall individuals have a weakness of connective tissue in the aortic wall produced by an inherited condition called Marfan's syndrome. The increased blood pressure produced by exercise may cause the aorta to rupture. In aortic valve stenosis, the narrowed aortic valve may not permit adequate cardiac output during exercise. Cerebrovascular accidents in young persons during exercise often are associated with the rupture of a blood vessel in the brain. Abnormalities of the cardiac conducting system and myocarditis probably cause sudden death by producing ventricular fibrillation.

All of the aforementioned abnormalities are extremely rare, as is sudden death during exertion in young people. Nevertheless, certain warning signs should alert the exercise leader. A history of syncope or chest discomfort during exercise, even in a young person, may be associated with hypertrophic cardiomyopathy, anomalous coronary artery origin, aortic stenosis, or conducting system abnormalities. Professionals supervising sports in which height is an advantage should be aware of the characteristics of Marfan's syndrome: tallness, long fingers and arms, sternal deformity, and nearsightedness. With any of these symptoms or with the characteristics of Marfan's syndrome, the subject should be evaluated by a physician before exercise. Also, because myocarditis may be part of a generalized disease, exercise training should probably be restricted during the febrile period of any illness.

INCIDENCE OF CARDIAC COMPLICATIONS DURING EXERCISE

EXERCISE TESTING

In 1969, Rochmis and Blackburn surveyed 130 facilities to determine the risk of exercise testing.[8] Responses were received from the staff of 55% of facilities, yielding a total of 170,000 tests. Eight deaths (0.5 deaths per 10,000 tests) occurred within 1 hour of exercise and an additional eight deaths were attributed to the exercise test over the next 4 days. This rate of 1 death per 10,000 tests is a convenient figure for estimating the mortality of exercise testing. An additional 3 patients per 10,000 tests were admitted to the hospital for medical treatment. In only 34% of the surveyed test facilities were maximal tests routinely performed.

Stuart and Ellestad mailed questionnaires to 6000 possible exercise test facilities.[9] Professionals from 33% of the institutions replied, for a total of 518,448 tests. Respondents included hospital and office-based facilities. Seventy percent of the respondents used a symptom-limited maximal test. Data showed that only 0.5 deaths, 3.58 myocardial infarctions, and 4.78 arrhythmias requiring intravenous medication

or cardioversion occurred per 10,000 tests. The authors did not specify the time after exercise examined or the number of patients admitted to the hospital after exercise testing.

Atterhög, Jonsson, and Samuelsson prospectively determined the incidence of cardiac complications in 20 Swedish test facilities in which 50,000 tests were performed during an 18-month period.[10] Only 0.4 deaths, 1.4 myocardial infarctions, and 5.2 hospital admissions occurred per 10,000 tests.

In all of the aforementioned studies, those facilities examined conducted exercise testing in the usual clinical situation. Consequently, the risk of such testing is 1 or fewer deaths, 4 or fewer myocardial infarctions, and approximately 5 hospital admissions (including the infarctions) per 10,000 exercise tests—roughly 1 major problem for every 1000 clinical exercise tests. The risk of exercise testing varies with the patient population. Facilities in which those subjects tested are predominantly healthy should experience fewer problems than facilities in which testing primarily involves subjects with severe cardiac disease.[11]

EXERCISE TRAINING IN THE GENERAL POPULATION

Few studies of cardiac complications in the general population have been conducted. Thompson et al. determined the incidence of death during jogging in Rhode Island from 1975 through 1980.[12] Statistics relating to sudden death were collected by the Medical Examiner, who is required by law to investigate all sudden deaths. The number of Rhode Island men jogging at least twice weekly was determined by using a random-digit telephone survey and population estimates. Results showed only 1 death per year for every 7620 joggers aged 30 through 64 years (95% confidence limits: 1 death per 2000 to 13,000 joggers). Nevertheless, the hourly death rate during jogging was seven times that during more sedentary activities (95% confidence limits: 4 to 26 times). The association of exercise with sudden death, therefore, is rare but is probably more than coincidental. If men with known heart disease are excluded and certain assumptions are made, the death rate for healthy men in Rhode Island was only 1 death per year for every 15,200 middle-aged joggers.

Similar results were reported in a case control study of cardiac arrests during vigorous exercise in Seattle.[13] Only one episode of cardiac arrest occurred per year during exercise for every 18,000 healthy men. Once again, the death rate during vigorous exercise exceeded that at other times, especially for men unaccustomed to vigorous activity.

We do not know of studies of the general population in which researchers have quantified the risk of myocardial infarction during vigorous exercise. Consequently, the previous estimates of death during exercise underestimate the total risk of cardiac complications. Nevertheless, one can estimate a risk of 1 death per year during exercise for every 15,000 to 20,000 healthy men. The risk of sudden death is much lower among women because of the lower incidence of heart disease in young and middle-aged women.

CARDIAC REHABILITATION

Several investigators have examined the incidence of cardiac complications during cardiac rehabilitation.[14] In one of the most comprehensive studies, researchers obtained information from the directors of 30 cardiac rehabilitation programs.[15] The results were based on 13,500 patients and more than 1.6 million hours of exercise. Only 61 major cardiovascular complications, including 50 cardiac arrests, occurred during or soon after exercise, yielding an incidence of only 1 arrest and 1 death per 33,000 hours and 120,000 patient-hours of activity, respectively.

INDICATIONS TO LIMIT EXERCISE

Historic evidence of exercise-induced angina, syncope, or cardiac arrhythmias in any participant warrants further evaluation before exercise training. Most fitness leaders know the importance of exercise-induced chest discomfort. Cardiac ischemia may also manifest as jaw, neck, arm, shoulder, or back discomfort or as an uncomfortable shortness of breath. Some middle-aged patients join exercise programs just to "prove" that such symptoms are not evidence of heart disease. It is useful, therefore, to know whether new symptoms have prompted the initiation of an exercise program. Subjects who

feel ill or are febrile should be prohibited from training. Similarly, persons returning from a *major* illness should first be evaluated by a physician. The cardiac rehabilitation leader should ensure that the patients have not developed new or progressive symptoms since their last exercise session.

During exercise, significant symptoms, including new or worsening angina, palpitations, dizziness, weakness, unusual and extreme fatigue, or excessive air hunger, should indicate the end of the exercise session for any subject. Subjects who experience such symptoms during exercise should be promptly evaluated by a physician either at the exercise facility or after transport to an emergency room.

The major cause of important cardiovascular complications during exercise is CAD. Consequently, the risk of exercise complications increases with the prevalence of CAD in the exercising population. The risk is extremely small among healthy young adults and nonsmoking women, is higher among groups with CAD risk factors, and is highest among persons with known disease. The *absolute* risk for cardiac complications in the general population is small. Nevertheless, the exercise leader should be aware of individuals that may be at increased risk and should take appropriate precautions.

REFERENCES

1. Thompson PD: Cardiovascular hazards of physical activity. In *Exercise and Sport Sciences Reviews.* Edited by RL Terjung. Philadelphia: Franklin Institute Press, 1982.
2. McHenry PL, Fisch C, Jordan JW, Corya BR: Cardiac arrhythmias observed during maximal exercise testing in clinically normal men. *Am J Cardiol, 29:*331, 1972.
3. Green LH, Cohen SI, Kurland G: Fatal myocardial infarction in marathon racing. *Ann Intern Med, 84:*704, 1976.
4. Chan KL, Davies RA, Chambers RJ: Coronary thrombosis and subsequent lysis after a marathon. *J Am Coll Cardiol, 4:*1322, 1984.
5. Gertz SD, et al.: Endothelial cell damage and thrombus formation after partial arterial constriction: Relevance to the role of coronary artery spasm in the pathogenesis of myocardial infarction. *Circulation, 63:*476, 1981.
6. Ragosta M, Crabtree J, Sturner WQ, Thompson PD: Death during recreational exercise in the State of Rhode Island. *Med Sci Sports Exerc, 16:*339, 1984.
7. Demak R: Marfan syndrome: A silent killer. *Sports Illustrated, February 17:*30, 1986.

8. Rochmis P, Blackburn H: Exercise tests: A survey of procedures, safety, and litigation experience in approximately 170,000 tests. *JAMA, 217*:1061, 1971.

9. Stuart RJ Jr, Ellestad MH: National survey of exercise stress testing facilities. *Chest, 77*:94, 1980.

10. Atterhög J-H., Jonsson B, Samuelsson R: Exercise testing: A prospective study of complication rates. *Am Heart J, 98*:572, 1979.

11. Young DZ, Lampert S, Graboys TB, Lown B: Safety of maximal exercise testing in patients at high risk for ventricular arrhythmia. *Circulation, 70*:184, 1984.

12. Thompson PD, Funk EJ, Carleton RA, Sturner WQ: Incidence of death during jogging in Rhode Island from 1975 through 1980. *JAMA, 247*:2535, 1982.

13. Siscovick DS, Weiss NS, Fletcher RH, Lasky T: The incidence of primary cardiac arrest during vigorous exercise. *N Engl J Med, 311*:874, 1984.

14. Thompson PD: The cardiovascular risks of cardiac rehabilitation. *J Cardiopul Rehabil, 5*:321, 1985.

15. Haskell WL: Cardiovascular complications during exercise training of cardiac patients. *Circulation, 57*:920, 1978.

CHAPTER 30

EMERGENCY PLANS AND PROCEDURES FOR AN EXERCISE FACILITY*

WILLIAM E. STRAUSS,
MICHAEL S. SCARAMUZZI,
DIANE PANTON-LAPSLEY,
AND KEVIN M. MCINTYRE

All exercise programs, be they exercise testing, cardiac rehabilitation, or supervised aerobic exercise, should ideally be free of risk. Obviously, however, this is not the case; although the benefits are potentially much greater, the finite risk of a patient developing a problem during exercise does exist. In the following section, we explore this risk and what can be done to reduce it. Many of the guidelines we propose are simple common sense. The central and most important point we stress is the need for an organized, written plan delineating how different levels of patient-related problems are handled *in that facility*. Many different types of exercise facilities exist and the health and degree of wellness of the patients or clients, the equipment present, and the expertise of the employees vary considerably. Instead of trying to propose plans and procedures for all, or even many, of these different exercise facilities, we propose certain guidelines that hopefully can be models or templates for the exercise technologist, exercise specialist, or program director to use as a stepping stone in modifying the plans to an individual situation. Many references could be cited; instead, we include "suggested reading" that may be used as further reference material or as one of many examples we have used to make a point.

RISKS AND BENEFITS OF EXERCISE

The pros and cons of exercise have been controversial for more than 30 years. Results of epidemiologic studies suggest that vigorous exercise is associated with a reduced risk of cardiovascular events and mortality. In addition, a large segment of our population has correctly or incorrectly over the last decade become enamoured with the overall sense of well-being and health associated with frequent exercise. On the other hand, myocardial ischemia and death have been observed to occur during strenuous exercise. The trade-offs of the risks and benefits of exercise can perhaps be put in perspective by an excellent study performed by Siscovick and colleagues. They examined the exercise habits of a group of previously healthy men who sustained a cardiac arrest and compared them with a random sample of similar men who had not had sudden death. The study confirmed that the risk of cardiac arrest did increase transiently during vigorous exercise, al-

* Supported by the Medical Research Service of the US Veterans Administration.

though those men who had a high level of habitual exercise had a far lower risk of cardiac arrest during exercise than those men with a low level of weekly exercise. Although vigorous physical activity was associated with an increased risk of sudden death, habitual participation in such aerobic activity was associated in an overall reduction in the risk of experiencing sudden death. The overall incidence of sudden death can be approximated from a review of the 13-year experience with 2500 patients participating in supervised exercise programs in Seattle: 0.6 episodes occurred for every 10,000 hours of exercise.

One of the basic premises of this section is that the frequency of cardiac arrest and other serious complications, as well as their ultimate outcome, can be improved. The risk of the development of such events hopefully can be decreased by screening to identify high-risk patients. In addition, the likelihood of surviving those episodes that do occur can be enhanced if trained personnel have developed appropriate plans and procedures ahead of time.

A part of pre-exercise screening involves common sense—patients or clients should be excluded if they have unstable symptoms or major uncontrolled illnesses. In addition, some markers can help to identify the high-risk patient. In a review of their experience with supervised exercise training, Hossack and Hartwig not only provided the data concerning cardiac arrest incidence, but also they delineated clinical findings more likely to be associated with the development of sudden death: myocardial ischemia during exercise and non-compliance with the exercise prescription. Patients with sudden death had more ST depression on the electrocardiogram during pretraining exercise tolerance testing, a reliable manifestation of exercise-induced ischemia. The sudden death patients not only had more normal exercise capacities pretraining than those individuals who did not experience sudden death, but also they exceeded their prescribed training heart rate range more than twice as frequently. Thus, a high-risk participant may be considered as having continued exercise-related ischemia and a propensity to "push" himself during training.

Despite the ability to screen and to observe high-risk patients more closely, some untoward events continue to happen. In the following sections, we outline guidelines for personnel, equipment, and finally plans or procedures to be put into effect.

CLINICAL KNOWLEDGE REQUIRED OF PERSONNEL IN AN EXERCISE FACILITY

SAFE CONDUCT OF AN EXERCISE PROGRAM

Having the capability of conducting a safe exercise program may help to prevent a serious problem from developing, or if such a situation occurs, to be aware of circumstances surrounding the incident. The degree to which each of these criteria are met must be consistent with the program of each particular facility.

1. Obtain an accurate and complete medical history, and include any physical and emotional limitations.
2. Understand fully the principles of exercise and conditioning, such as frequency, duration, intensity, and type of exercise.
3. Recognize clinical signs and symptoms and differentiate between normal and abnormal responses to exercise.
4. Understand the physiologic effects of environmental factors as related to heat and cold on the body, both during and after exercise.
5. Be aware of the pre-exercise habits of the exercise participant as they relate to eating, drinking, clothing, and activity.
6. Know the medication a participant is taking and the effects of that medication.
7. Be able to take vital signs and know what values are appropriate for a particular level of activity.
8. Know how to operate, maintain, and calibrate equipment.

CONTRAINDICATIONS TO EXERCISE

The importance of being fully aware of the contraindications to exercise cannot be overstated. We refer the reader to Tables 2–4 and 2–5 in *Guidelines for Exercise Testing and Prescription* (3rd Ed. Lea & Febiger, 1986) for a detailed summary of these contraindications.

REASONS FOR TERMINATING EXERCISE

The reasons for terminating exercise are listed in Table 2–9 in *Guidelines for Exercise*

Testing and Prescription (3rd Ed. Lea & Febiger, 1986) and are not repeated here, although we stress the value of being well acquainted with these reasons.

EMERGENCY PLAN

Not only having an emergency plan but also knowing the plan without having to read it is of utmost importance in any emergency situation. Each facility must have a plan conducive to their particular setting. All personnel must know the plan and review it regularly.

1. Know how to activate the emergency plan (i.e., wall switch, telephone, or the like).
2. Know the location of all necessary communication equipment (i.e., telephone, including a dime if necessary; the telephone number to call; warning alarm).
3. Know how to describe the location of the incident, how to get there, and the location of the exits.
4. Know the location of all emergency equipment (i.e., defibrillator, crash cart, and backboard).
5. Know the responsibilities for people assisting with the incident.
6. Be able to provide first responder assistance.
7. Know how to prepare crash cart and defibrillator for use by those trained to use it (if applicable).
8. Prepare an accurate account of the incident and what was done.

CARDIOPULMONARY RESUSCITATION

We recommend strongly that all personnel involved in the exercise program be certified in Basic Life Support (BLS) and demonstrate competency in the execution of the skills involved in cardiopulmonary resuscitation (CPR). Consult your local American Heart Association or American Red Cross for further information.

USE OF EQUIPMENT BY PERSONNEL IN AN EXERCISE FACILITY

The safe operation of an exercise facility depends on the condition of the equipment and the expertise of the staff in its use. Not all facilities have all the following equipment, yet all personnel in every facility should be competent in the use and care of their equipment.

EXERCISE LABORATORY

1. Climate control is necessary to monitor environmental factors of heat and cold as may be affected by the summer and winter months. Caution is also required if some exercise sessions are held out of doors.
2. Floors should not be slippery. Carpeting or non-slip finishes on hardwood or tile helps to reduce the incidence of falls.
3. All running/walking tracks or lanes should be designed to ensure one-way travel or traffic patterns.
4. Care is needed in locker rooms or swimming areas to prevent falls and also to provide a dry area in the event of an emergency requiring defibrillation.
5. Any isolated area that is used for exercise should have a warning system to alert others in the event of an emergency situation.

EXERCISE EQUIPMENT

All exercise equipment must be properly maintained and calibrated to assure accurate performance. The staff should know how to operate all the equipment in the exercise facility.

Treadmill. If electrically operated, it must be grounded and the control panel should be positioned to allow for easy access. An emergency shutoff switch is sometimes mounted on the treadmill itself for quick shutoff. Regular maintenance, including calibration and belt inspection, should be routinely performed.

Cycle ergometer. Handlebars and seat should be adjustable for proper positioning. Calibration of the resistance mechanism is of utmost importance to provide for accurate workloads.

Rowing machine. All moving parts, including the handles and seat, should be properly maintained for smooth movement and proper resistance.

Swimming pool. Routine checks for proper pH and chlorine levels should be made. Life preservers and Shepherd's crooks should be spaced around the pool.

MONITORING EQUIPMENT

1. Proper skin preparation and electrode placement are necessary to ensure good contact of electrodes for accurate ECG recording.
2. The ECG monitor should be of the type designed for exercise testing because that allows for easy hookup to electrodes. The choice of hardwire models or telemetry units depends upon the facility's particular program. Expertise is needed to be able to recognize, analyze, and interpret ECG changes and arrhythmias both on an oscilloscope and on ECG paper.
3. Quick look ECGs can be obtained from the paddles of certain monitor-defibrillators. It is imperative that personnel understand fully how to select the proper mode on the defibrillator and where to place the paddles.
4. Blood pressure cuffs should be readily available. Personnel should be trained to take accurate readings while a participant is exercising or at rest.

EMERGENCY EQUIPMENT (TABLE 30–1)

Emergency equipment includes a crash cart complete with drugs (Table 30–2), suctioning apparatus, oxygen, and a defibrillator. Personnel of facilities with such equipment should not be involved with its use unless they are trained in Advanced Cardiac Life Support or some comparable level of training. In an emergency situation, however, having such equipment available and prepared for use when the proper personnel arrive at the scene is of great value. Other equipment that may prove useful in an emergency situation includes an alarm to summon help, a clock to note length of time, and a backboard to provide a firm surface for the victim or to remove someone from a swimming pool.

Table 30–1. Emergency Equipment

Defibrillator (portable synchronized)
Oxygen tanks
Airways (oral and endotracheal tubes)
Laryngoscope and intubation equipment
Bag-valve-mask hand respirator (Ambu bag)
Syringes and needles
Intravenous tubing and solutions
Intravenous stand
Adhesive tape
Suction apparatus and supplies (tubing, gloves, etc.)

Table 30–2. Emergency Drugs

The American Heart Association's classification of drugs most commonly used in a life-threatening emergency include:

1. Drugs to correct hypoxemia and metabolic acidosis:
   Oxygen
   Sodium bicarbonate
2. Drugs to increase heart rate:
   Atropine
   Isoproterenol
3. Drugs to correct ventricular dysrhythmias:
   Lidocaine
   Bretylium
   Procainamide
4. Drugs to decrease supraventricular tachycardia:
   Verapamil
5. Drugs to raise blood pressure and cardiac output:
   Epinephrine
   Norepinephrine
   Dopamine
   Dobutamine
6. Intravenous fluids
   D_5W
   Saline (0.9%)
7. Miscellaneous (depending on facility):
   Nitroglycerine: oral or intravenous use
   Diuretics (i.e., Lasix)
   Morphine sulfate
   Sodium nitroprusside

EMERGENCY ACTION PLANS

Having a "plan" in case of an emergency situation is necessary. In this section, emergencies are divided into life-threatening, potentially life-threatening, and non-emergency situations. Remember also that the exercise sessions may be held in a variety of settings: from "Basic" (i.e., an area that has only the basic equipment of a clock and nearby telephone) to "Intermediate" (i.e., a facility that may also have an emergency defibrillator and possibly a "start up" kit containing a few essential drugs, intravenous lines, an oxygen tank, and a mask hand ventilator) to "High" level, which has all necessary emergency equipment available.

Guidelines for each level of emergency are presented within the particular setting of the exercise program. These guidelines are intended for use as models that each staff should modify to fit individual needs. Remember, having a basic plan of action for your individual facility and following this plan is most important when an emergency arises.

Throughout this section, we discuss the role of the first, second, and third rescuer. Certainly, instances occur when only a single rescuer or more than three rescuers are involved. For a single rescuer only in a life-threatening emergency (CPR being performed), the rescuer follows the AHA guideline that states "CPR must be performed for one full minute" before interruption to call the emergency number if no second rescuer is available. In all instances, the first rescuer stays with the victim, calls for help, and performs CPR, if necessary. The second rescuer activates the emergency medical system (EMS) for the facility, waits for the emergency team to direct them to the scene, or returns to the scene and provides assistance. The third (or more) rescuer provides assistance at the scene or waits at a common location to direct the emergency team to the scene.

The level of education and training in emergency care of those persons involved with exercise programs varies greatly. No one should do any more than one is trained to do. All recommendations state that *all* personnel involved with exercise training should be certified in BLS. Common sense is a must for any non-emergency or potential life-threatening emergency situation. Any additional skills (i.e., pulse or blood pressure taking, reading monitors, and administering first aid) are, of course, helpful to any situation. When called upon to "assist a physician," your assistance would be of greater value if you:

a. Know the exact time and nature of the emergency.
b. Know all the pertinent information leading up to the emergency situation to be able to provide a history.
c. Have any available data at hand for review (e.g., vital signs or ECG strip).
d. Are able to administer BLS.
e. Are familiar with the contents of an emergency cart/box to give to the physician.
f. Are familiar with the operation of all emergency equipment to set up for use by the physician (i.e., ECG machine or defibrillator).

In summary, the aforementioned guidelines are meant to be models for the many and varied types of exercise facilities and personnel so that they may develop appropriate and specific plans for their individual needs. Outlined examples of emergency plans follow; however, of paramount importance is that each facility have its own structured emergency plan developed in parallel as exercise programs are developed. These written and specific plans must be prepared *in advance* and then included in the orientation and training for all personnel. "An ounce of prevention is worth a pound of cure!"

EXAMPLES OF EMERGENCY PLANS

NON-EMERGENCY SITUATION

The victim complains of angina or not feeling well, has nausea/vomiting, fever, dizziness or shortness of breath during exercise, and exhibits a drop or excessive rise in blood pressure (B/P) during exercise or an excessive rise or a fall in pulse with exercise.

LEVEL: Basic	Intermediate	High
First Rescuer 1. Instruct victim to stop activity. 2. Remain with victim until symptoms subside. a. If symptoms worsen, follow steps of Potential Life-Threatening Emergency. b. If symptoms do not subside, bring victim to the ER/MD office for evaluation. 3. Advise victim to seek medical advice before future activity. *Second Rescuer* 1. Assist rescuer #1, drive victim to ER/MD office if necessary.	*First Rescuer* Same as Basic level #1–3. Add: 4. Take vital signs. 5. Monitor and record rhythm. 6. Bring record of vital signs and strip to ER/MD office if symptoms do not subside and visit is necessary. *Second Rescuer* Same as Basic level #1. Add: 2. Bring B/P cuff, monitor to site. 3. Assist with taking and monitoring vital signs.	*First Rescuer* *In-patient Facility* Same as Intermediate level #1–5. Add: 6. Call for RN if on ward or for RN or MD if in clinic to evaluate. 7. Notify primary MD. 8. Document in record. 9. Request new consult from MD to resume exercise if more than 3 consecutive exercise programs are interrupted for same complaint. *Third Rescuer* Same as Intermediate level #1–3.

POTENTIALLY LIFE-THREATENING SITUATION

Any event in which the victim suddenly loses consciousness (respirations and pulse present), seizure activity, an accident with large blood loss, complains of chest pressure/pain with activity or angina symptoms that are unrelieved by 3 nitroglycerine tablets (TNG). This type of situation *may* lead to a life-threatening emergency if action is not taken immediately.

LEVEL:	Basic	Intermediate	High
	First Rescuer	*First Rescuer*	*First Rescuer*
	1. Establish responsiveness	Same as Basic level #1 and 2.	Same as Intermediate level
	a. Responsive:	Add:	#1–5.
	Instruct victim to sit.	3. Apply monitor to victim and	*Also* may adapt/add:
	Call for help.	record rhythm. Monitor	*In-patient program:*
	Direct rescuer #2 to call	continuously.	1. Call RN on ward.
	EMS.	4. Take vital signs every 1–5 min.	2. Call RN/MD if off ward.
	Stay with victim until EMS	5. Document vital signs and	3. Document in patient record.
	team arrives.	rhythms. Note time and victim	*Outpatient program:*
	Note time of incident.	complaints.	1. Request rescuer #2 to call
	Apply pressure to any		ER.
	bleeding, if necessary.	*Second Rescuer*	2. Bring to ER if in same building.
	Keep victim comfortable.	Same as Basic level #1–3.	3. Notify primary MD as soon
	Note if victim takes any	Add:	as possible.
	medication (i.e., TNG).	4. Bring all emergency equipment	
	Offer reassurance.	and	*Second Rescuer*
	Take pulse.	a. place victim on monitor.	Same as Intermediate level
	b. Unresponsive:	b. run strip.	#1–4.
	Place victim supine.	c. take vital signs.	
	Open airway.		*Third Rescuer*
	Call for help.	*Third Rescuer*	Same as Intermediate level #1
	Check respirations. If	Same as Basic level #1 and 2.	and 2.
	absent, go to Life-		
	threatening section.		
	Maintain open airway.		
	Check pulse. If absent, go		
	to Life-threatening		
	section.		
	Direct rescuer #2 to call		
	EMS.		
	Stay with victim, continue		
	to monitor respiration		
	and pulse.		
	2. Other considerations		
	a. If bleeding, compress area to		
	decrease/stop bleeding.		
	b. Suspected neck fracture:		
	open airway with a jaw-		
	thrust maneuver. Do *not*		
	hyperextend the neck.		
	c. If seizing: prevent injury by		
	removing harmful objects.		
	Place something under the		
	head (if possible). Turn victim		
	on side once seizure activity		
	stops to help drain secretions.		
	Second Rescuer		
	1. Call EMS.		
	2. Wait to direct emergency team		
	to scene or		
	3. Return to scene to assist.		
	Third Rescuer		
	1. Direct emergency team to		
	scene or		
	2. Assist rescuer #1.		

LIFE-THREATENING SITUATION

Any event accompanied by unresponsiveness or absence of respirations and/or pulse.

LEVEL: Basic	Intermediate	High
At a YMCA pool or a park without emergency equipment.	At a gym or other outside facility with basic equipment plus defibrillator and possibly a small "start-up" kit with drugs.	Hospital or hospital-adjunct with all the equipment of Intermediate Level plus a "code cart" containing emergency drugs, equipment for intravenous drug administration, intubation, drawing arterial blood gas samples, and suctioning. Victim may be in-patient or outpatient.

First Rescuer
1. Position victim (pull from pool if necessary) and place supine.
2. Call for help.
3. Open airway; look, listen, and feel for air.
4. Give 2 ventilations if no respirations.
5. Check pulse (carotid artery).
6. Administer 15:2 compression/ventilation ratio if no pulse.
7. Continue ventilation every 5 sec if pulse present.

Second Rescuer
1. Locate nearest phone and call EMS.
2. Return to scene and help with 2-man CPR, or
3. Remain at designated area and direct emergency team to location.

Third Rescuer
1. Assist with 2-man CPR or
2. Help direct emergency team to site.
3. Help clear area.

First Rescuer
Step #1–7 for Basic level.

Second Rescuer
Step #1–3 of Basic level.
Add:
4. Return to scene, bringing defibrillator; take "quick look" at rhythm. Document rhythm [you are *not* to defibrillate a victim unless certified to do so (i.e., ACLS)]
5. Place monitor leads on patient and monitor rhythm during CPR.
6. Bring emergency drug kit if available:
   a. Open oxygen equipment and use Ambu bag with oxygen at 10 L if trained to do so.
   b. Open drug kit and prepare intravenous line and drug administration. (These steps must only be done by trained, licensed professionals.)
   c. Keep equipment at scene for use by emergency personnel.

Third Rescuer:
Same as Basic level.

First Rescuer
In-patient program:
Step #1–7 of Basic level.
Outpatient program:
Step #1–7 of Basic level.

Second Rescuer
In-patient program:
Step #1–6 of Intermediate level.
Outpatient program:
Step #1–6 of Intermediate level.

Third Rescuer
In-patient program:
Step #1–3 of Basic level.
Outpatient program:
Step #1–3 of Basic level.

SELECTED READING

RISK OF EXERCISE

1. Hossack KF, Hartwig R: Cardiac arrest during cardiac rehabilitation. Identification of high risk patients. *Am J Cardiol, 49*:915, 1982.
2. Siscovick DS, Weiss NS, Fletcher RH, Lasky T: The incidence of primary cardiac arrest during vigorous exercise. *N Engl J Med, 311*:974, 1984.

REFERENCE GUIDELINES FOR EXERCISE FACILITIES AND EQUIPMENT

3. Ellestad MH, Blomqvist CG, Naughton JP: Standards for adult exercise testing laboratories. *Circulation, 59*:421A, 1979.
4. Hellerstein HK: Specifications for exercise testing equipment. Circulation Standards and Guidelines for Cardiopulmonary Care and Resuscitation (CPR) and Emergency Cardiac Care (ECC). *JAMA, 255*:2905, 1986.
5. Standards and guidelines for cardiopulmonary resuscitation (CPR) and Emergency Cardiac Care (ECC). *JAMA, 255*:2905, June 6, 1986.

MEDICOLEGAL

6. Alexander J, Holder AR, Wolfson S: Legal implications of exercise testing. *J Cardiovasc Med, 3*:1137, 1978.
7. *Textbook of Advanced Cardiac Life Support.* Dallas, TX, American Heart Association, 1987.

CHAPTER 31

MUSCULOSKELETAL INJURY: RISKS, PREVENTION, AND FIRST AID

BRUCE H. JONES,
PAUL B. ROCK, AND
MICHAEL P. MOORE

Musculoskeletal injury is an inherent risk of any vigorous physical activity, including exercise testing and training. Although the risk of injury can never be completely eliminated, many potential injuries may be prevented by eliminating specific risk factors and using "common sense" during exercising. If injuries occur in spite of preventive measures, early recognition and appropriate treatment can help to limit the extent of the injury and its impact on further activity.

RISK OF INJURY

To prevent injury, risks must be identified and then modified or circumvented. Although much information exists on the treatment of exercise-related injuries, little information is available concerning risk factors, even for common injuries. In a statistical sense, the relative risks are determined by comparing the injury rate (number of individuals injured divided by the total number of injured and uninjured individuals) of groups exposed to a putative risk factor with similar groups that have not been exposed. Most authors purporting to identify risk factors describe "case series" studies in which they report only the number of injured and, therefore, do not permit calculation of injury rates for comparison.

In spite of the lack of information needed for clear documentation of risks associated with various physical activities, factors have been identified that probably constitute risks for injury during exercise. The focus of this section is on the risks of injury associated with aerobic activities such as walking and running, but the general principles and strategies discussed can be applied to all repetitive weight-bearing activities, including such games and sports as tennis and soccer. Management of risks are discussed, but because of our imprecise knowledge of risk factors, only general preventive strategies are outlined.

Extrinsic and intrinsic risk factors for musculoskeletal or "biomechanical" injuries are listed in Table 31–1. Extrinsic risk factors are variables outside the individual (such as environmental factors, terrain features, and equipment); intrinsic factors are inherent characteristics of the individual (age, sex, weight, and percent body fat). Of all the variables associated with exercise, training factors — particularly frequency and duration of exercise — are the most amenable to modification and may be the most important variables to adjust to prevent injury. In untrained individuals, a

Table 31–1. Risk Factors for Musculoskeletal Injuries Associated with Weight-Bearing Physical Training

Extrinsic risk factors
1. Training parameters: increase in intensity, duration, or frequency of training.
2. Equipment (shoes, boots): poor quality, maintenance, or fit.
3. Training surfaces (roads): hard, irregular, and sloping.

Intrinsic risk factors
1. Level of fitness: low level (aerobic and/or strength).
2. Anatomy: malalignment (flat feet, high arches, or bowed legs).
3. Body composition: obesity.
4. Gender: women.
5. Age: elderly.
6. Prior injury: serious injury (torn cartilage, severe sprain).
7. Musculoskeletal disease: arthritis, disc disease, and the like.

frequency of exercise above 3 days per week, and/or durations of greater than 30 min per session are associated with greatly increased rates of injury and minimal gains in aerobic capacity (Table 31–2). Injury rates among distance runners and joggers increase with increasing mileage, even though fewer injuries per mile occur for the high mileage runners. Exercise intensity (level of effort) is undoubtedly also a significant risk factor, but the relationship has not been clearly documented.

No good data are available on the effects of playing surface or terrain on injury rates. Common sense suggests that different surfaces are associated with different risks of injury. For runners, there may be a trade off between the increased shock absorbency of grass or dirt trails and the increased risk of traumatic injuries from the irregularity of these surfaces. Common sense and practicality should dictate the choice of where to exercise.

In regard to footwear, again, no experimental or epidemiologic data are available to demonstrate that any one type of footwear (athletic or running shoe) protects the wearer from injury. We find it difficult to believe, however, that today's better designed shoes are not protective.

One intrinsic factor that may predispose athletes to injury is low fitness level. Evidence to support this conclusion comes from military data, which suggest that men and women who are in the lowest two quartiles of aerobic fitness, as measured by entry level mile-run times, are more likely than their more physically fit counterparts to be injured (2.5 and 1.5 times, respectively). Data such as these suggest that sedentary, relatively "unfit" individuals are more likely to suffer injuries when exposed to routine high intensity (relative to the current fitness level) physical training.

Body composition is thought to increase injury rates because the increased fat relative to lean body mass (muscle and bone) causes greater physiologic and biomechanical stress during weight-bearing exercise. Although the relationship has not been quantified, it seems reasonable that careful structuring of exercise routines would limit the risks of injury for this group. In some instances, non–weight-bearing activities, such as swimming or biking, may be preferable initially. Weight reduction to decrease the fat to lean body ratios may also help prevent injuries. A combination of dieting and exercise is recommended to ensure weight reduction programs are effective (see American College of Sports Medicine Position Statement on Proper and Improper Weight Loss Programs).

Gender has also been implicated as a risk factor for training injuries in women, but the data are not clear. Results of military studies indicate that female recruits engaged in "total fitness" programs similar to those for men seek medical attention for musculoskeletal injuries almost twice as often as male recruits (see Table 31–3). Also, more women than men runners have re-

Table 31–2. Effects of Training Frequency and Duration on Incidence of Injury and Improvement in $\dot{V}O_{2\,max}$ among Previously Sedentary Men*

	Effect of frequency (30 min/session for 20 weeks)			Effect of duration (3 days/wk for 20 weeks)	
Days/week	Injuries (%)	$\dot{V}O_{2\,max}$ (% increase)	Min/day	Injuries (%)	$\dot{V}O_{2\,max}$ (% increase)
1	0	8.3	15	22	8.6
3	12	12.9	30	24	16.1
5	39	17.4	45	54	16.9

* Adapted from Pollock ML, et al.: Effects of frequency and duration of training on attrition and incidence of injury. *Med Sci Sports Exerc*, 9:31–36, 1977.

Table 31-3. Risks of Exercise-Associated Musculoskeletal Injuries by Gender

	"Total fitness"* (Military)	Running† (Civilian)	
Injury Interval	Seen on sick call 8 weeks	Reported only 1 year	Seen by doctor
Female risk	42%	38%	17%
Male risk	23%	37%	13%
Risk ratio	1.8‡	1	1.3

* Adapted from Bensel CK: Lower extremity disorders among men and women in Army Basic Training and effects of two types of boots. US Army Natick Research, Development and Engineering Laboratories, Natick, MA. Tech. Report Natick/tr-83/06, Jan. 1983.
† Adapted from Koplan JP, et al.: An epidemiologic study of the benefits and risks of running. JAMA, 248:3118-3121, 1982.
‡ $p < 0.05$.

quested medical attention for acute musculoskeletal injuries after the Boston Marathon in the last several years. In a recent survey from the Centers for Disease Control, however, overall injury rates were similar for women and men runners (38% per year). Women did seek medical care more frequently than men over a 1-year period, which indicates that women may be more likely than men to seek medical attention for similar conditions or that the injuries that they suffer are more serious. Lower physical fitness levels, higher levels of body fat, and perhaps some anatomic factors may also explain the excess number of injuries among women. Whatever the cause, modulating exercise in accord with the individual's fitness level and body composition should help to minimize any apparent excess risk.

Age is another purported risk factor for injury that has not been documented. Although aerobic capacity and other fitness parameters decrease with increasing age, injury rates do not increase systematically among older exercise participants. Several authors studying medical casualties during marathons have shown just the opposite, i.e., acute musculoskeletal injury rates after these races decrease consistently with increasing age (Table 31-4). These data may reflect judicious pacing and a greater inclination to stop exercise when warning signs are perceived in older individuals. Age is clearly *not* a contraindication to vigorous exercise, although discretion should be used in programming intensity and other training parameters for older individuals.

Among the most frequently cited intrinsic causes of injury are anatomic variants, such as flat feet (pes planus), high arches (pes cavus), and bowed legs (genu varum). Ironically, no clear documentation exists to show any of the conditions confer excess risk; circumstantial evidence that they do, however, is strong. Unless an individual with an anatomic variant is bothered by discomfort or pain, no reason exists to seek medical consultation or to curtail activity for one of these anomalies. In some instances, orthopedic or podiatric interventions, such as orthotics, may be appropriate.

The role of minor injuries in causing other injuries is also not well documented, but the effect is probably small. Clearly, however, serious or severe past injuries (i.e., torn cartilage or ligaments, severely sprained ankles, and fractures) may result in residual structural weaknesses that undoubtedly predispose to re-injury. Common sense and the presence of discomfort should dictate the level and amount of exercise in persons with recent injuries.

As more older individuals begin to exercise, the question of how degenerative joint diseases,

Table 31-4. Percentage Risks of Musculoskeletal (MSK) and Total Casualties for Male (M) and Female (F) Runners

Age	Boston 1984 (M)* [Cool 7°C (45°F)]		Bostonfest 1983 (M)† [Cool 10°C (50°F)]	Scheffield 1982 (M&F)‡ [Warm 24°C (75°F)]	
	% MSK	% Total	% Total	% MSK	% Total
<30	3.4	6.5	16.5	12.4	19.0
30-39	2.4	5.5	10.3	10.3	16.0
>40	1.5	3.5	8.5	9.1	13.0

* Extracted from unpublished data.
† Adapted from Jones BH, et al.: Medical complaints after a cool weather marathon. *Phys Sportsmed, 13:*103-110, 1985.
‡ Adapted from Nicholl JP, Williams BT: Injuries sustained by runners during a popular marathon. *Br J Sports Med, 17:*10-15, 1983.

such as osteoarthritis and rheumatoid arthritis, affect injury rates and exercise tolerance becomes increasingly important. Exercise is not precluded in either of these conditions, although weight-bearing activities may be contraindicated. The prescription of non–weight-bearing exercise for these individuals is perhaps best. Furthermore, individuals with impaired functional activities as a result of these and similar conditions should seek medical advice before initiating an exercise routine.

INJURY PREVENTION STRATEGIES

Although certain intrinsic or extrinsic factors appear to increase the risk of injury during exercise, we still have a very limited understanding of the underlying causal mechanisms. For this reason, devising precise preventive measures for specific injuries is difficult. A general preventive strategy aimed at broad categories of risk and a variety of injuries must therefore suffice. This strategy includes individualized exercise programs based on fitness and risk assessment; monitoring for signs of impending injury; appropriate use of warm-up, stretching, and cool-down periods; and use of proper equipment.

INDIVIDUALIZATION OF EXERCISE

Risk factors must be taken into account in tailoring an exercise program. The type of exercise and its intensity, duration, and frequency must all be considered along with the person's exercise goals and ability to tolerate both physiologic and biomechanical stress.

Special care is needed for very sedentary or obese individuals. Prudence dictates that initial training in particular should be of low intensity and duration to give both the cardiovascular and musculoskeletal systems time to accommodate to the new stresses of exercise (see Chapter 3 in *Guidelines for Exercise Testing and Prescription*). For individuals with limiting mechanical risk factors (i.e., anatomic malalignment, injury, arthritis, or obesity), a wise recommendation may be non–weight-bearing physical activities such as swimming or biking.

WARNING SIGNS

Exercising individuals should routinely monitor themselves for signs of impending injury.

Fatigue and lack of enthusiasm for training are frequently indicators that exercise has been too intense or that rest and recovery have been inadequate. The remedy is increased rest and decreased intensity of training.

Pain is another important warning sign, and usually indicates that a body part is overstressed. Pain that develops precipitously and is severe, or that gradually but consistently increases on successive days, should be heeded and training should be curtailed until the pain improves or abates. Also, discomfort accompanied by changes in function (e.g., limping gait) requires modification of the exercise program. Individuals with recent severe injuries, musculoskeletal disease, or clear anatomic malalignment should pay particular attention to these warning signs.

WARM-UP, STRETCHING, AND COOL-DOWN

Although clear-cut evidence of its efficacy is lacking, warming up is recommended as a means of preventing injury and increasing performance. Current opinion is that the warm-up should involve the major muscle groups used in the physical activity. The warm-up should increase gradually in intensity to levels near that of the proposed work-out. Five to ten minutes of steady-state exercise are usually required to raise muscle temperature to optimal levels. At the end of the 5 or 10 min of initial warm-up (walking or slow running), another 5 to 10 min of calisthenics may be beneficial.

Non-ballistic (non-bouncing) stretching exercise are also recommended, even though their efficacy has also not been proven. For individuals performing weight-bearing activity, the focus of this stretching should be the lower back, hamstrings (posterior thigh), and the calf muscles of the leg (gastroc-soleus complex). A textbook or training manual for the particular sport of interest should be consulted for specific stretching routines.

The cool-down, like the warm-up, is thought to be beneficial in preventing injuries. This phase should allow gradual cooling of the major muscle groups involved in prior exercise. This cooling allows the blood vessels to contract gradually, decreasing the likelihood of fainting as a result of blood pooling in the leg muscles when exercise suddenly stops. The cool-down, coupled with gentle stretching, is also thought to help decrease post-exercise muscle soreness and stiffness.

EQUIPMENT

The most important piece of equipment for weight-bearing activities (walking, running, tennis, and soccer) is a good shoe. Shoes are now specifically designed and engineered for particular sports, with the goal of improving performance and preventing injuries. Footwear is particularly important for running, because each foot may impact with the pavement 1000 times per mile. According to current thinking, a good running shoe should have a durable, flexible, and shock-absorbent sole; an elevated, stable heel counter; and a comfortable insole. Most importantly, the shoe should fit the individual's foot (see article by Bates concerning the choice of a good shoe). Maintenance of shoes is also important in injury prevention. Wearing shoes with excessive wear on the outside or inside of the heels is comparable to having an anatomic defect of the foot. Badly worn shoes should be replaced.

ACUTE AND CHRONIC INJURIES

Exercise-induced injuries can be broadly classified as either acute (traumatic) or chronic ("overuse") injuries. Acute injuries result when ligaments, bones, or muscle-tendon units are subjected to an abrupt force that exceeds their stress-strain threshold or yield point. Forces that exceed that yield point cause mechanical deformation of the structure resulting in failure and injury. Acute injuries usually result from single violent events such as twisting an ankle in a pot hole or breaking a bone in a collision between two soccer players.

Overuse injuries result from small repetitive overload forces on the structural (bones, ligaments, and tendons) and force-generating (muscles) elements of the body. With weight-bearing activities like running, microtraumatic events that slightly exceed the body's ability to repair itself accumulate foot-step after foot-step, mile after mile. Eventually, the accumulation of these slight insults results in a noticeable injury. Because overloading of not only the cardiovascular but also the musculoskeletal system is necessary to achieve a training effect, these injuries are bound to occur to some extent with any exercise program. Most overuse injuries to the musculoskeletal system are soft-tissue injuries.

ACUTE INJURIES

The two most common traumatic injuries encountered in the exercise setting are sprains (ligament) and strains (muscle).

Sprains

Injuries to ligaments are termed "sprains." Ligaments are fibrous connective tissue that connect bones or cartilage providing support and strength to joints. Sprains are conventionally classified into three categories — first, second, and third degree — depending on the severity of ligament tearing. First-degree sprains result from minimal tearing of the ligament and are characterized by microfailure of collagen fibers within the ligament. No associated joint instability results and pain and swelling are minimal. Second-degree sprains are more severe, with partial tearing of the ligament and possibly the joint capsule. Second-degree sprains may be associated with varying degrees of joint instability, although instability may not be apparent if muscle spasm occurs. Damage to the collagen fiber is substantial, and loss of strength of the ligament is considerable with second-degree sprains. These injuries are characterized by severe pain and marked swelling. A second-degree sprain that is inadequately treated may result in further injury or complete tearing of the ligament.

Third-degree sprains result from a complete tear of the ligament. These injuries are characterized by severe pain at the time of injury and obvious joint instability. Injuries of this severity often require surgical reconstruction and stabilization.

Strains

Strains are commonly referred to as "muscle pulls" and generally result from stretching or tearing of muscle. They are classified by the severity of muscle damage and resulting loss of function. First-degree strains produce only mild signs and symptoms, with minimal local pain that increases with passive stretch or vigorous contraction of the injured muscle. Often with mild strains, only a sensation of muscle tightness with activity is present. Second-degree strain is a more severe injury, with partial tearing of the injured muscle. Pain is substantial and loss of function is considerable. With second-degree strains, varying degrees of hemorrhage and discoloration from bruising are noted. Third-degree muscle strains cause marked muscle disruption and possible avulsion of the muscle-tendon unit. These injuries may require surgical intervention and should be promptly evaluated by an orthopedic surgeon.

Muscle strains are common injuries, particularly in the lower extremities; the hamstring musculature and the calf muscles are the groups most often injured. Most strains of the lower extremity are mild to moderately severe but may require as many as 3 weeks for recovery. More severe muscle strains may require several months to heal. Muscle strains often recur, particularly if rehabilitation was inadequate, because the inelastic scar tissue that forms at the site of injury impairs flexibility. For this reason, both flexibility and strength of the injured muscle are perhaps best restored to near normal function before the return to previous levels of activity.

Other Acute Injuries

More serious, but less frequent acute injuries include fractures (broken bones) and dislocations (separation of joints). These injuries result in severe pain, swelling, and weakness. Suspected fractures should be immobilized (splinted) to prevent both further separation of bone fragments and damage to blood vessels and nerves. Dislocated joints should also be immobilized. Individuals with these ailments should then be transported immediately to a hospital for evaluation and treatment.

OVERUSE AND CHRONIC INJURIES

Overuse injuries can affect the bursae (bursitis), tendons (tendinitis and tenosynovitis), muscles (strains), ligaments (sprains), and bones (stress fractures).

Bursitis

Bursitis is the presence of inflammation of a known bursa. A bursa is a fluid-filled sac that functions to reduce friction between adjacent tissues, it is located where muscle or tendon passes over a bony prominence. The key symptoms of bursitis are pain and limitation of motion. Signs of bursitis include point tenderness over the bursa, swelling, and limited motion. Occasionally, an inflamed bursa appears red

(erythematous) and warm. Bursitis usually results from acute and/or chronic mechanical irritations or trauma, although acute septic bursitis, which requires antibiotic therapy, should also be considered. Treatment of bursitis consists of rest, ice application, and anti-inflammatory medication.

Tendinitis

Tendinitis is the painful inflammation of a tendon. This condition may be acute or chronic and results from repetitive stress of forceful muscle contractions, which leads to overload of the tendon and "mechanical fatigue" with micro-tears (microfailure). Excessively violent force may cause a complete tear or rupture of the tendon. Overload of tendons is greater with eccentric (lengthening) muscle contractions, such as occurs while running downhill or lowering a weight, than with concentric contractions (shortening).

Force overload is believed to be a major etiologic factor in the development of such conditions as achilles tendinitis, tennis elbow (lateral epicondylitis), rotator cuff tendinitis, and jumper's knee (patellar tendinitis). Tendinitis may be classified by the presence or absence of activity-related pain and its severity. In the initial stage, the primary complaint is pain. Repeated stress results in progressive inflammation, which is characterized by mild pain before activity that improves with exercise and frequently reappears after activity. This stage is characterized by varying degrees of point tenderness of the tendon at the site of injury and pain with passive stretching. Progressive inflammation results in continuous activity pain, which heralds more serious pathologic changes in the tendon. If recovery does not occur, pain frequently prohibits the individual from participation in exercise or sports. This degree of inflammation is characterized by swelling, point tenderness, and considerable pain with stretching of the tendon. Treatment consists of rest, ice massage of the tendon, and anti-inflammatory medication. The goal of treatment is pain-free activity and restored flexibility.

Patellofemoral Syndrome

A frequently encountered overuse injury is knee pain. The most common cause of overuse knee pain is the patellofemoral pain syndrome, which affects, in particular, those individuals participating in running programs ("runner's knee"). The term chondromalacia is often inappropriately used to describe overuse knee pain. Chondromalacia rather literally means "soft cartilage" and specifically describes the pathologic state and appearance of deteriorating cartilage.

The etiology of patellofemoral syndrome is complex, but is thought to be related to abnormal patellofemoral (thigh-knee) mechanics. Multiple biomechanical factors have been described as predisposing to this injury. Among the most common are femoral ante-version, "squinting" patella, shallow femoral groove, and excessive Q-angle. The amount of exercise, however, may be of greater importance. The syndrome is often associated with abrupt increases in training mileage and/or intensity of running; hill running is often cited as an exacerbatory factor. The lay term "runner's knee" is testament to the role of exercise in its development.

The primary symptom of patellofermoral syndrome is pain that is noted in the region below or around the patella and increases with activity. Activities such as running downhill, ascending-descending stairs, and prolonged sitting with the knee flexed typically intensify the symptoms. Frequently, the individual complains of instability or of the knee "giving way." A sensation of grating behind the knee cap also may be associated with this syndrome, as well as pain noted with compression of the knee cap. Treatment for this syndrome consists of rest, ice, and anti-inflammatory medications.

Sprains and Strains

Although many sprains and strains are acute injuries, they may also result from or be aggravated by overuse. These injuries therefore may be classified as chronic injuries. Whatever the cause, the symptoms are the same as those noted for acute traumatic sprains and strains, except that the symptoms are generally milder. The treatment of these injuries is also the same.

Stress Fractures

Most stress fractures occur in the lower extremities (tibia of the leg and metatarsals of the foot) and do so in two successive stages in response to repetitive overloading of bones during activities such as running, walking, or marching. The first stage is a normal physiologic response called "remodeling," in which the body attempts to strengthen stressed bone by removal of old bone and the laying down of new bone. This response is called a stress reaction if it is excessive and can be documented with bone scans and occasionally with radiography. If the stress of weight-bearing continues, the repair process may actually weaken the bone if more old bone is removed than new bone is laid down. The weakened bone is more susceptible to mechanical failure and the second stage occurs when the weakened bone fractures. Because of the potentially serious consequences of stress reactions of bone, any individual with aching "bone" pain associated with exercise that does not abate in a few days or worsens should be evaluated by an appropriate medical practitioner.

Lower Back Injuries

A complete discussion of lower back injuries is beyond the scope of this book. Low back pain is such a common symptom of injury, however, either associated with or exacerbated by exercise, that a few generalities about the causes, treatment, and prevention of back injuries merit mention.

Low back pain as a result of musculoskeletal injury may be a symptom of damage to the bony structural elements of the spine (vertebrae), the shock-absorbing discs between the vertebrae, the ligaments connecting vertebrae, or the supportive musculature of the back and abdomen. These injuries include vertebral fractures and stress fractures, ruptured discs, torn or sprained ligaments, and muscle strains or spasms. Unless neurologic symptoms accompany the low back pain, differentiating between serious causes of discomfort, such as a ruptured disc and less serious ones such as muscle strains, may be difficult. If symptoms of neurologic involvement such as pain radiating into the buttocks or down one or both legs, numbness or tingling of the legs, or weakness occur, a physician should be consulted. Chronic back pain of unknown origin or severe pain are other reasons to consult a physician.

The most common causes of low back pain are sprains or strains of the soft tissues connecting and supporting elements of the vertebral column. Initial treatment for these consists of rest, ice application, and pain-relieving and anti-inflammatory medication, such as aspirin. A few days of bed rest may also be beneficial, although longer periods of complete rest may be counterproductive.

Flexibility and strengthening exercises are also frequently prescribed for both rehabilitation and prevention of lower back injuries. No one set of exercises has proven efficiency, however, and what specific exercises should be done is still the subject of some debate. The best strategy for preventing strains and sprains of the back is probably a general overall conditioning program that includes some non-ballistic exercises to stretch the back muscles, hamstrings, and hip muscles, and calisthenics designed specifically to strengthen not only the back but also the abdomen. Exercises that involve excessive flexion or rotational motions should be avoided, especially by individuals over the age of 40 years.

INFLAMMATION

A basic understanding of inflammation is essential to ensure proper treatment of musculoskeletal injuries, because inflammation underlies most musculoskeletal injuries. Inflammation is the result of a complex series of physiologic reactions to injury. The initial swelling or edema associated with injury results from bleeding and leakage of plasma fluid from the capillaries supplying the injured area. Oozing of fluid from capillaries results from the release of biochemical substances that cause increased vascular permeability. Direct trauma may cause tearing of small blood vessels with resultant hemorrhage or bruising. White blood cells are attracted to the site by chemical substances released by damaged tissues. They function to clean up debris from the injury, but their digestive enzymes (lysozymes) may leak into the area, damaging healthy tissues and contributing to a self-perpetuating cycle of chronic inflammation unless appropriate interventions are initiated.

The end result of the inflammatory process is the classic set of signs and symptoms of musculoskeletal inflammation—swelling, redness, loss of function, warmth, and pain. These signs and symptoms vary depending on the severity of the injury and whether it is acute or chronic in nature. Excessive and persistent swelling

from inflammation impairs the healing response. Swelling and bleeding also cause pain by mechanical stimulation of free nerve endings. In an attempt to splint (protect) the injured area, secondary muscle spasm may occur, which further aggravates the pain from other causes. Thus, a major goal of initial treatment of musculoskeletal injuries is to minimize swelling and edema, which also ameliorates other associated symptoms.

FIRST AID FOR BIOMECHANICAL INJURIES

The purpose of initial treatment of exercise-related injuries is to decrease pain, to limit swelling and excessive inflammation that might retard healing, and to prevent further injury. In the setting of acute injuries, these objectives may be accomplished by a combination of rest, ice application, compression, and elevation of the injured part. The acronym "RICE" is used to refer to this treatment protocol (R-rest, I-ice, C-compression, E-elevation). Chronic injuries may require additional forms of treatment, including physical therapy techniques. The use of anti-inflammatory medication may be helpful for persons with chronic or acute injuries.

REST

Severe injuries may require not only immediate rest to prevent further injury but also several days to weeks of complete rest for healing. For mild acute and chronic conditions, rest may be relative, requiring only a decrease in the intensity, duration, and frequency of exercise. Normal exercise may be resumed when pain-free activity is possible.

ICE (CRYOTHERAPY)

Ice is applied to reduce swelling, bleeding, inflammation, and pain. Cold causes local constriction of blood vessels, which limits bleeding and escape of fluid into the area. It also decreases pain by reducing nerve conduction velocity and reduces muscle spasm.

Cold may be applied in the form of ice packs, gel packs, or chemical cold packs. Ice in plastic bags is probably the simplest way to apply cold. Crushed or chipped ice in plastic bags wrapped with an elastic bandage conforms to the contour of the injured part better than ice cubes. Gel packs also conform well to injured areas when wrapped with an elastic pressure bandage, but they lose their cooling properties rapidly. Gel packs must not come in direct contact with the skin because they may be much colder than ice and can cause frostbite. Chemical cold packs are expensive and are not reusable. Some injuries, especially those to the hands or feet, may be treated by immersing the area in a water bath made cold by adding ice to cold water until a temperature of 13 to 18°C (55 to 65°F) is reached. For chronic injuries, ice massage with chunks of ice or ice frozen in paper cups is an effective way to apply cold.

Cold therapy is especially crucial in the first 24 to 48 hours after acute injuries. This therapy is also helpful in limiting the inflammatory process in chronic injuries, particularly when daily activities reaggravate the injury routinely. Cold should be applied for only 20 to 30 min at a time; otherwise, reflex vascular dilatation may result in increased swelling and bleeding. Acute cold can be applied for 20 to 30 min each hour for the first several hours, but later two applications per day is optimal. Cold therapy should not be used for individuals with peripheral circulatory problems or cold hypersensitivity, such as Raynaud's syndrome.

COMPRESSION

Compression also helps to reduce swelling and bleeding and is achieved by using elastic wraps and sleeves. Compression and ice may be applied simultaneously by wrapping an ice pack within an elastic bandage over the injured area.

ELEVATION

Elevation of the injured part decreases blood flow and blood pressure to the injured area, and allows gravity to assist drainage from the area, thus decreasing swelling. For treatment to be effective, an injured extremity should be raised above the level of the heart and placed on a comfortable padded surface.

HEAT

Heat, a popular means for treatment, has a limited role in treating musculoskeletol injuries. Heat should not be used for acute injuries. Heat is most beneficial for relief of muscle and joint stiffness after the acute period (first 24 to 48 hours) of injury. Furthermore, heat should not be applied when swelling and bleeding persist, and it may aggravate some inflammatory conditions.

ANTI-INFLAMMATORY MEDICATIONS

Anti-inflammatory medications are useful adjuncts to the treatment of acute and chronic exercise related-injuries. These medications are best for relief of such chronic inflammatory conditions as tendinitis and bursitis, but they are also good pain relievers. Because aspirin-like compounds decrease the ability of blood to form clots, their use is discouraged for acute injuries while bleeding persists (first 24 hours). Anti-inflammatory medications may cause heartburn (gastritis) and bleeding of the gastrointestinal tract in some individuals, so they should always be taken with meals or snacks. As an aside, acetaminophen is a good pain reliever, but it lacks the anti-inflammatory properties of such drugs as aspirin.

Most training injuries result from inappropriate intensity, duration, or frequency of activity for the existing intrinsic condition of the participant or the extrinsic environmental conditions. The use of good judgment and moderation may be sufficient to prevent most exercise-related injuries. Training routines should be based on an objective assessment of the individual's physical fitness level and other susceptibility (risk) factors. Periodic re-evaluation of training is warranted, especially if warning signs of injury such as pain, dysfunction, or decreased performance occur. If these measures fail to prevent injury, first aid should be instituted promptly. Finally, medical attention should be sought whenever the extent of injury is sufficiently severe or if the need for professional medical intervention is uncertain.

REFERENCES

ARTICLES

1. American College of Sports Medicine: Position statement on the Recommended Quantity and Quality of Exercise for Developing and Maintaining Fitness in Healthy Adults. *Med Sci Sports Exerc, 10:*VII–IX 1978.
2. American College of Sports Medicine: Position state-

ment on the Proper and Improper Weight Loss Programs. *Med Sci Sports Exerc, 15:*IX–XIII, 1983.

3. American College of Sports Medicine: Position statement on the Participation of the Female Athlete in Long Distance Running. *Med Sci Sports Exerc, 11:*IX–XI, 1979.

4. Bates WT: Selecting a running shoe. *Phys Sportsmed, 10:*154–155, 1982.

5. Brody DM: Running injuries. *Ciba Found Symp, 32:*2–36, 1980.

6. Koplan JP, et al.: An epidemiologic study of the benefits and risks of running. *JAMA, 248:*3118, 1982.

7. Powell KE, Kohl HW, Caspersen CJ, Blair SN: An epidemiologic perspective on the causes of running injuries. *Phys Sportsmed, 14:*100–114, 1986.

BOOKS

1. Brooks GA, Fahey TD: *Exercise Physiology: Human Bioenergetics and Its Applications.* New York: John Wiley & Sons, 1984.

2. Ellison AE (ed): *Athletic Training and Sportsmedicine.* Chicago: American Academy of Orthopedic Surgeons, 1984.

3. McArdle WD, Katch FI, Katch VL: Exercise Physiology: Energy, Nutrition, and Human Performance. 2nd Ed. Philadelphia: Lea & Febiger, 1986.

4. Pollock ML, Wilmore JH, Fox SM: *Exercise in Health and Disease.* Philadelphia: WB Saunders, 1984.

HUMAN DEVELOPMENT AND AGING

32

PHYSIOLOGIC CHANGES OVER THE YEARS

ROY J. SHEPHARD

In considering physiologic changes over the years, we consider normal physiologic changes in heart rate, maximal oxygen intake ($\dot{V}o_{2\,max}$), skeletal muscles, bones, flexibility, and overall body composition. We then examine orthopedic problems in relation to age, and finally this discussion includes the effects of acute and chronic exercise, smoking and substance abuse, and pathologic changes and conditions such as hypertension and obesity. Our aim is to cover the broad spectrum of growth and aging from the toddler through the adolescent to middle and old age, while recognizing that much of the available information pertains to changes in young adults.

NORMAL PHYSIOLOGIC CHANGES

HEART RATE

Age-related changes in resting and maximal heart rate are important when prescribing exercise, when conducting a maximal effort test, and when attempting a prediction of maximal oxygen intake from submaximal data. In a child, a heart rate of 170 beats/min, as developed in the PWC_{170} test, corresponds to about 80% of maximal aerobic power. By the age of 65

years, however, this value is the maximal heart rate.

The child has what has been described as a hypokinetic circulation, with a small stroke volume in relation to size.[1] In part because of this disparity and in part because of a high resting metabolism and some anxiety exhibited during evaluation, the resting heart rate of a young child is often quite high (typically 80 beats/min, and sometimes as high as 100 beats/min). The resting heart rate of the adult depends greatly upon the individual's physical condition. In well-trained subjects with a large stroke volume, rates as low as 26 beats/min have been described. Usually, some loss of condition occurs with aging, and the resting heart rate may thus increase by a small amount over the adult span. In many older people, this tendency is exacerbated by a decrease in stroke volume, which seems associated with coronary vascular narrowing and becomes particularly evident at higher work rates (when oxygen supply is no longer meeting cardiac demand).[2]

The maximal heart rate is usually quoted as $220 - \text{age (years)}$. In young children, some authors have seen maximal values of 210 to 215 beats/min, but 195 to 200 beats/min is a more common finding. The lower maxima may reflect difficulty in motivating the young child to sustain anaerobic effort. A maximum of 195 beats/min is typical of a 25-year-old adult, but at age 65 years, the estimate of 155 beats/min obtained from the classic formula is too low, particularly during treadmill exercise when the true maximum seems to be at least 170 beats/min.[3] The main reason for the decrease in maximal rate with aging is increased "stiffness" of the ventricular walls and slowing of ventricular filling.

Exercise prescription assumes a linear relationship between heart rate and oxygen consumption. In the young adult, this relationship has been demonstrated between 50 and 100% of maximal oxygen intake, $\dot{V}O_{2\,max}$ (from 128 to 195 beats/min in men and from 135 to 198 beats/min in women). What heart rate corresponds to 50% of $\dot{V}O_{2\,max}$ in an older subject, is less clear, however, or indeed, whether the linear relationship continues to apply. Although the child and the young adult maintain a fairly constant stroke volume between 50 and 100% of $\dot{V}O_{2\,max}$, the stroke volume of an older person tends to decrease as maximal effort is approached.[4] Thus, the heart rate comes closer to its maximal value at any given fraction of the $\dot{V}O_{2\,max}$. The situation in an ever increasing proportion of elderly individuals is further complicated by the administration of beta-blocking drugs. These drugs are prescribed to treat hypertension and various arrhythmias, and for the prophylaxis of arrhythmia in "post-coronary" patients. Such agents greatly limit the normal exercise-induced increase of heart rate. Occasionally, a "post-coronary" patient may also develop a "sick-sinus syndrome," in which ischemia or secondary fibrosis of the sinus region restricts the normal exercise-induced increase of heart rate.

MAXIMAL OXYGEN INTAKE ($\dot{V}O_{2\,max}$)

The most appropriate method of expressing $\dot{V}O_{2\,max}$ at various ages has been the topic of much discussion.[5] In the growing child, theoretic arguments favor relating $\dot{V}O_{2\,max}$ to the square of standing height.[6] This type of standard would be difficult to apply in an older person, however, for whom height is progressively decreased by: (1) kyphosis; (2) compression of intervertebral discs; and (3) sometimes frank vertebral collapse. One widely used alternative is to relate the number of milliliters of O_2 transported per minute to body mass. The same units can then be applied at various ages. The

relative aerobic power (ml $\cdot$ kg^{-1} $\cdot$ min^{-1}) is an appropriate method of gauging the ability to perform most types of aerobic exercise, because the energy cost of most forms of movement is also roughly proportional to body mass. Weight-supported exercises (on chairs or in the pool), however, are popular among the elderly population, and in such circumstances the absolute aerobic power becomes a more appropriate index of condition than of the relative figure. Notice that a low relative $\dot{V}O_{2\,max}$ may reflect poor oxygen transport or excessive accumulation of body fat.

The ideal measuring device for a very young child is an adaptation of a toy such as a pedal car. From age 6 or 7 years through to old age, however, the $\dot{V}O_{2\,max}$ is best determined by progressive uphill treadmill exercise.[5] The young child is liable to stumble, and a safety harness is then desirable. Beyond the age of 50 to 60 years, problems may be encountered with unstable knee joints. The subject may then rest the hands lightly on the supporting rail, and walking becomes a preferable form of exercise to running. The cycle ergometer places a heavy load on a single muscle group (the quadriceps), and perhaps for this reason as many as 50% of children fail to reach a plateau of oxygen consumption during this type of exercise. The cycle ergometer has some attraction as a safe means of evaluating an older person with unstable knees, but the net mechanical efficiency of operation of the ergometer (the work performed per unit of oxygen intake) drops from around 23% in a young adult to about 21.5% in a 65-year-old adult. This effect of aging must be noted if the oxygen consumption is not measured but is estimated from the work performed (for example, when using the work scale of the Astrand nomogram) to predict $\dot{V}O_{2\,max}$.

Because of changes in mechanical efficiency as well as substantial interindividual variations in the decrease of maximal heart rate with age, the prediction of $\dot{V}O_{2\,max}$ values by using submaximal tests becomes increasingly difficult as a person ages. Both in children and in older adults, a low efficiency of running also limits the possibility of gauging condition from the distance run in 12 min.[7]

The relative $\dot{V}O_{2\,max}$ value of a fit male subject is fairly constant from young childhood to early adult life—about 50 ml $\cdot$ kg^{-1} $\cdot$ min^{-1}. In those persons selected and trained for endurance sports, figures of 80 to 85 ml $\cdot$ kg^{-1} $\cdot$ min^{-1} are possible. In sedentary and somewhat obese subjects, oxygen transport can drop to 40 ml $\cdot$ kg^{-1} $\cdot$ min^{-1} or lower. Typically, a loss of 5 ml $\cdot$ kg^{-1} $\cdot$ min^{-1} occurs per decade from age 25 to 65 years; however, how much of this loss is inevitable and how much must be attributed to a reduction of habitual activity or to subclinical disease of the myocardium is unclear. After the age of 65 years, the rate of functional loss is thought to accelerate, although the subjects studied in this age range are few and are highly selected.

In theory, no apparent reason exists why the relative $\dot{V}o_{2\,max}$ value of a young girl should not match that of a boy, although in practice (probably because of social conditioning to a less active lifestyle), figures of 40 to 45 ml $\cdot$ kg^{-1} $\cdot$ min^{-1} are usually observed in female subjects. As an adolescent and a young adult, the relative aerobic power of the female subject is further restricted by a high percentage of body fat and a low hemoglobin level. Values for female subjects are typically in the range of 35 to 40 ml $\cdot$ kg^{-1} $\cdot$ min^{-1} from adolescence through about 35 years of age. A steady decline, to about 25 ml $\cdot$ kg^{-1} $\cdot$ min^{-1}, occurs at the age of 65 years, with an accelerating loss of function thereafter.[7]

SKELETAL MUSCLES

The relative proportions of slow- and fast-twitch fibers are apparently determined at birth (although vigorous endurance training can cause some conversion of fast glycolytic to fast oxidative and glycolytic fibers). The number of muscle fibers is also fixed at an early age, although considerable enlargement of muscles remains possible by fiber splitting and hypertrophy of existing fibers.

As with $\dot{V}o_{2\,max}$, some authors argue that muscle strength should be related to the square of stature.[6] In practice, however, growth is more closely related to the third power of height;[8] because often the force must be used to displace body mass, standardization of results for the growing child per kilogram of body mass is more convenient. In male subjects, rapid hypertrophy of muscle occurs coincident with the adolescent growth spurt, with a parallel increase in the maximum of absolute muscle force. Maximal levels of both muscle tissue quantity and strength are reached in the early twenties. A plateau of strength is maintained until about 40 to 45 years of age, thereafter

followed by an accelerating loss of lean tissue and an associated decrease in strength.[7] By the age of 65 years, most muscle groups show an 18 to 20% loss of maximal force. Again, how much of this loss is an inevitable consequence of aging and how much is a reflection of a decrease in habitual activity with advancing years is unclear.

Girls do not show any disproportionate development of their muscles at puberty. Thus, although the strength of a young girl is similar to that of a boy, the young woman has only about 60% of the strength of her male counterpart.[9] The discrepancy by gender in maximal force is greater for the arms than for the legs. About one half of the difference seems attributable to the shorter stature of women. Of the difference, one part probably reflects a lesser secretion of androgens in the female subject and another part is an expression of sex differences in patterns of habitual activity. The adult woman also tends to a plateau of strength between 20 and 45 years, followed by an accelerating decline of function in later life. At all ages, however, women seem somewhat more vulnerable to loss of lean tissue than are men. With any tendency toward anorexia, muscle weakness may appear in adolescence or in early adult life.

The anaerobic power, as measured by a staircase sprint (Margaria test) or 5 sec of all-out cycle ergometer exercise (Bar-Or test), deteriorates substantially during adult life (45 to 60% decrease between 25 and 65 years). Part of this loss is attributable to the decreased mass of lean tissue, and part to a selective loss of fast-twitch (type II) muscle fibers.[10] Other important factors are decreased coordination of the muscle contraction, decreased motivation, decreased efficiency of movement, and (in the case of the staircase sprint) fear of stumbling. The peak anaerobic capacity of the young adult corresponds to a blood lactate level of 10 to 11 mmol/L. In a child of either sex, the peak blood lactate concentration is 8 to 9 mmol/L. Some authors attributed this difference in tolerance of anaerobic effort to a deficiency of glycolytic enzymes, such as phosphofructokinase, in the muscles of a growing child.[11] A second, important consideration, however, is a smaller ratio of muscle mass to total blood volume. The latter factor also affects the performance of a 65-year-old person; at this age, blood lactate levels rarely exceed 8 to 9 mmol/L after an all-out test, even if the individual concerned is well motivated.

BONES

In the child, because the long bones are still growing, the epiphyses are not yet united with the shafts. Two practical problems result: (1) a traction epiphysitis may develop through over use, for example, at the medial epicondyle of the humerus (baseball thrower's elbow), less commonly at the upper epiphyseal plate of the humerus (baseball shoulder), or at the tibial tubercle in young jumpers; and (2) fractures developed during contact sports may pass through the epiphyseal plate, leading to a disruption in normal growth.[12]

The dangers of osteoporosis are gaining increasing recognition.[13] The amenorrheic female adolescent may already be at some risk, but the calcium content of the bones begins to diminish progressively in most women, beginning between 20 and 30 years of age. The rate of calcium loss becomes more rapid after menopause, but it can be checked if not reversed by a program of progressive weight-bearing exercise. In men, the process usually begins somewhat later and develops less rapidly. Toward the end of a working career, however, sufficient calcium loss has occurred to increase vulnerability to fractures.

Damage to and degeneration of the articular cartilages causes a progressive increase in the incidence of osteoarthritis with aging. By 50 to 60 years of age, radiographs of the spine show characteristic lesions in 70 to 80% of subjects, although only a small proportion of individuals (15 to 20%) complain of specific symptoms.[14] Because of degenerative changes in the knee, hip, and spine, walking or water-supported exercises are often a more appropriate prescription for the elderly than jogging. A fast walk can develop the same energy expenditure as a slow jog, while exposing the knee joint to only one third the amount of impact stress.

FLEXIBILITY

Collagen, which provides the structural basis of tendons, undergoes progressive degeneration with advancing age. A cross-linkage develops between individual fibers, reducing flexibility and increasing the liability to injury if excessive force is applied.[15] The extent of the functional loss has been studied most fully for flexion of the hips and spine, as measured by the Dillon sit-and-reach test. About a 20% decrease in the range of movement on this test

occurs between the ages of 25 and 65 years. The rate of deterioration probably accelerates beyond the age of 65 years, the process being exacerbated by other structural changes, including ankylosis of fibrocartilaginous joints and osteoarthritis.

An important fact to note is that the relationship between flexibility and function is not linear, but rather shows important discontinuities when the range of movement is no longer adequate to allow the performance of specific tasks, such as climbing into or out of a bath. Likewise, if a small increase in the range of movement can be developed by an appropriate training regimen, a large gain in the quality of life may result.

BODY COMPOSITION

Although many methods for the analysis of body composition have assumed a two compartment model (fat and lean tissue), in reality the overall body density depends on both the relative amounts and the respective densities of three body components: fat, bone, and other lean tissue (especially muscle).

In young children, the amount of fat is fairly small (10 to 15%), although (probably for cultural reasons) even prepubertal girls carry slightly more fat than boys of the same age. In boys, some increase in percentage of body fat occurs with the decreasing activity of adolescence; a figure of 15 to 20% is typical by the age of 20 to 30 years. A further accumulation of 5 to 10 kg of fat is common by middle age (40 to 49 years), bringing the percentage of fat to 25 to 30%. Body mass begins to decline again by the final decade of working life (55 to 65 years), but this decrease reflects a loss of lean tissue rather than a decrease of body fat.[7] In girls, the effects of decreasing physical activity are supplemented by an accumulation of fat in the breasts and around the hips at puberty, so that a figure of 20 to 25% body fat is typical of adolescence and early adult life. A further build-up of adipose tissue after menopause brings many older women to a figure of 30 to 35% body fat.

Changes in lean tissue (other than bone) usually reflect the course of muscular strength, the boys showing a large increase of muscle protein at puberty and both sexes progressively losing muscle after age 40 to 45 years. The loss of bone mass in men is about 10% at age 65 years, and is about 20% by the age of 80 years. In women, the loss averages about 20% by 65 years of age and 30% by the age of 80 years.

These various alterations of body composition complicate the assessment process. A gain of body mass over the course of the adult life (in the absence of specific training) generally reflects an accumulation of fat, but a loss of mass may be attributable to fat, muscle, or bone. The relationship between skinfold readings and body density changes with age, in part because the skin component of the fold (4 mm in a young adult) becomes thinner with aging, and in part because the density of the lean tissue compartment decreases with bone loss. Even underwater weighing, widely regarded as the "gold standard" of body composition determinations, has only limited validity, because the two-component models that are used fail to accommodate interindividual differences in the density of lean tissue.

Attempts to assess lean body mass from percentage body fat and body mass determinations are even less satisfactory. Estimates of lean tissue based on body water or ^{40}K are complicated by age-related changes in the water and mineral content of the cells; if an accurate measure of body protein or bone calcium levels is required, the recourse is neutron activation and whole-body counter technology. Although safe and accurate, such procedures are expensive and are still available only in major hospitals.[16]

ORTHOPEDIC PROBLEMS IN RELATION TO AGE

Orthopedic problems can arise from excessive exercise at any age. In the growing child, the most frequent problem is inflammation of the epiphyseal regions through repeated overloading of the tendon, for example, the medial epicondylar inflammation noted with repeated throwing of "curved" balls by a little-league baseball player, or inflammation of the tibial tubercle through overly frequent repetition of running and jumping. In both cases, lesions can be avoided by moderating the intensity of the effort demanded until closure of the epiphyses is complete, with less severe competition, shorter training periods, age classification of players, and careful examination of any children reporting symptoms.[12]

In middle age, many exercise programs have an alarming toll of injuries, particularly among recent recruits. As many as 50% of participants have developed incapacitating musculoskeletal injuries because of such factors as inadequate warm-up, poorly developed muscle strength, sudden violent movements, and overrapid progression of the exercise prescription. Surprisingly, such injuries do not always have a negative impact upon subsequent intentions to exercise; perhaps for some subjects the excitement associated with the risk of injury is (at least subconsciously) a desired aspect of exercise. This way of thinking naturally complicates the task of prevention (G. Godin and R. Shephard, unpublished results).

The incidence of muscle tears can be reduced by a preliminary phase of gentle stretching of the limbs and an adequate warm-up period (at least 5 min of exercise) at a moderate pace. In middle-aged and older individuals, the latter precaution also helps to reduce the frequency of cardiac arrhythmias during the early phases of exercise.[17]

Swelling of the knees and an exacerbation of previous back injuries are common complications of jogging, particularly when the exercise is performed on a hard or an uneven surface. Even mild symptoms are an indication for moderation of the prescription; physical activity should leave the individual no more than pleasantly tired the following day. The likelihood of problems can be reduced by the use of well-cushioned shoes, a strengthening of the knee and back muscles, and a reduction of body mass. If symptoms persist or worsen, the only alternative may be to adopt some other form of exercise, such as fast walking, cycling, swimming, or aqua-fitness classes.

Tendoachilles injuries and "shin splints" are also common early complications of increased physical activity. A hard or uneven running surface and inadequately cushioned shoes are again a factor in such injuries. The tendoachilles can be damaged by allowing the heel to drop too far, and problems thus arise if the shoe that is worn for exercise has an inadequate heel. Shin splints and other orthopedic problems of the ankle and foot commonly reflect an inappropriate angulation of the knee and ankle joints, and can be countered by simple orthotic devices.[18]

Currently, many middle-aged and older individuals are preparing for marathon and even longer races. Plainly, a minimum mileage is an essential component of preparation for such events, but a mileage ceiling should also be set, perhaps 40 to 50 miles/week. If athletes in training exceed this limit, the time for normal, recuperative processes is inadequate, and injuries (including stress fractures of bones such as the metatarsals) become increasingly frequent. In one series of Master's track and field competitors, we found that 50% had sustained injuries over the past year, and in one third of the injured group, the lesion had been sufficiently severe to interrupt training for 1 month or more. Such athletes frequently take vitamin C, in the belief that it will either protect them against injury or speed their recovery; however, we find this makes no difference in either the incidence of injuries or the duration of disability.[19]

As a person ages, osteoarthritis increases the likelihood of knee and back problems. The prime reason for osteoarthritis is an injury to the hyaline cartilage of the articular surface. Few formal studies have been performed, yet trauma experienced during contact sports such as ice hockey at an earlier age is undoubtedly a significant etiologic factor. Nevertheless, a surprising divergence exists between the extent of symptoms and the radiographic appearances.[14]

A second, important factor, which in part is a function of personality, is the conservation of muscle and ligamentous strength about the joint by a combination of passive and active movements, plus isometric contractions of the principal muscles. If the knee can no longer be fully extended and has thus become unstable, a cane can be provided. Use of such an aid limits activity, however, and encourages an unnatural pattern of motion. The cane should thus be regarded as a temporary expedient to keep the person active while the quadriceps muscles are being strengthened. Aspirin can also be given to relieve pain, and in the event that limitation of movement at the hip is already extensive, an artificial prosthesis can be considered.

Corns and calluses develop more frequently in the elderly. Although simply treated by a trained chiropodist, they also, if ignored, can lead to abnormal movement patterns and a worsening of condition at deteriorating joints.

Lastly, demineralization renders the older person vulnerable to fractures of the long bones, hips, and pelvis.[13] This risk increases with obesity, a deterioration of equilibrium, poor eyesight, a reduced leg lift, and a tendency to develop postural hypotension.[20] A heavy person is at slightly decreased risk because although the individual falls more heavily, sub-

cutaneous fat may protect the limbs against trauma. Clearly, the older person should avoid contact sports, activities that involve the danger of collision with stationary objects, and slippery surfaces.

AGE-RELATED EFFECTS

ACUTE AND CHRONIC EXERCISE

Children have difficulty paying attention for long bouts of exercise, and a nominal hour of gymnastics too readily is dissipated in changing, showering, and theoretic instruction. A good immediate training response can be obtained, however, if at least one 6-min period of each weekday is allocated to exercise at 80% of maximal oxygen intake.[21] In the adult, a more usual approach is to hold the intensity of training below the anaerobic threshold of perhaps 70% of maximal oxygen intake. Therefore, at least three 30-min sessions of such activity per week are required if training is to occur.[7]

The extent of the training response in an older person depends greatly upon motivation. Authors have described sedentary subjects in their 40s and 50s who have largely restored both the strength and the aerobic power that they enjoyed in their early 20s, but these individuals are exceptional. At the age of 65 years, a more usual finding is the same *percentage* gain that would be seen in a younger person, but about one half of the absolute response.[22] By this age, many subjects lack the initial condition to commence regular 30-min sessions of exercise at 70% of maximal oxygen intake. Thus, to note that a slower but useful response is observed in a sedentary person with sustained exercise at 50 to 60% of maximal oxygen intake is encouraging (for example, encouraging the subject to undertake fast walking over a progressively extended distance).

SMOKING AND SUBSTANCE ABUSE

Persuading a person to stop smoking undoubtedly has as much or more of an effect upon health as involvement in regular physical activity. In the teenage years, the initial impulse to smoke is thought to come from parental example and peer pressure. Active, athletic parents and peers who are committed to endurance sports thus exert a strong counterinfluence against the insidious pressures of adolescent society.

About 75% of young adults who smoke wish that they did not, and some evidence is available that individuals who become involved in endurance events are more successful in abandoning the habit than those who do not.[23] As the coronary-prone years approach, smoking increases the risk of arrhythmia, and the wisdom of encouraging exercise in a person who is "unable" to stop smoking may be questioned. Certainly, care is needed to avoid the sudden, violent activities that might provoke a ventricular tachycardia or fibrillation; however most investigators suggest that more moderate exercise is beneficial to the prognosis, even of those individuals who continue to smoke. Particular encouragement must be given to their exercise adherence; the onset of smoking is often indicative of a poor body image, and many smokers quickly become discouraged when they are recruited to a class of healthy nonsmokers who do not become dyspneic during exercise.[24] They can be assured that some of the acute effects on the chest will be reversed with a few days of abstinence, and further resolution of chronic bronchitis will ensue over the next several years. Destruction of lung tissue, however, cannot be reversed.

Some middle-aged women complain that they gain weight if they stop smoking. We recommend linking advice concerning diet to the process of smoking withdrawal, and emphasizing that the weight gain is usually temporary, exercise helps to restore energy balance, and the impact of 2 to 3 kg of fat on health is far less serious than the smoking of even 5 cigarettes per day.[25]

Interactions between substance abuse and exercise have been studied less thoroughly. Again, acquisition of a drug habit is often a matter of peer pressure, and such peers are less likely to be found in a physically active milieu. A second factor in drug addiction is a poor body image; again, an appropriate exercise program can help in developing a more positive body image. Finally, cynics argue that the endurance athlete obtains a comparable "high" through stimulation of an endogenous production of β-endorphins.[26]

HYPERTENSION

Authors of studies conducted in Canada show that as many as 20% of the adult population have been told at some time by their physicians that their blood pressure is too high.[27] Often, however, the blood pressure is temporarily elevated under the anxiety-provoking circumstances of a medical consultation.

The systemic blood pressure reading at rest shows a steady rise from early adulthood to the age of 65 years, with a minimal increase thereafter. The main cause of high blood pressure in old age is "benign essential hypertension." The separation of normal from abnormal is arbitrary, however, and a small rise in systolic readings may be no more than an exaggeration of normal aging.

Evidence is now abundant that regular exercise reduces the resting blood pressure by 5 to 10 mm Hg in both normotensive and hypertensive patients.[28] At first inspection, this response seems small, but on a population basis, it compares favorably with most available drugs while lacking their unpleasant side effects. During exercise, the well-trained individual is able to develop a somewhat higher systolic pressure, because stroke volume is increased.

OBESITY

Exercise plays an important role in the control of obesity at all ages. Exercise prescription is positive advice, in contrast to the usually restrictive tone of a dietary recommendation; its mood-elevating tendency counters the depression normally encountered with dietary restriction; it tends to replace adipose tissue with protein; and it establishes a new lifestyle that helps to avoid the all-too-common recidivism once dietary objectives are attained.[7]

If the obesity is severe, the subject is frequently embarrassed to exercise in the presence of the opposite sex. The initial tolerance of exercise is also quite limited, and overenthusiastic demands on the part of the instructor can lead to poor program compliance, with further deterioration of body image. The heavy body mass places a severe strain on the back and the knees, particularly in an older person with arthritic joints; walking or weight-supported exercise is initially more practical than jogging or calisthenics. The low body density and good insulation makes swimming particularly agreeable for such subjects. Sometimes the required daily energy expenditure is best attained by two or even three relatively brief exercise sessions in the course of a day. This schedule not only reduces the liability to fatigue, but also avoids an excessive rise of core temperature; heat elimination is necessarily made more difficult by the insulation of subcutaneous fat. The energy cost of most tasks is increased by obesity, and allowance must be made for this increased cost when using standard MET tables in exercise prescription. Likewise, the assumption of 23% mechanical efficiency for a cycle ergometer or 16% efficiency for a step test is incorrect.

Finally, with all types of exercise, obese persons tend to be more clumsy and fall heavily. They are then at increased risk of bone injury, particularly older individuals with some osteoporosis.

FURTHER READING

1. Shephard RJ: *Physical Activity and Aging.* London: Croom Helm, 1978.
2. Shephard RJ: *Physical Activity and Growth.* Chicago: Year Book, 1982.
3. Shephard RJ: *Physiology and Biochemistry of Exercise.* New York: Praeger, 1982.

REFERENCES

1. Bar-Or O, Shephard RJ, Allen CL: Cardiac output of 10–13 year old boys and girls during submaximal exercise. *J Appl Physiol, 30:*219, 1971.
2. Weisfeldt ML, Gerstenblith G, Lakatta EG: Alterations in circulatory function. In *Principles of Geriatric Medicine.* Edited by R Andres, EL Bierman, and WR Hazzard. New York: McGraw-Hill, 1985.
3. Lester FM, Sheffield LT, Reeves TJ: Electrocardiographic changes in clinically normal older men following maximal and near-maximal exercise. *Circulation, 36:*5, 1967.
4. Niinimaa V, Shephard RJ: Training and oxygen conductance in the elderly. II. The cardiovascular system. *J Gerontol, 33:*362–367, 1978.
5. Cumming GR: Body size and the assessment of physical performance. In *Physical Fitness Assessment. Principles, Practice and Application.* Edited by H Lavallée and RJ Shephard. Springfield, IL: Charles C Thomas, 1978.
6. Von Döbeln W: Kroppsstorlek, Energieomsattning och Kondition. In *Handbok: Ergonomi.* Edited by G Luthman, U Aberg, and N Lundgren. Stockholm: Almqvist and Wiksell, 1966.
7. Shephard RJ: *Endurance Fitness.* 2nd Ed. Toronto: University of Toronto Press, 1977.
8. Shephard RJ, et al.: On the basis of data standardiza-
9. Celentano E, Nottrodt J: Analysing physically demanding jobs: The Canadian Forces approach. In *Proceedings of the 1984 International Conference on Occupational Ergonomics.* Edited by DA Attwood and C McCann. Toronto: Human Factors Association of Canada, 1984.
10. Davies CTM, White MJ: Contractile properties of elderly triceps surae. *Gerontology, 29:*19–25, 1983.
11. Eriksson BO, Saltin B: Muscle metabolism during exercise in boys aged 11 to 16 years compared to adults. *Acta Paediatr Belg, 28* (Suppl):257, 1974.
12. Larson RL: Physical activity and the growth and development of bone and joint structures. In *Physical Activity, Human Growth and Development.* Edited by GL Rarick. New York: Academic Press, 1973.
13. Smith E: Bone—a dynamic tissue and exercise and age. In *Proceedings of the 2nd International Conference on Physical Activity and Aging.* Edited by R Harris. Albany NY: Center for the Study of Aging, 1985.
14. Hult L: Cervical, dorsal and lumbar spinal syndromes. *Acta Orthop Scand [Suppl], 17:*7, 1954.
15. Bjorksten J: Cross-linkage and the aging process. In *Theoretical Aspects of Aging.* Edited by M Rockstein. New York: Academic Press, 1974.
16. Mernagh JR, et al.: Composition of lean tissue in healthy volunteers for nutritional studies in health and disease. *Nutr Res 6:*499–507, 1986.
17. Barnard RJ, MacAlpin RN, Kattus AA, Buckberg GD: Ischemic response to sudden strenuous exercise in healthy men. *Circulation, 48:*936–942, 1973.
18. Nigg BM: Biomechanics, load analysis and sports injuries in the lower extremities. *Sports Med, 2:*367–379, 1985.
19. Kavanagh T, Shephard RJ: The effects of continued training on the aging process. *Ann NY Acad Sci, 301:*656, 1977.
20. Overstall PW, et al.: Falls in the elderly related to postural imbalance. *Br Med J i:*261–264, 1977.
21. Goode RC, et al.: Effects of a short period of physical activity in adolescent boys and girls. *Can J Appl Sport Sci, 1:*241, 1976.
22. Sidney KH, Shephard RJ: Frequency and intensity of exercise training for elderly subjects. *Med Sci Sports Exerc, 10:*125, 1978.
23. Morgan P, Gildiner M, Wright GR: Smoking reduction of adults who take up exercise: A survey of a running club for adults. *CAHPER J, 42:*39, 1976.
24. Massie JF, Shephard RJ: Physiological and psychological effects of training. *Med Sci Sports Exerc, 3:*110, 1971.
25. Rode A, Ross R, Shephard RJ: Smoking withdrawal program. *Arch Environ Health 24:*27, 1972.
26. Harber VJ, Sutton J: Endorphins and exercise. *Sports Med, 1:*154, 1984.
27. Shephard RJ, Cox M, Simper K: An analysis of PAR-Q responses in an office population. *Can J Public Health, 72:*37, 1981.
28. Tipton C: Exercise, training and hypertension. *Exerc Sport Sci Rev, 12:*245, 1984.

33

DEVELOPMENTAL PSYCHOLOGY

JAVAID SHEIKH

This chapter is an overview of the psychologic development of human beings over the life cycle. The concept of the life cycle is based on the assumption that an underlying order exists in the human life course from conception through old age. The life of any given individual may differ from that of another individual based on differences in biologic, psychologic, and social conditions, yet everyone goes through common developmental phases or sequence of events.

These phases can have pronounced effects on the psychologic meanings of particular events and relationships. No consensus so far exists among researchers concerning how to divide these segments of life. Levinson and colleagues, for example, conceive of the life cycle as a sequence of four eras; preadulthood (0–22 years), early adulthood (22–45 years), middle adulthood (40–65 years), and late adulthood (over age 60 years).[1] Each era has its own biopsychosocial character, thereby making its distinctive contribution to the whole.[2] The idea of such age-linked eras and periods, however, is quite new and needs further investigation. For the purposes of this chapter, we follow the traditional wisdom of organizing the life cycle after infancy into the stages of a toddler, childhood, adolescence, young adulthood, middle age, and old age.

TODDLER

This period is usually considered to last from the age of 18 months to 3 years. The major feature of this period is the development of language skills. By the age of 3 years, most children are able to talk in sentences. They can also tell stories and communicate clearly. Another important feature of this period is the development of social behavior, which usually means an attempt to imitate parents (caretakers) in every way possible. Important elements in the outcome of such attempts are learning to feed oneself and toilet training. These children also make a gradual shift from being in their own world to playing with other children. The establishment of a sense of maleness or femaleness, a gender identity, also occurs during this phase.

CHILDHOOD

This period spans ages 3 to 12 years and includes both the preschool child and the juvenile. During the preschool period, the child learns to accept his or her place as a child member of the family and prepares to invest energies in schooling and in activities with peer groups. The juvenile spends increasing amounts of time in school-related activities and with the neighborhood peer group. The child's concept of self thus begins to crystallize in relation to the way teachers and peers relate to him. This period is quite important in the ultimate development of peoples' identification with their society and their commitment to values and ethics, as contrasted with a deep-seated sense of alienation.[3]

ADOLESCENCE

Adolescence spans the ages of 13 to 18 years. Puberty marks the beginning of adolescence at the age of 13 years and is an important milestone between childhood and adolescence. With important hormonal changes taking place in the body, manifesting as menarche in girls and the onset of nocturnal emissions in boys, along with the development of secondary sexual characteristics, this period is one of rapid physiologic and psychologic change for both sexes. Salient features of important psychologic changes beginning during puberty and continuing into adolescence follow:

1. Individuals tend to become "moody," including increases or decreases in subjectively experienced feelings of depression, guilt, stress or anxiety, irritability, shame, erotic arousability, pleasure, pride, and so forth.
2. Behavioral changes in the realm of heterosexual interactions occur; specifically, individuals start manifesting interest in members of the opposite sex and in dating.
3. Relationship with parents and other authority figures, such as teachers and coaches, begins to change, with adolescents wanting more autonomy.
4. A common occurrence is the development of specific areas of psychologic conflict concerning sexual motives, masturbation, menstruation, body appearance, and the like.
5. Adolescents tend to be sensitive about self-esteem and show rapid fluctuations in their self-perception.

Psychologic adaptation to puberty and adolescence is considered to occur along two broad lines:

Direct effects model. One assumption of this model is that psychologic changes occur in direct response to the above-mentioned physiologic changes. A high degree of psychologic conflict, moodiness, and stress are thus considered inescapable results of hormonal development, and any individual differences are attributed to variation within antecedent biologic variables, for example, "the strength of the drives."[4,5] A review of the literature, however, demonstrates that direct evidence of such a relationship with hormonal effects is lacking.

Mediated effects model. With this model, the effects of adolescent changes on psychologic development are presumed to be mediated by intervening variables or to be moderated by other external factors. Such factors include sociocultural effects and socialization practices as well as endogenous personality characteristics, such as patterns of thoughts and feelings, attitudes toward growing up and adulthood, self-esteem, anxiety about acceptability, and degree of autonomy from need for external approval.[6,7]

Overall, the adolescent struggle represents attempts to gain freedom from dependence on parents. This struggle is usually manifest in nonconformist or rebellious behavior. Vacillation between following the crowd (as a substitute for following the parents), and trying to resist peer pressure without regressing to becoming mother's "model child," characterizes the attitudes and behavior of the high school student. Toward the end of adolescence, there is an increasing tendency toward emotional maturity, acceptance of one's identity, and goal-oriented thinking.

YOUNG ADULTHOOD

The period between the ages of 18 to 28 years is usually considered to represent young adulthood. The length of the time required for an individual to make the transition from adolescence to young adulthood depends to a considerable extent on the attitudes of parents, teachers, and other important adults. A general assumption is that by the end of this period, certain developmental tasks should have been accomplished and early adulthood is achieved.[8]

Early adulthood brings a set of challenges that are unique to that stage in life. This period is different in many ways from the previous decade. No longer can protection from others be expressed in statements like: "He is too young to understand." Total responsibility must be taken for all actions. The people in the world outside expect young adults to know where they are headed and to possess convictions they can define, be sure about, and are able to defend logically if called upon to do so. Young adults have to look within themselves for answers to questions about sex, religion, career, and loyalty to friends, as well as about political and cultural morality. Choices about going home for Christmas or skiing with friends, whether to date a boyfriend's roommate, for instance, may cause confusion, and this confusion can be embarrassing.

Erickson postulates that commitment is the primary task for the young adult.[9] If this challenge cannot be met, an individual feels immature and inadequate and probably experiences a developmental lag. Events that occur in childhood and adolescence bear importantly on the ability to make healthy commitments as an adult. Among the most important areas in which these commitments are to be made are: (1) problem solving, (2) sexuality, (3) career choice, and (4) intimacy.

MIDDLE AGE

Middle age is usually considered to span the ages of 40 to 65 years. Like entering the adult world in the twenties, the beginning of middle age marks the start of a new era. A working definition of middle age was proposed by Mogul as a period in which, "previous choices in important life areas and the ensuing successes, failures, satisfactions, and disappointments are reviewed and reworked in the context of old aspirations and wishes, the current recognition of limitations in oneself, and the finiteness of opportunities and of time itself."[10] Until recently, important issues in middle age for men and women differed considerably, a phenomenon that quite likely will change in the future. For example, one belief is that a most important event for married women during this period is the movement of children away from home, giving rise to an "empty nest syndrome." A positive side of such a phenomenon, however, is the freedom to pursue their own inter-

ests or to return to work because the responsibility of caring for the children is no longer their own. In addition, the loss of reproductive capacity for women who do not have a family is thought to be a source of major concern and a sense of loss. With increasing numbers of women interested in pursuing their careers, these issues may no longer create the disparity between the concerns of men and women in the middle stages of the life cycle.

The important issues for men during this time usually surround their careers. Men are supposed to be at the pinnacle of their careers during this period, and hence their perception of success or failure in achieving their career goals determines to great extent their satisfactory adjustment to this phase of life.

OLD AGE

Psychologic theories of old age are complicated by the fact that, as humans pass through their life experiences, they become increasingly different rather than similar. Infants at 6 months of age are more similar than children at age 12 years. This divergence continues throughout life as a response to a large array of possible learning and living experiences. As a consequence, no unified theory of the psychology of aging has been developed. One fact, however, is well recognized, that psychologic development during old age is closely tied to biologic and social influences. Examples of such influences include a decline in physical functioning, the development of multiple medical problems, and multiple losses, including the death of a spouse and close friends. Personalities maintain their characteristics in middle and late life, and any changes or disintegration are not related to age per se but rather to losses, particularly those involving health and social support systems.

A common belief is that certain personality traits in late life are gender related. For example, men are more affiliative, that is, they ally themselves with groups of men in male group identity. In contrast, women become more individualistic, egocentric, and more aggressive.[11] In addition, a difference in life expectancy between men and women creates a sex ratio imbalance and has profound effects on attitudes, behavior, social opportunities, and expectations. For example, most older men are married, whereas most older women are widows. Of men 65 years of age and over, two thirds live with wives, whereas only one third of all elderly women have husbands.

An important component of the psychology of aging, particularly in men, is adjustment to retirement. It is essential for most individuals to feel needed and to feel that they can contribute to the well-being of others. Those individuals who continue to be involved in meaningful activities after retirement tend to cope better with retirement than those who are not so involved. Lastly, an important factor in determining how elderly people cope with old age and retirement is financial security. People in the higher socioeconomic group tend to use this time as an opportunity to pursue their long postponed interests, whereas elderly persons who are not well off financially may experience difficulties in adjusting to a lower income.

In conclusion, the concept of the life cycle presented here suggests that psychologic development continues throughout life and provides useful information about the meaning of particular events in any given phase of this cycle. A study of different phases of the life cycle maps the universal order as well as the general developmental principles underlying such segments. Such a framework can be helpful in understanding psychologic meaning of different life events and the process of adaptation to such events.

REFERENCES

1. Levinson DJ, et al.: *The Seasons of a Man's Life.* New York: Alfred A. Knopf, 1978.
2. Levinson DJ, Gooden WE: The life cycle. In *Comprehensive Text Book of Psychiatry.* 4th Ed. Edited by HI Kaplan and BJ Sadock. Baltimore: Williams & Wilkins, 1985.
3. Lidz T: The life cycle. In *American Handbook of Psychiatry.* Vol. 1. 2nd Ed. Edited by S Arieti. New York: Basic Books, 1974.
4. Freud A: Adolescence. In *Psychoanalytic Study of the Child.* Vol. 13. Edited by RS Eissler, et al. New York: International Universities Press, 1958.
5. Freud A: *The Ego and the Mechanisms of Defense.* New York: International Universities Press, 1946.
6. Clausen JA: The social meaning of differential physical and sexual maturation. In *Adolescence in the Life Cycle.* Edited by SE Dragastin and GH Elder, Jr. New York: Halsted, 1975.
7. Schonfeld W: Adolescent development: Biological, psychological, and sociological determinants. In *Adolescent Psychiatry.* Vol. 1. Edited by S Feinstein, P Giovacchini, and A Miller. New York: Basic Books, 1971.
8. Blaine GB Jr, Farnsworth DL: Personality development in the young adult. In *The Course of Life: Psychoanalytic Contributions Toward Understanding Personality Development.* Vol. 11. Edited by SI Greenspan and GH Pollock. Washington, DC, NIMH, 1980.
9. Erikson EH: *Childhood and Society.* New York: W.W. Norton, 1950.
10. Mogul KM: Women in Midlife: Decisions, rewards, and conflicts related to work and careers. Am J Psychiatry, 136:1139, 1979.
11. Busse EW: Old age. In *The Course of Life: Psychoanalytic Contributions Toward Understanding Personality Development.* Vol. III. Adulthood and the Aging Process. Edited by SI Greenspan and GH Pollock. Washington, DC, NIMH, 1980.

CHAPTER 34

EXERCISE PRESCRIPTION FOR CHILDREN

LINDA D. ZWIREN

PHYSIOLOGIC ASPECTS

Major differences in physiologic responses to exercise exist between children and adults. These differences and the implications for exercise are presented in Table 34–1. Apart from low economy of locomotion and limitations of exercising in climatic extremes no apparent underlying *physiologic* factor has been identified that would make children less suitable than adults for prolonged, continuous activities. The American Academy of Pediatrics (AAP) states, however, that: "Under no circumstances should a full marathon be attempted by immature youths (less than Tanner Stage 5 sexual maturity rating.)"[7]

Although children can perform exercise over a wide variety of intensities and durations, children *spontaneously* prefer short-term intermittent activities with a high recreational component and variety rather than monotonous, prolonged activities. In accordance with their physiologic profile and from a psychologic viewpoint, children seem best suited to repeated activities that last a few seconds, interspersed with short rest periods. The least suitable forms of exercise for children, from a physiologic viewpoint, are highly intense activities lasting 10 to 90 sec.[1]

PRECAUTIONS FOR EXERCISING IN CLIMATIC EXTREMES

Because children have a higher metabolic level at a given submaximal walking or running speed, children produce excessive body heat. This higher metabolic load in addition to a poor sweating capacity, large surface-to-mass ratio, and immature cardiovascular system (Table 34–1), causes children to have shorter tolerance for exercising in hot climates and greater susceptibility to heat stress.[1] The AAP recommends: "Clothing should be light weight, limited to one layer of absorbent material in order to facilitate evaporation of sweat and to expose as much skin as possible. Sweat-saturated garments should be replaced by dry ones. Rubberized sweat suits should never be used to produce loss of weight."[8]

Children have low tolerance to extreme heat; they thermoregulate as effectively as adults, however, when exercising in neutral or moderately warm climates.[2] The AAP recommends that activities lasting 30 min or more should be reduced whenever relative humidity

Table 34−1. Physiologic Characteristics of the Exercising Child

Function	Comparison to adults	Implications for exercise prescription
METABOLIC:		
Aerobic		
$\dot{V}O_{2max}$ (L $\cdot$ min^{-1})	Lower (function of body mass)	
$\dot{V}O_{2max}$ (ml $\cdot$ kg^{-1} $\cdot$ min^{-1})	Similar	Can perform endurance tasks reasonably well
Submaximal oxygen demand (economy)	Cycling: similar (18−30% mechanical efficiency); walking and running: higher metabolic cost	Greater fatiguability in prolonged high-intensity tasks (running and walking); greater heat production in children at a given speed of walking or running
Anaerobic		
Glycogen stores	Lower concentration and rate of utilization of muscle glycogen	
Phosphofructokinase (PFK concentration)	Glycolysis limited because of low level of PFK. Breakdown of ATP and creatine phosphate is the same	Ability of children to perform *intense* anaerobic tasks that last 10 to 90 sec is distinctly lower than adults
LA_{max}	Lower maximal blood lactate levels	
Oxygen transient	Faster reaching of steady state than adults. Shorter half-time of oxygen increase in children	Children reach metabolic steady-state faster. Children contract a lower oxygen deficit. Faster recovery. Children, therefore, are well suited to intermittent activities
CARDIOVASCULAR		
Maximal cardiac output ($\dot{Q}_{max}$)	Lower due to size difference	Immature cardiovascular system means child is limited in bringing internal heat to surface for dissipation when exercising intensely in the heat
$\dot{Q}$ at a given $\dot{V}O_2$	Somewhat lower	
Maximal stroke volume (SV_{max})	Lower due to size and heart volume difference	
SV at a given $\dot{V}O_2$	Lower	
Maximal heart rate (HR_{max})	Higher	Up to maturity HR_{max} is between 195 and 215 beats/min
HR at submax work	At given absolute power output and at relative metabolic load, child has higher HR	Higher HR compensates for lower SV
Oxygen carrying capacity	Blood volume, hemoglobin concentration, and total hemoglobin are lower in children	
O_2 in arterial and venous supplies (CaO_2 and CvO_2)	Somewhat higher	Potential deficiency of peripheral blood supply during maximal exertion in hot climates
Blood flow to active muscle	Higher	
Systolic and diastolic pressures	Lower maximal and submaximal	No known beneficial or detrimental effects on working capacity of child
PULMONARY RESPONSE:		
Maximal minute ventilation $\dot{V}_{Emax}$ (L $\cdot$ min^{-1})	Smaller	Early fatiguability in tasks that require large respiratory minute volumes
$\dot{V}_{Emax}$ (ml $\cdot$ kg^{-1} $\cdot$ min^{-1})	Same as adolescents and young adults	
$V_{Esubmax}$ ventilatory equivalent	V_E at any given $\dot{V}O_2$ is higher in children	Less efficient ventilation would mean a greater oxygen cost of ventilation. May explain the relatively higher metabolic cost of submaximal exercise
Respiratory frequency and tidal volume	Marked by higher rate, tachypnea and shallow breathing response	Children's physiologic dead space is smaller than adults; therefore, alveolar ventilation is still adequate for gas exchange
Perception (RPE: rating of perceived exertion)	Exercising at a given physiologic strain is perceived to be easier by children	Implications for initial phase of heat acclimatization
THERMOREGULATORY:		
Surface area (SA)	Per unit mass is approximately 36% greater in children	Greater ratio of heat exchange between skin and environment. In climatic extremes, children are at increased risk of stress

Table 34–1. Physiologic Characteristics of the Exercising Child *(Continued)*

Function	Comparison to adults	Implications for exercise prescription
THERMOREGULATORY:		
Sweating rate	Lower absolute amount and per unit of SA. Greater increase in core temperature required to start sweating	Greater risk of heat-related illness on hot humid days due to reduced capacity to evaporate sweat. Lower tolerance time in extreme heat
Acclimatization to heat	Slower physiologically; faster subjectively	Children require longer and more gradual program of acclimatization; special attention during early stages of acclimatization
Body cooling in water	Faster cooling due to higher SA per heat, producing unit mass; lower thickness of subcutaneous fat	Potential hypothermia
Body core heating during dehydration	Greater	Prolonged activity: hydrate well before and enforce fluid intake during activity

(Adapted from Bar-Or O: Exercise in Childhood. In *Current Therapy in Sport Medicine, 1985–1986*. Edited by RP Walsh and RJ Shephard. Toronto: C.V. Mosby, 1985, with information from related references.[2–6])

and air temperature are above critical levels (Table 34–2).[8]

ACCLIMATIZATION

Children tend to lag behind adults in the *rate* of physiologic acclimatization and, therefore, should be involved in a longer and more gradual program. The AAP recommends: ". . . that intensity and duration of exercise should be restrained initially and then gradually increased over a period of 10 to 14 days to accomplish acclimatization to the effects of heat."[8] Children can acclimate, to some extent, when they exercise in *neutral* environments, and when they *rest* in hot climates; however, they acclimatize *subjectively* faster than adults. Therefore, children, especially at the early stages of acclimatization, may *feel* quite capable of performing physical exercise in the heat, despite a marked physiologic heat stress.[9]

FLUID REPLACEMENT

During continuous activity of more than 30 min duration, fluid replacement should be 100

to 150 ml every 15 to 30 min, even when the child is not thirsty.[2,8] Bar-Or recommends that replacement fluids for children should not exceed 5 mEq/L Na^+ (0.3 g/L NaCl), 4 mEq/L K^+ (0.28 g/L KCl), and 25 g/L sugar. Haymes and Wells suggest that a child weighing 40 kg should ingest 150 ml of cold tap water every 30 min during activity.[4]

OVERUSE INJURY

The recent increases in overuse injuries in children have been attributed to the increase in children who compete and train intensely. Children may be more anatomically susceptible to overuse injuries than adults because of the presence of growth tissue.[10] Risk factors include:

- Abrupt change in intensity, duration, or frequency of training (intensity should not be increased more than 10% per week).
- Musculotendinous imbalance in strength and flexibility.
- Anatomic malalignment of lower extremities.
- Footwear and running surface.

Table 34–2. Weather Guide for Prevention of Heat Illness

Air temperature (°F)	Danger zone (% Relative humidity)	Critical zone (% Relative humidity)
70	80	100
75	70	100
80	50	80
85	40	68
90	30	55
95	20	40
100	10	30

(From Haymes EM, Wells CL: *Environment and Human Performance*. Champaign, IL: Human Kinetics, 1986, with permission.)

EXERCISE PRESCRIPTION

Although positive scientific verification is still lacking, the recommended guidelines for exercising adults, in terms of frequency, duration, and intensity, can be used for children.[2,7,11,12] Some controversy remains, however, as to whether the use of adult guidelines for children will increase the level of maximal oxygen intake ($\dot{V}o_{2max}$) beyond that level asso-

Table 34–3. Exercise Prescription in the Management of Specific Pediatric Diseases

Disease	Purposes of program	Recommended activities
Anorexia nervosa	Means for behavioral modification; educate regarding lean mass versus fat	Various; emphasize those with low energy demand
Bronchial asthma	Conditioning; possible reduction of exercise-induced bronchospasm; instill confidence	Aquatic, intermittent, long warm-up
Cerebral palsy	Increase maximal aerobic power, range of motion, and ambulation; control of body mass	Depend on residual ability
Cystic fibrosis	Improve mucus clearance, training of respiratory muscles	Jogging, swimming
Diabetes mellitus	Help in metabolic control; control of body mass	Various; attempt equal daily energy output
Hemophilia	Prevent muscle atrophy, contractures, and possible bleeding into joints	Swimming, cycling; avoid contact sports
Mental retardation	Socialization; increase self-esteem; prevent detraining	Recreational, intermittent, large variety
Muscular dystrophies	Increase muscle strength and endurance; prevent contractures; prolong ambulatory phase	Swimming, calisthenics, wheelchair sports
Neurocirculatory disease	Increase effort tolerance; improve orthostatic response	Various; emphasize endurance-type activities
Obesity	Reduction of body mass and fat; conditioning; socialization and improved self-esteem	High in calorie uptake but feasible to child; emphasize swimming
Rheumatoid arthritis	Prevent contractures and muscle atrophy; increase daily function	Swimming, calisthenics, cycling, sailing
Spina bifida	Strengthen upper body; control of body mass and fat; increase maximal aerobic power	Arm shoulder resistance training, wheelchair sports (including endurance)

(From Bar-Or O: Exercise in childhood. In *Current Therapy in Sport Medicine, 1985–1986.* Edited by RP Walsh and RJ Shephard. Toronto: C.V. Mosby, 1985, with permission.)

ciated with growth.[2,6,11-13] Because some evidence exists that health benefits in the adult are related to activity level, perhaps the best prescription for children involves keeping them active, with less concern for increasing $\dot{V}o_{2max}$.

Children with an illness or disability with resultant hypoactivity may require specific exercise prescription (Table 34–3). A specific prescription may also be advised for those children who are identified as having two or more risk factors for coronary artery disease.

GRADED EXERCISE TESTS

RATIONALE FOR EXERCISE TESTING

The various reasons for using exercise testing in pediatric diagnosis are listed in Table 34–4. Application of graded exercise testing (GXT) to specific diseases or problems is beyond the scope of this monograph, and we refer the reader to other references for more detailed information.[2,14,15] In many cases, the GXT is used most successfully as an affirmation to the child and parents that exercise can be performed at high intensity with no ill effects.

Table 34–4. Rationale for Exercise Testing in Pediatric Diagnosis

Measure physical working capacity
1. Assess daily function—establish whether daily activities are within physiologic functioning level
2. Identify deficiency in specific fitness component— muscular endurance and strength may limit daily performance rather than aerobic capacity (e.g., muscular dystrophy)
3. Establish a baseline before the onset of an intervention program
4. Assess the effectiveness of an exercise prescription
5. Chart the course of a progressive disease (e.g., cystic fibrosis, Duchenne muscular dystrophy)

Exercise as a provocation test
1. Amplify pathophysiologic changes
2. Trigger changes otherwise not seen in the resting child

Exercise as an adjunct diagnostic test
1. Noninvasive exercise test can be used for screening to determine the need for an invasive test
2. Assessing the severity of dysrhythmias
3. Assessing the functional success of surgical correction
4. Assessing the adequacy of drug regimens at varying exercise intensities

Assessment and differentiation of symptoms: chest pains (asthma from myocardial infarction), breathlessness (bronchoconstriction from low physical capacity), coughing, easy fatiguability

Instill confidence in child and parent

Motivation or compliance in intervention program

(Adapted from Bar-Or O: Exercise in pediatric assessment and diagnosis. *Scand J Sport Sci,* 7:35–39, 1985.)

ERGOMETERS

The same types of ergometer can be used with children and adults, although preferably children, especially those younger than age 7 years, would be tested on a treadmill. Premature local muscle fatigue and the inability to maintain a specific cadence prevent many children from reaching maximal values on the cycle ergometer. Cardiorespiratory measurements must be directly assessed on the treadmill. Prediction of maximal values from submaximal $\dot{V}o_2$ are not applicable with children because the efficiency of a child's gaits is so variable.[2]

If a cycle ergometer is used, an electronically braked cycle ergometer is preferred, because power output is not dependent on a given pedal rate.[15] On mechanically braked ergometers, pedal rates of 50 to 60 rev $\cdot$ min^{-1} are recommended.[2] If children ages 8 or 9 years old or younger are to be tested, special pediatric models should be used or existing cycle ergometers should be modified. The handlebars should be lengthened, the seat height must be adjusted so that the angle of the knee joint at extension is 15°, and the pedal crank length should be reduced (13 cm for age 6 years; 15 cm for age 8 to 10 years).[2,16] In addition, because smaller resistance increments may be needed, resistance unit indicators on the cycle ergometer should be in 5-w gradations. Testing of children with diseases that involve the legs may require the use of arm ergometers.

PROTOCOL

A variety of exercise protocols are available for children who are symptomatic.[2,14,16–18] Some protocols are very similar to those used with adults. In some instances, protocols are modified so that the initial power output and subsequent incremental increases are lowered. The specific protocol selected depends on the specific question(s) to be answered, measurements to be obtained, whether submaximal and/or maximal data are needed, and on the abilities and limitations of the patient. A GXT is not required when evaluating asymptomatic children.

SUPERVISORY PERSONNEL

During GXT, a technician and/or nurse should be present, and a physician should be available within 30 to 60 sec. For the following conditions, a physician should be actively involved in the testing:[2,15]

- Serious rhythm disorders
- Aortic stenosis with anticipated gradients over 50 mm Hg
- Myocardial disease
- Cyanotic heart disease
- Advanced pulmonary vascular disease
- Ventricular dysrhythmia with heart disease
- Coronary arterial disease

CONTRAINDICATIONS

In addition to the contraindications listed in the *Guidelines,* the contraindications for testing pediatric patients follow:

1. Asthmatic child who is dyspneic at rest or whose 1-min forced expiratory volume (FEV_1) or peak expiratory flow is less than 60% of predicted value
2. Acute renal disease
3. Hepatitis
4. Insulin-dependent diabetic who did not take prescribed quantity of insulin or who is ketoacidotic[2]

CRITERIA FOR TERMINATION OF TEST

Criteria for stopping an exercise test are similar to those for adults included in the *Guidelines.*[19]

Attainment of Maximal Values

Maximal Oxygen Uptake ($\dot{V}O_{2max}$). The evidence of a plateau is less common in children than in adults.[2,13] Data on intraindividual variation in $\dot{V}o_{2max}$ indicate, however, that acceptable data can be obtained even if criteria for identifying a plateau in $\dot{V}o_{2max}$ are not always satisfied.[13]

Maximal Heart Rate. Children with peripheral musculature that is weak or atrophied (e.g., muscular dystrophy or cerebral palsy) are not able to generate enough force to reach maximal heart rates associated with other children their age (Table 34–1). In addition, children with congenital complete heart block (and a number of other congenital heart defects), anorexic children, and children receiving beta-blocker therapy also may have reduced maximal heart rates.[2,15]

EXERCISE PRESCRIPTION FOR PEDIATRIC CARDIAC PATIENTS

The concept of following adult guidelines for exercise prescription in terms of intensity, frequency, and duration can also be used successfully in pediatric cardiac patients.[2] Exercise prescription should be based on the results of a GXT, the limitations of specific disease conditions, and information obtained from an activity questionnaire that elicits information as to the child's activities, the activity habits of other family members, and the parental attitudes toward activity.[2]

REFERENCES

1. Bar-Or O: Exercise in childhood. In *Current Therapy in Sport Medicine, 1985–1986*. Edited by RP Walsh and RJ Shephard. Toronto: C.V. Mosby, 1985.
2. Bar-Or O: *Pediatric Sports Medicine for the Practitioner: From Physiologic Principles to Clinical Applications.* New York: Springer, 1983.
3. Bar-Or O: The child athlete and thermoregulation. In *Exercise and Sport Biology.* Edited by P Komi. Champaign, IL: Human Kinetics, 1982.
4. Haymes EM, Wells CL: *Environment and Human Performance.* Champaign, IL; Human Kinetics, 1986.
5. Inbar O, Bar-Or O: Anaerobic characteristics in male children and adolescents. *Med Sci Sport Exerc,* 18:264–269, 1986.
6. Wells CL: The effects of physical activity on cardiorespiratory fitness in children. In *American Academy of Physical Education Papers No. 19.* Edited by GA Stull and HM Eckert. Champaign, IL: Human Kinetics, 1986.
7. American Academy of Pediatrics: Risks in long-distance running for children. *Phys Sportmed,* 10:82, 86, 1982.
8. American Academy of Pediatrics: Climatic heat stress and the exercising child. *Phys Sportmed,* 11:155, 159, 1983.
9. Inbar O: Exercise in the heat. In *Current Therapy in Sport Medicine, 1985–1986.* Edited by RP Walsh and RJ Shephard. Toronto: C.V. Mosby, 1985.
10. Micheli L: Pediatric and adolescent sport injuries: Recent trends. *Exerc Sport Sci Rev,* 14:359–374, 1986.
11. Rowland TW: Aerobic response to endurance training in pre-pubescent children: A critical analysis. *Med Sci Sport Exerc,* 17:493–497, 1985.
12. Sady SP: Cardiorespiratory exercise in children. In *Clinics in Sports Medicine.* Vol. 5. Edited by F Katch and PF Freedson. Philadelphia: WB Saunders, 1986.
13. Krahenbuhl GS, Skinner JS, Kohrt WM: Developmental aspects of maximal aerobic power in children. *Exerc Sport Sci Rev,* 13:503–538, 1985.
14. American Heart Association Council on Cardiovascular Disease in the Young: Standards for exercise testing in the pediatric age group. *Circulation,* 66:1377A–1397A, 1982.
15. Cumming GR: Exercise tests in pediatric cardiology. In *Current Therapy in Sport Medicine 1985–1986.* Edited by RP Walsh and RJ Shephard. Toronto: CV Mosby, 1985.
16. Klimt F, Voight GB: Investigations on the standardization of ergometry in children. *Acta Paediatr Scand [Suppl],* 217:35–36, 1971.
17. Cumming GR, Langsford S: Comparison of nine exercise tests used in pediatric cardiology. In *Children and Exercise.* Edited by RA Binkhorst, HCG Kemper, and WHM Saris. Champaign, IL: Human Kinetics, 1985.
18. Godfrey S: *Exercise Testing in Children. Applications in Health and Disease.* Philadelphia: WB Saunders, 1974.
19. American College of Sports Medicine: *Guidelines for Exercise Testing and Prescription.* 3rd Ed. Philadelphia: Lea & Febiger, 1986.
20. Bar-Or O: Exercise in pediatric assessment and diagnosis. *Scand J Sport Sci,* 7:35–39, 1985.

CHAPTER 35

EXERCISE PROGRAMMING FOR THE OLDER ADULT

GREGORY W. HEATH

Individuals who engage in regular vigorous physical activity have an increased physical working capacity, decreased body fat, increased lean body tissue, increased bone density, and lower rates of coronary artery disease (CAD), hypertension, and cancer. Increased physical activity is also associated with greater longevity. The benefits of regular physical activity and exercise can also assist older adults in enhancing their quality of life, improving their capacity for work and recreation, and altering their rate of decline in functional status.

When designing and prescribing exercise programs for older adults, a number of physiologic, anatomic, and psychologic characteristics should be considered to ensure a safe, effective, and enjoyable exercise experience.

CHARACTERISTICS THAT AFFECT PROGRAM DESIGN

CARDIOVASCULAR SYSTEM[1]

Aging is associated with changes in the cardiovascular system. Resting heart rate shows little or no change with increasing age; however, maximal exercise heart rate shows a decline. This decline is related in part to a decline

in sensitivity to catecholamines noted with advancing age. Functional and structural changes take place that affect the myocardium. One such change is a reduction in resting cardiac output, which in part results from a fall in resting stroke volume that occurs with myocardial hypertrophy. When comparing older and younger individuals, we note submaximal exercise leads to similar increases in stroke volume and cardiac output. At maximal exercise intensities, however, older individuals have cardiac outputs that are 20 to 30% less than those of younger individuals.

Elasticity of the major blood vessels declines with aging. Higher resting and exercise blood pressure determinations result. The increase in blood pressure both at rest and exercise often peaks at age 65 to 70 years, with little or no further change beyond this age level.

Maximal oxygen uptake ($\dot{V}O_{2max}$) shows a steady decline with age. The level of physical activity, however, dramatically influences this change. The decline in $\dot{V}O_{2max}$ that can be attributed to aging per se is primarily due to changes in the myocardium that are related to maximal cardiac output (expressed as the product of maximal stroke volume and maximal heart rate). A decrease in myocardial sensitivity to catecholamines with age appears to be the most likely explanation for the decline in heart rate. Peripheral vascular changes and the ability of the skeletal muscle to extract oxygen are minimally involved in this decline.

A major threat to cardiovascular health in the elderly is CAD. This disease, with its underlying process of atherosclerosis, is the most prevalent chronic disorder found in older individuals. Many of the limitations within the cardiovascular system that appear to be associated with aging are often a result of CAD and its complications. Atherosclerosis can also affect the arteries of the brain and kidneys as well as the peripheral vascular system. These effects should be understood in light of the physiology of aging and the desired effects of regular physical activity.

Older individuals can obtain cardiovascular endurance benefits from regular endurance exercise training that are similar to those benefits observed in younger adults. The degree of $\dot{V}O_{2max}$ can increase in sedentary older persons with regular endurance activity. Lower heart rate, blood pressure, and blood lactate levels at submaximal exercise can be demonstrated with regular endurance exercise.

RESPIRATORY SYSTEM[2]

Changes in the lung and respiratory system occur with aging. The residual volume increases 30 to 50%; the vital capacity decreases 40 to 50% by the age of 70 years. Therefore, as individuals age, they show a greater dependency on increased respiratory frequency rather than increased tidal volume during exercise. This dependency increases the overall work in breathing. Respiratory function does not limit exercise capacity unless function is significantly impaired such as with chronic obstructive pulmonary disease (e.g., emphysema, chronic bronchitis). The ventilatory changes that are seen with aging do not interfere with the ability of the individual to manifest significant improvements in $\dot{V}O_{2max}$ after training.

NERVOUS SYSTEM[3,4]

Significant changes occur in the central and peripheral nervous system with age. Reaction times become slower and the velocity of nerve conduction slows by 10 to 15% by age 70 years. More specifically, sensory defects increase in incidence with increasing age. Mechanical and neurologic changes occur in the auditory system of older individuals. These changes are responsible for impaired auditory activity and decreased sound discrimination.

The visual system also undergoes significant change with increasing age. The lens undergoes a yellowing and in some cases, lens opacity occurs (cataracts). The number of rods and cones is usually reduced. The iris loses the ability to open as wide as occurs in younger individuals. These changes are responsible for the common complaint of impaired night vision in the elderly as well as the general need for better visual conditions, such as improved lighting. Regular lifetime physical activity appears to delay the slowing of reaction times with aging; however, results of studies in which scientists examined these variables in response to regular exercise in previously sedentary older individuals are inconclusive. Although few researchers have documented positive or negative effects of regular exercise on neurologic function, some investigators report the possibly decreased level of anxiety in older regular exercisers and the consistent finding of an increased sense of well-being in older participants with regular exercise.

MUSCULOSKELETAL SYSTEM[5-9]

A 20% decline in muscle strength usually occurs between the ages of 22 and 65 years. This decline in strength is attributed not only to advancing age but also to the effects of disuse. A progressive loss in bone mass occurs with aging. This loss is particularly evident in women, but it also occurs in men. Women over the age of 35 years lose bone mass at a rate of approximately 1% per year. Men begin to sustain bone loss at about age 55 years and usually lose 10 to 15% by age 70 years. Bone loss can be exacerbated in the elderly subject by an inadequate dietary calcium intake, diabetes mellitus, lack of supplemental estrogen and progestin in postmenopausal women, renal impairment, or immobility. Bone loss with resultant loss of bone strength predisposes many older individuals to fractures, particularly of the hip, vertebrae, and forearm. These injuries are a significant cause of morbidity and mortality (hip) in the elderly.

Older adults can have significant limitations in flexibility. Changes that occur with aging have not been well documented; however, investigators found the major cause of declining flexibility is the lack of movement with joints that are not usually used in daily activities. The aging joint is generally less flexible and mobile. Connective tissue changes in muscles, ligaments, joint capsules, and tendons appear responsible for most of the loss of flexibility and mobility.

Regular strength training in older individuals can result in increased strength with mild to moderate muscle hypertrophy. Regular weight-bearing exercise can cause an increase in bone density in middle-aged and older women; men who exercise regularly have reportedly higher bone densities than their sedentary counterparts. Exercise programming for the elderly that emphasizes flexibility activities has brought about significant improvements in these individuals in regard to joint range of motion, including the neck, shoulder, wrist, back, hip, knee, and ankle.

OTHER SYSTEMS[10]

Renal function declines by about 30 to 50% between the ages of 30 and 70 years. Along with the decline in kidney function is decreased acid-base control, glucose tolerance, and drug clearance. A general reduction in total cellular water occurs with aging, with a decline of 10 to 50% in total body water. This change predisposes the older individual to more rapid dehydration when confronted with a hot environment, burns, or diarrhea. Evaporative water losses and perspiration must be considered when older adults exercise.

METABOLISM[11]

Basal metabolic rate gradually decreases with age, as does $\dot{V}O_{2max}$. Sedentary men have exhibited decreases in their $\dot{V}O_{2max}$ of 9% per decade, with regularly active men showing only a 5% per decade decline. Glucose tolerance is diminished with increasing age, accompanied by an increasing likelihood of developing non–insulin-dependent diabetes mellitus. Lean body mass decreases, and body fat percentage increases.

Regular physical activity can increase $\dot{V}O_{2max}$, increase lean body mass, and decrease percentage body fat. Alterations in glucose and lipid metabolism have also occurred in older individuals who engage in regular endurance activities, with some researchers reporting apparently improved glycemic control in diabetic persons. The pharmacologic needs of older adults warrant consideration. Certain medicines for diseases that commonly affect the elderly influence an individual's response to exercise (e.g., beta blockers). Vigorous exercise will affect the action of some medicines (e.g., decreased insulin requirement, increased sensitivity to dehydration from diuretics).

PSYCHOSOCIAL ELEMENTS[12]

In American society, retirement often marks the end of the productive period of life. Certain attitudes have led most of society to relegate the older adult to a sedentary lifestyle. Regular physical activity can be an effective tool in maintaining functional ability and promoting an enhanced sense of well-being in the older adult.

EXERCISE PROGRAMMING

MEDICAL HISTORY AND CLEARANCE[13]

Exercise programming for the elderly may be offered on three different levels: (1) a program-based level that consists primarily of supervised exercise training; (2) exercise counseling and exercise prescription followed by a self-monitored exercise program; and (3) community-based exercise programming that is self directed and self monitored.

Within supervised exercise programs and programs offering exercise counseling and prescription, participants should complete a brief medical history and risk factor questionnaire. From the questionnaire, important information regarding potential limitations and restrictions for the individual participant's activity program can be made. Exercise leaders do well to require their senior participants to have had a physical examination with a physician within 2 years of the start of a vigorous exercise program. Participants should be encouraged to consult a physician if they have any questions regarding their medical status.

After an appropriate medical history is gathered, potential participants should undergo a preprogram evaluation in which flexibility, endurance capacity (aerobic), and strength are assessed. The primary purpose of the preprogram evaluation is to document baseline measures of flexibility, cardiorespiratory endurance, and strength. These baseline values not only assist the exercise leader in prescribing an appropriate physical activity level, but also provide feedback to participants regarding progress when the evaluation is repeated periodically. The evaluation measures need not be sophisticated. Flexibility may be assessed with sit-and-reach assessments, both on the floor and in a chair.

The use of a goniometer is helpful in determining limitations in joint flexibility and mobility. Observation of gait and movement from a seated to standing position provides insight into sensory impairment, impaired equilibrium, or orthostatic hypotension. Strength testing may take the form of simple grip strength testing combined with modified pushup and situp performance. Cardiorespiratory endurance capacity may be assessed by appropriate field tests, such as a walking speed test for 12 min or the chair step test. Submaximal bicycle testing with pulse palpation and blood pressure measurements may also be employed. The previously mentioned cardiorespiratory tests are intended to be functional evaluations that are at submaximal levels and in appropriately screened individuals are relatively safe and effective while providing data for exercise prescription and physical activity education.

Potential participants with documented CHD, diabetes mellitus, or known risk factors for these diseases should be recommended for diagnostic exercise tolerance testing as well as functional assessment. The testing and evaluation should be directed by a physician. Typical methods of exercise tolerance testing include graded treadmill exercise testing with continuous electrocardiographic (ECG) monitoring and simultaneous measurement of heart rate and blood pressure. Exercise tolerance testing often involves a symptom-limited testing protocol through which an estimation of $\dot{V}o_{2max}$ can be made. A number of appropriate treadmill testing protocols are currently in use. The modified Balke and modified Bruce protocols, in which the speed and grade are initially at less than 2.5 METS with gradual increases in workload of 1 to 2 METS every 2 to 3 min, are examples of appropriate testing protocols.

An alternative to treadmill testing is bicycle ergometry. The principles of ECG, heart rate, and blood pressure monitoring are the same. The most common reason for employing the bike is selected medical contraindications for the use of the treadmill, including the presence of osteoarthritis or an artificial limb, as well as an unstable gait or severe obesity. The use of the bike has one major disadvantage in symptom-limited testing — the common experience of localized muscle fatigue in the legs. This result sometimes interferes with the participant's ability to achieve sufficiently high heart rates as to be of diagnostic value.

When developing a community-based, self-directed program, medical clearance is left to the judgment of the individual participant. An active physical activity promotion campaign in the community seeks to educate the senior population regarding precautions and recommendations for moderate and vigorous physical activity. These messages should provide steps for seniors to follow before beginning a regular vigorous physical activity program. These steps should include:

1. Awareness of pre-existing medical problems (i.e., CHD, arthritis, osteoporosis, or diabetes mellitus)
2. Consultation before starting a program, with a physician or other appropriate health professional if any of the above-mentioned problems are suspected
3. Appropriate mode of activity and tips on different types of activities
4. Principles of training intensity and general guidelines as to rating perceived exertion (RPE) and training heart rate (THR)
5. Progression of activity and principles of starting slowly and gradually increasing activity time and intensity
6. Principles of monitoring symptoms of excessive fatigue
7. Making exercise fun and enjoyable

ADAPTATIONS OF THE EXERCISE PRESCRIPTION[14]

Mode of Activity. Many older individuals who wish to participate in regular exercise programming have significant limitations. Degenerative joint disease, including osteoarthritis, is common in this age group. The mode of exercise must be appropriately modified to accommodate these participants. Emphasis on minimal or non–weight-bearing activities, such as cycling, swimming, and chair and floor exercises, may be the most appropriate. For participants with difficulty in joint mobility of the knees and hips, movement down to and up from the floor may be initially contraindicated. Generally, most seniors are able to engage in moderate walking activities. Individualization of the mode of activity is important, including variation of activity as well as adjustments for participant bias and preference. Prescribing calisthenics for individuals suffering from degenerative joint changes should be done with care. Modified stretching and strengthening exercises should be included when indicated.

Frequency. Emphasis on more frequent activity (5 to 7 days per week) is important. This recommended increase in frequency has physiologic relevance for the maintenance of endurance capacity as well as flexibility. In addition, the greater frequency enhances compliance and leads to a greater probability of the subject assimilating physical activity into the daily routine.

Duration. An appropriate goal for most seniors is 20 to 40 min of endurance activity per session. Because of physiologic and pathophysiologic limitations, however, lower levels of exercise intensity are often necessary. Therefore, a session that approaches 1 hour in duration may be most effective for older adults.

Intensity. Because of the general medical and physiologic limitations often seen in older individuals, the intensity of activity is of critical importance. For participants with a history of CAD or who are at high risk for CAD, the exercise prescription should be based on the results of a recent ECG-monitored exercise evaluation. An appropriate target heart rate based on the formula of Karvonen can be calculated, as well as an appropriate MET level, both of which are adjusted for symptoms and/or ECG changes noted in the exercise test. Usually young-old ($\leq$75 years) individuals can have peak work capacities of 7 METS or greater, whereas the old-old ($>$75 years) participants usually have peak levels that do not exceed 4 METS. Unfortunately, the medical status and physical activity status of participants can vary considerably, so that generalization of workloads often becomes difficult. When an individual's work capacity has been assessed, the use of MET levels in calculating an appropriate intensity is useful. Use of the principles of RPE have proven helpful in regulating intensity in exercising older individuals. Usually a level of 12 to 15 on a scale of 6 to 20 is adequate for most conditioning activities. When participants are well oriented to this method, it becomes a useful self-monitoring mechanism for regulating intensity of exercise.

Progression of Activity. A gradual approach to increasing activity levels is most appropriate. With initiation of exercise, a 4- to 6-week period is usually necessary for seniors to progress from a moderate to vigorous conditioning level. Another 4 to 6 weeks is often necessary to achieve an appropriate maintenance level. Individual variability in fitness and adaptation to the exercise usually dictate the appropriate progression of activity.

LEADING AN EXERCISE PROGRAM FOR OLDER PARTICIPANTS[15]

PLANNING

Community-based exercise programs require adequate research before implementation. Focus groups with seniors is an appropriate approach to assessing the physical activity needs of older individuals. Facilities and environmental settings can then be adequately planned. Types of supervised programming should be well researched. Seniors should have adequate input regarding the types of activities for the program; community surveys of senior groups can provide invaluable information regarding the perceived exercise needs of the population. The promotion of the exercise programming should be focused, often with differing messages aimed at particular target groups. This step is important in exercise program leadership to ensure that an adequate subset of the senior community is involved in physical activity programming, whether supervised or self directed.

FACILITIES

When selecting facilities for supervised exercise programming, consider the previously mentioned limitations of older individuals. A facility with adequate lighting and ventilation is important. Ideally, a facility should limit background noise as much as possible because of the greater prevalence of hearing impairment in the elderly. A resilient surface is necessary and well-cushioned mats for floor exercise are important.

PROGRAMMING

The program should offer a good variety of activities that are designed not only for conditioning effects, but also for fun and enjoyment. Well-trained and amiable personnel are critical. Many programs succeed without the best of facilities or equipment because the staff members are empathetic, knowledgeable, and fun. Knowledge of the community and its resources are important in the promotion of programming. Selection of sites for programming should be convenient and easily accessible.

EMERGENCY SKILLS

All staff members involved in supervised programming should be certified in cardiopulmonary resuscitation and knowledgeable about basic first aid. Familiarity with the major medical disorders of the elderly (i.e., CAD, diabetes, arthritis, and hypoglycemia) ensures a safer environment for exercise. Participants in supervised programming or for whom exercise counseling and prescription is provided should have a basic knowledge of their medical and pharmaceutical regimens and how these might influence their response to exercise.

An appropriate emergency plan is essential in supervised programs. A file card for each participant, with important emergency phone numbers as well as the name and phone number of their physician, should be readily available. A pattern of referral for medical consultation should also be provided in the event that participants are without a primary physician and are in need of medical evaluation and treatment.

REFERENCES

1. Fleg JL: Alterations in cardiovascular structure and function with advancing age. *Am J Cardiol, 57*:33c–44c, 1986.
2. DeVries HA, Adams GM: Comparison of exercise responses in old and young men. II. Ventilatory mechanics. *J Gerontol, 27*:344–348, 1972.
3. Smith EL: Special considerations in developing exercise programs for the older adult. In *Behavioral Health: A Handbook of Health Enhancement and Disease Prevention.* Edited by JD Matarazzo, SM Weiss, JA Herd, NE Miller, and SM Weiss. New York: John Wiley & Sons, 1984.
4. Barry AJ, et al.: Effects of physical conditioning on older individuals: Motor performance and cognitive function. *J Gerontol, 21*:192–199, 1966.
5. Smith DM, et al.: Age and activity effects on rate of bone mineral loss. *J Clin Invest, 58*:716–721, 1976.
6. Johns RJ, Wright U: Relative importance of various tissues in joint stiffness. *J Appl Physiol, 17*:824–828, 1962.
7. Spirduso WW: Reaction and movement time as a function of age and physical activity. *J Gerontol, 30*:435–440, 1975.
8. Munns K: Effects of exercise on the range of joint motion. In *Exercise and Aging: The Scientific Basis.* Edited by EL Smith and RC Serfass. Hillside, NJ: Enslow Publishers, 1981.
9. Moritani T: Training adaptations in the muscles of older men. In *Exercise and Aging: The Scientific Basis.* Edited by EL Smith and RC Serfass. Hillside, NJ: Enslow Publishers, 1981.
10. Rowe JW, Shock NW, Defronzo RA: The influence of age on the renal response to water deprivation in man. *Nephron, 17*:270–278, 1976.
11. Heath GW, et al.: A physiological comparison of young and older endurance athletes. *J Appl Physiol, 51*:634–640, 1981.
12. Sidney KH, Shephard RJ: Attitudes towards health and physical activity in the elderly: Effects of a physical training program. *Med Sci Sports Exerc, 8*:246–252, 1977.
13. Fitzgerald PL: Exercise for the elderly. *Med Clin North Am, 69*:189–196, 1985.
14. Smith EL, Gilligan C: Physical activity prescription for the older adult. *Phys Sportsmed, 11*:91–101, 1983.
15. Smith EL, Stoedefalke KG, Gilligan C: *Aging and Exercise: Freedom through Fitness.* Biogerontology Laboratory, Department of Preventive Medicine, University of Wisconsin, Madison, Wisconsin, 1980.

VIII

HUMAN BEHAVIOR/ PSYCHOLOGY

CHAPTER 36

PRINCIPLES OF HEALTH BEHAVIOR CHANGE

C. BARR TAYLOR,
NANCY HOUSTON MILLER, AND
JUNE FLORA

Helping people begin and maintain health behavior change is a challenge for the most experienced counselor. In many settings, instructors have little time or opportunity to help participants make behavior changes. Nevertheless, behavioral scientists have identified some strategies that if systematically applied are useful in helping an individual begin and sustain health behavior change. We describe one model for health behavior change that includes some practical approaches. This is derived from social learning theory, a comprehensive analysis of human functioning in which human behavior is assumed to be developed and maintained on the basis of three interacting systems: behavioral, cognitive, and environmental.[1,2] Social learning theory emphasizes the human capacity for self-directed behavior change. Willingness to change is related to self-efficacy, which is influenced by four main factors: persuasion from an authority, observation of others, successful performance of the behavior, and physiologic feedback. Social learning theory is a useful model to help in the understanding of why people change; behavioral therapy provides the methods and strategies for effecting and maintaining behavior change.[3] Many excellent and detailed discussions of behavior change programs are available.[4-6]

In this chapter, the person helping another person make a health behavior change — a physician, nurse, exercise specialist, fitness instructor, or health educator — is the *instructor*; the person making the changes is the *participant*.

HEALTH BEHAVIOR CHANGE MODEL

Health behavior change can be conceptualized as occurring in stages, arbitrarily divided into the antecedent, adoption, and maintenance phases (Fig. 36–1). Antecedents refer to all conditions that exist that can help initiate, hinder, or support change. Adoption refers to the early phases at the start of a behavior change program. Maintenance applies to later phases when the participant is already undergoing behavior change.

ANTECEDENTS

People sometimes decide to change for reasons that even they do not understand or that are beyond their control. A chance encounter with a friend who has made important changes and looks better for it; an illness; a caustic remark from a co-worker; and clothes, once loose

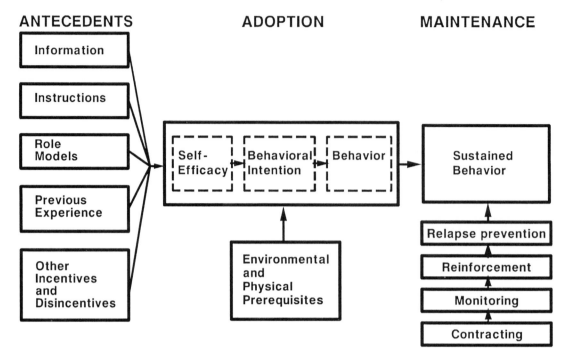

ANTECEDENTS   **ADOPTION**   **MAINTENANCE**

FIGURE 36–1. Stages of health behavior change.

that become tight fitting, are all events that may push a person to adopt a health behavior. Such chance occurrences, life experiences, and opportunities are often critical factors in instigating change. Nevertheless, social learning theory predicts that certain antecedents to behavior change can be identified that are useful in increasing a person's intention to change. We prefer to use the phrase "intention to change" rather than motivation, the customary term describing a person's willingness to change, because motivation implies dichotomy (the individual will or will not change), whereas intention implies a continuous psychologic state. If you ask a person to rate their intention on a scale from 0 to 10 in which 0 indicates no intention to change and 10 indicates certainty, people with little intention are not likely to change, whereas those persons with higher "scores" of intentions are more likely to change. Intentions frequently change and can be influenced by the factors listed in Figure 36–1.

Information. Intention to change often begins with information that should be presented in simple and clear ways, with the use of language or writing that is understandable to the audience. Keep in mind that 30 to 40% of the American public reads at a 7th grade level or lower. Information is most effective when com-

bined with instructions on how to make the changes. Although pamphlets, self-help books, and hand-outs are often used to communicate health information, most people read only 10 to 15% of such material, unless they are extremely interested in the topic or are held accountable for it. Some audiences that would seem to benefit most from information tend to ignore it: for instance, smokers tend to ignore messages describing the risks of smoking and nonexercisers know less about the benefits of physical activity than exercisers. Any knowledge critical for behavior change should be tested.

Instructions. Persuasion from a person of authority, e.g., instructions to change a particular behavior, is a powerful source of behavior change. Health care professionals are considered the most credible source of information by the public. Persuasion from an authoritative figure should occur in a kind but firm manner. People reluctant to make health behavior changes listen for ambivalence in a health professional's message. They are not, for example, likely to follow this message, "Smoking is bad for your health; you should think about stopping." They are more likely to be affected by, "You must stop smoking." Instructions should be clear, achievable, and accompanied by the necessary information about how to bring about changes. In addition, they should be reinforced by reminders and feedback. Participants should be asked to repeat the critical information.

Models.   Role models, whether family, friends, or other credible sources (e.g., health professionals), can facilitate change by allowing the participant to see how other individuals make changes, react to those changes, generalize those changes to different types of situations (e.g., how people practice food changes at home, in restaurants, and in grocery stores), and cope with difficult situations to maintain their healthy habits. People undergoing health behavior change can benefit from being asked by their instructors to think of those persons they know or admire who have made changes like the ones they want to make. Videotapes or films demonstrating how individuals have made changes and the effect of these changes can be effective in increasing intention to change.

Previous Experience.   Previous experience is a major factor in determining whether we begin a new health behavior. We are more likely to take an aspirin for a headache, for instance, if it was helpful in the past. Previous experience also leads to many superstitious health traps. If we happen to take an extra vitamin C tablet at a time when a cold seemed to resolve more rapidly than usual, we are likely to take an extra dose of vitamin C the next time we get a cold, whether or not it is really helpful. The level of our confidence to try a new behavior is largely determined by our previous experience. In helping a person change a health care behavior, have them review their previous success or failure with it. If they started exercise, for instance, but then quit, an important step is to determine why they quit last time and what they can do differently if the same problem occurs. As another example, a participant might fail to adopt a new diet because they feel unable to prepare the meals they are expected to prepare. People often need to develop new skills to be and feel more effective before change can occur. Developing new skills leads to increased confidence and increased intention to change.

Other Incentives and Disincentives.   Other incentives and disincentives are also important antecedents for health behavior change. Incentives should be built into the program and should outweigh the disincentives. Clients should be encouraged to answer the question, "How can I make sure that I benefit from this program?" Some of the benefits may be obvious, e.g., exercising to feel and look better; other benefits may not be as obvious, e.g., exercising to prevent disease. Reducing the disincentives anticipated with beginning a health program are equally important. Many people begin exercising at an inconvenient time, in a place that does not appeal to them, and with an activity they do not enjoy. Such disincentives almost ensure that the program will be short-lived.

Careful attention to these antecedents can influence a person's intention to adopt behavior change. With sufficient information; compelling instructions; appropriate models to change; positive physiologic feedback; increased confidence to change; and maximized incentives and minimized disincentives, a person is more likely to adopt a health behavior change.

An examination of the antecedents for change answers the questions: What does the participant need to know about the reasons for and methods of bringing about the desired change? What instructions has the participant been given from significant people in his life about the importance of making these changes? What are existing and potential models for change? What has been the participant's success with making this and comparable changes in the past? How confident does the participant feel that he can make the changes this time? What can be done to increase the participant's confidence? What are the potential incentives and disincentives for change?

ADOPTION

Once a person intends to make a behavior change and has high confidence that they will be able to succeed with the change, the adoption of the health change is often precipitated by "cues to action." For instance, many people begin a health care program on the basis of their symptoms or how they are feeling. Such physiologic and emotional feedback both cues people to change and is critical as to whether a program is sustained. Smoking relapse often occurs in the first few days after quitting because tobacco withdrawal symptoms may overwhelm intentions to stop. Poorly conditioned people may stop exercising in the first days of a new exercise program because of unpleasant feelings of being out of breath.

Certain environmental and physical prerequisites are often necessary for health behavior change and should be discussed with participants. Such prerequisites for exercising include such things as clothing, equipment, access to facilities, necessary written materials, and a release from a physician.

The early stages of change are often the most difficult. Replacing one activity, even a self-destructive one, with another involves many subtle and important shifts in peoples lives. Cigarette smokers often say they feel as though they have lost a good friend when they stop. The instructor should be particularly available and supportive at such times.

MAINTENANCE

Once a behavior is adopted, different factors determine whether it is maintained. Behaviors generally are maintained if they are satisfying (reinforcing) or if not doing them causes more discomfort than doing them. Four strategies have proven useful in enhancing maintenance: (1) the activity is monitored and feedback of change occurs (monitoring); (2) the activity is made as satisfying as possible (reinforcement); (3) relapse or interruptions are anticipated (see *Relapse Prevention*); and (4) commitment is formalized (see *Contracts*).

Monitoring. Self-report, diary, physiologic, or other types of monitoring are useful to sustain behavior change and to help instructors determine the progress made by their participants. Monitoring forms can be used by instructors for review and problem solving. In addition, monitoring through the use of self-report forms and diaries provides the participant with important feedback that may increase the likelihood that the behavior is maintained.

Many monitoring forms have been developed. In general, they should be simple and convenient to use. Chapter 38 provides an example of several exercise monitoring forms.

Reinforcement. Reinforcement is a powerful factor in sustaining behavior. An event is considered a reinforcer of a previous event if it increases the frequency of a previous event. Many environmental stimuli are natural reinforcers, for example, food, water, sexual activity, and warmth. Other activities are social or symbolic reinforcers, such as attention, praise, money, and diamonds. When considering reinforcers, it is necessary to bear in mind that reinforcers are idiosyncratic, that is, what is reinforcing to one person may not be reinforcing to another person. An example would be attempt-

ing to reinforce jogging behavior with cigarettes in a nonsmoker. Several excellent references are available concerning how to use reinforcement for health behavior change.[3-7]

Relapse Prevention. Various techniques are used to help participants avoid slips (lapses) that may lead to relapse or to prepare for interruptions or other events that may cause discontinuation of a program. The relapse prevention model is derived from studies of alcoholics and smokers trying to quit. Marlatt and colleagues observed that even one cigarette might lead to total relapse, and that preparation for the situations in which the cigarette urges are strongest (e.g., while drinking or experiencing stress) could help to prevent this relapse.[8] The model can be applied to other behaviors, such as exercise. For instance, to help exercisers continue with their program, the Stanford Cardiac Rehabilitation Program staff encourages people to monitor their exercise (see Fig. 36–2); to identify clear relapse danger signals, such as an actual or anticipated reduction in exercise frequency; and to develop strategies to deal with these potential relapses. When beginning an exercise program, for example, participants are encouraged to write down what they will do when illness, injury, or changes in work schedule interrupt their exercise program. They might ask a jogging partner for a telephone call to remind them to exercise as soon as they return from a vacation, leave a money "deposit" with a friend refundable when they have starting exercise again after an illness, or ask the instructor to call them periodically to determine if they are exercising.

Contracts. Written contracts with the participants themselves, a friend, or the instructor are also extremely useful to maintain change and to help people continue with a program. Instructors should not have participants write contracts that are unrealistic or unlikely to be achieved. Clients should feel they are at least 70% confident (on a scale, for example, ranging from 0 = no confidence to 100 = complete certainty) that they can fulfill the contract. An example of a contract is provided in Figure 36–2.

DEVELOPING A PROGRAM

A program consists of two parts: the adoption and maintenance components and how they are sequenced and integrated; and the interaction with the instructor. An example of the components integrated into the Stanford exer-

LOCKHEED/STANFORD EXERCISE TRAINING PROGRAM

Self-Monitoring Exercise Chart

Exercise Sessions / Week

4+	4+	4+	4+	4+	4+	4+	4+	4+	4+	4+	4+
3	3	3	3	3	3	3	3	3	3	3	3
2	2	2	2	2	2	2	2	2	2	2	2
1	1	1	1	1	1	1	1	1	1	1	1
0	0	0	0	0	0	0	0	0	0	0	0
WEEK ENDING											

> Enter date in "week ending" boxes.
> Mark your exercise sessions at the end of each week.
> Return by mail when chart is complete.
> Feel free to write in additional comments.

Name _____

FIGURE 36–2. Exercise contract.

cise studies of moderate exercise is detailed in Table 36–1.[9]

Organization. The components listed in Table 36–1 can be readily organized into a step-by-step approach. The first step is to ask the participant to consider making a change. Often people intend to adopt a behavior, but sometimes an important step is to recommend additional changes, for instance, to advise and help an exerciser to stop smoking. Suggesting such changes can be difficult, but few people resent a thoughtful attempt to help them improve their health. The second step, and perhaps part of asking a participant to consider making a change, is to provide information, instructions, and models; to review past experiences; to build confidence to change; and reduce disincentives and increase incentives to

change. The third step is to request a commitment that is specific in time and place as to when the new behavior or the first step in a chain of events leading to that behavior will occur. The fourth step is to develop with the participant a way to monitor progress with the new behavior and to determine when and how their progress will be reviewed. Early in the adoption phase, the participant should be trained in relapse prevention. Problem solving should be used as necessary to help overcome difficulties.

Instructor Qualities. Different instructors achieve different outcomes, even when the same program is used. The characteristics of an effective instructor are the subject of much debate and the ideal profile remains elusive. Instructors seem to be more effective if the partici-

Table 36-1. Elements of Exercise Program Design

ANTECEDENTS AND ADOPTION
  Written description of benefits of exercise
  Assessment of expectations; review of expectations to make them realistic
  Assessment of confidence; skills training to enhance confidence
  Videotape instruction on how to warmup and keep heart rate within guidelines
  Physical examination, treadmill, weight, and skinfold assessment
  Experimentation to identify most enjoyable locations

MAINTENANCE
  Monitoring
    Weekly diaries of exercise duration and intensity
    Heart rate monitor with auditory feedback
  Reinforcement
    Social: Biweekly phone calls from staff; group meetings
    Monetary: None built into program
    Physical: Three and six-month treadmill test and weight assessment
    Symbolic: T-shirts
    Accomplishment: Monitoring of confidence, psychologic variables
  Contracts
    None built into program
  Relapse prevention
    Participant develops own plans for interruptions to exercise

pant feels that the instructor is competent and likes, understands, and is interested in the participant. This relationship translates into a bond between the instructor and the participant that makes the program effective. Role-playing of typical participant situations with peers and receiving feedback is a particularly good way to develop interpersonal skills.

Instructors commonly make two errors that undermine the effectiveness of health care programs and lead to frustration. The first error is *overpersistence.* Some instructors continue to work with a participant who, through poor adherence, indicates little interest in changing. Instructors who take too much responsibility for the actions of another person are particularly likely to be overpersistent. Unfortunately, overpersistent instructors often begin to resent their participants inaction, to feel chronic frustration, or to devote too much time to that person. To avoid these problems of overpersistence, instructors must have or develop clear guidelines as to when a program or request for change is discontinued. In one YMCA program, participants meet with the nurse coordinator to review reasons for their noncompliance, to solve problems, and to set measurable compliance goals. A second meeting is scheduled if the client continues to be noncompliant. If they fail after the second meeting, a termination meeting is scheduled to drop the participant from the program. During the termination meeting, the nurse coordinator explains that this program is not appropriate for that person, and that in light of the dangers of noncompliance both to the participant and to persons who might be influenced by noncompliance (e.g., overexerting), the participant should not continue in the program.

The second problem undermining the effectiveness of a program is *underpersistence.* For these instructors, minimal effort, particularly minimal planned effort, is put into helping a client adopt or maintain a program. A plan should be developed to determine how each area of behavior change is undertaken in a program, perhaps by using the approaches outlined in other chapters in this text or in other publications.

Social learning theory is the basis for a model for understanding behavior change; behavior therapy helps to develop many effective change procedures. Information, instructions, models, increasing confidence negatively affected by previous experiences, as well as maximizing incentives and minimizing disincentives can increase intentions to change and lead to actual adoption of health behavior change. Once adopted, maintenance can be improved by monitoring and feedback, reinforcement, relapse prevention, and the use of contracts.

REFERENCES

1. Bandura A: Self-efficacy: Toward a unifying theory of behavioral change. Psychol Rev, *84*:191–215, 1977.
2. Bandura A: *Social Learning Theory.* Englewood Cliffs, NJ: Prentice-Hall, 1977.
3. Agras WS, Kazdin AE, Wilson GT: Behavior therapy: Toward an applied clinical science. San Francisco: WH Freeman, 1979.
4. Melamed BG, Siegel LJ: *Behavioral Medicine: Practical Applications in Health Care.* New York: Springer, 1980.
5. Watson DL, Tharp RG: *Self-directed Behavior Change.* Monterey: Brooks/Cole, 1981.
6. Goldfried M, Davison GC: *Clinical Behavior Therapy.* New York: Holt, Rinehart and Winston, 1976.
7. Cautela JR, Kastenbaum RA: Reinforcement survey schedule for use in therapy, training, and research. *Psychol Rep, 29*:115–130, 1967.
8. Marlatt GA, Gordon JR (eds): *Relapse Prevention: Maintenance Strategies in the Treatment of Addiction.* New York: Guilford Press, 1985.
9. Gossard D, et al.: Effects of low and high intensity home exercise training on functional capacity in healthy middle-aged men. *Am J Cardiol, 57*:446–449, 1986.

CHAPTER 37

BASIC PSYCHOLOGIC PRINCIPLES RELATED TO GROUP EXERCISE PROGRAMS

C. BARR TAYLOR AND NANCY HOUSTON MILLER

When conducting exercise programs, exercise program personnel encounter a variety of psychologic issues and problems. Therefore, these professionals should be familiar with basic psychologic principles and ideas to manage their clients and groups most effectively. The following discussion is a brief overview of some of the psychologic principles that affect exercise participants. The topic areas reflect those areas of concern frequently encountered by exercise instructors, and address the learning objectives in the *Guidelines for Exercise Testing and Prescription* (3rd Ed.).

CRISIS MANAGEMENT/FAILURE TO COPE

A crisis is a period, usually brief, of life when demands from an event exceed the ability and resources to cope, leading to distress.[1] People in crisis feel hopeless and extremely anxious and tense. Other common feelings are fear, anger, guilt, embarrassment, and shame. The high level of anxiety often impedes thinking and paradoxically impairs coping.

The most common crises are situational: premature delivery, status and role change, rape, physical illness, physical abuse, divorce, or loss of a loved one. Maturation, however, may also precipitate crises as a new stage in life requires new coping responses. People in crises should not be considered mentally ill, yet their distress should be taken seriously. Crisis management follows four broad steps:

1. *Psychosocial assessment of the individual in crisis.* Always determine if individual is capable of suicide or assault to other persons.
2. *Development of a plan.* Usually involves referral to an expert in crisis management.
3. *Implementation of the plan.* Involves drawing on the person's personal, social, and material resources.
4. *Follow-up.* Continued support and reinforcement of patient's actions (when appropriate) are important.

The exercise instructor is involved with the first two steps, and needs to continue to ascertain the status of the participants during the final two steps.

PSYCHOSOCIAL ASSESSMENT

The purpose of assessment is to determine the origin of the problem, the risk of suicide or assault, and if the participant is able to take care of himself or herself. If the instructor in any way suspects that a participant is depressed or upset, or for other reasons is suicidal, the instructor should approach the participant as to whether suicide is contemplated. Any suggestion that suicide is a possibility should be followed to determine the seriousness of the intent. Participants with physical illness, who feel helpless and hopeless, are at particularly high risk of suicide. A common belief is that asking about suicide may plant the idea; the opposite is true. An open discussion about suicidal feeling is both helpful in and of itself and can set the stage for referral. Participants who are suicidal or dangerous and unable to take care of themselves should be referred for immediate professional help. Suicide crisis centers and community mental health centers exist in all large communities and have capable staff members who can provide advice and recommendations as to how and where to refer a person. Participants can also be taken to hospital emergency rooms where the staff is familiar in dealing with crises. Make sure that the participant has an immediate place to go and a way to get there. Suicidal and disabled individuals should be accompanied by police, mental health staff, family, or friends to the place of referral.

Most crises, however, do not lead to nor are accompanied by emergency situations. Further assessment includes answering questions like these: To what extent has the crisis disrupted normal life patterns? Is the individual able to hold a job? Can the person handle the responsibility of daily living? Has the crisis disrupted the lives of others? Has the crisis distorted the individual's perception of reality? Is the usual support system present, absent, or exhausted? What are the available resources?

MANAGEMENT PLAN

Development and implementation of a crisis management plan is not appropriate for most exercise instructors; however, follow-up contact is appropriate. People in crisis appreciate the concern of other persons and often can benefit substantially from such concern.

COMMUNICATION SKILLS

Certain basic interviewing skills are useful for obtaining information and for establishing a

Table 37–1. Facilitative Communication Behaviors

Noncommittal acknowledgment (verbal and nonverbal). Brief expressions that communicate understanding acceptance, and empathy, such as: "Oh," "I see," "Mm-hmmm," head nodding, focused posture.

Door openers. Invitations to expand or continue the expressions of thoughts and feelings (without specifying the content), such as "Could I hear more?" "Please go on," "I don't quite understand," "Please pursue that," "and (use some of the last words the patient said.)."

Content paraphrase. Rephrasing the factual portion of the message and send it back to check your accuracy in understanding.

positive relationship with an individual.[2,3] In acquiring information from patients and in problem solving and making recommendations for change, the use of facilitative or neutral communication skills is important, i.e., skills that encourage the participant to speak openly and to avoid disruptive communication behaviors. Definitions of some facilitative communication behaviors are provided in Table 37–1.

Confronting the individual is sometimes necessary. Confrontation involves directing attention to something that the client may not be aware of or is reluctant to admit. Confrontation should only address observable facts and not make inferences about the patient's motives or specific emotional state. For example, a post-myocardial infarction participant who is intoxicated at the time of an exercise session and is disruptive may need to be confronted about the behavior. An example of an inappropriate confrontation follows:

Exercise instructor: You have been drinking. You had better not drink before you come here.

An appropriate confrontation might be:

Exercise instructor: You seem to be acting funny today. Have you been drinking?
Participant: Nah.
Exercise instructor: I can smell alcohol on your breath. When did you last have something to drink?
Participant: Oh, a couple of beers about an hour ago.
Exercise instructor: I can't allow people to exercise here if they have been drinking. Will you make sure you have not been drinking before you come next time?

Most of us are uncomfortable with direct confrontation, but it is often necessary as well as useful.

PSYCHOPATHOLOGY

The *Diagnostic and Statistical Manual of the American Psychiatric Association* lists over 100 diagnostic categories.[4] Only the few general problems the exercise leader is likely to encounter, however, are discussed in this section.

DEPRESSION

Depression affects 5 to 10% of adults at one time or another.[5] In addition to feeling "down," depression is often accompanied by somatic symptoms, including weight loss or gain, loss of appetite, sleep disturbance (particularly early morning waking with trouble getting back to sleep), loss of energy and fatigue, and loss of interest in usual activities. Depressed patients may exhibit psychomotor retardation, easy crying, and a sad face. Depressed patients often feel helpless and hopeless and exhibit self-reproach. Most importantly from an assessment standpoint, depression is frequently accompanied by suicidal feelings. Suicidal feelings in depressed patients should be assessed directly, and such patients should be referred for care, following the aforementioned guidelines for emergency crises. Screening questions for depression are provided in Table 37–2.

Hospitalization for psychiatric care is sometimes necessary, but more often depressed patients recover with professional help, medication, and the passage of time. The symptomatology of depression makes exercising diffi-cult, but exercise appears to be beneficial in removing many of the symptoms of depression.[6] Depressed patients may benefit from structured exercise programs and from exercise with other people.

ANXIETY DISORDERS

Anxiety affects everyone at one time or another. Severe anxiety, however, can lead to avoidance and restriction of life's activities, and can be associated with severe depression and terrifying panic attacks. Acute anxiety can usually be resolved with reassurance or brief periods of psychotherapy.

Chronic anxiety is usually secondary to depression, but it may represent a primary anxiety disorder. The three most prevalent primary anxiety disorders are Generalized Anxiety Disorder, Panic Disorder, and Agoraphobia.[7] Generalized Anxiety Disorder is characterized by excessive worry and anxiety and signs of motor tension (e.g., trembling, muscle tension, restlessness); autonomic hyperactivity (e.g., sweating, dry mouth, and frequent urination); vigilance; and scanning (e.g., feeling keyed up or on edge all the time.) Panic disorder is characterized by recurrent panic attacks, which are discrete periods of apprehension of fear accompanied by such symptoms as dyspnea, palpitations, choking, chest pain or discomfort, sweating, dizziness, fear of going crazy, and/or doing something uncontrolled. The first panic attack occurs usually in the early 20s and comes "out of the blue." Agoraphobic patients have panic attacks and they also have extensive avoidance. An agoraphobic patient would not likely be able to participate in an exercise class or program, but doing so would be of great ben-

Table 37–2. Depression Screen

Circle a number from the scale below to show how much you are troubled by feeling miserable or depressed:

0	1	2	3	4	5	6	7	8
Not at all		Slightly troublesome		Definitely troublesome		Markedly troublesome		Very severely troublesome

If you have been feeling depressed:

	Yes	No
a. Have you had poor appetite or significant weight loss?	___	___
b. Have you had trouble falling asleep, waking frequently, trouble staying asleep, waking too early, or sleeping too much?	___	___
c. Have you lost interest or pleasure in your usual activities?	___	___
d. Have you been having trouble thinking or concentrating?	___	___
e. Have you been thinking about death or about hurting yourself?	___	___

Interpretation

Patients who score 4 or higher and have two of the items a–e marked yes may be seriously depressed.

efit. Chronic anxiety can occur secondary to psychiatric problems besides depression, such as alcoholism, drug abuse, and schizophrenia. It can also be caused by medical problems, most commonly hyperthyroidism, pheochromocytoma, hypoglycemia, and temporal lobe epilepsy.[8]

Some patients with anxiety may report unpleasant symptoms with exercise. In fact, in several studies conducted in the 1950s, scientists reported that anxious patients produced more lactate with exercise and were exercise intolerant. These early observations have not been confirmed in more recent studies; however, mitral valve prolapse occurs more commonly in anxious patients. One group of researchers found that mitral valve prolapse patients have evidence of adrenergic dysregulation, for instance they are orthostatic on rising and are hypovolemic.[9] Use of a treadmill can help reassure anxious patients that exercise is safe and can help the exercise instructor identify any contraindications to exercise.[10]

ALCOHOL AND DRUG ABUSE

Drug and alcohol abuse are more common than depression and anxiety. When the instructor suspects alcohol abuse, e.g., the patient smells of alcohol, reports black-out periods, and seems preoccupied with alcohol, the instructor may need to confront the participant about alcohol use. The Michigan Alcohol Screening Test (MAST) can be used to collect more information about the clients alcohol use (see Table 37–3).[11]

If heavy alcohol use is noted in patients before participation in an exercise session, the participant warrants confrontation about their behavior as well as the physiologic effects of alcohol on the heart. The participant's behavior may also be destructive in a group setting; referral to outside services should be offered.

ANOREXIA NERVOSA

Anorexia nervosa is a potentially life-threatening eating disorder; the clinical picture of this condition is listed in Table 37–4.[12,13] Although it is a relatively rare condition, the incidence of anorexia appears to be increasing. Most anorexics exercise to excess. If anorexia is suspected, a weight and dietary history should be

Table 37–3. Michigan Alcohol Screening Test

	Yes	No
Do you drink alcohol?	——	——
If yes:		
1. Do you feel you are a normal drinker?	——0	——2
2. Do friends or relatives think you are a normal drinker?	——0	——2
3. Have you ever attended a meeting of Alcoholics Anonymous (AA)?	——5	——0
4. Have you ever lost friends or girlfriends/boyfriends because of drinking?	——2	——0
5. Have you ever gotten into trouble at work because of drinking?	——2	——0
6. Have you ever neglected your obligations, your family or your work for two or more days in a row because you were drinking?	——2	——0
7. Have you ever had delirium tremens (DTs), severe shaking, heard voices, or seen things that were not there after heavy drinking?	——2	——0
8. Have you ever been in a hospital because of drinking?	——5	——0
9. Have you ever gone to anyone for help about your drinking?	——5	——0
10. Have you ever been arrested for drunk driving or driving after drinking?	——2	——0
TOTAL	——	——

Interpretation

This instrument represents a revised form of the shortened Michigan Alcohol Screening Test. Scores 6 or greater indicate past or present problems with excessive alcohol abuse.

obtained, and if possible percentage of body fat should be measured.

Anorectic patients are best helped by professionals specializing in eating disorders, but the exercise specialist can play an important role in their care by confronting the patient as to the seriousness of the disorder and by insisting that the patient seek help. Once the patient has begun therapy, the exercise instructor can help the patient design a normal eating and activity pattern, emphasizing health and proper nutrition, not weight; and in general providing support.

Table 37–4. Clinical Picture of Anorexia Nervosa

Loss of more than 25% premorbid body weight
Distorted body image
Fears of weight gain or of loss of eating control
Adolescent and young adult women primarily affected
Perfectionist behavior
Refusal to maintain normal body weight
No known physical illness to account for weight loss

GROUP DYNAMICS

Because many exercise programs are conducted in groups, an understanding not only of how to handle individual problems but also of the effects of certain behaviors on the group is important. Several good references are available concerning group dynamics.[14]

Within any group are chronic complainers, comedians, disruptive individuals, noncompliers, and participants who overexert themselves. If not addressed early in the program, such individuals can dominate group time and make extraordinary demands on staff members.

When dealing with behaviors that may cause significant reactions by both the staff and the group, important points to assess are: (1) how you are feeling about the patient; (2) what the patient is doing or saying; and (3) what are the dynamics of the interaction itself, especially how to manage the situation from the start to avoid problems that ultimately influence the entire group.

CHRONIC COMPLAINERS

Typical initial reactions to the chronic complainer are feelings of avoidance, impatience, and anger. Anger is especially common if the patient continually criticizes people or things that you admire. In managing such an individual, first determine whether the patient is simply looking for a sympathetic ear and is really not complaining, or whether this problem is constant. Accordingly, appropriate steps to follow are

1. Listen attentively
2. Acknowledge what the patient has said and how the patient must feel about the situation, interrupting if necessary
3. Do not agree with the patient; this implies acceptance
4. Set limits regarding staff time
5. Agree upon how the situation should be stopped

DISRUPTORS/COMEDIANS

Disruptors and comedians have many of the same characteristics, and may be handled somewhat the same in a group setting. The disruptor may cause feelings of impatience, frustration, and anger, whereas initial reactions to the comedian may be mild. If, however, the comedian's humor becomes disruptive, your reaction may be the same as that to the disruptor. In addition, the comedian's senseless humor may lead to avoidance. The disruptor and the comedian often feel insecure or unappreciated, or are in need of attention. Although staff members may need to spend more time with these individuals to ascertain their needs, the added time may help to resolve the problems. If continued disruptive behavior occurs, however, limits must be set, with goals for changing the behavior. If the disruptive behavior persists, dropping the patient from the group warrants consideration to avoid unpleasant reactions that may develop from other group members.

NONCOMPLIERS

The noncompliant participant in a group exercise program is at risk when exercising haphazardly, and detracts from the sense of cohesion necessary to ensure positive group dynamics. The leader of a group exercise session should keep in mind the following points when handling noncompliance.

1. Assess the intention of the patient's behavior
2. Determine the barriers to attendance
3. Provide positive reinforcement
4. Problem-solve solutions to the lack of attendance
5. Set incremental goals
6. Choose methods to enhance compliance, such as contracting, self-rewards, and telephone prompts
7. Monitor change in the behavior
8. Consider dropping the participant from the program if person is unwilling to cooperate

OVEREXERTERS

Instructors often find a participant in an exercise program who is unwilling to listen to instructions about target heart rates and the necessity for maintaining these heart rates. This person tends to exhibit characteristics of the type A personality (competitive attitude, underlying hostility, and time urgency). The overexerciser foolishly undertakes bursts of exercise at high heart rates, and may disrupt the class with behavior similar to that of the disruptor. Because maintenance of heart rate is critical to the safety of any program, this person must be addressed immediately upon ascertaining the negative behavior. By the following steps, the instructor can counteract the behavior and ensure increased safety for the participant.

1. Identify for the participant the type of behavior exhibited and the effects regarding safety (participant is often unaware and has not listened)
2. Reinforce for the participant that this type of behavior is unacceptable
3. Set limits regarding the consequences of continued behavior
4. Positively reinforce the participant when exercising appropriately
5. Consider dropping the participant if unwillingness to comply with instructions persists

This brief overview of some psychologic issues relevant to exercise programs is only a starting point. Exercise instructors should identify mental health professionals in their communities with whom they can consult as well as to whom they can refer clients in need of care.

Acknowledgments

We thank Kathy Berra for her helpful comments.

REFERENCES

1. Hoff LA: *People in Crisis.* 2nd Ed. Menlo Park: Addison-Wesley, 1984.
2. Enelow AJ, Swisher SN: *Interviewing and Patient Care.* New York: Oxford, 1979.
3. Froelich RE, Bishop EM: *Medical Interviewing: A Programmed Text.* St. Louis: C.V. Mosby, 1969.
4. American Psychiatric Association: *Diagnostic and Statistical Manual of Mental Disorders.* 3rd Ed. Washington, D.C.: American Psychiatric Association, 1980.
5. Rush AJ, Altshuler EZ (eds): *Depression: Basic Mechanisms, Biology and Treatments.* New York: Guilford, 1986.
6. Taylor CB, Sallis JF, Needle R: The relation of physical activity and exercise to mental health. *Public Health Rep, 100:*195–201, 1985.
7. Klein D: *The Anxiety Disorders. Psychiatry Update.* Vol. III. Washington, D.C.: American Psychiatric Press, 1984.
8. Stein MB: Panic disorder and medical illness. *Psychosomatics, 27:*833–838, 1986.
9. Gaffney FA, et al.: Abnormal cardiovascular regulation: The mitral valve prolapse syndrome. *Am J Cardiol, 52:*316–320, 1983.
10. Taylor CB, et al.: Treadmill exercise test and ambulatory measures in patients with panic attacks. *Am J Cardiol, 60:*48J–52J, 1987.
11. Hedlund JL, Vieweg BW: The Michigan Alcoholism Screening Test (MAST): A comprehensive review. *J Operat Psychol, 15:*65, 1984.
12. Garfinkel PE, Garner DM: *Anorexia Nervosa: A Multidimensional Perspective.* New York: Brunner/Mazel, 1982.
13. Harris RT: Bulimarexia and related serious eating disorders with medical complications. *Ann Intern Med, 99:*800–807, 1983.
14. Yalom ID: *The Theory and Practice of Group Psychotherapy.* 3rd Ed. New York: Basic Books, 1985.

38

ADHERENCE TO EXERCISE

ABBY C. KING AND JOHN E. MARTIN

EXTENT OF THE PROBLEM

Over the past few decades, we have witnessed a virtual explosion of interest by the American public and health professionals alike in physical activity as a means for achieving a variety of goals, including better health. Despite this increased interest, as well as the belief by most adults that they would benefit personally from additional physical activity, available evidence indicates that about 66% of Americans do not exercise regularly (i.e., weekly) and between 28 and 45% do not exercise at all. During the past decade, participation in all types of physical activity has shown an increase of only 10%, with this increase primarily limited to such population segments as young adults and individuals belonging to high socioeconomic groups. Population segments that are notably under-represented among the ranks of those engaging in exercise include older individuals (particularly women); the less educated; blue-collar workers; smokers; and overweight individuals. For the less than 10% of sedentary adults likely to begin a regular exercise program within a year, and those already participating in group or individual exercise, approximately one half can be expected to drop out within 3 to 6 months. For individuals enrolled in secondary prevention programs, a 50% dropout by 12 months is typical.

The aforementioned statistics indicate that helping many individuals stay regularly involved in a physical activity program is a challenge requiring creativity and patience on the part of the health professional. We can be helped in our efforts by taking advantage of the current public enthusiasm for becoming more active as well as the growing wealth of findings suggesting the types of strategies that can be effective in enhancing physical activity participation.

REASONS FOR THE ADHERENCE PROBLEM

A belief that is gaining popularity is that in at least some ways physical activity may be a unique health behavior, governed by factors that differ somewhat from other health behaviors.[1-4] Certainly the demand for regularity in performing physical activity so to continue to reap health benefits throughout life calls for innovative methods of studying the *process* of making regular exercise a habit. Another fact receiving attention is that the factors influencing initial adoption and early participation in exercise may differ from those affecting subsequent maintenance. These factors are discussed subsequently.

CURRENT KNOWLEDGE

Although no one theory allows investigators to explain fully why individuals become or stay active, researchers have been helped in their efforts to understand such health behaviors by placing them in the context of a *social learning model* of health behavior change. This social learning approach, broadly defined, views such behaviors as being initiated and maintained through a complex interaction of personal, behavioral, and environmental factors and conditions. Put another way, an individual's past experiences with physical activity, how they view physical activity in general and different forms of activity in particular, the extent of their current activity-related knowledge and skills, and how the surrounding environment either helps or hinders their efforts to increase activity levels, all play a role in influencing how active the individual currently is and will remain.

Personal Factors

In addition to *demographic* and *health* factors, such as age and smoking status, variables influencing participation in regular physical activity include *past experiences* with physical activity; an individual's *perceptions* of *health status* as well as exercise ability and skills; feelings of *personal responsibility* for one's own health; the *perceived physical demands* of activity; and an understanding of how increased activity will *personally benefit* the individual, both in the short term as well as in the long term. In addition, a person's rating of *self-motivation* is related to continued maintenance of an exercise regimen. Importantly, when "self-motivation" is defined as the ability to find rewards for behavior independent of external rewards available for that behavior, it is something that conceivably can be *learned* by the individual. This concept is preferable to definitions of motivation that place the blame for nonadherence on internal processes related to "personality" and similar constructs. These latter definitions, aside from being unfair to the individual by ignoring extrapersonal influences on behavior (e.g., the environment), do not provide the health professional with a firm direction for intervention.

Although many of the abovementioned factors are associated to some extent with *initial participation* in physical activity, relatively few appear to influence substantially how long an individual maintains an exercise regimen.

Behavioral Factors

Behavioral factors include the actual *skills* an individual possesses to carry out physical activity to maximize exercise-related benefits while minimizing injury, boredom, and other impediments to maintenance. Such skills include the knowledge and use of behavioral and psychologic strategies that help the individual to negotiate the barriers and pitfalls that inevitably interfere with being active on a regular basis.

Environmental/Program Factors

A number of environmental and program-based factors can influence initial participation as well as adherence, including: *family influences* and support, with individuals who report their spouses to be neutral or unsupportive of their physical activity more likely to drop out; *access to facilities*, for those individuals preferring facility-based activities; *weather; regimen flexibility;* the *convenience* of the activity (either real or perceived); immediate *cues and prompts* in the environment promoting physical activity (e.g., reminders to exercise); as well as the *immediate consequences* of the activity for the individual.

Immediate consequences, including observance of physical activity-related benefits and enjoyability of the activity itself, are factors that are likely to have a strong impact on subsequent adherence. Conversely, the sedentary person persists in this unhealthy pattern principally because it is immediately reinforcing, and any attempts to become physically active have met with immediate aversive consequences. Thus, it is the task of the health professional to ensure that initial attempts to exercise are painless, enjoyable, and highly reinforcing (see later discussion). Although time constraints are typically noted as a major reason for inactivity, regular exercisers complain as much about time-related difficulties as those persons who are not regularly active. Thus, perceived available time may reflect in large part the priority the individual places on being physically active rather than actual time limitations per se.

Several points must be made concerning the

identification of the factors influencing physical activity adoption and adherence. First, as mentioned previously, the factors that most strongly influence initial adoption are most likely different than those that affect how well activity is maintained once started. Second, the currently noted variables clearly constitute only part of all the factors relevant in affecting activity levels, many of which have yet to be identified. Because of the complex inter-relationships among these variables, many individuals may have difficulty reporting why they are having difficulty starting or maintaining a physical activity program unless they actually *monitor* their activities. Third, some factors that have been identified as predictive of inactivity (e.g., smoking status; being overweight) indicate that those individuals who can reap the most health benefits from regular physical activity, in terms of reducing health risks, are those persons who currently are least likely to adopt or maintain an activity program. Finally, the variety of factors implicated indicates the importance of developing programs and strategies that fit the needs and preferences of different groups of individuals. This matching or *"tailoring"* approach can be contrasted with the more typical method of trying to get individuals to "fit into" ongoing, already existing programs. By tailoring physical activity approaches to fit population or individual needs more closely, health professionals may be able to decrease the drop-out rate during the initial "critical period" (i.e., the first 3 to 6 months), when reduced participation or dropping out typically occurs.

CHANGING PHYSICAL ACTIVITY PATTERNS

INCREASING ADOPTION AND EARLY ADHERENCE

Adoption of increased activity patterns can be enhanced through paying particular attention to factors in each of the aforementioned personal, behavioral, and environmental/program spheres.

Personal and Behavioral Factors

In terms of personal factors, previous experiences with physical activity should be explored, along with any unreasonable beliefs and misconceptions the individual may harbor toward activity (e.g., "no pain, no gain;" older individuals should not be active, i.e., they need to "conserve their energy"). For example, many would-be exercisers believe that exercise is an inherently painful and aversive process; these individuals not only must be told but also must be shown that this statement is absolutely untrue. The utility of more moderate activities of daily living (e.g., brisk walking) is often unknown to many sedentary individuals, and may for many persons be more appealing than more structured, vigorous activity regimens. Behaviorally, many sedentary individuals can benefit from specific instruction (accompanied by actual rehearsal and feedback) on appropriate ways of performing specific activities (e.g., jogging, striding, cycling, and warmup exercises) so to obtain health-related benefits while avoiding injury.

In addition to activity-related attitudes, knowledge, and skills, a physical activity program should be made *personally relevant* for the individual, both in terms of the type of activity or activities chosen and the goals of the program. For instance, if stress reduction is a motivating factor for an individual, then activities that can be helpful in reducing stress (i.e., not overly competitive, noisy, or demanding) should be targeted. Examples of such activities include brisk walking, jogging, or bicycling programs conducted outdoors in pleasant surroundings, which could allow the individual time to "get away from it all."

Additionally, a useful measure is to structure appropriate *expectations* concerning physical activity and what it can and cannot do as early as possible, to stress the varied benefits of making the change for the individual, as well as exploring any perceived *barriers* to increasing activity (e.g., unreasonable expectations; fear of embarrassment, failure, boredom). A simple questionnaire regarding expectations for the individual can provide the health professional with early clues as to where such expectations may lie.

Environmental/Program Factors

Numerous environmental and program-related factors can enhance initial adoption and early adherence to physical activity.

Convenience. Three convenience factors relate importantly to the successful initiation and maintenance of an exercise program. First, researchers clearly demonstrated that the greater the effort required to prepare for doing physical activity, such as a long drive to and from an exercise facility, the greater the potential for drop-out (up to twice the drop-out and one half the initial participation rates for inconvenient facilities). Facilities should be within easy access to the individual. Alternatively, encouraging methods of being physically active in or around the home (the place where many individuals report preferring to exercise) can make convenience less of a potential deterrent to adherence. Care is needed to ensure the prescription to or encouragement for participation in an exercise program (i.e., joining Spa or Health Club) that is close to the home or workplace or is conveniently in between these locations.

Along with the physical convenience of the activity is the second convenience factor of exercise — time. If the program being offered utilizes a class structure, offering several time options can be helpful. For some members of groups with extreme time constraints, such as working mothers, discussing alternatives to a class format is often necessary. Alternatively, some health programs and establishments, as well as worksite settings, now offer childcare services.

The third convenience of exercise factor concerns the exercise mode itself. If the exercise selected requires special, costly, or time-consuming preparation, such as skiing or possibly even swimming, the level of exercise adherence can be expected to be potentially lower. Thus, the selection of the exercise type or mode, the location or facility, and the time of day, can be of critical importance in the early stages of acquisition of the exercise habit. Each choice should therefore be evaluated carefully by both the exerciser and health professional before embarking on any systematic program.

Behavior Shaping. For sedentary individuals, the major objective is to establish a physical activity habit through allowing the individual *success* in accomplishing activity goals while decreasing opportunities for failure. Therefore, the initial activity prescription should be one that, although less rigorous than the health professional might prefer, is easily *doable* given the person's current preferences, motivation, skills, and present life circumstances. For some individuals, this shaping may translate into an initial increase simply in activities of daily living (e.g., walking more at work and at home; taking stairs). For other individuals, the initial prescription may involve structured aerobic ac-

tivities twice a week, with a concomitant increase in routine activities, until the individual is ready to move on to a more vigorous activity schedule.

The key consideration in all exercise programs and prescriptions should be the *gradual shaping* of successive approximations of the ultimate exercise and/or fitness goal. When this important behavior shaping principle is violated, such as starting exercisers at too high an intensity, frequency, or duration, adherence is almost always negatively affected. For example, when beginning exercisers are exposed to exercise intensities greater than 85% of aerobic capacity, exercise frequencies greater than or equal to 5 days per week, and/or exercise sessions of more than 45 min duration, the rate of injuries and dropping out significantly increases, affecting as many as one-half the participants.

Thus, the exercise regimen should be *easy* and *gradually incremented*, ensuring success at each stage. Most importantly, health professionals and beginning exercisers should focus primarily on shaping and maintaining the *exercise habit* for about the first 6 to 12 weeks, rather than on rapid establishment of the optimal regimen for desired benefits. The health professional must always keep in mind that any benefits of even the most successful physical training program are lost completely unless the exercise habit foundation is solidly established. This approach of first establishing behavioral control of the exercise habit implies that health professionals should encourage early participants to "just show up" (e.g., "No matter how little you may feel like doing or are able to do . . . remember, we are working on reinforcing the habit of exercising, the benefits will definitely come, and stay, if you can master this first 'habit step' ").

Several methods might be considered for use in properly shaping exercise and to avoid overextending the early participants. Exercisers should be encouraged to maintain an intensity level at which they can still comfortably talk without breathing or sweating heavily. This level can be easily monitored by the participant as well as the health professional. Exercising with other participants and talking throughout the session is an excellent method of controlling the intensity. Heart rate is a good physiologic index of intensity: exercisers can monitor pulse rates during the exercise (this assessment can also be done by using portable heart rate monitors with preset alarms). The Borg Scale, or rating of perceived exertion (RPE), is excellent for tracking the perception of exercise intensity (in many ways just as important as the actual physical work output).[6] In practice, these measures can be used together. For example, in the more sedentary and unfit participants, an RPE no higher than 12 and a heart rate of less than 70% maximum would be recommended for optimal enjoyment and lifetime habit establishment, whether the form of exercise is routine activities such as walking or programmed aerobic training. Figure 38–1 is an example of individual monitoring of heart rate within an "effective comfort zone" of 60 to 75% maximum, representing an optimal training intensity for both motivational and physical benefit.[6]

Enjoyability. That the individual in some way enjoy or reap some immediate benefits from doing an activity is critical if the activity is to be continued. The physical discomfort that often accompanies the early stages of increased activity must in some way be minimized or offset by positive factors if the person is to be kept from dropping out. Ways of enhancing enjoya-

bility include the tailoring of the type(s) of activity, the actual activity regimen, and the format of the regimen (group or alone; class or home-based) to individual preferences. For instance, does the individual prefer a group aerobics class with music, or would a walking/jogging program augmented with a portable stereo cassette player fit better with the person's work schedule and personal preferences? Discomfort can be minimized by, again, gradually shaping the regimen from mild (e.g., RPE below 13) to more challenging; again, the individual can monitor whether the regimen is too demanding by focusing on ease of breathing and talking during the activity. Individuals can also be taught distraction techniques, when relevant, to help them to refocus their attention away from what are for some individuals aversive aspects of activity (i.e., increased exertion and sweating). One method of assessing enjoyability of the exercise session is to ask participants to note their level of enjoyment on self-monitoring records that reflect a range of values from "very unenjoyable" to "very enjoyable" (e.g., 1 to 5 scale). If two or more sessions are in the

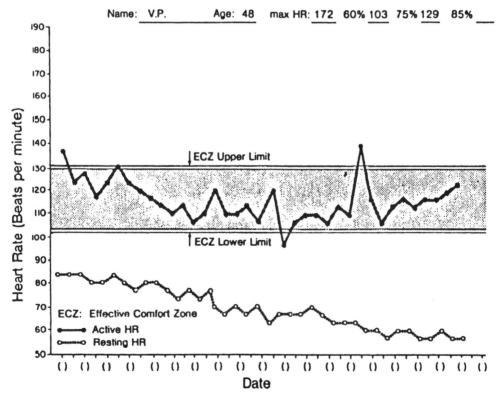

FIGURE 38–1. Heart rate and adherence graph.

"unenjoyable" range, the exercise regimen might best be modified or varied, perhaps with more reinforcement provided.

External Rewards and Incentives. As noted previously, the initial steps involved in becoming more physically active for many individuals are often found to be anything but rewarding. Often it is not until several months into a regular physical activity program that individuals begin to report experiencing positive benefits from physical activity on a regular basis. In fact, the longer the period of inactivity and the more unfit the individual (e.g., obese smoker), the longer the period is likely to be before any physical activity becomes intrinsically reinforcing (i.e., feels good). Therefore, beginners need external rewards early in their program, to help to encourage and motivate them. For our highly unfit overweight smoker, "beginner" status might extend to 6 months or 1 year, and special external incentives may need to be programmed throughout that time period. For other, more fit individuals, this "beginner" phase may need to occur for only a short time.

One extremely valuable form of reward is *social support.* Social support has proven to be a powerful motivator for many people. Social support can be delivered in many forms, including through a class instructor, exercise partners, and family members who encourage increased activity regardless of whether they themselves actually participate, as well as through phone calls and letter prompts from a caring health professional. *Praise* is a critical component of social support. To be most effective, this vocal encouragement should be both immediate (during or very shortly after the exercise) and specific. For example: "Your effort level is great . . . you'll be able to keep that pace for some time!"; "Great going, your attendance has been perfect over the past month!" The praise of exercise therapists, family members, and fellow participants should occur consistently and frequently during the early stages of acquisition of the exercise habit. Families of the neophyte exercisers might also be encouraged to exercise with them, or at least accompany them whenever possible to enhance this support. When this support from significant others is active and ongoing, exercisers are two to three times more likely than those with little or no family support to persist in their physical activity program. Therapists, family members, and "helpers" alike should be cautioned, however, against even the best-intentioned nagging or employment of any other aversive procedure (e.g., inviting guilt for failure to exercise) designed to induce the recalcitrant person to exercise. These counterproductive actions almost inevitably increase the punishing characteristics of the exercise, further upsetting the delicate balance between motivation to exercise and remaining pleasantly inactive.

The use of social support can also be extended and formalized by using written *contracts* between the individual and a significant person in the environment. Contracts are written, signed agreements that help to specify the person's activity-related *goals* in a public format (Fig. 38–2). They typically specify short-term, concrete goals and the types of positive consequences that will occur upon reaching the goals. The contract should have some flexibility in daily goal-setting, such that the individual is not faced with rigid daily goals that are difficult or impossible to meet, thereby providing frequent failure experiences (see following section). Thus, in the earlier stages of the program, an appropriate goal might be related to attendance rather than performance within the session. These contracts often work best if developed in tandem with an interested person or "helper" in the individual's environment. Such contracts can help to increase an individual's personal responsibility and commitment to the program. An alternative to the value-exchange contract is the written agreement, through which the participant agrees in writing to perform certain behaviors. Although not as effective as the formal contract, the agreement can be useful for those persons who refuse to go so far as to sign a contract.

The use of appropriate and consistent exercise *models* in the individual's environment (i.e., other individuals the person can observe exercising) can also motivate individuals to begin and to continue to exercise. These models should be as similar as possible to the targeted individuals (some programs use successful graduates as future participant-assistants) for maximal effectiveness. Furthermore, whenever possible, the health professional or therapist should set an appropriate example by exercising along with the program participants.

Another type of incentive occurs in the form of *feedback* to the individual concerning how they are doing on what they deem as relevant or important dimensions. Such feedback can be delivered by another person or it can be gener-

Two-Week Contract:

Plan to Increase Amount of Brisk Walking

<u>My Responsibilities:</u>

1. To focus on increasing my brisk walking while at work, especially during my lunch hour.

2. To reward myself on each day that I reach 2 1/2 miles on my pedometer with thirty minutes (or more) of reading for my own enjoyment.

3. To record my data in my exercise journal at 10:00 each night.

<u>My Helper's Responsibilities:</u>

1. To prompt me during work to do my activity.

2. In return, I will prompt him concerning a behavior of his choice, as desired.

This contract will be evaluated in two weeks, on *(date)*.

Signed:

_____

_____ (helper)

_____ (health provider)

_____ (date)

_____ (date)

_____ (date)

FIGURE 38 – 2. Sample contract.

ated by the individual through the use of self-recorded monitoring sheets, an activity diary (see Fig. 38 – 3), and/or a graph showing progress in one or more variables (e.g., see Fig. 38 – 1, plotted heart rates, and attendance/adherence across time). Computer-generated feedback letters currently show promise as an efficient, systematic method for providing personalized feedback to participants on a regular basis. When used in conjunction with *goals* that are reasonable, personally relevant, and short-term, feedback can be a powerful motivating factor.

Behavioral Success. A key factor in adherence is recognizing that continued adherence is typically a consequence of *behavioral success,* rather than the education or instruction that constitutes the early portions of most programs. In other words, often the feelings of success and accomplishment that accompany actually *doing* an activity on a regular basis are what shape our beliefs and attitudes about continuing the activity rather than vice versa. This fact helps to explain why many individuals, despite being

very knowledgeable concerning physical activity, are not currently active. Health professionals can help this process along by pointing out to individuals the changes and gains they have made, no matter how modest. Individuals should be "shaped" such that they engage in the exercise no matter how they feel (barring illness or injury) or what their attitude. Eventually, this regular and successful participation produces appropriate feelings of mastery, if not enjoyment, as well as positive attitudes toward their own exercise program—a process that enhances the probabilities of sticking with the exercise program over the long run.

Self-management. Success in behavioral change correlates with building in, early on, training in *self-management strategies* and an understanding of the importance of taking *personal responsibility* for physical activity. Individuals must recognize the importance of taking charge of their physical activity as a lifelong goal rather than as something that occurs only so long as their 12-week class or program lasts. Such programs are a *vehicle* for establishing

Name_____   Social Security #: _____   Exercise Goal_____
Date:_____

	Sun.	Mon.	Tues.	Wed.	Thurs.	Fri.	Sat.
Activity Type:							
Total Time:							
Distance:							
Heart Rate Before exercise:							
During exercise:							
After exercise:							
Enjoyment 1. very enjoyable 2. somewhat enjoyable 3. neutral 4. somewhat enjoyable 5. very enjoyable	1 2 3 4 5	1 2 3 4 5	1 2 3 4 5	1 2 3 4 5	1 2 3 4 5	1 2 3 4 5	1 2 3 4 5
Where did you exercise?							
With whom did you exercise?							

FIGURE 38–3. Activity record.

the lifelong habit, and are not the sole means by which physical activity is defined. Early in all programs, individuals should be taught methods of being able to prompt and successfully engage in activity in a variety of settings and under a variety of circumstances, e.g., specific instruction on how to set the occasion for exercise (e.g., carry exercise clothes in car, or lay by the bed; spend time with exercise "buffs"; park car and walk) and what to do if an exercise class or episode is missed or a relapse has occurred (e.g., admit responsibility for "slip," set restart plan, call exercise "buddy," arrange reinforcement, simplify or change regimen).

ENHANCING MAINTENANCE

In addition to those sedentary individuals who have difficulty starting a physical activity program, some individuals spend much of their time *restarting* activity programs that they terminated for various reasons. Often they stopped the program completely after an inevitable "break" in the activity schedule because of illness or injury, travel, holidays, inclement weather, or increased demands at work. There-

fore, a useful step is to prepare individuals, both psychologically as well as behaviorally, for breaks or "slips" in their activity that can lead to a full-blown relapse and return to their previous sedentary ways.[7] Individuals should first be warned that such breaks are inevitable and do not indicate the person is hopelessly lazy or is a failure. Having individuals identify their own types of "high-risk situations" that lead to inactivity, and also devise strategies to prepare for them ahead of time, can be profitable.

RECOMMENDED STRATEGIES

Useful plans include identifying types of alternate activities (e.g., brisk walking), planning to exercise as soon as possible after the break in the schedule, arranging to exercise with someone else, and resetting goals to an easier level so to avoid discouragement.

Other methods can be used for enhancing maintenance.

Reminders of Benefits. Provision of continued evidence of relevant personal benefits from regular activity (in the physical, social, and psychologic arenas) is important. The professional staff should ask individuals on a regular basis what types of benefits and positive consequences they are reaping from their current physical activity. For some individuals at particular risk for dropping out, such questioning might be posed frequently (e.g., one or more times a month). If an individual cannot define positive aspects of the exercise or can provide a list of negative aspects that is twice as long, then that participant is at serious risk of dropping out and should be targeted for increased attention.

Generalization Training. Directors of exercise programs or classes should try to avoid halting the program abruptly, especially if no generalization training has been conducted. To ensure continued adherence, the exercise habit must be generalized or re-established in the new (e.g., home) environment before programmed sessions are discontinued in the old setting. This generalization might be accomplished in one of several ways, including requiring unsupervised, home exercise sessions from the beginning or an earlier stage of the program; including family or significant others in exercise sessions for a period before cessation of the more formal program; and adding additional exercises before "graduation" that are more easily maintained in the home environment. Ideally, session supervision, reinforcement, and feedback characteristics should fade gradually as the change date approaches so to approximate more closely the conditions the exerciser is likely to experience in the new (maintenance) setting.

Reassessment of Goals. Such reassessment provides the opportunity to verify that they are still relevant, realistic, and motivating. Again, goals that are too long-term or are vague do not provide enough motivation to maintain the individual through trying or rough periods. During the early stages of an exercise program (i.e., the first 3 to 6 months), goals should be adjusted frequently if necessary (i.e., once every 2 weeks), to keep the individual on course.

Social Support. Its continued use in as many forms as possible is valuable. If the format of the physical activity is a class situation or group headed by an exercise leader, the exercise leader should take responsibility for calling individuals on the telephone who miss two classes in a row (one class, if the person has been targeted as someone at high risk for dropping out). The purpose of the phone call is not to scold or in any way to make these individuals feel guilty for not attending, but rather to let

them know that they were missed and that other participants noticed and care about them. Other individuals in the class can assume this type of responsibility as well (a "buddy system"). If the exercise program is conducted outside of a formal class or group, the health professional can continue support in the form of periodic phone calls, letters, and newsletters. Family members, co-workers, and friends of the individual should continue to encourage and support the individual's exercise efforts as well.

Relevant Rewards. When used for physical activity behavior and achievements in conjunction with the person's activity goals, such rewards should change periodically so to maintain their motivating impact. Rewards may include "points" that are accumulated as the person continues to exercise and that can be totaled to obtain a large reward (e.g., a new exercise outfit; dinner out; a small trip), or small rewards in such areas as "time off" (to read or engage in other enjoyable activities).

Feedback. Self-monitoring and other forms of *feedback* are useful for noting progress and enhancing motivation. For some individuals, this feedback may take the additional form of professionally or self-administered exercise or fitness *assessments*. Such fitness assessments involve setting up aspects of the individual's immediate environment as a standardized exercise "course" so the individual can measure current fitness levels against past performance. Frequently, individuals see how fast they can complete a specified distance, or note their rapid heart rate during the completion of a specific amount of work done over a specified amount of time.

Contracts. As noted previously, contracts should frequently be updated and changed, if warranted, and should include specified goals, rewards, and helpers. Contracts that are too easy do not provide the challenge needed to motivate many individuals. In contrast, contracts that are too difficult lead to frustration and discouragement (as well as injury, in some cases).

Avoidance of Boredom. Individuals should be encouraged to monitor the amount of enjoyment they derive from their activity, and to take responsibility for making it more enjoyable, if it is not currently meeting their needs. The health professional should work collaboratively with the individual to achieve this goal (e.g., through implementation of new activities, environments, goals, and partners). With the wide variety of aerobic activities from which to choose, and the diversity of settings currently available in which to conduct such activities, the "I'm bored" response should not be allowed for long. For some individuals, boredom may be licked by coaching them in an exercise regimen that involves a variety of activities. For other participants, one activity conducted in varied settings and formats may be more appropriate or preferable. Some form of enjoyable competition (e.g., fun runs) may also stimulate exercise maintenance.

Importance of Routine Activities. For many individuals, particularly as they age, an increase in activities of daily living can provide a useful "backdrop" of activity that can keep them loose and "peppy," even during those times when they are not in more vigorous activity. Individuals need to understand that the health benefits obtained from an active lifestyle include becoming more active in a variety of ways—both within and outside of formal programs.

Helping individuals to begin and maintain increased levels of physical activity undoubtedly can be a challenge to even the most enterprising health professional. Such a task requires continued creativity and flexibility in developing and modifying programs to meet the changing needs of participants. Health professionals can be helped in their efforts by remembering the guidelines to changing and maintaining behavior that behavioral scientists have found are particularly useful. A summary of some of the more general guidelines follows.

1. Behavior (including physical activity) is strongly influenced by its immediate consequences for the individual.
2. To increase the likelihood that a behavior will occur, increase the immediately rewarding aspects of the behavior, and decrease the negative or punishing aspects.
3. Rewards, used to reinforce behavior change and to motivate future behavior, are in the "eye of the beholder." Let the individual choose those rewards that are personally motivating.
4. Set appropriate activity-related goals, and modify these goals as necessary. Encourage individual tailoring of and flexibility in exercise goal-setting, emphasizing adherence/attendance at first rather than performance per se.

5. Provide relevant feedback whenever possible. Encourage (teach) exercisers to plot their progress (e.g., heart rate, time exercising) on graphs for visual motivation purposes.
6. Gradually "shape" an initially difficult behavior; have individuals start with less demanding activity goals to help "ease" them into the habit of being physically active.
7. Structure appropriate expectations in the *early* stages of the program.

In addition, health professionals should keep in mind the usefulness of a *public health perspective* in attacking exercise adoption and adherence problems with their clients. This perspective emphasizes the importance of inspiring as many individuals as possible in a community to engage in *some* physical activity, rather than a relatively small number doing a large amount. Although use of the traditional prescription of "3 times per week, for at least 30 min at a time at an aerobic heart rate" is certainly a useful general goal, for many individuals in our society this goal is currently unreachable. Alternatively, striving to motivate the very sedentary among us to increase their general activity levels through more moderate, convenient activities of daily living can be a worthwhile endeavor that should not be ignored. Health professionals must remain open to the various options available in enhancing physical activity levels in their clients, particularly on a community-wide, cost-efficient basis.

REFERENCES

1. Dishman RK: Compliance/adherence in health-related exercise. *Health Psychol*, 1:237–267, 1982.
2. Oldridge NB: Compliance and exercise in primary or secondary prevention of coronary heart disease: A review. *Prev Med*, 11:56–70, 1982.
3. Martin JE, Dubbert PM: Behavioral management strategies for improving health and fitness. *Cardiac Rehab*, 4:200–208, 1984.
4. Martin JE, Dubbert PM: Exercise adherence. *Exerc Sport Sci Rev*, 13:137–167, 1985.
5. Martin JE, Dubbert PM: Exercise promotion. In *Applications in Behavioral Medicine and Health Psychology: A Clinician's Source Book*. Edited by JA Blumenthal and DC McKee. Sarasota, FL, Professional Resource Exchange, 1986.
6. Borg GV: Perceived exertion as an indicator of somatic stress. *Scand J Rehabil Med*, 2:92–98, 1970.
7. King AC, Frederiksen LW: Low-cost strategies for increasing exercise behavior: The effects of relapse preparation training and social supports. *Behav Modif*, 4:3–21, 1984.

CHAPTER 39

NUTRITION

KELLY D. BROWNELL AND
SUZANNE NELSON STEEN

An adequate and balanced diet is essential for normal functioning. What we eat influences our work, play, psychologic status, and health. Considering the abundance of food in industrialized societies, the continued existence of nutrient deficiencies is surprising. The more significant problem, however, is that of *overnutrition.* The excessive consumption of calories, fat, cholesterol, and sodium has been linked to coronary heart disease, certain forms of cancer, obesity, and other diseases.

In the average American diet, approximately 12% of calories are acquired from protein, 46% from carbohydrate, and 42% from fat.[6] The protein intake is at the recommended level but progress is needed to attain the recommended levels of carbohydrate (58%) and fat (30%).[6] Some authorities suggest that fat intake should be reduced further, especially in persons at high risk for coronary artery disease and cancer.

Changing the diet of an individual is not always easy. Food preferences are strongly ingrained and are influenced by family and by culture. Ethnic groups who migrate to another culture are likely to change language, customs, and even religious practices before changing food preferences. Food acquires symbolic meaning when mothers feed children, families assemble for meals, holidays are celebrated with feasts, and so forth. The hectic lifestyle led by many people also influences food choices. The fast food that is an easy solution to a busy schedule tends to be high in fat, sodium, and calories. What then, constitutes a balanced diet, and how can health professionals encourage positive changes?

THE FOUR FOOD GROUPS—STILL THE BEST CHOICE

Six classes of nutrients are necessary in daily intake: protein, carbohydrate, fat, vitamins, minerals, and water. The Food and Nutrition Board has determined Recommended Dietary Allowances (RDAs) that represent the levels of essential nutrients necessary for healthy persons (Table 39–1). These levels are used by the Food and Drug Administration for the USRDA, which is the basis for nutrition labeling.

On the basis of their similar nutrient content, foods can be classified into four food groups. The four groups, along with the number of recommended daily servings, are shown in Tables 39–2 and 39–3.

If a person consumes the recommended number of servings from the four groups, and maintains a balanced selection of foods within each group, he or she is likely to have an ade-

Table 39-1. Food and Nutrition Board, National Academy of Sciences—National Research Council Recommended Daily Dietary Allowances,[a] Revised 1980

	Age (years)	Weight (kg)	Weight (lb)	Height (cm)	Height (in)	Protein (g)	Fat-soluble vitamins Vitamin A (μg RE)[b]	Vitamin D (μg)[c]	Vitamin E (mg α-TE)[d]	Water-soluble vitamins Vitamin C (mg)	Thiamine (mg)	Riboflavin (mg)	Niacin (mg NE)[e]	Vitamin B6 (mg)	Folacin (μg)	Vitamin B12 (μg)	Minerals Calcium (mg)	Phosphorus (mg)	Magnesium (mg)	Iron (mg)	Zinc (mg)	Iodine (μg)
Infants	0.0-0.5	6	13	60	24	kg × 2.2	420	10	3	35	0.3	0.4	6	0.3	30	0.5[g]	360	240	50	10	3	40
	0.5-1.0	9	20	71	28	kg × 2.0	400	10	4	35	0.5	0.6	8	0.6	45	1.5	540	360	70	15	5	50
Children	1-3	13	29	90	35	23	400	10	5	45	0.7	0.8	9	0.9	100	2.0	800	800	150	15	10	70
	4-6	20	44	112	44	30	500	10	6	45	0.9	1.0	11	1.3	200	2.5	800	800	200	10	10	90
	7-10	28	62	132	52	34	700	10	7	45	1.2	1.4	16	1.6	300	3.0	800	800	250	10	10	120
Males	11-14	45	99	157	62	45	1000	10	8	50	1.4	1.6	18	1.8	400	3.0	1200	1200	350	18	15	150
	15-18	66	145	176	69	56	1000	10	10	60	1.4	1.7	18	2.0	400	3.0	1200	1200	400	18	15	150
	19-22	70	154	177	70	56	1000	7.5	10	60	1.5	1.7	19	2.2	400	3.0	800	800	350	10	15	150
	23-50	70	154	178	70	56	1000	5	10	60	1.4	1.6	18	2.2	400	3.0	800	800	350	10	15	150
	51+	70	154	178	70	56	1000	5	10	60	1.2	1.4	16	2.2	400	3.0	800	800	350	10	15	150
Females	11-14	46	101	157	62	46	800	10	8	50	1.1	1.3	15	1.8	400	3.0	1200	1200	300	18	15	150
	15-18	55	120	163	64	46	800	10	8	60	1.1	1.3	14	2.0	400	3.0	1200	1200	300	18	15	150
	19-22	55	120	163	64	44	800	7.5	8	60	1.1	1.3	14	2.0	400	3.0	800	800	300	18	15	150
	23-50	55	120	163	64	44	800	5	8	60	1.0	1.2	13	2.0	400	3.0	800	800	300	18	15	150
	51+	55	120	163	64	44	800	5	8	60	1.0	1.2	13	2.0	400	3.0	800	800	300	10	15	150
Pregnant						+30	+200	+5	+2	+20	+0.4	+0.3	+2	+0.6	+400	+1.0	+400	+400	+150	h	+5	+25
Lactating						+20	+400	+5	+3	+40	+0.5	+0.5	+5	+0.5	+100	+1.0	+400	+400	+150	h	+10	+50

[a] The allowances are intended to provide for individual variations among most normal persons as they live in the United States under usual environmental stresses. Diets should be based on a variety of common foods in order to provide other nutrients for which human requirements have been less well defined.
[b] Retinol equivalents. 1 retinol equivalent = 1 μg retinol or 6 μg β carotene.
[c] As cholecalciferol. 10 μg cholecalciferol = 400 iu of vitamin D.
[d] α-tocopherol equivalents. 1 mg d-α tocopherol = 1 α-TE.
[e] 1 NE (niacin equivalent) is equal to 1 mg of niacin or 60 mg of dietary tryptophan.
[f] The folacin allowances refer to dietary sources as determined by Lactobacillus casei assay after treatment with enzymes (conjugases) to make polyglutamyl forms of the vitamin available to the test organism.
[g] The recommended dietary allowance for vitamin B_{12} in infants is based on average concentration of the vitamin in human milk. The allowances after weaning are based on energy intake (as recommended by the American Academy of Pediatrics) and consideration of other factors, such as intestinal absorption.
[h] The increased requirement during pregnancy cannot be met by the iron content of habitual American diets nor by the existing iron stores of many women; therefore the use of 30-60 mg of supplemental iron is recommended. Iron needs during lactation are not substantially different from those of nonpregnant women, but continued supplementation of the mother for 2-3 months after parturition is advisable in order to replenish stores depleted by pregnancy.

346

Table 39–2. Representative Foods from the Four Food Groups

Food groups			
Milk	Bread and cereal	Fruit and vegetable	Meat
Milk	Bread	Oranges	Chicken
Yogurt	Rolls	Apples	Pork
Cheese	Pasta	Strawberries	Beef
Ice cream	Rice	Pears	Veal
Cottage cheese	Grain products	Grapefruit	Turkey
	Cold cereals	Peas	Lamb
	Hot cereals	Corn	Processed meats
		Broccoli	Tuna
		Squash	Fish
		Carrots	Nuts
			Dried beans

quate diet. Supplementation with vitamins, minerals, protein, or other nutrients is necessary only in special cases, despite claims to the contrary from health food and nutrition stores, lay health and nutrition magazines, and many of the special magazines for athletes.

SPECIFIC NUTRIENTS

To communicate with other professionals and with the public, an understanding of sev-

eral facts about basic nutrients and what changes are indicated for certain individuals is helpful.

FATS AND CHOLESTEROL

Confusion often centers around dietary fat and body fat. When a person consumes more energy than needed, whether from protein, carbohydrate, or fat, the excess is stored in adipose tissue (body fat). The goal of weight reduction is to maximize the loss of body fat while

Table 39–3. Nutrients in the Four Food Groups and the Recommended Number of Servings

		Recommended servings				
		Child	Teen	Adult	Pregnancy	Lactation
Milk Group		3	4	2	4	4
Provides:	protein, calcium, riboflavin, phosphorus					
Foods:	8 oz milk or yogurt					
	1½ slice cheese					
	1½ c ice cream					
	1½ c cottage cheese					
Meat Group		2	2	2	3	2
Provides:	protein, niacin, iron, thiamine					
Foods:	2 oz fish, lean meat, or poultry					
	2 eggs					
	1 c dried beans or peas					
	5–6 oz tofu					
	4 tbsp peanut butter					
Fruit and Vegetable Group		4	4	4	4	4
Provides:	Vitamins A and C					
Foods:	½ c cooked or juice					
	1 c raw					
	1 med vegetable or fruit					
Bread/Cereal/Grain Group		4	4	4	4	4
Provides:	carbohydrate, iron, thiamine, niacin					
Foods:	1 slice bread, roll, biscuit, tortilla, pancake, waffle					
	½ c cooked cereal, pasta, rice					
	¾ c cold cereal					

preserving or even building muscle (lean body mass).

Dietary fat refers to the fat we eat. It is hidden in many foods and is a concentrated source of calories. Fat contains 9 calories/g, roughly twice the calories in the same amount of protein or carbohydrate. Therefore, the common notion that dieters should eat less starch (carbohydrate) should give way to the exhortation to eat less fat. Some fat in the diet is necessary, because it provides essential fatty acids and carries fat-soluble vitamins, but in most persons, fat intake is excessive.

Most fat in foods is in the form of triglycerides, which in turn are composed of fatty acids and glycerol. Fatty acids are saturated or unsaturated. Herein lies a crucial link between diet and health. Saturated fats increase serum cholesterol levels, which enhances the risk of cardiovascular disease. These fats are solid at room temperature and are typically from animal sources. Examples of saturated fats are butter, cream, cheese, meat fat, and lard. The three plant sources of saturated fat are coconut oil, palm oil, and cocoa butter. These hidden fats are widely used in commercially prepared foods and can easily become a significant source of saturated fat in the diet.

Unsaturated fats are liquid at room temperature and are usually found in plant products. Examples are oils from corn, safflower, and soy. These fats are associated with lower levels of serum cholesterol. As a consequence, not only is consideration of the total fat content in the diet important, but also the kind of fat consumed. Saturated fat should account for 10% of total energy intake, balanced with polyunsaturated and monounsaturated fats, each of which should account for about 10%.

Dietary fat from animal sources also contains cholesterol. It is essential for normal functioning, but when consumed in excess, or when the body manufactures excessive cholesterol itself, atherosclerosis may result. Cholesterol is transported in the blood by lipoproteins. Low-density lipoproteins (LDL) are a major carrier of cholesterol in the blood and have an affinity for arterial walls. High-density lipoproteins (HDL) are a major transporter of cholesterol and appear to play a protective role by carrying cholesterol away from the arterial walls to the liver, where it is converted to bile and excreted. Very low density proteins (VLDL) are synthesized from LDL and are a major carrier of triglycerides in the blood. A high ratio of HDL to LDL is

desirable. Exercise can favorably alter this ratio. Saturated fats, not dietary cholesterol, have the greatest nutritional impact on total and LDL blood cholesterol levels.

Prudent dietary recommendations for fat involve no more than 30% of total calories from fat, a P : S (polyunsaturated/saturated) ratio of 1 : 1, and daily cholesterol intake of no more than 300 mg. The following changes may help achieve these goals: (1) use lean meat, poultry, and fish; (2) trim visible fat off meats; (3) substitute lowfat and nonfat products for whole fat products when buying cheese, yogurt, ice cream, and milk; (4) use unsaturated oils in cooking and preparing meals; (5) decrease foods high in cholesterol, including egg yolks, organ meats, and butter; and (6) bake, boil, or broil rather than fry.

CARBOHYDRATES AND FIBER

Simple carbohydrates are made of glucose, sucrose (table sugar), and fructose (found in fruits, vegetables, and honey). Double sugars (disaccharides) are galactose, maltose, and lactose (found in milk). The complex carbohydrates are made up of long chains of the simple sugars, and are found in cereals, grains, pastas, peanuts, potatoes, carrots, beans, and other starchy foods.

The typical diet contains more than the recommended amount of simple sugars and too few complex carbohydrates. The simple sugars are generally found in processed and refined foods such as candy, jelly, soda, and desserts. These foods supply only "empty calories" accompanied by few useful nutrients. Complex carbohydrates tend to be high in vitamins, minerals, and fiber. Given the recommendation that 58% of daily calories should be from carbohydrate, 48% should come from complex carbohydrates and only 10% from simple sugars.

Fiber is the nondigestible portion of carbohydrate. It is found in foods high in complex carbohydrates and aids in the elimination process by adding water and bulk to the stool. Fiber may play a role in the prevention and treatment of diabetes, colon cancer, diverticulosis, irritable bowel syndrome, cardiovascular disease, and hemorrhoids. It may also benefit dieters by creating a feeling of fullness without a high level of calories. The recommended fiber intake is 25 to 50 g/day, compared with the current average intake of 10 to 20 g/day. Cooked legumes provide approximately 9 g/½ cup; corn and peas have 5 g/½ cup; and bran cereal with raisins has 4 g/1.3 oz.

PROTEIN

Proteins are composed of amino acids and are found in both plant and animal sources. Eight (9 in children) of the 20 amino acids found in proteins are essential, i.e., they cannot be synthesized by the body and must be supplied in the diet. Proteins from animal sources generally contain all the essential amino acids and are considered "complete." Protein from plant sources is "incomplete" in that one or more of the essential amino acids are missing. Vegetarians must be careful to complement their sources of protein to ensure consumption of all essential amino acids.

The percentage of calories from protein should be approximately 12%. The RDA for protein is based on body weight, with increased amounts required during times of growth, certain disease states, pregnancy, and lactation. For the average man, the recommended intake is 0.8 g/kg body weight. This requirement can be met with 8 oz of meat or poultry.

VITAMINS

Vitamins are essential for life and cannot be manufactured by the body. The *fat-soluble* vitamins, vitamins A, D, E, and K, are stored in the body. Overconsumption can lead to toxicity because the body retains excess amounts in the fat. *Water-soluble* vitamins are not stored in the body, so excess amounts are generally excreted in the urine. These vitamins are C, thiamine, riboflavin, B_6, niacin, folacin, B_{12}, biotin, and pantothenic acid. Complications have been reported from large doses ("pharmacologic" levels of 10 times or more of the RDA) for vitamin C, niacin, and vitamin B_6.

American consumers spend as much as $500 million annually on vitamins, which reflects the unfounded belief that vitamins cure and prevent disease, increase energy level, improve athletic performance, enhance sexual potency, and reduce stress. Some vitamin producers are marketing general purpose multivitamins as meeting the special needs of active people, individuals with stressful lifestyles, and so forth, and health food establishments promote "natural vitamins." The vitamin hysteria has also been promoted in books by nutrition "experts"

who claim expertise in sports nutrition or other areas. Miraculous benefits are often promised, including a longer life. What is fact and what is fallacy?

Vitamins have not been shown to prevent or cure any illness (including the common cold) except when specific deficiencies exist. Some vitamins aid in energy metabolism, but they do not themselves provide energy. Essentially no difference exists between a vitamin synthesized in a laboratory and a "natural" vitamin from plants or animals. Overuse of vitamins is not advisable. Eating a balanced diet should meet the vitamin requirements of most persons.

MINERALS

Minerals exist in the body in minute amounts, but they are vital. Fifteen minerals have been identified, but dietary allowances have been established for only six (calcium, phosphorus, magnesium, iron, zinc, and iodine). The RDA levels for minerals are shown in Table 39–1.

SPECIAL DIETARY CONSIDERATIONS

Certain medical conditions or lifestyles dictate changes from the described standard, balanced diet. Several of the more notable cases are briefly discussed. We refer the reader to the resource material provided at the end of this chapter for more detailed discussions.

OSTEOPOROSIS

This condition exists when bone mass decreases excessively. It afflicts one of every four elderly women. As a natural part of the aging process, the body takes calcium from the bones more easily than it can be replaced. After menopause, calcium is removed at an even more rapid rate because of decreased quantities of estrogen. The bones then become porous and thin, and are susceptible to fracture. Lack of exercise and smoking may contribute to osteoporosis, as may excessive intake of vitamins A and D, caffeine, and alcohol.

The average intake of calcium is 550 to 600 mg/day. In postmenopausal women, this quantity should increase to 1000 to 1200 mg/day. Any of the following foods provides about 300 mg of calcium: 8 oz of milk, 1 cup of yogurt, 1 oz of Swiss cheese, 2.5 oz of sardines, and 1.5 cups of ice cream. If an insufficient quantity of calcium is consumed in the diet, supplementation may be necessary. Many supplements are available, but they vary widely in elemental calcium. The best supplement is one that supplies the highest concentration of calcium, is inexpensive, and is free from toxins, like those found in dolomite and bone meal. By these guidelines, calcium carbonate is the best choice.

HYPERTENSION

Sodium plays a major role in the maintenance of blood volume and pressure, but a high intake may contribute to high blood pressure. Hypertension is a condition related to the development of heart disease, stroke, and kidney disease. The average intake of sodium is 2 to 3 times the recommended amount of 1100 to 3300 mg. Many people are surprised by the foods high in sodium, including canned soups, cheeses, processed meats, and soy sauce. The sodium content in fresh fruits, vegetables, meats, and poultry, along with grains and some cereals, is low.

CARDIOVASCULAR DISEASE

Many of the above recommended changes may reduce the risk for cardiovascular disease. Reducing saturated fat, cholesterol, and sodium; increasing fiber intake and the P : S ratio; and maintaining normal weight levels may aid in this effort. These changes may influence several of the coronary risk factors, including serum cholesterol level, the HDL to LDL ratio, blood pressure, diabetes, and obesity.

NUTRITION FOR ATHLETES

Athletes do not require "special foods" to improve performance. A well-balanced diet can meet the nutritional needs of most athletes. Highly competitive athletes often require special dietary advice, if they are to perform at their peak, however, that goes beyond the dietary needs of less active or sedentary individuals. Carefully planned nutrition is needed to support the athlete during prolonged competition or intense athletic efforts, in addition to the daily training regimen. Caloric requirements depend on the individual and the demands of the sport. About 55 to 60% of total caloric intake should be from carbohydrates to ensure adequate repletion of glycogen stores for energy and to protect lean body mass. In contrast to a high-fat or a mixed diet, a high-carbohydrate diet is associated with both higher muscle glycogen concentration and a greater time to exhaustion. For elevated carbohydrate intake to be effective, the caloric consumption of the athlete must be equivalent to total energy expenditure. Athletes in negative calorie balance compromise their ability to synthesize glycogen.

Approximately 15% of the total caloric intake should be from high-quality protein. Contrary to popular belief, the athlete can meet protein needs with diet and does not need protein supplements. Excess protein does not increase muscle mass or potential for strength development. Although fat is a valuable metabolic fuel for muscle activity, fat intake should not exceed 30%. Vitamin and mineral supplements are not necessary if the athlete is consuming a balanced diet. Supplementation should be given only after appropriate diagnosis and screening.

The pre-event meal should be consumed 3 to 4 hours before competition and should include readily digested foods and fluid. These requirements can be met by including foods high in complex carbohydrates and low in fat and protein. Ingestion of salty, high fiber, or gaseous foods should be minimized before competition. Liberal intake of fluids should be encouraged for adequate hydration.

ASSESSING DIETARY INTAKE

The evaluation of a person's dietary intake is a challenging aspect of nutritional assessment. To obtain dietary information about an individual without influencing it is difficult, and the report of food intake may depend on what the person believes the professional wants to see or hear. Some individuals may have difficulty recording or remembering types and amounts of foods eaten. In addition, data regarding the nutrient composition of foods are incomplete for certain nutrients (e.g., magnesium and B_6). To obtain an accurate description of nutrient intake and dietary patterns, objectivity and skill on the part of the health professional are required. Several techniques for assessment may be used.

TWENTY-FOUR-HOUR RECALL

Twenty-four-hour recall is simple and rapid, and is particularly useful for surveying large population groups. The individual is asked to recall the foods and beverages consumed within the previous 24 hours. Pertinent information concerning portion size, food preparation, alcohol consumption, and vitamin and mineral supplementation are obtained. Foods least accurately reported are sauces, gravies, and snack items. Limitations of the 24-hour recall include (1) the intake reported may not be representative of typical intake; (2) the person may be unable to recall the amounts of food eaten; and (3) the person may be unwilling to respond truthfully.

FOOD INTAKE RECORD

A more complete picture of food intake can be obtained from a food record in which the individual records all foods and beverages consumed during a specified length of time, usually 3 or 7 days. The 3-day records, which include 2 weekdays and 1 weekend day, are representative for most people. The individual is instructed to carry the food record at all times and to record food items immediately after eating. To increase the accuracy of the data, respondents should be advised about portion sizes by use of plastic food models, utensils, or a description of household measures. Limitations are: (1) compliance depends on the person's motivation; (2) incorrect estimation of portion sizes; (3) failure to record all items leading to underestimation of nutrient intake; and (4) the days chosen may not be representative of typical intake.

FOOD FREQUENCY

A food frequency record evaluates the number of times per day, week, or month an individual consumes particular foods and beverages. This information can be used as a crosscheck for the 24-hour recall and helps to clarify patterns of food consumption. The food frequency analysis may include questions about all foods or it may be selective for specific foods suspected of being deficient or excessive in the diet (e.g., foods high in fat or sodium). The food frequency typically provides only qualitative data and relies upon the individual's memory.

DIET HISTORY

A diet history is a more complete assessment that includes a 24-hour recall and food frequency. In addition, individuals supply information about economic status, physical activity, ethnic background, appetite, dental and oral health, gastrointestinal function, chronic disease, medications, supplements, and recent weight changes.

OBSERVED FOOD INTAKE

Observation of food intake is the most accurate method, but it is also the most time consuming, expensive, and tedious. It requires that the amount and types of food given to the person are known and that the amount actually eaten is recorded in a nonintrusive manner. This method is most easily used in a controlled setting, such as in a hospital or nursing home. The ideal setting for determining dietary intake is the metabolic unit in which a weighed portion of food is given to the individual, the uneaten food is weighed, and the recorded difference is the amount eaten. Limitations include time, expense, and subject compliance.

INTERPRETING DIETARY INTAKE

Two methods can be used to evaluate dietary intake for nutrient adequacy. The first method is a fast, crude estimate that involves estimating the number of servings from the four food groups that were consumed during the day recorded, and comparing them to what is recommended (see Table 39–3). Low intake of protein, iron, calcium, riboflavin, and vitamins A and C can be detected this way. The dietary goals can be used for rough evaluation of nutrients consumed in excess, such as fat, cholesterol, sugar, and sodium.

The second method is more accurate and involves calculating the nutrients present in every food consumed. This process can be done by hand, with the use of USDA food composition books and information from manufacturers and food labels, or with a computerized nutrient data bank or computer software program. (The sources used for nutrient composition vary for computer programs and each should be evaluated carefully before a choice is made for analysis.)

After determining the nutrient composition

for each food, the nutrient composition of the total diet can be calculated. A comparison can be made to a desired standard such as that of the RDA. From food intake data, statements can be made regarding the adequacy of the diet for various nutrients as compared to the RDA. The assumption cannot be made, however, that if an individual has a low or inadequate intake of a certain nutrient that they are deficient in that nutrient. The individual must give a thorough history, be examined for clinical signs of a deficiency, and undergo appropriate biochemical tests performed before a deficiency can be confirmed.

FACILITATING CHANGES IN DIETARY BEHAVIOR

Professionals tend to believe that providing nutritional information changes eating behavior. This assumption is probably faulty. Dietary habits in the United States would be altered dramatically if individuals simply practiced what most of us learned before we were teenagers — that we should eat a balanced diet from the four food groups.

Culture, psychology, and physiology must be considered along with the delivery of information if we aim to alter eating practices. We are bombarded by temptations to eat, and for most people, highly palatable foods that are high in fat and sugar are readily available. Preference for some foods of this type may be of biologic origin. In addition, culture shapes strong preferences for some foods and dislike for others, so the persistence of habits is not surprising.

Balanced against this pessimistic picture, however, is evidence of clear changes in dietary behavior. Per capita consumption of whole milk and red meat has declined, and the rate of consumption of skim milk and chicken has increased. Millions of people are concerned about what they eat, read food labels, and seek out restaurants with lighter foods, salad bars, and the like. The climate is right for encouraging even broader changes. What skills are necessary?

GENERAL PRINCIPLES OF BEHAVIOR CHANGE

Specific steps can aid an individual in changing general dietary practices or in altering specific nutrient intake (e.g., salt, fat). The first step is to assess motivation for change. Some individuals are ready to change and can be guided through certain steps. Other individuals may require more encouragement.

An analysis of current eating patterns can help to provide a clear picture of areas in need of change. Instruction is the next step so the person works with proper information. Goal setting, reinforcement, and altering the eating environment can follow.

Analyzing Eating Patterns

Changing dietary behavior is greatly facilitated by an analysis of the individual's eating patterns. Methods for assessing the types and amounts of food were discussed previously. This information can be helpful in identifying likely nutrient deficiencies and in gauging how the diet compares to the recommended diet. Other patterns, such as time of eating, association of eating with certain moods, and problems with specific foods can be highlighted with a diet diary, which is a more global version of the diet record discussed previously. The person simply writes down what he or she eats, the time, location, mood, and other information deemed important by the person or professional. Patterns typically emerge from keeping such a record for several weeks. The information can be motivational and can provide specific targets for change.

Instruction

Relevant information can be provided concerning types and amounts of food that should be part of a healthy diet. The information could be general or specific, depending on the individual. For someone with no special dietary needs, general information can include advice discussed in previous parts of this chapter. For persons with known problems, such as diabetes, hypercholesterolemia, or hypertension, more detailed aid is needed. Special meal plans, focused cookbooks, and food preparation classes may be helpful.

In general, focusing on increases in positive behavior rather than decreases in negative behavior is preferable. For instance, advising a person to eat more fruits and vegetables may be more acceptable than asking for deletion of favored foods from the diet. If individuals learn to be creative with healthy foods, intake of unhealthy foods usually decreases. The complexity and volume of the information presented should be tailored to the person's levels of knowledge, education, and motivation for change.

Goal Setting

The establishment of reasonable goals is important. A person suddenly motivated to eat a healthier diet because of pressure from family, doctor's orders, or social pressure may begin with a burst of motivation. Wholesale changes in the diet are the rule for such people, but the changes tend to be transient. A man told by his physician that his family history of heart disease is a reason to reduce fat in the diet may hear tales of dramatic improvement in people on strict diets such as the Pritikin plan. He may forsake his favorite foods and begin eating foods he may not enjoy, a difficult plan to follow. A more sensible plan for him might be to drop his fat consumption in 5% increments until compliance begins to suffer.

In this context, the principle of shaping, making gradual steps toward the ultimate goal, can be helpful. Each step is taken only when the previous step is mastered. In the case cited in the previous paragraph, the man may reduce his fat intake by 5% and only move to the next step when the first 5% change is part of his lifestyle. If the next 5% change is difficult, an intermediate goal would be selected.

Reinforcing the Changes

Dietary changes are more likely imitated and sustained if they are reinforced. The individual can reinforce changes by praising himself or herself for making gradual changes and by avoiding self-condemnation in the face of slips or mistakes. Approval from the health professional and from family and friends can be helpful.

Altering the Eating Environment

Structuring the eating environment can take several forms. Keeping healthy foods available and problem foods out of the house can reduce temptation and curb automatic or compulsive eating. The individual can benefit from instruction about how to shop for food in a careful and planned manner and to store, prepare, and

Table 39–4. Recommended Dietary Goals and Dietary Changes from the U.S. Senate Select Committee on Nutrition and Human Needs (1977)

Recommended Dietary Goals

1. To avoid overweight, consume only as much energy (calories) as expended; if overweight, decrease energy intake and increase energy expenditure
2. Increase consumption of complex carbohydrates and "naturally occurring" sugars from about 28% of energy intake to about 48% of energy intake
3. Reduce overall fat consumption from approximately 40 to 30% of energy intake
4. Reduce saturated fat consumption to account for about 10% of total energy intake; balance that reduction with polyunsaturated and monounsaturated fats, each of which should account for about 10% of energy intake
5. Reduce cholesterol consumption to about 300 mg/day
6. Reduce consumption of refined and processed sugars by about 45% to account for about 10% of total energy intake
7. Decrease consumption of salt and foods high in salt content

Recommended Dietary Changes

1. Increase consumption of fruits, vegetables, and whole grains
2. Decrease consumption of animal fat and substitute poultry and fish, which decrease saturated fat
3. Decrease consumption of foods high in total fat and partially replace saturated with polyunsaturated fat
4. Except for young children, substitute lowfat and nonfat milk for whole milk, and substitute lowfat dairy products for high-fat products
5. Decrease consumption of butterfat, eggs, and other high cholesterol sources
6. Decrease consumption of refined and other processed sugars and foods high in such sugars
7. Decrease consumption of salt and foods high in salt content

serve food in ways that promote better eating. (Additional information and resources are listed in Chapter 40, concerning weight management.)

Nutrition is an important aspect of healthy living. Dietary fads are common, yet the best advice for most individuals is straightforward and can be conveyed in several basic messages. The seven dietary goals and the corresponding dietary changes recommended by the Senate Select Committee on Nutrition and Human Needs provide a comprehensive summary (Table 39–4).

RECOMMENDED REFERENCE MATERIALS

1. Committee on Dietary Allowances, Food and Nutrition Board: *Recommended Dietary Allowances*. 9th Ed. Washington, D.C.: National Academy of Sciences, 1980.

2. Shils ME, Young VR: *Modern Nutrition in Health and Disease.* 7th Ed. Philadelphia: Lea & Febiger, 1988.
3. Guthrie HA: *Introductory Nutrition.* 5th Ed. St. Louis: C.V. Mosby, 1983.
4. Krause ME, Mahan LK: *Food, Nutrition, and Diet Therapy.* 7th Ed. Philadelphia: W.B. Saunders, 1984.
5. McArdle WD, Katch FI, Katch VL: *Exercise Physiology: Energy, Nutrition, and Human Performance.* 2nd Ed. Philadelphia: Lea & Febiger, 1986.
6. Senate Select Committee on Nutrition and Human Needs: *Dietary Goals for the United States.* 2nd Ed. Washington, D.C.: Government Printing Office, 1977.

CHAPTER 40

WEIGHT MANAGEMENT AND BODY COMPOSITION

KELLY D. BROWNELL

Dieting is an activity common to millions of people in the Western world. Estimates are that 80% of American women diet every year. Persistent dieting has been documented in children in the 4th grade. This focus on dieting is in part a rational response to the high prevalence of obesity, but it also reflects obsessive concern about body shape. The typical female American, for example, aspires to the figure of a fashion model. Having so little body fat may be physiologically possible for few women, and even then it may occur at the cost of constant dietary vigilance.

Some of the casualties of this ubiquitous pressure to be thin are thin indeed, but they have the eating disorders of anorexia nervosa or bulimia. Other individuals are obese. This discussion of weight management and body composition, therefore, applies to people in all weight categories — millions of overweight persons along with millions who are at or close to normal weight but fight to maintain desirable body size.

BODY WEIGHT AND HEALTH

For many years, concepts about weight and health were based on the familiar tables from the Metropolitan Life Insurance Company, which were developed in 1959. The proposed linear relationship between weight and mortality has been called into question in recent years. Most people who read this chapter are familiar with this debate over whether it is harmful to be overweight because the topic is played out in the media and in professional publications. The debate is not likely to end soon because the epidemiologic data that bear on the issue are complex and are open to interpretation.

I believe the evidence indicates that obesity is a dangerous medical condition. It increases the risk for coronary heart disease through its influence on blood pressure, lipids, and lipoproteins, as well as for diabetes. Even aside from these effects, obesity is probably an independent risk factor. The precise point at which increasing weight exceeds the threshold of safety is not clear. At the NIH Consensus Conference on the Health Risks of Obesity in 1985, the figure of 20% overweight was determined to be the point at which risk begins to increase. Furthermore, results of clinical studies show that the coronary risk factors associated with obesity improve with weight reduction.

An important new development in this area is the study of distribution of body fat. Fat distributed in the abdomen, called upper-body or android-type obesity because it occurs most often in men, is associated with greater morbidity and mortality than is body fat distributed below the waist, called lower body or gynoid obesity. The simple ratio of waist to hip circumference is a stronger predictor of cardiovascular risk than is body weight, body fat, or the familiar body mass index (weight/height).[2] This finding implies that people vary in risk depending on the distribution of their body fat.

Health risks are different and are less severe for underweight individuals, unless the low weight is caused by disease or an eating disorder. The low weights and low percentages of body fat demanded in some sports may have positive or negative effects on health; more research is necessary to draw specific conclusions.

ARE WEIGHT PROBLEMS PHYSIOLOGIC OR PSYCHOLOGIC?

The public, along with most health professionals, believe being overweight reflects lack of willpower, poor self-concept, and deep-seated psychologic problems. Research findings show this supposition is incorrect. Excess weight results from a complex interaction of cultural, genetic, physiologic, and psychologic factors. Even when studies show psychologic distress in overweight persons, and these results are noted in the minority of studies, the distress could be the consequence rather than the cause of their condition.

Much of the interest in physiologic factors has focused on the concept of a body weight "set point." The set point is the "natural weight" of each individual, i.e., the weight the body seeks to protect against pressures to be too heavy or too thin. If some people have a set point above the ideal societal level, they are destined to fight their physiology to lose weight.

The set point theory may or may not stand the test of time. If the body does regulate around some biologic ideal, a range of comfortable weights is more likely to exist than a single point, and these comfortable weights are probably higher than those we see in fashion models and actresses.

In contrast to obesity, the eating disorders of anorexia and bulimia owe more to psychologic patterns than to physiology. Certainly physiology is changed from disordered eating, but specific psychologic, cultural, and familial patterns are thought to create these disorders. I do not mean to imply that all thin people have an eating disorder. Quite the contrary, maintaining ideal weight with a sensible program of nutrition and exercise is desirable. When disordered eating occurs, however, either with or without low weight, the pattern is reason for concern. Extreme dieting patterns and excessive levels of exercise are hidden within some people who appear to be engaging in healthy practices.

THE ENERGY BALANCE CONCEPT

A simple rule, and one that most people know, is that weight loss occurs when energy expenditure exceeds energy intake (negative energy balance). This principle leads to the common exhortation from health professionals to "eat less or exercise more." This is, of course, the only solution to a weight problem, but the tendency is to oversimplify a complex system and to assume that heavy people could be thin if they were only like thin people.

Many complex factors influence what happens to ingested energy and to calories expended through exercise and metabolic needs. Think for a moment of people you know. We all know people who eat large amounts and remain thin and other persons who gain weight if they vary even slightly from their constant dieting. These individuals defy explanation by a simple concept of energy balance, and show that a person's weight is determined by more than the number of calories they eat and expend.

Is it true, therefore, that 3500 calories equals a pound? People have been told for years that if they reduce their calorie intake by 500 per day (3500/week), they will lose 1 pound each week. This calculation is valid only when intakes and expenditures are averaged across many people. For persons who have a "thrifty" metabolic system, very low intakes (sometimes less than 800 calories per day) are needed for weight loss. Keeping a dietary record is therefore useful to determine their maintenance level of calories.

IMPORTANCE OF EXERCISE IN WEIGHT CONTROL

BENEFITS OF EXERCISE

Exercise has been prescribed as a component of weight control programs for years, but only as a formality. Professionals held little hope for compliance because they knew how daunting the prospect of exercise could be to someone with the physical burden of excess weight. The picture can look even more gloomy when the dieter considers running more than 12 miles to expend the calories in a single fast food meal of a jumbo hamburger, French fries, and a soft drink. Compelling reasons exist, however, to emphasize physical activity.

1. *Exercise expends energy.* Exercise does use calories, but some dieters make the mistake of believing they can burn enough calories from low-level activity to permit increased food intake. The cumulative effects of exercise over long periods can be substantial, so even modest levels of activity can be beneficial.

2. *Exercise may suppress appetite.* This issue has been studied more in animals than in humans, but exercise may help to suppress appetite in some persons. Other individuals may increase intake enough to offset the increased expenditure, so the effects of exercise on appetite are either neutral or positive for the dieter. Some people find scheduling exercise at times when they typically overeat to be helpful in weight control effects.

3. *Exercise can counteract the ill effects of obesity.* Exercise can have positive effects on blood pressure, serum cholesterol levels, body composition, and cardiorespiratory function. Obese persons are at increased risk for abnormalities in each of these areas. Exercise can provide these benefits independent of weight loss.

4. *Exercise can improve psychologic functioning.* Changes in anxiety, depression, general mood, and self-concept are noted in people who begin and maintain an exercise program. In someone attempting to lose weight, the psychologic changes can enhance dietary compliance. Exercise may have this effect by increasing a general sense of personal control.

5. *Exercise may minimize loss of lean body mass.* As much as 25% of the weight lost by dieting alone can be lean body mass (LBM). Overweight people typically have increased LBM as well as fat, but the loss of LBM during dieting is considered potentially dangerous if the body depletes protein reserves in essential areas of the body. The percentage of LBM lost decreases when exercise is combined with diet. Researchers have not studied formally what seems intuitively correct —that strength training exercise protects LBM more than endurance activities. Because endurance activities are more likely part of most exercise prescriptions, this potential for accelerating or decelerating loss of LBM is an important area for further research.

6. *Exercise may counter the metabolic decline produced by dieting.* Calorie restriction produces a rapid reduction in resting metabolic rate (RMR). The decline can be as much as 20%, and because RMR accounts for 60 to 70% of total energy expenditure, such a decline is noteworthy. This RMR reduction may account in part for the "plateau" reached by most dieters when weight loss slows or stops even when calorie intake remains stable. Exercise is known to increase the RMR, but the magnitude and duration of the increase are controversial. How the type, frequency, intensity, and duration of the exercise can be altered to offset the metabolic decline produced by dieting is not clear.

Professionals should be aware of these benefits of exercise and can be enthusiastic about exercise as one aspect of weight control. Describing the benefits to dieters can be an added incentive to become more physically active.

EVIDENCE SUPPORTING THE VALUE OF EXERCISE

Several lines of evidence demonstrate the importance of exercise in weight control. First, overweight persons rarely are among the ranks of the physically active, but the inactivity of overweight persons could be either the cause or the consequence of their weight problem. The second line of evidence comes from the finding that people in weight loss programs who maintain their loss tend to be those persons who exercise. The most convincing evidence, however, comes from studies in which dieters are randomly assigned to groups that do or do not receive an exercise program to accompany dietary change. Only a few such studies exist, but they point to a consistent conclusion—that exercise facilitates long-term weight loss. This effect of exercise could occur for any or all of the abovementioned reasons, but the fact that it does occur is reason to favor programs that include exercise.

THE MYTH OF SPOT REDUCING

Many people exercise to improve their appearance. In dieters, this effort may take the form of countless situps to "flatten the tummy" or leg exercises to trim the thighs. The well-known fact remains, however, that exercises cannot rid the body of fat in specific places. Muscle tone *can* be improved in some areas of the body and thus may help to improve appearance somewhat. In choosing an activity, however, the focus should be on calorie expenditure and enjoyment (to promote compliance) rather than spot reducing.

BARRIERS TO EXERCISE

BARRIERS RELATED TO WEIGHT

When inactive people state what prevents them from exercising, they usually say they are too busy. This barrier can often be overcome by creative scheduling and by alerting people to the many benefits of exercise. The "busy schedule" reason, however, often masks other, more important barriers. One such barrier is the physical burden of excess weight. Becoming active can be difficult, tiring, and painful when the body carries an extra load. People must be instructed to set reasonable exercise goals and to expect some time to elapse before they can do high levels of activity.

Another obstacle to exercise involves the negative associations that plague many people, particularly those persons who have been overweight since childhood. They are likely to be self-conscious and embarrassed about their bodies, because they have been teased, have been picked last for teams, and have suffered from poor performance at sports and games. When the mere prospect of exercise evokes such negative feelings, care is necessary to prescribe levels of activity consistent with abilities and fitness level, and to work with individuals to select activities they enjoy.

WARNING: AN EXERCISE "THRESHOLD"

When professionals encourage individuals to exercise, a common question is, "How much should I do?" Too often the response is well-meaning, but is automatic and perhaps counterproductive. Individuals are told of the famous, three-part equation involving *frequency, intensity,* and *duration.* A typical prescription from this equation is that exercise should be done 3 times per week at 70% maximal heart rate for at least 15 min each time. This equation is born from extensive research efforts that yielded results showing such exercise is necessary to improve cardiorespiratory conditioning. This goal is important but it is not the only goal of exercise.

Use of this equation implies an exercise "threshold." Inherent in this threshold is the notion that exercise must be done at specific levels to have any value. If an activity meets or exceeds the levels dictated by the equation, an individual is thought to have exercised "enough," having incurred some physiologic benefit. If the effort falls below this level, people often assume they have not profited. This threshold may be a useful incentive for some individuals but represent a deterrent to other persons.

Professionals should make a specific point about exercise, especially to individuals who are not fit or who are overweight. *Any exercise is better than no exercise.* When a person asks if walking one block is "enough," tell them it is far better than some of the alternatives, such as watching reruns of "McHale's Navy" and eating Fritos. The threshold should be reserved for people in reasonable condition. Other individuals should begin at low levels and progress gradually.

DIET, EXERCISE, AND BODY COMPOSITION

The object of weight loss is to maximize fat loss and minimize loss of LBM. As mentioned previously, dieting is typically associated with some loss of lean tissue. The loss can be large or small depending on the individual, type of diet, and exercise program. Protein depletion and the accompanying loss of LBM can be dangerous.

Protein loss is most pronounced on strict diets. Large losses of LBM can occur from a prolonged fast or from a very-low-calorie diet (less than 800 calories/day). Researchers have experimented with supplementing such diets with protein to prevent the body from using its lean stores for fuel. The loss of LBM can be minimized if a very-low-calorie diet is supplemented with 1.5 g of protein of high biologic value (i.e., from meat, fish, and fowl) per kilogram of ideal (not actual) body weight. This supplementation is less crucial in a diet of more calories, but maintaining a balanced diet, e.g., foods from the basic food groups, is always important (see Chapter 39).

Exercise also may prevent the loss of LBM during weight reduction. This benefit of exercise was noted by several investigators using endurance exercise, which is unlikely to build much muscle. Therefore, the mechanism for preservation of LBM is unknown.

For people of normal weight who maintain that level through exercise, a sensible diet combined with an exercise program appears to be the safest and most healthy way to remain thin. Endurance exercises such as running, cycling, and swimming produce the greatest calorie losses and the greatest health benefits.

Body composition is important to consider in people in all weight categories. The rate of lean to fat varies between the sexes and among participants in different sports. For example, football players in some positions tend to have a higher percentage of body fat than other athletes such as runners, gymnasts, and figure skaters. The body fat levels for athletes in various sports are presented in Table 40–1. These percentages are thought to be related to performance and may have positive or negative health consequences; the evidence is not clear, however, on either matter.

Some coaches encourage athletes to decrease their percentage body fat to the lowest possible levels, with the hope of providing a competitive advantage. In wrestling, severe weight loss has become an institution. As a result, concerned researchers developed the concept of "minimum wrestling weight" based on body composition measures. Athletes with low percentages of body fat are probably below the level they would be were it not for the rigorous training imposed by their sport. Whether this reduced level is harmful or may actually reduce the risk for chronic disease is not known.

A COMPREHENSIVE APPROACH TO WEIGHT CONTROL

Weight problems are not easily remedied by simple advice for people to "eat less and exercise more." Not surprisingly, most programs display the bias of the professionals who run them, i.e., programs conducted by dietitians tend to focus on nutrition, programs run by psychologists emphasize behavior, and so forth. Important elements of programs should have a broad base with consideration of at least three factors: nutrition, exercise, and behavior change, with the assumption that each area is done well. This breadth of focus is not easy because most professionals are expert in only one area. Commercial groups such as Weight Watchers, self-help groups like Overeaters Anonymous, professional counseling, and most other approaches are successful for some people. Therefore, educated referrals are an important aspect of work with overweight persons. Unfortunately, we must rely on clinical judgment for making such referrals, because research has not yet provided the necessary guidelines.

The program at the University of Pennsylvania School of Medicine contains five primary components. I present these, not because this is the only approach, but because it typifies comprehensive programs assembled by multidisciplinary teams. The five components form the acronym LEARN.

L   Lifestyle
E   Exercise
A   Attitudes
R   Relationships
N   Nutrition

The importance of changes in lifestyle, exercise, and nutrition is clear to most professionals. The attitude area is a relatively new, but critical part of the program. It deals with thoughts, feelings, and emotional reactions to weight, dieting, and exercise. Attitudes are one determinant of whether people can adhere to a diet and also whether the inevitable slips and mistakes that occur during dieting are used to increase control or to abandon control and thus relapse. Relationships refers to the social support that can be obtained from family members, friends, and co-workers, an important aid to some dieters.

A written guide or manual is helpful when used in conjunction with whatever program the professional employs. Individuals thus have access to accurate and detailed information in all aspects of weight information. Such a resource is especially important for the areas in which the professional is not expert. Most im-

Table 40–1. Weight and Percent Body Fat of Male and Female Athletes*

Activity	Males		Females	
	Weight (kg)	% Fat	Weight (kg)	% Fat
Baseball	83–90	10–16	—	—
Basketball	84–109	7–11	63–68	21–27
Bicycling	67	9	61	15
Canoeing	76–80	10–12	—	—
Dancing, ballet and general	—	—	48–51	16–21
Football				
Defensive back	77–85	10–12	—	—
Offensive back	80–91	9–12	—	—
Linebacker	87–102	13–14	—	—
Offensive lineman	99–113	16–19	—	—
Defensive lineman	98–117	18–19	—	—
Quarterback, kicker	90	14		
Golf	—	—	62	24
Gymnastics	69	5	50–58	10–24
Ice hockey	77–87	13–15	—	—
Jockeys	50	14	—	—
Orienteering	72	16	58	19
Pentathlon	—	—	65	11
Racquetball	71–80	8–9	68	14
Rowing	93	7	—	—
Rugby	86	9	—	—
Skiing				
Alpine	66–78	7–14	59	21
Cross-country	67–73	8–13	56–59	16–22
Nordic	70	9–11	—	—
Ski jumping	70	14	—	—
Soccer	72–76	9–11	—	—
Skating				
Figure	60	9	49	13
Speed	74–77	9–11	—	—
Swimming	59–79	5–11	57–67	15–26
Tennis	77	15–16	56	20
Track and Field				
Runners				
Distance	63–72	5–18	53–57	15–19
Middle distance	72	7–12	—	—
Sprint	73–74	5–17	57	19
Cross-country	—	—	51	15
Discus	105–111	16	71	25
Jumpers, hurdlers	—	—	59	21
Shot put	113–126	17–20	78	28
Triathlon	—	7	—	13
Volleyball	86	12	60–71	18–25
Weight lifting				
Power	77–92	16–20	—	—
Olympic	88	12	—	—
Body Builders	83–88	8	54	13
Wrestling	66–82	4–14	—	—

* Data adapted from Wilmore JH, Costill DL: *Training for Sport and Activity: Physiological Basis of the Conditioning Process.* 3rd Ed. Boston: Allyn & Bacon, 1987. When more than one study was available, the minimum and maximum values for weight and body fat are presented. The studies reviewed by Wilmore and Costill varied in techniques for measuring body fat. These numbers therefore provide a general range for various groups of athletes, but do not necessarily reflect the weights or fat levels at which performance is maximized.

portantly, the guide can be used by the individual after the program ends. Several available manuals and books for weight control are cited in the reference section of this chapter.

Obesity and overweight are significant problems in modern society. Complex physiologic, genetic, cultural, and psychologic factors cause the problem, so it should not be automatically attributed to weak willpower or personal deficits. Exercise is an important predictor of success at weight reduction, so increased physical activity is one of the key aims in working with people who wish to reduce. Compliance is jeopardized, however, if the special physical and psychologic burdens of being overweight are not considered. A comprehensive program in which consideration of behavior, attitudes, social support, and nutrition, in addition to exercise, are integral factors appears to hold the greatest promise for long-term results.

RECOMMENDED READINGS

1. Bray GA: *The Obese Patient.* Philadelphia: W.B. Saunders, 1976.
2. Brownell KD: *The LEARN Program for Weight Control.* 1987. (Available from the author: Department of Psychiatry, University of Pennsylvania, 133 So. 36th Street, Philadelphia, PA 19104).
3. Brownell KD, Foreyt JF (eds): *Handbook of Eating Disorders: Physiology, Psychology, and Treatment of Obesity, Anorexia, and Obesity.* New York: Basic Books, 1986.
4. DeBakey ME, Gotto AM, Scott LW, Foreyt JP: *The Living Heart Diet.* New York: Simon & Schuster, 1984.
5. Garrow JS: *Treat Obesity Seriously: A Clinical Manual.* London: Churchill Livingstone, 1981.
6. McArdle WD, Katch FI, Katch VL: *Exercise Physiology: Energy, Nutrition, and Human Performance.* Philadelphia: Lea & Febiger, 1981.
7. Wilmore JH: *Sensible Fitness.* Champaign, IL: Leisure Press, 1986.
8. Wilmore JH, Costill DL: *Training for Sport and Activity: Physiological Basis of the Conditioning Process.* 3rd Ed. Boston: Allyn & Bacon, 1987.

CHAPTER 41

SMOKING CESSATION

ANDREW M. GOTTLIEB AND
DAVID P.L. SACHS

HEALTH RISKS OF SMOKING

Cigarette smoking is one of the key risk factors for premature death from heart disease, lung disease, and cancer. Of 50 million Americans who smoke regularly, about 325,000 die of premature illness each year. Although most people are aware of the link between smoking and cancer, far fewer individuals understand the causal relationship between smoking and heart disease.

The risk of heart disease is directly related to the number of cigarettes smoked. Smoking one pack per day doubles the risk compared to nonsmoking; smoking more than one pack per day triples the risk. The main mechanisms that affect the development of heart disease are the effects of nicotine and the effects of carbon monoxide. Nicotine causes increases in heart rate and blood pressure, which lead to increased work for the heart. It also may increase platelet adhesiveness, changing blood viscosity inside blood vessels. Carbon monoxide interferes with the ability of red blood cells to carry oxygen, thereby reducing the oxygen supply delivered to the heart muscle.

HEALTH BENEFITS OF QUITTING SMOKING

Although the risks from smoking are cumulative, the increased risk of cancer and heart disease drops rapidly after stopping smoking, even when the person has smoked for many years.[1,2] After 2½ years of nonsmoking, the risk of lung cancer is reduced by 50% and the risk of heart disease decreases by 25%. Within 5 to 10 years after cessation, the risk of major health problems decreases to levels only slightly greater than those of people who have never smoked. Besides the obvious major health benefits, many other benefits result, including increased energy, better complexion, and the ability to exercise more easily.

WHY PEOPLE SMOKE

To counsel smokers effectively, an understanding of some of the mechanisms that drive smoking behavior is useful. A major factor is physical dependency on nicotine. Each cigarette puff delivers a "hit" of nicotine to the brain within 7 sec, making smoking one of the most effective drug delivery systems known. The average smoker may self-administer 50,000 to 70,000 nicotine doses a year. Nicotine appears to have both stimulating and tranquilizing effects, depending on dosage. Evidence exists that nicotine may increase the production of brain hormones, such as β-endorphins. This effect may explain why nicotine can reduce the perception of pain and increase feelings of well-being. The smoker can "fine-tune" emotional responses by varying the puff rate and puff depth to control the amount of nicotine delivered to the brain. Thus, the smoker literally has fingertip control of emotional and physical responses, reducing the need for other coping techniques. Once a person becomes dependent on these effects of smoking to function normally, quitting becomes extremely difficult.

Although nicotine dependence is important, it does not fully explain why people smoke. Smoking appears to also have a second major component: psychologic dependence. Because smokers tend to become conditioned to certain smoking cues, these cues tend to stimulate the desire for a cigarette. Some cues are situational, such as drinking coffee, talking on the phone, or driving. Other cues involve negative emotions, such as anger or frustration, which tend to trigger smoking.

CESSATION

THE QUITTING PROCESS

If you have never smoked, you need to understand the quitting process to provide the right support for your students or clients who are trying to quit. Withdrawal from nicotine produces a variety of effects, including craving for tobacco, increased anxiety, increased irritability, increased restlessness, difficulty concentrating, headache, drowsiness, and gastrointestinal disturbances. These symptoms are most intense for the first 2 to 3 days after cessation, decrease over the first week, increase somewhat in the second week, and decrease gradually thereafter. The acute phase of smoking withdrawal is generally over within 2 to 4 weeks, although periodic urges to smoke can continue for months. Most smokers who re-

lapse do so within the first 6 months, although the risk of relapse does not disappear completely after that. A small proportion of ex-smokers will relapse even years after cessation.

EVALUATING VARIOUS TECHNIQUES

To help the person who wishes to quit smoking, you need to know the most effective approaches to smoking cessation.[3] The number of smoking cessation programs is extensive. How does one counsel the person who asks which method is effective? Understanding how to evaluate a smoking cessation approach is important. Because relapse is a serious problem in smoking cessation, the important criterion for effectiveness is the long-term quit rate, or the percentage of people who have maintained abstinence for at least 1 year. The quit rate at the end of treatment is less important, because some programs boast high initial quit rates but also have high relapse rates.

Smoking cessation techniques can be divided into four categories: (1) pharmacologic interventions; (2) behavioral interventions; (3) a combination of these two types; and (4) "other," such as acupuncture and hypnosis. Hundreds of studies have been conducted in evaluating various smoking cessation approaches, allowing us to identify with some confidence the approaches that work and those that do not work.

Pharmacologic or Medication Treatments

Early pharmacologic interventions included Pronicotyl, a spice tablet, and silver acetate. Both of these substances were supposed to make cigarettes taste foul when inhaled, but both proved ineffective. Another early drug approach was the use of the nicotine analogue, lobeline (sold as Bantron or Nicoban). Unfortunately, this substance also failed to have any advantage over placebo.

A more recent pharmacologic approach is the use of nicotine polacrilex (Nicorette), which is a medication available by prescription that has nicotine bound to a resin base. When chewed, the medication releases nicotine, which is absorbed through the oral mucosa. The rationale for this treatment is to provide a partial substitute for the nicotine in cigarettes, making the initial phase of tobacco withdrawal less unpleasant. This substitute helps the person through the early phase of quitting, allowing the subject to learn new ways of coping with the psychologic dependence factors. Nicotine polacrilex is used for a limited time after quitting, usually 3 to 6 months.

Although studies of nicotine polacrilex show that it is not a panacea for smoking, it is clearly more effective than placebo. When physicians administer this medication with initial counseling but no follow-up assessment, 1-year abstinence rates generally double from 4 to 8%. When minimal follow-up contact is provided, cessation rates rise to greater than 25%. When nicotine polacrilex use is combined with an extensive behavioral treatment program that focuses on psychologic dependency, but without physician involvement, quit rates of 30 to 50% are reported. When advising a patient, therefore, an important step is to steer the individual either to a behavioral program in which nicotine polacrilex use is an integral part or to a physician who provides good follow-up care along with this medication.

Behavioral Treatments

Another category of smoking cessation techniques involves behavioral approaches. One of the most effective techniques is rapid smoking; when properly administered, this approach yields long-term abstinence rates of 64 to 70%. Rapid smoking is a multicomponent treatment that involves several different elements, including relapse prevention training (see subsequent discussion) and rapid smoking, in which the patient inhales smoke from his own cigarette every 6 sec until he no longer wants to take another puff. The procedure creates an aversion to smoking that, when combined with skills training, leads to good cessation outcomes. Although the procedure involves heavy smoking, it has been shown to be safe even for patients with pre-existing cardiac and pulmonary disease. Abstinence rates of 50% at 2 years have been achieved in patients with cardiac or pulmonary disease. This technique must not be attempted without proper support and guidance from a therapist.

MAINTENANCE

The most recent advance in behavioral approaches to maintaining smoking cessation is an approach called relapse prevention. Developed by Alan Marlatt and Judith Gordon at the University of Washington, relapse prevention teaches people to anticipate those situations in which they will be tempted to smoke, and to develop new coping methods for avoiding relapse in these situations.[4] Simple questionnaires developed by Edward Lichtenstein at the University of Oregon can be used to measure a smoker's confidence with his ability to resist smoking during exposure to high-risk situations.[5] These questionnaires can be helpful in determining on what types of coping skills to focus attention.

The relapse prevention approach is particularly valuable in smoking cessation. Quitting is easy; it is staying "quit" that is difficult. Or as Mark Twain said, "Quitting smoking is easy, I have done it many times." Studies in which investigators combine relapse prevention approaches with nicotine polacrilex use produce outstanding abstinence rates, ranging from 40 to 70%.

SELF-HELP PROGRAMS

Self-help programs are available from the American Lung Association, as well as a number of self-help books. Data on these programs are scarce, but one study of the American Lung Association's *Freedom from Smoking in 20 Days* program revealed a 1-year quit rate of 5% in contrast to a control condition of 2%. Thus, self-help programs are apparently not as effective as other approaches, but they may be a good "minimal intervention" approach.

COMMERCIAL AND OTHER PROGRAMS

A variety of other smoking cessation approaches are currently used, some are commercial programs. Data on the effectiveness of many of these programs are lacking. The SmokEnders program appears to be a behavior modification approach, administered in a group format. Serious design problems have been noted with studies on this program, but when these problems are considered and adjustments are made, the long-term quit rate is probably about 25%.

Acupuncture is another popular smoking cessation technique. Unfortunately, controlled studies have failed to show any positive correlation between acupuncture and smoking cessation. Another very popular technique is hypnosis. Most studies of hypnosis have lacked the use of control groups, making an accurate estimation of effectiveness impossible. But this technique appears to have some efficacy, particularly when combined with group therapy.

Other commercial programs, such as Shick Clinics, are numerous, but most have not allowed independent evaluations of their effectiveness, so any judgment of their success rate is impossible.

SUMMARY OF QUITTING TECHNIQUES

In summary, the two most effective cessation approaches appear to be nicotine polacrilex use combined with behavioral skills training and relapse prevention, and the multicomponent rapid smoking treatment. Long-term quit rates as high as 50 to 70% are documented with these approaches. The use of nicotine polacrilex with follow-up care by a physician but no specific behavioral intervention is moderately effective, yielding 1-year rates of 27%. Behavioral programs without rapid smoking or nicotine polacrilex use yield quit rates of 16 to 20%; with nicotine polacrilex use, the rate is 38%. Self-help approaches and physician-initiated nicotine polacrilex use without follow-up care yield low but significant quit rates of 5 to 10%. Acupuncture has no demonstrable efficacy.

HOW TO HELP SOMEONE STOP SMOKING

Exercise leaders are often asked to help someone stop smoking. A number of guidelines are useful in helping someone to quit smoking. First, recognize that advice to quit from someone with good rapport with the patient, such as yourself, may have substantial impact. For example, studies with physicians show that as few as 60 sec of definitive counseling regarding quitting smoking has a substantial impact on long-term quit rates. With regard to advice-giving, remember that your advice should be definitive. Be clear, succinct, and unequivocal regarding the importance and benefit to that individual of stopping smoking. Provide infor-

mation such as that presented in this chapter concerning the dangers of smoking and the benefits of quitting. In addition, if you can time your discussion to occur when your client is experiencing symptoms caused by smoking, such as shortness of breath or angina-type pain, your advice is likely to be more effective. Another fact to remember is to avoid being moralistic or punitive. Emphasize the positive health benefits that your client will experience after quitting. Finally, do not advise the smoker simply to cut down or switch to a pipe, cigars, snuff, or chewing tobacco. Recent evidence shows that even large decreases in cigarette consumption translate to very small changes in risk factors. In addition, few smokers can successfully smoke in a limited way. The best advice is complete abstinence.

Once you have provided advice to quit, aid the person in deciding when and how to quit. A review of prior quitting attempts is valuable to evaluate what helped and what created pitfalls. Frame past failures in a positive light by emphasizing how each previous quit attempt can teach your client something useful. Setting a quit date is important. A firm commitment to quit on a specific date helps the person to prepare for nonsmoking.

The next step involves working with the person to develop a specific plan for cessation. In many cases, this step involves giving a list of programs and available resources to the client. Information should include the phone number, address, cost, success rate, and type of program. You may wish to include some of the information in this chapter on relative efficacy of various programs.

Once your client has entered a program and is going through the quitting process, be helpful in encouraging the quit efforts and providing support through difficult times. In addition, help to motivate the patient to maintain cessation by asking for a report of any positive health benefits they have noticed since quitting — increased stamina, better breathing, less coughing, and the like. After the person has successfully quit, relapse becomes a real threat. You can help to prepare the patient for possible threats to abstinence. Ask the person to identify situations that may be difficult and help develop coping strategies for those situations.

For individuals that do not want to quit, remember that at some later time they may change their mind. Someone who does not want to quit may be concerned about the negative impact of quitting—smoking withdrawal, weight gain, and so forth. Determining the main factors behind this reluctance to quit, and addressing these factors by educating your client about ways of coping with these problems, can often lead to a decision to quit. Almost all smokers would like to quit if they thought they could do so without undue negative consequences. Even if someone is clear about not wishing to quit now, a gentle but firm continued reminder about the importance of quitting can influence the motivation to quit.

REFERENCES

1. Sachs DPL: Cigarette smoking: Health effects and cessation strategies. *Clin Geriatr Med,* 2:337–362, 1986.
2. Schuman LM: The benefits of cessation of smoking. *Chest,* 59:421–427, 1971.
3. Sachs DPL: Smoking cessation: What are your referral options? *J Respir Dis,* 5(3):49–57, 1984.
4. Marlatt GA, Gordon J: *Relapse Prevention: Maintenance Strategies in the Treatment of Addictive Behaviors.* New York: Guilford Press, 1985.
5. Condiotte MM, Lichtenstein E: Self-efficacy and relapse in smoking cessation programs. *J Consult Clin Psychol,* 49:648–658, 1981.

CHAPTER 42

STRESS MANAGEMENT APPLICATIONS IN THE PREVENTION AND REHABILITATION OF CORONARY HEART DISEASE

WESLEY E. SIME AND
MARK E. MCKINNEY

The etiology of coronary heart disease (CHD), although studied extensively, remains only partially revealed. Standard risk factors are noted in only about one half of reported new cases of CHD.[1] One hypothesis is that emotional stress also plays a role in the development of CHD and sudden coronary death, with certain common factors noted within the person/environment interface.[2-6]

Rather than attempting to quantify stress based upon the attendant environmental events, stress is defined in this chapter in terms of the response elicited by certain standardized events within any one individual. In this manner, stress or the reaction to stress can be measured and quantified within the framework of individual difference analysis. This suggestion is based in part on observations that simple tasks such as quizzes, mental arithmetic tasks, and cold pressor tests cause dramatic changes in the cardiovascular functioning of certain individuals.[7-11] Furthermore, these changes are reflective of the activation of various neuroendocrine mechanisms that are known to have pathophysiologic consequences.

More specifically, stress is defined as any physical, psychologic, or cognitive event, of either a negative (adverse) or positive (exhilarating) nature, that elicits a physiologic response requiring significant homeostatic adaptation. When this adaptation is either excessive or prolonged, the deviation from baseline levels can be referred to as "strain." In addition, these strain responses, resulting from stressful stimuli, may yield pathophysiologic consequences if they are experienced with great intensity and/or with high frequency over time. The nature of the pathophysiologic findings is determined primarily by individual factors that predispose a person to one or more of a variety of stress-related illnesses.

The physiologic changes caused by stress exposure include increased blood pressure, which in turn can have pathophysiologic consequences through increased shearing forces on the arterial wall; increased circulating catecholamine levels, which can damage the arterial wall and the myocardium; and increased incidence of ventricular arrhythmia, a known risk factor for sudden coronary death.[7,12-14] In addition, such stress leads to increased levels of free fatty acid and serum cholesterol related to sympathetic activation of the liver, as well as increased platelet adhesion and aggregation in the arteries, because of elevated catecholamine levels.[15,16] Such a combination could set the stage for the development of atheromatous plaques in the coronary arteries, which in turn may potentiate CHD. Emotional stress of this type can also lead to increases in sodium levels and thus fluid retention in humans; in addition, release of epinephrine leads to loss of plasma potassium.[17,18] This combination of sodium retention and plasma potassium loss could lead to important ion imbalances, which set the stage for the aforementioned ventricular arrhythmias.

Stress management in patients with CHD begins with assessment. The details of assessment are beyond the space limitations of this article, but are found elsewhere.[19]

After the assessment phase, an important point in stress management is to recognize that the exercise routinely used in cardiac rehabilitation to improve cardiovascular function is also a potent means of muscle tension reduction. As such, a stress management program for cardiac rehabilitation should be designed to capitalize upon the side benefits of the exercise component. Logistically, therefore, a short relaxation training session should occur as soon after each exercise session as possible. The reason we recommend this sequential format is because cardiac patients do not learn relaxation easily or quickly. The physiologic concomitants of a truly relaxed hypometabolic state include decreased heart rate, blood pressure, oxygen consumption, muscle tension (EMG), electrodermal response, increased skin temperature, and numerous other neurohormonal changes in response to parasympathetic activation.[20] If the patient happens to be among the large percentage of postinfarct patients who are of type A personality, they are literally programmed for constant, habitual, high-tension activities. As such, they have long since forgotten what constitutes a truly relaxed experience. They block out early signs of pain or muscle tension in deference to the higher priority need for achievement or dominance. Because of these considerations, providing an extremely conducive, facilitating environment is necessary to have any chance that the patient will experience a hypometabolic relaxation response. Exercise is one paradoxic precursor that facilitates the relaxation experience. Evidence is considerable in documenting the role of aerobic exercise (moderate intensity and duration) in reducing muscle tension acutely.[21,22] Thus, exercise is an excellent facilitating prelude for relaxation training in individuals who are particularly tense. Relaxation training is apparently more likely to succeed if training can be scheduled soon after each exercise session. The added advantage, of course, is one of safety. Because a large proportion of exercise-related cardiac complications occur in the post-exercise period (during the shower or on the way home), the longer the cardiac rehabilitation staff can monitor patients after exercise (without simply wasting their time), the more efficacious the safety element in rehabilitation.

Another benefit of a regular exercise program appears to be a reduction in the characteristics of type A behavior. Fifty men and women suffering from cardiovascular disease engaged in a 10-week supervised aerobic exercise program.[23] At the end of the program, these subjects were scored as significantly less type A on the Jenkins Activity Survey, primarily because of a reduction in their hard-driving tendencies. In this study, Blumenthal and colleagues showed significant decreases in blood pressure and weight with exercise, as well as a marginally significant increase in HDL.[23] Although the cardiac rehabilitation patient might be characteristically more type A and less amenable to change, these results are certainly encouraging and add support to the use of exercise as a stress management tool. In addition, however, counseling should be considered, given results of a randomized study involving infarction patients for whom type A counseling was more effective than traditional cardiac rehabilitation in reducing the risk of recurrent infarction.[24]

One other important consideration is the reciprocal relationship between exercise and relaxation. Although exercise seems to have a facilitating effect on the relaxation experience, a reciprocal benefit from the relaxation also occurs during exercise. Benson and other investigators demonstrated that oxygen consumption at a fixed workload was significantly lower (4%) when subjects utilized a relaxation response technique during exercise on a bicycle ergometer.[25] Comparisons were made in a within-subject experimental design under carefully controlled conditions wherein maximal oxygen uptake was significantly lower during trials than during the comparable pre-trial and post-trial periods at a predetermined standardized workload. Similar results were observed in a study in which heart rate biofeedback training during exercise was used. Subjects received beat-to-beat heart rate feedback during five 10-min trials of walking on a treadmill at 2.5 mph, 10% grade with the instruction to try to lower their heart rate.[26] After 5 weeks, the feedback group showed significantly lower mean heart rate (97 versus 109 beats/min), systolic blood pressure (114 versus 131 mm Hg), and rate pressure product (11.1×10^3 versus 14.3×10^3 beats/min-mm Hg) during exercise than the control group. These differences were maintained after the cross-over of feedback provision for an additional 5 weeks. Increased muscular and cardiopulmonary efficiency probably accounts for these observations.

Because most cardiac patients are electrocardiographically monitored during exercise, it is technically feasible to include heart rate biofeedback training in most cardiac rehabilitation programs.

The acceptance of all patients into a stress management program is usually appropriate. A new patient may, however, have a special need for selected aspects of a program. For example, a patient who has severe anxiety and neurosis associated with specific life stress conditions, including recent cardiovascular health problems, might be directed immediately to a counselor for action-oriented solutions or for cognitive restructuring strategies to alleviate the self-perception of stress. Regarding the other basic self-regulation (relaxation) strategies, it is important to include all patients in a systematic, structured program.

SPECIFIC STRESS MANAGEMENT TECHNIQUES FOR CARDIAC REHABILITATION

BIOFEEDBACK-ASSISTED RELAXATION TRAINING

We believe that all patients should be offered one or two sessions of biofeedback. Some additional cost is involved for equipment and technician time, but the advantages far outweigh these costs. The health professional can illustrate vividly with digital displays, graphic displays, and auditory feedback the tremendous impact even small bouts of emotional arousal have on physiologic functions such as heart rate, blood pressure, skin temperature, and palmar sweating.[27] Many cardiac patients are hard-driving and somatically imperceptive. Although their perception of exertion may be somewhat vague, their perception of emotional response is often totally absent. The use of biofeedback equipment to demonstrate their highly specific and individualistic responsive-

ness can be invaluable as a motivational tool for biofeedback itself or for any of the other stress management techniques. In clinical programs wherein biofeedback equipment and technician time are limited, a feasible approach might be to include a short session of biofeedback as an extension of the psychophysiologic stress testing session.

Biofeedback is a tool to facilitate learning to control voluntary and involuntary physiologic functions.[27] In simplest terms, it involves the transfer of analogue signals of recorded physiologic functioning into a visual or auditory mode. Thus, by a trial and error process, the patients develop cognitive strategies for controlling physiologic functions. In most cases the purpose is to learn to diminish responses; however, stroke patients and other neuromuscular rehabilitation patients utilize biofeedback to aid in regaining function in muscles that have been nonfunctional.

The most relevant biofeedback parameters for cardiac rehabilitation are heart rate, electromyography (EMG), electrodermal response (palmar sweating), and peripheral blood flow (skin temperature). Blood pressure (BP) feedback is feasible but complicated by technical problems. By using the standard cuff method, feedback can be obtained only at 1-min intervals. Alternative methods involve the use of special equipment with constant cuff pressure, or indirect estimate with a pulse-wave velocity system, both of which involve considerable additional cost.[28,29] Electroencephalographic (brain wave) feedback and stroke volume feedback procedures are technically feasible but they are not commonly used in cardiac rehabilitation programs.

Biofeedback is usually used in conjunction with one of several other self-regulation strategies discussed herein. Sessions are of 25- to 50-min duration and are repeated 1 or 2 times weekly for a period of 4 to 12 weeks, depending on the individual needs of the patient. Patients with hypertension and cardiac arrhythmias are especially good candidates for biofeedback. This method of treatment can be the core of a comprehensive stress management program because the objective measurement of individual progress can be documented.

PROGRESSIVE RELAXATION

Progressive relaxation, a technique developed by Edmund Jacobson, is the oldest and most prominent Western method of self-regulation and stress management.[30] The technique involves the use of muscle contraction instructions for isolated muscle groups at varying levels of intensity for the purpose of enhancing sensory perception therein. Signal detection theory underlies this procedure, in that patients learn to recognize smaller and smaller differences in muscle tension and the resultant awareness presumably enhances control and subsequent relaxation of muscles at will. The key premise is that very tense patients do not recognize the proprioceptive sensations associated with muscle contraction.

Procedures for teaching progressive relaxation according to Jacobson's classic methodology are laid out in a step-by-step procedure.[30] The patient is instructed to contract a specific, isolated muscle or muscle group and to hold that contraction until a clear and distinct sensation of effort can be distinguished in the belly of the muscle, not in the surrounding joints or in the antagonist muscle. With the instruction to stop the contraction, the patient is expected to notice the clear distinction between tension and the relative absence thereof after the release. A residual level of tension always remains and hopefully declines over time. Initially, patients often are not able to perceive these signals accurately and need a repeated trial and error process to become more perceptive. Once the sensations associated with a high magnitude contraction are perceived accurately, the patient is asked to produce that contraction at progressively lower levels of intensity, thus developing an acute awareness of tension. Even with observable movement in the selected muscle or joint, the perceptive patient learns to recognize very low levels of premovement contraction. With this newly acquired awareness of small changes in muscle tension, the patient presumably becomes much more efficient in utilizing tension only by choice (not by emotion or by anxiety) and also uses only the minimal required level of tension for a given task. For example, the driver of a car can hold the steering wheel efficiently with modest effort or grip it excessively in a very tense and inefficient manner. Learning this technique requires regular practice in a systematic program focusing upon each of the major muscle groups progressively from day to day.

We caution the practitioner, however, that not all progressive muscle relaxation programs currently available are identical. Many efforts have been made to modify the original Jacobson program, yet research evidence shows these modified programs may not be as efficacious as the original.[31] Therefore, the original Jacobson work is the superior reference when implementing such a program.[32]

AUTOGENIC TRAINING

Luthe and Schultz founded Autogenic Training in the same era as Jacobson, but with a completely different psychophysiologic basis.[33] Their premise was that man has an inherent homeostatic mechanism to regulate all physiologic functions. When one or more of these functions goes awry in a pathologic state, it is possible to use self-suggestion to achieve self-regulatory neutralization. Six basic exercises cover the areas of heaviness, warmth, heart, respiration, solar plexus, and forehead. In each case, the patient is instructed to utilize subvocal suggestive phrases to achieve the desired physiologic changes. Examples of the phrases include: "my right arm is very heavy" . . . "my left arm is very heavy" . . . "my right arm is very warm," and so forth. In an autogenic training session, the patient is asked to repeat one of the phrases over and over subvocally. Subsequently, these individual phrases may be combined into consecutive and more lengthy phrases. Progression to new exercises occurs only after the patient has successfully achieved the outcome (sensation of heaviness, warmth). Thermal biofeedback is often used in conjunction with autogenic training to provide reinforcement and objective assessment attendant on progress in increasing peripheral blood flow, which is attendant on the increased hand temperature. In addition to group or individual training sessions with an instructor, the patient is asked to repeat the autogenic experience in shorter periods several times throughout the day. This technique is fairly complicated and the prospective instructor should seek practical training from a trained professional and should use one of several instructional manuals.[33,34]

BREATHING STRATEGIES

Inherent in most relaxation techniques is the attention paid to efficient breathing strategies. Patients who have tension problems almost always exhibit some form of dysfunctional breathing as well.[35] Usually, a form of reverse breathing is noted, wherein a chest breathing pattern prevails over abdominal breathing. The patient may even suck in the abdominal area while taking in a breath, thus exhibiting the most inefficient form of breathing.

In a relaxed state, the patient should breathe in a regular pattern of 8 to 12 breaths per minute. The abdomen should rise (when the patient is supine) with each inhalation and fall with the exhalation. The patient's chest should barely move and only after the abdominal shift appears. Patients often err by trying to breathe too deeply and in so doing they tend to hold the air in for a short while at the peak of inhalation. The pause, if any, should occur at the end of exhalation in a short rest period. Patients also tend to hold their breath or restrict breathing drastically during periods of excitement or anxiety. This pattern can be observed particularly during conversation, interview, or other test procedures. The classic signs appear in a patient who "sighs" frequently. The sigh is a homeostatic recovery phenomena associated with periodic breath-holding behavior. Additional information on dysfunctional breathing and appropriate breathing strategies is available.[35]

QUIETING REFLEX TRAINING

The Quieting Reflex procedure is an eclectic technique originated by Charles Stroebel that involves a combination of progressive relaxation, autogenic training, and a therapeutic breathing strategy in a simplified, quick exercise.[36] The patient is taught to initiate the 6-sec procedure upon stimulus cueing at numerous times through the day. The 6-sec technique is a basic 4-step procedure that may be individually tailored to the prescribed stress and tension needs of the patient. The four basic elements include:

1. Smile inwardly and say to yourself, "alert mind, calm body"
2. Take an easy, natural abdominal breath and let all the air flow out, followed by several more smooth regular breaths
3. As you exhale, let jaw, tongue, and shoulders go loose
4. As you exhale, imagine a wave of warmth and heaviness flowing from head to toes

Although this procedure is terribly incomplete by the purist standards of Edmund Jacobson in Progressive Relaxation or of Luthe and Schultz in Autogenic Training, its great strength lies in the option of being repeated hundreds of times daily in the face of mild and intensely stressful situations, thus averting the progressive build-up of residual tension and mental fatigue.

COGNITIVE RESTRUCTURING

Cognitive Restructuring is a stress management procedure aimed at identifying and changing self-defeating and self-destructive thinking. It is based on the general principles of Rational Emotive Therapy as outlined by Ellis, and has been popularized in several books, including an excellent text by Maultsby.[37,38] Several derivations of this procedure include one developed particularly for patients with stress-related disorders, including cardiovascular disease (H. Witte, personal communication). This procedure is aimed at promoting emotional control by attacking the negative self-talk of the patient. One important concept is to bring the patient to acknowledge, "I upset myself." The natural tendency is for patients to claim that "It upsets me." The "It" is usually a stressful event such as a divorce, death of a loved one, or loss of job. Although these events may be real stressors, too often the "it" is conceived and embellished in the mind of the patient. That we "make mountains out of mole hills" is a common experience that exacerbates the stress response. The end product of cognitive restructuring is to change a thin-skinned (easily disturbed) person into a more thick-skinned (emotionally stable) person who can better cope with the perception or the reality of any stressor.

SENSORY AWARENESS: A PRACTICAL SELF-ASSESSMENT TOOL

A stress management technique that can be a useful adjunct to any of the aforementioned techniques is Sensory Awareness Relaxation Training (SART), practical self-assessment strategy devised by Sime.[39] It is most effective when interjected periodically throughout a relaxation session (progressive relaxation) or during a biofeedback session. After a substantial period of relaxation (10 to 20 min), the instructor or therapist poses to the patient a series of questions aimed at noting the presence or absence of proprioceptive sensations.

The basis of this approach is the fact that sensation of pressure (feeling of contact with objects, support, and the like) diminishes gradually as the relaxation experience develops. Ultimately, patients who are completely relaxed do not feel any proprioceptive contact with such things as ring, watch, collar, belt, and shoes. As such, the progressive loss of these sensations from distal to proximal areas of the body can be a simple "yardstick" measure of the success or failure of the experience. Inherent in the entire process is that the patient must forego trying hard and simply allow the process to occur. A common denominator of failure is trying too hard. The patient should be encouraged to allow the relaxation to develop.

SPECIAL CONSIDERATIONS FOR STRESS MANAGEMENT IN CARDIAC REHABILITATION

SUPERVISION AND LEADERSHIP

Staff members providing stress management training should have a clear understanding of the physiologic and psychologic aspects of emotional stress, as well as the ability to communicate these principles to patients individually or in groups. Furthermore, they should have personal training and experience in one or more of the aforementioned stress management strategies. The stress management leader should also be an integral part of the cardiac rehabilitation team, be informed of the patient's current medical status, and be prepared to handle any medical emergency.

ORGANIZATION

The program can be operated on a group or individual basis. Relaxation training sessions should be held at least 2 times per week immediately after the exercise session and a third session should be scheduled for support group discussions and/or lecture presentations on sources of stress and action-oriented solutions. The latter sessions are specifically designed to provide information on the physiology of stress, the role of stress in disease, and the theoretic basis of the stress management techniques. In the support group discussions, patients are encouraged to relate their personal stress experiences and their recent successes and/or failures in coping.

The stress management program should be of 6 to 12 weeks' duration (20 to 40-min sessions, 3 times per week) for minimum benefits in the typical cardiac population with relatively deep-seated stress and tension habit patterns. Ideally, an individual biofeedback program could be initiated simultaneously or consecutively with the group stress management program. Biofeedback should be provided by a certified therapist at a frequency of 1 to 2 sessions per week for 6 to 12 weeks, with daily home training exercises.[40] The Biofeedback Certification Institute of America (10200 W. 44th, Wheat Ridge, CO) is the source for information for individuals seeking training and certification in biofeedback.

PRACTICAL ASPECTS OF RELAXATION TRAINING

After completing the exercise session, patients should go to an area that is conducive to a relaxation experience. Patients should have the opportunity to sit or lie down comfortably. Gymnasium mats are a valuable asset. In addition, we recommend placing foam cushions (10 × 12 × 14 in.) at a comfortable height under the lower legs of patients who are supine. This positioning relieves the strain on the lower back imposed by tight ileopsoas muscles.

Patients should wear loose clothing and should remove such obtrusive items as gum from the mouth or contacts from eyes. Lighting should be dimmed gradually to a semi-darkened state. The noise level should be minimized as much as possible; use of soft background music may be necessary to muffle any sharp or loud distracting noises from surrounding rooms. The temperature of the room should be between 72 and 78°F or be adjusted to the comfort level of the patients given their dress and metabolic level after exercise. Sometimes, individual patients may need sheets, blankets, or pillows to adapt to specific temperature or anatomic position problems. The leader should exercise control over the session by using mellow voice quality necessary to facilitate relaxation while communicating instructions effectively.

Some patients are inclined to fall asleep during the relaxation session. These individuals are probably short on sleep and should be encouraged to improve the quality or quantity of sleep. Another appropriate step is to move patients from a recumbent to a sitting position to avert the tendency to fall asleep, as well as to provide further challenge as the patient's relaxation skills develop.

Stress management in cardiac rehabilitation is designed to facilitate a hypometabolic, trophotropic experience in direct opposition to the ergotropic state experienced during exercise or intense emotional upset. Ironically, moderate exercise provides a healthy metabolic release of the skeletal muscle and neurohormonal components of emotional upset, and, in effect, facilitates progress toward relaxation. Biofeedback is a valuable adjunctive (or primary) therapeutic tool to illustrate vividly the physiologic arousal that accompanies various cognitive experiences of either anxiety or excitement; audiovisual feedback of heart rate, muscle tension, electrodermal response (palmar sweating) and skin temperature are the most common biofeedback modalities. Progressive relaxation, autogenic training, cognitive restructuring, systematic (efficient) breathing, and quieting reflex strategies provide the basic foundation for high-quality stress management programs. The health professional must coordinate all stress management activities with the exercise component to achieve integration with the overall cardiac rehabilitation program. Contraindications for stress management are few, but routine precautions are advisable for high-risk patients. Prescriptive recommendations for stress management are much like those for exercise therapy, i.e., the frequency should be at least three times a week, with home exercises daily; the duration of each session should be 20 to 40 min; and the intensity (quality) of each session should be judged on the motivation of the patient to "allow" the relaxation experience to occur and on the skill of the instructor (therapist) in facilitating a high-quality experience.

REFERENCES

1. Corday E, Corday SR: Prevention of heart disease by control of risk factors: The time has come to face the facts. *Am J Cardiol, 35:*330–333, 1975.
2. Engel G: Sudden and rapid death during psychological stress. *Ann Intern Med, 74:*771–785, 1971.
3. Burch GE, Giles T: Aspects of the influence of psychic stress on angina pectoris. *Am J Cardiol, 31:*108–110, 1973.
4. Engel G: Psychologic stress, vasodepressor (vasovagal) syncope, and sudden death. *Ann Intern Med 89:*403–412, 1978.
5. Buell JC, Eliot RS: Stress and cardiovascular disease. *Mod Concepts Cardiovasc Dis, 4:*19–24, 1979.
6. Crisp AH, Queenan M, D'Souza MF: Myocardial infarction and the emotional climate. *Lancet, 1:*616–619, 1984.
7. Shiffer F, Hartley LH, Schulman CL, Abelman WH: The quiz electrocardiogram: A new diagnostic and research technique for evaluating the relation between emotional stress and ischemic heart disease. *Am J Cardiol, 37:*41–47, 1976.
8. Brod J, Fencl V, Hejl Z, Jirka J: Circulatory changes underlying blood pressure elevation during acute emotional stress (mental arithmetic) in normotensive and hypertensive subjects. *Clin Sci, 78:*269–279, 1959.
9. Williams RB Jr, et al.: Type A behavior and elevated physiological and neuroendocrine responses to cognitive tasks. *Science, 218:*483–484, 1982.
10. Hines EA, Brown GE: The cold pressor test for measuring the reactibility of blood pressure: Data concerning 571 normal and hypertensive subjects. *Am Heart J, 11:*1–9, 1936.
11. Lovallo W: The cold pressor test and autonomic function: A review and integration. *Psychophysiology, 12:*268–282, 1975.
12. Eliot RS, Buell JC, Dembroski TM: "Biobehavioral perspectives on coronary heart disease, hypertension and sudden cardiac death. *Acta Med Scand [Suppl], 660:*203–213, 1982.
13. Raab W, Stark E, MacMillan WH, Gigee WR: Sympathetic origin and antiadrenergic prevention of stress-induced myocardial lesions. *Am J Cardiol, 8:*203–211, 1961.
14. Todd GL, Pieper GM, Clayton FC, Eliot RS: Histopathologic animal correlates of clinical sudden cardiac death and acute myocardial infarction. *Fed Proc, 36:*1073, 1977 (Abstract).
15. Dimsdale JE, Herd JA: Variability of plasma lipids in response to emotional arousal. *Psychosom Med, 44:*413–430, 1982.
16. Glass DC: Stress, behavior patterns, and coronary disease. *Am Sci, 65:*177–187, 1977.
17. Light KC, Koepke JP, Obrist PA, Willis PW: Psychological stress induces sodium and fluid retention in men at high risk for hypertension. *Science, 220:*429–431, 1983.
18. Limm M, Linton RAF, Bard DM: Continuous intravascular monitoring of epinephrine-induced changes in plasma potassium. *Anesthesiology, 57:*272–278, 1982.
19. Sime WE, Buell JC, Elliot R: Psychological emotional stress testing for assessing coronary risk. *J Cardiovasc Pulmon Tech, 8:*27–36, 1980.
20. Brener J: A general model of voluntary control applied to the phenomena of learned cardiovascular change. In *Cardiovascular Psychophysiology.* Edited by PA Obrist, AH Black, J Brener, and LV DiCara. Chicago: Aldine Publishing, 1974.
21. DeVries H, Hams G: Electromyographic comparison of single doses of exercise and meprobamate as to effects on muscular relaxation. *Am J Phys Med, 51:*130–141, 1972.
22. Sime W: *Acute Relief of Emotional Stress. Proceedings of the American Association for the Advancement of Tension Control.* Blacksburg, VA: University Publications, 1978.
23. Blumenthal JA, Williams S, Williams RB Jr., Wallace AG: Effects of exercise on the type A (coronary prone) behavior pattern. *Psychosom Med, 42:*289–296, 1980.
24. Friedman M: Behavior modification and MI recurrence. *Prim Cardiol, 11:*37–49, May, 1985.

25. Benson H, Dryer T, Hartley H: Decreased Vo_2 consumption during exercise with elicitation of the relaxation response. *J Human Stress,* 4:38–42, 1978.

26. Goldstein D, Ross R, Brady J: Biofeedback heart rate training during exercise. *Biofeedback Self-Regul,* 2:107–125, 1977.

27. Schwartz MS: *Biofeedback: A Practitioners Guide.* New York, Guilford Press, 1987.

28. Tursky B, Shapiro D, Schwartz GE: Automated constant cuff-pressure system to measure systolic and diastolic blood pressure in man. *IEEE Trans Biomed Eng,* 19:271–276, 1972.

29. Steptoe A: Blood pressure control: A comparison of feedback and instructions using pulse wave velocity measurements. *Psychophysiology,* 13:528–535, 1976.

30. Jacobson E: *Self-Operations Control: A Manual of Tension Control.* Chicago: National Foundation for Progressive Relaxation, 1964.

31. Lehrer PM: How to relax and how not to relax: A reevaluation of the work of Edmund Jacobson. Presented at the annual meeting of the Biofeedback Society of America, Chicago, 1982.

32. Jacobson E, McGuigan FJ: *Principles and Practice of Progressive Relaxation.* BMA Audio Cassettes, New York, Guilford Press, 1982.

33. Luthe W, Schultz J: *Autogenic Therapy: Medical Applications.* New York: Grune and Stratton, 1970.

34. Luthe W: *Introductions to the Methods of Autogenic Therapy.* Wheat Ridge, CO: Biofeedback Society of America, 1979.

35. Fried R: *The Hyperventilation Syndrome.* Baltimore, MD, Johns Hopkins University Press, 1987.

36. Stroebel C: *QR: The Quieting Reflex.* New York: G.P. Putnam, 1982.

37. Ellis A, Harper R: *A New Guide to Rational Living.* Hollywood: Wilshire Book, 1979.

38. Maultsby MC Jr.: *Help Yourself to Happiness Through Rational Self-Counseling.* New York: Institute for Rational Living, 1975.

39. Sime W: *Cognitive Strategies and Subjective Report of Tension in Relaxation Training. Proceedings of the American Association for the Advancement of Tension Control.* Blacksburg, VA: University Publications, 1977.

40. Schwartz MS: Biofeedback Certification Institute of America: Blueprint knowledge statements. *Biofeedback Self-Regul,* 6:253–262, 1981.

ADMINISTRATIVE CONCERNS

43

MANAGEMENT SKILLS REQUIRED FOR EXERCISE PROGRAMS

LARRY R. GETTMAN

MANAGEMENT SKILLS

This chapter provides general information on the management skills required for the administration of exercise programs in a variety of settings. This information supplements the guidelines for program administration published in Chapter 7 of the ACSM *Guidelines for Exercise Testing and Prescription* (3rd Ed).[1]

A program administrator should possess the quality of being a good leader. Leadership is really the key to a successful program. Too often, organizations consider first the facilities to build and what equipment to purchase and then the staff needed to oversee the program. The priorities for a successful program should be exactly the reverse; qualified health and fitness professionals should be carefully selected, and these individuals then can plan and implement appropriate programs for the design and capabilities of the facilities and equipment.

The administrator of an exercise program is often a health/fitness professional with many roles to play at the same time—a manager, planner, supervisor, educator, exercise leader, motivator, counselor, promoter, assessor, and evaluator.[2] The 10 roles are delineated in Table 43–1. Ideally, all staff members of an exercise

program should possess some qualities of all 10 roles.

MANAGEMENT BY OBJECTIVES

Perhaps the administrative technique used most often in the United States today is a system called management by objectives. It is intended to keep program goals and objectives foremost while respecting the needs, interests, and problems of the individual staff members. Problems are handled more easily if all staff members understand the goals set for the program and are willing to cooperate with the program manager in accomplishing the goals.

The management philosophy promoted in this system is to lead, guide, and advise staff members as opposed to drive, demand, and threaten them. The manager must respect the importance of each person as a human being while achieving the goals and objectives set for the program. The manager should strive to maintain an atmosphere in the program in which staff members can achieve individual goals and aspirations along with those of the entire group. Individuals accomplish most when they care the most. If the staff members recognize that the manager really cares about

Table 43–1. Characteristic Duties of the Health/Fitness Practitioner

Manager	**Motivator**
Administer daily operation	Give impetus to program
Design program activities	Persuade participants
Control program	Influence participants
Guide and direct staff	Induce changes in
Purchase equipment	participants
Maintain facilities	Incite action
Regulate budget	
Schedule activities	**Counselor**
Communicate with staff	Advise participants
and participants	Suggest changes
Cooperate with other	Express opinions
departments	Judge effectiveness of
	actions
Planner	Recommend action
Assess organization needs	Consult with participants
Establish goals for program	
Design program	**Promoter**
Organize resources	Design marketing
Arrange schedule	techniques
	Encourage participation
Supervisor	Use sales techniques
Hire and dismiss staff	Advance program
Oversee program and staff	advantages
Coordinate staff and	
program	**Assessor**
Motivate staff	Conduct participant tests
Evaluate staff	Interpret test results
	Follow safe procedures
Educator	
Train staff	**Evaluator**
Instruct participants	Design program-evaluation
Evaluate learning	procedures
Develop curricula	Perform statistical analyses
	Interpret results
Exercise Leader	Analyze program trends
Guide participants	Convey reports to
Conduct classes	management
Use safe techniques	
Provide a role model	

(From Patton RW, Corry JM, Gettman LR, Graf J: *Implementing Health/Fitness Programs.* Champaign, IL: Human Kinetics, 1986.)

them, they will care more about their jobs and strive to do better.

THE MANAGEMENT PROCESS

Effective management of exercise programs involves a four-stage recyclable process that includes information input, planning, implementation, and evaluation. The process is illustrated in Figure 43–1.

Information Input

The first stage in the management process is gathering information, which helps to determine what the needs are, what the clients want, and what the organization is interested in pro-

viding. Input information defines where the organization is now and where it wants to be in the future.

Input data should be collected from both clients (participants) and management and then merged for comparing needs and interests. Several methods may be used to gather input information and include interviews with participants; meetings with management, advisors, and staff; and surveys of potential participants.

A structured approach should be part of the interview technique to obtain the necessary information. This approach is much like conducting a written survey, but the personal interview format is used. The purpose of the personal interview is to determine what the clients really want and need.

Input information is also obtained by meeting with the organization's management to clarify the general philosophy of the program and what the management is willing to offer. Questions to be answered include: (1) How does management view the program? (2) How does the exercise program fit in with goals and the mission of the sponsoring organization? (3) Does management's philosophy of the organization match with the philosophy of the exercise program?

Another channel for information input is to form a program advisory committee. Meeting with the committee provides a forum to obtain their ideas on how they view the program, what should be offered, and how it should be conducted. The advisors may be representatives from the organization's staff and participants and/or outside professionals who have an interest in helping the program.

Meetings with existing staff (if any) are also important sources of input information. If the program is new, prospective staff members may be interviewed to get their ideas on program concepts. Staff ideas are sources of information that should not be overlooked.

Written surveys may also be used to gather information, for submitting objective reports to management. A sample survey form is provided in Figure 43–2. Ask for program ideas concerning only those programs you know can be offered. If questions are posed about programs that the organization is unable to provide, the participants will surely express interest in those programs and will be disappointed.

After the input information is gathered, analyze it to determine where the program is and

1. Information Input

    a. Participant Interviews
    b. Meetings with Management
    c. Meetings with Advisors
    d. Meetings with Staff
    e. Written Surveys

2. Planning

    a. Summarize Input
    b. Establish Goals
    c. Define Tasks

4. Evaluation

    a. Process Evaluation
    b. Outcome Evaluation

3. Implementation

    a. Assign Tasks
    b. Implement Tasks
    c. Supervise the Program

FIGURE 43–1. Four-stage management process for exercise programs.

where it should be. With this preparation, go to step 2, which involves planning how to implement the needed programs.

Planning

The second stage in the management process is planning. A summary of the input information is examined and the goals and objectives for the program are planned accordingly. We recommended that both short-term (1-month) and long-term (5-year) goals be planned.

Some questions to answer in planning a program for implementation include:

- What are your resources?
- What are your staffing needs?
- What are your options?
- What are the anticipated obstacles?
- What is the budget?

- What programs can be offered within the budget?
- How will you keep the participants motivated?
- How will you document the program's effectiveness?
- How will records be kept?

The objectives for the program should be placed in order of priority and the tasks necessary to meet those objectives need to be defined. The next step in the management process is to assign those tasks to staff members and implement the program.

Implementation

The implementation stage of the management process involves four steps: (1) review the

1. Your age _____
      sex _____
      job classification _____

2. The following exercise programs are offered by *XYZ Program.* Rank the programs you would use in order of 1 = first choice, 2 = second choice, etc.
   _____ Medical screening
   _____ Fitness testing
   _____ Walking
   _____ Jogging
   _____ Stationary Cycling
   _____ Outdoor cycling
   _____ Swimming
   _____ Dance Classes
   _____ Weight training
   _____ Tennis
   _____ Racquetball
   _____ Basketball
   _____ Volleyball
   _____ Walleyball
   _____ Circuit Programs
   _____ Calisthenic Classes

3. What are the best times during the day for you to use program? (rank 1 = best, 2 = next best, etc.)
   _____ 6:00 am
   _____ 7:00
   _____ 8:00
   _____ 9:00
   _____ 10:00
   _____ 11:00
   _____ 12:00 noon
   _____ 1:00 pm
   _____ 2:00
   _____ 3:00
   _____ 4:00
   _____ 5:00
   _____ 6:00
   _____ 7:00
   _____ 8:00

4. What are the best days during the week for you to use the program? (rank 1 = best, 2 = next best, etc.)
   _____ Monday   _____ Saturday
   _____ Tuesday
   _____ Wednesday
   _____ Thursday
   _____ Friday

FIGURE 43–2. Survey for gathering input information.

planned objectives and tasks; (2) assign the tasks to staff members; (3) have the staff members complete the tasks; and (4) supervise the implementation of the tasks. This series is initiated on the assumption that the program staff members have been hired and are available to implement the tasks assigned to them. Review-ing the planned objectives and tasks with the staff members helps to increase communication between management and staff and improves the understanding that everyone is working for the same goals.

When assigning the program tasks, the manager is faced with some important decisions:[2]

- Who will develop and supervise the budget?
- Who will develop the time line for the implementation procedures?
- How and when will the participants be enrolled?
- Who will supervise the different areas of the program? (For example, testing, individual exercise, exercise classes, follow-up, etc.)
- What facility resources will be used or developed?
- Who will supervise the maintenance of facilities and equipment?
- How and when will the participants be medically screened?
- How and when will other health and fitness tests be administered?
- How and when will the exercise programs be implemented?
- What educational strategies will be used in the program?
- What motivational techniques will be used?
- How will feedback be given to the participants?
- What special events will be conducted and when?
- How will emergencies be handled?

After implementation, the fourth step in the management process, which is evaluation, follows.

Evaluation

Evaluation of the exercise program involves two methods: process evaluation and outcome evaluation. Process evaluation involves verifying if the assigned tasks have been accomplished. Outcome evaluation determines if the objectives of the program were met.

During process evaluation, the manager should monitor the program activities to ensure the:

- operation of the program was efficient
- tasks assigned were reasonable
- time schedule was realistic
- staff members were prepared to perform and actually did complete the tasks
- staff members were dependable and enthusiastic
- proper resources were available for effective programming
- budget was adequate
- program was fun, accessible, and personalized

The facts collected for outcome evaluation include:

- the number of participants starting a program
- the number of participants completing a program
- a survey of participants and management to determine if the program objectives were met
- a cost/benefit or cost-effective analysis

The findings of the process and outcome evaluations are then combined and the overall effectiveness of the program is determined. If the program was effective, the participants should exhibit positive changes:

1. *Exercise behaviors* — increased activity levels
2. *Health* — more energy, disease risks reduced, health care costs reduced
3. *Fitness* — improved cardiovascular endurance, fat to lean body weight ratio, flexibility, and strength
4. *Knowledge* — health and fitness concepts understood
5. *Attitudes* — improved morale and self-confidence

Managers of exercise programs increase their chances for success if they consider seriously the aforementioned four-step recyclable process.

TIME MANAGEMENT

Time management is a useful technique that can be used by managers and all staff members to make better use of their time. Quite often employees express that they spend a lot of time doing several things but they feel as though they never accomplish anything. This recurring situation can lead to negative stress, anxiety, tension, and low work productivity. Some helpful techniques to make better use of work time include:

- Finish the project that was started
- Make a plan for future work and stick to that schedule
- Make and follow "to do" lists
- Prioritize work and complete priority one before proceeding to priority two
- Design a filing system so information can be retrieved quickly
- Delegate tasks (if appropriate) for an efficient work plan
- Anticipate problems with contingency plans

- Develop a simple and reliable management information reporting system to keep everyone informed of work tasks and to avoid duplication
- Use an uninterrupted "quiet hour" each day to review the schedule and priorities and to plan for the next day
- Balance the work day with exercise and relaxation for optimal performance

A well-organized, efficiently run exercise program is a likely result of a good time-management system.

ORGANIZATIONAL STRUCTURES

Two examples of organizational structures for exercise programs appear in Figures 43–3 and 43–4. Medical supervision of participants in a program can be provided in several different ways. The organizational structure in Figure 43–3 illustrates that a personal physician may be involved in medically clearing the participant for the exercise program or the personal physician may be involved in referring the participant to the program. In either case, a medical director is in charge of the exercise program and may have an additional medical advisory committee or a governing body associated with the program. The medical advisory committee or

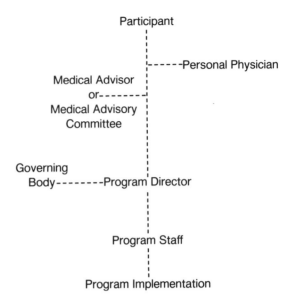

FIGURE 43 – 4. Organizational structure of exercise program with medical advisors.

governing body comprises professionals who contribute collective knowledge toward development and operation of the program.[1] In some instances, they help to establish administrative policy.

The responsibilities of the medical director are to manage and supervise the program and to ensure that medically safe procedures are followed. In some cases, the medical director assumes the ultimate medical liability for the program.

An example of organizational structure with the use of medical advisors to the exercise program is illustrated in Figure 34 – 4. The program director in this structure manages and supervises the program and receives consultative help from a medical advisor or medical advisory committee. The personal physician of the participant may again be involved in medically clearing the participant for exercise. The program director may also receive administrative policy help from a governing body. Other organizational structures for exercise programs exist but these two examples provide guidelines for emerging programs to follow.

STAFF RELATIONSHIPS

The exercise program staff, all under the supervision of the program director, may consist of a variety of health/fitness professionals, in-

FIGURE 43 – 3. Organizational structure of exercise program with medical director.

cluding exercise specialists, fitness instructors, physical educators, health educators, recreation specialists, nurses, physical therapists, dance instructors, and coaches. Support staff of the program include receptionists, secretaries, clerical workers, and custodians.

The organizational relationships and specialties among program staff depend on the size of the program and the exact mission of the organization. For example, some commercial and community-based exercise programs have strong recreational purposes and therefore have a predominance of recreation specialists on the professional staff. The staff of clinically based programs typically comprises health educators, nurses, or exercise physiologists. In the corporate setting, a wide variety of staff specialties are found. Some companies have recreation-based programs, others have medical departments, and still others blend a mix of medical and health education professionals with recreation and exercise specialists.

STAFFING CONSIDERATIONS

As described previously, expertise can vary widely. When staffing an exercise program with members of various specialities, a manager should consider having written job descriptions, following standard selection procedures, establishing staff training and development programs, following good supervising principles, evaluating personnel, and contracting with outside resources.

JOB DESCRIPTIONS

Good administrative policy includes having job descriptions for each position, including management, in a program. The program director should define what job positions exist in the program and then have descriptions written cooperatively by existing staff, if any, and the director. This process establishes, in writing, the responsibilities of each staff member so that each person knows what to expect and what is expected by management. A useful job description should be specific and should detail what the person in the job should accomplish. The job description should reflect a complete range of duties and responsibilities.

Program managers may have to coordinate many people, such as professional and support staff, advisory board members, student interns, consultants, subcontractors, and volunteers. Written job descriptions for all of these positions helps the program director delineate the responsibilities of each team member and blend this variety of expertise into an efficient and effective program. Written job descriptions also help the staff members to understand their own responsibilities in relation to those of other individuals. The written descriptions are excellent guides in the orientation and training of new staff members.

SELECTION/INTERVIEWS

Nothing is more important to a program than the selection of a competent staff who are committed to doing a good job. Selecting the right person for the right job helps to avoid many potential problems in the implementation of the program. Some personnel problems that do arise result from poor selection of staff. The wrong person is often placed in the wrong position. Effective personnel selection involves (1) defining the needs of the program; (2) identifying the qualifications needed for the open position that will meet the needs of the program; (3) reviewing and ranking the candidates for the open position; and (4) interviewing the top candidates. Personal characteristics or special skills that are required for certain jobs should be identified. A person with these abilities can then be sought. The criteria characteristics can be written and can form the basis for the interview and selection process. The criteria can be weighted so that candidates receive a score in the selection process.

When evaluating a candidate, the manager should use (1) written information from the candidate; (2) references listed by the candidate; and (3) conclusions and information from a personal interview of the candidate. The skills and level of knowledge of the candidate can be determined from these sources.

The manager should carefully examine the written information from the candidate to assess communication skills. The application letter itself reveals originality, creativity, grammar, spelling, and accuracy. The manager should contact those persons listed as references by the candidate so to discuss the qualifications of the candidate. Personal attributes of the candidate can also be discussed with references.

The personal interview is the final step in the selection process and should be designed to:

- Allow discussion of program objectives from the candidate's point of view. The applicant then has input into the selection process
- Allow the candidate to put forth his or her best impression
- Reveal the candidate's feelings about the job
- Validate the information on the candidate's application form
- Describe the benefits of the organization to the candidate

Good interviews are carefully planned. The manager should be very familiar with the available job, review the candidate's application in advance, and plan what occurs during the interview. When planning an interview, points to consider include:

- Amount of time spent
- General format
- Atmosphere of the interview
- Allow the candidate an opportunity to describe how he or she can contribute to the organization
- Explain how the manager sees the candidate contributing to the organization
- Outline what commitments the organization is willing to make

Avoid yes and no answers in the interview. Use an open question format. Let the candidate express answers freely. An interview should be a two-way exchange. The manager should not reveal what is expected from the outset because the candidate will simply agree with those expectations without exploring them creatively. By asking questions carefully, the manager can have the candidate describe his or her qualifications and talent and explain exactly how those attributes fit into the organization. The manager should keep the meeting on track and not let the discussion wander, yet interrupting or cutting off a response by the candidate should be avoided.

Compatibility of the candidate with the manager and the organization is an important consideration, but so is objective job performance. The manager should glean the opinions of co-workers by having other members of the staff interview the candidates. Use of the team approach in the selection process yields the greatest likelihood of revealing the best candidate.

We recommend practicing the interview process. Examples of some questions to ask during an interview are listed in Table 43–2.

Five key characteristics of candidates for the manager to assess when hiring exercise program staff are:[2]

1. Positive image of good health—exercises regularly, is not overweight, does not smoke
2. Fitness level—scores well on fitness tests
3. Enthusiasm—has a positive, contagious attitude that motivates people to action!
4. Dependability—on-time for appointments, meets commitments, maintains confidentiality of participants
5. Growth—active in professional organizations and is willing to learn more to grow in job

TRAINING/DEVELOPMENT

Regardless of the quality of the staff selection process, some training of staff members is usually necessary. The training process involves orientation of new staff members to the new work environment, to other staff members, to

Table 43–2. Sample Questions for Job Interview

1. What interests you about the announced job opening?
2. Why are you making a change from your present position?
3. What are some of your more important accomplishments?
4. What part of your job do you like the best?
5. What duties do you like the least?
6. How would you apply what you have learned in past jobs to the current position?
7. How would you lead an exercise program under the following circumstances? (interviewer should list some common characteristics of the current program to determine how the candidate would handle the situation)
8. Do you have examples of how you attempt to communicate and motivate?
9. What have you done to develop your skills and experience in the past few years?
10. Describe your relationship with your past three supervisors.
11. What are your strengths in relating to other people?
12. Do you have an example of a situation in which you might not have been effective in relating to others? What would you do differently?
13. Some people are quick-tempered and impatient. How would you describe yourself?
14. Have you encountered any health problems?
15. Would you describe one or two new ideas, projects, or innovations of which you are particularly proud?
16. How do you feel about your career progress?
17. What are your future aspirations?
18. Are there any conditions that would limit your ability to take the new job?

the policies and procedures of the organization, to the job responsibilities of staff members, and to the staff reporting relationships. Several ways to provide continuing development of staff members include: continuing education/training courses; involvement in professional associations and committees; attendance at professional conferences; and assignments as understudies to more experienced staff members.

SUPERVISION

The responsibilities of a supervisor include hiring staff, helping to develop the potential of each staff member, delegating tasks, directing and coordinating staff, monitoring staff performances, motivating staff, evaluating staff, and making recommendations. Good communication is a key to being a good supervisor.

Good communication means understanding as well as being understood. Two-way communication takes more time but is better than one-way communication. In two-way communication, the sender solicits a response and feedback from the receiver. Tools to improve two-way communication include:

- *Active listening:* pay attention and attempt to understand what is said and meant by the other person
- *Paraphrase:* check for understanding of what is being said by paraphrasing what was heard
- *Check feelings:* ask the other person how he or she feels. This step helps to improve understanding of the other person's communication
- *Describe behavior:* tell the other person what you see
- *Give constructive feedback:* express constructive feedback positively, even if it regards a negative situation. Feedback provides information to help the other person improve performance in achieving goals

A good supervisor is a good delegator. A good delegator clarifies expected results, keeps track of the progress of all subordinates, is accessible for questions and guidance, gives feedback, and recognizes the accomplishments of the staff. Three popular and effective techniques for successful supervision were promoted by Blanchard and Johnson:[3]

1. *One-minute goal setting.* Have regular staff meetings and delineate short, simple goals.

Review these goals often and analyze accomplishments, problems, and strategies to solve problems.
2. *One-minute praising.* Praise staff immediately for doing things right, and be consistent.
3. *One-minute reprimand.* First, confirm the facts. Then, state the reprimand firmly, and attack the mistake, not the person.

PERSONNEL EVALUATION

The purpose of evaluating staff members is to improve their performances. Managers should be positive and objective in their evaluations and each evaluation should be personal and confidential. Areas covered in staff performance evaluations are listed in Table 43–3.

CONTRACTING OUTSIDE RESOURCES

Several resources surrounding a program are available to help the program accomplish its operational tasks. Some of those resources include part-time consultants, subcontractors, student interns, and volunteers. Consultants and subcontractors may be available to provide certain aspects of the program, such as medical/fitness testing, exercise class leadership, or educational seminars. The use of outside consultants and services may reduce the compensation and overhead costs of having permanent staff on the payroll. Use of outside resources may also free in-house staff to spend more time

Table 43–3. Areas for Assessment through Staff Performance Evaluations

Job knowledge, training, and experience
Willingness to accept responsibility
Planning and organization of work
Quality and quantity of work
Cost consciousness and control
Relationships with others
Leadership qualities
Initiative and resourcefulness
Originality and creativeness
Soundness of judgment
Dependability
Personal appearance, speech, habits
Attendance and punctuality
Support for organization goals and policies
Career objectives

(From Patton RW, Corry JM, Gettman LR, Graf J: *Implementing Health/Fitness Programs.* Champaign, IL: Human Kinetics, 1986.)

counseling participants and preparing for other aspects of the program.

Most students in the health/fitness field must complete an internship during their bachelor's or master's degree program, and they may be available to help in the program at low to moderate costs. Consult authorities at a nearby college or university for internship possibilities.

In some instances, participant volunteers may help to recruit, encourage, and motivate other participants. Volunteers are usually used to help with special events, such as fun-runs, fitness days, tournaments, and seminars. Volunteers represent a no-cost but tremendous source of talent to help the program achieve some of its objectives. Volunteers may be located by word of mouth, newsletters, or in-house announcements.

PROGRAM ADMINISTRATION

Prompting consumers to use the program involves not only good management processes and staffing but also good marketing and implementation procedures. Regardless of the quality of the staff and programs, they will not be used unless the consumer knows about their availability.

MARKETING

Although marketing methods have gained a certain mystique, the definition of marketing is quite simple: determine or create the wants of the people and satisfy them. For commercial exercise programs, an additional statement can be made—and make a profit doing it. Cleary summarized six guidelines for effective marketing:[4]

1. Define and concentrate on the best market
2. Keep the price credible—then make it affordable
3. Find the right distribution channel
4. Help sellers sell
5. Make advertising a faithful extension of the product itself
6. Never betray the customer's trust

Successful marketing of an exercise program must serve a consumer need or desire and must do so in an honest, reliable way.[4] Otherwise, the program will not win repeat participants and referrals. Ultimately, the participant-provider relationship lives or dies on the basis of mutual respect and trust.

In providing a credible exercise program, the staff, program, and facilities must be professional and well organized. Separate staff should be hired to market the exercise program if the purpose of the program is to expand widely and/or to make a profit. For the technical personnel in a program to also be the marketing staff is a difficult; there simply is not enough time in the day to be thoroughly effective at both tasks. If marketing is of prime importance to the program, full-time marketing personnel should be hired. Marketing staff should have full knowledge of all details of the program, with familiarity of technical aspects of the program as well.

Public Relations

One major function of marketing is to build a good relationship with clients (potential participants). A good relationship with the media (radio, TV, newspaper) may also help to promote programs. Good public relations is a foundation for soliciting program participants and building a referral network.

Marketing Plan

A good marketing system for an exercise program involves development of a marketing strategy, implementation of that marketing plan, and evaluation of the results. The development phase requires a description of the marketplace in terms of the geographic, demographic, and economic characteristics of the potential users. The marketing plan should include a description of the competition, with a comparison of "their" services to those of the current program. The needs of the users should be identified in the marketing plan by surveying the market; Figure 43–2 illustrates such a survey example.

After the market has been described thoroughly, special groups should be targeted so to begin the promotional plan outlined for the exercise program. The initiation of market trials before a full market plan is implemented is advisable. Market trials could first include program employees and spouses. Volunteers from the program can also be used. As feedback is received from the market trials, the marketing plan is adjusted to provide the most effective strategy for obtaining program participants.

After implementation of a full marketing plan, its effectiveness should be evaluated. Strengths and weaknesses of the plan are identified and the results are used to design new marketing plans for the future.

Advertising Techniques

A good marketing plan includes some form of advertising. Examples of pertinent advertising techniques include:

- Word of mouth
- Media releases
- Print advertising
- Radio announcements
- Staff speaking engagements
- Direct mail
- Brochures
- Audio and video tapes
- Free memberships

MANAGING EXERCISE FACILITIES

Several features of an exercise facility make it successful. The most important is *convenience* to the participants. A close second choice is the degree of cleanliness of the facility.

The facility should be configured to save the participants time. It should have a good traffic flow pattern so that users are not confused and do not bump into each other. Optimal size for exercise circuit areas of a facility is reported to be 60 sq ft for each participant.[5]

In addition to convenience and traffic flow, the manager should ensure that the facility has ventilation, temperature control, and regular maintenance for safety and cleanliness. Good ventilation minimizes odors and enhances evaporative cooling for the exercising participants. The heat and humidity in the locker rooms should be controlled at a comfortable 70°F and 40% relative humidity.

The facility should be cleaned daily to provide a safe, clean, and attractive environment for the participants. The program staff can be scheduled to help maintain and service the facilities and equipment and oversee the cleaning schedule. A safe, clean, and attractive facility enhances program participation and success!

BUDGETING ISSUES

One required skill of the manager of an exercise program is budgeting. Budgeting is the projection of how much money will be spent during a 1-year period and the allocation of the money to various program components. Planning and controlling a budget helps to analyze the program's cost effectiveness; helps to determine the importance of each program component; reveals high-quality results of some program components; and helps to evaluate the overall financial health of the sponsoring organization.

A well-designed budget is a good decision-making guide. Management can select components for future programs on the basis of which programs produce the best participation and/or revenue. The program budget must be flexible so managers can transfer monies to areas of need or best use.

When planning a budget, the increase or decrease in the operations of the existing programs must be estimated. Then, the cost of developing new programs is projected. After the projected budget is reviewed by the management, the program director may have to negotiate for the final design of the budget. The program director should be a good budget negotiator.

Because a typical exercise program is a service provided by people, staff costs are usually a high proportion of the budget. Sometimes the management attempts to trim budgets by cutting the essential core of the service, that is, the staff. The program director should remind the personnel in management who are in control of the budget that staff services are essential to the program.

The program director has the responsibility of being a source of information to management and presenting the budget in a positive manner. A good budget presentation includes an analysis of the program operations and suggestions for how to improve operations in the new budget.

The program director must monitor the budget and compare actual expenditures with projections. This analysis can be done on a monthly, quarterly, and annual basis. If the difference between expenditures and projections is large, the budget should be re-evaluated to determine the reasons for the difference. The program director should find areas of savings and should emphasize this positive finding.

Table 43–4. Sample Line-item Budget

Item	1985 projected costs ($)	1984 costs ($)	1983 costs ($)
Staff salaries and fringe			
Director	50,000	45,450	41,318
Exercise specialists	30,000	27,273	24,794
Secretaries/clerical	27,000	24,545	22,314
Facilities			
Rent	200,000	200,000	200,000
Amortization construction	23,333	23,333	23,333
Utilities	30,000	27,900	25,947
Maintenance	30,000	28,500	27,075
Equipment			
New purchases	10,000	9,091	8,265
Amortization purchases	3,333	3,000	2,727
Maintenance	2,000	1,860	1,730
Supplies			
Testing	8,000	7,440	6,919
Educational	2,500	2,325	2,162
Exercise/sports	5,000	4,750	4,513
Office	2,500	2,325	2,162
Miscellaneous			
Special events	5,000	4,850	4,753
Publications and dues	2,000	1,960	1,901
Printing	4,500	4,320	4,234
Travel	3,000	2,940	2,852
Program promotion	1,000	950	931

(From Patton RW, Corry JM, Gettman LR, Graf J: *Implementing Health/Fitness Programs.* Champaign, IL: Human Kinetics, 1986.)

Table 43–5. Sample Functional-area Budget

Item	1985 projected costs ($)	1984 costs($)	1983 costs ($)
Program promotion			
Staff time	11,888	10,807	9,825
Materials	6,500	6,280	6,135
Advertising	5,000	4,850	4,753
Public relations	11,888	10,807	9,825
Other	1,000	950	931
Program management			
Staff supervision	11,888	10,807	9,825
Staff training	14,888	13,747	12,677
Financial management	11,888	10,807	9,825
Program planning	11,888	10,807	9,825
Facilities and equipment			
Rental	200,000	200,000	200,000
Amortization	26,666	26,333	26,060
Maintenance	32,000	30,360	28,805
Supplies	5,000	4,750	4,513
Services			
Testing	19,888	18,247	16,744
Classes	16,888	15,457	14,150
Counseling	11,888	10,807	9,825

(From Patton RW, Corry JM, Gettman LR, Graf J: *Implementing Health/Fitness Programs.* Champaign, IL: Human Kinetics, 1986.)

Table 43–6. Sample Impact-area Budget

Item	1985 projected costs ($)	1984 costs($)	1983 costs ($)
Evaluation			
Medical examinations	14,916	8,105	7,368
Fitness tests	4,972	2,702	2,457
Prescription			
Exercise	10,166	9,267	8,450
Nutrition	7,319	6,672	6,084
Weight control	7,319	6,672	6,084
Blood pressure	6,100	5,560	5,070
Smoking cessation	4,066	3,707	3,380
Stress management	3,660	3,336	3,042
Substance-abuse elimination	2,033	1,853	1,690
Follow-up counseling	11,888	10,807	9,825
Education and communication			
Newsletter	3,500	3,326	3,189
Materials	3,125	2,970	2,847
Audiovisual	2,750	2,613	2,505
Advertising	1,250	1,188	1,139
Public relations	1,250	1,188	1,139
Other	625	594	569
Motivation			
Special events	2,500	2,425	2,376
Awards	2,500	2,425	2,376
Documentation			
Computer	1,000	930	865

(From Patton RW, Corry JM, Gettman LR, Graf J: *Implementing Health/Fitness Programs*. Champaign, IL: Human Kinetics, 1986.)

Budget formats vary widely. Examples of line-item, functional-area, and impact-area budgets are illustrated in Tables 43–4, 43–5, and 43–6. Of the three types, line-item budgets are the easiest to use; each item of expenditure is logged into a general ledger and items are grouped into logical categories in the line-item budget.

Organizing items into functional areas of the program, such as promotion, management, facilities, equipment, and services, is an example of compiling a functional-area budget. An impact-area budget categorizes the budget into program components, such as evaluation, prescription, counseling, education, motivation, and documentation. Keeping careful records is part of accurate budgeting, but it also helps meet legal requirements for tax purposes and safeguards the organization's assets.

OFFICE ADMINISTRATION

Clerical and secretarial details, maintenance, and custodial services are often overlooked or taken for granted in a program. These positions are important to the success of a program. For example, the receptionist/secretary is often considered a low-paid, low-priority position. Yet, in an exercise program, this person is quite often the first line of communication with the participants. This person is therefore an important key to the program. The receptionist/secretary should have good "people" skills and should be friendly, courteous, and personal. This person should be efficient when making appointments, have good typing and word processing skills, be careful about keeping accurate files, and be well organized.

REFERENCES

1. American College of Sports Medicine: *Guidelines for Exercise Testing and Prescription*. 3rd Ed. Philadelphia: Lea & Febiger, 1986.
2. Patton RW, Corry JM, Gettman LR, Graf J: *Implementing Health/Fitness Programs*. Champaign, IL: Human Kinetics, 1986.
3. Blanchard K, Johnson S: *The One Minute Manager*. New York: Berkley Books, 1982.
4. Cleary DP: Learning from America's Great Marketers. *In Business*. May–June: 35–36, 1981.
5. O'Donnell MP, Ainsworth T: *Health Promotion in the Workplace*. New York: John Wiley & Sons, 1984.

CHAPTER 44

BUDGET CONSIDERATIONS

JOSEPHINE WILL MUSSER

The budget responsibilities of the Program Director (PD) and Health and Fitness Director (HFD) vary according to the employment setting. The HFD who is owner/manager of a free-standing health club has greater responsibilities, with more in-depth, direct knowledge of budgeting than the director who is a departmental manager in the multilayered organization of a corporation or nonprofit hospital. Ultimate budget responsibility varies, depending on the structure of the organization. Individuals with any one of several titles — chief operating officer, chief financial officer, accountant, president, division manager — may be ultimately responsible. The HFD and PD may be a line or staff position, which can be at any level of the organizational chart. Regardless of the organization, the HFD and PD should understand the budgeting process so the program can be developed efficiently and implemented in a cost-effective manner.

Many processes and philosophies on developing and using budgets have been described, with varying language, depending on the organization. Understanding of the process is gained best by working through several cycles and under the direction of those individuals who are ultimately responsible for the financial status of the organization.

TYPES AND USES OF BUDGETS

A budget may be simply a historic recording of revenues collected and expenses incurred. Accountants use this type of financial budget to maintain accounts and prepare periodic financial statements, such as balance sheets and funds flow statements for owners and management. Some organizations, including hospitals and other nonprofit institutions, use budgets and the budgeting process in an expanded role as a management tool. In this way, operating budgets are used in addition to historic costs. Operating budgets record current and past data, which are then compared and analyzed to plan for the future. Used in this way, a budget becomes a tool to aid in coordination and implementation and helps to quantify a plan of action.

ROLE OF BUDGETING

The budget process should assist the manager in making operating decisions as well as financial decisions. The budget process should ultimately assist the manager in efforts to make plans, evaluate performance, coordinate activities, motivate subordinates, communicate, implement plans, and authorize action. These functions fall into two categories—controlling functions and planning functions.

The control function of a budget is a framework for setting targets (activity or revenue) based on the goals and objectives of an organization. This system involves linking costs with each activity or product, and provides performance criteria for evaluating success and for planning future activities.

A variety of budget systems can be utilized. A budget system may be developed or purchased. It can describe a small subunit or the entire organization. The components of the system should be matched to the level of management control and responsibility. For example, the manager with no direct control over revenues, as in a hospital setting with third-party reimbursement, should work with a budget system that focuses on expenses and cost control.

Budget analysis is an essential managerial activity. Budget systems must provide frequent feedback, weekly or monthly reports, and accurate, up-to-date records for review and analysis. Periodic review of the budget is necessary for controlling costs, motivating staff, and periodic evaluation of the financial success of programs, products, or services.

LANGUAGE AND PROCESS OF BUDGETING

The budgeting process has two distinctly separate but related components—capital budgeting and operations budgeting. Some organizations develop separate staffing budgets. *Capital budgeting* and planning is used to plan for major development or improvement expenses, such as equipment purchases or facilities construction or remodeling, for which payment comes of revenues set aside for business development. Capital budgets are usually prepared annually and reviewed quarterly. Capital investment decisions are based on criteria such as *net present value* and *discounted cash flow*, which are beyond the scope of this discussion. Capital investment decisions are usually based on retained earnings and long-range plans, whereas operating decisions are based on current and short-term (up to 1 year) cash flow. Operating

budgets describe all activity and each source of revenue and expense, usually on a monthly basis. Operating budgets are prepared annually and usually are reviewed monthly, often weekly. Operating budgets are usually prepared for each subunit of an organization, e.g., division or department. Optimally, they should include a description of each discrete work group, and should be prepared and reviewed by the lowest-level supervisor of the work group who has direct control over costs.

A *profit center* is any organizational unit or segment, activity or product, to which all the components of revenue and costs can be assigned to determine the net profit or loss. Organizations that are designated nonprofit entities also identify profit centers and measure profits with the same formula as for profit enterprises:

$$Profit = Revenue - Costs$$

In nonprofit accounting, the terms "surplus" and "deficit" are typically substituted for "profit" and "loss."

The entire business operation is a profit center. Profit center budgeting is most useful at upper levels of management, where control over revenues and costs can be exerted. The profit center budgeting typically is broken into a *cost center* budgeting, which permits identification of all the costs associated with a discrete organizational subunit, activity, or product.

BUDGET PREPARATION

ACTIVITY FORECAST

The steps in preparing an operating budget for a manufacturing or retail organization usually begin with a sales forecast, followed by a production budget. In service organizations, such as fitness centers, these two steps must be carefully modified and combined to become the activity forecast, which is the foundation of the entire budget. The activity forecast must reflect the best combined information provided by the marketing, sales, and programming staff.

COSTS

When the activity forecast is established, costs are assigned to each revenue-generating activity. *Cost accounting* is the system of allocating costs to the appropriate revenue-producing unit, activity, or product. It may be referred to as *managerial accounting*, because of its usefulness to first-line managers who have responsibility and control of activity. Direct costs such as *direct material* (DM) and *direct labor* (DL) are so named because they are easily linked to the entity that produces revenue. By contrast, *indirect costs* such as clerical salaries (indirect labor) and office supplies (indirect materials) often cannot be tied exclusively to one activity or product, but rather are allocated by percentage use over several activities or products.

All operating expenses are either fixed or variable, whereas capital expenses are always fixed expenses. *Fixed costs* (FC), such as rent and taxes, do not vary with activity levels, whereas *variable costs* (VC), such as utilities and some supply costs (towels, electrodes, etc.) increase and decrease according to activity and hours of operation. Direct costs are always VC, indirect costs may be either FC or VC. Selling and general administrative costs (SGA) may be either of the fixed type, such as advertising and supervisory expenses, or of the variable type, such as sales commissions. The most important feature in any cost accounting system is that *every* cost is identified and allocated in a consistent manner.

After each cost is identified and multiplied by its associated item(s) in the activity forecast, the projected expenses for the total year can be listed in a *budget schedule* by month. For example, three accounts, (1) Subscriptions and Professional Books, (2) "Patient" Education Materials, and (3) Office Supplies, are shown in Table 44 – 1.

REVENUE

Expense accounts must be balanced by a schedule of the incoming revenue stream to ensure a sufficient positive cash flow. If major expenses are incurred in the first quarter but the sales during that period do not generate cash for 90 days, the payroll cannot be met without suf-

Table 44 – 2. Revenue and Expense Budget Projections by Month*

OPERATING REVENUES (Jan to Dec)	Total
Product W: Membership sales	
Product X: Cardiac rehabilitation visits	
Product Y: Fitness assessments	
Product Z: Smoking cessation programs	
Other	===
Total Revenues	_____
OPERATING EXPENSES	
Salaries	
Managerial (SGA)	
Professional (DL)	
Clerical (IDL)	
Sales commissions (SGA)	
Materials	
Stress test supplies (DM)	
Educational materials for smoking program (DM)	
Office supplies (IDM)	
Towels (DM)	
Other	
Overhead	
Telephone (fixed)†	
Maintenance (fixed)†	
Heat (variable)	
Rent (fixed)	
Other	===
Total Expenses	
NET INCOME	_____

* Examples of direct materials (DM), direct labor (DL), indirect materials (IDM), indirect labor (IDL), and sales, general, and administrative (SGA) costs.

† May be defined as variable or fixed.

ficient reserve. This potential disaster becomes apparent if a cash flow schedule (analysis) is prepared during the budget planning process.

Table 44 – 2 illustrates a partially complete example of a detailed schedule format containing the information gathered in the budget process. Many other types of accounts are encountered.

BUDGET ANALYSIS

End-of-month reports can be compiled for review only after a detailed schedule is prepared, such as is shown in Table 44 – 3. Each

Table 44 – 1. Partial Budget Schedule by Month

	Jan	Feb	Mar	Apr	May	Jun	Jul	Aug	Sep	Oct	Nov	Dec
Subscriptions	0	0	0	0	0	60	0	100	0	0	0	0
Patient education	0	0	0	0	0	2000	0	0	0	0	0	2000
General office	115*	115	115	115	115	115	115	115	115	115	115	115

*Office supplies average $115.00 each month; other two accounts incur expenses only during 2 months of the year.

Table 44-3. End-of-Month Report

	For June			Year-to-Date		
	Budgeted	Actual	Variance	Budgeted	Actual	Variance
Revenue Projection						
Product W	5000	6000	1000	30,000	38,000	8000
Product X	4000	3980	(20)	24,000	28,900	4900
Product Y	3000	1500	(1500)	18,000	17,100	(900)
Product Z	8000	6300	(1700)	64,000	64,000	0
Total Revenues	20,000	17,780	2220	136,000	148,000	12,000
Expense Projection						
Salaries	18,000	19,500	(1500)	120,000	128,000	(8000)
Materials	4,000	4,300	(300)	24,000	25,000	(1000)
Overhead	11,000	12,400	(1400)	78,000	79,000	(1000)
Total Expenses	33,000	36,200	(3200)	222,000	232,000	(10,000)

item from the budget is listed, along with projected, actual, and year-to-date figures for cumulative totals.

The example demonstrated in Table 44-3 shows a cost overrun of $3200 for the month and a year-to-date figure of $10,000 greater than was budgeted. Revenues, however, were $12,000 greater than anticipated. These figures are negative and positive *variances* from budget. A thorough manager reviews these figures to determine to what extent the $10,000 cost overrun is appropriate for the $12,000 increase in revenue, and thus identifies the point at which this planning was erroneous. If the manager is dealing with a *fixed budget,* the variance continues to adjust, accumulating to year's end. If the budget system provides *flexible budgets,* a range of best-estimated projections should have been prepared by developing (usually) three separate budgets for three estimates of projected activity.

THE BOTTOM LINE

Two methods are often used to arrive at "the bottom line," or net profit for each unit, activity, or product. One method calculates *Gross Margin.* Gross Margin (GM) is equivalent to sales (e.g., revenues from fitness assessments) minus all costs except fixed sales and general administrative (SGA) costs. For instances in which variable SGA costs exist (e.g., the commissions paid for selling fitness assessments), the calculation of *Contribution Margin* (CM) is more useful than GM. The calculation of CM is essential in making decisions as to whether to continue specific programs or product lines (Table 44-4).

The CM method allows the manager to determine if a product is covering its VC, which affects the decision as to whether to continue sales in the short run. In the long run, the product must cover its FC as well as its VC to contribute to the net profit.

Breakeven analysis (or more appropriately, cost, volume, profit analysis) is a useful activity. The breakeven point is the point of activity at which total revenues and total expenses are equal. Several methods are available for use in calculating the breakeven point, both by equation and graphically. On a micro level, the relevant issue may be, "How many enrollments must I sell?" Again the CM method is used.

Table 44-4. Summary of Gross Margin (GM) and Contribution Margin (CM) Method of Arriving at the "Bottom Line"

CM method for product X	GM method for product X
Revenues	Revenues
minus	minus
Variable Costs*	Variable Costs
Contribution Margin	minus
minus	Fixed Costs
Fixed Costs†	Gross Margin
Net Income	minus
	Sales and Administrative (SGA) Costs
	Net Income

* Includes variable SGA costs.
† Includes fixed SGA costs.

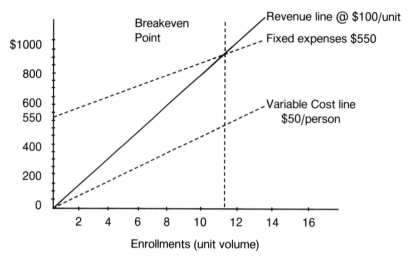

FIGURE 44-1. Determining breakeven point.

1. Unit CM = Unit revenue − unit variable expense

2. Breakeven point = $\dfrac{\text{Fixed expenses}}{\text{Unit CM}}$

In a smoking cessation program, for which the enrollment price is $100.00, VC are $50.00 per person, and total fixed expenses associated with the program are $550.00:

1. Per person CM = $100.00 − $50.00 = $50.00

2. Breakeven point = $\dfrac{\$550.00}{50}$ = 11 enrollments

A graphic example is provided in Figure 44-1.

The purpose of this discussion is not to present a comprehensive course in budgeting, but rather to provide the foundation upon which to build knowledge based on experience and future study. Health and fitness products and services have become highly competitive and important components of many businesses, necessitating that PDs and HFDs ac-quire the necessary information and skills to guide programs that not only have high standards of care and service, but also are financially responsible and sound. We recommend strongly that directors access available resources in the business library, Small Business Administration, workshops, and seminars, and whenever possible seek the assistance and guidance of experienced financial managers, including PDs and HFDs.

REFERENCES

1. Dewhurst RFJ: *Business Cost-Benefit Analysis.* London: McGraw Hill, 1972.
2. Horngren, CT: *Cost Accounting, A Managerial Emphasis.* Englewood Cliffs, NJ: Prentice-Hall, 1982.
3. Matthews LM: *Practical Operating Budgeting.* New York, McGraw Hill, 1977.
4. O'Donnell, MP, Ainsworth TH: *Health Promotion in the Workplace.* New York: John Wiley & Sons, 1984.
5. Ramsey JE, Ramsey IL: *Budgeting Basics.* New York: Franklin Watts, 1985.

CHAPTER 45

LEGAL CONSIDERATIONS

WILLIAM G. HERBERT AND
DAVID L. HERBERT

Legal considerations abound for professionals who provide exercise testing, prescription, and physical training programs for adults. These concerns encompass the professional-patient relationship and the activities performed within the legal confines of that relationship; the setting within which program activities are conducted; the purpose for which such activities are performed; and the procedures employed by the professional in providing services to the exercise client. The law influences exercise personnel in each of these domains. Despite the fact that jurisdictional variations exist, some principles in law have broad application to exercise testing, prescription, and leadership. Preventive and rehabilitative exercise program personnel should be cognizant of these principles and endeavor to develop practices to reduce risk of negligence-type litigation and, concomitantly, to maintain safe care of their clientele.

Although statistical data indicate a rather low risk of serious cardiovascular accidents among adults who participate in moderate-vigorous exercise, untoward events can and do occur, especially with diseased or high-risk patients.[1] Only a small fraction of these cases have ever resulted in legal claims against exercise professionals, but such claims are decidedly being processed through the legal system and thus forecast an ever increasing risk of claim and suit.[2,3]

TERMINOLOGY AND CONCEPTS

Almost invariably, legal claims against exercise professionals center on either alleged violations of contract law or tort principles. These two broad legal concepts, along with written and statutory laws, define and govern most legal relationships between individuals.

CONTRACT LAW

The law of contracts defines those undertakings that may be specified among individuals. A legal contract is simply a promise or performance bargained for and given in exchange for another promise or performance, all of which is supported by adequate consideration, i.e., something of value. In examining exercise testing and prescription activities, the law of contracts impacts the relationship established between exercise professionals and their clients. In effect, the conditions of the contract are satisfied in that both parties bargain for performance, which is supported by something of value. The client may receive physical fitness information and recommendations on exercise training; likewise, the professional may perform exercise testing services in exchange for payment, reimbursement, or some other valuable consideration. This contract relationship also encompasses any related activities that occur before and after exercise testing, such as health screening and exercise prescription. If expectations during this relationship are not fulfilled, law suit for breach of contract *may* be instituted. At the core of such a suit is alleged nonfulfillment of certain promises or alleged warranties, including implied warranties that the law sometimes imposes upon many contractual relationships.

INFORMED CONSENT

Aside from breach of contract claims arising from a lack of promise fulfillment, claims against exercise professionals can also be based on breach of contract for failure to obtain adequate informed consent from exercise participants. Although claims based on lack of informed consent, which are founded upon contract principles, are somewhat archaic, suits promulgated upon such failures can still be put forth in some jurisdictions. More frequently, however, such claims are brought forth in connection with negligence actions rather than breach of contract suits. To subject another individual to a specific exercise procedure both properly and lawfully, the client must give *informed* consent to the procedure with full knowledge of the material risks and benefits associated with that activity. This consent can be expressed (written) or implied by law arising out of the conduct of the parties. To give consent validly to a procedure, the individual must be of lawful age; not be mentally incapacitated; know and fully understand the importance and relevance of the material risks; and give consent voluntarily and not under any mistake of fact or duress.[4]

In many jurisdictions, the *participant* is required to know and understand the risks and circumstances associated with the procedure. In such states, a so-called subjective test is utilized to determine whether the particular person involved (as opposed to a reasonable man) understood and comprehended the risks and the procedures associated with the matter at hand. Other states have adopted a less rigid rule and provide an objective test to determine an individual's consent to a procedure or treatment.

Under this test, the legal determination centers on whether this person, as a reasonable and ordinary man, understood the facts and circumstances associated with the procedure so as to give a voluntary consent. In any case, exercise personnel must give special attention to the legal requirements of the informed consent process so that participants may freely decide whether to proceed with any particular test or programmatic activity.

Suits arising from the informed consent process can also occur in which an injured party claims that a professional was negligent in the explanation of the procedure including the risks, and that the participant would not, but for the negligence of the professional, have undergone the procedure. These cases are often decided upon the testimony of expert witnesses who determine whether the professional engaged in substandard conduct in securing the informed consent. These informed consent cases can involve claims relating to contract law, warranties, negligence, and malpractice.

TORT LAW

A tort in law is simply a type of civil wrong. Most tort claims affecting the exercise professional are based on allegations of either negligence or malpractice.

NEGLIGENCE

Negligence, although incapable of precise legal definition, may be regarded as a failure to conform one's conduct to a generally accepted standard or duty. A legal cause of action for negligence may be established given proof of certain facts, namely, that one person failed to provide *due care* to protect another person to whom the former owed some duty or responsibility, and that such failure proximately caused some injury to this latter person.[4]

MALPRACTICE

Malpractice is a specific type of negligence action involving claims against professionals arising from the course of their relationship with a patient or client. Malpractice actions generally involve claims against certain *statutorily defined* professionals for alleged breach of professional duties and responsibilities toward patients or other persons to whom they owed a particular standard of care or duty.[4] Historically, malpractice claims have been confined to actions against physicians and lawyers. By statute or case law, however, some states have expanded this group to include nurses, physical therapists, dentists, psychologists, and other health professionals.

DEFENSES TO NEGLIGENCE/ MALPRACTICE ACTIONS

If properly given, consents can sometimes be utilized as legal defenses to claims based on either tort or contract principles. In such cases, defense counsel may seek to characterize a consent as an *assumption of the risks by the plaintiff*. Assumption of the risks of a procedure, however, is often difficult to establish without an explicit written statement or clear conduct that demonstrates such an assumption. In addition, an assumption of the risks never relieves the exercise professional of the duty to perform in a competent and professional manner. Even when a valid informed consent/assumption of the risks is obtained, a participant's spouse, children, and/or heirs can file suits against the exercise professional for loss of consortium-type claims (even when the participant could not have asserted those claims because of his or her own assumption of the risks.[5] Recent trends in this area may indicate a need to obtain a consent from a participant, the participant's spouse, and perhaps in a limited number of states, to make it binding on any children. Certainly such consents should be binding on the patients' estates if certain of these negligence/ malpractice claims are to be avoided successfully from those quarters.

Informed consents are often confused with so-called "releases." Releases are statements sometimes written into consent documents that contain exculpatory language professing to relieve a party from any legal responsibility in the event of a participant's injury or death due to the professional's negligence. These releases are prospective waivers of responsibility and are generally disfavored in legal practice. Moreover, in a medical setting, the use of such releases has, with certain exceptions, been declared invalid as being against public policy. In nonmedical settings, however, particularly with certain ultrahazardous as well as other activities (e.g., auto racing and sky diving), the use

of such releases can be valid in some jurisdictions and under certain circumstances if properly drafted and obtained by a program.

Several other defenses to claims of negligence or malpractice are also available. In some states, for example, proof of a participant's negligence, referred to in law as *contributory negligence*, can preclude any recovery of damages from the defendant. In many states, however, this rule has been modified to adopt a so-called system of *comparative negligence*. Under this latter rule, the negligence of the injured party is compared with the negligence of all defendants in the case. Then, if the negligence of the injured party is found to be less than that of all defendants in the case, the plaintiff is allowed to recover, although in an amount that is reduced by the sum of the injured party's own negligence.[4]

STANDARDS OF PRACTICE FOR EXERCISE PROFESSIONALS

Standards of practice have been promulgated by several prominent professional associations that should be regarded as benchmarks of competency that would certainly be used in a court of law to assess a professional's performance in given situations. In fact, the use of these standards in certain cases dealing with exercise testing and exercise leadership has already occurred.[3] The standards developed by the American College of Sports Medicine, the American Heart Association, the American Medical Association, the National Council of YMCAs, the American Physical Therapy Association, and the Aerobics & Fitness Association of America, among others, provide guidelines of professional conduct for persons engaged in exercise programs for healthy adults as well as patients.[6-16] Unfortunately, these guidelines are not entirely uniform and in the event of participant injury or death, may create more confusion than provide a solution as to the benchmarks of professional behavior in a particular exercise setting. For example, in the area of exercise testing, the standards of the American Heart Association (AHA) and those of the American College of Sports Medicine (ACSM) are somewhat inconsistent in that the former imply that the physical presence of a physician is necessary during any graded exercise test, especially with diseased patients or individuals at risk.[7,9] In contrast, the ACSM guidelines are more liberal and do not mandate the presence of a physician except when testing higher risk or diseased individuals.[6]

The AHA guidelines and those of ACSM are also at variance relative to some aspects of professional authority for exercise prescription. The AHA guidelines reserve exercise prescription activities exclusively for physicians, particularly if the participant is at a higher-risk level or has heart disease.[7-9] In the ACSM guidelines, the emphasis for prescription is clearly with the qualified and certified Exercise Specialist or Program Director.[6]

UNAUTHORIZED PRACTICE OF MEDICINE AND OTHER ALLIED HEALTH PROFESSIONAL STATUTES

The modern trend in medicine is to utilize certain para-professionals in ever-increasingly important and expanded treatment roles. In fact, various states have undertaken efforts to expand nursing practice and other medical practice laws beyond mere observation, reporting, and recording of patient signs/symptoms. Various physician assistant or similar paraprofessional laws allow more nonphysicians expanded treatment authority when dealing with patients. Until this on-going process is completed, however, some nonphysicians who engage in certain practices that might be characterized as the practice of medicine or some other statutorily defined and controlled allied health profession, run the risk of engaging in unauthorized practices. This practice could lead to both criminal and civil sanctions. Many states have defined the practice of medicine broadly so that persons engaged in exercise testing and prescription activities could, under some circumstances, fall within the ambits of such statutes. Thus, without the presence or assistance of a licensed physician or other allied health professional for certain aspects of these exercise services, claims as to the unauthorized practice of medicine could be put forth. Under some of these state statutes, such practices are often classified as crimes, usually misdemeanors, punishable by imprisonment for less than 1 year and/or a fine.

In addition, a person found to have engaged in the unauthorized practice of medicine or some other allied health profession faces (after the fact) the legal expectation to provide an elevated standard of care in the event of participant injury or death. Under this rule, the exercise professional's actions are compared to an assumed standard of care of a physician or other allied health professional acting under the same or similar circumstances. In the event that the professional's actions do not meet this standard (which the non-physician or allied health professional cannot meet due to inadequacies of knowledge, skill, authorization, or experience), liability may result.

COMMON AREAS OF POTENTIAL LIABILITY AND EXPOSURE

In the course of conducting exercise programs, certain common claims seem to be the most likely sources of litigation. A summary follows:

1. Failure to monitor an exercise test properly and/or to stop an exercise test in the application of competent professional judgment
2. Failure to evaluate the participant's physical capabilities or impairments competently, factors that would proscribe or limit certain types of exercise
3. Failure to prescribe a safe exercise intensity in terms of cardiovascular, metabolic, and musculoskeletal demands
4. Failure to instruct participants adequately as to safe performance of the recommended physical activities or as to the proper use of exercise equipment
5. Failure to supervise properly the participant's exercise during program sessions or to advise individuals regarding any restrictions or modifications that should be imposed in performing conditioning activities during unsupervised periods
6. Failure to assign specific participants to an exercise setting with a level of physiologic monitoring, supervision, and emergency medical support commensurate with their health status
7. Failure to perform or render performance in a negligent manner in a variety of other situations[4]
8. Rendition of advice to a participant that is later construed to represent diagnosis of a medical condition or is deemed tantamount to medical prescription to relieve a

disease condition and that subsequently and/or proximately causes injury and/or deterioration of health and/or death

9. Failure to refer a participant to a physician or other appropriately licensed professional in response to the appearance of signs or symptoms suggestive of health problems requiring medical or other professional attention

10. Failure to maintain proper and confidential records documenting the informed consent process, the adequacy of participant instructions with regard to performance of program activities, and the adequacy of their physical responses to physical activity regimens[4]

This discussion is but an overview of the potential legal problems that face the exercise professional. As more and more participants are exposed to organized exercise programs, the actual number of untoward, as well as avoidable, events will inevitably rise. Increased numbers of these occurrences will result in negligence-type claims that will ultimately find resolution in court. The probabilities of such traumatic actions are quite low, particularly for those individuals and organizations that operate programs in a manner commensurate with professional standards. Awareness of the areas of special legal vulnerability and the adoption of legally sensitive practices in response, however, will keep the risks of litigation low and concurrently lead to safer and more efficacious programs.

REFERENCES

1. Rochmis P, Blackburn H: Exercise tests: A survey of procedures, safety and litigation experience in approximately 170,000 tests. *JAMA, 217*:1061–66, 1971.
2. *DeRouen vs. Holiday Spa Health Clubs of California.* Superior Court of County of Los Angeles, Case No. C346987 (Dismissed upon settlement 1985).
3. *Tart vs. McGann.* U.S. District Court, Southern District of New York, Case No. 81-CIVIL-3899 (ELP 1981). *Cited in* 697 F. 2d 75 (2d Cir. 1982).
4. Herbert DL, Herbert WG: *Legal Aspects of Preventive and Rehabilitative Exercise Programs.* Canton, OH: Professional and Executive Reports & Publications, 1985.
5. Child Sues for "Loss of Consortium." *Lawyers Alert,* 3:249, 1984.
6. American College of Sports Medicine: *Guidelines for Exercise Testing and Prescription.* 3rd Ed. Philadelphia: Lea & Febiger, 1986.
7. American Heart Association, The Committee on Exercise: *Exercise Testing and Training of Apparently Healthy Individuals: A Handbook for Physicians.* Dallas: American Heart Association, 1972.
8. American Heart Association, The Committee on Exercise: *Exercise Testing and Training of Individuals With Heart Disease or at High Risk for its Development: Handbook for Physicians.* Dallas: American Heart Association, 1975.
9. American Heart Association: *The Exercise Standards Book* (Reprinted from *Circulation,* 59:421A, 1979; *Circulation,* 59:849A, 1979; *Circulation,* 59:1084A, 1979; *Circulation,* 62:699A, 1980). Dallas: American Heart Association, 1980.
10. American Medical Association, Committee on Exercise and Physical Fitness: Evaluation for exercise participation: The apparently healthy individual. *JAMA, 219*:900–901, 1972.
11. American Medical Association, Council on Scientific Affairs: Indications and contraindications for exercise testing (A council report). *JAMA, 246*:1015–1018, 1981.
12. American Medical Association: Standards and Guidelines for Cardiopulmonary Resuscitation (CPR) and Emergency Cardiac Care (ECC). *JAMA, 244*:453–509, 1980.
13. Golding, L, Myers C, Sinning W, (eds): *The Y's Way to Physical Fitness (revised): A Guidebook for Instructors.* Rosemont, IL: Program Resources Office for the National Board of YMCA of the USA, 1982.
14. American Physical Therapy Association, Cardiopulmonary Specialty Council: *Specialty Competencies in Physical Therapy: Cardiopulmonary.* Manhattan Beach, CA: Board for Certification of Advanced Clinical Competence, American Physical Therapy Association, 1983.
15. Cooper PG (ed): *Aerobics Theory & Practice.* Sherman Oaks, CA: Aerobics and Fitness Association of America, 1985.
16. Herbert WG, Herbert DL: Exercise testing in adults: Legal and procedural considerations for the physical educator and exercise professionals. *JOHPER, 46*:17–18, 1975.

CHAPTER 46

REIMBURSEMENT FOR CLINICAL EXERCISE PROGRAMS

G. CURT MEYERS

Preventive and rehabilitative exercise programs can and do encompass a variety of clinical disciplines that either individually or collectively include physical therapy, occupational therapy, recreation therapy, respiratory therapy, exercise physiology, athletic training, nursing, nutrition, behavioral medicine, and physician services. Each discipline is unique in its education, certification process, and means of receiving payment from third-party carriers. Therefore, to review and discuss the areas of reimbursement of clinical programs is difficult without discussing in detail the relationship of each discipline as well as each service to the insurance payment mechanism. One reminder is that reimbursement for clinical services is in a state of revision at this time, and may change in the near future. Another important point is that payment for various services differs between states and between insurance companies.

INSURANCE COMPANY REVIEW

Presently, more than 188 million Americans are protected by one or more forms of health care insurance.[1] Health insurance organizations can be classified into two distinct parts: the private sector and the public sector. The private sector is primarily composed of the Blue Cross, Blue Shield, private commercial insurance companies (e.g., Aetna, Travellers and others), health maintenance organizations (HMOs), and preferred provider organizations (PPOs). Most of the private sector companies offer basic coverage, with major medical coverage provided at an additional cost. The public sector encompasses government-administered insurers such as Medicare, Medicaid, Civilian Health and Medical Program of the Uniformed Services (CHAMPUS), Indian Health Services, Workers' Compensation Medical Care, and the Bureau of Vocational Rehabilitation (BVR). Table 46-1 illustrates how the public and private sectors are related to inpatient and outpatient care.

Most preventive and rehabilitative exercise programs occur on an outpatient basis. Payment for this type of service usually comes from those sources listed in Table 46-1 for outpatient care. These services are covered due to the subscribers' claim against health care, workmen's compensation, disability, and/or in few cases, prevention coverage. The current outpatient prevention and rehabilitation payment mechanism is changing rapidly as the health care consumer and employers increase their financial commitment to the prevention of disease as a means of controlling costs.

Table 46–1. Payment Mechanism for Clinical Prevention and Rehabilitative Services

	Public Sector	Private Sector
Inpatient care	Medicare Part A	Blue Cross
	Medicaid	HMOs
	CHAMPUS	PPOs
	Indian Health Service	Most private insurance companies
		Private payment
Outpatient care	Medicare Part B	Blue Shield
	Medicare Part A (CORF)	Major Medical
	Medicaid	HMOs
	CHAMPUS	PPOs
	BVR	Most private insurance companies
	65 Special (Medicare)	Private payment

THIRD-PARTY PAYMENT FOR PREVENTION OF CHRONIC DISEASE THROUGH EXERCISE PROGRAMS

Health insurance companies as well as employers play an important role in programs that are designed to reduce absenteeism, improve productivity, and lower health claims and workmen's compensation costs by increasing the well-being of the working population and society. The insurance industry must solve specific problems before preventive programs are covered as a rule rather than the exception:

1. Due to the means of data collection, most carriers are unable to determine a cost versus benefits comparison. Therefore, the price of the premium for such service is difficult to ascertain.
2. The decision as to which disciplines and services should be covered is difficult.
3. A significant lack of agreement exists concerning which providers of specific services should be covered. Historically, third-party payors have required that a licensed or state-certified individual provide service to receive payment. During the past years, however, members of certain disciplines, such as exercise physiologists, have provided service without a license or state certification process, other than the certification of the American College of Sports Medicine. The lack of understanding of this certification process on the part of the insurance industry typically results in nonpayment. A teaching process from the provider to third-party payors would help solve this problem.
4. The amount of time required to achieve prevention is difficult to determine.
5. The value of the time spent with each member of various disciplines is undefined; therefore, payment for each service should be determined jointly. The chances for receiving payment for preventive exercise programs may increase as more data on effectiveness and cost benefits are available.

REIMBURSEMENT FOR REHABILITATIVE EXERCISE PROGRAMS

Most rehabilitative exercise programs focus on the secondary prevention and progression of chronic disease. Diseases such as atherosclerosis, chronic obstructive pulmonary disease (COPD), osteoarthritis, renal disease, obesity, hypertension, osteoporosis, and diabetes usually involve exercise in the treatment plan. As such, treatment through rehabilitative medicine usually includes one or more of the disciplines mentioned at the beginning of this chapter. An example of the coverage provided by major private sector providers (Blue Cross, Blue Shield, and Blue Cross Major Medical) for rehabilitative programs in the Pennsylvania area for Capital Blue Cross and Pennsylvania Blue Shield is provided in Table 46–2 (Brundt, correspondence by letter, Feb 9, 1984). We recommend that the exercise professional obtain similar information from insurers in their particular state before billing for services.

Public payment for outpatient services is well defined through the regulation of the Health Care Financing Administration (HCFA). An example of the criteria used for coverage can be found in the Comprehensive Outpatient Rehabilitation Facility Survey Report Form — 360.[2] The following areas are reviewed within these guidelines to determine coverage.

Table 46–2. Coverage by Major Private Sector Providers for Rehabilitative Programs*

Programs and Services	Basic Blue Cross			Major Medical			Blue Shield
	Outpatient	MD Office	Clinic	Outpatient	MD Office	Clinic	
Cardiac rehabilitation	Not covered	Not covered	Not covered	Covered → 12 wk	Covered → 12 wk	Covered → 12 wk	Covered → 12 wk
Cardiac exercise stress test	Covered if patient not in CRP. If in CRP, initial test only	Not covered	Not covered	Covered	Covered	Covered	Covered
Diabetic day care Smoking cessation Patient evaluation Dietary counseling	Covers diagnostic testing, emergency medical services. Instructional support services not covered.	Not covered	Not covered	Same as Basic outpatient	Not covered	Not covered	Not covered
Nursing services	Not covered as chargeable service	Not covered	Not covered	Covered if private duty nurse → 240 hr per year	Not covered	Not covered	Not covered
Physician services	Covered if hospital-based	Not covered	Not covered	Covered	Covered	Covered	Covered
Physical therapy	Covered to maximum improved potential, except diapulse, diathermy, ultrasound chest treatment for pulmonary conditions	Covered in plan	Covered in plan	Same as Basic	Same as Basic if provided by registered therapist	Same as MD office	Same as MD office
Respiratory therapy, general	Covered	Not covered	Not covered	Covered	Covered if provided by licensed therapist	Same as MD office	Same as MD office
Respiratory therapy, pulmonary rehabilitation	Not covered	Not covered	Not covered	Not covered	Not covered	Not covered	Not covered
Psychologic services	Not covered	Not covered	Not covered	Covered if provided by licensed psychologist or psychiatrist	Same as Outpatient	Same as Outpatient	Same as Outpatient

* Programs in the Pennsylvania area for Capital Blue Cross and Pennsylvania Blue Shield, as of 1986. CRP: cardiac rehabilitation program.

1. Condition of participation—compliance with state and local laws.
   a. Licensure of facility
   b. Licensure of personnel
2. Governing body and administration
   a. Ownership
   b. Administration
   c. Professional personnel
   d. Institutional budget
   e. Patient care policies
   f. Organizational chart
3. Patient services
   a. Plan of treatment
   b. Coordination of services
   c. Scope and site of services
   d. Patient assessment
4. Clinical records
   a. Content
   b. Protection of information
   c. Retention and preservation
5. Safety and comfort of patients
   a. Fire and safety codes
   b. Fire alarms
   c. Evacuation plan
6. Sanitary environment
   a. Infection control
   b. Cleaning standards
7. Equipment maintenance
8. Physical access for the handicapped
   a. Toilet facilities
   b. Doorways, stairwells, and passageways
   c. Elevators
   d. Parking
9. Drills and staff training
   a. Fire and disaster
   b. CPR
10. Utilization review
    a. Admissions
    b. Treatment plan
    c. Clinical practice
    d. Discharges

Review of these standards provides the clinician with an understanding of the requirements needed to obtain payment for services such as physical therapy, pulmonary rehabilitation, skilled nursing facilities, and durable medical equipment.

Medicare Part B also pays for outpatient services. Outpatient cardiovascular rehabilitation programs are primarily covered under this payment plan. Currently, Medicare covers 12 weeks of outpatient hospital or clinic-based cardiac rehabilitation. The criteria for coverage are:

1. The patient must have a documented diagnosis of acute myocardial infarction within the preceding 12 months or have had coronary bypass surgery and/or stable angina pectoris.
2. The therapy must be ordered by the patient's physician.
3. The program is provided in a hospital or clinic setting.
4. The facility must be directed by a physician, with a physician available at all times to perform duties while the facility provides cardiac rehabilitation.
5. The facility must have the necessary cardiopulmonary emergency, diagnostic, and therapeutic lifesaving equipment considered medically necessary available for immediate use at all times.
6. The program must be conducted in an area of exclusive use and must be staffed by the personnel necessary to conduct the program safely and effectively.
7. The nonphysician personnel must be employees of the physician or clinic directing the program, and their services must be incidental to a physician's professional service. When these criteria are met, Medicare usually pays 80% of the charge after the insured client has met their deductible.[3]

PAYMENT FOR SERVICES

Because of the various services and payors, and the differences that exist between states and third-party payors, a review of the amount of payment for each service rendered under clinical preventive and rehabilitative programs is difficult, if not impossible. The following guidelines may be used to obtain payment for services.

Diagnosis. This aspect is important when submitting a claim for payment. Most carriers utilize the *International Classification of Diseases* (9th Revision, Clinical Modification [ICDM-9-CM]) book published by the U.S. Department of Health and Human Services Public Health Service-Health Care Financing Administration.[4] Communication with the director of Provider Relations of the insurance company can result in a better understanding of what services are covered when certain diagnoses are used. As an example, the treatment for obesity can occur when the diagnosis of hypothyroidism, Cushing's disease, and hypothalamic lesions

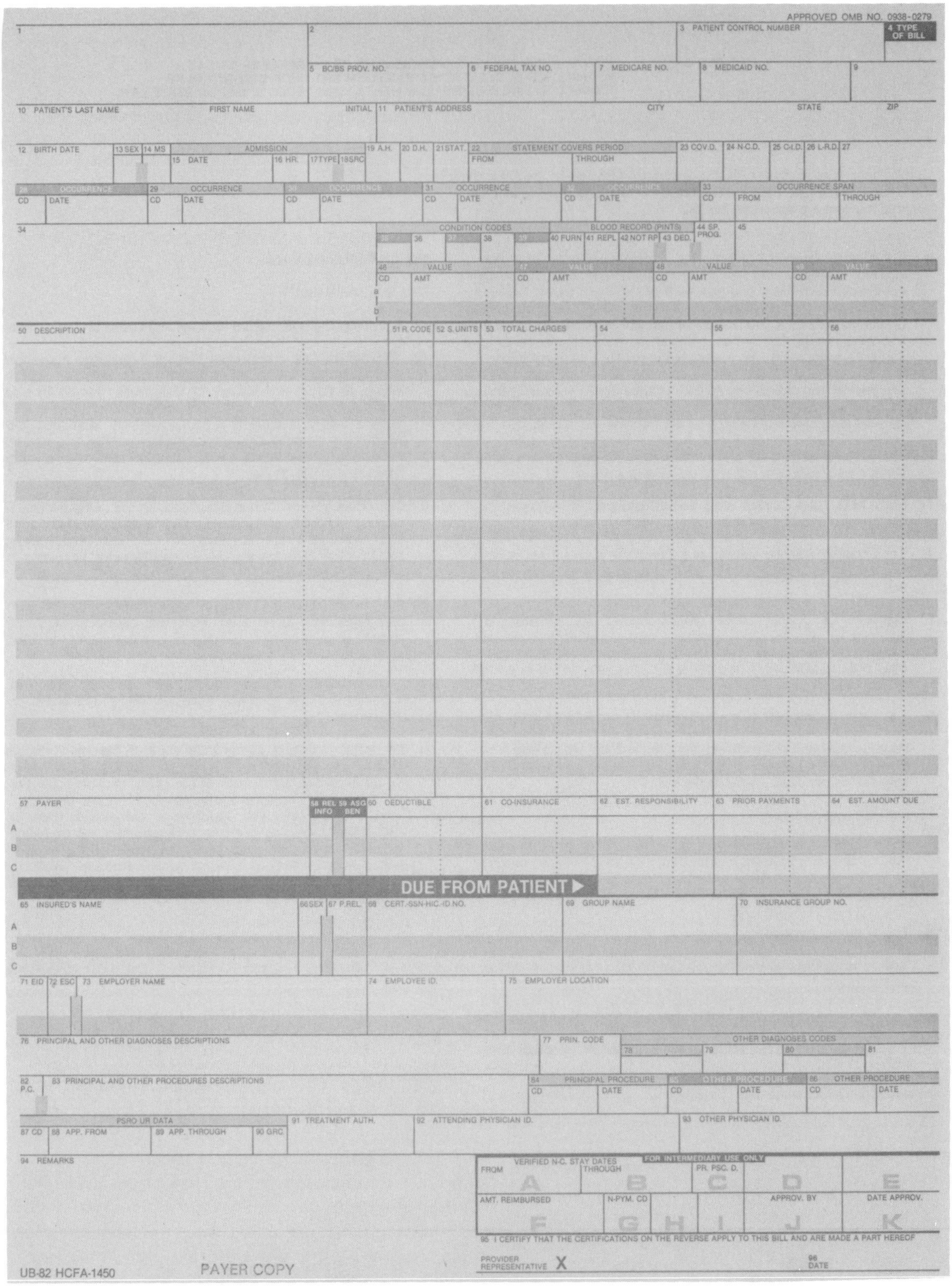
APPROVED OMB NO. 0938-0279

1 | 2 | 3 PATIENT CONTROL NUMBER | 4 TYPE OF BILL

5 BC/BS PROV. NO. | 6 FEDERAL TAX NO. | 7 MEDICARE NO. | 8 MEDICAID NO. | 9

10 PATIENT'S LAST NAME | FIRST NAME | INITIAL | 11 PATIENT'S ADDRESS | CITY | STATE | ZIP

12 BIRTH DATE | 13 SEX | 14 MS | ADMISSION 15 DATE | 16 HR. | 17 TYPE | 18 SRC | 19 A.H. | 20 D.H. | 21 STAT. | 22 STATEMENT COVERS PERIOD FROM | THROUGH | 23 COV.D. | 24 N-C.D. | 25 C-I.D. | 26 L-R.D. | 27

28 OCCURRENCE CD DATE | 29 OCCURRENCE CD DATE | 30 OCCURRENCE CD DATE | 31 OCCURRENCE CD DATE | 32 OCCURRENCE CD DATE | 33 OCCURRENCE SPAN CD FROM THROUGH

34 | CONDITION CODES 35 36 37 38 39 | BLOOD RECORD (PINTS) 40 FURN 41 REPL 42 NOT RP 43 DED. | 44 SP. PROG. | 45

46 VALUE CD AMT | 47 VALUE CD AMT | 48 VALUE CD AMT | 49 VALUE CD AMT
a
b

50 DESCRIPTION | 51 R. CODE | 52 S. UNITS | 53 TOTAL CHARGES | 54 | 55 | 56

57 PAYER | 58 REL INFO | 59 ASG BEN | 60 DEDUCTIBLE | 61 CO-INSURANCE | 62 EST. RESPONSIBILITY | 63 PRIOR PAYMENTS | 64 EST. AMOUNT DUE
A
B
C

DUE FROM PATIENT ▶

65 INSURED'S NAME | 66 SEX | 67 P. REL. | 68 CERT.-SSN-HIC.-ID NO. | 69 GROUP NAME | 70 INSURANCE GROUP NO.
A
B
C

71 EID | 72 ESC | 73 EMPLOYER NAME | 74 EMPLOYEE ID. | 75 EMPLOYER LOCATION

76 PRINCIPAL AND OTHER DIAGNOSES DESCRIPTIONS | 77 PRIN. CODE | OTHER DIAGNOSES CODES 78 79 80 81

82 P.C. | 83 PRINCIPAL AND OTHER PROCEDURES DESCRIPTIONS | 84 PRINCIPAL PROCEDURE CD DATE | 85 OTHER PROCEDURE CD DATE | 86 OTHER PROCEDURE CD DATE

PSRO UR DATA 87 CD | 88 APP. FROM | 89 APP. THROUGH | 90 GRC | 91 TREATMENT AUTH. | 92 ATTENDING PHYSICIAN ID. | 93 OTHER PHYSICIAN ID.

94 REMARKS | FOR INTERMEDIARY USE ONLY: VERIFIED N-C. STAY DATES FROM A | THROUGH B | PR. PSC. D. C | D | E | AMT. REIMBURSED F | N-PYM. CD G | H | I | APPROV. BY J | DATE APPROV. K

95 I CERTIFY THAT THE CERTIFICATIONS ON THE REVERSE APPLY TO THIS BILL AND ARE MADE A PART HEREOF

PROVIDER REPRESENTATIVE X | 96 DATE

UB-82 HCFA-1450 PAYER COPY

FIGURE 46-1. Example of billing form.

are utilized. Blue Shield may also cover treatment of obesity in the event of an underlying diagnosis of cardiac disease, respiratory disease, diabetes, and hypertension.[6]

Procedure. Each type of therapy should have a procedure that is used in the treatment plan of the patient. It is important that the correct procedure is indicated on the billing form, which is usually the UB-82 form (Fig. 46-1).

All procedures for treatment used by therapists are coded and listed in the current procedural terminology book.[5] An example for cardiovascular and pulmonary rehabilitation would include the following:

CARDIAC REHABILITATION
( ) 90020 Initial Visit
( ) 90060 Interim Visit

PULMONARY REHABILITATION
( ) 90020-1 Initial Visit
( ) 90060-1 Interim Visit

PHYSICIAN SERVICES
( ) 90040-1 Brief Visit, Est. Pt.
( ) 90020-2 Initial Visit

TESTING
( ) 93000   12-Lead ECG—Cardiac
( ) 93000-1   12-Lead ECG—Pulmonary
( ) 93000-2   12-Lead ECG—Diagnostic
( ) 93015   ETT—Cardiac
( ) 93015-1   ETT—Pulmonary
( ) 93015-2   ETT—Diagnostic
( ) 93040   2-Lead Rhythm ECG
( ) 93274   24-Hour ECG
( ) 94010   Spirometry with MVV
( ) 94681   Expired Gas Analysis
                B/A bronchodilator
( ) 82792   Oximetry, Rest
( ) 82792-22 Oximetry, Rest and Exercise
( ) 94240   Residual Capacity
( ) 94664   Aerosol Therapy (Initial)
( ) 94665   Aerosol Therapy (Subsequent)
( ) 94667   CPT (Initial)
( ) 94668   CPT (Subsequent)
( ) 36600   Arterial Blood Gas
( ) 08001   Nutritional Conference
( ) 94720   Carbon Monoxide
                Diffusing Capacity
( ) 01001   Conditioning
( ) 01002   Phase III Rehabilitation
( ) 36425   Venipuncture

Third-party utilization review guidelines. Payment also can be obtained more readily when the plan of treatment and length of treatment occur within the guidelines of utilization review as published by the third-party carrier. For example, physical therapy or sports medicine care of a dislocated shoulder must demonstrate progress in the range of motion, decrease in pain, and increase in strength. Without documentation of progress, payment is usually terminated because of the lack of rehabilitative potential or entrance into a maintenance treatment program.

Personnel licensure requirements. Finally, payment from third parties may occur only if a licensed or certified therapist co-signs the treatment chart. In the case of sports medicine, a certified athletic trainer, in some instances, is not recognized as a reimbursable provider without a co-signature from a licensed or registered physical therapist.

In summary, to receive payment for clinical exercise programs, the program director must be cognizant of the rules and regulations as set forth by the third-party carriers. As expansion of programs take place, more communication must take place between the provider of service and the payer.

REFERENCES

1. Health Insurance Association of America: *Source Book of Health Insurance Data 1983–84.* Available from authors: 1850 K. St. N.W. Washington, D.C. 20006.
2. Department of Health and Human Services: *Health Care Financing Administration: Part IV. Medicare Program; Comprehensive Outpatient Rehabilitation Facility Services.* Final rule 47 (241) Wednesday, December 15, 1982.
3. National Association of Rehabilitation Facilities: NARF Tech Brief. Brief 8, August 27, 1985. Available from authors: P.O. Box 17675, Washington, D.C. 20041.
4. U.S. Department of Health and Human Services-Public Health Service-Health Care Financing Administration: *International Classification of Diseases.* 9th Revision. Clinical Modification DHHS Publication No. (PHS) 80-1260, September 1980.
5. American Medical Association: *Physician's Current Procedural Terminology.* 4th Ed. Chicago, American Medical Association, 1983.
6. Pennsylvania Blue Shield: *Procedure Terminology Manual.* Camp Hill, PA, January, 1985.

CHAPTER 47

THE EXERCISE TESTING LABORATORY

EDWARD T. HOWLEY

The specifications of the exercise testing laboratory dictate the type of testing to be performed, the types of persons to be tested, and the complexity of the measurements to be made. Laboratories designed for testing elite athletes differ from the facilities in YMCAs, and the testing facilities located in hospitals offering a complete cardiac rehabilitation program differ from those found in a physician's office. Testing of elite athletes might include direct measurement of maximal aerobic power ($\dot{V}O_{2\,max}$) and the lactate threshold, with little concern for electrocardiographic (ECG) changes. The YMCA recommends the use of a submaximal fitness test to evaluate fitness before and after a fitness program in which heart rate is the primary measurement. In contrast, the staff of the exercise testing facility in a hospital typically monitors a 12-lead ECG during a graded exercise test (GXT) to obtain as much information as possible about the ECG changes related to the diagnosis of heart disease. The following sections outline facilities and equipment associated with submaximal fitness testing, diagnostic maximal clinical tests, and the testing of elite athletes.

FACILITY DESIGN

The exercise testing area should be apart from any other aspect of the facility or program. This separation ensures that the equipment used in testing is always available for testing, and that with less use and movement, the calibration of each piece of equipment is maintained more easily. A locker room and showering area in close proximity to the exercise testing area is recommended for the convenience of clients and test subjects and to allow monitoring of the person after testing.

Testing facilities may accommodate one or more individuals at a time. In a multitest facility, the testing area is designed around a central monitoring and observation area in which the physician can evaluate the ECG response to each of the tests. An exercise test technologist conducts the tests and maintains the necessary communication with the physician regarding signs and symptoms. Given the cost of physician time, this multitest design is an economical way to schedule the testing area and keep the overall cost of a GXT to a minimum. Both the single and multitest facility should have a "waiting" area or room in which to meet the subject, assign a locker in the changing/showering room, and have the individual fill out standard health history forms, if they have not already done so. Resting data (heart rate (HR), blood pressure (BP), 12-lead ECG, blood samples for a lipid profile and pulmonary function) may then be obtained in a separate area that should be kept quiet (block out noise from the treadmill) and relaxing to help obtain "true" resting data. At the completion of the resting measurements, the subject is prepared with electrodes and BP cuff to take the exercise test.

The exercise testing room must have the necessary equipment used for testing (treadmill or cycle ergometer) and monitoring (ECG, sphygmomanometer, stethoscope, gas analyzers, and volume flow meters) of the subject. Each piece of equipment should be calibrated on a regular basis (monthly for the cycle ergometer, treadmill, and volume flow meter; before and after each test for the ECG and gas analyzers). This room should also be equipped so that subjects may assume sitting or supine positions after the cool-down phase and during the recording of recovery measurements.

SELECTION OF EQUIPMENT

The mission of the testing facility determines the test type and, consequently, the equipment required. When equipment is selected, the emphasis must be on the quality of the equipment needed to maintain calibration and to provide for repeatability of the exercise stress from one test to the next. The following section is a summary of equipment typically used in testing centers involved with submaximal fitness tests, diagnostic sign/symptom-limited tests, or performance tests on athletes.

Submaximal fitness tests are used to evaluate HR, BP, and rating of perceived exertion (RPE) responses to a series of progressive work rates. The end point of the test is usually at 70 to 85% of estimated maximal HR. These data are then extrapolated to the age-adjusted maximal HR to estimate what the work rate or $\dot{V}O_2$ would be at that point. The equipment and supplies used for such a test include:

1. Cycle ergometer (and metronome) or treadmill

2. Sphygmomanometer and stethoscope
3. Clock or stop watch
4. RPE chart
5. Recording forms

Diagnostic sign/symptom-limited tests are used to evaluate cardiovascular function by imposing a series of continuous (or discontinuous) work rates while monitoring ECG changes, HR and BP responses, and specific signs and symptoms. These tests can be either maximal or submaximal; we refer the reader to pages 16 and 17 of *Guidelines for Exercise Testing and Prescription (3rd Ed.)* for further discussion of this issue. The equipment used in diagnostic tests include:

1. Treadmill, cycle ergometer, or arm ergometer (and metronome)
2. Sphygmomanometer and stethoscope
3. ECG—for monitoring a single or 12 leads
4. Clock or stop watch
5. Equipment/drugs for cardiac emergency (see *Guidelines for Exercise Testing and Prescription* for specific suggestions)
6. RPE chart
7. Recording forms

Exercise testing of athletes varies depending on the purpose of the tests. The tests might include the measurement of maximal aerobic power, lactate threshold, or anaerobic power (Margaria step test or the Wingate test). The level of monitoring and the personnel supervising these tests typically differ from that associated with the aforementioned tests.

CALIBRATION OF EQUIPMENT

This discussion of the calibration of the equipment used in exercise testing is meant to be instructive and is not a replacement for the specific procedures recommended by the manufacturer.

TREADMILL

The treadmill is one of the most common pieces of equipment used to study exercise responses. The intensity of the exercise can be altered by changing the speed and/or grade.

Speed Calibration

Method 1. In some older treadmills (A.R. Young), a mechanical counter was attached to the rear of the treadmill with a microswitch suspended over the treadmill belt. As the belt moved around the drums, an elevated surface on the outside edge of the belt would trigger the switch. If you knew the belt length (meters) and the number of times the belt moved past the switch per minute, you could obtain the belt speed in meters per minute. Use of the same procedure is possible on any treadmill by following certain steps:

1. Measure exact length of the belt in meters, and record the value.
2. Place a small piece of tape on the belt surface near the edge, or mark the surface with a pen.
3. Turn on the treadmill to a given speed using the speed control.
4. Count the number of belt revolutions in 1 min by counting the number of times the piece of tape on the belt passes a fixed point. (Note: start counting with zero and start your watch as the tape first moves past the fixed point.)
5. Convert the number of revolutions to revolutions per minute. For example, if the belt made 33 complete revolutions in 58 sec: 58 sec ÷ 60 sec · min^{-1} = 0.967 min. So, 33 rev ÷ 0.967 min = 34.14 rev · min^{-1}.
6. Multiply the calculated rev · min^{-1} (step 5) times the belt length (step 1). This product is the belt speed (m · min^{-1}). For example, if the belt length is 2.532 m: 34.14 rev · min^{-1} × 2.532 m · rev^{-1} = 86.4 m · min^{-1}.
7. To convert meters per minute to miles per hour (mph), divide the answer in step 6 by 26.8 m · min^{-1} per mph: 86.4 m · min^{-1} ÷ 26.8 m · min^{-1} per mph^{-1} = 3.22 mph.
8. The value obtained in step 7 is the actual treadmill speed (in mph). If the speed indicator does not agree with this value, adjust the meter to the proper reading. The calibration adjustment is accessible on most treadmills through a small hole in the front of the control panel.
9. Repeat for a number of different speeds to assure accuracy across the speeds used in test protocols.

Method 2. If your treadmill is equipped with a device to count the revolutions of one of the drums (like the Quinton 24-72 model), the counter may be used to check the accuracy of the speedometer. Simply set the counter to zero, set the treadmill to the desired speed, and operate the counter for exactly 1 min. For the 24-72 treadmill, 21 rev · min^{-1} is equal to 1 mph, and 210 counts · min^{-1} is equal to 10 mph. Check the manual for your treadmill to make sure of the relationship between the revolutions per minute and speed (in mph). This method is accurate only if the treadmill belt is properly adjusted and does not slip.

Elevation Calibration

The manual that comes with the treadmill describes how to calibrate the grade with a simple "carpenter's level" and a "square." This calibration procedure follows.

1. Use a carpenter's level to make sure that the treadmill is level and check the zero on the grade meter under these conditions (with the treadmill electronics "on"). If the meter does not read zero, follow instructions to make the adjustment (usually the small screw on the face of the meter).
2. Elevate the treadmill so that the percent grade meter reads approximately 20%. Measure the exact incline of the treadmill as shown in Figure 47–1. When the bubble of the level is exactly in the center of the tube, the "rise" measurement is obtained. Calculate the grade as the "rise" over the "run" (tangent θ), and adjust the treadmill meter to read that exact grade. For example, if the "rise" is 4.5 in. to the 22.5 in. of the run, the fractional grade is:

$$\text{Grade} = \text{tangent } \theta = \text{rise} \div \text{run}$$
$$= 4.5 \text{ in.} \div 22.5 \text{ in.} = 0.20 = 20\%$$

3. Repeat this process at grades between 0 and 20° (0 to 34%) to make sure the meter is correct.

This "rise" over the "run" method is a typical engineering method for calculating grade — the vertical rise divided by the horizontal run. This method gives the tangent of the angle (the opposite side divided by the horizontal distance, as shown in Figure 47–1). Although this tangent method is not exactly correct, it is a good approximation for grades less than 20% or 12° (see Table 47–1).

The "correct" method expresses grade as the sine of the angle (sin θ), in which sin θ equals the vertical rise (opposite side) over the hypote-

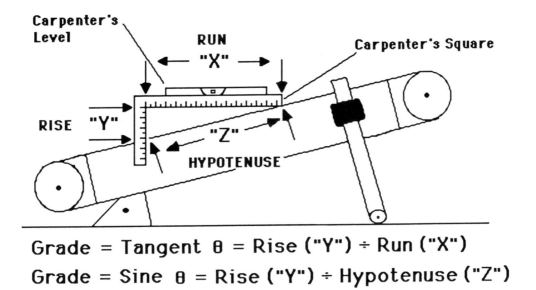

$$\text{Grade} = \text{Tangent } \theta = \text{Rise ("Y")} \div \text{Run ("X")}$$
$$\text{Grade} = \text{Sine } \theta = \text{Rise ("Y")} \div \text{Hypotenuse ("Z")}$$

FIGURE 47–1. Calibration of grade by tangent method (rise ÷ run) with carpenter's square and level.

nuse [sin θ = rise ÷ hypotenuse (see Fig. 47–1)]. This method should be used to calculate very steep grades (> 20%). The vertical rise can be calculated very simply for a treadmill with a fixed rear axle. Simply measure the change in the height of the front axle above the horizontal (rise). Divide this value by the axle-to-axle length (hypotenuse), and the quotient is the grade, expressed as a fraction (Fig. 47–2).

For the large treadmill with moveable rear and front axles, the vertical rise is equal to the sum of the rise of the front axle and the drop of the rear axle (Fig. 47–3). When this total is divided by the axle-to-axle length, the quotient is the grade, expressed as a fraction. For example, if the front axle height is 0.327 m on the level (0% grade) and 0.612 m at the unknown grade, then the front axle rise is $0.612 - 0.327 = 0.285$ m. Similarly, if the rear axle height is 0.324 m at 0% grade and 0.299 m at the unknown grade, the drop is 0.025 m. The total vertical rise then is equal to the "rise" plus "drop" or $0.285 + 0.025 = 0.31$ m. If the axle-to-axle length (hypotenuse) is 2.095 m, then the grade can be calculated as:

$$\text{Grade} = \text{total rise} \div \text{hypotenuse}$$
$$= 0.31 \text{ m} \div 2.095 \text{ m} = 0.148 = 14.8\%$$

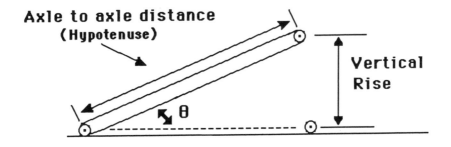

Fixed rear axle treadmill

$$\text{Grade} = \text{Sine } \theta = \text{Rise} \div \text{Hypotenuse}$$

FIGURE 47–2. Calibration of grade for fixed rear axle treadmill by sine method (rise ÷ hypotenuse).

Table 47–1. Table of Natural Sines and Tangents

Degrees	Sine	% Grade	Tangent	% Grade
0	0.0000	0.0	0.0000	0.0
1	0.0175	1.7	0.0175	1.7
2	0.0349	3.5	0.0349	3.5
3	0.0523	5.2	0.0524	5.2
4	0.0698	7.0	0.0699	7.0
5	0.0872	8.7	0.0875	8.7
6	0.1045	10.4	0.1051	10.5
7	0.1219	12.2	0.1228	12.3
8	0.1392	13.9	0.1405	14.0
9	0.1564	15.6	0.1584	15.8
10	0.1736	17.4	0.1763	17.6
11	0.1908	19.1	0.1944	19.4
12	0.2079	20.8	0.2126	21.3
13	0.2250	22.5	0.2309	23.1
14	0.2419	24.2	0.2493	24.9
15	0.2588	25.9	0.2679	26.8
20	0.3420	34.2	0.3640	36.4
25	0.4067	40.7	0.4452	44.5

Note: For low grades (<20%), the sine method gives a value that is nearly equal to the tangent method, so the choice of method is irrelevant (see Table 47–1). For steep grades, the "rise" over the "run" method (using the carpenter's square) can be used to obtain a proper sine value for treadmill grade. After obtaining a tangent value, simply look across Table 47–1 to the sine column to obtain the correct sine value to set on the treadmill dial. For example, if the "rise" over the "run" method yielded 0.268 or 26.8% (tangent), the "correct" setting would be 25.9% (sine). The latter value is set on the grade dial of the treadmill.

CYCLE ERGOMETER

GENERAL CONCEPTS

Work rate or power output is expressed in a variety of ways. To make some sense of this calculation, the basic units of measurement are presented. Mechanics involves three "undefinables," measures that cannot be defined in any other units. These measures are length, time, and mass. In the metric system, length is measured in meters (m), time in seconds (sec), and mass in kilograms (kg).

Work is equal to force times the distance through which the force acts: $W = F \cdot d$. Force is equal to the product of the mass of an object and its acceleration: $F = m \cdot a$. The basic unit of force is the newton (N); it is that force that when applied to a 1-k mass gives it an acceleration of $1 \, m \cdot sec^{-2}$.

Whereas mass is a measure of the quantity of matter an object contains, its weight is the *force* with which it is attracted toward the center of the earth. Weight is appropriately expressed in newtons (N). If we return to our formula for work: $W = F \cdot d$ (with distance in meters) then, Work $= F(N) \cdot d(m) = Nm$. One Nm (Newton meter) is equal to 1 joule (J), which is the basic unit of work. A common unit used to express force is the kilopond, not the kilogram (mass unit). The kilopond is the force acting on the mass of 1 kg at the normal acceleration of gravity, and is equal to 9.80665 N.

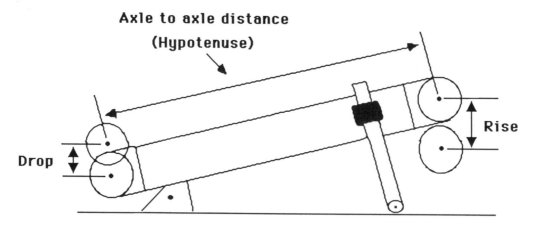

Axle to axle distance

(Hypotenuse)

Rise

Drop

Total Vertical Rise = Rise + Drop

Grade = sine θ = Total Vertical Rise ÷ Hypotenuse

FIGURE 47–3. Calibration of grade for moveable rear axle treadmill by sine method (rise ÷ hypotenuse).

On the Monark cycle ergometer, a force (kp) is moved through a distance (meters), so work is expressed in kp · m. Because work is accomplished over some period of time (minutes), the activity is known as a work *rate*, not a workload. Another name for work rate is *power*. In the preceding example work rate is expressed in kp · m · min^{-1}.

The wheel on the Monark cycle ergometer travels 6 m per pedal revolution, so at 50 rev · min^{-1}, the wheel travels 300 m · min^{-1} (i.e., 6 m · rev^{-1} · 50 rev · min^{-1} = 300 m · min^{-1}). If a force of 1 kp hangs from that wheel, the work rate or power output is 300 kp · m · min^{-1} (i.e., 1 kp · 300 m · min^{-1} = 300 kp · m · min^{-1}). The distance the wheel travels per minute is easy to measure because you can count pedal revolutions. Although the force exerted on the wheel is easily set and maintained, calibration of the force values on the scale is necessary to assure that the work rate is what it appears to be. The following steps outline the procedures to follow in the calibration of the Monark cycle ergometer scale.

1. With a carpenter's level, adjust a table to ensure that it is *level*, and put the ergometer on it.
2. Disconnect the "belt" at the spring.
3. Adjust the set screw on the front of the bike against which the numerical scale rests, so that the vertical mark on the pendulum weight is matched with "0" kp on the weight scale. The pendulum must be free-swinging. Lock the adjustment screw.
4. Suspend a 0.5-kg weight from the spring so that no contact is made with the flywheel; note if the pendulum moves to the 0.5-kp mark. If not, place tape over the scale and make a mark in line with the pendulum.
5. Systematically add weight to the spring. The pendulum mark should match the weight scale mark for each weight. If the marks do not match, put tape over the marks and numbers on the weight scale, and label the taped scale appropriately. Note: Be sure to calibrate the ergometer through the range of values to be used in your tests.
6. Reassemble the cycle ergometer.

In some laboratories, the aforementioned procedure is modified to reduce the chance that the weight might contact the flywheel. The rear of the cycle ergometer is raised by about 3 in. by means of a 2 × 4. The scale is set to 0 and the weights are added as described previously. When the scale is calibrated, the 2 × 4 is removed, and the scale is again set to 0. The cycle ergometer is now calibrated.

Other Facts about Cycle Ergometers

The work rate is expressed in many different units, but some units are preferred. Dividing the work rate in kp · m · min^{-1} by 6.12 yields the work rate in watts (1 watt = 6.12 kp · m · min^{-1}). The work rate can also be expressed in kcal per minute (1 kcal = 427 kp · m) or in kilojoules (kJ) per minute (1 kcal = 4.19 kJ). The reason for presenting these units is that the authors of most research papers and textbooks use watts and kJ/min to express work rate.

SPHYGMOMANOMETER

A sphygmomanometer is a blood pressure measurement system composed of an inflatable rubber bladder, an instrument to indicate the applied pressure, an inflation bulb to create pressure, and an adjustable valve to deflate the system. The cuff and the measuring instrument are the most crucial in terms of measurement accuracy. The width of the cuff should be about 20% wider than the diameter of the limb to which it is applied; when inflated, the bladder should not cause a bulging or displacement. Choose the cuff size carefully. The pressure measuring device can be an anaeroid or a mercury type. The mercury type is the "standard" and is easily maintained. The mercury column should rise and fall smoothly, form a clear meniscus, and read zero when the bladder is deflated. If the mercury sticks in the tube, remove the cap and swab out the inside. If it is very dirty, the tube should be removed and cleaned (detergent, water rinse, and alcohol for drying). If the mercury column falls below zero, the simple addition of mercury restores the instrument's accuracy.

The anaeroid gauge contains a bellows assembly that transmits pressure through gears to an indicator. A spring attached to the pointer moves the pointer downscale to zero when the bladder is deflated. This gauge should be calibrated annually at a variety of settings, with the use of the mercury column described previously. A simple "y-tube" is used to connect the two systems. When the pressure is raised in the mercury column, the reading is checked on the anaeroid device (Fig. 47–4).

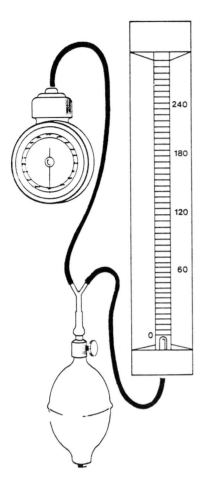

FIGURE 47–4. Calibration of aneroid manometer with mercury manometer. (From Kirkendall WM et al: Recommendations for human blood pressure determination by sphygmomanometer. *Circulation,* 62:1146A–1155A, 1980, with permission.)

Table 47–2. Tasks to Complete Before Patient/Client Arrival

Availability of physician (if appropriate)
Phone call to patient/client to:
- Find out if they will be coming as scheduled
- Remind to bring comfortable walking, running shoes
- Remember to wear jogging clothes or loose-fitting pants/front button shirt
- Remember to bring all medications
- Inquire about allergies
- Instruct not to eat after midnight (for nuclear testing), or to have had something light to eat at least 3 hours before a regular GXT
- Remind to stop by the office to register on computer

Inventory of supplies: electrodes, tape, ECG paper, cuffs, forms, and pens
Calibrate the equipment

Note: detail varies with submaximal fitness tests, compared to maximal diagnostic GXT protocols.

Table 47–3. Emergency Equipment Check List

Defibrillator
  Batteries
  Charge/discharge
  Monitor and printout

Crash cart
  Drugs; present and up-to-date
  O_2 delivery system
    Pressure in cylinder
    Ambu bag is present and working
    Suction is working
  Intravenous equipment, lines, and D_5W

Table 47–4. Check List for the Testing Setting

☐ Greet patient/client
☐ Obtain consent (oral and written)
☐ Have person explain why he or she is here
☐ Evaluate medications; ask if other drugs are taken
☐ Ask about allergies
☐ Record age, and measure height and weight. Calculate and record estimated HR_{max} and 70 to 85% of HR_{max}
☐ Send to dressing room
☐ Full 12-lead hook-up, plus cuff (I.V. if needed for nuclear studies)
  • Prepare skin with suitable abrasive material
  • Check electrodes to be sure they are fresh (not dried out)
  • For women, tape over electrodes in "cross your heart" pattern with 2-in. hypoallergenic tape.
  • Wrap chest with 6-in. self-adhesive wrap
☐ Obtain resting HR, BP, and ECG while sitting/ standing or lying/standing, depending on post-test positions
☐ Instruct client on how to walk on the treadmill
  • Hold onto railing, get "feel" of belt speed by putting one foot on the belt, keeping up with belt speed
  • Step on, keep eyes ahead, back straight, walk relaxed with arms swinging
  • Initially, person can hold on for balance, then use just finger or back of hand to *touch* railing

OR

☐ Instruct on how to use the cycle ergometer
  • Adjust seat height so the knee is slightly flexed when the foot is at the bottom of the pedal swing and parallel to the floor
  • Keep pace with the metronome
  • Do not hold tightly onto the handlebars; release hold when blood pressure is taken
☐ Follow test protocol
  • Advise person to talk during the test about how they feel
  • Follow criteria for termination of the test (see Table 2–9 of *Guidelines for Exercise Testing and Prescription (3rd Ed.)*

Note: for fitness evaluations, HR, BP, and RPE are the usual variables measured.

Table 47–5. Post-test Protocol

Cool down is programmed per physician and other
post-treadmill tests
Sit down or lie down depending on post-tests (nuclear)
Monitor HR, BP, and ECG immediately and after 1, 2, 4,
and 6 min
Remove cuff and electrodes when double product
(HR × systolic BP) is close to pretest value
Provide instructions for showering
Wait for about 30 min
Move around in shower, use warm (not hot) water
Check for return of person from shower
Organize test data and discuss test results with person

ELECTROCARDIOGRAPHS

Electrocardiographs require calibration before and after a GXT to ensure that the deflection of the pen or stylus corresponds to the proper voltage: 1 cm/mV. A regular (annual) maintenance check-up includes paper speed, electric isolation of the patient, operator protection from electric shock, and a variety of performance checks.

EVENTS IN A TYPICAL TESTING DAY

The events in a typical testing day, and the steps needed to attend to them, before, during, and after an exercise test are listed in Tables 47–2 through 47–5. These lists are general steps to follow, with the understanding that the exact steps vary with the purpose and location of the submaximal fitness, maximal diagnostic, or performance test.

Acknowledgments

I thank Pat Checka of the Cardiac Rehabilitation Outpatient Program in Fort Sanders Hospital for her help with the day-to-day lists associated with testing; and Robert Holly (University of California, Davis) and Patricia Painter for their review of this manuscript.

REFERENCES

1. Åstrand P-O: Work Test with the Bicycle Ergometer. Varberg, Sweden: Monark-Cresent AB.
2. American College of Sports Medicine: *Guidelines for Exercise Testing and Prescription.* 3rd Ed. Philadelphia: Lea & Febiger, 1986.
3. Quinton Instruments Instruction Manual—Model 24-72. Seattle, WA: Quinton Instruments, 1970.
4. *Sphygmomanometers, Principles and Precepts.* W. A. Baum Co., Inc., New York, 1961.
5. Kirkendall WM, Feinlieb M, Freis ED, Mark AL: Recommendations for human blood pressure determination by sphygmomanometers. *Circulation,* 62:1146A–1155A, 1980.

CHAPTER 48

EVALUATION OF PREVENTIVE AND REHABILITATIVE EXERCISE PROGRAMS

BRENDA S. MITCHELL AND
STEVEN N. BLAIR

In this chapter, we introduce concepts associated with planning and conducting evaluations of preventive and rehabilitative exercise programs. We hope the overview and outline provided will encourage program directors to become both consumers and producers of evaluation studies.

To the inexperienced evaluator, the evaluation process briefly described in this chapter may seem formidable. Indeed, evaluation can be complicated and extensive. We recommend that program managers not be intimidated by the evaluation process, but take initiative to develop plans for program evaluation. All program managers evaluate; however, some managers do not follow systematic procedures nor obtain good data. Inadequate evaluation procedures lead to poor decision making by managers. The program manager should carefully build an evaluation plan so that over time better decisions can be made. A complete evaluation plan does not have to be established at the outset (although that is ideal), rather it can be broadened or elaborated upon as time and resources permit.

WHY EVALUATE?

For most programs (or products), evaluation provides a framework for answering questions about goals, activities, outcomes, and costs. Anyone who needs information regarding the merits of a program is a potential user of evaluation findings. For example, the board of directors of a cardiac rehabilitation program may want to know how effective the programs are in returning patients to work. A company president may be interested in the extent of employee participation in a preventive exercise program.

Evaluations can be described in several ways. Altman describes a framework organized around three broad stages of evaluation: (1) evaluation of process; (2) evaluation of physiologic, psychologic, and social effects; and (3) evaluation of social relevance.[1] In this model, the evaluation moves through the three stages, addressing key issues or factors at each stage. Examples of issues that might be pertinent in each stage of an evaluation of preven-

Table 48–1. Evaluation Stages

Evaluation of Process	Evaluation of physiologic, psychologic, and social effects	Evaluation of social relevance
Participation/adherence rates	Increased physical fitness	Cost-effectiveness
Cointervention	Improved job satisfaction	Return to work
Referral patterns		
Qualitative analysis	Reduction in anxiety	Reduction in absenteeism

tive and rehabilitative exercise are presented in Table 48–1.

The following sections include descriptions of components that are part of the evaluation process. An example of a plan for evaluating a preventive and rehabilitative exercise program is developed to illustrate the process. The plan follows a model developed by Fink and Kosecoff.[2]

FORMULATING CREDIBLE QUESTIONS

The questions to be answered are the heart of the evaluation, and all activities must be organized so that the questions can be answered efficiently. The number of possible questions depends upon the money, time, and resources available, and the priorities of the consumer of the evaluation results.

A thorough description of the program, especially its goals and objectives, must be prepared before questions can be stated. Sources of information about the program may be obtained from written proposals, annual reports, brochures, products produced by the program, organizational structure, and staff. A program description (example in Table 48–2) should be prepared that states the program's goals and activities and provides at least some evidence of program merit for each activity and goal.

The main source of information for formulating the evaluation questions is the evidence of program merit in the program description. This

information can be easily translated into questions. Examples of evaluation questions might include:

- What is the change in physical work capacity (PWC) in program participants after 6 months of exercise conditioning?
- What percentage of overweight individuals achieve target weight?
- What percentage of hypertensive subjects have their blood pressure under control?

The evaluation may also include questions based on general considerations and not derived directly from the program description. Once a preliminary draft of the evaluation questions is prepared, the program staff should meet to establish priorities for the questions, add or delete questions, and ensure that all questions can be answered within the time period, given the resources available.

CONSTRUCTING EVALUATION DESIGNS

The evaluation design specifies the ways that participants are grouped and variables are manipulated to answer one or more evaluation questions. In some evaluations, a single design is used to answer all questions, whereas in other evaluations several designs are required.

Internal and external validity are the criteria used to decide how accurately the evaluation design provides answers to the evaluation

Table 48–2. Example of a Program Description

Goal*	Activity	Evidence of Merit
Improve physical work capacity (PWC)	Exercise program	Increased PWC
Weight control	Weight loss counseling	Weight loss in overweight participants
Blood pressure control	Nutrition counseling, exercise program, drug therapy	Improved blood pressure in participants
Return to work (post-myocardial infarction)	Total rehabilitation program	Return to work by most patients

* For all goals, additional evidence of merit is provided by behavior change or adherence to therapeutic regimens.

questions. Internal validity means that an evaluation design can distinguish between changes caused by the program and those resulting from other sources.[3] Campbell and Stanley identified seven factors that can threaten internal validity:

- *History.* Changes in the environment that occur at the time of the program.
- *Maturation.* Changes within the individuals participating in the program that result from natural biologic or psychologic development.
- *Testing.* Effects of taking a pretest on subsequent post-tests.
- *Instrumentation.* Changes in the calibration of an instrument, or changes in the observers, scores, or the measuring instruments used from one time to the next.
- *Statistical regression.* Performance on the post-test that is too high or too low because of selection for entering a program on the basis of an extremely high or low pretest score.
- *Selection bias.* Results when assignment produces groups with innately different characteristics.
- *Mortality.* Changes in the results because of participants dropping out of the evaluation.

External validity is the criterion for deciding whether the evaluation findings hold true for other people in other settings.[3] Threats to external validity include:

- *Reactive effects of testing.* Occurs because of pretest sensitization to a program.
- *Interactive effects of selection bias.* Results do not follow for different participants in another location.
- *Reactive effects of innovation.* Better performance because of taking part in an innovative or special program (Hawthorne effect).
- *Multiple program interference.* Changes result from the combined effect of two different programs.

Numerous designs for program evaluations are available. A summary of each of five designs that are frequently used to evaluate preventive and rehabilitative exercise programs follows.[4]

- *One group pretest and post-test.* Weakest design because of lack of a comparison group. Many threats to validity. Even with shortcomings, still useful for some evaluation questions for exercise programs because obtaining control groups is frequently difficult or impossible. Use extreme care when interpreting results.

- *Nonequivalent control group.* Can be very useful when evaluating exercise programs if selection bias is avoided.
- *Time series.* Requires many data points spaced at equal intervals over a sufficient period of time. History is the principal threat to internal validity.
- *Multiple time series.* Involves study of outcomes at different points in time for a treatment and a comparison group. Appropriate for situations in which retrospective and prospective data bases are easily accessible or an individual(s) from an organization can observe program participants periodically.
- *Randomized trial with control group.* Strongest design, allows best control of the several threats to internal and external validity. Numerous variations of this design are available.

An evaluation design should be selected that can offset the most likely threats to internal and external validity. A plan can be prepared that summarizes information about the design strategies selected for an evaluation. For each evaluation question, the plan should specify the type of design strategy, the independent and dependent variables, the sampling procedures, and the threats to internal and external validity. Independent variables form the structure of the design and are the factors that are manipulated in an evaluation. Dependent variables are the factors that are observed and measured to determine the results of manipulating the independent variables.

The ways in which participants are selected for an evaluation study vary. Three common methods for obtaining representative samples are:

- *Simple random sample.* A lottery system is used to select an appropriate number of subjects from the total population.
- *Stratified random sample.* The total population is divided into subgroups (e.g., sex or age categories), and a certain number of subjects is randomly selected from each subgroup.
- *Purposive sample.* Individuals or groups are deliberately selected for a particular reason.

Sampling has important implications for the way that the evaluation results are interpreted. We recommend seeking the assistance of a biostatistical consultant because of the complexity of determining sample size and selecting appropriate analytic techniques.

A design strategy for answering the evalua-

Table 48–3. Example of an Evaluation Design Strategy

| Evaluation Questions | Design Strategy | | | |
	Type	Independent/Dependent Variables	Sampling	Threats to Validity
Change in physical work capacity (PWC)	One group pretest-post-test	$\dot{V}O_{2\,max}$ or PWC (dependent): age, sex, disease state, smoking status; body weight (independent)	Purposive (all participants)	History, maturation, mortality
Return to work	Nonequivalent controls	Employed rate (dependent); demographics/health status (independent)	Random sample of controls and participants	Selection, reactive effects, multiple program interference

tion questions posed in the preceding example above is provided in Table 48–3.

PLANNING INFORMATION COLLECTION

An information collection plan should be developed to ensure that each evaluation question is answered. Each evaluation question, together with the information collection techniques and a list of any limitations imposed by the evaluation's schedule, design, or sampling procedures, are listed subsequently. Specific information about the instruments, time and place for information collection, who is included in the sample, and who will collect the information is also included. An example of an information collection plan is provided in Table 48–4.

Common techniques for information collection, including their advantages and disadvantages, follow:

- *Performance tests.* An individual or group performs an activity or task and the quality of the performance is assessed. Examples include exercise tests, laboratory values, and weight loss. Advantage: it relies on objective data. Disadvantage: it is usually time consuming and expensive.
- *Rating and ranking scales.* These scales can be

used for self-assessment or to assess other people, events, or products on a given dimension. Examples include feelings of well-being and life satisfaction. Advantages: they are relatively inexpensive to construct and administer, they are usually easily understood, and the information they provide readily lends itself to analysis. Disadvantage: they are subject to many types of bias.
- *Existing records.* This technique refers to collecting evaluation information from program-related documents. Examples include reviewing patient charts for information that is not included in the computer data base or reviewing past medical or employment records. Advantage: it does not interfere with the program being evaluated and it is relatively inexpensive. Disadvantages: legal problems associated with obtaining and using records, and the possibility that program documents may be disorganized or unavailable.
- *Observations.* Information collected by observers can be reported by check lists, rating scales, narrative records, and summary reports. Examples include rating program staff on communications skills. Advantages: (1) they help the information collectors become familiar with and sensitive to the program; and (2) they are often the only feasible and economical way to gather certain kinds of information. Disadvantages: (1) it is costly to train information collectors; (2) the people

Table 48–4. Example of an Information Collection Plan

Evaluation questions	Collection technique/ instruments	Time/place	Limitations	Who will collect
Improve physical work capacity	Exercise tests	Baseline and follow-up care	Expense of testing	Laboratory staff
Return to work	Questionnaire	1–2 years after program	Difficulty in tracking, subjective response	Program administrative staff

observed may not behave normally because of the presence of the observer; and (3) several observations may be needed to obtain consistent results.

- *Interviews.* In an interview, a person talks with another person or group and records information on narrative records, structured interview forms, summary reports, or other related forms. Examples include diet recalls, exercise histories, or family issues and problems. Advantage: they permit in-depth probes of sensitive subjects, like attitudes and values. Disadvantages: they are usually time consuming and costly, and interviewers must be specially trained.
- *Questionnaires.* Self-administered survey forms that consist of a set of questions for which answers may be either free responses or forced choices. Examples include health behavior inventories, medical histories, and psychologic factors. Advantages: they are less expensive to construct and administer than most measures, and the resulting information is relatively easy to analyze. Disadvantage: the kind of information obtained is sometimes limited.

Selecting an instrument for collecting information involves reviewing currently available measures and then choosing or adapting the most appropriate choice. Advantages of selecting an existing information collection instrument are that it is less expensive than developing a new one, and technical information about the validity, reliability, and applicability of the instrument usually is available. Instruments appropriate for answering the evaluation questions are not always readily available, however, and searching through existing instruments can be time consuming.

New information collection tools may be developed by combining the features of several instruments. This approach can save time and money, but may require obtaining permission for use and a study to validate the hybrid instrument. Designing and validating an evaluation instrument is the best guarantee for obtaining the necessary information, but this process requires considerable skill and time.

COLLECTING EVALUATION INFORMATION

The major activities related to the collection of evaluation information include: validating the information collection instruments and procedures, training information collectors, implementing the information collection plan, and organizing evaluation information for analysis.

Pilot testing takes additional time and effort and program managers may be tempted to omit this step. Thorough pilot testing is ideal and may not always be possible, but problems may be avoided if time is allotted for a pilot test. Pilot testing of the instruments and procedures can answer questions such as:

- Are certain words or questions used in the instruments redundant or misleading?
- Are the instruments appropriate for the audience?
- Can the information collectors administer, collect, and report information in a standardized manner using the written directions and special coding forms?
- How consistent is the information obtained by the instruments (reliability)?
- How accurate is the information obtained with the instruments (validity)?

The ideal pilot test should be conducted following these guidelines:

- Conduct all activities under conditions that are identical to those followed in the evaluation.
- Include a representative sample of the participants in the pilot study.
- Omit participants in the pilot test from any subsequent evaluation activities because they will be familiar with the evaluation measures (threat to internal validity).
- Have experts review the information collection plan, the instruments, and other evaluation guidelines.
- Revise the instruments and procedures if necessary.
- Repeat the pilot testing until you are confident that the evaluation instruments and procedures are feasible and yield credible information.

Before beginning the information collection activities, data collectors should learn as much as possible about the program, the evaluation questions, and the specific information collection activities they will conduct. They should receive detailed training about how to obtain, record, and communicate information.

Most information collection activities are subject to legal restrictions and may require clearance or approval from an Institutional Review Board or other groups. Matters of confidentiality and informed consent must be incorporated into the information collection plan.

PLANNING AND CONDUCTING INFORMATION ANALYSES

Even before the information collection begins, the analyses should be planned so that the evaluation questions can be answered directly. The evaluation design and information collection plan must be coordinated with the information analyses. Choices of analyses are always guided by the appropriateness of the method to be used.

The results of analyses are numbers, descriptions, explanations, justifications of events, and statistical statements. Interpreting the results means using the findings of the analyses to answer each of the evaluation questions. When all questions have been answered, the results may be considered collectively to evaluate the program as a whole and to provide recommendations and offer suggestions as to how to document the merits of the program or how to improve the program.

When making interpretations, important precautions are as follows: (1) Be sensitive to personal bias; (2) Do not extrapolate beyond the limits of the results; and (3) Report only information that is related to the evaluation questions or the evidence of program merit.

REPORTING EVALUATION INFORMATION

An evaluation report provides the answers to the evaluation questions and explains the procedures used to obtain the answers. Whether informal or formal, written or oral, the report should include the following components:

1. Title page
2. Executive summary (abstract)
3. Table of contents
4. Introduction
   A. Program description
   B. Evaluation questions
5. Design strategy
   A. Sampling procedures
   B. Limitations

6. Information collection techniques
   A. Instruments
   B. Schedule of activities
7. Data analysis
8. Findings and summary of conclusions
9. Recommendations

MANAGING AN EVALUATION

Of critical importance is that evaluation activities are coordinated so that the information is ready when needed for decision making. Directors of evaluation studies must give attention to establishing schedules, assigning staff and monitoring their activities, and budgeting. Establishing evaluation schedules requires attention to the specific evaluation activities, deadlines for completing activities, and the total amount of time to be given to each activity. The evaluator should decide the skills needed to perform each activity so that the staff members with those skills can be assigned appropriately. These tasks are usually addressed during the planning stages and are incorporated into the original proposal.

Managing an evaluation also means monitoring the efficiency of the staff in performing the evaluation activities. Information collected should describe the amount of time spent on each activity, how thoroughly each activity has been accomplished, and any problems encountered. Frequent informal meetings or reports to the project staff are helpful.

Evaluation budgets vary in form and detail; they are usually part of the planning process. An evaluation usually has a given amount of money and must be accomplished without exceeding the amount. A thorough understanding of the available resources (staff, time, equipment, and money) must be considered when making decisions about the overall program and evaluation plan. Programs planned well in advance with appropriate evaluation activities generally have a higher likelihood of success than unplanned evaluation activities.

REFERENCES

1. Altman DG: A framework for evaluating community-based heart disease prevention programs. *Soc Sci Med,* 22:4, 1986.
2. Fink A, Kosecoff J: *An Evaluation Primer.* Washington, D.C.: Capitol, 1978.

3. Campbell DT, Stanley JC: *Experimental and Quasi-Experimental Designs for Research.* Chicago: Rand McNally, 1966.

4. Windsor RA, Baranowski T, Clark N, Cutter G: *Evaluation of Health Promotion and Education Programs.* Palo Alto: Mayfield, 1984.

5. Guttentag M, Struening EL: *Handbook of Evaluation Research.* Beverly Hills: Sage, 1975.

6. Kerlinger F: *Foundations of Behavioral Research.* 2nd Ed. New York: Holt, Rinehart and Winston, 1973.

7. Nunnally JC: *Psychometric Theory.* 2nd Ed. New York: McGraw-Hill, 1978.

8. Daniel WW: *Biostatistics; A Foundation for Analysis in the Health Sciences.* New York: John Wiley & Sons, 1974.

9. Cronbach LJ, et al.: *Toward Reform of Program Evaluation.* San Francisco: Jossey-Bass, 1980.

10. Cronbach LJ: *Designing Evaluations of Educational and Social Programs.* San Francisco: Jossey-Bass, 1982.

11. Rossi PH, Freeman HE, Wright SR: *Evaluation—A Systematic Approach.* Beverly Hills: Sage, 1979

12. Morell JA: *Program Evaluation in Social Research.* New York: Pergamon Press, 1979.

13. Posavac EJ, Carey RG: *Program Evaluation: Methods and Case Studies.* Englewood Cliffs, NJ: Prentice-Hall, 1980.

14. Green LW, Lewis FM: *Measurement and Evaluation in Health Education and Health Promotion.* Palo Alto: Mayfield, 1986.

15. Fitz-Gibbon CT, Morris LL: *How to Design a Program Evaluation.* Beverly Hills: Sage, 1978.

16. Schulberg HC, Baker F: *Program Evaluation in the Health Fields.* New York: Human Sciences Press, 1979.

INDEX